Butterworths Local Government Finance

Butterworths Local Government Finance

William Birtles LLM (London and Harvard)
Barrister

Anna Forge BA
Solicitor

Contributing Editors
Tony Child LLB
Solicitor

Peter Steiner BA
Solicitor

Butterworths
London, Edinburgh, Dublin
2000

United Kingdom	Butterworths, a Division of Reed Elsevier (UK) Ltd, Halsbury House, 35 Chancery Lane, LONDON WC2A 1EL and 4 Hill Street, EDINBURGH EH2 3JZ
Australia	Butterworths, a Division of Reed International Books Australia Pty Ltd, CHATSWOOD, New South Wales
Canada	Butterworths Canada Ltd, MARKHAM, Ontario
Hong Kong	Butterworths Hong Kong, a Division of Reed Elsevier (Greater China) Ltd, HONG KONG
India	Butterworths India, NEW DELHI
Ireland	Butterworth (Ireland) Ltd, DUBLIN
Malaysia	Malayan Law Journal Sdn Bhd, KUALA LUMPUR
New Zealand	Butterworths of New Zealand Ltd, WELLINGTON
Singapore	Butterworths Asia, SINGAPORE
South Africa	Butterworths Publishers (Pty) Ltd, DURBAN
USA	Lexis Law Publishing, CHARLOTTESVILLE, Virginia

A CIP Catalogue record for this book is available from the British Library.

ISBN 0 406 90013 2

Typeset by B & J Whitcombe, Nr Diss, Norfolk, IP22 2LP
Printed and bound by Bookcraft (Bath) Ltd, Midsomer Norton, Avon

Foreword

Peel back the outer layers of any successful local authority and you will invariably find highly regarded finance and legal staff working behind the front line. They are two of the 'must have' ingredients which are absolutely critical to the chemistry of an effective council.

But what exactly are the distinctive contributions which the accountants and lawyers bring to the organisation? Many would describe them using terms like 'professionalism' and 'corporate control'—the people who set and police the rules, the people who decide what can and can't be done, the professionals who exemplify the integrity we associate with our best public institutions. There is no doubt that these are important, if sometimes unglamorous, parts of the role. But in the best organisations finance and legal staff would also be at least as strongly associated with terms like 'creativity', 'innovation' and 'leadership'—the people who shape some of the big ideas, the people who make a difference and make things happen.

Life in the local authorities of the twenty-first century will be far from easy. We shall need to work hard on the control levers—discipline, focus, stewardship, accountability, ethics—and harder still to develop and deliver the right innovative responses to the ever more complex problems which society faces. Overriding all we shall need strong leadership which is bold enough to paint an ambitious vision for a better future, and brave and skilful enough to turn the vision into reality.

I am sure that this book will be an invaluable aid to the lawyers and accountants as they ply their trade. I am equally sure that they will rise to and be a match for the huge challenges which the future presents.

Mike Weaver
President of CIPFA

The Alexander Maxwell Law Scholarship Trust

Maurice W Maxwell whose family founded Sweet & Maxwell, the law publishers, by his Will established a charitable trust to be known as the Alexander Maxwell Law Scholarship Trust in memory of both his great-great-grandfather and great-grandfather. The Trust is committed to promoting legal research and writing at various levels by providing financial assistance to authors whether they be experienced legal practitioners, those in the early years of legal practice or at postgraduate level.

The authors of this book received financial assistance from the Trust to enable them to complete the work.

The Trust calls for applications for awards from time to time. Anyone interested in its work should write to The Clerk to the Trustees, Alexander Maxwell Law Scholarship Trust, c/o Sweet & Maxwell, 100 Avenue Road, Swiss Cottage, London NW3 3PF.

The Trust will shortly be launching a website at:

http://www.amlst.org.uk

Preface

Local government finance law is often regarded as an obscure and arcane area of law, but it is one which is of vital importance to the working of local government. Yet there is a dearth of accessible literature on the subject and this book is designed to fill that gap. It is an area of law which is undergoing considerable change, along with the wider statutory framework for local government. Indeed, at the time of writing a Government Green Paper outlining proposals for the complete replacement of the capital finance system for local government is expected imminently.

We intend to provide an analytical account of the main areas of local government finance law and to highlight areas undergoing reform, in a way which is readable and will be of assistance to those practising in this area. This book is primarily aimed at lawyers employed in, or acting for, local and central government and those who deal with local authorities. Although the book does not approach the subject from an accountant's perspective, we hope that those working in local government finance departments and accountants involved with local government will use it and benefit from it.

We are conscious that a new book of this kind could well run into many hundreds of pages and cover every aspect of the subject in great detail. We could, for example, have filled out the length of the book with appendices containing legislation, government and other relevant guidance. We have chosen not to do so because we think that there is a need for a portable work of reasonable size and price. We do not deal with rating and local taxation, as these areas are more than adequately covered in the present standard works.

We have divided the book into four parts. Part I is an introduction to the local government finance regime, intended to set the scene. It outlines recent changes and proposals for change which have an impact on virtually every chapter of the book. After a basic description of the legal structure of local government relevant to financial matters, we move to consider the main sources of income and spending power and the various funds, accounts and budgets which local authorities operate. Part II of the book deals with general financial control and accountability and begins with a discussion of the essential legal principles and general expenditure powers. We then cover the responsibilities of officers and members before turning to a consideration of the new 'best value' regime, audit and the functions of external auditors to local government. Part III of the book deals with capital finance, covering the various controls and reliefs and recent developments. Part IV deals with selected aspects of local government finance. Of necessity, we have chosen those areas which we think are topical and of practical significance. Thus we discuss the Private Finance Initiative for local government, local authority interests in companies, local economic development and Value Added Tax, and (although aspects of these matters are dealt with extensively elsewhere) no book on local government finance law would be complete without chapters on housing and education finance.

Finally, we have included a glossary of some of the expressions which are commonly encountered in connection with local government finance, with basic explanations and references to more detailed information.

We are grateful to David Abbott and Lisa Plitt who helped us in the early stages of the book and to Stephen Hughes, Director of Finance at the London Borough of Brent, for his helpful comments on the Glossary.

In addition, we gratefully acknowledge the support of the Alexander Maxwell Law Scholarship Trust for financial support in the preparation of this book.

The law is stated as at 7 August 2000, but subsequent changes have been noted where possible.

William Birtles

Anna Forge

7 August 2000

Contents

Foreword v
Preface ix
Abbreviations xvii
Table of statutes xix
Table of statutory instruments xxxiii
Table of cases xli

PART I INTRODUCTION TO THE LOCAL GOVERNMENT FINANCE REGIME 1

Chapter 1 An introduction to local government and current proposals for reform 3
A Introduction 3
B Reform of public finance and local government 12

Chapter 2 Central government support 22
A Grants 22
B Credit approvals 25
C Council tax 25
D Non-domestic rate 30

Chapter 3 Funds and accounts 35
A Funds 35
B Accounts 46
C Supply of goods and services 50
D Publicity accounts 51
E Other accounts 52

PART II FINANCIAL CONTROL AND ACCOUNTABILITY 55

Chapter 4 Basic legal principles 57
A Ultra vires 57
B 'Wednesbury unreasonableness' 58
C Quasi-fiduciary duty 58
D Financial motives, levying charges and trading for profit 59
E Unlawful fetters on discretion and failure to exercise discretion 60
F Improper purposes 62
G Unlawful delegation 63

H Annual accounting and forward funding 63
I The scope of Local Government Act 1971, s 111 64
J The scope of Local Government Act 1972, s 137 66

Chapter 5 Financial responsibilities of officers 70
A Introduction 70
B The statutory duty for proper administration 71
C Appointment of the Chief Finance Officer 71
D The monitoring officer 74
E The head of the paid service 76
F Code of conduct for local government employees 76

Chapter 6 Financial responsibilities of members 77
A Specific statutory duties 77
B Access to documents 77
C Monetary payments 77
D Pecuniary and non-pecuniary interests 80
E The National Code of Local Government Conduct 82
F The Nolan Report 84

Chapter 7 Best value 92
A Introduction 92
B The duty to secure best value 95
C Securing compliance 107
D Ancillary matters 109
E Conclusions 113

Chapter 8 Audit 114
A Introduction 114
B Internal audit 114
C District audit; the Audit Commission; bodies subject to audit; the appointment of auditors 116
D Functions, role and liabilities of external auditors 120
E The audit process 127

Chapter 9 Specific powers of auditors to deal with financial irregularities 143
A Introduction 143
B Declaration that an item of account is contrary to law 144
C Duty to certify for failure to account or loss through wilful misconduct 153
D Prohibition orders 160
E Advisory notices 163
F Judicial review 164

PART III CAPITAL FINANCE 167

Chapter 10 Introduction to capital finance 169
A Background to the current system under the LGHA 1989, Pt IV 170
B Importance of subordinate legislation 170
C Introduction to controls under Pt IV of the LGHA 1989 171
D Expenditure to be charged to revenue account 172

E Exceptions to the obligation to charge to revenue account 173
F Expenditure for capital purposes: definition 174
G Approved investments 175
H Overview of the controls under Pt IV of the LGHA 1989 177
I Special treatment of debt-free authorities 178
J Special treatment of European Community grants 181

Chapter 11 Credit approvals, limits and provision for credit liabilities 182
A Credit approvals 182
B Limits on credit 188
C Provision for credit liabilities 193

Chapter 12 Credit arrangements 201
A Introduction 201
B Categories of credit arrangement 203
C Exceptions—arrangements which are not credit arrangements 214
D Initial and subsequent cost of credit arrangements 217
E Special rules for certain credit arrangements under the LA(CF)R 1997 224
F Variation of credit arrangements 232
G Limits on powers to enter into credit arrangements 237

Chapter 13 Borrowing 239
A General borrowing powers 239
B Permitted means of borrowing 240
C Loan instruments and register of loan instruments and loans 241
D Security for money borrowed, remedies and protection for creditors 242
E Limits on borrowing 243
F Short-term borrowing 245
G Debt management powers 246
H The Public Works Loan Board 247

Chapter 14 Capital receipts and notional capital receipts 250
A Capital receipts 250
B Notional capital receipts 253
C Exceptions: items which are not capital receipts 255
D Reserved part 257
E Usable part of capital receipts 263
F Reliefs in respect of capital receipts under the LA(CF)R 1997 263
G Reliefs in respect of notional capital receipts 269

PART IV SELECTED ASPECTS OF LOCAL GOVERNMENT FINANCE 273

Chapter 15 Private finance transactions and the Local Government (Contracts) Act 1997 275
A Background to the Private Finance Initiative 275
B Evolution of the PFI for local government and initial capital finance measures 278
C Definition of private finance transaction 282
D Reduced or nil initial cost for private finance transactions 283

E Leases as part of a private finance transaction 290
F Notional capital receipts in connection with private finance transactions 291
G Special arrangements for 'debt-free' authorities 292
H Administration of revenue support for local government PFI schemes 292
I Local Government (Contracts) Act 1997 296

Chapter 16 Local authorities' interests in companies 309
A Background 309
B Provisions expressly authorising local authority participation in companies 311
C Assumptions regarding local authority participation in companies 313
D Case law on powers to set up and participate in external bodies 314
E Local Government and Housing Act 1989, Pt V 318
F Council members and officers as company directors 337
G The concept of shadow director 339
H Proposals for change and recent developments 340

Chapter 17 Local economic development 343
A Context 343
B Background to the Local Government and Housing Act 1989, Pt III 344
C Local Government and Housing Act 1989, Pt III 345
D Extent of powers envisaged by LGHA 1989, Pt III 345
E Restrictions on powers to promote economic development 347
F Accounting requirements and conditions of assistance 350
G Relationship with the financial provisions of Local Government and Housing Act 1989, Pt IV 350
H Notification of state aids 351
I The Local Government Act 2000 352

Chapter 18 Value Added Tax 356
A The basis of VAT and its administration 356
B Basic outline of the tax 357
C Local authorities and VAT 358
D VATA 1994, s 33 refunds and the de minimis threshold 359
E VAT and local authority land transactions and construction 363
F Appeals concerning VAT 368

Chapter 19 Housing finance 370
A Introduction 370
B The housing revenue account 370
C The housing repairs account 371
D Practice and procedure 372
E Special rules 376
F The budget 377
G Housing subsidies 378
H Capital finance for public sector housing 380
I Proposals for reform 381

Chapter 20 Local education finance 384
A Before the School Standards and Framework Act 1998 384
B Under the School Standards and Framework Act 1998 385
C The Secretary of State and funding authorities 394

D Local education authorities 394
E Delegated budget responsibility 395
F Grants 397
G Payment of schools fees and expenses 399
H Recoupment 399

Glossary 401

Index 419

Abbreviations

LGA 1963	Local Government Act 1963
LGA 1972	Local Government Act 1972
LGPLA 1980	Local Government, Planning and Land Act 1980
LGFA 1982	Local Government Finance Act 1982
CA 1985	Companies Act 1985
LGA 1985	Local Government Act 1985
LGA 1988	Local Government Act 1988
LGFA 1988	Local Government Finance Act 1988
LGHA 1989	Local Government and Housing Act 1989
LAR 1990	Local Authorities (Capital Finance) (Approved Investments) Regulations 1990, SI 1990/426
LG(PED)R 1990	Local Government (Promotion of Economic Development) Regulations 1990, SI 1990/789
LGFA 1992	Local Government Finance Act 1992
VATA 1994	Value Added Tax Act 1994
LACO 1995	Local Authorities (Companies) Order 1995, SI 1995/849
EA 1996	Education Act 1996
LGCA 1997	Local Government (Contracts) Act 1997
LA(CF)R 1997	Local Authorities (Capital Finance) Regulations 1997, SI 1997/319
ACA 1998	Audit Commission Act 1998
SSFA 1998	School Standards and Framework Act 1998
LGA 1999	Local Government Act 1999
LGA 2000	Local Government Act 2000

Table of statutes

PARA

Airports Act 1986
s 13 ... 16.14
14 ... 16.14
Audit Commission Act 1998 ... 1.21, 1.45, 6.35, 7.42, 8.3, 8.22, 8.23, 8.24, 8.38, 8.41, 8.51, 8.55, 8.56, 8.82, 8.90, 8.107, 8.116, 9.2, 9.4, 9.67, 9.78, 9.80, 16.100, 16.101
s 1 ... 8.12, 8.13
2 ... 1.20
(1) ... 8.57
(a), (b) ... 8.23
3 ... 7.37, 8.36, 8.49, 15.90, 15.102
(1), (3) ... 8.26
(7) ... 8.27
4 ... 8.15, 8.17
(3)–(6) ... 7.41
5 ... 8.31, 8.61
(1) ... 8.109
(2) ... 8.32, 8.36
6 ... 8.122
(1) ... 8.54, 8.117
(2), (4) ... 8.117
(5) ... 8.123, 8.125
(6) ... 8.118, 8.121
7 ... 8.113, 8.124
(3)–(8) ... 7.42
8 ... 8.33, 8.43, 8.50, 8.60, 8.65, 8.68, 8.72, 8.73, 8.74, 8.76, 8.77, 8.91, 8.93, 8.94, 8.100, 8.106
9 ... 8.57, 8.62
10(1) ... 8.69
(a) ... 8.74
(2) ... 8.69
(4) ... 8.73
11(3) ... 8.67, 8.72, 8.74, 8.76
(4) ... 8.72
(5) ... 8.72, 8.75
(6) ... 8.72
(8) ... 8.72
12(1) ... 8.74
(2)(a), (b) ... 8.75
(3) ... 8.75
13(5), (6) ... 8.77

PARA

Audit Commission Act 1998—*contd*
s 14 ... 8.57, 8.79, 8.84, 8.86, 8.113
(3) ... 8.85
15 ... 8.57, 8.113
(1) ... 8.57, 8.78, 8.86, 8.67, 8.89
(2) ... 8.57, 8.79, 8.87, 8.89
(3), (5) ... 8.43, 8.81
16 ... 8.57, 8.60, 8.65, 8.79, 8.101
(1) ... 8.57, 8.91, 8.92, 8.98
(a) ... 8.102, 9.40
17 ... 5.10, 8.33, 8.43, 8.46, 8.48, 8.60, 8.65, 8.91, 8.94, 8.100, 8.108, 9.10, 9.38, 9.39, 9.73, 15.90
(1) ... 9.7, 9.13, 9.40
(b) ... 9.5
(2) ... 9.6
(a) ... 9.3, 9.46
(b) ... 9.3
(c) ... 9.37
(3) ... 9.5
(4) ... 8.104, 9.40
18 ... 5.10, 8.33, 8.43, 8.44, 8.46, 8.60, 8.65, 8.91, 8.93, 8.94, 8.100, 8.101, 8.108, 9.3, 9.36, 9.55, 9.76, 9.79, 15.90
(1) ... 9.41
(a) ... 9.52
(2) ... 9.74
(3) ... 9.77
(5) ... 8.105
(7) ... 9.73
(8) ... 9.74
(9) ... 9.75
19A ... 9.95
19B ... 9.95
(1), (2) ... 9.96
(3)(d) ... 9.96
19C(1), (2) ... 9.95
20 ... 8.33, 9.3, 9.84, 9.85, 15.90, 15.102a
(1) ... 9.87, 9.95
(2)–(5) ... 9.87
(6) ... 9.91
(8) ... 9.87, 9.90

PARA

Audit Commission Act 1998—*contd*
s 21 .... 9.85, 9.89
22 .... 9.85, 15.90
(1) 9.90
(2) 9.90
(a) 9.87
22(3) 9.91, 9.92, 15.103
(4) 9.92
(5) 9.88
23 .... 1.45, 9.85
(1) 9.93
(2) 9.92, 9.94
24 .... 8.33, 8.65, 9.86, 9.98, 9.99, 9.100, 9.104
25 .... 8.87, 8.91
(1), (2) 8.110
(5) 8.113
27 .... 8.4, 8.31
33–35 .... 8.18
35A 8.18
36 .... 8.18
37 .... 8.18
(6) 8.40
38 .... 8.18
40 .... 8.18, 8.40
41(4) 8.40
44 .... 7.19, 7.32, 8.14, 8.19, 8.31
45 .... 8.14, 8.19
46 .... 7.19, 7.32, 8.14, 8.19
47 .... 8.14, 8.19
48(3) 8.17
49 .... 8.20, 8.42
(1) 8.40
(a) 8.42
(b) 8.43
(3) 8.39
53(1) 15.90
(2) 8.22, 8.82
54(1) 15.90
Sch 1 .... 8.13, 8.22
para 1, 2 .... 8.13
3 .... 8.36
Sch 2 .... 1.20, 8.21
Sch 3 .... 15.90
Banking Act 1987
s 39 .... 8.121
42 .... 8.121
Building Societies Act 1987
s 97 .... 10.24
Charities Act 1993 .... 20.11, 20.23
Civil Defence Act 1948
s 2 .... 15.44
Companies Act 1980
s 1 .... 16.26
Companies Act 1985 .... 12.50, 16.13, 16.14
s 152(2) 16.44
227 .... 16.59, 16.61
(6) 16.61
229(3)(a), (c) 16.59
248 .... 16.59

PARA

Companies Act 1985—*contd*
s 258 .... 16.53, 16.54
(2)(c) 16.55
(4)(a) 16.56, 16.62
262(1) 16.87
310(1) 16.112
(3) 16.111, 16.112
375 .... 16.92
736 .... 16.35
Sch 4
para 77 .... 16.44
Sch 10A 16.55
Deregulation and Contracting Out Act 1994 .... 7.10, 15.83
s 18 .... 1.43
19 .... 1.44
70 .... 1.43, 7.68, 15.115
Education Act 1944 .... 17.27
Education Act 1993
s 305 .... 16.17
Education Act 1986
s 1(1) 20.46
Education Act 1994
s 1, 2 .... 20.47
13 .... 20.47
Education Act 1996 .... 20.7
s 10, 11 .... 20.32
12 .... 20.28
13 .... 20.34
14 .... 20.8, 20.28
Pt II 20.1
s 31–33 .... 20.2
34 .... 20.4
60 .... 20.4
Pt III 20.1
s 183 .... 20.2
s 482 .... 20.49, 20.50
Pt VIII (ss 484–494) 20.36
s 484 .... 20.48, 20.51
485 .... 20.49, 20.51
486 .... 20.52
487 .... 20.53
488 .... 20.54
489 .... 20.46
490 .... 20.56
491 .... 20.57
493 .... 20.58
494 .... 20.59
579(1) 20.58
Education Act 1997
s 57(1) 20.58
Sch 7 .... 20.58
Education (No 2) Act 1986
s 50 .... 20.46, 20.47
Education (Schools) Act 1997 .... 20.57
Education Reform Act 1988 .... 1.6
s 74 .... 16.20
210 .... 20.54
211 .... 20.56
Employment and Training Act 1973
s 8, 9 .... 16.17

PARA

Environment Act 1995
s 48 .... 12.54
76 .... 12.54
(3) 12.99
Environmental Protection Act 1990
s 32 .... 4.22, 14.30
(2) 16.12
(9) 16.12, 16.38
Sch 2
para 1 .... 16.12
Finance Act 1990 .... 13.42
Fire Services Act 1947 .... 10.8, 12.54, 12.87, 18.22
Further Education Act 1985
s 2 .... 3.61, 16.4
(2)(c) 16.15
(8) 16.15
3(4), (5) 3.61
28 .... 20.49
Government of Wales Act 1998 .... 1.65
Greater London Authority Act 1999 .... 1.68
s 34(1) 15.95
82 .... 1.17
133 .... 8.14
325 .... 15.82
405 .... 17.51
409(2) 14.11, 14.30
Sch 8 .... 8.14
Sch 10
para 1(3) 15.95
Sch 27
para 116 .... 15.82
Sch 34
Pt VII 15.82
Health Act 1999
s 26–30 .... 1.33
31 .... 1.33, 7.69
32 .... 1.33
Highways Act 1980 .... 18.61
s 97 .... 12.111
214(1) 3.69
270 .... 12.111
Housing Act 1985
s 1–2 .... 19.3
9 .... 16.20
10, 11 .... 19.11
32, 43 .... 14.31, 14.55
56 .... 14.27
Pt II 14.30, 14.34, 19.3, 19.4
s 99A, 99B 19.20
100 .... 19.20
115 .... 19.6
164 .... 1.14
183 .... 14.55
192 .... 19.4
421(1) 19.42
422–427 .... 19.42
622 .... 14.27
Pt IV 12.56, 12.92
Pt V 14.30, 14.34, 14.58
Pt XIII 19.1
Sch 6A 14.12, 14.27, 14.30

PARA

Housing Act 1988
s 100 .... 12.53
Housing Act 1996
s 22 .... 16.4
56 .... 8.40
s 140D(2) 19.14
Pt VII (ss 175–218) 12.92
Sch 18
para 4(1) 19.8
Housing Associations Act 1985 .... 7.43
s 58 .... 16.4, 16.20
(4) 16.11
Housing (Rural Workers) Act 1926 .... 19.4
Human Rights Act 1998 .... 6.35, 8.47
Income and Corporation Taxes Act 1988
s 591(1) 3.28
(2)(h) 3.28
Industrial and Provident Societies Act 1965 .... 16.25, 16.51
Insolvency Act 1986
s 214 .... 16.110, 16.113
(3) 16.107
(7) 16.113
251 .... 16.114
Justices of the Peace Act 1997
s 39 .... 8.18
Land Compensation Act 1973
s 42 .... 19.13
Landlord and Tenant Act 1954
Pt II 20.23
s 24 .... 12.71, 12.102, 12.127, 12.133
Leasehold Reform Housing and Urban Development Act 1993
s 122 .... 19.20
127 .... 19.9
136 .... 11.40
Local Authorities (Goods and Services) Act 1970 .... 3.43, 3.47, 3.49, 3.60, 4.10, 7.69, 18.24
s 1 .... 3.60
(4) 3.49, 4.10
(5) 4.10
2(2) 3.60
Local Authorities (Land) Act 1963
s 2, 3 .... 17.4
Local Authority Social Services Act 1970 .... 15.44
s 2 .... 4.22
Sch 1 .... 1.10
Local Government (Access to Information) Act 1985 .... 6.2
s 1 .... 6.2
Local Government (County Boroughs and Adjustments) Act 1926 .... 1.2
Local Government (Contracts) Act 1997 .... 15.113, 15.116
s 1 .... 15.13, 15.81, 15.88, 15.115
(1) 15.84, 15.87
(2) 15.86, 15.87, 15.95
(3) 15.82, 15.83
(4), (5) 15.85
2 .... 15.83, 15.88, 15.89, 15.92
(1) 15.106, 15.107

PARA

Local Government (Contracts) Act 1997—*contd*
s 2(2) 15.101
(3) 15.93
(4) 15.104
(5) 15.93, 15.101
(6), (7) 15.107
3 . . . . . 15.83, 15.88, 15.89, 15.92, 15.94, 15.95
(1) 15.101
(c) 15.88
(2) 15.92, 15.95
(e), (f) 15.94, 15.95
(g) 15.95
(3) 15.94, 15.97
(4) 15.99
4 . . . . . 15.83, 15.88, 15.89, 15.92
(1) 15.92, 15.100, 15.101
(2) 15.105
(3), (4) 15.88, 15.95
(5) 15.88
5 . . . . . 15.83, 15.88, 15.89, 15.90
(1), (2) 15.107
(3) 15.114
(4) 15.90
6 . . . . . 15.83, 15.88, 15.89, 15.90
(1) 15.111
(2)(a), (b) 15.110
(3) 15.109
(4) 15.112
7 . . . . . 15.83, 15.88, 15.89, 15.90
(1) 15.112
(3) 15.111, 15.112
8 . . . . . 15.83, 15.88, 15.89, 15.90
(2) 15.103
9 . . . . . 15.83, 15.88, 15.89
(3)(c) 15.115
12(2) 15.82
(3) 15.82, 15.93, 15.101
Local Government (Miscellaneous Provisions) Act 1976
s 11 . . . . . 3.68
12(4) 3.68
19 . . . . . 16.5, 16.20, 16.21
39 . . . . . 16.110
Local Government (Miscellaneous Provisions) Act 1982 . . . . . 1.10
s 2 . . . . . 4.17
Sch 3 . . . . . 4.17
Local Government (Scotland) Act 1973 . . 15.90
Pt II (ss 21–32) 5.18
s 83 . . . . . 17.4
235(1) 15.82
Local Government (Wales) Act 1994: 1.15, 10.8, 12.54, 12.97
s 5 . . . . . 1.15
17–26 . . . . . 1.15
38(1)–(4) 3.2, 3.5
(5) 3.2
(7)–(10) 3.2
Pt V (ss 39–45) 1.15
s 39 . . . . . 12.53

PARA

Local Government Act 1888 . . . . . 1.1
Local Government Act 1894 . . . . . 1.1
Local Government Act 1929 . . . . . 2.1
Local Government Act 1933 . . . . . 1.1, 8.54
Local Government Act 1948
s 136 . . . . . 4.45
Local Government Act 1958 . . . . . 1.2
Local Government Act 1963 . . . . . 1.4, 11.37
s 23(3) 14.12
84 . . . . . 14.12
Sch 1 . . . . . 1.3
Local Government Act 1966 . . . . . 2.1
Local Government Act 1972 . . . 1.4, 1.10, 1.14, 4.30, 6.3, 8.11, 8.25, 8.54, 8.57, 9.37, 9.60, 10.8, 11.37
s 2 . . . . . 1.8
10(4), (5) 8.73
13 . . . . . 1.8
20(4) 1.3
33 . . . . . 1.8, 17.34
51(2) 14.12
58(1)(b) 16.17
(2) 14.12
59(3) 16.17
67(1), (2), (4) 14.12
80, 81 . . . . . 16.66, 16.92
83 . . . . . 6.24
94 . . . . . 6.8, 6.9
(1) 6.9
(5) 6.11
95 . . . . . 6.8
96 . . . . . 6.9
97(4)–(6) 6.8
98 . . . . . 6.8
(1A) 6.8
100 . . . . . 6.2
100F 6.2
101 . . . . . 15.115, 16.20
(6) 13.30
(9), (10) 4.22
111 . . . . . 1.67, 4.10, 4.27, 4.28, 9.19, 9.76, 10.21, 13.39, 15.87, 15.95, 16.4, 16.5, 16.19, 16.21, 16.117, 17.15
(1) 15.84, 16.20
(2) 4.32
(3) 4.31, 4.32
112 . . . . . 9.20, 16.111
114(1), (2) 5.14
115 . . . . . 5.14
123 . . . . . 14.31, 14.39, 14.40, 14.58, 16.20, 17.14, 17.20
(2) 14.41
(7) 17.20
127 . . . . . 3.38
135(4) 9.21
137 . . . . . 4.34, 4.35, 4.36, 4.39, 4.43, 16.5, 17.2, 17.4, 17.6, 17.34
(1) 4.38, 4.40
(2) 4.44, 4.48

PARA
Local Government Act 1972—*contd*
s 137(2A–2C) 17.34
(2D) 17.34
(3) 4.45, 4.48
(4) 4.46
(7) 3.67
137A 4.48, 17.34
139 .... 3.38
144 .... 16.5, 16.21, 17.4
145 .... 16.4, 16.17, 17.4
148 .... 3.7
(5A), (5B) 3.8
151 .... 1.23, 5.1, 5.3, 5.7, 5.8, 8.4, 8.9, 10.21, 15.97
173 .... 6.5
(1) 6.5, 6.6
(2) 6.5
(3) 6.5
(4) 6.5, 6.6
(6) 6.5
173A 6.5
174 .... 6.5, 6.6
175 .... 6.5, 6.6
176 .... 6.5, 6.7
177(1) 6.5
178 .... 6.5
Pt IX (ss 179–215) 1.10
s 179(4) 1.10
228 .... 6.4
245(10) 1.2
254 .... 14.13
270 .... 5.2, 8.22
(1) 8.82
Sch 1 .... 1.3
Pt V 1.3
Sch 4
Pt I 1.3
Sch 12A
Pt I 6.2
Sch 13 .... 10.5, 13.40
para 11(1)–(3) 13.19
15 .... 11.36
16 .... 14.11
21 .... 13.19
Sch 17 .... 10.8
Local Government Act 1974
Pt III (ss 23–34) 5.18
s 26(8) 5.18
Sch 5
para 4 .... 5.18
Local Government Act 1985 .... 1.8, 11.37, 11.56
s 10 .... 3.46, 10.8
Pt III (ss 18–22) 1.4, 3.4
Pt IV (ss 23–42) 1.4, 3.4, 3.45, 3.63, 10.8
s 58–63 .... 1.4
66 .... 3.23
(1) 14.12
67 .... 3.23
(3) 5.5, 14.12

PARA
Local Government Act 1985—*contd*
s 72(1) 3.4
73 .... 5.3, 15.97
85 .... 1.4, 2.6
105(1) 5.3
Sch 14
para 13 .... 6.8
18–20 .... 6.5
24 .... 6.4
Sch 17 .... 6.5
Local Government Act 1986
s 2 .... 16.66
5(1) 3.64
(2), (3) 3.66
(5) 3.65
6(2), (3) 3.63
(4) 3.62
Local Government Act 1988 .... 3.44
Pt I (ss 1–16) 1.42, 7.7, 9.21
s 3(2)–(4) 3.44
9 .... 3.58
(1)–(4) 3.55
10 .... 3.57
11(2)(a) 3.57
(3) 3.57
(7) 3.57
13, 14 .... 3.58
Pt II 7.73
s 17 .... 1.44, 7.73, 15.108
(1) 15.107
19 .... 7.73
30 .... 9.86
32 .... 1.42
33 .... 16.18
Pt VIII (ss 111–116) 5.6
s 111(1) 5.6
112 .... 5.4
113(3) 5.9, 5.13
114 .... 5.15
(2)(a)–(c) 5.11
(3), (3a) 5.12
(4)–(6) 5.13
115(2), (3) 5.14
(5)–(8) 5.14
116(1), (2) 5.14
Sch 6 .... 1.42
Local Government Act 1992 .... 1.7, 1.9, 1.17, 8.14, 12.54
s 2–3 .... 1.16
5 .... 1.22
8–11 .... 1.42, 7.7
Pt II 12.97
s 12 .... 1.7
13 .... 1.7, 2.8
14 .... 1.7
17 .... 3.8
40 .... 1.17
41 .... 1.17
66(1) 1.17
91(8) 3.8
101 .... 4.22

PARA

Local Government Act 1992—*contd*
s 245A ... 1.15
594 ... 4.22
Sch 1 ... 1.42
Local Government Act 1999 ... 1.39, 7.3, 7.29, 7.58, 7.63
Pt I (ss 1–29) ... 1.36, 1.40, 3.43, 7.1, 7.4, 7.6, 7.7, 7.12, 7.14, 7.17, 7.53, 7.54, 7.56, 7.64, 7.65, 7.72, 7.74, 7.80, 9.21, 16.18
s 1 ... 8.18
(1) ... 7.77
(a) ... 7.12
(b)–(j) ... 7.12
(2), (3) ... 7.12
2(2)–(3) ... 7.13
(4) ... 7.12, 7.13
(5) ... 7.14
3 ... 1.41, 7.8, 7.12, 7.14, 9.21, 16.118
(1) ... 7.15, 7.16, 7.17
(2), (4) ... 7.17
4 ... 7.8, 7.14, 7.20, 7.21
(3) ... 7.19
(4) ... 7.19
(5) ... 7.18
5 ... 7.8, 7.14, 7.32, 7.33
(2)(c) ... 7.24
(3)(a) ... 7.23
(4) ... 7.26
(6)(b) ... 7.22
(7) ... 7.22
6 ... 7.14, 7.19, 7.38
(1) ... 7.37
(2) ... 7.32, 7.37
(3) ... 7.8, 7.32
(4) ... 7.37, 7.79
(5)–(7) ... 7.37
7 ... 8.64, 9.21
(1)–(2) ... 7.37
(3) ... 7.37
(4) ... 7.38
(e) ... 7.47
(f) ... 7.61
(5) ... 7.39
(6) ... 7.8, 7.39
(7)–(9) ... 7.37
8 ... 7.8, 7.37, 8.16
(2) ... 7.8, 7.41, 7.42, 7.41
(3) ... 7.41
(4)–(6) ... 7.42
9 ... 7.8
(1) ... 7.39
(2) ... 7.61
(3) ... 7.34, 7.40
(4) ... 7.40
(5) ... 7.34, 7.40
(6) ... 7.40
10 ... 7.8, 7.38, 7.44, 7.49, 7.51, 8.34, 9.21
(1), (2) ... 7.45

PARA

Local Government Act 1999—*contd*
s 10(3) ... 7.46
(4) ... 7.47
(b) ... 7.79
(5) ... 7.50
11(1)(a) ... 7.49
(3) ... 7.50
(4) ... 7.50
(7) ... 7.49
12 ... 7.52
13(2)(b) ... 7.51, 7.60
(4) ... 7.51
(5) ... 7.34, 7.51
14 ... 7.53
15 ... 7.8, 7.38, 7.39, 7.60, 8.34, 9.21
(2)–(5 ... 7.57
(6)(a) ... 7.57
(7) ... 1.41, 7.57, 7.59, 7.64
(8) ... 1.41, 7.57, 7.64
(9) ... 7.62
(10) ... 7.40, 7.61, 7.62
(11), (12) ... 7.62
(13) ... 7.56
16 ... 1.41, 1.55, 7.11, 7.64, 7.69, 7.72, 16.118, 17.51
(1) ... 7.65
(2) ... 7.66, 7.67, 7.70
(4) ... 7.71
(5) ... 7.67
17 ... 7.11, 7.69, 7.71, 7.72
(1) ... 9.22
(b) ... 9.23
(2) ... 9.27, 9.28
(a) ... 9.29, 9.30, 9.31
(b) ... 9.29, 9.34
(3) ... 9.29, 9.35
18 ... 7.11, 7.68, 7.69, 7.72, 9.35
(1) ... 9.34
(a) ... 9.23
(7) ... 9.34
19 ... 1.44, 7.73, 15.108
20 ... 7.77
21 ... 1.42, 7.8
(2) ... 7.75
22 ... 1.45, 7.43
(7) ... 7.43
23 ... 1.45, 7.76
24(2), (3) ... 7.54
25(1) ... 7.48, 7.55
(2) ... 7.48, 7.55, 7.78
26 ... 7.78, 7.79
(4) ... 7.78
27 ... 1.47
29(2)(a) ... 7.11
(b) ... 7.10, 7.72
(3) ... 7.10
(4) ... 7.59
Pt II (ss 30–31) ... 1.24, 1.46, 10.26
s 34 ... 7.8, 7.75
Sch 2 ... 7.75

PARA

Local Government Act 2000 . . . 1.36, 1.48, 1.52, 1.53, 1.54, 1.55, 1.57, 8.34, 8.101, 8.105, 9.35, 9.79, 9.81, 9.97, 9.100, 9.105, 16.1, 16.5, 16.9
Pt I (ss 1–9) . . . 1.49, 17.3, 17.45, 17.53
s 2 . . . 17.6, 17.53
(1) . . . 17.46, 17.49, 17.50, 17.51
(2), (3) . . . 17.46
(4) . . . 1.49, 17.47
(d), (e) . . . 17.47
(5) . . . 17.46
(6) . . . 17.47
3 . . . 1.49
(1) . . . 17.49, 17.53
(3) . . . 17.48
(7) . . . 17.49
4(5) . . . 17.50
5 . . . 1.55, 7.70 , 16.119, 17.51
(5) . . . 17.51
6(1) . . . 1.55
(6) . . . 17.51
8 . . . 4.34, 16.5, 17.6
Pt II (ss 10–48) . . . 1.48, 1.50, 4.22, 8.9
s 11 . . . 1.51
18 . . . 9.26
Pt III (ss 49–83) . . . 1.56, 9.81
s 49 . . . 9.81
(1), (2) . . . 6.21
(3)–(5) . . . 6.22
(6) . . . 6.23, 6.24
50 . . . 6.21, 9.81
51(1) . . . 6.23
52 . . . 6.24
53 . . . 6.25, 6.26
54(2) . . . 9.81
(4)–(7) . . . 6.27
57 . . . 6.28, 9.81
58 . . . 6.30, 9.81
59 . . . 6.31, 9.81
60 . . . 6.32
61 . . . 6.33
62(10) . . . 6.34, 6.42, 9.82
63 . . . 6.35
(4) . . . 6.36, 9.82
64 . . . 6.37, 9.81
(2)–(3) . . . 6.38
65 . . . 6.39, 9.81
66(2) . . . 9.81
68–74 . . . 6.28, 9.81
75 . . . 6.40
(1) . . . 9.81
76 . . . 6.41, 9.81
77(7) . . . 6.42
78 . . . 6.39
(1)(b) . . . 9.81
(4) . . . 9.81
(10) . . . 9.81
79 . . . 6.43, 9.81
(15) . . . 9.81
82 . . . 5.27, 9.81

PARA

Local Government Act 2000—*contd*
90 . . . 8.104, 9.3, 9.5, 15.90
(2) . . . 8.91
(a) . . . 9.26
(b) . . . 9.29, 9.40
(c) . . . 9.29
(3) . . . 9.26, 9.80
91 . . . 9.3, 15.90
(1) . . . 9.95
(2) . . . 9.85, 15.102
99–100 . . . 6.3
105(5) . . . 6.21
107 . . . 8.91, 8.104, 9.3, 9.5, 17.51
108(1), (2) . . . 17.45
(3) . . . 9.5, 17.45
(a) . . . 9.3, 9.91
(4) . . . 9.81, 17.45
(5)(d) . . . 9.81, 17.45
(6)(b) . . . 9.81, 17.45
Sch 4 . . . 9.81
Sch 5 . . . 17.52
para 28 . . . 9.81
Sch 6 . . . 8.91, 8.104, 9.3, 9.5
Local Government and Housing Act 1989 . . . 3.1, 4.48, 10.28, 11.27, 14.49, 16.28, 16.50
s 1(1) . . . 5.9
2(6), (7) . . . 15.97
4(1) . . . 15.97
(b) . . . 5.22
(2) . . . 5.23
(3) . . . 5.23
(d) . . . 5.18
(4), (5) . . . 5.24
5 . . . 1.23, 5.20, 8.9, 8.76, 9.81, 9.96
(1) . . . 5.1, 5.17, 15.95
(2) . . . 5.18
(3)(a) . . . 5.18
(d) . . . 5.19
(4) . . . 5.19
(5)(a), (b) . . . 5.21
(6) . . . 5.21
6 . . . 15.97
(1) . . . 5.5
7(1) . . . 5.9
(2)(e) . . . 5.9
15 . . . 1.52
18 . . . 6.3
19(4)(a) . . . 6.9
(5) . . . 6.9
21 . . . 6.6
31 . . . 6.13
Pt III (ss 33–38) . . . 3.71, 8.71, 16.9, 17.5, 17.6, 17.41, 17.45
s 33 . . . 4.3, 14.60, 17.6, 17.7, 17.8, 17.9, 17.12, 17.15, 17.15, 17.32, 17.38, 17.52
(2) . . . 16.9, 17.12
(3) . . . 17.14, 17.48
(a) . . . 17.22

PARA

Local Government and Housing Act 1989—*contd*
s 33(3)(b) . . . 3.71, 17.22
(c) . . . 17.22
(e) . . . 13.3, 16.9
(f) . . . 17.8, 17.14
(4) . . . 17.8
34 . . . 17.3, 17.6, 17.52
(1) . . . 17.8, 17.16, 17.18, 17.21, 17.26
(2) . . . 17.8
(5) . . . 17.8
35 . . . 17.3, 17.32, 17.50, 17.52
(1) . . . 17.29
(2) . . . 17.30, 17.31
(3) . . . 17.26, 17.31
(4) . . . 17.30, 17.31
36 . . . 17.6
(4) . . . 4.46, 17.34
Pt IV (ss 39–66) . . . 2.10, 8.57, 10.4, 10.5, 10.7, 10.8, 10.9, 11.29, 11.45, 11.61, 12.2, 12.43, 12.51, 12.78, 13.13, 14.1, 14.2, 14.3, 14.40, 15.13, 16.16, 16.17, 16.69, 16.72, 16.76, 16.78, 16.102, 17.37
s 39(1), (3) . . . 10.8
(5)–(7) . . . 16.22
40 . . . 10.14, 14.6, 14.8
(2) . . . 10.16, 19.43
(b) . . . 11.58
(3) . . . 19.20, 19.43
(4) . . . 10.16, 10.22
(5) . . . 10.19, 10.20, 12.40
(6) . . . 10.19, 10.20, 11.15
41 . . . 19.43
42 . . . 10.13, 19.43
(2) . . . 10.14
(b) . . . 13.3
(c) . . . 11.1, 13.5
(d) . . . 10.22
(f) . . . 14.18
(g) . . . 10.37, 14.18
(h), (i) . . . 11.32
43 . . . 13.24
(1) . . . 13.2
(2) . . . 10.7, 13.7, 13.8, 13.11
(a), (b) . . . 13.16
(3) . . . 10.7, 13.10, 13.11
(4) . . . 13.11, 13.14
(5) . . . 13.11, 13.14, 13.15
43(6), (7) . . . 13.11
44 . . . 12.79, 13.24
(1) . . . 11.30, 11.31, 13.22, 13.23, 13.24
(2) . . . 13.22, 13.25
(3) . . . 11.28, 13.22, 13.28, 13.36
(4), (5) . . . 13.24
(6) . . . 12.137, 13.21
45 . . . 13.26, 13.28, 13.37

PARA

Local Government and Housing Act 1989—*contd*
s 45(1) . . . 13.30
(b) . . . 13.36
(c) . . . 13.6
(3) . . . 11.28, 13.29, 13.30
(4) . . . 13.30
(5) . . . 13.30
(6) . . . 13.27
46(1) . . . 13.15
(3) . . . 13.16
(9) . . . 13.16, 13.17
47(1)–(3) . . . 13.19
(7) . . . 13.18
48 . . . 10.14, 12.22, 12.54, 12.113, 16.71
(1) . . . 12.4, 12.21, 12.37
(a) . . . 12.11, 12.12, 12.13. 12.14, 12.15, 12.31, 12.35, 12.39, 12.42, 12.44, 12.44, 12.73, 12.83, 12.126, 12.135
(b) . . . 12.11, 12.13, 12.13, 12.16, 12.19, 12.21, 12.23, 12.26, 12.28, 12.29, 12.31, 12.35, 12.39, 12.42, 12.56, 12.73, 12.74, 12.76, 12.83, 12.108, 12.135, 15.25, 17.37
(c) . . . 10.35, 12.4, 12.11, 12.29, 12.30, 12.31, 12.32, 12.39, 12.41, 12.42, 12.73, 12.74, 12.76, 12.84, 12.135, 15.25, 15.26
(2) . . . 12.17, 12.19
(3) . . . 12.5, 12.19, 12.43, 12.74, 12.78, 12.135
(b) . . . 12.15
(c) . . . 12.41
(4) . . . 12.20, 12.113
(5) . . . 12.6, 12.47, 12.48, 12.86
(6) . . . 12.24
(7) . . . 12.23, 12.75, 12.114
(8) . . . 12.19, 12.20
49 . . . 11.30, 12.61, 12.73, 12.75, 12.80, 12.113, 15.70
(1) . . . 12.11, 12.74, 15.32
(2) . . . 11.58, 12.11, 12.60, 12.62, 12.65, 12.74, 12.76, 12.87, 12.101, 12.107, 12.117, 12.118, 12.124, 12.125, 12.129, 12.133, 15.32, 15.35, 15.40
49(3) . . . 12.60, 12.74, 12.76, 12.117, 12.124, 12.125
(4) . . . 12.11, 12.79, 12.124
(5) . . . 12.23, 12.114, 12.114
(b) . . . 12.75
50 . . . 12.3, 12.7, 12.80, 12.115, 12.134
(1) . . . 12.17, 12.40, 12.135, 13.5, 15.26

PARA

Local Government and Housing Act 1989—*contd*

s 50(2) ... 11.5, 12.11, 12.89, 12.135, 12.136, 12.137
(3) ... 12.9, 12.120, 12.135, 12.136, 12.137
(b) ... 11.39, 11.41, 11.42, 11.60
(c) ... 11.5, 11.39, 11.41, 11.60
(4) ... 11.31, 12.135
(5) ... 11.5, 12.120, 12.136
(6) ... 12.138
51 ... 12.15, 12.20, 12.26, 12.80, 12.113, 12.126, 12.134, 15.39
(1) ... 12.105, 12.112, 12.121, 12.124, 15.38, 15.41, 16.71
(2) ... 12.114, 12.122, 15.38
(3) ... 11.31, 12.121, 12.122, 12.135, 15.41
(4) ... 11.60, 12.11, 12.115, 12.120, 12.122, 15.41, 16.76
(a) ... 15.41
(b) ... 12.123
(5) ... 12.11, 12.116, 12.117, 12.125, 15.40
(6) ... 12.116, 12.117, 12.118, 12.125, 15.40
(7) ... 12.117, 12.125, 15.40
(8) ... 12.11, 12.124
(9) ... 12.123
(10) ... 12.105, 12.112, 12.124
52 ... 11.37, 12.44, 12.134
(1) ... 12.42, 12.138
(2) ... 12.44
(3) ... 12.11, 12.42
(a) ... 12.80
(b) ... 12.11, 12.80, 12.138
53 ... 2.10, 10.14, 11.12, 12.9, 16.79, 16.80, 19.44
(1) ... 10.7
(4), (5) ... 11.13
54 ... 10.14, 10.37, 10.39, 11.14, 12.9, 15.60, 15.69, 16.79
(1) ... 10.7
(2) ... 11.11
(5) ... 11.15, 11.54
55 ... 2.10, 11.17, 11.20
(2)(a), (b) ... 11.18
(3), (4) ... 11.19
56 ... 2.10, 12.9
(1) ... 11.5, 11.6, 13.6
(a) ... 10.14, 11.1, 11.40
(b) ... 11.1, 11.40, 11.42
(2) ... 11.8
(3) ... 11.7
(a) ... 11.5
57(1) ... 11.9
(2) ... 11.6
(4)–(6) ... 11.7
58(1) ... 14.5, 14.14
(a) ... 14.6, 14.10, 14.12, 14.23
(b) ... 10.22, 14.7, 14.10, 14.20, 14.60

PARA

Local Government and Housing Act 1989—*contd*

s 58(1)(c) ... 14.8, 14.23, 17.36
(d) ... 14.9, 17.36
(2) ... 14.21
(4)–(6) ... 14.11
(7) ... 14.22
(8) ... 14.19, 14.49, 14.53
(9) ... 14.4
(b) ... 14.18, 14.23, 14.45
59 ... 3.38, 11.19, 14.23, 14.30, 14.44, 14.51, 14.57, 16.76
(1) ... 11.41, 11.47, 11.60, 14.3, 14.24
(2) ... 14.25, 14.31
(a), (b) ... 14.27
(3) ... 14.25, 14.26, 14.31, 14.45
(4) ... 14.45, 14.48
(6) ... 14.25, 14.31, 14.36, 14.45
(7) ... 10.14, 11.20, 14.24, 14.32
(8) ... 10.14, 11.20, 14.24, 14.33
(9) ... 10.14, 11.20, 14.24, 14.34
60 ... 14.42
(2) ... 10.14, 11.61, 12.9, 12.120, 14.43
(a) ... 12.40, 15.26
(b) ... 11.41, 12.136
61 ... 11.19, 14.13, 14.14, 14.21, 14.44, 14.56, 14.59, 15.57
(1) ... 14.15
(a)–(c) ... 14.14, 14.16
(2) ... 14.15, 14.40
(3) ... 14.15
(4) ... 11.41, 11.47, 11.60, 14.30, 14.35, 14.36, 14.45, 14.45, 14.57, 15.58, 16.76
(5) ... 14.37
62 ... 11.29, 11.32, 12.135, 15.41
(1)(a), (b) ... 13.36
(2) ... 11.36
(3), (4) ... 11.32, 13.33
(5) ... 10.37, 10.39, 11.32, 13.34
(6) ... 11.32
63(1) ... 10.30, 11.41, 11.42, 11.47, 11.50, 11.60
(2), (3) ... 11.9, 11.41, 11.60
(4) ... 10.37, 10.39, 11.41, 11.60, 16.71, 16.76
64(1)(a)–(b) ... 11.42, 11.62
(c) ... 11.42, 11.62, 13.12, 13.47
(2) ... 10.30, 11.40, 11.63
(a) ... 11.40, 11.63
(b) ... 11.63, 11.66
(3) ... 11.67
(4) ... 11.63
66(1)(a) ... 10.14, 10.23, 13.35, 14.20
(b) ... 16.76
(3)(a) ... 12.27, 12.66, 12.78
(4) ... 8.31, 8.57, 15.36
(b) ... 3.43
(5) ... 8.31, 8.57

PARA

Local Government and Housing Act 1989—*contd*
s 66(7) 13.24
Pt V (ss 67–73) 4.3, 15.15, 16.2, 16.19, 16.24, 16.26, 16.31, 16.116
s 67 16.2, 16.7
(1), (2) 16.24
(4) 16.22
68 16.2, 16.7, 16.39, 16.47
(1) 16.29, 16.39, 16.49
(5) 16.48
(6) 16.12, 16.32, 16.37
69 16.2, 16.7, 16.32, 16.33
(1) 16.29, 16.39, 16.42, 16.45, 16.49
(a) 16.43, 16.96
(3) 16.36, 16.45, 16.49, 16.96
(4) 16.36, 16.44
(5) 16.36, 16.40
70 16.2, 16.7
(1) 16.22, 16.31, 16.100
(2) 16.100
(a) 16.38
(5) 16.22
71 16.31, 16.49
(1) 16.32, 16.47
(b) 16.22
(2) 16.2, 16.7, 16.47
(3) 16.2, 16.47
(4) 16.47, 16.92
(5)(a) 16.47, 16.92
(b) 16.2, 16.47
(6) 16.47, 16.92
(7) 16.2, 16.47
(8) 16.47
72 16.2, 16.27
73 16.2, 16.34, 16.65, 16.94
(1) 16.95
(2) 16.96
(3) 16.96, 19.5
Pt VI (ss 74–80) 19.1, 19.2
s 74 14.27, 14.30, 15.23, 15.24, 19.3
(1) 12.93, 19.3, 19.4
(2) 19.4
(4) 19.6
(5)(b) 19.6
75 19.9
76 4.3
(2) 19.30
(3)–(9) 19.31
77(1)–(5) 19.7
78A–B 19.8
79 19.32
80 19.33
(2) 19.24
87 19.33
88 19.33
(1) 19.3
157 11.9, 11.41, 11.42, 11.60

PARA

Local Government and Housing Act 1989—*contd*
s 157(1)(b) 11.41
(7)(b) 11.40
190 17.8
191(1) 17.8
Sch 2 4.34
Sch 3
para 2 11.7
8 11.37
9 11.37
(1)(b) 11.39
11 11.30, 11.49
(1) 11.40
(2) 10.35, 11.39, 11.42, 11.45, 12.45, 12.46, 15.60
12(1) 11.41
(2) 11.39
(a) 11.41, 11.42, 12.46
(c) 11.42
13 11.40
14(1) 11.41
(2) 11.40
Pt IV 11.47, 11.50,
para 15(1)(b) 11.39, 12.46
(2) 10.30, 11.48
18 11.43
19 11.58
Sch 4 19.1, 19.9
Pt I 19.10
Pt II 19.20
Pt III 19.29
para 2 19.19
3, 3A 19.19
4–7 19.19
Sch 11 6.5
para 28(1)–(3) 6.6
Sch 12 6.5
Local Government Finance Act 1982: 8.25, 8.52, 8.53, 17.33
s 11 8.12
12(1) 3.40
15(3) 1.22, 8.51
19 9.10
23 3.61, 3.66, 3.72, 8.4
24 3.67, 9.105
30 8.115
90(2) 1.17
Pt III 16.66
Local Government Finance Act 1988: 2.1, 2.7, 2.11, 2.23, 2.27, 2.30
s 12A 2.5
41 2.31
42 2.31
43 2.21, 2.26
(3) 2.30
45 2.21, 2.26, 2.28
(5) 2.30
49 2.29
47 2.26

PARA

Local Government Finance Act 1988—
contd
s 51 ..... 2.22, 2.25, 2.27
53 ..... 2.31
55 ..... 2.31
56 ..... 2.30
59(4) 3.1
61 ..... 2.31
64(4), (8) 2.21
74 ..... 1.18
75 ..... 1.18
Pt V (ss 76–88B) 2.2, 20.36
s 78A 2.2, 11.27
82(2) 2.6
83(2) 2.6
84A(1), (2) 2.6
85(1) 2.6
87 ..... 2.8
88(3) 2.8
88A(1) 2.8
88B 1.65, 2.9, 11.16, 15.64
89(1) 3.9
(3) 3.9
(4) 3.17
(5) 3.17, 10.21, 13.3
90(1) 1.17, 3.10
(2) 3.18
91(1), (2) 3.3
(4) 3.3
(5) 3.4
(8) 3.8
92 ..... 3.3
93(1) 3.6
94 ..... 3.6
97 ..... 3.14
(1) 3.3, 3.11, 3.18
(2) 3.11, 3.16
(3) 3.3, 3.11, 3.18
(4) 3.11
98(4) 3.18
(5) 3.12, 3.17
99(3) 3.10, 3.18
(6) 3.12
112 ..... 15.97
114 ..... 5.1, 8.76, 9.89, 9.96
(2), (3) 1.23
(7) 5.17
115 ..... 1.23, 5.1
(5), (6) 9.89
118 ..... 1.18
136 ..... 2.32
144(2) 3.9
Sch 5 ..... 2.22, 2.25, 2.27
Sch 6 ..... 2.30
Sch 9
para 5–7 ..... 2.31
Sch 22 ..... 2.32
Local Government Finance Act 1992: 1.16, 3.18
Pt I (ss 1–69) 10.26
s 1 ..... 2.12
(2) 3.3
3 ..... 2.12

PARA

Local Government Finance Act 1992—
contd
Ch IVA, V 1.46
s 4 ..... 2.12
5 ..... 2.13
(1) 2.17
(2) 1.16
6 ..... 1.16, 2.14
(6) 2.14
11 ..... 1.16, 2.14
14 ..... 2.18
15 ..... 2.32
16 ..... 2.19
20 ..... 2.13
24 ..... 2.13
26 ..... 2.13
27(4)–(5) 2.13
(7) 2.13
30 ..... 1.26
32 ..... 2.12
33 ..... 2.17
(2) 2.12
34, 35 ..... 2.17
38(2), (3) 2.18
(8), (9) 3.5
40 ..... 2.17
41 ..... 2.17
44 ..... 2.17
45, 46 ..... 2.17
106 ..... 6.13
Sch 1 ..... 2.16
Sch 2, 4 ..... 2.18
Sch 10 ..... 2.9
Sch 13
para 32 ..... 6.9
Local Government Finance (Supplementary Credit Approvals) Act 1997 ..... 11.20
s 1 ..... 11.19
2 ..... 11.15
Local Government, Planning and Land Act 1980 ..... 3.45, 3.59, 10.9, 10.24, 11.37, 14.48
s 2 ..... 7.77
Pt III (ss 5–23) 1.42, 7.7
s 5 ..... 3.43
8 ..... 3.43
9(2) 3.51
10 ..... 3.54
(1) 3.45, 3.46
(ii) 3.46
(3) 3.48
(6) 3.49
11(1), (2) 3.50
12 ..... 3.54
(1) 3.51
13 ..... 3.54
(1) 3.52
(2)(b) 3.52
(4) 3.52
(5) 3.52
16 ..... 3.52
18 ..... 3.53

PARA
Local Government, Planning and Land Act 1980—*contd*
s 19A, 19B 3.55
20(1) 3.45
(2)–(4) 3.49
24 .... 6.5
25 .... 6.5
(1), (2) 6.6
(3) 6.6
26 .... 6.5
80(11), (12) 12.44
80A(1) 12.44
(7) 12.44
135 .... 3.46
Pt VIII 9.104, 10.5
Sch 12
para 4 .... 12.44
Sch 34 .... 6.6
Lotteries and Amusements Act 1976 .... 3.38
Miscellaneous Financial Provisions Act 1983
s 7 .... 6.5
National Health Service Act 1977
s 28A(1) 20.36
(2)(c) 20.36
National Health Service and Community Care Act 1990
s 20 .... 8.14
National Health Service (Private Finance) Act 1997 .... 15.81
National Loans Act 1968 .... 13.42
s 4 .... 13.44
Sch 4
para 1 .... 13.43
New Towns Act 1981 .... 3.45
Newspaper Libel and Registration Act 1881
s 1 .... 17.18
Norfolk and Suffolk Broads Act 1988
Sch 6
para 10(1) 6.8
Nursery Education and Grant– Maintained Schools Act 1996
s 1, 2 .... 20.55
Parochial Assessment Act 1836 .... 2.11
Pensions (Increase) Act 1974 .... 3.37
Pension Schemes Act 1993 .... 3.37
Police Act 1964 .... 1.13
Police Act 1996 .... 1.13, 3.45, 10.8, 12.54
s 1(2) 1.13
3 .... 1.13, 5.4, 8.21, 10.8
4 .... 1.13
14(1)–(3) 3.39
54, 55 .... 7.54
Police Act 1997 .... 12.54
s 67 .... 10.8
Police and Magistrates' Courts Act 1994: 12.54
Sch 4
para 7 .... 6.8
Poor Law Amendment Act 1844 .... 8.11
Poor Relief Act 1601 .... 2.11
Public Bodies (Admission to Meetings) Act 1960 .... 8.73

PARA
Public Health Act 1875 .... 16.110
s 161 .... 12.111
247(7) 9.10
265 .... 16.111
Public Health Act 1936
s 310 .... 13.19
Public Libraries and Museums Act 1964
s 12 .... 3.38
Sch 2
para 4 .... 10.21
Public Works Loans Act 1875 .... 13.42
s 9 .... 13.43
Road Traffic Regulation Act 1984
s 45 .... 3.70
55(1)–(4) 3.70
School Standards and Framework Act 1998 .... 20.1, 20.19
s 19 .... 20.24
Pt II (ss 20–83) 20.39
s 20 .... 20.8, 20.28
21 .... 20.11
22(3) 20.13
29 .... 20.24
30 .... 20.24, 20.26
35 .... 20.26
37 .... 20.10
47 .... 20.38
48(2)(b) 20.31
49 .... 20.41
(5) 20.21
50 .... 20.42
51 .... 20.21, 20.43, 20.44
52 .... 20.45
53 .... 20.45
76 .... 20.23, 20.25
77 .... 20.23
Sch 2 .... 20.7, 20.28
Sch 3
Pt II 20.16
para 2(6), (7) 20.15
Sch 6 .... 20.24
Sch 8
para 3 .... 20.26
Sch 9 .... 20.10, 20.29
Sch 10
para 3(c) 20.31
Sch 12 .... 20.10
Sch 15 .... 20.21, 20.44
Sch 22 .... 20.23, 20.25
Social Security Administration Act 1992
s 134(8) 19.37
139A(1), (2) 7.53
139C(1) 7.53
Social Security and Housing Benefits Act 1982 .... 6.10
Solicitors Act 1957 .... 8.121
Superannuation Act 1972 .... 9.19, 14.21
s 7(1) 3.21
9 .... 3.25
Supreme Court Act 1981
s 31(3) 9.99

PARA
Town and Country Planning Act 1990 ... 1.10, 1.12, 10.8
s 2 ... 1.12
(1B) ... 10.8
106 ... 14.23, 18.62
233 ... 14.58
Sch 1 ... 1.12
Transport Act 1985
s 67 ... 16.13
72 ... 16.30
Tribunals and Inquiries act 1992
s 11 ... 18.65
Value Added Tax Act 1994 ... 18.1
s 4(2) ... 18.6
19(2) ... 18.6
33 ... 18.14, 18.17, 18.25, 18.26, 18.30, 18.34, 18.39, 18.43
(1) ... 18.22, 18.24
(2) ... 18.27
(3) ... 18.22, 18.27
42 ... 18.17
58 ... 18.2

PARA
Value Added Tax Act 1994—*contd*
s 82–84 ... 18.64
86 ... 18.65
94(1) ... 18.16
96(4) ... 18.17, 18.22
Sch 8
Group 5 ... 18.35
Sch 9
Group 1 ... 18.35, 18.51
Sch 10 ... 18.35
Sch 11
para 1(1) ... 18.2
Sch 12 ... 18.64
Water Act 1973
s 34 ... 14.12
Sch 6 ... 14.12
Weights and Measures Act 1985
s 95 ... 17.4

Northern Ireland
Industrial and Provident Societies Act 1969 ... 16.51

Table of statutory instruments

PARA

Accounts and Audit Regulations 1996, SI 1996/590 . . . . 8.31, 8.56, 8.57, 8.58, 8.90
reg 5 . . . . .8.4, 8.5
6 . . . . 8.84
(1) 8.57
8(1)–(3) 8.57
9 . . . . 8.57, 8.86
11 . . . . 8.57, 8.59, 8.92
12 . . . . 8.57
13 . . . . 9.38
14 . . . . 8.57
15 . . . . 8.93
16 . . . . 8.57
19 . . . . 8.59
Banking Coordination (Second Council Directive) Regulations 1992, SI 1992/3218 . . . . 10.23
reg 4 . . . . 3.31
6(3)–(6) 3.31
7(5)(a) 3.32
(8) 3.32
8 . . . . 3.32
77(1)(a) 3.33
(2) 3.33
(3)–(6) 3.34
(9), (10) 3.33
79(2) 3.35
(4), (5) 3.35
80 . . . . 3.35
81(1) 3.35
(d) 3.36
(2) 3.35, 3.36
90–92 . . . . 3.37
Civil Procedure Rules 1998, SI 1998/3132
Pt 52 . . . . 8.103, 18.65
r 52.1(3)(c) 9.78
52.4(2) 8.103
52.11 . . . . 8.103, 9.78
Rules of the Supreme Court
Ord 53
r 4 . . . . 9.102
Ord 55 . . . . 8.103
r 3 . . . . 8.47
Ord 7 . . . . 8.103
Ord 98 . . . . 8.103

PARA

Civil Procedure (Amendment No 4) Rules 2000, SI 2000/2092 . . . . 8.103
Coal Industry Act 1994 (Consequential Modifications of Subordinate Legislation) Order 1994, SI 1994/2567 . . . 10.23
Common Council and New Successor Bodies (Chief Finance Officer) Regulations 1991, SI 1991/445 . . . . 5.6
Community Charge Tribunals Regulations 1989, SI 1989/479 . . . . 2.32
Council Tax (Administration and Enforcement) Regulations 1992, SI 1992/613
reg 21 . . . . 2.18
36 . . . . 2.18
52 . . . . 2.18
53(2) 2.18
56 . . . . 2.18
Council Tax (Alteration of Lists and Appeals) Regulations 1993, SI 1993/290 . . . . 2.13
Council Tax (Exempt Dwellings) Order 1992, SI 1992/558 . . . . 2.12
Council Tax (Liability of Owners) Regulations 1992, SI 1992/551 . . . . 2.14
Council Tax (Situation and Valuation of Dwellings) Regulations 1992, SI 1992/550 . . . . 2.13
Council Tax (Transitional Deduction Scheme) England Regulations 1995, SI 1995/209 . . . . 2.8
Education (Budget Statements) (England) Regulations 2000, SI 2000/516 . . . . 20.45
Education (Change of Category of Maintained Schools) (Wales) Regulations 1999, SI 1999/2633 . . . . 20.7
Education (Grants for Education Support and Training) (England) Regulations 1997, SI 1997/514 . . . . 20.48
Education (Grants for Education Support and Training) (Wales) Regulations 1998, SI 1998/392 . . . . 20.48
Education Standards Fund (England) Regulations 2000, SI 2000/703 . . . . 20.46
Financing of Maintained Schools (England) Regulations 2000, SI 2000/478 . . . . 20.31
reg 3(1) 20.20
4(d) 20.20

PARA

Financing of Maintained Schools (England) (No 2) Regulations 2000, SI 2000/1090 .... 20.20
Greater London Authority Act 1999 (Commencement No 3 and Transitional Finance Provisions) Order 1999, SI 1999/3434 .... 8.14
Greater London Authority Act 1999 (Consequential Amendments of Subordinate Legislation) (Fire etc Authority) Order 2000, SI 2000/1553: 14.1
Housing Benefit (General) Regulations 1987, SI 1987/1971
reg 72(15) 19.37
Local Authorities (Borrowing) Regulations 1990, SI 1990/767 .... 13.14, 13.15
Local Authorities (Borrowing) (Amendment) Regulations 1991, SI 1991/551 .... 13.16
Local Authorities (Calculation of Council Tax Base) Regulations 1992, SI 1992/612: 2.12
Local Authorities (Capital Finance) Regulations 1990, SI 1990/432 .... 15.18
reg 7 .... 12.67
(6) 12.132
8 .... 12.128
13(1) 14.23
15, 18 .... 14.48
26(1)(a) 12.81
(2)(c) 12.81
Local Authorities (Capital Finance) Regulations 1997, SI 1997/319: 10.7, 10.23, 11.30, 12.32, 12.61, 12.81, 14.1, 16.17
reg 2–7 .... 10.18, 14.6
8 .... 10.2, 10.18, 14.6, 15.26
(2) 12.17
8A 10.20
9, 10 .... 10.18
13 .... 15.23, 15.24
(1) 12.93, 12.97
14 .... 12.64, 12.87
(2) 12.130
15(2) 12.51, 12.66
(3) 12.83
16 .... 10.20, 10.35, 12.84, 12.109, 15.18, 15.22, 15.23, 15.25, 15.38, 15.39, 15.72
(1) 15.23, 15.24
(2)(c) 15.55
17 .... 12.11, 12.17, 12.39, 12.41, 15.25
18 .... 12.86
(2)(a) 12.50
(b) 12.49
19 .... 12.49, 12.51, 12.83, 12.86
20 .... 12.86
(1), (2) 12.52
21 .... 12.86
(1)(a), (b) 12.53
22 .... 12.49, 12.86
(1) 12.56, 14.55
23 .... 12.49, 12.86

PARA

Local Authorities (Capital Finance) Regulations 1997, SI 1997/319—*contd*
reg 24 .... 12.49, 12.86
(1)(a), (b) 12.54
(2)(a)–(e) 12.54
25 .... 12.49, 12.86
26 .... 12.60, 12.62, 12.73, 12.87, 12.116, 12.129, 12.135
27 .... 12.11, 12.15, 12.60, 12.62, 12.101, 12.135
28 .... 12.11, 12.15, 12.60, 12.62, 12.63, 12.67, 12.102, 12.135, 15.52, 15.53
29 .... 12.11, 12.15, 12.60, 12.62, 12.63, 12.67, 12.93, 12.102, 12.131, 12.135
30 .... 12.11, 12.15, 12.60, 12.62, 12.63, 12.67, 12.102, 12.131,12.135
31 .... 12.11, 12.15, 12.60, 12.62, 12.63, 12.67, 12.102, 12.135
32 .... 12.11, 12.15, 12.60, 12.62, 12.63, 12.67, 12.102, 12.131, 12.135
33 .... 12.11, 12.15, 12.60, 12.62, 12.63, 12.67, 12.102, 12.135
34 .... 12.11, 12.15, 12.60, 12.62, 12.63, 12.67, 12.135
(1) 12.99, 12.102
(3) 12.100
35 .... 12.11, 12.15, 12.60, 12.62, 12.63, 12.67, 12.68, 12.70, 12.72, 12.102, 12.104, 12.132, 12.133, 12.135
36 .... 12.11, 12.15, 12.60, 12.62, 12.63, 12.66, 12.70, 12.72, 12.85, 12.104, 12.135
37 .... 12.11, 12.15, 12.60, 12.62, 12.63, 12.68, 12.69, 12.70, 12.72, 12.103, 12.104, 12.135, 15.54
38 .... 12.11, 12.15, 12.60, 12.62, 12.63, 12.70, 12.103, 12.104, 12.135, 15.52
(3)(a), (b) 12.105
(4) 12.105
39 .... 12.11, 12.15, 12.60, 12.62, 12.72, 12.135
Pt IV 12.59, 12.73
reg 40 .... 12.11, 12.60, 12.73, 12.87, 12.90, 12.106, 12.116, 12.135, 14.60, 15.22, 15.27, 15.29, 15.33, 15.34, 15.35, 15.36, 15.37, 15.38, 15.39, 15.42, 15.43, 15.45, 15.46, 15.49, 15.53, 15.55, 15.56, 15.58, 15.61, 15.66, 15.67, 15.69, 15.71, 15.72

PARA

Local Authorities (Capital Finance) Regulations 1997, SI 1997/319—*contd*
reg 40(2)(b) ... 15.32
41 ... 12.60, 12.63, 12.69, 12.90, 12.106, 12.116, 12.135, 14.60, 15.19, 15.22, 15.43, 15.44, 15.45, 15.46, 15.47, 15.49, 15.51, 15.54, 15.58
(1) ... 15.46
(3)(b) ... 15.46
(4) ... 12.11
(5) ... 15.47
(6) ... 12.11
(7) ... 15.48, 15,58
42 ... 12.60, 12.63, 12.69, 12.73, 12.90, 12.106, 12.116, 12.135, 14.60, 15.19, 15.22, 15.43, 15.49, 15.51, 15.54, 15.58
(4), (5) ... 12.11
(6) ... 15.50, 15.58
43 ... 12.60, 12.73, 12.107, 12.108, 12.110, 12.116, 12.135, 15.19, 15.51
44 ... 12.60, 12.73, 12.107, 12.108, 12.111, 12.116, 12.135, 15.19, 15.51
(1)(b) ... 12.46
45 ... 12.60, 12.108, 12.135, 15.19, 15.51
(2), (3) ... 12.11
46 ... 12.15, 12.101, 12.105, 12.116, 12.129, 15.40
47 ... 12.11, 12.15, 12.71, 12.102, 12.116, 12.129, 12.130, 12.131, 12.132
(2) ... 12.130, 12.133
48 ... 12.11, 12.15, 12.102, 12.116, 12.127, 12.129, 12.131, 15.40
49 ... 12.11, 12.15, 12.71, 12.102, 12.116, 12.129, 12.133, 15.40
50 ... 12.11, 12.15, 12.71, 12.102, 12.116, 12.127, 12.129, 15.40
51 ... 12.11, 12.15, 12.116, 12.129, 15.40
Pt V (regs 52–55) ... 11.9
reg 56, 57 ... 14.12
Pt VI ... 14.4
reg 58 ... 11.56, 14.12
58A ... 14.12
59 ... 14.12
61 ... 16.78
63 ... 14.8, 14.23, 14.46, 17.36
64(1)(b) ... 12.46
64A ... 10.34, 14.13, 14.26, 14.36, 14.46, 16.70, 17.36, 17.38
65 ... 10.34, 10.35, 14.30, 15.60
(1) ... 14.30

PARA

Local Authorities (Capital Finance) Regulations 1997, SI 1997/319—*contd*
reg 66 ... 10.34, 14.30, 16.17
(1) ... 16.17
(2)(a)–(d) ... 14.30, 15.18
(e) ... 14.30, 15.18
(ii) ... 17.36
(f)–(g) ... 14.30, 15.18
(3), (4) ... 14.44
66A ... 10.34
67 ... 10.34, 14.29, 14.30
68 ... 11.54, 14.30
68A ... 10.34, 14.30
69 ... 10.34, 14.29, 14.30
70 ... 14.30
72 ... 10.34, 14.27
76–78 ... 14.28
82 ... 14.54
83 ... 14.54
84 ... 14.52, 14.53, 14.55
85–87 ... 14.55
93 ... 14.55
94, 95 ... 14.33, 14.55
96 ... 14.48, 14.55, 15.16
97 ... 12.55, 14.55
98 ... 14.55
99 ... 14.48, 14.55, 15.16
100–104A ... 14.55
106 ... 14.57, 14.59
(2) ... 14.54, 14.60
110, 111 ... 15.18, 15.19
112 ... 14.60, 15.58, 15.59
114 ... 14.60
118 ... 11.40
119 ... 10.32
(3) ... 11.42
122 ... 10.14, 12.45, 12.87
123 ... 10.14, 10.35, 12.45, 15.60
126–129 ... 11.43
132 ... 11.51, 11.52
(2) ... 11.44
133 ... 11.51, 11.52
134 ... 11.51, 11.54
135 ... 11.51, 11.56
136 ... 11.51, 11.54
137 ... 11.51, 11.56, 12.89
138 ... 11.44, 11.57, 11.70
139 ... 11.44
139–145 ... 11.44
146 ... 11.44, 11.55
147–149 ... 11.44
150 ... 11.44, 11.55
155 ... 11.40, 11.64
156 ... 10.31, 11.40, 11.64
(1), (2) ... 11.64
157 ... 10.33, 11.40, 11.65, 11.70
158 ... 11.40, 11.66
Pt XI ... 11.43
Pt XIII ... 11.63

PARA

Local Authorities (Capital Finance) Regulations 1997, SI 1997/319—*contd*
Sch 1 . . . . . 15.44
para 1–6 . . . . . 15.46
8, 9 . . . . . 15.46
Sch 2
Pt II 11.57, 11.70
Local Authorities (Capital Finance) (Amendment) Regulations 1997, SI 1997/848 . . . . . 10.7, 12.11, 14.1, 15.58, 16.17
Local Authorities (Capital Finance) (Amendment) Regulations 1998, SI 1998/371 . . . . . 10.7, 10.20, 12.11, 14.1, 15.23, 16.17
Local Authorities (Capital Finance) (Amendment) (No 2) Regulations 1998, SI 1998/602 . . . . . 10.7, 12.11, 14.1, 16.17
Local Authorities (Capital Finance) (Amendment No 3) Regulations 1996, SI 1996/2539 . . . . . 12.131, 15.17
Local Authorities (Capital Finance) (Amendment No 3) Regulations 1998, SI 1998/1937 . . . . . 10.7, 10.26, 12.11, 14.1, 14.26, 15.18, 15.57, 16.70, 17.36, 17.38
reg 4 . . . . . 14.12
6 . . . . . 10.34, 14.13
Local Authorities (Capital Finance) (Amendment) (No 4) Regulations 1992, SI 1992/3257 . . . . . 12.131
Local Authorities (Capital Finance) (Amendment) Regulations 1999, SI 1999/501 . . . . . 10.7, 10.29, 12.11, 14.1, 14.55, 16.17
Local Authorities (Capital Finance) (Amendment) (England) Regulations 1999, SI 1999/3423 . . . . . 14.1, 15.34, 16.17
Local Authorities (Capital Finance) (Amendment) (England) Regulations 2000, SI 2000/1773 . . . . . 14.1
Local Authorities (Capital Finance) (Amendment) (Wales) Regulations 2000, SI 2000/992 . . . . . 15.34, 15.43
reg 2 . . . . . 12.106
Local Authorities (Capital Finance) (Approved Investments) Regulations 1990, SI 1990/426 . . . . . 10.14, 10.23, 15.15
reg 1(2) 10.24
2 . . . . . 10.24
3(3) 10.29
(4) 10.25
13(1) 14.23
15, 18 . . . . . 15.16
Schedule
Pt I 10.24
Local Authorities (Capital Finance) (Approved Investments) (Amendment) Regulations 1991 SI 1991/501 . . . . . 10.23

PARA

Local Authorities (Capital Finance) (Approved Investments) (Amendment) Regulations 1992, SI 1992/1353 . . . . . 10.23, 10.29
Local Authorities (Capital Finance and Approved Investments) (Amendment) Regulations 1995, SI 1995/850 . . . . . 10.23, 10.29, 12.132, 15.15
Local Authorities (Capital Finance and Approved Investments) (Amendment No 2) Order 1995, SI 1995/1982 . . . . . 10.23, 10.29, 15.15
Local Authorities (Capital Finance and Approved Investments) (Amendment) Regulations 1996, SI 1996/568 . . . . . 10.23, 10.29, 12.32, 12.131, 12.132, 15.16
Local Authorities (Capital Finance and Approved Investments) (Amendment) Regulations 1999, SI 1999/1852 . . . . . 10.7, 12.11, 12.33, 12.94, 12.96, 14.1, 15.23, 16.17
Local Authorities (Capital Finance, Approved Investments and Contracts) (Amendment) Regulations 2000, SI 2000/1033 . . . . . 10.23, 14.1
Local Authorities (Capital Finance) (Prescribed Bodies)Regulations 1990, SI 1990/404 . . . . . 10.8
Local Authorities (Capital Finance) (Rate of Discount for 1999/2000) Regulations 1999, SI 1999/453 . . . . . 11.58, 12.65
reg 2 . . . . . 12.77, 12.118
Local Authorities (Capital Finance) (Rate of Discount for 2000/2001) (England) Regulations 2000, SI 2000/259 . . . . . 12.65, 12.77, 12.118
Local Authorities (Capital Finance) (Rate of Discount for 2000/2001) (Wales) Regulations 2000, SI 2000/825 . . . . . 12.65, 12.77, 12.118
Local Authorities (Companies) Order 1995, SI 1995/849 . . . . . 10.36, 12.56, 14.54, 15.15, 15.18, 16.2, 16.23, 16.31, 16.46, 16.91
art 1(4) 16.51, 16.65
(a) 16.36
(b) 16.46
(5) 16.51, 16.52, 16.53, 16.58, 16.62, 16.63
(6) 16.53
(7) 16.51, 16.52, 16.59, 16.62, 16.63
(8) 16.59
4 . . . . . 16.66
5 . . . . . 16.66
6 . . . . . 16.66
7 . . . . . 16.66
8 . . . . . 16.66
(1) 16.69

PARA

Local Authorities (Companies) Order 1995, SI 1995/849—*contd*
art 9 . . . 16.67
10 . . . 16.38, 16.68
11 . . . 16.32, 16.48, 16.49, 16.92
12(1) . . . 16.69, 16.71, 16.74
(2) . . . 16.71, 16.74
13 . . . 16.73, 16.76, 16.86
(1) . . . 16.72
(2) . . . 16.73
(3), (4) . . . 16.75
14 . . . 11.43, 16.76, 16.81, 16.82, 16.86
(1)(a) . . . 16.78
(2)(a) . . . 14.30, 16.76
(3) . . . 16.76
(4) . . . 16.77
(5) . . . 16.79
(a) . . . 10.36, 11.41, 11.60
(b) . . . 10.36, 11.6
15 . . . 16.76, 16.81, 16.83
16 . . . 16.80, 16.89
(1)(a) . . . 16.18
(bb) . . . 16.89
(i) . . . 16.87
(3) . . . 16.71, 16.76
(4) . . . 16.71, 16.80
(5) . . . 16.88
(5A) . . . 16.84, 16.88
(5B) . . . 16.88
(6)–(7) . . . 16.84
18 . . . 16.97
(4) . . . 16.98
Pt V . . . 14.46, 16.101
Local Authorities (Companies) (Amendment) Order 1996, SI 1996/621 . . . 12.56, 15.15, 16.2, 16.23, 16.69, 16.89
Local Authorities (Contracts) Regulations 1997, SI 1997/2862 . . . 15.94, 15.101
reg 3–5 . . . 15.95
6 . . . 15.95
7(2), (3) . . . 15.97
8 . . . 15.97
Local Authorities (Discretionary Expenditure) (Relevant Population) Regulations 1993, SI 1993/40 . . . 16.5
Local Authorities (Discretionary Expenditure Limits) Order 1993, SI 1993/41 . . . 16.5
Local Authorities (Funds) (England) Regulations 1992, SI 1992/2428 . . . 3.12
reg 2(2) . . . 3.14, 3.19, 3.20
3(1) . . . 3.13, 3.19, 3.20
(2), (3) . . . 3.14, 3.20
(4), (5) . . . 3.16
(6)–(8) . . . 3.19
4(2)–(5) . . . 3.15
5, 6 . . . 3.15
11, 12 . . . 3.13

PARA

Local Authorities (Funds) (England) Regulations 1992, SI 1992/2428 —*contd*
reg 13 . . . 10.21
(1)–(4) . . . 3.17
Sch 1 . . . 3.15
Sch 2 . . . 3.13
Sch 3 . . . 3.17
para 2 . . . 3.21
Local Authorities (Members' Allowances) Regulations 1991, SI 1991/351 . . . 6.4
reg 2 . . . 6.6
9(1) . . . 6.4
10(3), (3A) . . . 6.4
(4) . . . 6.4
16 . . . 6.7
17(2) . . . 6.6
18 . . . 6.6
19 . . . 6.6
Local Authorities (Members' Allowances) (Amendment) Regulations 1995, SI 1995/553 . . . 6.4
Local Authorities (Members' Allowances) (Amendment) Regulations 1996, SI 1996/469 . . . 6.4
reg 2 . . . 6.6
Local Authorities (Members' Interests) Regulations 1992, SI 1992/618 . . . 6.9
Local Authorities (Members' Interests) (Amendment) Regulations 1996, SI 1996/1215 . . . 6.9
Local Authorities (Precepts) (Wales) Regulations 1995, SI 1995/2562 . . . 3.2, 3.5
Local Authorities (Publicity Account) (Exemption) Order 1987, SI 1987/2004 . . . 3.65
Local Authorities (Standing Orders) Regulations 1993, SI 1993/202
reg 1(2)(c) . . . 5.9
Sch 1 . . . 5.9
Local Government Act 1999 (Commencement No 1) Order 1999, SI 1999/2169 . . . 1.47, 7.7
art 2(2) . . . 7.8
3 . . . 7.8
4 . . . 7.8
5(1) . . . 7.8
Sch 1 . . . 7.8
Sch 2 . . . 7.8
Local Government Act 1999 (Commencement No 3) (England) Order 2000, SI 2000/1724 . . . 1.47
Local Government Act 1999 (Commencement) (Wales) Order 1999, SI 1999/2815 . . . 1.47, 7.7
art 2 . . . 7.8
Local Government Act 2000 (Commencement No 1) Order 2000, SI 2000/2187 . . . 1.48
Local Government and Housing Act 1989 (Commencement No 3) Order 1989, SI 1989/2445 . . . 16.2, 16.47

PARA
Local Government and Housing Act 1989 (Commencement No 8 and Transitional Provisions) Order 1990, SI 1990/1274 .... 16.47
Local Government and Housing Act 1989 (Commencement No 8 and Transitional Provisions) (Amendment) Order 1990, SI 1990/1335 .... 16.47
Local Government and Housing Act 1989 (Commencement No 16) Order 1993, SI 1993/2410 .... 16.2
Local Government and Housing Act 1989 (Commencement No 17) Order 1995, SI 1995/841 .... 15.15, 16.47
Local Government and Housing Act 1989 (Commencement No 11 and Savings) Order 1991, SI 1999/344 .... 6.6
Local Government (Best Value) (Exemption) (England) Order 2000, SI 2000/339 .... 7.14
Local Government (Best Value) (Exemption) (Wales) Order 2000, SI 2000/1029 .... 7.14
Local Government (Best Value) (Performance Indicators) Order 2000, SI 2000/896 .... 7.20
Local Government (Best Value) (Performance Indicators) (Wales) Order 2000, SI 2000/1030 .... 7.20
Local Government (Best Value) (Performance Plans and Reviews Order 1999, SI 1999/3251 .... 7.56
art 1(2) 7.22
3(1) 7.32
(d) 7.24
(e) 7.22
4(2) 7.33
(d) 7.21
(f)–(h) 7.22
5 .... 7.24, 7.32, 7.33
6 .... 7.32, 7.33
(1) 7.26
Sch 1 .... 7.32
Local Government (Best Value) (Reviews and Performance Plans) (Wales) Order 2000, SI 2000/1271 ..... 7.21, 7.39
art 1 .... 7.33
3 .... 7.26
4 .... 7.32
5 .... 7.8, 7.32
6 .... 7.8
Local Government (Contracts) Act 1997 (Commencement No 1) Order 1997, SI 1997/2843 .... 15.83
Local Government Changes for England (Payment to Designated Authorities) (Minimum Revenue Provision) Regulations 1995, SI 1995/2894
reg 8, 9 .... 14.12
Local Government (Direct Labour Organisations) (Specified Number of Employed Persons)Order 1989, SI 1989/1589 .... 3.50
Local Government Changes for England (Property Transfer and Transitional Payments) Regulations 1995, SI 1995/402 .... 12.54
Local Government Finance Act 1988 (Miscellaneous Amendments and Repeals) Order 1990, SI 1990/10 ... 6.8
Local Government (Grants from Structural Funds) Regulations 2000, SI 2000/589 .... 10.14, 13.34, 16.71, 16.76
Local Government Pension Scheme (Management and Investment of Funds) Regulations 1998, SI 1998/1831
reg 2 .... 3.30
3 .... 3.29
5(2) 3.27
(6) 3.28
6(6) 3.30
9 .... 10.21
(1), (3) 3.29
12 .... 3.29
Local Government Pension Scheme Regulations 1995, SI 1995/1019 .... 3.22
Local Government Pension Scheme Regulations 1997, SI 1997/1612 .... 3.22, 3.23, 3.24
reg 5 .... 3.26
74 .... 3.25
75 .... 3.26
Sch 2, 5 .... 3.25
Local Government (Prescribed Expenditure) (Consolidation and Amendment) Regulations 1987, SI 1987/2186 .... 12.44
Local Government (Prescribed Expenditure) (Amendment) (No 2) Regulations 1988, SI 1988/1534 .... 12.44
Local Government (Promotion of Economic Development) Regulations 1990, SI 1990/763 .... 3.71, 17.35
reg 9(1), (2) 3.72
Pt III 17.10
reg 4 .... 17.14
5 .... 17.14, 17.18
(2) 17.19
6(2) 17.23
(3) 17.25
9 .... 17.33
Sch 1 .... 17.17
Sch 2
para 1 .... 17.18
2 .... 17.14, 17.20
Local Government (Promotion of Economic Development) (Amendment) Regulations 1990, SI 1990/789 .... 17.10

	PARA
Local Government (Promotion of Economic Development) (Amendment) Regulations 1991, SI 1991/473	17.10
Local Government (Promotion of Economic Development) (Amendment) Regulations 1995, SI 1995/556	17.10, 17.17
Local Government Reorganisation (Pensions) Order 1989, SI 1989/1815:	1.5
London Government Reorganisation (Pensions etc) (Amendment) Order 1990, SI 1990/198	1.5
Local Government Reorganisation (Wales) (Capital Finance) Order 1995, SI 1995/1041	10.23, 10.29
Local Government Reorganisation (Wales) (Consequential Amendments) Order 1996, SI 1996/532	12.54
Local Government Residuary Body (England) Order 1995, SI 1995/401	12.53
Local Government Superannuation Regulations 1986, SI 1986/24	3.22
Sch 1	3.24
Metropolitan Police (Capital Finance) Order 2000, SI 2000/1474	14.1, 14.12
National Assembly for Wales (Transfer of Functions) Order 1999, SI 1999/672	8.40, 10.7, 20.7
art 2	10.7, 11.12
Sch 1	10.7, 11.12
National Assembly for Wales (Transfer of Functions) Order 2000, SI 2000/253	20.7
National Park Authorities (England) Order 1996, SI 1996/1243	
art 2	12.99
15	12.100
Non-Domestic Rating (Collection and Enforcement) Regulations 1989, SI 1989/1058	
reg 7	2.25
12	2.25
20	2.25
Police and Magistrates' Courts Act 1994 (Commencement No 5 and Transitional Provisions) Order 1994, SI 1994/3262	
art 9	12.54
Public Airport Companies (Capital Finance) Order 1996, SI 1996/604	16.30
Public Airport Companies (Capital Finance) (Amendment) Order 1999, SI 1999/554	16.30
Public Airport Companies (Capital Finance) (Second Amendment) Order 1999, SI 1999/2125	16.30
Public Services Contracts Regulations 1993, SI 1993/3228	15.63
Public Supply Contracts Regulations 1995, SI 1995/201	15.63
Public Works Contracts Regulations 1991, SI 1991/2680	15.63
Residuary Body for Wales (Appointed Body) Order 1995, SI 1995/102	1.15
Residuary Body for Wales (Appointed Day) Order 1995, SI 1995/103	12.53
Revenue Support Grant (Specified Bodies) Regulations 1992, SI 1992/89	20.36
Secure Tenants of Local Authorities (Compensation for Improvements) Regulations 1994, SI 1994/613	19.20
Teachers' Superannuation (Consolidation) Regulations 1988, SI 1988/1652	3.25
Transfer of Undertakings (Protection of Employment) Regulations 1981, SI 1981/1794	1.44
Value Added Tax (Refund of Tax) (No 2) Order 1986, SI 1986/532	18.22
Value Added Tax (Refund of Tax) (No 2) Order 1995, SI 1995/2999	18.22
Waste Regulation and Disposal (Authorities) Order 1985, SI 1985/1884	
reg 9	5.3

Table of cases

PARA

A

A v B Bank (Bank of England intervening) [1993] QB 311, [1992] 1 All ER 778, [1992] 3 WLR 705, 135 Sol Jo 11 .... 8.121
Allsop v North Tyneside Metropolitan Borough Council (1992) 90 LGR 462, [1992] ICR 639, [1992] RVR 104, CA 9.19
Asher v Lacey [1973] 3 All ER 1008, [1973] 1 WLR 1412, 72 LGR 66, 117 Sol Jo 697: 9.57, 9.63, 9.65
Asher v Secretary of State for the Environment [1974] Ch 208, [1974] 2 All ER 156, [1974] 2 WLR 466, 72 LGR 333, 118 Sol Jo 258, CA 8.29, 9.70
Associated Provincial Picture Houses Ltd v Wednesbury Corpn [1948] 1 KB 223, [1947] 2 All ER 680, 45 LGR 635, 112 JP 55, [1948] LJR 190, 92 Sol Jo 26, 177 LT 641, 63 TLR 623, CA 4.6, 8.48, 9.15
A-G v Aspinall (1837) 1 JP 4, 2 My & Cr 613, 1 Jur 812, [1835–42] All ER Rep 525, sub nom A-G v Liverpool Corpn, A-G v Aspinall 7 LJ Ch 51 .... 9.66
A-G v Belfast Corpn (1855) 4 Ir Ch R 119 .... 9.14, 9.33, 9.67
A-G v Crayford UDC [1962] Ch 575, [1962] 2 All ER 147, [1962] 2 WLR 998, 60 LGR 261, [1962] 1 Lloyd's Rep 163, 126 JP 308, 106 Sol Jo 175, CA 8.107
A-G v De Winton [1906] 2 Ch 106, 4 LGR 549, 70 JP 368, 75 LJ Ch 612, 54 WR 499, 50 Sol Jo 405, 22 TLR 446 .... 8.11, 9.66, 9.69
A-G v East Barnet Valley UDC (1911) 9 LGR 913, 75 JP 484 .... 9.24
A-G v Great Eastern Rly Co (1880) 5 App Cas 473, 44 JP 648, 49 LJ Ch 545, 28 WR 769, 42 LT 810, [1874–80] All ER Rep Ext 1459, HL 4.27
A-G v Smethwick Corpn [1932] 1 Ch 562, 30 LGR 117, 96 JP 105, 101 LJ Ch 137, [1932] All ER Rep 304, 146 LT 480, 48 TLR 227, CA 4.29
A-G v Tottenham Local Board of Health (1872) 27 LT 440 .... 9.32
A-G v Wilson (1840) Cr & Ph 1, 10 LJ Ch 53, 4 Jur 1174, 47 RR 173 .... 9.67

B

Baird, Re [1989] NI 56 .... 9.78
Bank of England v Riley [1992] Ch 475, [1992] 1 All ER 769, [1992] 2 WLR 840, CA 8.121
Barrs v Bethell [1982] Ch 294, [1982] 1 All ER 106, [1981] 3 WLR 874, 80 LGR 269, 125 Sol Jo 808 .... 9.66
Beecham v Metropolitan District Auditor (1976) 75 LGR 79 .... 9.13, 9.21
Birkdale District Electric Supply Co Ltd v Southport Corpn [1926] AC 355, 24 LGR 157, 90 JP 77, 95 LJ Ch 587, 134 LT 673, 42 TLR 303, [1926] All ER Rep Ext 714, HL 4.13
Boardman v Portman (22 May 2000, unreported) 9.78
Bookbinder v Tebbit (No 2) [1992] 1 WLR 217 .... 8.42
Bradford Metropolitan City Council v Anderton (1991) 89 LGR 681, [1991] RA 45, 135 Sol Jo 251, [1991] COD 313 .... 2.14
Bromley London Borough Council v Greater London Council [1983] 1 AC 768, [1982] 1 All ER 129, sub nom R v Greater London Council, ex p Bromley London Borough Council [1982] 2 WLR 62, 80 LGR 1, [1982] RA 87, 125 Sol Jo 809, CA; affd sub nom Bromley London Borough Council v Greater London Council [1983] 1 AC 768, [1982] 1 All ER 153, [1982] 2 WLR 62, 80 LGR 1, [1982] RA 47, 126 Sol Jo 16, HL 4.8, 9.10
Brown v DPP [1956] 2 QB 369, [1956] 2 All ER 189, [1956] 2 WLR 1087, 54 LGR 266, 120 JP 303, 100 Sol Jo 369 .... 6.9

PARA

Bryan v United Kingdom (1995) 21 EHRR 342, [1996] 1 PLR 47, [1996] 2 EGLR 123, [1996] 28 EG 137, ECtHR 8.48
Buckingham v Shackleton (1981) 79 LGR 484, DC 6.2
Burgoine v Waltham Forest London Borough Council (1996) 95 LGR 520, [1997] 2 BCLC 612, [1997] BCC 347 .... 16.110

C

Camden London Borough v Secretary of State for the Environment and Barker (1993) 67 P & CR 59, [1993] EGCS 83 .... 4.17
Colton v District Auditor for Wembley Borough Council (1962) 60 LGR 247 .... 8.114
Commission for Local Authority Accounts in Scotland v Stirling District Council 1984 SLT 442: 9.22
Coomber (Surveyor of Taxes) v Berkshire Justices (1883) 9 App Cas 61, 2 TC 1, 48 JP 421, 53 LJQB 239, 32 WR 525, 50 LT 405, [1881–5] All ER Rep Ext 1457, HL 2.23
Council of Civil Service Unions v Minister for the Civil Service [1985] AC 374, [1984] 3 All ER 935, [1984] 3 WLR 1174, [1985] ICR 14, 128 Sol Jo 837, [1985] LS Gaz R 437, sub nom R v Secretary of State for Foreign and Commonwealth Affairs, ex p Council of Civil Service Unions [1985] IRLR 28, HL 4.1, 4.7
Crédit Suisse v Allerdale Borough Council [1995] 1 Lloyd's Rep 315; affd [1997] QB 306, [1996] 4 All ER 129, [1996] 3 WLR 894, [1996] 2 Lloyd's Rep 241, CA.... 4.10, 4.20, 4.21, 15.12, 16.5, 16.20, 16.106, 17.15
Crédit Suisse v Waltham Forest London Borough Council [1997] QB 362, [1996] 4 All ER 176, [1996] 3 WLR 943, 29 HLR 115, CA 15.75, 16.5, 16.20, 17.15
Customs and Excise Comrs v Cantor Fitzgerald International [1998] STC 948 .... 18.57
Customs and Excise Comrs v Harz [1967] 1 AC 760, sub nom R v Harz [1966] 3 All ER 433, [1966] 3 WLR 1241, 110 Sol Jo 565, CCA; affd sub nom Customs and Excise Comrs v Harz [1967] 1 AC 760, [1967] 1 All ER 177, [1967] 2 WLR 297, 51 Cr App Rep 123, 131 JP 146, 111 Sol Jo 15, HL 8.121

D

Davies v Cowperthwaite [1938] 2 All ER 685, 36 LGR 459, 102 JP 405, 159 LT 43, DC ... 9.21, 9.59
Dickson, Re [1948] 2 KB 95, [1948] 1 All ER 713, 64 TLR 233, sub nom Dickson v Hurle-Hobbs 46 LGR 175, 112 JP 232, [1948] LJR 1119, 92 Sol Jo 244, CA 9.30, 9.44
DPP v Burton (1995) Times, 8 June 6.12
Dowty Boulton Paul Ltd v Wolverhampton Corpn [1971] 2 All ER 277, [1971] 1 WLR 204, 69 LGR 192, 135 JP 333, 115 Sol Jo 76 .... 4.14

E

Ebbw Vale UDC v South Wales Traffic Area Licensing Authority [1951] 2 KB 366, 95 Sol Jo 334, [1951] 1 TLR 742, sub nom R v South Wales Traffic Licensing Authority, ex p Ebbw Vale UDC [1951] 1 All ER 806, 49 LGR 515, 115 JP 278, CA 16.20

F

Farmer (Valuation Officer) v Buxted Poultry Ltd [1993] AC 369, [1993] 1 All ER 117, [1993] 2 WLR 34, 91 LGR 121, [1993] RA 1, [1993] 1 EGLR 155, [1993] 10 LS Gaz R 36, [1993] NLJR 51, [1993] 11 EG 124, 137 Sol Jo LB 39, HL 2.25
Fleming v Lees [1991] COD 50 .... 9.36, 9.47

G

Garton v Hunter (Valuation Officer) [1969] 2 QB 37, [1969] 1 All ER 451, [1969] 2 WLR 86, 67 LGR 229, [1969] RA 11, 14 RRC 136, 133 JP 162, 112 Sol Jo 924, 208 Estates Gazette 1087, CA 2.30
Gerrard (Thomas) & Son Ltd, Re [1968] Ch 455, [1967] 2 All ER 525, [1967] 3 WLR 84, 111 Sol Jo 329 .... 8.29
Giddens v Harlow District Auditor (1972) 70 LGR 485, DC 8.48
Graham v Teesdale (1981) 81 LGR 117 .... 9.53
Grainger v Liverpool Corpn [1954] 1 QB 351, [1954] 1 All ER 333, 52 LGR 152, 118 JP 136, 98 Sol Jo 113 .... 4.29
Grunwick Processing Laboratories Ltd v Advisory Conciliation and Arbitration Service [1978] AC 655, [1978] 1 All ER 338, [1978] 2 WLR 277, [1978] ICR 231, CA; affd [1978] AC 655, [1978] 1 All ER 338, [1978] 2 WLR 277, [1978] ICR 231, 122 Sol Jo 46, sub nom Advisory Conciliation and Arbitration Service v Grunwick Processing Laboratories Ltd [1977] IRLR 38, HL 9.15

PARA

H

Hall & Co Ltd v Shoreham-by-Sea UDC [1964] 1 All ER 1, [1964] 1 WLR 240, 62 LGR 206, 15 P & CR 119, 128 JP 120, 107 Sol Jo 1001, CA 4.9
Haringey London Borough Council v Customs and Excise Comrs [1995] STC 830 .... 18.28
Hazell v Hammersmith and Fulham London Borough Council [1990] 2 QB 697, [1990] 3 All ER 33, [1990] 2 WLR 17, 88 LGR 433, 134 Sol Jo 21, [1990] 2 LS Gaz R 36, [1989] RVR 188; on appeal [1990] 2 QB 697, [1990] 3 All ER 33, [1990] 2 WLR 1038, 88 LGR 433, 134 Sol Jo 637, [1990] 20 LS Gaz R 36, [1990] RVR 140, CA; affd [1992] 2 AC 1, [1991] 1 All ER 545, [1991] 2 WLR 372, 89 LGR 271, [1991] RVR 28, HL 4.1, 4.10, 4.30, 5.8, 7.16, 8.48, 9.10, 9.21, 9.22, 9.37, 13.38, 13.39, 15.78, 15.84, 16.5, 16.20, 17.15
Hillingdon London Borough Council v Paulssen [1977] JPL 518 .... 8.80
Hinckley and Bosworth Borough Council v Shaw [2000] BLGR 9 .... 9.20
Hopson v Devon County Council [1978] 1 All ER 1205, [1978] 1 WLR 553, 76 LGR 509, 142 JP 277, 121 Sol Jo 760 .... 6.5
Hurle-Hobbs, Re, ex p Riley (1944) unreported 9.60
Hurle-Hobbs's Decision, Re [1944] 2 All ER 261, 42 LGR 285, 108 JP 200, CA 8.119, 9.17, 9.21, 9.68

J

Joint Stock Discount Co v Brown (1869) LR 8 Eq 381, 17 WR 1037, sub nom London Joint-Stock Discount Co Ltd v Brown 20 LT 844 .... 9.33

K

Kingston Cotton Mill Co (No 2), Re [1896] 2 Ch 279, 65 LJ Ch 673, 3 Mans 171, 40 Sol Jo 531, 74 LT 568, 12 TLR 430, CA 8.29
Kleinwort Benson Ltd v Lincoln City Council [1999] 2 AC 349, [1998] 4 All ER 513, [1998] 3 WLR 1095, [1998] NLJR 1674, [1998] RVR 315, 142 Sol Jo LB 279, HL 15.78
Kuwait Asia Bank EC v National Mutual Life Nominees Ltd [1991] 1 AC 187, [1990] 3 All ER 404, [1990] 3 WLR 297, [1990] 2 Lloyd's Rep 95, [1990] BCLC 868, [1990] BCC 567, [1990] 26 LS Gaz R 40, PC 16.104

L

Laing (John) & Son Ltd v Kingswood Assessment Area Assessment Committee [1949] 1 KB 344, [1949] 1 All ER 224, 47 LGR 64, 42 R & IT 15, 113 JP 111, 93 Sol Jo 26, 65 TLR 80, CA ... 2.21
Leicester City Council v District Auditor for Leicester. See R v District Auditor for Leicester, ex p Leicester City Council
Lever Finance Ltd v Westminster (City) London Borough Council [1971] 1 QB 222, [1970] 3 All ER 496, [1970] 3 WLR 732, 68 LGR 757, 21 P & CR 778, 134 JP 692, 114 Sol Jo 651, 216 Estates Gazette 721, CA 4.17
Lloyd v McMahon [1987] AC 625, [1987] 1 All ER 1118, [1987] 2 WLR 821, 85 LGR 545, 131 Sol Jo 409, [1987] LS Gaz R 1240, [1987] NLJ Rep 265, [1987] RVR 58, HL 5.8
Lloyd v McMahon. See Smith v Skinner
Lobenstein v Hackney London Borough Council [1980] LGC 1292 .... 4.42
LCC v Erith Parish (Churchwardens and Overseers of the Poor) and Dartford Union Assessment Committee [1893] AC 562, Ryde Rat App (1891–93) 382, 57 JP 821, 63 LJMC 9, 6 R 22, 42 WR 330, [1891–4] All ER Rep 577, 69 LT 725, 10 TLR 1, HL 2.30
Luby v Newcastle-under-Lyme Corpn [1964] 2 QB 64, [1964] 1 All ER 84, [1964] 2 WLR 475, 62 LGR 140, 128 JP 138, 107 Sol Jo 983; affd [1965] 1 QB 214, [1964] 3 All ER 169, [1964] 3 WLR 500, 62 LGR 622, 128 JP 536, 108 Sol Jo 541, [1964] RVR 708, 191 Estates Gazette 121, CA 4.8, 9.11

M

McCarthy & Stone (Developments) Ltd v Richmond upon Thames London Borough Council. See R v Richmond upon Thames London Borough Council, ex p McCarthy & Stone (Developments) Ltd
Magrath, Re [1934] 2 KB 415, 103 LJKB 660, [1934] All ER Rep 440, 78 Sol Jo 586, sub nom Lee v McGrath 32 LGR 380, 151 LT 553, 50 TLR 518, CA 9.12, 9.16
Manchester City Council v Greater Manchester Metropolitan County Council (1979) 78 LGR 71, CA; affd (1980) 78 LGR 560, HL 4.15, 4.25, 4.38, 16.19, 16.20
Meriden and Solihull Rating Authority v Tyacke [1950] 1 All ER 939, 48 LGR 349, 114 JP 269, 66 (pt 1) TLR 1197 .... 2.25

PARA

Mersey Docks and Harbour Board v Jones (1861) 25 JP 391, 9 CBNS 812, 30 LJMC 185, 9 WR 484, 4 LT 53; on appeal sub nom Jones v Mersey Docks and Harbour Board (1865) 29 JP 483, 11 HL Cas 443, 20 CBNS 56, 35 LJMC 1, 11 Jur NS 746, 6 New Rep 378, 13 WR 1069, [1861–73] All ER Rep 78, 12 LT 643 .... 2.21
Mirror Group plc v Customs and Excise Comrs [1998] SWTI 1056, [1998] BVC 2180 .... 18.57
Murphy v Middleton (1974) unreported 9.13

N

Nell v Longbottom [1894] 1 QB 767, 38 Sol Jo 309, 10 TLR 344, sub nom Louth Municipal Election, Re, Nell v Longbottom 63 LJQB 490, 10 R 193, 70 LT 499 .... 6.11
Newbold v Leicester City Council [1999] ICR 1182, [1999] 31 LS Gaz R 38, 143 Sol Jo LB 211, CA 9.14

P

Padfield v Minister of Agriculture, Fisheries and Food [1968] AC 997, [1968] 2 WLR 924, 110 Sol Jo 604, CA; revsd [1968] AC 997, [1968] 1 All ER 694, [1968] 2 WLR 924, 112 Sol Jo 171, HL 4.20, 4.21, 4.41, 9.15
Parr v A-G (1842) 8 Cl & Fin 409, 6 Jur 245, HL 9.66
Parry-Jones v Law Society [1969] 1 Ch 1, [1968] 1 All ER 177, [1968] 2 WLR 397, 111 Sol Jo 910, CA 8.121
Pickwell v Camden London Borough Council [1983] QB 962, [1983] 1 All ER 602, [1983] 2 WLR 583, 80 LGR 798, 126 Sol Jo 397, [1982] RVR 140 .... 9.14, 9.15
Pooley v District Auditor No 8 Audit District (1964) 63 LGR 60; on appeal sub nom Pooley v District Auditor No 8 District (1965) 63 LGR 236, CA 9.62, 9.70
Porter v Magill (1997) 96 LGR 157, 30 HLR 997; revsd [2000] 2 WLR 1420, 97 LGR 375, 31 HLR 823, [1999] 21 LS Gaz R 39, 143 Sol Jo LB 147, CA 8.47, 8.48, 8.122, 9.71, 9.78
Prescott v Birmingham Corpn [1955] Ch 210, [1954] 3 All ER 698, 53 LGR 68, 119 JP 48, 98 Sol Jo 886, CA 4.8, 9.10
Provident Mutual Life Assurance Association v Derby City Council [1981] 1 WLR 173, 79 LGR 297, [1981] RA 117, 125 Sol Jo 134, HL 5.8, 5.15

R

R v Brent London Borough Council, ex p Gunning (1985) 84 LGR 168 .... 17.31
R v Brent London Borough Council, ex p O'Malley (1997) 30 HLR 328; affd (1997) 30 HLR 328, CA 10.4, 14.15, 14.35, 14.40
R (Duckett) v Calvert [1898] 2 IR 511 .... 9.21
R v Carson Roberts [1908] 1 KB 407, 6 LGR 268, 72 JP 81, 77 LJKB 281, 52 Sol Jo 171, 98 LT 154, 24 TLR 226, CA 9.10, 9.70
R v District Auditor for Gateshead, ex p Judge (18 June 1996, unreported) 8.103
R v District Auditor for Isle of Anglesey County Council, ex p Jones (1999) LGLR 626; on appeal (23 July 1999, unreported), CA 8.51
R v District Auditor for Isle of Anglesey County Council, ex p Owen (13 October 1999, unreported) 8.51
R v District Auditor for Leicester, ex p Leicester City Council [1985] RVR 191; on appeal sub nom Leicester City Council v District Auditor for Leicester [1989] RVR 162, CA 4.43, 8.50
R v District Auditor No 3 Audit District of West Yorkshire Metropolitan County Council, ex p West Yorkshire Metropolitan County Council [1986] RVR 24 .... 4.40, 8.50, 8.106
R v Dolby [1892] 2 QB 301 .... 9.36
R v Drury [1894] 2 IR 489 .... 8.35, 9.14
R (Inglis) v Drury [1898] 2 IR 527 .... 9.12
R v Dublin Corpn (1878) 2 LR Ir 371 .... 9.14
R v Ealing London Borough Council, ex p Lewis (1992) 90 LGR 571, 24 HLR 484, CA 19.20, 19.29
R v Gloucester Corpn (1859) 23 JP 709 .... 9.17
R v Grain, ex p Wandsworth Guardians [1927] 2 KB 205, 25 LGR 231, 91 JP 71, 96 LJKB 563, 71 Sol Jo 308, 136 LT 776, 43 TLR 342, CA 9.24
R v Greater London Council, ex p London Residuary Body (1986) 19 HLR 175 .... 4.26
R v Greater London Council, ex p Westminster City Council (1985) Times, 22 January 4.31
R v Hackney London Borough Council, ex p Secretary of State for the Environment (1989) 88 LGR 96 .... 3.49

PARA

R v Hendon RDC, ex p Chorley [1933] 2 KB 696, 31 LGR 332, 97 JP 210, 102 LJKB 658, [1933] All ER Rep 20, 149 LT 535, 49 TLR 482 .... 6.11, 9.32
R v Hertfordshire County Council, ex p Green Environmental Industries Ltd [2000] 1 All ER 773, [2000] 2 WLR 373, [2000] 09 LS Gaz R 42, [2000] NLJR 277, [2000] EGCS 27, HL 8.121
R v Hurle-Hobbs, ex p Simmons [1945] KB 165, [1945] 1 All ER 273, 43 LGR 45, 109 JP 63, 114 LJKB 225, 173 LT 59, 61 TLR 135 .... 8.119, 8.120
R (O'Carroll) v King (1910) 50 ILTR 193 .... 9.48, 9.49
R v Liverpool Corpn, ex p Liverpool Taxi Fleet Operators' Association [1972] 2 QB 299, [1972] 2 WLR 1262, 71 LGR 387, 116 Sol Jo 201, sub nom Re Liverpool Taxi Owners' Association [1972] 2 All ER 589, CA 4.16
R v Local Comr for Administration in North and North East England, ex p Liverpool City Council [2000] 3 CL 474, Times, 3 March, CA 6.15
R v LCC, ex p Akkersdyk, ex p Fermenia [1892] 1 QB 190, 56 JP 8, 61 LJMC 75, 40 WR 285, [1891–4] All ER Rep 509, 66 LT 168, 8 TLR 175, DC 6.11
R v Lord President of the Privy Council, ex p Page [1993] AC 682, [1992] 3 WLR 1112, [1993] ICR 114, [1993] 10 LS Gaz R 33, 137 Sol Jo LB 45, sub nom Page v Hull University Visitor [1993] 1 All ER 97, [1993] NLJR 15, HL 9.15
R v Middlesbrough, ex p Frostree Ltd (16 December 1988, unreported) 14.39, 14.58
R v Monmouthshire County Council, ex p Smith (1935) 33 LGR 279, 99 JP 246, 79 Sol Jo 383, 153 LT 338, 51 TLR 435, DC 8.80
R (Jackson) v Newell [1898] 2 IR 530, 31 ILTR 8 .... 9.12
R (King-Kerr) v Newell (1903) 3 NIJR 93, [1903] 2 IR 335, 37 ILTR 45 .... 9.8
R v Philip Reid [1973] 3 All ER 1020, [1973] 1 WLR 1283, 57 Cr App Rep 807, 138 JP 51, 117 Sol Jo 681, 137 JP Jo 697, CA 8.118
R v Reed (1880) 5 QBD 483, 44 JP 633, 49 LJQB 600, 28 WR 787, 42 LT 835, CA 9.14
R v Richmond upon Thames London Borough Council, ex p McCarthy & Stone (Developments) Ltd (1989) 58 P & CR 434, [1989] 2 PLR 22, [1990] JPL 41; affd [1992] 2 AC 48, [1990] 2 All ER 852, [1990] 2 WLR 1294, 60 P & CR 174, [1990] 27 LS Gaz R 41, [1990] NLJR 362, CA; revsd sub nom McCarthy & Stone (Developments) Ltd v Richmond upon Thames London Borough Council [1992] 2 AC 48, [1991] 4 All ER 897, [1991] 3 WLR 941, 90 LGR 1, 63 P & CR 234, [1992] 3 LS Gaz R 33, [1992] JPL 467, 135 Sol Jo LB 206, HL 4.9, 4.31
R v Roberts [1901] 2 KB 117, 65 JP 359, 70 LJKB 590, 49 WR 488, 45 Sol Jo 424, 84 LT 530, 17 TLR 426 .... 9.48
R v Roberts, ex p Scurr [1924] 1 KB 514; on appeal [1924] 2 KB 695, CA; revsd sub nom Roberts v Hopwood [1925] AC 578, 23 LGR 337, 89 JP 105, 94 LJKB 542, [1925] All ER Rep 24, 69 Sol Jo 475, 133 LT 289, 41 TLR 436, HL 4.8, 4.21, 9.8, 9.10, 9.14, 9.15, 9.32, 9.70
R v St Pancras Assessment Committee (1877) 2 QBD 581, Ryde Rat App [1871–85] 188, 41 JP 662, 46 LJMC 243, 25 WR 827, sub nom Willing v St Pancras Assessment Committee 37 LT 126 .... 2.21
R v Saunders (1854) 3 E & B 763 .... 9.69
R v Secretary of State for the Environment, ex p Avon County Council (1990) 89 LGR 498 .... 2.7
R v Secretary of State for the Environment, ex p Camden London Borough Council [1998] 1 All ER 937, [1998] 1 WLR 615, 96 LGR 460, 31 HLR 242, [1998] 16 LS Gaz R 26, [1998] NLJR 401, [1998] RVR 199, 142 Sol Jo LB 110, HL 19.3
R v Secretary of State for the Environment, ex p Enfield London Borough Council (1993) 26 HLR 51, CA; affd (1994) 92 LGR 525, 27 HLR 132, HL 19.36
R v Secretary of State for the Environment, ex p Hammersmith and Fulham London Borough Council [1991] 1 AC 521, [1990] 3 WLR 898, 89 LGR 129, [1990] RVR 188, sub nom Hammersmith and Fulham London Borough Council v Secretary of State for the Environment [1990] 3 All ER 589; on appeal sub nom R v Secretary of State for the Environment, ex p Hammersmith and Fulham London Borough Council [1991] 1 AC 521, [1990] 3 WLR 898, 89 LGR 129, [1990] RVR 188, sub nom Hammersmith and Fulham London Borough Council v Secretary of State for the Environment [1990] 3 All ER 589, CA 2.7
R v Secretary of State for the Environment, ex p London Borough of Greenwich (1990) 22 HLR 543 .... 19.33
R v Tameside Metropolitan Borough Council, ex p Governors of Audenshaw High School (1990) Times, 27 June 16.20
R v Tower Hamlets London Borough Council, ex p Chetnik Developments Ltd [1988] AC 858, [1988] 2 WLR 654, 86 LGR 321, [1988] RA 45, 132 Sol Jo 462, [1988] 2 EGLR 195, [1988] 16 LS Gaz R 44, [1988] NLJR 89, [1988] 28 EG 69, sub nom Tower Hamlets London Borough Council v Chetnik Developments Ltd [1988] 1 All ER 961, HL 4.20

PARA
R v Walsall Metropolitan Borough Council, ex p Yapp (1993) 92 LGR 110, [1994] ICR 528, CA 4.16
R v Waltham Forest London Borough Council, ex p Baxter [1988] QB 419, [1987] 3 All ER 671, [1988] 2 WLR 257, 86 LGR 254, 132 Sol Jo 227, [1988] LS Gaz R 36, [1987] NLJ Rep 947, [1988] RVR 6, CA 4.18
R v Westminster City Council, ex p Legg (2000) Times, 13 June 9.76, 16.110
R v Westminster City Council, ex p Union of Managerial and Professional Officers (2000) Times, 13 June 9.76, 16.110
R v Wirral Metropolitan Borough Council, ex p Milstead (1989) 87 LGR 611, [1989] RVR 66 .... 9.104
R v Yorkshire Purchasing Organisation, ex p British Educational Suppliers Ltd (1996) 95 LGR 413, [1997] COD 210; on appeal (1997) 95 LGR 727, [1998] ELR 195, [1997] COD 473, CA 4.10, 20.21
Rands v Oldroyd [1959] 1 QB 204, [1958] 3 All ER 344, [1958] 3 WLR 583, 56 LGR 429, 123 JP 1, 102 Sol Jo 811 .... 6.9
Ransom & Luck Ltd v Surbiton Borough Council [1949] Ch 180, [1949] 1 All ER 185, 47 LGR 467, 113 JP 95, [1949] LJR 809, 93 Sol Jo 41, 65 TLR 57, CA 4.13
Reading v A-G [1951] AC 507, [1951] 1 All ER 617, 95 Sol Jo 155, [1951] 1 TLR 480, HL 9.51
Readman v DPP (1991) Times, 4 March 6.10
Rhondda Cynon Taff County Borough Council v Customs and Excise Comrs LON/99/670 .... 18.18
Roberts v Hopwood. See R v Roberts, ex p Scurr
Rothnie v Dearne UDC (1951) 50 LGR 123 .... 9.12, 9.16, 9.32

S

Sagnata Investments Ltd v Norwich Corpn [1971] 2 QB 614, [1971] 2 All ER 1441, [1971] 3 WLR 133, 69 LGR 471, 115 Sol Jo 406, CA 4.17
Secretary of State for Education and Science v Tameside Metropolitan Borough Council [1977] AC 1014, [1976] 3 All ER 665, [1976] 3 WLR 641, 120 Sol Jo 539 CA; on appeal [1977] AC 1014, [1976] 3 All ER 665, [1976] 3 WLR 641, 75 LGR 190, 120 Sol Jo 735, HL 4.4
Secretary of State for the Environment v Cumbria County Council (1983) 81 LGR 241, [1983] ICR 52, HL 3.25
Secretary of State for Trade and Industry v Deverell [2000] 2 All ER 365, [2000] 2 WLR 907, [2000] 03 LS Gaz R 35, 144 Sol Jo LB 49 .... 16.115
Shah v Barnet London Borough Council [1983] 2 AC 309, [1983] 1 All ER 226, [1983] 2 WLR 16, 81 LGR 305, 127 Sol Jo 36, HL 2.14
Shelley v LCC [1949] AC 56, [1948] 2 All ER 898, 47 LGR 93, 113 JP 1, [1949] LJR 57, 93 Sol Jo 101, 64 TLR 600, HL 19.20
Smith v Skinner [1986] RVR 45; on appeal sub nom Lloyd v McMahon [1987] AC 625, [1987] 1 All ER 1118, [1987] 2 WLR 821, 85 LGR 545, 130 Sol Jo 696, [1986] RVR 188, CA; affd [1987] AC 625, [1987] 1 All ER 1118, [1987] 2 WLR 821, 85 LGR 545, 131 Sol Jo 409, [1987] LS Gaz R 1240, [1987] NLJ Rep 265, [1987] RVR 58, HL 5.8, 8.46, 8.98, 8.115, 9.54, 9.55, 9.58, 9.63, 9.65, 9.71, 9.78
Smith and Fawcett Ltd, Re [1942] Ch 304, [1942] 1 All ER 542, 111 LJ Ch 265, 86 Sol Jo 147, 166 LT 279, CA 16.103, 16.104
Southend-on-Sea Corpn v Hodgson (Wickford) Ltd [1962] 1 QB 416, [1961] 2 All ER 46, [1961] 2 WLR 806, 59 LGR 193, 12 P & CR 165, 125 JP 348, 105 Sol Jo 181 .... 4.16
State v Moran (1953) ILTR 37 .... 8.49
Stockdale v Haringey London Borough Council (1989) 88 LGR 7, [1989] RVR 107, CA 9.13, 9.37
Storehire (UK) Ltd v Wojcik [1991] RA 39 .... 2.21
Stringer v Minister of Housing and Local Government [1971] 1 All ER 65, [1970] 1 WLR 1281, 68 LGR 788, 22 P & CR 255, 114 Sol Jo 753, [1970] RVR 481, [1971] JPL 114 .... 4.13, 4.17
Sutton London Borough Council v Morgan Grenfell & Co Ltd (1996) 95 LGR 574, 29 HLR 608, CA 15.75, 15.76, 17.15

T

Taylor v Munrow [1960] 1 All ER 455, [1960] 1 WLR 151, 58 LGR 135, 124 JP 207, 104 Sol Jo 169 .... 4.8, 9.9, 9.14
Thomas v Devonport Corpn [1900] 1 QB 16, 63 JP 740, 69 LJQB 51, 48 WR 89, 81 LT 427, 16 TLR 9, CA 9.10

PARA

W

West Cheshire Water Board v Crowe [1940] 1 KB 793, [1940] 2 All ER 351, 38 LGR 243, 104 JP 231, 109 LJKB 590, 84 Sol Jo 416, 163 LT 155, 56 TLR 603, DC 9.18
West Wiltshire District Council v Garland [1995] Ch 297, [1995] 2 All ER 17, [1995] 2 WLR 439, [1995] 03 LS Gaz R 38, [1994] NLJR 1733, [1995] RVR 97, sub nom West Wiltshire District Council v Garland (Cond, third party) 93 LGR 235, CA 8.52
Western Fish Products Ltd v Penwith District Council [1981] 2 All ER 204, 77 LGR 185, 38 P & CR 7, 122 Sol Jo 471, [1978] JPL 623, CA 4.16
Westminster City Council, Re [1986] AC 668, [1986] 2 WLR 807, 84 LGR 665, 130 Sol Jo 341, [1986] LS Gaz R 1554, sub nom Westminster City Council v Greater London Council [1986] 2 All ER 278, HL 4.25
Westminster City Council v Woodbury (Valuation Officer) and the Yard Arm Club Ltd [1992] RA 1, [1991] 2 EGLR 173, [1991] 48 EG 129, CA 2.21
Wheeler v Leicester City Council [1985] AC 1054, [1985] 2 All ER 151, 83 LGR 725, 129 Sol Jo 332, [1985] LS Gaz R 1710, [1985] NLJ Rep 413, CA; revsd [1985] AC 1054, [1985] 2 All ER 1106, [1985] 3 WLR 335, 83 LGR 725, 129 Sol Jo 558, [1985] LS Gaz R 3175, [1985] NLJ Rep 781, HL 4.21
Wilkinson v Doncaster Metropolitan Borough Council (1985) 84 LGR 257, CA........... 9.9, 9.13

PART I

Introduction to the local government finance regime

CHAPTER 1

An introduction to local government and current proposals for reform

A Introduction

1.1 Local government stretches back into the early middle ages but the true ancestor of the modern system is probably that of the justices which was established in the fifteenth century[1]. This system developed into a complete administrative structure along with the commissioners for sewers and the network of boroughs. The zenith of this system came after the revolution of 1688 and in response to the excesses of the Stuart regime. A system of independent local government was established then and some writers have called this the 'Golden Age' of local government[2]. The modern system evolved from the nineteenth century Local Government Acts[3] which moved a long way towards establishing single body multi-purpose authorities and the two-tier system of local government which remains the basis of local government today. A greatly simplified structure emerged and achieved a degree of uniformity that was able to be codified in the Local Government Act 1933. Today's equivalent differs in many ways. Much of the independence of the earlier system is lost, although this process has been in place since the seventeenth century. At the centre of the question of dependence is the financing of local government and it is in this sphere that central government has drawn its hold on local government even tighter. In discussing local government, this chapter seeks to set out its basic structure and an outline of the system of local government finance.

1 *Holdsworth's History of English Law*, vol iv.
2 Wade, for example, gives this title: H W R Wade and C F Forsyth *Administrative Law* (7th edn, 1994) p 110. If one values the independence of local government it was certainly a high point.
3 The Local Government Acts 1888 and 1894.

1 THE TYPES AND FUNCTIONS OF LOCAL AUTHORITIES

(a) The structure of local government

1.2 Local Government Acts in the late nineteenth century established an elected county council for each county and each city which contained in excess of 50,000 inhabitants[1]. This was further divided into urban and rural districts. In the larger parishes of rural districts parish councils were organised. This entire structure was codified in the Local Government Act 1933. Non-county and district borough councils were sanitary, housing and rating authorities, whilst county councils were responsible for education, planning, the fire service and some welfare and health services[2]. With central government taking on more responsibility for areas such as health, the poor law and transport, the two spheres of authority no longer had well defined parameters. With the added problem of increase in population leading to great disparities between the boroughs it soon became clear that reform was necessary.

This reform took the shape of the Local Government Act 1972, which restructured local government in England and Wales. It gave effect to the proposals in the Consultation Paper 'Local Government in England: Government Proposals for Reorganisation'[3]. It greatly simplified the law relating to the structure and function of local authorities. The Act replaced the Local Government Act 1933 and incorporated the provisions of the London Government Act 1963. The LGA 1972 came into force on 1 April 1974[4].

1 This was raised to 75,000 in 1926 (Local Government (County Boroughs and Adjustments) Act 1926) and 100,000 in 1958 (Local Government Act 1958) to accommodate the growth in population. It is also interesting to note when one talks of 'cities' that such nomenclature has no significance except as a title of honour. A city will call itself such on the basis of royal charter or time honoured tradition. Legally the title has no distinction from 'Borough'. Section 245(10) of the Local Government Act 1972 deals with this point.
2 H W R Wade and C F Forsyth *Administrative Law* (7th edn, 1994), p 113.
3 Cmnd 4584 (1971).
4 This is an important date in local government history as the water authorities and the National Health Service were simultaneously reformed.

1.3 In England the Act created six metropolitan counties which were divided into 36 metropolitan districts, and 39 non-metropolitan counties divided into 296 districts[1]. In Wales eight counties are divided into 36 districts[2]. The non-metropolitan counties are for the most part larger than their predecessors, the old counties. This reflects the attempt by the LGA 1972 to reduce the fragmentation of local government administration. Not all local governments have changed though. In England the former parishes continue to exist as parishes, although not in urban areas, where parishes were abolished in 1933, and the Secretary of State has the power to constitute new parishes[3]. In Wales, however, a new method of organising this level of local government has been adopted. A system of communities is in place, one for each of the former boroughs, urban districts and rural parishes[4]. Each parish must have a parish meeting at least once a year and a parish council may or must—depending on status—be established by the district council. In order to maintain an element of flexibility in the organisation of local government, Boundary Commissions are in place in England and Wales and may propose alterations to the boundaries of local government areas. In this way the government can respond effectively to changes in the population of any particular area either due to population growth or to migration from one centre to another.

1 Local Government Act 1972, Sch 1.
2 LGA 1972, Sch 4, Pt I.
3 LGA 1972, Sch 1, Pt V.
4 LGA 1972, s 20(4).

(b) London government

1.4 Whilst these important changes to the structure of local government were taking place in the rest of the country in 1974, the structure of London government was not materially affected. The London Government Act of 1963, which was incorporated into the LGA 1972, had established the Greater London Council and the London Borough Councils. The administrative area of London comprises 32

London Boroughs[1], the City of London and the Temples[2]. The LGA 1963 abolished the old London and Middlesex County Councils and all other local authorities within the area of Greater London. The Greater London Council's main responsibilities were for roads, traffic management, refuse disposal, the fire service, land drainage and education in the inner London area. It shared planning and housing matters with the London borough councils[3].

The Local Government Act 1985 made great changes in the administration of Greater London. It abolished the Greater London Council and the metropolitan county councils[4]. Under the Act the functions of the abolished bodies were transferred to the London borough councils and the metropolitan district councils. The Act effectively reduced London to a one-tier system. It is important to note that LGA 1985, Pt III established the Inner London Education Authority as a directly elected authority. LGA 1985, Pt IV provided for separate Joint Authorities to organise police, fire, civil defence and passenger transport in the metropolitan authorities and fire and civil defence in London. LGA 1985, s 85 established a Residuary Body to deal with residual matters. It was made up of five to ten members all of whom are appointed by the Secretary of State. It was abolished with effect from 29 March 1996.

Its functions were as follows[5]:

(1) to assume the rights and liabilities of the external debt of the Greater London Council;
(2) to make redundancy payments to former Greater London Council staff;
(3) to administer the Superannuation Fund transferred from the Greater London Council and the payment of pensions;
(4) to take over the property rights and liabilities of the Greater London Council, but only where no provision has been made for them elsewhere: such may well have been passed on to the relevant London Borough; and
(5) to wind up the accounts of the Greater London Council and present those accounts for audit.

1 The London Boroughs are listed in Schedule 1 to the London Government Act 1963.
2 Inner Temple and Middle Temple are ancient authorities but do not have many administrative functions.
3 *Cross on Local Government* (8th edn, 1997) at Appendix G–O1.
4 Local Government Act 1985.
5 LGA 1985, ss 58–63.

1.5 By the London Government Reorganisation (Pensions) Order 1989[1] the London Residuary Body transferred its pensions and superannuation fund functions to the newly created London Pensions Fund. It comprises between seven and eleven members appointed by the Secretary of State. It has the power to make levies on London Boroughs and the Common Council.

1 SI 1989/1815, as amended by SI 1990/198.

1.6 This system of London local governance was again changed in part by the Education Reform Act 1988. This abolished the Inner London Education Authority in April 1990. The Act provided for the transfer of most of its functions to the councils of the inner London boroughs. The Secretary of State retained the power to designate which schools would be administered by the local authority and for the transfer of property rights and staff and for any liabilities. He also had control for five years over the management structure of local education authority functions established by each Authority.

1.7 The Local Government Act 1992 has brought substantial change to the organisation of local government in England and Wales[1]. Unitary authorities are established to replace a large number of the non-metropolitan authorities. Two-tier authorities are retained in the others, whilst some large cities will be given unitary status[2].

1 Local Government Act 1992, ss 12–14.
2 The government's policy on this matter is contained in the document Local Government Reviews: The Structure of Local Government: a Consultation Paper (1991).

(c) Local authorities as corporations

1.8 It is a feature common to all local authorities that they are corporate bodies and enjoy corporate status. That corporation takes legal shape as one individual taking rights and duties and being capable of suing and making contracts. These rules are enshrined in statute for local authorities. The Local Government Act 1972, s 2 provides that a principal council shall be a body corporate. Sections 13 and 33 apply the same principle to parish and community councils. The Local Government Act 1985 further grants corporate status to joint authorities and residuary bodies.

(d) The functions of local government

1.9 The allocation of functions between local authorities is a complex matter in a state of constant flux. As if to underline this point, the Local Government Act 1992 changes matters again with the introduction of single-tier authorities which will take on all the functions listed below.

1.10 The functions of local government in the rest of the country are allocated by a series of provisions in the LGA 1972[1]. Only in the case of the parishes was no reallocation required[2]. They inherited their functions from their predecessors. The allocation of these functions is best explained by means of a simple list[3].

County Councils are responsible for the following:

- education, town and country planning[4], social services[5], food and drugs, roads (for the most part), refuse disposal, libraries, highways, traffic, public transport, recreation, the police and the fire service.

District Councils are responsible for the following:

- housing, town and country planning, public health and sanitary services, food and drugs, minor urban roads, refuse collection, entertainment, recreation, rating, coast protection and local licensing[6].

Parish Councils are then left to deal with the following functions:

- footpaths, allotments, bus shelters, recreation grounds, village greens, burial grounds, parking spaces for motor cycles and bicycles.

1 Local Government Act 1972, Pt IX.
2 LGA 1972, s 179(4).
3 A fuller description is contained in the Department of the Environment Circular 121/72, Annexe A.
4 This involves the making of plans, enforcement of planning policy and the carrying out of duties under the Town and Country Planning Act 1990 as amended.
5 The Local Authority Social Services Act 1970, Sch1 outlines the local authority social services responsibilities.
6 Licensing powers are numerous. Many of the local authority powers of licensing are contained in the Local Government (Miscellaneous Provisions) Act 1982.

1.11 In the large metropolitan areas after the abolition of the metropolitan county councils the district authorities inherited the planning, roads, waste disposal, the administration of justice, land drainage and other miscellaneous functions. Three joint authorities were established to take charge of civil defence, police and fire service and passenger transport.

In London, after it was reduced to a one-tier system following the abolition of the Greater London Council, the London Fire and Civil Defence Authority was established as a joint authority. The other functions were controlled by the London Boroughs.

1.12 Where there are special reasons for one authority to administer a larger area than a normal local government area a statutory joint board may be established by ministerial order. These powers are established for example under the Town and Country Planning Act 1990[1] (joint planning boards). These joint boards have their own corporate identity and their own powers, including the power to issue their own precepts for raising revenue through rates.

1 Section 2 and the First Schedule.

(e) The administration of police functions

1.13 The organisation of local government functions has undergone another change with the introduction of the Police Act 1996. New arrangements for police authorities were introduced by this Act which has made significant amendments to the Police Act 1964. The Act came into effect on 1 April 1995. The organisation of police authorities is now as follows.

England and Wales are divided into 41 police areas, the City of London police area and the Metropolitan police district[1]. There is a police authority for each corresponding police area[2]. Importantly, all police authorities are now authorities in their own right and are not annexed to a local authority. Each authority is normally made up of 17 members[3]. Three of those members are magistrates, five are independent members and seven are members of 'relevant' councils for the area. A 'relevant council' for the purposes of a police authority is a council for a county, district, county borough or London borough which is wholly within the police authority's area. Where there is more than one relevant council for the area a joint committee must be established. That committee will then appoint members to the police authority. These appointments should reflect the political makeup of the councils from which they have come. Independent members are appointed by the other members of the police authority. The names from which the other council members choose the independent members are taken from a short list prepared by the Secretary of State.

1 Police Act 1996, s 1(2).
2 PA 1996, s 3.
3 PA 1996, s 4.

1.14 When outlining the functions of local government it is important to note, however briefly, the extent of central government influence and control. Local government is subject to central government in numerous ways. The Local Government Finance Acts have given central government a stranglehold on local government income and expenditure. In many other matters ministers give mandatory directions. Departmental inspectors are appointed to review schools, the fire service and the police. Many local government appointments are subject to central control. There is also the final sanction of the default power. If the minister considers that a local authority is failing to perform its functions, he can make a legally enforceable order instructing the authority to carry out a particular act or policy. There is no general default power under the LGA 1972 but such powers are a feature of individual Acts, for example the Housing Act 1985, s 164 concerning the right of council tenants to buy their homes. Here the Secretary of State may force the local authority, should they be unwilling or tardy in their sale of council houses to tenants, to speed the process up.

1.15 Further legislation has altered local government in Wales. The Local Government (Wales) Act 1994, Pt II[1] provides for the transfer of functions to the new unitary authorities. LG(W)A 1994, Pt V[2] establishes the residuary body for Wales[3].

Local Government Act 1972, s 245A—as substituted by Local Government (Wales) Act 1994, s 5—provides that a county council in Wales may petition for the conferral by the Queen by charter of county borough status. This status does not affect the powers and duties of the council but allows the chairman to assume the status of mayor.

The constitution and functions of the Welsh Assembly are outside the scope of this book but are referred to at para **7.10**.

1 Sections 17–26.
2 Sections 39–45.
3 Its name in Welsh is Corff Gweddilliol Cymru. It is established by the Residuary Body for Wales (appointed Body) Order 1995, SI 1995/102.

2 BILLING, PRECEPTING AND CHARGING AUTHORITIES, LEVYING BODIES AND SPECIAL CASES

(a) Billing authorities

1.16 The revenue which local authorities raise for themselves comes in part from their powers of taxation. It scarcely needs mentioning that in the past these taxes have been a cause of some controversy. The much criticised rates gave way in 1988 to the community charge which became even more unpopular on account of its regressive flat rate. This was replaced under the Local Government Finance Act 1992 by the council tax. The council tax is levied on chargeable dwellings on a daily basis[1]. Under the LGFA 1992 a dwelling is to be placed in one of eight bands of property based upon its value[2]. The band the property is in determines the rate of taxation. Where there is only one person resident in the property the tax is subject to a 25% discount[3]. The tax is imposed on the resident in the dwelling. Where there are more than one resident then the tax is payable by those with the most interest in the property[4]. The task of drawing up valuation lists and allocating houses to bands is not a local function[5]. The collection of the tax is undertaken by the district councils and these are known as the billing authorities. An aggrieved person can appeal against the decision of the billing authority that one's dwelling is chargeable or that the person in question is liable to pay the tax or that the calculation of the relevant amount of taxation is incorrect to the local valuation tribunal[6].

1 Local Government Finance Act 1992, s 2–3.
2 LGFA 1992, s 5(2).
3 LGFA 1992, s 11.
4 LGFA 1992, s 6.
5 This task is undertaken by the Commissioners of Inland Revenue and is thus a central government function.
6 For a full discussion see Chapter 2.

(b) Precepting authorities

1.17 The billing authorities collect the tax not only for themselves but also on behalf of the precepting authorities. From 1993–94 receipts in respect of council tax and non-domestic rates are to be paid into a Collection Fund[1]. From that Fund the authorities make payments of precepts to major precepting authorities and payment to the Secretary of State in respect of non-domestic rates[2]. Major precepting authorities (primarily the county councils and bodies such as fire authorities or civil defence authorities which cover more than one local area) do not include parish councils, which are defined as local precepting authorities. These authorities—a major precepting authority *must*, a minor precepting authority *may*—issue precepts to the billing authorities indicating the amount of revenue they require for their budgets[3]. The precept must be issued by 1 March of the preceding financial year. Failure to do this will not, however, make the precept invalid. These figures are then built into the billing authority's calculation of the tax. Neither the billing nor the precepting authorities have a free hand in calculating the amount which they will charge. They must follow strict guidelines set down in the Local Government Act 1992 and are judicially reviewable upon the use of those guidelines[4]. The council tax must be set at the level which bridges the gap between the authority's budget requirement and the expected income from domestic rates and the revenue support grant. Note that the Greater London Authority is a major precepting authority from 1 May 2000: Greater London Authority Act 1999, s 82.

1 The Collection Fund is established under s 90(1) of the Local Government Finance Act 1988. For a full discussion see Chapter 3.
2 Local Government Finance Act 1982, s 90(2).
3 Local Government Act 1992, ss 40–41.
4 1992 Act, s 66(1) states that judicial review is the only possible form of action here.

(c) Levying bodies

1.18 Local Government Finance Act 1988, s 74 defines a levying body as a statutory body other than a precepting authority which has the power to raise its expenses from a local authority. The pre-existing powers of these bodies were abolished by LGFA 1988, s 117, but s 74 enables the Secretary of State to make regulations conferring powers to issue levies on the councils concerned, which may be either billing or precepting authorities. Levies are charged to the General Fund and become a component of the authority's own budgeting.

Local Government Finance Act 1988, s 75 deals with special levies. This section applies to any body which has no power to levy a rate by virtue of regulations under LGFA 1988, s 118, or a body whose power to levy a rate is modified under s 118. The Minister may make regulations conferring on that body the power to issue a special levy.

3 CENTRAL—LOCAL GOVERNMENT RELATIONS

(a) Public expenditure planning

1.19 It is clear that the relationship between local and central government is of the utmost importance. Local expenditure must be seen in the context of overall government expenditure. As local authorities are funded mainly by central government then the block grant given must take its place alongside the other expenditure of government, central government must therefore have some control over local government expenditure and play a large part in its planning. To this end there can be no general expenditure by local government without central government approval. There are several points at which the government must be consulted or gain authorisation for particular expenditure.

The most obvious point at which the government has control over the expenditure of local government is in the setting of the council tax. As we have seen a council must send its proposed rates to the Secretary of State who may then decide the rate of taxation is too high. This may then be followed by the capping procedure which is described below.

(b) Audit

1.20 A further system of control of local government is that of audit. Section 2 and Sch 2 of the Audit Commission Act 1998 requires the listed local authorities to submit their accounts for audit to the district auditor who is appointed or approved by the Secretary of State. The system is designed to ensure that in the matter of expenditure and general financial practice the local authority keeps within the law. It is the auditor's job, inter alia, to see that expenditure was authorised by statute, that statutory limits on expenditure have not been exceeded and that statutory scales have been observed.

1.21 Under the ACA 1998 auditors are given a greater degree of independence than before and are no longer appointed by the Secretary of State. The Audit Commission which controls the audit system is itself, however, still appointed by the Secretary of State.

1.22 Auditors should not be seen as creatures of central government. They are independent in their task of ensuring that economy, efficiency and effectiveness are maximised by local government. The Local Government Act 1992, s 5 places a duty on the local authority to consider the auditor's report under Local Government Act Finance Act 1982, s 15(3) and to any written recommendations by an auditor which is contained therein.

Local audit is discussed in much greater detail in Chapter 8. It is obvious from this section that the opinion of the district auditor is of key importance when a local authority is considering its expenditure.

1.23 LGA 1972, s 151 appoints a chief finance officer of each authority. The Local Government Finance Act 1988, s 114 places a duty on him to make a report to the Secretary of State if it appears to him that the local authority is about to incur unlawful expenditure which is in excess of its resources[1]. The local authority must then consider the report at a meeting within 21 days and is prohibited from taking the relevant action until the meeting has been held[2].

The Local Government and Housing Act 1989, s 5 requires a local authority to appoint a monitoring officer. The duties of the two officers seem to overlap. The monitoring officer is required to report on any proposal which may give rise to a contravention of the law or lead to maladministration.

1 Subsections (2) and (3).
2 Section 115.

4 STATUTORY FRAMEWORK FOR LOCAL GOVERNMENT EXPENDITURE PLANNING

(a) Key processes

1.24 There are several identifiable key processes which are central to planning the expenditure of a local authority. First, the Local Government Finance Report sets out the available grant for a local authority for a particular financial year. This document tells a local authority how much it has to spend. Of great importance to the local authority is the capping procedure where the Secretary of State limits a local authority's expenditure if he feels its expenditure plans are excessive: the present law relating to capping is contained in Pt II of the Local Government Act 1999. This process has been much used by the last Conservative government and partially reformed by the present Labour government (see para **1.46**ff below). Last, important dates such as the deadline for announcing the council tax for that year are also important. These subjects are dealt with later in this book.

(b) The timetable for setting the council tax

1.25 The deadline for setting the council tax is a key date in the expenditure planning timetable. It is beyond this date that the decision on whether to cap an authority's budget is taken.

1.26 The Local Government Finance Act 1992, s 30 provides that a local authority must have set the level of council tax by the 11 March of each financial year. Failure to do this, though, is not fatal to any tax level set after this date. Precepting authorities are required to issue their precepts before 1 March. Again, failure to do this will not be fatal to any precept issued after this date. The total amount of council tax may not be set before the earlier of 1 March of the preceding financial year or of the precepting authority issuing its precept to the billing authority.

5 THE ANNUAL PROCESS FOR LOCAL GOVERNMENT EXPENDITURE PLANNING

1.27 A key forum for discussion between central and local government on financial matters is the Consultative Council on Local Government Finance (CCLGF). This non-statutory body is chaired by the Secretary of State for the Environment (or his deputy) and comprises ministers and civil servants from every department concerned with local government and members selected by local authority associations. The Council's business is decided upon after detailed consideration by the Official Steering Group. This group is made up of civil servants, the secretary of each local authority association, officer advisers and the specialist professional staff of each association. The Council has undoubtedly brought the local authority associations into closer contact and provided a better organised basis for consultation between central and local government. Some writers, however, feel that the expectations of the body as a productive forum for negotiation have not been fulfilled. Indeed the efficacy of the Council as a consultative body has been questioned by others who feel that it is little more than a platform for the announcement of decisions by central government[1].

1 See eg *Cross on Local Government Law* (8th edn, 1997) at paras 2-11 to 2-33.

1.28 This body is by no means the only means for consultation, however. Consultation is written into many Acts. Discussions do also take place between central government and the local authority associations about a whole range of issues.

B Reform of public finance and local government

1.29 Reform of public finance and the modernisation of local government are key aspects of current government policy. At the time of writing, local government is in the midst of changes and proposals for reform which affect virtually every aspect of its activities and organisation, including the financial affairs dealt with in this book. Three years on, many of the proposals for modernisation of local government announced since the general election in May 1997 are being implemented through two major new Acts for local government and others are at various stages of formulation or implementation. The following summarises some of the key developments affecting local authorities in England and Wales, many of which are referred to later in this work.

1 COMPREHENSIVE SPENDING REVIEW

1.30 In June 1997, shortly after its election, the government commenced a fundamental review of all public spending, described as 'the Comprehensive Spending Review' ('CSR'), aimed at examining government spending and priorities across the board and establishing a new planning framework for public expenditure. The review covered all government departments, agencies and non-departmental bodies and included local government. 'A fair and just finance system for local government' was said to be vital to a 'renewed and vigorous local democracy'[1].

1 Speech by Local Government Minister, 25 July 1997.

1.31 The Chancellor of the Exchequer announced the first stage of the results of the review in June 1998 in his Economic and Fiscal Strategy Report[1]. In addition to announcing an end to the annual spending round, to be replaced with three year spending plans for government departments, he outlined four key elements of reform:

(a) two fiscal rules: the 'golden rule' that over the 'economic cycle' current spending should be covered by revenues; and the 'sustainable investment rule' that there must be a prudent ratio between debt and national income (the Gross Domestic Product);
(b) a radical reassessment of what government does and how its money is spent, eradicating areas where it should not act;
(c) a radical change in government policy towards investment and publicly owned assets;
(d) that spending on public services should be explicitly linked to modernisation and reform of government departments, with any additional resources being linked to specific outputs.

1 Stability and Investment for the Long Term—Economic and Fiscal Strategy Report (11 June 1998) Cm 3978.

1.32 Many of the themes of the Chancellor's statement to the House of Commons in June 1998 have been carried through into specific changes for the local government sector[1]. For example, the need to ensure 'best value' for money and the most efficient use of public resources, the emphasis on clear outputs and the use of efficiency and performance targets, the impetus to dispose of surplus public assets in order to fund new investment and the aim of nurturing effective public private partnerships to maximise investment in the renewal of infrastructure. Added to this, there is the consistent message, that resources for local government would be conditional upon reform.

1 These themes had also been foreshadowed in the series of six interrelated consultation papers published by the Department of the Environment, Transport and the Regions ('DETR') on modernisation of local government earlier in 1998 (see para **1.35** below).

1.33 The second stage announcement of the results of the CSR was made in July 1998, with the publication of public spending plans for 1999–2002[1]. Of particular importance to local government was the prioritisation of spending on education and health (with subsequent legislative reform aimed at encouraging local authorities and health bodies to work together more closely[2]. Other features included increased resources to encourage the development of the Private Finance Initiative ('PFI') for local government[3] and to tackle deprived neighbourhoods under the New Deal for Communities initiative[4]. In addition, proposals were announced for a new system of local government finance to be set out in a White Paper which would ensure:

(a) an end to 'universal' council tax capping, whilst indicating that there would be an alternative framework for central government to control excessive council tax;
(b) a commitment to focus on efficient and effective council services through the Best Value initiative;
(c) a commitment to reinvigorate local democracy by ensuring that local politicians would be more accountable to the local electorate;
(d) reform of the system of subsidy to councils for council tax benefit; and
(e) a commitment to provide local authorities with greater flexibility and increased incentives to manage their assets more efficiently.

In July 2000, the Chancellor announced the Spending Review 2000 to set Departmental budgets for the financial years 2001–2002 to 2003–2004, including an average 11% increase for housing, the regions and the environment (and a further £4.2 billion for transport). Some £4 billion is to be allocated for local authority PFI projects over the three-year period.

1 Modern Public Services for Britain: Investing in Reform, Comprehensive Spending Review: New Public Spending Plans 1999–2002 (14 July 1998) Cm 4011. See now, Prudent for a Purpose: Building Opportunity and Security for All. Spending Review 2000. New Public Spending Plans 2001–2004. Cm 4807.
2 See Health Act 1999, ss 26–32, on 'partnership', intended to establish closer working arrangements between health service bodies and local authorities, including provisions to enable the pooling of resources and prescribed joint working arrangements.
3 See Chapter 15.
4 £800 million over three years from April 1999 was earmarked by the government to assist the most deprived neighbourhoods. The initiative is targeted initially at 17 'pathfinder' neighbourhoods, bringing together housing and regeneration programmes to enhance economic and employment opportunities. 'Local partnerships' apply for funding for up to 10 years.

1.34 One important aspect of (e) in para **1.33** which did not require new legislation was the announcement of proposals to end 'set-aside' on most non-housing capital receipts as from September 1998 in order to allow local authorities to reinvest most of the proceeds of asset sales, other than those from housing land. The means of achieving this change was, in technical terms, minor, but the practical effects were to simplify significantly many local government transactions, especially those involving the disposal of local authority land. The effect of these changes is outlined in Chapter 14.

2 WHITE PAPER—MODERN LOCAL GOVERNMENT

1.35 A series of six consultation papers[1] issued by the Department of the Environment, Transport and the Regions ('the DETR') in February and March 1998, including three specifically addressing financial issues, considered options for changes for local government and promised a Government White Paper to 'contain a detailed programme of the changes needed to give to this country a modern local government well able to face the challenges and needs of the 21st Century'.

1 The 'Modernising Local Government' green papers published for consultation by the Department of the Environment, Transport and the Regions during February and March 1998: 'Local democracy and community leadership'; 'A new ethical framework'; 'Improving local services through best value'; 'Capital Finance'; 'Business rates' and 'Improving local financial accountability'.

1.36 The White Paper, entitled 'Modern Local Government—In Touch with the People'[1] was published in July 1998 ('the White Paper'). The proposals outlined in the White Paper entail a radical and wide ranging review of local government. They included reforms of the legal and administrative arrangements concerning local authority finance[2]. If implemented in their entirety, certain of the proposals would have implications for the vires of local authorities discussed in this book. Most of the White Paper proposals required new primary legislation. This is being tackled in stages, with no comprehensive timetable or end-date for reform. However, significant progress has already been made. The LGA 1999 received Royal Assent on 27 July 1999, implementing a first tranche of measures (see para **1.39**ff). The LGA 2000, not yet fully in force, was enacted on 28 July 2000 (see para **1.48**ff).

1 Cm 4014.
2 Certain changes on capital finance were introduced immediately (to end set-aside on most capital receipts). Whilst these changes were significant, they did not require new primary legislation.

1.37 The major areas of proposed change covered by the White Paper which explicitly concern finance comprised:

(a) improvements to financial accountability, including the abolition of 'crude and universal capping';
(b) simplification of the capital finance system; and
(c) amendment of the regime for business rates.

Other broad areas of proposed reform outlined in the White Paper are of equal, if less direct, relevance to this book:

(d) the 'best value' initiative to improve local services;
(e) new political structures for local government;
(f) a new framework for ethics in local government;
(g) improvements to local democracy;
(h) new functions for local authorities to promote the economic, social and environmental well-being of their areas;
(i) the concept of 'beacon councils': the best-performing local authorities who might eventually be rewarded with additional resources and, possibly, with additional legal powers or freedom from constraints.

1.38 The following summarises the progress which has been made with implementation of these initiatives to date.

3 LOCAL GOVERNMENT ACT 1999

1.39 A Local Government Bill to address certain of the proposals in the White Paper (known informally as the 'Best Value and Capping Bill') was introduced at the beginning of the Parliamentary session in November 1998 and received Royal Assent on 27 July 1999. The Local Government Act 1999 is in two parts.

(a) Best value

1.40 LGA 1999, Pt I deals with 'best value' and is referred to in Chapter 7. It creates the concept of 'best value authorities' (ie local and other authorities in England and Wales, including the recently created Greater London Authority in respect of functions exercised by the Mayor).

1.41 Best value authorities are under a duty to make arrangements to secure continuous improvement in the way in which their functions are exercised, 'having regard to a combination of economy, efficiency and effectiveness'[1]. This duty is supplemented by detailed provisions concerning local consultation, performance indicators and standards to be specified by the Secretary of State, requirements for authorities to prepare performance plans and conduct regular reviews, and involves external audit checks and powers of the Secretary of State to intervene to ensure compliance. There are also new powers for the Secretary of State, by statutory instrument, to amend or repeal existing enactments and to confer new powers on best value authorities to assist them to comply with their new duties under LGA 1999, Pt I[2].

1 See the Local Government Act 1999, s 3.

2 LGA 1999, s 16. The form of the Secretary of State's new powers is at first sight extensive, albeit limited in effect by the nature of the duties under Part I to which they are explicitly linked. See also the powers of the Secretary of State to amend primary legislation through regulations made under ss 15(7) and (8) of the 1999 Act.

1.42 LGA 1999, Pt I (s 21) made provision for the legislation on compulsory competitive tendering[1] to cease to have effect on 2 January 2000. The Secretary of State was given power to issue guidance to best value authorities on the exercise of their functions during the transitional period before the new 'best value' regime took effect in April 2000.

1 Under the Local Government, Planning and Land Act 1980, Pt III; the Local Government Act 1988, Pt I, s 32 and Sch 6; and the Local Government Act 1992, ss 8–11 and Sch 1.

1.43 There are also explicit powers for the Secretary of State to make orders under Deregulation and Contracting Out Act 1994, s 70 in respect of 'best value authorities', to enable such authorities to delegate specified functions to an external body: LGA 1999, s 18.

1.44 Additional powers are given to the Secretary of State (under s 19) in respect of the 'non-commercial' matters which local authorities are bound to disregard, under Local Government Act 1988, s 17, when awarding certain supply and works contracts. In respect of best value authorities, the Secretary of State may now specify by order that a matter is to cease to be a 'non-commercial matter'. The LGA 1988 itself only enables the Secretary of State to specify *additional* non-commercial matters by order[1]. At the time of writing, the DETR is consulting on a draft order[2] under LGA 1999, s 19 which proposes that 'workforce matters' should cease to be non-commercial matters for the purposes of LGA 1988, s 17, where such matters are relevant to the achievement of best value, and in circumstances where the Transfer of Undertakings (Protection of Employment) Regulations 1981 (SI 1981/1794 as amended) would apply.

1 This follows through from the government's support for the failed Local Authorities Tenders Bill 1998 and a commitment in the White Paper. General principles of administrative law and the EC Treaty place independent constraints on the 'non-commercial' or other matters authorities can take into account in awarding contracts.
2 Letter from the DETR to Chief Executives of Best Value Authorities in England, 11 April 2000.

1.45 Amendments are made to the Audit Commission Act 1998, to take account of the Commissioner's new functions in connection with best value authorities (LGA 1999, s 22) and the Secretary of State is empowered to make regulations regarding the accounts to be kept by best value authorities: LGA 1999, s 23.

(b) Council tax capping

1.46 LGA 1999, Pt II deals with council tax capping, the means by which central government regulates increases in local taxation. Part II gives effect to Schedule 1 to the Act which is to govern the limitation of council tax and precepts for the financial years beginning on or after 1 April 2000[1]. This Schedule also repeals the current system of 'universal' capping under Part I, Chapter V of the Local Government Finance Act 1992. From 1 April 2000, the Secretary of State has more flexible (and no less extensive) powers to select individual authorities for capping, and to address their budget requirements over a number of years.

1 By inserting a new Chapter IVA into Pt I of the Local Government Finance Act 1992.

1.47 The LGA 1999 has been brought into force in stages[1], with many of the key provisions taking effect on 1 April 2000. In readiness for that time, provisions concerning preparatory matters such as certain consultation requirements and definitions came into effect on 10 August 1999, and the powers of the Secretary of State to make orders and prepare guidance and the obligation of the Audit Commission to prepare a code of practice for auditors came into force on 27 September 1999.

1 See LGA 1999, s 27 and the Local Government Act 1999 (Commencement No 1) Order 1999, SI 1999/2169; Local Government Act 1999 (Commencement) (Wales) Order 1999, SI 1999/2815; and Local Government Act 1999 (Commencement No 3) (England) Order 2000, SI 2000/1724.

4 LOCAL GOVERNMENT ACT 2000[1]

1.48 On 25 November 1999 a Bill was introduced in the House of Lords containing the government's proposals for political reform and the promotion of economic, social or environmental well-being in for local authorities in England and Wales. The Bill received the Royal Assent on 28 July 2000, but is not yet fully in force.

1 The Act is to be brought into force by statutory instrument. Much of Pt II was brought into force on 7 August 2000 by the Local Government Act 2000 (Commencement No 1) Order 2000, SI 2000/2187.

(a) Economic, social or environmental well-being

1.49 Local Government Act 2000, Pt I[1] provides for a new discretionary power for local authorities to take steps they consider likely to promote the economic, social or environmental well-being of the area and of those who live, work, and visit there. Section 2(4) of the Act gives specific authority for the new functions to be discharged by working in partnership with other bodies. For example, it allows authorities to assist other statutory bodies to discharge their functions, or to exercise those functions on their behalf. This is intended to help local authorities and other statutory service providers to work together to provide services in ways which meet the needs of communities. Section 3 of the Act prevents authorities from using the power in s 2 to raise money. It permits the Secretary of State to issue guidance to authorities on the exercise of the power and allows him to prevent authorities from using the power to do anything that he might specify by order that they should not do. Before issuing any guidance, the Secretary of State will have to consult local government and others.

1 See Chapter 17.

(b) Political structures

1.50 Part II of the LGA 2000 draws on proposals contained in the failed Local Government (Experimental Arrangements) Bill (known as the Hunt Bill) aimed at enabling local authorities to experiment with different types of political structure[1].

1 Part II will require all local authorities to make proposals for political management structures with a separate executive, and sets out three initial broad forms of executive within which local authorities' proposals must be framed. The objective of this policy is to deliver greater efficiency, transparency and accountability of local authorities. Separation of the executive is intended to ensure that decisions can be taken more quickly and efficiently than in the existing committee system, but the individuals responsible for decision-making can be more readily identified by the public, and that those decision-makers can be held to account in public by overview and scrutiny committees. The Act allows the Secretary of State to add further forms of executive at a later date. The Act, or subordinate legislation made under it, are to require local authorities to hold a referendum:
- where their proposal includes a directly-elected mayor (or other form of executive specified in regulations);
- where 5% or more of the council's electorate petition for a directly-elected mayor (or for another form of executive requiring a referendum); or
- where the Secretary of State requires an authority to hold a referendum on one of the forms of executive available under the Act.

1.51 Under LGA 2000, s 11, the 'executive of a local authority' must take one of the following forms:

(a) a directly elected mayor who appoints an executive of two or more councillors;
(b) an executive leader elected by the full council who then either appoints an executive of two or more councillors drawn from the council, or heads an executive appointed by and drawn from the council;
(c) a directly elected mayor, with an officer of the authority, appointed by the council, as a council manager; or
(d) such further form of executive as the Secretary of State may specify in regulations.

1.52 The LGA 2000 prescribes the way in which 'a local authority executive' is to discharge its executive functions, dependent upon which of the three forms the executive takes. The requirements for political balance under LGHA 1989, s 15 do not apply to the executive or its committees.

1.53 The LGA 2000 requires each authority to establish one or more 'overview and scrutiny committees' as part of the executive arrangements, in order to 'hold the executive to account'. The composition of the overview and scrutiny committee would need to reflect the political balance of the full council. Members of the executive could not sit on the overview and scrutiny committees. There is still to be a chairman of the council who is independent of the executive.

1.54 The provisions of the LGA 2000 incorporate requirements for public consultation. Executive arrangements involving an elected mayor would require the favourable outcome of a referendum prior to implementation. The Secretary of State would have power, by regulations, to specify circumstances in which an authority would be required to hold a referendum on whether the council should operate executive arrangements under one of the prescribed models. Elected mayors would hold office for four years (subject to any alternative period specified by the Secretary of State in regulations).

1.55 In similar vein to the LGA 1999[1], the Local Government Act 2000 gives the Secretary of State power, by regulations, to modify enactments (whenever passed or made). In the case of the LGA 2000, this power to modify primary and subordinate legislation through subordinate legislation would apply if the Secretary of State thinks that an enactment (whenever passed or made) prevents or obstructs local authorities in exercising their power to promote economic, social or environmental wellbeing within its area: s 5. However, there is no power (as under LGA 1999, s 16) to confer *new* powers through subordinate legislation). The Secretary of State also has power to modify any enactment (whenever passed or made) which requires a local authority to prepare, produce or publish any plan or strategy relating to any particular matter: s 6(1). All these powers are, potentially, of wide application.

1 See Local Government Act 1999, s 16.

(c) Ethics

1.56 LGA 2000, Pt III deals with the conduct of local authority members and officers (see Chapters 6 and 9). It builds on the recommendations in the Third Report of the Nolan Committee on Standards in Public Life, which addressed local government[1]. The requirements of Pt III, once in force, include:

(a) the creation of a statutory obligation for local authorities to adopt a code of conduct for members, underpinned by general principles to be approved by Parliament and incorporated in a model code of conduct for members issued by order by the Secretary of State;
(b) the creation of a duty for local authorities to establish standards committees with specified functions concerning the promotion of high standards of conduct by members and assisting members to observe the code of conduct;
(c) the creation of the Standards Board for England and the Adjudication Panel for England with separate arrangements for Wales, as part of an independent process for investigating, reporting on and adjudicating on any unethical conduct by local authority members; and
(d) the creation of a statutory code of conduct for local government officers,

issued by the Secretary of State, by order, which is to be deemed to be incorporated in their individual contracts of employment.

1 Third Report of the Committee on Standards in Public Life: Standards of Conduct in Local Government in England, Scotland and Wales, July 1997, Cm 3702.

(d) Audit

1.57 The LGA 2000 also includes a number of ancillary provisions relating to the audit framework for local government (set out in the Audit Commission Act 1998) (see Chapter 9). These include the repeal of the current surcharge provisions. They also cover the repeal of the Secretary of State's power to sanction items of account: this enables the Secretary of State to protect individuals from surcharge and becomes unnecessary once the surcharge is repealed. Finally, the Act includes arrangements to introduce a new system of advisory notices to enable auditors to seek a court decision about the legality of what the local authority wants to do. This would replace existing arrangements for auditors to issue a prohibition order. No commencement date has been set for these provisions at the time of writing.

5 SELECT COMMITTEE REPORT

1.58 The House of Commons Select Committee on Environment, Transport and Regional Affairs published its Eighth Report, which concerned local government finance, in March 1999. The recommendations in that Report concluded:

> 'We believe that without more radical reform of the local government finance system the aims of the White Paper, Modern Local Government—In Touch with the People, will not be achieved and will not contribute to an improvement in local accountability.'

1.59 The report was critical of many of the steps taken by the government to date. The recommendations included:

(a) an increase in the proportion of local government finance to be raised by local taxation, accompanied by greater accountability to the local electorate;
(b) a return of national non-domestic rates to the control of local authorities;
(c) legislation to introduce Business Improvement Districts[1];
(d) the government should investigate the anomalous situation whereby farm buildings and land are exempt from the non-domestic rate;
(e) a need to reconsider the current council tax bands, in order to increase the size of the local tax base;
(f) a detailed timetable for the government's review of the Standard Spending Assessment should be published and that the emphasis of reform should be fairness and equity (rather than simplicity);
(g) the development of a new and improved capital finance system, under which projects which ultimately pay for themselves should not be subject to public sector borrowing controls, and taking into account the Local Government Association's proposals for the removal of restrictions on borrowing to be replaced with prudential controls;
(h) the government should withdraw its proposals to restrict Council Tax Benefit Subsidy;
(i) council tax capping should be entirely abolished.

1 A concept derived from the United States, being areas in which businesses are able to secure enhanced services and environmental improvements in exchange for higher local taxation.

1.60 In its response published on 13 July 1999[1], the Government rejected the majority of the Select Committee's recommendations, but undertook to take account of the Committee's views in certain areas, such as revenue grant distribution.

1 Cm 4402, July 1999.

6 CAPITAL AND REVENUE FINANCE

1.61 At the time of writing, further government proposals for the reform of both capital and revenue finance are under consideration by the DETR. A Government Green Paper, reviewing each aspect, is expected to be issued for consultation in September 2000.

1.62 In relation to the grant distribution system the current grant formulae are being held constant, whilst a thorough review of the system is undertaken. Research is being undertaken on local authorities' views on the characteristics of allocation systems, on grant distribution systems used in other countries and into the issues relevant to a formulae-based system for all or part of the grant distribution method.

1.63 In relation to capital finance, there are plans to create a 'single capital pot' to take effect from the financial year 2002–03 in place of the various service-specific funding mechanisms which are currently used to allocate capital resources to councils. The 'single pot' is to be distributed between authorities partly on the basis of a needs based formula and partly by a competitive assessment of authorities' capital strategies and their performance in delivering them. It was said that the single capital pot approach would allow authorities greater flexibility in allocating resources internally between the various services, although it was made clear that the government's objectives for schools, in particular, would need to be safeguarded. In preparation for the implementation of the single capital pot, local authorities are being required to prepare, by November 2000, Asset Management Plans, which identify their assets and proposals to optimise their use.

1.64 Research by consultants has been commissioned into the possibility of a capital finance system which relies on 'prudential indicators' to control local authority debt and, separately, on the replacement of minimum revenue provision with a mandatory accounting code. It is to be expected that these issues will be addressed in the forthcoming Green Paper.

7 BEACON COUNCILS

1.65 A recurrent feature of the White Paper proposals is the concept that the best performing councils should be rewarded for their efforts (and that the Secretary of State should retain effective reserve powers to deal with authorities who 'fall behind'). One aspect of this 'encouragement to perform' is the beacon council scheme. The White Paper suggested that the best performing authorities, 'beacon councils', might be rewarded with additional financial resources and eventually with additional legal powers and freedom from constraints. Details of phase one of the Beacon Scheme, which does not require new legislation, were published by the DETR in February

1999[1]. This initial phase involves according recognition to the best performing authorities and disseminating information on best practice, for example through holding open days and entering into secondment and mentoring arrangements[2]. From April 1999, all local authorities were encouraged to seek 'beacon status' in a single service area (or 'cross-cutting service area', eg community safety), although they could apply in respect of up to three of the seven service areas identified for the first year of the scheme. 42 authorities were accorded 'beacon status' in December 1999 and a second tranche of councils are to be awarded beacon status in January 2001. 'Themes' for a third round are now under consideration.

1 See 'The Beacon Council Scheme: how will it work', DETR February 1999 and 'The Beacon Council Scheme: How to apply', DETR May 1999.
2 Councils selected as 'beacons' are to be eligible to receive Special Grants (under the Local Government Finance Act 1988, s 88B) to support their role.

8 FURTHER NEW POWERS

1.66 Phase two of the Beacon Scheme, said to entail beacon councils being given, and being a test bed for, new freedoms and flexibilities, would require new legislation. It is understood that further research is being undertaken before any new legislation is proposed and consulted upon in order to pursue this initiative.

1.67 The consultation paper which preceded the White Paper proposals for beacon councils[1] had raised the possibility of the need to replace the subsidiary power of local authorities under the Local Government Act 1972, s 111, which is referred to throughout this work, but this possibility was not mentioned explicitly in the White Paper itself or addressed in either of the two recent enactments and, at the time of writing, no concrete proposals to amend this power have emerged.

1 'Modernising local government: Local democracy and community leadership', DETR 1998.

9 NEW BODIES

1.68 Since the general election a number of new bodies have been created with functions relevant to this work. These include:

(a) the National Assembly for Wales[1], to which many of the functions of the Secretary of State for Wales were transferred on 1 July 1999;
(b) the Regional Development Agencies, eight of which commenced operations on 1 April 1999 and the ninth, the London Development Agency, which commenced operations on 3 July 2000 as one of the four functional bodies of the new Greater London Authority;
(c) the Greater London Authority (GLA), the Mayor for London and the four functional bodies commenced operations on 3 July 2000[2];
(d) non-statutory bodies, such as the Local Government Improvement and Development Agency, which was set up by the Local Government Association to assist local authorities in England and Wales to improve their performance and promote innovation and modernisation.

1 Established under the Government of Wales Act 1998. See SI 1999/672.
2 Established under the Greater London Authorities Act 1999.

CHAPTER 2

Central government support

A Grants

2.1 The system of block grants as a means of funding local government was first introduced by the Local Government Act 1929. The General Rate Grant was supplemented by what was called a Rate Deficiency Grant. Both types of grant were merged into a single Rate Support Grant in the Local Government Act 1966. The current system was introduced by the Local Government Finance Act 1988 as amended. The system is currently under review by DETR. Grants from the Exchequer to local authority services fall into two groups, namely Revenue Support Grant and specific grants. These will be dealt with in turn.

1 REVENUE SUPPORT GRANT

2.2 Revenue Support Grant was introduced with effect from 1 April 1990 by Local Government Finance Act 1988, Pt V. The new system replaced the much maligned Rate Support Grant[1].

The LGFA 1988[2] (as amended) grants the Secretary of State the power to lay before the House of Commons, for each financial year from 1990/1991 onwards, a report which outlines the total amount of grant for the year, how it is to be distributed amongst the receiving authorities and the calculations and information upon which these decisions were made. Receiving authorities in England are district councils, London borough councils, the Common Council of the City of London and the Council of the Isles of Scilly. In Wales they are county councils and district councils. First, the Secretary of State must consult such representatives of local government as appear to him to be necessary and gain the consent of the Treasury. Perhaps rather strangely, the Act does not specify the basis upon which the grant should be distributed. At the present time the needs of each authority are assessed by central government. The grant is then distributed in such a way that if every local authority spent at the level of their needs assessment they would all set the same council tax unless they are entitled to rebates. The LGFA 1988 is a framework statute which relies on the report the Secretary of State lays before the House of Commons to fill in the details[3].

1 For the history see *Cross on Local Government Law* 9-03 (8th edn, 1996).
2 Local Government Finance Act 1988, s 78A.
3 The most recent reports are the Local Government Finance Report (England) 2000/2001 HC Paper no 160; the Local Government Finance Report (England) 1998/1999: Amending Report 2000 HC Paper no 162; the Local Government Finance (England) Special Grant Report (No 52) HC Paper no 161.

(a) The Revenue Support Grant part

2.3 This states the total amount of revenue support grant available for that financial year, the individual amounts to be paid to specific bodies, and the balance which will be distributed amongst receiving authorities. Specified bodies are those specified in regulations made by the Secretary of State and providing services to local authorities, for example, the Fire Service College.

(b) The distribution part

2.4 This part outlines the basis upon which the Secretary of State plans to distribute the revenue support grant amongst the receiving authorities. The Secretary of State must inform such representatives of local government as appear to him to be appropriate of the contents of the Report. He is not, however, required by statute to consult those representatives. The distribution of the revenue support between local authorities is decided upon via the Standing Spending Assessment (SSA). The SSA for each local authority represents the amount of net revenue expenditure which it would be appropriate for the authority to incur in the financial year to provide a standard level of service.

The SSA for each local authority is drawn from an assessment of the cost of the services for which it is responsible. Differential factors for each local authority, such as the number of pupils in schools, are taken into account. There are thirteen components of the assessment covering all the services and the financing costs of capital expenditure. The method of calculation fixes a unit cost of providing each service and multiplies that by the number of consumers of that service. Adjustments are then made which take into account the variation of costs between authorities.

The resulting distribution of the grant is intended to ensure that if each charging and precepting authority spent at the level of their SSA they would all set the same level of taxation.

(c) The population part

2.5 Local Government Finance Act 1988, s 12A provided for the submission by the Secretary of State to the House of Commons of a Population Report containing the calculations for the 'relevant population' of local authorities. The figure which is calculated is used to assist in distributing the Revenue Support Grant.

2 THE PAYMENT OF THE GRANT

2.6 Once the Revenue Support Grant has been approved by the House of Commons the Secretary of State calculates the amounts payable to each authority in accordance with the Report[1]. He may request information from a local authority or take into account any other information supplied to him if the local authority fails to respond to his request[2]. The Secretary of State may also make one revised calculation of the amount payable to an authority[3]. The Secretary of State may pay the grant in whatever instalments and at whatever time he, with the consent of the Treasury, deems fit[4].

If fresh circumstances arise which affect the finances of local government, the Secretary of State may under LGFA 1988, s 85, with the consent of the Treasury, introduce to the House of Commons for approval a report detailing an additional grant to be paid to local authorities. The Secretary of State may also issue an amending report at any time before the end of the financial year following the financial year in question. He may thus change the basis of calculation of the Report[5]. Finally, the Secretary of State may approve an additional grant. If, during a financial year in respect of which a Report has already been made, the Secretary of State forms the view that fresh circumstances affecting the finances of local authorities have arisen since the approval of that Report, he may pay additional grant[6]. The procedure is the same as the procedure by which the Revenue Support Grant is determined.

1 Local Government Finance Act 1988, s 82.
2 LGFA 1988.
3 LGFA 1988, s 82(2).
4 LGFA 1988, s 83(2).
5 LGFA 1988, s 84A(1),(2).
6 LGFA 1988, s 85(1).

3 CHALLENGING THE GRANT

2.7 Challenge by judicial review is, of course, available but its scope in this instance is rather narrow. The withholding or underpayment of grants may be challenged. Interest cannot be awarded in such proceedings. The reality is that the courts are reluctant to intervene in matters of policy such as this: *R v Secretary of State for the Environment, ex p Avon County Council* (1990) 89 LGR 498 and *R v Secretary of State for the Environment, ex p Hammersmith and Fulham London Borough Council* [1991] 1 AC 521. The latter case was a challenge to the process of designation under s 100 of the Local Government Finance Act 1988, ie the process by which the Secretary of State controls budgets which seem to him to be excessive. The challenge failed. The House of Lords emphasised that the courts can only overturn decisions of this type, which involve questions of political judgment and are subject to the approval of the House of Commons, on grounds of 'bad faith, improper motive or manifest absurdity.'

After approval by the House of Commons the Secretary of State pays the approved amount to each local authority. It is central to this process that the level of rate support grant is in no way related to the level of the local authority's expenditure. The local authority cannot, therefore, increase its grant by over-spending in the previous year. This method of distributing the grant is entirely in line with the Government's policy of keeping a tight rein on local authority expenditure.

4 FURTHER GRANTS

2.8 Transport grants are payable under the Local Government Finance Act 1988, s 87. These are payable in connection with expenditure on highways or the regulation of traffic (where the council is in England), or on public transport (where the council is in Wales): Local Government Finance Act 1988, s 88(3).

Council tax grants are payable under LGFA 1988, s 88A. Their purpose is to mitigate the effects of the transition from the community charge to council tax. If the Secretary of State makes regulations under the Local Government Act 1992, s 13 to cushion the effects of the introduction of the council tax, the Secretary of

State may, with the consent of the Treasury, pay a grant to a local authority[1]. The Secretary of State has made such regulations: see eg the Council Tax (Transitional Deduction Scheme) England Regulations 1995, SI 1995/209.

1 Local Government Finance Act 1988, s 88A(1).

5 SPECIAL GRANTS

2.9 Local Government Finance Act 1988, s 88B grants the power to make special grants. This was amended by Local Government Finance Act 1992, Sch 10. These grants are made to local authorities for special purposes: for example, the police force.

The local authorities who are entitled to receive such a grant are as follows: billing authorities; major precepting authorities; metropolitan county passenger transport authorities. The principal councils in Wales may also receive such grants.

B Credit approvals

2.10 Under the new regime of capital finance for local authorities established by Local Government and Housing Act 1989, Pt IV the Secretary of State must issue each local authority with a basic credit approval[1]. This should cover all classes of capital expenditure with some narrow exceptions. When determining the amount of any credit approval the Secretary of State may take into account the local authority's usable capital receipts[2] and any expected contributions towards capital expenditure. The Secretary of State must not, however, take account of the local authority's ability to raise revenue[3].

Credit approvals may be used as authority to enter into credit arrangements or as authority to capitalise expenditure in accounts which increases the aggregate credit limit itself and thereby the powers of the local authority[4].

Credit approvals are considered in detail in Chapter 11.

1 Local Government and Housing Act 1989, s 53. See Chapter 11.
2 See Chapter 12 for usable capital receipts.
3 Local Government and Housing Act 1989, s 55.
4 Ibid, s 56. See Chapter 12.

C Council tax

2.11 Rating in England and Wales grew out of the Poor Relief Act of 1601. Liability fell on the residents and property owners of each parish to raise sums. There the tax was related to the visible estate of the ratepayer. This principle was underlined during the nineteenth century, in particular the Parochial Assessment Act 1836. It was not until 1988 that a radical new system was introduced in response to calls for change. The Local Government Finance Act 1988 produced the community charge. This became a controversial tax and one which was doomed to failure. This was in turn replaced by the present system, the council tax.

2.12 The council tax was brought into existence by the Local Government Finance Act 1992, s 1 of which establishes the basic duty of a billing authority to levy and collect the council tax in its area. The calculation of the amount of council tax required is the result of the calculation made by a local authority under Local Government Finance Act 1992, s 32, which contains the central calculation which a local authority must perform. If a result of the local authority's calculation is that anticipated outgoings exceed anticipated income, the difference is the local authority's budget requirement. In order to determine how much of that budget requirement will have to be funded by local taxation, the local authority must subtract from the budget requirements the amount which it anticipates receiving from redistributed non-domestic rates, Revenue Support Grant and additional grant. In practical terms, it is this final part of the calculation which will be the most difficult, because central funding of local government provides a far greater proportion of local government spending than does locally raised revenue. If after deducting the central funding from the budget requirement a positive figure remains, that is the amount which must be raised locally. If the resultant figure is negative, the authority must set a nil council tax: Local Government Finance Act 1992, s 33(2). Where a sum does need to be raised locally, that figure must be divided by the 'council tax base' in order to determine the 'basic amount of council tax'. The 'basic amount' is essentially an average for the council tax in an area. It corresponds to the sum which will be charged on a dwelling in Band D. The council tax base is essentially the constituency of council tax payers having regard to the fact that some persons will be entitled to reductions in council tax and others will be eligible for exemptions from payment. The council tax raised is calculated in accordance with the formula laid down in the Local Authorities (Calculation of Council Tax Base) Regulations 1992 as amended. This is discussed in more detail at para **2.14** below. Council tax is only payable on chargeable dwellings. A dwelling is defined as any property which would have been chargeable under the old rating system[1]. This included properties which are only partly used for domestic living. The Secretary of State has wide powers to amend the definition. A chargeable dwelling is defined as that which is not exempted by a class of dwelling specified by the Secretary of State[2]. The amount of tax chargeable depends upon the band in which the property is placed. The valuation bands are as follows (based on fair values as at 1 April 1991):

Band	**England**	**Wales**
A	up to £40,000	up to £30,000
B	£40,000 – £52,000	£30,000 – £39,000
C	£52,000 – £68,000	£39,000 – £51,000
D	£68,000 – £88,000	£51,000 – £66,000
E	£88,000 – £120,000	£66,000 – £90,000
F	£120,000 – £160,000	£90,000 – £120,000
G	£160,000 – £320,000	£120,000 – £240,000
H	£320,000 and over	£240,000 and over

Despite this 8-level band the properties in the top band will pay only three times what the properties in the lowest band will pay. The Secretary of State may change the banding values and proportions to each other by statutory instrument: LGFA 1992, s 5(4).

1 Local Government Finance Act 1992, s 3.
2 LGFA 1992, s 4 and Council Tax (Exempt Dwellings) Order 1992, SI 1992/558 as amended.

1 PLACING PROPERTIES IN A BAND

2.13 Listing officers are appointed[1] for each rating authority and they are charged with the compilation of the valuation list. Each valuation is based upon what the dwelling might have been expected to realise had it been placed on the open market and bought by a willing purchaser. It is presumed that the property was sold free of any encumbrances, freehold and was in a state of reasonable repair. Fixtures are not included in the valuation as this would obviously cause too much variation[2]. It is also presumed that the property had no development value other than that which comes from any normal permitted development[3]. The officer may enter the dwelling to inspect it providing three days' notice is given and written authority can be produced on request[4]. Notices requiring information may also be served. It is an offence for the owner of the property deliberately to give false statements in response to this or to refuse to reply[5]. The listing officer may in fact take into account other information, whatever its source[6].

The listing officer must then compile a valuation list. It is important the Billing Authority be able to comment and to that end it is sent a copy of the newly compiled list prior to publication. The list is then published and when the final list is sent to the Authority it is its duty to inform the people concerned as to where they are placed on the list. The Secretary of State has the power to make regulations concerning the alteration of the valuation lists. Conditions and procedures must be fulfilled before this can be done[7]. One of three factors must alter[8]. The first is the value of the dwelling. When the value of the property has increased the valuation list can only be altered where the property has been sold or a lease of seven years or longer has been granted. Where the value of the property has decreased then this must be due to some alteration in the locality of the property or even demolition of part of the property. The second factor is the opinion of the valuation officer. The valuation may be altered on the initiative of the listing officer or on request from the Billing Authority. These changes will be mostly due to clerical error. A person can apply to the listing officer stating his or her belief that the list is wrong and stating their reasons. The Secretary of State may alter the band under LGFA 1992, s 5.

1 By the Commissioners of Inland Revenue: Local Government Finance Act 1992, s 20.
2 These principles are contained in the Council Tax (Situation and Valuation of Dwellings) Regulations 1992, SI 1992/550.
3 Council Tax (Situation and Valuation of Dwellings) Regulations 1992, SI 1992/550. Permitted development is that for which no planning permission is needed.
4 Local Government Finance Act 1992, s 26.
5 LGFA 1992, s 27(4)–(5).
6 LGFA 1992, s 27(7). Presumably a decision based on ridiculous information would be open to judicial review on the grounds of unreasonableness.
7 Local Government Finance Act 1992, s 24.
8 The rules for these procedures are contained in Council Tax (Alteration of Lists and Appeals) Regulations 1993, SI 1993/290.

2 LIABILITY TO PAY

2.14 This depends upon whether the dwelling is a chargeable dwelling. The liability is the daily charge for that dwelling. There are a number of categories into which one may fall and be liable. The categories are based on interest in the property and residence. At the top of the list is the owner who is also resident. The list then goes through a number of residents who have varying legal interests, for example, leasehold. Where there is no residency then liability is established by ownership[1]. Where two people have equal legal interest they will be jointly and severally liable[2]. However, the terms being used here need some clarification. The term 'resident' is an individual of eighteen years of age who occupies the dwelling as the sole or main resident. This last phrase should be given its ordinary meaning[3]. If the owner has more than one dwelling the key factor will be how much time is spent at which dwelling. Other factors will be taken into consideration: for example, in *Bradford Metropolitan City Council v Anderton*[4] in deciding on the status of a seaman's residence the judge took into account where his wife lived and his legal interest in the house. An 'owner' is defined as someone with a material interest in the property[5]. There are circumstances where the Secretary of State may make regulations which enable the Billing Authority to determine that the owner be liable for the tax and not the resident. This is intended for situations such as hotels or nursing homes.

1 Local Government Finance Act 1992, s 6 and the Council Tax (Liability of Owners) Regulations 1992, SI 1992/551.
2 LGFA 1992.
3 *Shah v Barnet London Borough Council* [1983] 2 AC 309.
4 (1991) 89 LGR 681.
5 Section 6(6). This must be at least a leasehold which is granted for six months or more.

3 CALCULATION

2.15 The tax is calculated by multiplying the number of days in the year by the sum set for the band that the particular property is in. The amount may then be reduced by discount or in accordance with regulations made by the Secretary of State.

4 DISCOUNTS

2.16 Discounts arise in one of two situations[1]. The first is when all the residents of the property are to be disregarded, in which case the discount is 50%. The second is where one of the adults is to be disregarded, in which case the discount is 25%.

1 Discounts are covered by LGFA 1992, s 11 and Sch 1.

5 SETTING THE TAX

2.17 Each Billing Authority has a duty to set the amount of council tax for different dwellings depending on the band into which the dwelling falls. The calculation of the amount is reached by the aggregation of two sums. First, the amount which has been calculated by the Billing Authority per dwelling for its own purposes including precepts from minor precepting authorities. Second, the amount which has been calculated for the same purpose by the major precepting authority which it has issued to the Billing Authority. That precept states the amount of council tax applicable in each category of dwellings and the amount which the precepting authority calculates payable by the Billing Authority with respect to the precept for that financial year[1]. A minor precepting authority's precept must state the authority's budget requirement for the year and the amount payable to it by the Billing Authority. It is clear that each authority must calculate its budget requirement for the year. This is achieved by subtracting estimated income and estimated expenditure for the year. The basic amount of council tax must then be calculated. This is done by using the formula (R-P)T where R is the total budget requirement, P is the aggregate of the sums payable in respect of non-domestic rates and revenue support grant or additional grant and T is the council tax base for the year[2]. Special provision may be made with regard to special items[3]. Then the amount for the different calculation bands is calculated by the formula A x N/D. A is the amount calculated in accordance with the above formula, N is the proportion to be applied to the dwellings in the valuation band[4] and D is the number which in that proportion is applicable to the dwellings in the valuation band D. It is possible for an authority to make substitute calculations unless the basic amount of the council tax is larger than in the previous calculation or the authority does not comply with the requirement to use the same amount for the items specified in the calculation of the basic amount of tax. When this is completed a Billing Authority is required to publish the amount of tax in at least one newspaper circulating in the area[5].

1 LGFA 1992, ss 40 and 41 are relevant here, together with the Billing Authorities (Anticipation of Precepts) Regulations 1992, SI 1992/3239.
2 LGFA 1992, ss 33 and 44 and the Local Authorities (Calculation of Council Tax Base) Regulations 1992, SI 1992/612 (as amended).
3 Local Government Finance Act 1992, ss 34–35 and 45–46 respectively.
4 LGFA 1992, s 5(1) gives the proportions as 6:7:8:9:11:13:15:18.
5 LGFA 1992, s 38(2). Failure to do so does not make the amounts invalid: LGFA 1992, s 38(3).

6 THE COLLECTION OF THE TAX

2.18 The owner or occupier of property does not have to pay anything until they receive a demand notice from the rating authority. Once its notice has been served the person concerned must pay in a specified manner. The demand notice must be served as soon as is practicable after the completion of the process to determine the council tax described above. If a person fails to respond to the demand notice the Authority may seek an order in the magistrates' court[1].

The normal method of payment is by monthly instalments[2]. If the taxpayer continues to fail to pay seven days after the reminder notice has been served, then the balance of the complete estimated liability becomes payable. The local authority must serve a failure notice before they take any further steps to recover unpaid sums. If after seven days the order still remains unpaid then the rating authority may apply for a liability order from the magistrates' court. The application will be heard by at least two justices[3]. Once the order has been made the person in question must supply certain information in writing[4]. Failure to comply without reasonable excuse or knowingly or recklessly to provide false information is an offence[5]. The rating authority then has a number of options. It can make an attachment of earnings order or a winding up petition or a charging order. It is certainly possible for the rating authority to alternate if the first method proves unsuccessful[6]. Ultimately the rating authority may apply to the magistrates' court to issue a warrant to commit the debtor to prison, although the court must be convinced that the person in question is guilty of wilful refusal or culpable neglect.

1 Local Government Finance Act 1992, s 14 and Sch 2 and 4.
2 Council Tax (Administration and Enforcement) Regulations 1992, SI 1992/613 as amended, reg 21.
3 Council Tax (Administration and Enforcement) Regulations 1992, SI 1992/613 as amended, reg 53(2).
4 Council Tax (Administration and Enforcement) Regulations 1992, SI 1992/613 as amended, reg 36.
5 Council Tax (Administration and Enforcement) Regulations 1992, SI 1992/613 as amended, reg 56.
6 Council Tax (Administration and Enforcement) Regulations 1992, SI 1992/613 as amended, reg 52.

7 APPEALS

2.19 There can be an appeal under the council tax regime on a number of points. Appeals may be made:

(1) with regard to the alteration of the valuation list;
(2) regarding the penalty for supplying misinformation to the Billing or Levying Authority;
(3) against a completion notice;
(4) under LGFA 1992, s 16. Section 16 entitles the complainant to appeal to the Valuation Tribunal. This can take place in one of three circumstances –
    (i) if the person is not satisfied with the placement of their property in a certain band;
    (ii) if the person is unhappy with the decision that he lives in a chargeable dwelling;
    (iii) if the person disagrees with the actual calculation of the council tax pertaining to him.

In order for the appeal to go ahead the person must be dissatisfied with the written explanation that he has received from the rating authority. In the event of a full hearing any party may appear in person or be represented. The Tribunal consists of three members including a chairman. If the appellant fails to appear the Tribunal is likely to dismiss the appeal.

D Non-domestic rate

2.20 The second form of local taxation is the non-domestic rate ('the business rate'). This complex system of taxation will be considered under several heads: (1) the basis of rating, (2) exemptions, (3) liability and the setting of the rate, (4) valuation for rating and (5) collection of rates.

1 THE BASIS OF RATING

2.21 The rate is levied on the occupier of every non-domestic hereditament that is on the rating list[1]. The rate can also be levied on the owner of the property if it is unoccupied or if it is occupied by persons named on a central list, which covers ratings regarding people who work in more than one area[2]. Every relevant non-domestic hereditament must be entered on the local rating list. 'Relevant' is defined as property within the following list: lands, coal mines, other mines, sporting rights and advertising[3]. In *Westminster City Council v Woodbury (Valuation Officer)*[4] it was held that a vessel moored on the Victoria Embankment with no engine, connected to the mains and being used as a restaurant, was not a rateable hereditament in itself. It was a chattel and the Court of Appeal confirmed that while such cannot be rateable by itself it could be if occupied in conjunction with land. That land must in itself be rateable. The river bed of the Thames was not in this case such rateable land[5]. 'Non-domestic' is defined as an hereditament which consists entirely of property which is not domestic[6]. 'Domestic' is defined as property which is used entirely for the purpose of living accommodation. Another important question for the purposes of deciding rateability is what amounts to occupation. There is no statutory definition and the meaning is determined by case law. From the case law which is, in itself, complex some fairly clear principles have emerged[7]. Occupation must entail some form of possession, a term which is turn must entail some use or enjoyment. There must also be an element of permanence about the possession. The occupation must be beneficial. Lastly, the occupation must be exclusive as well as actual.

1 Local Government Finance Act 1988, s 43.
2 LGFA 1988, s 45.
3 LGFA 1988, s 64(4).
4 [1992] RA 1.
5 A case which is also cited for this point is *Storehire (UK) Ltd v Wojcik (Valuation Officer)* [1991] RA 39. In that case shipping containers used for storage were rateable.
6 Local Government Finance Act 1988, s 64(8).
7 The principles are based on the following cases: *R v Assessment Committee of St Pancras* (1877) 2 QBD 581; *Jones v Mersey Docks and Harbour Board* (1865) 11 HLC 443; *John Laing & Son Ltd v Kingswood Assessment Area Assessment Committee* [1949] 1 KB 344.

2 EXEMPTIONS

2.22 Several types of hereditament are exempt from rating or have their rate calculated on a different basis. LGFA 1988 introduces several cases where relief may be claimed by bodies or individuals[1].

1 Local Government Finance Act 1988, s 51 and Sch 5.

(a) Crown property

2.23 Crown properties are not rateable. This exemption is extended to property which is being used for the purposes of the Crown even though the occupants are not strictly servants of the Crown. This would include, for example, police stations[1]. LGFA 1988, however, excludes some properties from this exemption. Those are primarily places maintained for the purposes of the administration of justice, police purposes and other Crown services under a specified authority. These must be entered on the rating list.

1 *Coomber v Berkshire Justices* (1883) 9 App Cas 61.

(b) Places of public worship

2.24 Places of religious worship are exempted from rating as are buildings used in connection with any such place of worship. The latter includes buildings which are used for the administrative organisation of public religious worship.

(c) Agricultural land and buildings

2.25 LGFA 1988, Sch 5 gives total exemption from rates to agricultural land, agricultural buildings and fish farms[1]. A number of types of farm land are specified in the Act. It specifically excludes land used for sport or recreation. Agricultural buildings must be used solely in connection with agriculture. The word 'solely' is strictly interpreted in the case law and has restrictive effect on the exemptions in this area[2].

1 This is in conjunction with LGFA 1988, s 51.
2 There are a number of cases which serve as examples of this restrictive definition, eg *Meriden and Solihull Rating Authority v Tyacke* [1950] 1 All ER 939; *Farmer (Valuation Officer) v Buxted Poultry Ltd* [1993] AC 369.

(d) Charitable and other organisations

2.26 These bodies are eligible to receive rating relief in two ways. Firstly, under LGFA 1988, ss 43 and 45, charities only pay one-fifth of the non-domestic rate on the property. The qualifications for this are discussed above. Secondly, the rating authority may reduce the rates payable in relation to three types of organisation under LGFA 1988, s 47. The first is where the ratepayer is a charity or trustee of a charity and the hereditament is wholly or mainly used for charitable purposes. If this is the case then relief given may go beyond the stated 80%. The second type is where all or part of the hereditament is occupied for institutions which are not conducted for profit and whose main aim is charitable or philanthropic, religious or concerned with social welfare, science, literature or the fine arts. The third type covers hereditaments used wholly or mainly for the purposes of recreation and is part of an organisation which is not run for profit.

(e) Disabled persons

2.27 LGFA 1988 established a system of total exemption for property used wholly for specified purposes related to disabilities[1].

1 LGFA 1988, s 51 and Sch 5.

(f) Unoccupied property

2.28 Generally, under LGFA 1988, s 45 these properties are rateable. There are, however, some exceptions. These are hereditaments unoccupied for less than three months; when the owner is prohibited by law from occupying property; where the hereditament is vacant due to an action by the Crown; listed buildings; ancient monuments; industrial storage; electricity generation; small hereditaments where the rateable value is less than £1,000; where the occupier is only there as a representative of a deceased person; where there is a bankruptcy order on the owner's estate; where the owner is a company subject to a winding up order; where the owner is in possession only by virtue of being a liquidator and where the owner is in occupation only by virtue of being a trustee under a deed of arrangement.

(g) Personal reliefs

2.29 Under LGFA 1988, s 49 a rating authority has a general power to reduce or remit the payment if satisfied that the ratepayer would undergo hardship if it failed to do so and it is reasonable to do so in the interests of the council payers.

3 RATEABLE VALUE

2.30 The amount of tax which has to be paid on any non-domestic hereditament depends upon its rateable value. Rateable value is determined in accordance with Local Government Finance Act 1988, s 56 and Sch 6. The Act states this principle as:

> '... the rent at which it is estimated the hereditament might reasonably be expected to let from year to year if the tenant undertook to pay all usual tenant's rates and taxes and to bear the cost of repairs and insurance and the other expenses (if any) necessary to maintain the hereditament in a state to command that rent.'

The annual value for rating purposes is the rental value of year to year lettings. In *London County Council v Erith Parish (Churchwardens and Overseers of the Poor)*[1] Lord Herschall LC said that the rateable value is determined by what rent might be obtained for the vacant and to let property. In *Garton v Hunter (Valuation Officer)*[2] rent values were important but not decisive. Other relevant evidence should also be admitted.

The Secretary of State also has the power to substitute other considerations for hereditaments of a prescribed description. This is normally the case where rental values would be difficult to assess[3].

Under LGFA 1988 a multiplier is used to set the rate which is applied to the rateable value of property. The increase in the multiplier each year is linked to the retail prices index. All precepts are pooled centrally and then the Secretary of State redistributes to the local authorities.

The actual amount of liability is calculated on a daily basis. For occupied hereditaments liability is determined by the formula –

$$\frac{A \times B}{C}$$

where A is the rateable value, B is the multiplier for the year and C the number of days in the financial year[4]. If the ratepayer is a charity the formula is –

$$\frac{A \times B}{C \times 5}$$

(20% of the original amount)[5].

1 [1893] AC 562 at 588.
2 [1969] 2 QB 37.
3 Local Government Finance Act 1988, s 56, Sch 6.
4 LGFA 1988, s 43(3).
5 LGFA 1988, s 45(5).

4 RATING VALUATION

2.31 As has been already mentioned, non-domestic rating is based upon the rating list. There are both local and central rating lists. The Commissioners of the Inland Revenue are under a duty to appoint a valuation officer to compile each list[1]. The lists are compiled on 1 April every fifth year. The Valuation Officer is under a duty to take such steps as to ensure that the valuation list is compiled accurately, and pursuant to this he has the power to enter property and request information[2]. Once this list is compiled a copy must be sent to the local authority or the Secretary of State as soon as is reasonably practicable.

The local list must contain each hereditament which is non-domestic located within the local authority's area and is required to be included in the central rating list. Further, it is important that the list must distinguish between composite properties and those which are entirely non-domestic[3]. It must also show the rateable value of the property and which parts of that property, if any, are exempt from the rate. Under LGFA 1988, s 53 the central list must show the owner or occupier of the hereditament if it falls within a prescribed class.

The local rating list may be altered by the Valuation Officer either on his own initiative[4] or at the suggestion of a relevant authority or a ratepayer[5].

1 Local Government Finance Act 1988, s 61.
2 LGFA 1988, Sch 9, paras 5–7.

3 LGFA 1988, s 42.
4 This is impliedly authorised by the duty in LGFA 1988, s 41 to maintain the lists.
5 Local Government Finance Act 1988, s 55.

2.32 Appeals may be made against an alteration in the rating list and also in relation to completion notices and certification. These appeals are heard by Valuation Tribunals which were established by Local Government Finance Act 1988, s 136 and Sch 22. ('Valuation and Community Charge Tribunals'). These were retained by Local Government Finance Act 1992, s 15 as 'Valuations Tribunals'. Each area's Tribunal maintains permanent offices and clerk. Members are appointed by the relevant authorities. It is important to note that a member of a Billing Authority may not hear an appeal against a decision of the Registrar of that Authority.

Appeals may be dealt with, upon the agreement of all parties, by written representations. Both parties and the clerk to the Tribunal must follow the written representations procedure which is set out in regulations under the Act[1]. In the alternative, the appeal may proceed to a full hearing. A party may appear in person or be represented before a Tribunal consisting of three members, one of which is the chairman. The hearing takes place in public unless this would prejudice one of the parties. The Tribunal will determine its own procedure on the simple basis of efficacious clarification of the issues. The decision of the Tribunal may be by majority but can be remitted for the decision of another Tribunal if two of the members fail to agree. The decision may be reviewed on the following grounds:

(1) the decision was wrongly made as a result of clerical error;
(2) reasonable cause has been demonstrated for a party's failure to appear;
(3) the decision has been affected by an appeal from or decision of the High Court or Lands Tribunal where the case dealt with the hereditament concerned.

An appeal may be made by any party to the first appeal within four weeks or the original decision of the Lands Tribunal. The Lands Tribunal may make any order the original Tribunal could have made and can revoke, remit, set aside, confirm or vary the decision which has been appealed.

1 Valuation and Community Charge Tribunals Regulations 1989 as amended, SI 1989/479.

5 THE COLLECTION OF RATES

2.33 The Authority must serve a demand notice, which in essence is an estimate of liability for the year, on each ratepayer[1]. The normal method of payment is by monthly instalment but the ratepayer may organise other methods with the Authority's consent[2]. If, after receiving the service of a reminder notice the ratepayer fails to pay, the Authority has two options. First, they may raise an action for civil debt[3]. Second, enforcement by means of distress[4]. It seems unlikely that these remedies may be utilised concurrently.

1 Non-Domestic Rating (Collection and Enforcement) Regulations 1989, SI 1989/1058.
2 Non-Domestic Rating (Collection and Enforcement) Regulations 1989, SI 1989/1058, reg 7.
3 Non-Domestic Rating (Collection and Enforcement) Regulations 1989, SI 1989/1058, reg 20.
4 Non-Domestic Rating (Collection and Enforcement) Regulations 1989, SI 1989/1058, reg 12.

CHAPTER 3

Funds and accounts

A Funds

1 INTRODUCTION

3.1 Local authorities are statutorily required to establish and maintain a number of funds: the principal ones are the General Fund, the Collection Fund and the Superannuation Fund.

Apart from those sums which are to be paid into a local authority's Collection Fund or a Trust Fund, any sum received by a local authority must be paid into its General Fund: Local Government Finance Act 1988, s 59(4) ('LGFA 1988').

Local authorities may also continue to operate 'pooling' provisions: a consolidated loans pool, a consolidated advances and borrowing pool, and a central loans and investment account[1].

The consolidated loans pool continues the former practice of accounting for the acquisition and financing of fixed assets by individual services on a similar basis to the former Consolidated Loans Fund, adapted to the specific requirements of the Local Government and Housing Act 1989. The consolidated loans pool is an internal mechanism, borrowing externally on behalf of the local authority as a whole, and lending to individual services within it. The consolidated borrowing pool aggregates the transactions of different individual services. The central loans and investment account deals with income and expenditure in relation to interest.

1 See CIPFA Guidance on Capital Accounting Arrangements under Part IV, Local Government and Housing Act 1989—Revised Guidance Notes for Practitioners 1996.

3.2 The Local Government (Wales) Act 1994 introduced a new framework for the new principal councils in Wales from 1 April 1996. These principal councils must establish and maintain a fund, known as the Council Fund, into which all sums are received, and from which all payments must be paid, with the exception of transactions relating to trust funds[1]. A principal council may not delegate its functions in relation to the Council Fund[2]. Provision is made for general and special accounts within this fund, and for the Secretary of State to make regulations relating to separate funds within the Council Fund[3]. The Secretary of State may also make regulations[4] in relation to precepts of local and major precepting authorities[5].

1 Local Government (Wales) Act 1994, s 38(1)–(4).
2 Local Government (Wales) Act 1994, s 38(5).
3 Local Government (Wales) Act 1994, s 38(7)–(8).
4 See the Local Authorities (Precepts) (Wales) Regulations 1995, SI 1995/2562.
5 Local Authorities (Precepts) (Wales) Regulations 1995, SI 1995/2562, s 38(9)–(10).

2 GENERAL FUND

3.3 The requirement to establish and maintain a General Fund is applicable to 'billing authorities' as defined by the Local Government Finance Act 1992, s 1(2) (other than the City of London, which has its own provisions)[1]. The Secretary of State has power to make regulations about the relationship of the General Fund to any other fund of the local authority, and may require that any fund established by the local authority, other than the Collection Fund or a Trust Fund, shall be maintained as a separate fund within its General Fund[2].

All receipts must be paid into the local authority's General Fund, other than those payments which are required to be paid to the Collection Fund, or those required to be paid to a Trust Fund[3]. Transfers to the General Fund are transfers from the Collection Fund, principally those under LGFA 1988, s 97(1),(3). The main payments into the General Fund are (a) Revenue Support Grant, (b) charges, and (c) redistributed national non-domestic rates. This enables the local authority to meet its expenditure.

1 Local Government Finance Act 1988, s 91(1),(2).
2 LGFA 1988, s 92.
3 LGFA 1988, s 91(4).

3.4 All payments must be met from the local authority's General Fund, other than those payments which are required to be paid from the Collection Fund or those required to be paid from a Trust Fund[1]. As council tax goes into the Collection Fund and major precepts are paid out of the Collection Fund, the General Fund operates in relation to precepts only when there are substituted calculations or precepts, calling for adjustments to be made.

Local Government Act 1985, s 72(1) requires 'new authorities' ie those local authorities established under LGA 1985, Pt III or Pt IV to keep a fund known as the General Fund, and all receipts of that local authority must be carried to it and all liabilities discharged from it.

1 Local Government Finance Act 1988, s 91(5).

3 COUNCIL FUND

3.5 County and county borough councils established in Wales from 1 April 1996 must establish and maintain a Council Fund[1]. Sums received by those councils must be paid into the Fund and all payments met out of the Fund[2], except transactions applying to Trust Funds[3]. The Secretary of State for Wales has powers to make regulations concerning the establishment of separate funds and the liability of the councils to make payments from their Council Funds in respect of precepts issued under Chapter IV of Pt I of the Local Government Finance Act 1992[4]. The Local Authorities (Precepts) (Wales) Regulations 1995, SI 1995/2562, regs 3(1) and (4) make provision for sufficient funds to be transferred to meet the liabilities of the precepting authority and for payment to be made in accordance with a schedule of instalments.

1 Local Government (Wales) Act 1994, s 38(1).
2 Local Government (Wales) Act 1994, s 38(2),(3).
3 Local Government (Wales) Act 1994, s 38(4).
4 Local Government (Wales) Act 1994, s 38(8),(9).

4 CITY OF LONDON

3.6 The Common Council of the City of London has established and maintains a City Fund[1]. These provisions utilise and adapt the provisions governing the General Fund[2].

1 Local Government Finance Act 1988, s 93(1).
2 LGFA 1988, ss 93–94.

5 COUNTY FUND

3.7 County Councils are precepting authorities and do not engage in direct collection of council tax or non-domestic rates. Thus they are obliged to keep a single fund, the County Fund, to which all receipts are to be carried, and from which all liabilities are discharged[1].

1 Local Government Act 1972, s 148.

3.8 There is no obligation to keep a County Fund where the county council becomes a billing authority due to a structural change made by an order under the Local Government Act 1992, s 17. In such a case the county council must keep a Collection Fund and General Fund under the 1988 Act[1]. The assets held in the County Fund (other than assets forming part of a Trust Fund) are transferred to the General Fund on the date on which the structural change comes into force[2].

1 Local Government Act 1972, s 148(5A),(5B).
2 Local Government Finance Act 1988, s 91(8).

6 COLLECTION FUND

3.9 Billing Authorities have to establish and maintain a Collection Fund[1]. The functions in relation to its Collection Fund cannot be delegated[2].

1 Local Government Finance Act 1988, ss 89(1), 144(2).
2 LGFA 1988, s 89(3).

3.10 The 1988 Act, s 90(1) specifies what must be paid into the Collection Fund:

(i) council tax received (save penalties);
(ii) sums received by the local authority from a major precepting authority under regulations made by the Secretary of State under LGFA 1988, s 99(3);
(iii) sums received in respect of non-domestic rates;
(iv) sums received by way of repayment of provisional sums overpaid to the national non-domestic rate pool; and
(v) any other sums that the Secretary of State specifies are to be paid into the authority's Collection Fund[1].

1 The Collection Fund (General) (England) Specifications and Directions 1992 and the Collection Fund (Wales) Specifications and Directions 1993.

3.11 Payments into the Collection Fund will usually lead to transfers to the General Fund, with which to meet the local authority's expenditure. The main transfer is of a sum calculated by multiplying the basic amount of the local authority's council tax by the local authority's tax base for the year[1]. Where this calculation produces a negative amount, the equivalent amount must be transferred from the General Fund to the Collection Fund[2]. Similarly, where the Collection Fund for the previous year has shown a surplus, a proportion of that will be due to the General Fund[3]. Where the previous year's Collection Fund shows a deficit, then the General Fund must bear a proportion of the loss, and transfer a corresponding amount to the Collection Fund[4].

1 Local Government Finance Act 1988, s 97(1).
2 LGFA 1988, s 97(2).
3 LGFA 1988, s 97(3).
4 LGFA 1988, s 97(4).

3.12 The Secretary of State has power to make regulations governing the Collection and General Funds, including the liability to make transfers, how to calculate surpluses and deficits to the Collection Fund, their apportionment between billing authorities and precepting authorities, and to limit the amount which may stand to the credit of a Collection Fund at any time in a financial year[1]. Regulations[2] (other than regulations revoking earlier regulations, but otherwise including amending regulations) must come into force before 1 January in the year preceding that to which they are to apply[3].

The Secretary of State also has power to direct a transfer from the General Fund to the Collection Fund, in an amount (fixed or by reference to a method of calculation), and at such time, as he may direct[4].

1 Local Government Finance Act 1988, s 99.
2 Local Authorities (Funds) (England) Regulations 1992, SI 1992/2428 as amended ('The Funds Regulations').
3 Local Government Finance Act 1988, s 99(6).
4 LGFA 1988, s 98(5).

3.13 Payments from precepting authorities are payments of any deficit in respect of council tax in the Billing Authority's Collection Fund for the preceding financial year, calculated under the Funds Regulations, apportioned under reg 11 and Sch 2, and paid in accordance with reg 12 in no more than ten equal instalments.

3.14 The Collection Fund should have sufficient funds to meet its liabilities for the year in question, and funds must be transferred to it from the General Fund if necessary[1]. The word 'liabilities' here means obligations to meet major precepts, or to make payments or transfers from the Collection Fund in respect of the provisions of LGFA 1988, s 97[2].

The obligation to make the transfer during the year in question may not apply if the liability arises because of a re-calculation or a substituted precept which gives rise to any outstanding liability after the final instalment is to be paid by a precepting authority or transferred from the General Fund for the year in question, under a schedule of instalments[3]. In this case the transfer takes place as soon as reasonably practicable[4].

The Collection Fund (General) (England) Directions 1994 also govern the increased provision to be made for uncollected community charge and for the corresponding transfer from the Collection Fund to the General Fund in respect of community charge transitional relief grant and community charge transitional reduction scheme grant where community charges are written off or remain uncollected.

1 Local Authorities (Funds) (England) Regulations 1992, SI 1992/2428 as amended, reg 3(1).
2 LA(F)(E)R 1992, reg 2(2).
3 LA(F)(E)R 1992, reg 3(2).
4 LA(F)(E)R 1992, reg 3(3).

3.15 The Fund Regulations define the schedule of instalments as the schedule determined by the billing authority under LA(F)(E)R 1992, regs 4 and 6 and Sch 1[1]. The schedule must be determined before 31 January in the preceding financial year[2]. Billing Authorities may agree with all the major precepting authorities in their areas a schedule of instalments other than as determined under Sch 1, provided that there are no fewer than two instalments, which will discharge the whole of the Billing Authority's liabilities for that year[3]. If such an agreement is reached, then it becomes the schedule of instalments for other purposes. Billing Authorities have to notify precepting authorities of the schedule of instalments, in compliance with reg 5. The power to amend the schedule is contained in reg 6.

1 Local Authorities (Funds) (England) Regulations 1992, SI 1992/2428 as amended, reg 39(1).
2 LA(F)(E)R 1992, reg 4(2).
3 LA(F)(E)R 1992, reg 4(3)–(5).

3.16 A billing authority must transfer to the Collection Fund from the General Fund such amounts as will discharge the liability, during the financial year to which it relates, although this may be in such instalments as the billing authority determines[1]. This is subject to protection for a recalculation after the end of the financial year to which it relates, leading to a negative amount under LGFA 1988[2].

1 Local Authorities (Funds) (England) Regulations 1992, SI 1992/2428 as amended, reg 3(4),(5).
2 Local Government Finance Act 1988, s 97(2).

3.17 Sums paid into a Collection Fund can be used only to make payments to be met from the Fund, or transfers from it[1]. Pending such payment or transfer, any sums are to be held, invested or otherwise used as may be prescribed by the Secretary of State[2].

Such funds may either be held in cash, invested in an investment prescribed under Sch 3, or transferred to the General Fund, where they may be held in cash, invested in an investment prescribed by Sch 3, or used for the discharge or the Billing Authority's functions[3]. Where sums have been transferred to the General Fund under these provisions, they must be re-transferred if required to meet payments or make transfers from the Collection Fund, or otherwise as and when the Billing Authority thinks fit[4].

1 Local Government Finance Act 1988, s 89(4).
2 Local Government Finance Act 1988, s 89(5), s 98(5); Local Authorities (Funds) (England) Regulations 1992, SI 1992/2428 as amended, reg 13 and Sch 3.
3 Local Authorities (Funds) (England) Regulations 1992, SI 1992/2428 as amended, reg 13(1)–(3).
4 LA(F)(E)R 1992, reg 13(4).

3.18 The following sums *must* be paid from the Billing Authority's Collection Fund[1]:

(1) payments (other than by way of interest) in respect of a precept issued by a major precepting authority;
(2) payments to a major precepting authority in accordance with regulations made under LGFA 1988, s 99(3);
(3) payments to the Secretary of State in respect of non-domestic rate;
(4) repayments of excess receipts of non-domestic rate or council tax, pursuant to regulations under the 1988 and 1992 Acts; and
(5) any other payment that the Secretary of State specifies are to be paid from the Billing Authority's Collection Fund.

Payments into the Collection Fund will lead to transfers to the General Fund, with which to meet the Billing Authority's expenditure. The principal transfer is of a sum achieved by multiplying the basic amount of the Billing Authority's council tax by that authority's tax base for the year[2]. Where the Collection Fund for the previous year has shown a surplus, a proportion of that will be due to the General Fund[3].

The Secretary of State's general powers discussed above also apply to payments and transfers from the Collection Fund, including the method of payment of precepts.

The Secretary of State has the power to direct a transfer from the Collection Fund to the General Fund, in an amount (fixed or by reference to a method of calculation), and at such time, as he may direct[4].

1 Local Government Finance Act 1988, s 90(2) and the Collection Fund (General) (England) Directions 1994.
2 Local Government Finance Act 1988, s 97(1).
3 LGFA 1988, s 97(3).
4 LGFA 1988, s 98(4).

3.19 Payments to precepting authorities are those payable in respect of precepts, whether major or local[1]. Payments are made according to the schedule of instalments. There are also provisions concerning substitute precepts late in the financial year[2]. There is provision for payments from the Collection Fund to major precepting authorities in respect of their shares calculated in accordance with reg 11 of any prior year surplus calculated in accordance with reg 10, being a surplus in the Billing Authority's Collection Fund for the preceding financial year. This mirrors the obligation on a major precepting authority to pay the Collection Fund its share of any deficit[3].

1 Local Authorities (Funds) (England) Regulations 1992, SI 1992/2428 as amended, regs 2(2), 3(1).
2 LA(F)(E)R 1992, reg 3(3).
3 LA(F)(E)R 1992, reg 3(6)–(8).

3.20 The Collection Fund should transfer sufficient funds to meet the liabilities of the General Fund for the year in question[1]. 'Liabilities' is defined as meaning any obligation of the General Fund to meet local precepts, or to make payments or transfers from the General Fund in respect of the provisions of LGFA 1988, s 97[2].

The obligation to make such payments or transfers during the year in question may not apply if the liability arises because of a recalculation or a substituted precept, which gives rise to any outstanding liability after the final instalment is to be paid by a precepting authority or transferred from the General Fund for the year in question, under a schedule of instalments[3]. In such a case the payment need be made, and the transfer take place, only as soon as reasonably practicable[4].

1 Local Authorities (Funds) (England) Regulations 1992, SI 1992/2428 as amended, reg 3(1).
2 LA(F)(E)R 1992, reg 2(2).
3 LA(F)(E)R 1992, reg 3(2).
4 LA(F)(E)R 1992, reg 3(3).

7 PENSIONS AND OTHER SPECIAL FUNDS

3.21 The Secretary of State may, by regulation, make provision for pensions for persons, or classes of persons, employed in local government service[1]. These provisions may include the establishment and administration of superannuation funds the management and application of the assets of such funds, the amalgamation of all or any of such funds, and the winding up of, or other dealing with, any such fund[2].

1 Superannuation Act 1972 s 7(1).
2 Ibid, Sch 3, para 2.

3.22 The principal regulations governing superannuation are the Local Government Pension Scheme Regulations 1997, SI 1997/1612 ('LGPSR 1997'). Reference also needs to be made to the Local Government Pension Scheme Regulations 1995, SI 1995/1019 ('LGPSR 1995') and the Local Government Superannuation Regulations 1986, SI 1986/24 ('LGSR 1986'). See also the CIPFA Code of Practice on Local Authority Accounting 4.37–4.39.

3.23 Under the LGPSR 1997 all the Superannuation Funds maintained immediately prior to 2 May 1995 must continue to be maintained for the purposes of the LGPSR 1997 by the bodies then responsible for maintaining them. They are now known as Pension Funds.

The authorities required to maintain Superannuation Funds were as follows[1]:

(1) non-metropolitan county councils;
(2) the Common Council of the City of London;
(3) London borough councils;
(4) Councils designated under the Local Government Act 1985, s 66 in former metropolitan counties;
(5) bodies designated under the Local Government Act 1985, s 67 (ie on the winding up of residuary bodies);
(6) the London Pensions Authority;
(7) the Environment Agency;
(8) the West Midlands Passenger Transport Authority.

1 Local Government Superannuation Regulations 1986, SI 1986/24, reg P1(1).

3.24 These authorities were known as Administering Authorities[1], and remain so called under the LGPSR 1997.

1 Local Government Superannuation Regulations 1986, SI 1986/24, Sch 1.

3.25 Not all local authorities are obliged to maintain a Pension Fund, but all employees in local government service will be covered by an appropriate fund[1]. If it is not the Pension Fund maintained by their employer, it will be that maintained by a different authority in the geographical area in which they work, or in some cases, eg London, by a specific Pension Authority. The LGPSR 1997 apply to all pensionable employees of the bodies set out in Sch 2 (an LGPS employer) which as well as the Administering Authorities includes District Councils, Joint Boards or Committees, Fire Authorities and Police Authorities.

The term 'employees in local government service' does not include teachers, for whom there is a separate scheme under the Superannuation Act 1972, s 9[2]. Under this scheme, there is no requirement to maintain a separate Fund[3].

1 Local Government Pension Scheme Regulations 1997, SI 1997/1612, reg 74 and Sch 5.
2 See *Secretary of State for the Environment v Cumbria County Council* (1983) ICR 52, HL.
3 Teachers' Superannuation (Consolidation) Regulations 1988, SI 1988/1652.

3.26 Administering authorities may also make an agreement (an 'admissions agreement') with other bodies (broadly other statutory and non-statutory organisations connected with the provision of local government services)[1]. In such cases, the Administering Authority may establish an 'admission agreement fund' in addition to the 'main fund'[2].

1 Local Government Pension Scheme Regulations 1997, SI 1997/1612, reg 5.
2 LGPSR 1997, reg 75.

(a) Management and investment

3.27 Management and investment is governed by the Local Government Pension Scheme (Management and Investment of Funds) Regulations 1998, SI 1998/1831. The following sums must be credited each year to the Pension Fund[1]:

(1) employers' contributions;
(2) all members' contributions except additional voluntary contributions;
(3) all income arising during the year from the investment of the fund;
(4) all capital money deriving from such investment;
(5) all additional payments received by the authority under LGPSR 1997; and
(6) any other sums specified by LGPSR 1997.

1 Local Government Pension Scheme (Management and Investment of Funds) Regulations 1998, SI 1998/1831, reg 5(2).

3.28 An Administering Authority may pay out of the Fund any costs, charges and expenses incurred by it in administering the Fund[1]. This includes the costs of using and investing the money, and employing Fund managers. It does not include costs, charges and expenses incurred in connection with a retirement benefits scheme approved by the Commissioners of Inland Revenue under s 591(1),(2)(h) of the Income and Corporation Taxes Act 1988.

1 Local Government Pension Scheme (Management and Investment of Funds) Regulations 1998, SI 1998/1831, reg 5(6).

3.29 Investment of Fund monies that are not for the time being required to meet payments to be made out of the Fund. Such funds must be invested[1], and the Administering Authority has power to vary those investments[2]. Investment includes[3]:

(1) any contract entered into in the course of dealing in financial futures or traded options (as defined in the Regulations);
(2) use by the Administering Authority for any purpose for which they have a statutory borrowing power;
(3) certain insurance business;
(4) a stocklending arrangement (as defined in the Regulations);
(5) contributing to a limited partnership in an unquoted securities investment partnership;
(6) any sub-underwriting contract.

In discharging their investment function, Administering Authorities must have regard to the following matters[4]:

(1) the advisability of investing fund money in a wide variety of investments;
(2) the suitability of investments and types of investments;
(3) proper advice obtained at reasonable intervals.

Where administering authorities use funds for their own purposes, they must pay interest to the Fund on a daily basis at a rate no lower than the lowest rate at which that amount could have been borrowed at arms' length otherwise than by way of overdraft from a bank at 7 days' notice[5].

1 Local Government Pension Scheme (Management and Investment of Funds) Regulations 1998, SI 1998/1831, reg 9(1).
2 LGPS(MIF)R 1998, reg 3.
3 LGPS(MIF)R 1998, reg 3.
4 LGPS(MIF)R 1998, reg 9(3).
5 LGPS(MIF)R 1998, reg 12.

3.30 An Administering Authority must take 'proper advice'. This means the advice of a person, including an officer of the Administering Authority, who is reasonably believed by that Authority to be qualified by his ability in and practical experience of financial matters[1].

1 Local Government Pension Scheme (Management and Investment of Funds) Regulations 1998, SI 1998/1831, regs 2, 6(6).

3.31 One or more investment managers may be appointed to manage and invest the Fund monies[1]. An investment manager is a person authorised under the Financial Services Act 1986 to manage the assets of occupational pension schemes (or under an equivalent provision in a European state), or is a European institution carrying on home-regulated investment business in the UK[2].

An investment manager may only be appointed if the Administering Authority reasonably believes him to be suitably qualified and he is not an employee of the Authority[3]. No such appointment may be made unless the Authority has considered the value of the Fund to be managed by the manager or managers, has taken proper advice, and is satisfied that the value of the fund to be managed is not excessive, having regard to the desirability of securing diversification of the management of the Fund and the value of the assets[4].

1 Local Government Pension Scheme (Management and Investment of Funds) Regulations 1998, SI 1998/1831, reg 6(1).
2 Banking Coordination (Second Council Directive) Regulations 1992, SI 1992/3218; Local Government Pension Scheme (Management and Investment of Funds) Regulations 1998, SI 1998/1831, reg 4.
3 Local Government Pension Scheme (Management and Investment of Funds) Regulations 1998, SI 1998/1831, reg 6(3),(4).
4 LGPS(MIF)R 1998, reg 6(5),(6).

3.32 The appointment of an investment manager must include terms providing for termination by the Billing Authority on not more than one month's notice, for three-monthly reports by the investment manager, for that manager to comply with instructions given by the Authority and various other matters relating to the nature of investments[1]. When determining the terms of the appointment the Authority must have regard to proper advice[2].

Where an investment manager has been appointed the Authority must review the investments made by him/her at least every three months and, from time to time, consider the desirability of continuing or terminating the appointment[3]. In exercising this function the Authority must take proper advice –

(a) if LGPS(MIF)R 1998, reg 7(5)(a) applies, about the variety of the investments he has made; and

(b) about the suitability of those investments to the fund generally and as investments of their type.

1 Local Government Pension Scheme (Management and Investment of Funds) Regulations 1998, SI 1998/1831, reg 7.
2 LGPS(MIF)R 1998, reg 7(8).
3 LGPS(MIF)R 1998, reg 8.

3.33 After any audit of the Pension Fund, an Administering Authority must send copies of the Revenue Account and balance sheet of the Fund and any report by the auditor, to each body whose employees contribute to the Fund[1]. An actuarial valuation of the assets and liabilities of the Fund was required to be made on 31 March 1998 and must be made every three years thereafter[2]. The Authority must provide the actuary with the Consolidated Revenue Account of the Fund and such other information as he may require[3].

Unless the Secretary of State extends time, the valuation, a report and a rates and adjustment certificate must be obtained within 12 months of the date of the valuation[4]. Once received, copies of the valuation, report and certificate must be sent immediately to the Secretary of State, to each body whose employees contribute to the Fund, and to any other body liable to make payments to the Fund in respect of pensions[5]. The Secretary of State must also be sent a copy of the Consolidated Revenue Account and a summary of the assets of the Fund as at the date of valuation (unless this is already in the report)[6].

1 Local Government Pension Scheme (Management and Investment of Funds) Regulations 1998, SI 1998/1831, reg 76.
2 LGPS(MIF)R 1998, reg 77(1)(a).
3 LGPS(MIF)R 1998, reg 77(9).
4 LGPS(MIF)R 1998, reg 77(2).
5 LGPS(MIF)R 1998, reg 77(10).
6 LGPS(MIF)R 1998, reg 77(1).

(b) Definitions

3.34 The rates and adjustment certificate referred to above is a certificate specifying:

(1) the common rate of employer's contribution, and
(2) any individual adjustments

for each year of the period of three years beginning with 1 April in the year following that in which the valuation date falls[1]. The common rate of employer's contribution is the percentage of the pensionable employee's remuneration which should, in the actuary's opinion, be paid to the fund so as to ensure its solvency by all bodies whose employees contribute to it, having regard to[2]:

(1) the existing and prospective liabilities of the fund from circumstances common to all those bodies; and
(2) the desirability of maintaining as nearly constant a rate as possible.

Individual adjustments are defined as any percentage or amount by which, in the actuary's opinion, contributions at the common rate should, in the case of a particular body, be increased or reduced by reason of any circumstances peculiar to that body[3].

1 Local Government Pension Scheme (Management and Investment of Funds) Regulations 1998, SI 1998/1831, reg 77(3).
2 LGPS(MIF)R 1998, reg 77(4),(5).
3 LGPS(MIF)R 1998, reg 77(6).

3.35 For each year that a rates and adjustments certificate is required an employing authority must contribute to the appropriate fund a common percentage of the pay on which the contributions have, during that year, been paid to the fund by employees who are active members, increased or reduced by any individual adjustment specified in rates and adjustments certificate for that employer[1]. The common percentage is the common rate of employer's contributions specified in that certificate, expressed as a percentage[2].

Payments on account from non-administering authorities must be made at intervals determined by the Administering Authority[3]. If a payment on account is more than one month overdue, interest at one per cent above base rate (as defined) becomes payable, compounded at three-monthly intervals[4]. In certain circumstances, employers may be required to make further contributions[5].

1 Local Government Pension Scheme (Management and Investment of Funds) Regulations 1998, SI 1998/1831, reg 79(4).
2 LGPS(MIF)R 1998, reg 79(5).
3 LGPS(MIF)R 1998, regs 79(2), 81(1).
4 LGPS(MIF)R 1998, reg 81(2).
5 LGPS(MIF)R 1998, reg 80.

3.36 Employing authorities who are not Administering Authorities are required to make payments to Administering Authorities of employee contributions and other sums received by them in relation to the Fund, at such intervals (of 12 months or less) as may be determined by the Administering Authority[1]. These payments include contributions towards the cost of the administration of the Fund, except where the costs are themselves being met out of the Fund[2]. Interest is payable at a daily rate on payments which are more than a month overdue[3].

1 Local Government Pension Scheme (Management and Investment of Funds) Regulations 1998, SI 1998/1831, reg 81(1).
2 LGPS(MIF)R 1998, reg 81(1)(d),(2).
3 LGPS(MIF)R 1998, reg 81(1),(2).

3.37 The Fund must also make provision for pension increases and cash equivalents under the Pension Schemes Act 1993[1]. Pension increases under the Pensions (Increase) Act 1971 and the Pensions (Increase) Act 1974 are to be met out of the Fund[2]. Payments of premiums under the Pension Schemes Act 1993, s 55 are to be met out of the appropriate Pension Fund[3].

1 Local Government Pension Scheme (Management and Investment of Funds) Regulations 1998, SI 1998/1831, reg 90.
2 LGPS(MIF)R 1998, reg 91.
3 LGPS(MIF)R 1998, reg 92.

8 OTHER STATUTORY FUNDS

3.38 Apart from Trust Funds, local authorities may not maintain funds, save as provided for by statute. Examples of such specific statutory authority are under the Public Libraries and Museums Act 1964, s 12 (maintaining or proposing to provide a museum or art gallery) and the Lotteries and Amusements Act 1976, s 8 (the conducting of a local lottery).

Where there is no express authority in relation to establishing a Trust Fund, but there are a number of statutes which recognise that local authorities may hold funds as trustees, from which the power to establish such a fund may be inferred, examples are the Local Government Act 1972, ss 127, 139, and the Local Government and Housing Act 1989, s 59.

9 POLICE AUTHORITY FUNDS

3.39 Subject to limited exceptions all receipts of a Police Authority must be paid into the Police Fund and all expenditure paid out of it[1]. Accounts are required of all payments into or out of the Fund[2].

1 Police Act 1996, s 14(1),(2).
2 PA 1996, s 14(3).

B Accounts

3.40 Apart from the general statutory requirement to keep accounts in the Local Government Finance Act 1982, s 12(1), there are a number of other statutory provisions requiring separate accounts to be kept in relation to particular activities.

1 REVENUE ACCOUNT

3.41 This topic is dealt with in Chapter 2.

2 HOUSING REVENUE ACCOUNT

3.42 This topic is dealt with in Chapter 20.

3 DIRECT LABOUR AND SERVICE ORGANISATIONS

3.43 The Local Government, Planning and Land Act 1980 ('LGPLA 1980') required that certain works of construction and maintenance *must* be put out to tender. Local authorities could tender for such work themselves through their direct labour organisations. Where such work was carried out, it was known as 'functional work'[1]. Direct labour organisations can also carry out work for other local authorities or public bodies, eg under the Local Authorities (Goods and Services) Act 1970 ('LA(G&S)A 1970'), which arrangements are termed 'works contracts'[2]. Compulsory competitive tendering (CCT) was abolished with effect from 2 January 2000 when Pt I of the Local Government Act 1999 came into force. However, the accounting requirements will be relevant for some time to come. The 'proper practices' for local authority accounting now require local authorities to keep 'trading accounts' for nine headings of activity, one of which is their 'contracts' under the former CCT legislation with DLOs and DSOs. The 'proper practices' are contained in CIPFA's Best Value Accounting Code of Practice 2000, section 2 and Annex D (published 22 February 2000 and in force 1 April 2000): see LGHA 1989, s 66(4)(b).

1 Local Government, Planning and Land Act 1980, s 8.
2 LGPLA 1980, s 5.

3.44 The Local Government Finance Act 1988 ('LGFA 1988') introduced competitive tendering for a number of 'defined activities', eg refuse collection carried out by specific local authorities. The Local Government Act 1992, s 8 gave the Secretary of State extensive powers to extend and modify the provisions of LGFA 1988 in order to apply them to professional services, including legal and financial services. Local authorities could tender for work through in-house service organisations, in which case it was again referred to as 'functional work'[1], or for the work of other authorities or bodies, in which case it was again known as a 'works contract[2]'.

1 Local Government Finance Act 1988, s 3(4).
2 LGFA 1988, s 3(2),(3).

3.45 The accounting requirements of LGPLA 1980 applied to[1]:

(1) county councils;
(2) district councils;
(3) London borough councils;
(4) joint authorities[2];
(5) the Council of the Isles of Scilly;
(6) the Common Council of the City of London (in its capacity as a local authority or police authority);
(7) the Commission for New Towns;
(8) development corporations established under the New Towns Act 1981;
(9) county and county borough councils in Wales;
(10) police authorities[3].

1 Local Government, Planning and Land Act 1980, ss 10(1) and 20(1).
2 Local Government Act 1985, Pt IV.
3 Police Act 1996.

3.46 The requirements of the LGFA 1988 applied to a wider range of 'defined authorities', which are those listed above together with the following:

(1) parish councils;
(2) community councils;
(3) Urban Development Corporations[1];
(4) Combined Fire Authorities and Metropolitan County Fire and Civil Defence Authorities;
(5) the London Fire and Civil Defence Authority;
(6) Waste Disposal Authorities[2];
(7) Joint Education Authorities.

1 Local Government, Planning and Land Act 1980, s 135.
2 Local Government Act 1985, s 10.

(a) Direct labour organisations

3.47 Every local authority which undertook construction or maintenance work under works contracts or by way of functional work, and every development body which undertook construction or maintenance work by way of functional work should have kept in respect of each specified description of work a revenue account (the 'DLO revenue account')[1]. The Secretary of State also had power to direct that other accounts were kept[2].

1 Local Government, Planning and Land Act 1980, s 10(1).
2 LGPLA 1980, s 10(1)(ii).

3.48 Accounts had to be kept for:

(1) general highway works and works in connection with the construction or maintenance of a sewer;
(2) works of new construction (other than general highway or sewer works), the estimated cost of which exceeds £50,000;
(3) works of new construction (other than general highway or sewer works), the estimated cost of which does not exceed £50,000; and
(4) works of maintenance within the meaning of the Local Authorities (Goods and Services) Act 1970.

3.49 LGPLA 1980, s 10(3) defined 'general highway works' as meaning –

(1) the construction and maintenance work for the purpose of the laying out, construction, improvement, maintenance or repair of highways, other than work for the purpose of the construction of highways which is connected with the carrying out of other works of new construction;
(2) the gritting of or clearing of snow from highways; and
(3) the maintenance of street lighting.

3.50 LGPLA 1980, s 10(6) defined 'works of new construction' as meaning building or civil engineering works of any description which are not works of maintenance within LA(G&S)A 1970. The 1970 Act itself did not contain an extensive definition of 'maintenance work' but included within it 'minor renewals, minor improvements and minor extensions[1]'.

If maintenance work was genuinely such the reference to minor renewals, improvements and extensions provided power for added works (of these minor classes) as distinct from introducing the word 'minor' into the principal power, to undertake maintenance[2]. There were specific exclusions from the definition of construction and maintenance work in the 1980 Act[3].

1 Local Authorities (Goods and Services) Act 1970, s 1(4).
2 *R v Hackney London Borough Council, ex p Secretary of State for the Environment* (1989) 88 LGR 96.
3 Local Government, Planning and Land Act 1980, s 20(2)–(4).

3.51 A local authority was excluded from the accounting requirements if it did not at any one time in the previous financial year employ more than 15 persons who were engaged (wholly or partly) in carrying out construction or maintenance work of that particular description[1]. In counting the number of persons employed, those engaged wholly or mainly on work of 'design, development or control of construction or maintenance work' are to be excluded[2]. It should be emphasised that the GLC had full legal powers up to midnight on the eve of its abolition. This is relevant because many abolished bodies are transferring their functions to other bodies at the present time.

1 Local Government, Planning and Land Act 1980, s 11(1), as amended by the Local Government (Direct Labour Organisations) (Specified Number of Employed Persons) Order1989, SI 1989/1589.
2 Local Government, Planning and Land Act 1980, s 11(2).

(b) Practice

3.52 No amount could be credited to any DLO revenue account in respect of any functional work, in excess of the 'appropriate amount[1]'. Before undertaking functional work the local authority must have prepared a statement of either the amount it intended to credit to the DLO revenue account for the work, or a method by which the amount could be calculated. The appropriate amount was the sum identified by reference to this statement[2].

1 Local Government, Planning and Land Act 1980, s 12(1).
2 LGPLA 1980, s 9(2).

3.53 Every local authority which undertook construction or maintenance work, whether as functional work or under a works contract, and any development body which did such functional work, must—by 30 September of the following financial year—have prepared a written revenue account[1]. The account must show a 'true and fair view' of the financial result for each description of construction or maintenance work to which it relates[2]. Also needed was a statement on the rate of return which it was required to achieve by LGPLA 1980, s 16.

Where the account related to more than one description of work, it must show a true and fair view of the combined financial result of the authority or body of all the descriptions of work to which it relates[3].

1 Local Government, Planning and Land Act 1980, s 13(1), (2)(b).
2 See LGPLA 1980, s 13(4), as to 'true and fair view'.
3 LGPLA 1980, s 13(5).

3.54 A local authority which undertook construction or maintenance work, whether as functional work or under a works contract, and any development body which did such functional work, must—no later than 30 September in the financial year following that to which it related—have prepared a report which must include a statement which identified the work undertaken and the annual revenue account, and any other information which the Secretary of State may require, and must send a copy both to the Secretary of State, and to the local authority's or development body's auditor, no later than 31 October[1].

1 Local Government, Planning and Land Act 1980, s 18.

3.55 Where there is a failure to comply with the provisions of LGPLA 1980, ss 10, 12 and 13 (as well as other failures related to the statutory requirements of competitive tendering) then sanctions could be applied[1]. The Secretary of State could serve notice on a local authority or development requiring information from that local authority or development body. This could be followed by the issue of a direction under which the Secretary of State might require further tendering for contracts or might close down the direct labour organisation.

1 Local Government, Planning and Land Act 1980, s 19A, 19B.

(c) Accounts of direct service organisations

3.56 Where a defined authority carried out work within a defined activity, and the work was either a works contract or functional work, the authority must, for each financial year, have kept an account as regards all the work which fell within that activity[1].

Where the work was carried out under a works contract, the authority must have credited to the account the amount specified or ascertained under the contract, as the price for carrying out the work in that year[2]. Where the work was functional, there must be a credit or a debit to reflect the terms of the bid made by the direct service organisation[3].

1 Local Government Finance Act 1988, s 9(1),(2).
2 LGFA 1988, s 9(3).
3 LGFA 1988, s 9(4).

3.57 Local authorities and development bodies who have carried out any defined work in any year must have prepared an annual report. This must include a summary of the account kept for the year and the summary must present fairly the financial result[1]. The annual report must be prepared by 30 September in the financial year following that for which it is prepared, and a copy sent to the Secretary of State, and to the local authority's auditor, not later than 31 October[2]. The report must have included a statement on the rate of return which the authority was required to achieve by LGFA 1988, s 10.

1 Local Government Finance Act 1988, ss 11(2)(a), 11(3).
2 LGFA 1988, s 11(7).

3.58 Failure to comply with the requirements of LGFA 1988, s 9 (as well as other failures related to the statutory requirements of competitive tendering) brought sanctions equivalent to those under LGFA 1988[1].

1 Local Government Finance Act 1988, ss 13, 14.

3.59 Accounts must show a true and fair picture under LGPLA 1980 and a financial report which presents fairly the financial result under LGFA 1988. To do this local authorities needed to have regard to the relevant non-statutory guidance contained in the CIPFA Code of Practice on Local Authority Accounting in Great Britain, Statement of Recommended Practice in the CIPFA Code of Practice for Compulsory Competition 1995.

C Supply of goods and services

1 LOCAL AUTHORITIES (GOODS AND SERVICES) ACT 1970

3.60 The Local Authorities (Goods and Services) Act 1970 permits local authorities to enter into contracts for the supply of certain goods and services to other local authorities, and public bodies[1]. If a local authority enters into such an agreement, it must 'include a separate account in respect of the agreements'[2]. This requirement did not apply where the work was done by a direct labour organisation or direct service organisation under LGPLA 1980 and LGFA 1988.

1 Local Authorities (Goods and Services) Act 1970, s 1.
2 LA(G&S)A 1970, s 2(2).

2 FURTHER EDUCATION ACT 1985

3.61 The Further Education Act 1985 empowers local education authorities to supply goods and services through an institution maintained by them which provides higher and/or further education[1]. They may also lend money for the purposes of an agreement for the supply of goods or services to other institutes of higher and further education which are independent of themselves.

Any local education authority which exercises its powers under FEA 1985 must keep a general revenue account, and such other accounts and prepare such statement as the Secretary of State may direct[2]. No directions have yet been made. This is an additional requirement to those required under the Local Government Finance Act 1982, s 23. The revenue account and statement must show the full cost to the local authority of goods or services supplied under the Act and which are relevant to the account statement[3].

1 Further Education Act 1985, s 2.
2 FEA 1985, s 3(4).
3 FEA 1985, s 3(5).

D Publicity accounts

3.62 The Local Government Act 1986 introduced statutory restrictions on the use of publicity by local authorities. For these purposes 'publicity' refers to 'any communication in whatever form addressed to the public at large or to a section of the public'[1].

1 Local Government Act 1986, s 6(4).

3.63 The local authorities covered by the Local Government Act 1986 are[1]:

(1) county councils;
(2) district councils;
(3) London borough councils;
(4) the Broads Authority;
(5) a joint authority[2];
(6) the Council of the Isles of Scilly;
(7) a parish or community council;
(8) the Common Council of the City of London;
(9) county and county borough councils in Wales.

1 Local Government Act 1986, s 6(2),(3).
2 Local Government Act 1985, Pt IV.

3.64 Local authorities must keep a separate account of their expenditure on publicity[1].

1 Local Government Act 1986, s 5(1). Guidance on the keeping of this account is to be found in *Accounting for Publicity*, a guidance note produced jointly by the AETR and CIPFA.

3.65 The Secretary of State may exempt publicity and expenditure from the requirement[1] and by the Local Authorities (Publicity Account) (Exemption) Order 1987, SI 1987/2004 has exercised this power. Local authorities may choose to include exempt expenditure in the account[2]. As well as exempting expenditure of less than £3,000 per annum, expenditure where it is not easy to separate the expenditure on items of publicity from other activities, and certain other expenditure, the Order also provides a schedule of exempt publicity including to tenants, and to parents and pupils of educational establishments.

1 Local Government Act 1986, s 5(5).
2 *Accounting for Publicity*, para 5.

3.66 Any person interested is entitled to inspect the account and make copies of it at any reasonable time and without payment[1].

A person who has custody of the account (who may be an officer of the local authority or an external auditor), and who intentionally obstructs someone exercising rights of inspection and copying under subs (2), commits a summary offence[2]. The regulations made under the Local Government Finance Act 1982, s 23 apply to the right of inspection.

1 Local Government Act 1986, s 5(2).
2 LGA 1986, s 5(3).

E Other accounts

1 LOCAL GOVERNMENT ACT 1972, S 137

3.67 This section empowers local authorities to incur a limited amount of expenditure for certain purposes not otherwise authorised. Where such expenditure is incurred, the local authority must keep a separate account of it[1]. The right of inspection under the Local Government Finance Act 1982, s 24 applies to such accounts.

1 Local Government Act 1972, s 137(7).

2 LOCAL GOVERNMENT (MISCELLANEOUS PROVISIONS) ACT 1976, S 12

3.68 The Local Government (Miscellaneous Provisions) Act 1976, s 11 empowers local authorities in certain circumstances to provide heat, hot air, hot water or steam. Where any expenditure is incurred under this power, the local authority must keep a separate account[1].

1 Local Government (Miscellaneous Provisions) Act 1976, s 12(4).

3 HIGHWAYS ACT 1980, S 214

3.69 Under the Highways Act 1980 a Code has been established for the execution of works in private streets by certain local authorities. Such local authorities must keep separate accounts of all money expended and recovered by them in execution of the Private Street Works Code[1].

1 Highways Act 1980, s 214(1).

4 ROAD TRAFFIC REGULATION ACT 1984, S 55

3.70 The Road Traffic Regulation Act 1984, s 45 empowers local authorities to provide metered on-street parking. Local authorities must keep an account of their income and expenditure in respect of such parking places[1]. Any deficit on the account must be made good from the General Fund, and surpluses must be applied for designated purposes[2].

1 Road Traffic Regulation Act 1984, s 55(1).
2 RTRA 1984, s 55(2)–(4).

5 LOCAL GOVERNMENT AND HOUSING ACT 1989, PT III

3.71 The Local Government and Housing Act 1989, Pt III makes provision for local authorities to take appropriate steps for promoting economic development in their area, including the making of loans[1]. The Local Government (Promotion of Economic Development) Regulations 1990, SI 1990/763 regulate such loans.

1 Local Government and Housing Act 1989, s 33(3)(b).

3.72 Thus local authorities are permitted to make loans at a rate of interest which is more favourable than that reasonably obtainable on the open market. Where such a loan is made, and at any time when an amount of principal is outstanding, the local authority must keep a separate account of the amount of the loan, and of the difference between the amount of interest payable in respect of the loan and the amount that would have been payable at the prevailing market rate[1]. A statement of the account must be deposited with the proper officer of the local authority at the time which the statement of the local authority's accounts is published, in accordance with the regulations made under the Local Government Finance Act 1982, s 23[2].

1 Local Government (Promotion of Economic Development) Regulations 1990, SI 1990/763, reg 9(1).
2 LG(P of ED)R, reg 9(2).

PART II

Financial control and accountability

CHAPTER 4

Basic legal principles

A Ultra vires

4.1 This chapter concentrates on the relevance of the doctrine of ultra vires to the financial activities of local authorities. The object of the doctrine is said to be the protection of the public[1]. The fundamental principle, that a local authority may not act outside its powers, has two aspects. First, the local authority must have the express or implied authority of Parliament for all its actions. Second, the manner in which a local authority exercises its functions, and in particular the decision to use its powers, must not involve illegality, irrationality or procedural impropriety[2]. If it does, the local authority's action will be susceptible to judicial review and may be declared a nullity.

1 Lord Templeman in *Hazell v London Borough of Hammersmith and Fulham* [1992] 2 AC 1.
2 See the three-fold classification of the grounds for judicial review given by Lord Diplock in *Council of Civil Service Unions v Minister for the Civil Service* [1985] AC 374 at 410–11, which whilst not exhaustive, has been adopted in many subsequent cases.

4.2 Express statutory powers relating to the financial activities of local government are covered in detail throughout this book. Usually there is comparatively little difficulty in establishing whether a specific statutory power exists to authorise an activity. It is in the areas of implied authority and incidental powers that most problems in relation to 'statutory capacity' occur. This chapter concentrates on the second limb of the doctrine of ultra vires, namely matters which are generally relevant to the manner of exercise of statutory financial functions, especially where they entail the exercise of discretion by the local authority.

4.3 Statutory provisions which impose a specific financial duty on a local authority may leave no room for the exercise of discretion, eg to pay rent allowances at the prescribed rates where a valid claim is made under the housing benefit scheme. Some financial functions incorporate the use of both duties and discretions, eg to implement proposals to secure that a debit balance does not arise on the Housing Revenue Account under the Local Government and Housing Act 1989, s 76 which entails an obligation to achieve the particular result of preventing a deficit, but leaves some room for discretion in the method by which that result is to be achieved in terms of decisions which will affect items of income and expenditure on the Account. Other provisions allow the local authority a choice as to whether, and the extent and manner, in which it should exercise a function, eg to take steps to promote the economic development of its area under the Local Government and Housing Act 1989, s 33. Where the terms of the statute indicate a discretion, it will not be unlimited; the important question will be the breadth of that discretion.

4.4 The jurisdiction of the court to intervene in a local authority's decision making process by way of judicial review is not to take a different view on the facts[1] nor to act as an appellate body. The court is concerned only to see whether the local authority is acting in excess of the powers given to it by Parliament, whether in the form of 'simple' lack of statutory capacity, or arising from the manner of exercise of existing powers.

1 Although the court must enquire whether those facts exist and have been taken into account, per Lord Wilberforce in *Secretary of State for Education and Science v Tameside Metropolitan Borough Council* [1977] AC 1014 at 1047.

4.5 It is important to appreciate that the following are not clearly delineated rules, but broad principles, which tend to merge into one another. For example, there may well be an overlap between the application of the Wednesbury principles and certain of the other principles referred to below. Consideration of irrelevant factors may also entail the use of a statutory power for an improper purpose, or failure to observe the quasi-fiduciary duty may also be characterised as disregarding a relevant factor.

B 'Wednesbury unreasonableness'

4.6 The dicta of Lord Greene MR in *Associated Provincial Picture Houses Ltd v Wednesbury Corpn*[1], or the so-called Wednesbury principles of unreasonableness, are well-known and regularly cited:

> 'The Court is entitled to investigate the action of a local authority with a view to seeing whether or not they have taken into account matters which they ought not to have taken into account, or, conversely have refused to take into account or neglected to take into account matters which they ought to take into account. Once that question is answered in favour of the local authority, it may still be possible to say that, although the local authority had kept within the four corners of the matters they ought to consider, they have nevertheless come to a conclusion so unreasonable that no reasonable authority could ever have come to it. In such a case, again, I think that the court can interfere.'

The factors which are relevant and irrelevant to a particular decision will depend upon the statutory function under consideration.

1 [1948] 1 KB 223, [1947] 2 All ER 680.

4.7 The contemporary description of this principle[1] is 'irrationality':

> '... a decision so outrageous in its defiance of logic or accepted moral standards that no sensible person who had applied his mind to the question to be decided could have arrived at it.'

1 In *Council of Civil Service Unions v Minister for the Civil Service* [1985] AC 374 at 410, per Lord Diplock.

C Quasi-fiduciary duty

4.8 Whilst local authorities are not trustees of the funds they collect, they owe 'an analogous fiduciary duty' to those from whom they collect them[1]. All statutes must be construed in the light of this duty. The practical consequences of this principle are that in exercising any statutory discretion involving expenditure or the levying of charges, an authority is bound to have regard to the interests of its local tax payers. Local authorities must not act thriftlessly, indeed they should deploy their full financial resources to best advantage[2]. The interests of local taxpayers are not the sole determining factor in any decision, for example an authority should balance those interests against those of the recipients of a particular service intended to derive benefit from the decision (although the point has often been illustrated in cases where the balance was found to have weighed too heavily in favour of the individual recipients)[3].

1 *Prescott v Birmingham Corpn* [1955] Ch 210 and see the dicta of Lord Atkinson in *Roberts v Hopwood* [1925] AC 578 at 595–6, HL.
2 See the dicta of Lord Diplock in *Bromley London Borough Council v Greater London Council* [1983] 1 AC 768 at 829.
3 See eg *Roberts v Hopwood* [1925] AC 578 (excessive wages); *Prescott v Birmingham Corpn* [1955] Ch 210 (free travel scheme); *Taylor v Munrow* [1960] 1 All ER 455 (excessive rent subsidy); *Luby v Newcastle-under-Lyme Corpn* [1965] 1 QB 214 (failure to operate differential rent scheme based on individual tenants' means was not unlawful).

D Financial motives, levying charges and trading for profit

4.9 At the opposite end of the spectrum, an over-zealous approach to saving or generating finance for local government may also make a decision vulnerable to judicial review and potentially void.

For example, it would be improper for a planning authority to exact a 'price' from a planning applicant for the grant of a consent[1]. No charge may be made for the services a local authority provides, unless this is expressly authorised by statute or is a necessary implication of a statutory provision[2].

1 See eg *Hall & Co Ltd v Shoreham-by-Sea UDC* [1964] 1 All ER 1, where a planning condition purported to require the applicant to provide land for a road at his own expense.
2 *McCarthy & Stone Ltd v Richmond upon Thames London Borough Council* [1992] 2 AC 48 where the House of Lords held that charging a planning applicant for pre-application advice amounted to the 'incidental to the incidental' and was not authorised by Local Government Act 1972, s 111.

4.10 Local authorities have no implied power to engage in a trade or business for profit. Even if the intention is to apply the profits to some local government purpose, this would not render an activity intra vires which would otherwise be ultra vires[1]. Limited powers enabling local authorities to enter into agreements to supply goods and certain services to other local authorities and to 'public bodies[2]' are given by the Local Authorities (Goods and Services) Act 1970. Whilst the view was expressed on behalf of the Department of the Environment[3] that, within limits, these provisions encompass powers to trade for profit and to take on staff for the purposes of trading activities (and not merely to deploy surplus capacity), this view did not conform with advice previously given to auditors by the then solicitor to the Audit Commission[4]. There is now some authority on the point. In *R v Yorkshire Purchasing Organisation, ex p British Educational Suppliers Ltd*[5], it was argued on behalf of an applicant for judicial review that the 1970 Act did not authorise the respondent to conduct a trading enterprise, purchase large amounts of stock and engage in marketing activities, employ staff, and acquire stock prior to any specific agreement with another public body coming into being. The respondent, YPO, was a joint committee of twelve local authorities, running a substantial local authorities' supplies undertaking, which had an annual turnover of some £130 million in 1994. Owen J rejected the applicant's arguments, notwithstanding a strong presumption against a local authority's right to trade and found that YPO's activities were authorised under the 1970 Act.

1 Court of Appeal in *Hazell v London Borough of Hammersmith and Fulham* [1990] 2 QB 697, in relation to the use of interest rate swaps and in *Crédit Suisse v Allerdale Borough Council* [1996] 4 All ER 129 in relation to the intended use of the receipts from the sale of time share accommodation to finance the construction of a leisure pool.
2 As defined by the Local Authorities (Goods and Services) Act 1970, s 1(4) and in orders made by the Secretary of State under s 1(5). There are many such orders.
3 *Letters to Local Authority Associations* by P Rowsell dated 7 December 1995.
4 Audit Commission Technical Release 23/90.
5 (1996) 95 LGR 413. See decision on appeal: (1997) 95 LGR 727.

E Unlawful fetters on discretion and failure to exercise discretion

4.11 A local authority may not unlawfully fetter the exercise of its discretion. The authority must leave itself free to decide each case as the public interest requires at the time. Areas of particular concern are contracts and undertakings entered into by local authorities and any policy rules which they create.

4.12 What amounts to an 'unlawful' fetter is not always clear. If it is a necessary implication of the terms of a statute that an authorised activity will restrict the exercise of an authority's remaining functions, concurrently or in the future, then this will not be 'unlawful'. Further, the law acknowledges that certain 'fetters' are inevitable and are not automatically unlawful.

4.13 As far as local authority contracts are concerned, the general principle is that a public authority may not enter into a contract or other agreement which is incompatible with the due exercise of its powers, or the discharge of its duties, or which divests the authority of its statutory powers, or which obliges the authority not to exercise its powers[1]. Classical examples of impermissible contractual terms would be covenants to grant or refuse planning permission[2] in the future. But the position is not always so clear-cut and difficult questions of degree may be involved.

1 *Birkdale District Electric Supply Co Ltd v Southport Corpn* [1926] AC 355 in which the House of Lords rejected an argument which would have rendered invalid many ordinary contracts entered into by bodies exercising statutory powers in respect of the business management of their undertaking.
2 *Ransom & Luck Ltd v Surbiton Borough Council* [1949] Ch 180; *Stringer v Minister of Housing and Local Government* [1971] 1 All ER 65.

4.14 In order to discharge its statutory functions a local authority will need to enter into contracts with outside bodies, often covering a number of years. In doing so the authority will, inevitably, limit its ability to act to some degree. In *Dowty Bolton Paul Ltd v Wolverhampton Corpn*[1], the Corporation granted the company the right to use the municipal airport for certain purposes connected with the company's business for a term of years. Before the term had expired, the Corporation wished to develop the airfield as a housing estate and sought to argue that the contract with the company could not have the effect of fettering the Corporation's statutory powers. Pennycuick VC held that the Corporation was not entitled to override the right it had granted to the company:

> 'The cases are not concerned with a statutory power which has been validly exercised. Obviously, where a power is exercised in such a manner as to

create a right extending over a term of years, the existence of that right pro tanto excludes the exercise of other statutory powers in respect of the same subject matter, but there is no authority and I can see no principle upon which that sort of exercise could be held to be invalid as a fetter on the future exercise of powers[2].'

It has been said that the important question is whether there is incompatibility between the purposes of the statutory powers and the purposes for which the contract is entered into[3].

1 [1971] 1 WLR 204.
2 At 210.
3 Wade *Administrative Law* (7th edn, 1997) 367.

4.15 The courts have acknowledged that a financial commitment may outlive the currently elected body[1].

Unfortunately the position is not always clear, particularly where a contract, agreement or undertaking covers a number of financial years. To take a practical example, an agreement with a voluntary body under which the authority is to promise to make discretionary grants annually for a period of years may be important both to the proposed recipient body and to the local authority, but such an agreement may be vulnerable to challenge on the grounds of fettering the authority's statutory discretion as to the making of grants in each year or may offend the principles of annual accounting referred to below, unless the terms of the statute which authorise the particular grant envisage a long-term commitment from the authority.

1 Browne LJ in *Manchester City Council v Greater Manchester Metropolitan County Council* (1979) 78 LGR 71, affd (1980) 78 LGR 560.

4.16 On a number of occasions[1] the courts have considered the extent to which a local authority may consider itself bound by non-contractual undertakings or informal representations concerning the exercise of its statutory discretions in the future, or may be estopped from acting otherwise than in accordance with such undertakings or representations. The basic principle, that estoppel cannot be raised to hinder the exercise of a statutory discretion[2], appears to be subject to limited exceptions[3]. Further, any informal undertakings or representations previously given to affected parties may well be a relevant consideration for the local authority when it eventually exercises its discretion. They may lead to those parties having a 'legitimate expectation' of being afforded an opportunity to make representations before a decision is reached. It may even be found to be '*Wednesbury* unreasonable' or irrational to act inconsistently with a prior undertaking or representation, or a breach of the duty to act fairly[4].

1 Especially in the context of planning law.
2 See for example *Southend-on-Sea Corpn v Hodgson (Wickford) Ltd* [1962] 1 QB 416.
3 In *Western Fish Products Ltd v Penwith District Council* [1981] 2 All ER 204 the local authority was not bound by representations in a letter from an officer which appeared to confirm the existence of an established use and was entitled to refuse subsequent applications for planning consent and established use certificate. On the other hand, in *Lever Finance Ltd v Westminster (City) London Borough Council* [1971] 1 QB 222 and in *London Borough of Camden v Secretary of State for the Environment* (1993) 67 P&CR 59 the local authorities were bound by representations within the ostensible authority of an officer and acted upon by planning applicants that variations to plans were not material so as to require fresh planning permission.
4 *R v Liverpool Corpn, ex p Liverpool Taxi Fleet Operators' Association* [1972] 2 QB 299. See also the decision

of the Court of Appeal in *R v Walsall Metropolitan Borough Council, ex p Yapp* (1993) 92 LGR 110: local authority employees had legitimate expectations that they would be consulted prior to a decision to seek fresh tenders for building works previously awarded to the workforce and that the Council would only vary its previous resolution on rational grounds, but the authority was not in breach of its duty to act fairly towards them in deciding to seek fresh tenders.

4.17 Local authorities may adopt their own policies as to how their discretionary powers are to be used, provided, of course, that those policies are based on relevant considerations. However, (unless authorised by the particular statute in question)[1] any policies which are adopted must not be so rigidly applied as to prevent the authority 'applying its mind' to individual cases and considering whether there are grounds for an exception to be made. Slavish adherence to policy, to the point where the authority fails to consider all the matters relevant to the merits of an individual case and refuses to listen to objections would amount to an unlawful fetter on the exercise of a discretion[2].

1 See for example Local Government (Miscellaneous Provisions) Act 1982, s 2 and Sch 3.
2 See for example *Sagnata Investments Ltd v Norwich Corpn* [1971] 2 QB 614 and *Stringer v Minister for Housing and Local Government* [1971] 1 All ER 65.

4.18 The courts[1] have considered the role of a party political discipline in local government decision-making. In determining factual matters, an election manifesto or the party whip would have no relevance. But in deciding matters of policy, party loyalty and policy may be taken into consideration by individual members, provided that those factors do not dominate so as to preclude consideration of other factors; councillors must not breach their duty to make up their own minds as to how to vote. In *R v Waltham Forest London Borough Council, ex p Baxter*[2] the Court of Appeal found that members of the majority group who, at a private group meeting had voted against a particular rate increase which the group as a whole then agreed to support, had not fettered their discretion when they voted in favour of that increase at the council meeting. The existence of the sanction of withdrawal of the party whip for voting against group decisions did not in itself lead to such an inference.

1 The Widdecombe Committee on the Conduct of Local Government Business, Cmnd 9797 (1986).
2 [1988] QB 419.

4.19 Related aspects of the obligation to exercise statutory discretion fully are the prohibitions on delegating a decision-making function otherwise than in accordance with statute (see below) and on acting under the dictation of another body unless authorised by statute. Whilst a local authority may, and often should, take account of the views and advice of outside bodies and individuals, generally it must retain for itself the ultimate power to decide. It must not consider itself bound to act as an outside body requires or desires, unless authorised by statute to do so.

F Improper purposes

4.20 The statutory powers conferred on local authorities to be exercised for public purposes can only validly be used if they are used in the way in which Parliament, when conferring the powers, is presumed to have intended[1]. It has been said that they are not conferred absolutely, but upon trust[2]. The discretion local authorities are given by statute must be used to promote the policy and objects of the particular Act and not to thwart or run counter to them[3].

1 See Lord Bridge in *R v Tower Hamlets London Borough Council, ex p Chetnik Developments Ltd* [1988] AC 858 at 872, approving a passage from Wade *Administrative Law* (5th edn).
2 Ibid and see Neill LJ in *Crédit Suisse v Allerdale Borough Council* [1997] QB 306.
3 *Padfield v Minister of Agriculture, Fisheries and Food* [1968] AC 997.

4.21 Examples of the application of this principle include *Padfield v Minister of Agriculture, Fisheries and Food*[1] (improper reasons for a minister's refusal to direct a committee of investigation to act); *Wheeler v Leicester City Council*[2] (use of statutory powers of management to punish a rugby football club); *Roberts v Hopwood*[3] (misplaced philanthropy in setting employees' wages) and *Crédit Suisse v Allerdale Borough Council*[4] (scheme designed to circumvent statutory controls on local authority finance).

1 [1968] AC 997.
2 [1985] AC 1054.
3 [1925] AC 578.
4 [1997] QB 306.

G Unlawful delegation

4.22 The Local Government Act 1972, s 101 deals with the general ability of local authorities to delegate their functions to committees, sub-committees, officers and other local authorities. Functions with respect to levying, or issuing a precept for a rate may only be discharged by the authority itself. Certain functions may only be discharged by a specified committee[1]. Individual statutes may preclude delegation under s 101. For example, a local authority's duty to consider a report or recommendation made by an auditor under the Local Government Act 1992, s 5 cannot be delegated[2]. Alternatively, a particular statutory provision may expressly authorise delegation outside s 101[3].

1 See Local Authority Social Services Act 1970, s 2 and Local Government Act 1972, s 101(9) and (10).
2 LGA 1992, s 59(4).
3 For example, the obligation to transfer certain waste disposal functions to specially formed companies under the Environmental Protection Act 1990, s 32. See also LGA 2000, Pt II which authorises the new executive arrangements (not in force as of 7 August 2000).

H Annual accounting and forward funding

4.23 The general proposition that local government finance must be conducted on an annual basis has been accepted in a number of leading cases, but the practical effects of this principle require further explanation. The annual basis for accounting revolves around a local authority's obligation to levy council tax to meet the authority's budgeted expenditure for the year.

4.24 The principle of annual accounting does not mean that the purpose for which money is spent must be fulfilled within the year. Nor does it prohibit capital as opposed to revenue spending. For example, a local authority may spend money on a capital asset which will bring benefit in future years, or possibly make a lump sum payment in advance under a contract which is to be carried out over several years (provided that such a decision is 'reasonable' and represents a balance between the interest of current and future local tax payers).

4.25 In *Re Westminster City Council*[1] Lord Oliver explained the test in the following terms:

> 'The test of whether any given expenditure can properly be included in the budget for the year in respect of which a rate is to be levied is whether it is necessary to or consequent upon the exercise or carrying out during the year in question of the authority's powers and functions.'

In that case, the decision of the shortly to be abolished Greater London Council to provide 'forward funding' for the administrative expenses of a number of voluntary organisations in the year following the demise of the local authority, through grants to be paid to 'umbrella bodies' consisting of those organisations, was found to be ultra vires. Lord Oliver distinguished the House of Lords' decision in *Manchester City Council v Greater Manchester County Council*[2], where a trust fund established to provide bursaries for certain school children throughout a seven year curriculum was found to be intra vires, on the basis that on the facts of the *Manchester* case, the money paid to establish the trust was expenditure which 'fell to be defrayed' in the year in which it was paid over to the trust. The Council had intended to provide for the education of children of the requisite age and ability *in that year*. The power could only properly be exercised if, at the same time, secure provision was made for the future years of the curriculum. The voluntary organisations intended to benefit from the GLC decision had all received their grants for the year prior to abolition and the grants proposed to be paid to the umbrella bodies clearly related to the running expenses of the voluntary organisations for the following year. The grants for future years were not necessary or consequent upon the grants already made for the year in question, nor on anything other than the GLC's determination to make them.

1 [1986] AC 668 at 714.
2 (1980) 78 LGR 560.

4.26 In *R v Greater London Council, ex p London Residuary Body*[1] Macpherson J distinguished the decision in *Re Westminster* and upheld the validity of the decision of the GLC to make payments to a company to fund works to housing stock transferred to the boroughs, even though some of those works were to be commenced and completed after abolition. The payments made to the company were capital payments which at once 'soaked up' a substantial slice of immediately necessary works, programmed and fully identified, which were part of the GLC's instant duty to perform under its obligations which persisted until the 'death' of the authority. The Council's power and indeed its duty to fund the housing stock remained alive until the last minute. It should be emphasised that the GLC had full legal powers up to midnight on the eve of its abolition. This is relevant because many abolished bodies are transferring their functions to other bodies at the present time.

1 (1986) 19 HLR 175.

I The scope of Local Government Act 1971, s 111

4.27 A local authority is a corporation and as such is subject to the doctrine of ultra vires. The courts have held that in addition to things for which they have express or implied authority, corporations may do what is reasonably incidental to the doing of those things. This was established in *A-G v Great Eastern Rly*[1]. This common law rule has been given statutory force by the Local Government Act 1972, s 111.

1 (1880) 5 App Cas 473.

4.28 LGA 1972, s 111 states that a local authority shall have the power to do anything which is 'calculated to facilitate, or is conducive or incidental to, the discharge of any of their functions.'

The wording of this section has been subject to much litigation and resulting precise interpretation. This has revolved mostly around the meaning of the terms 'incidental to' and 'functions'. Each term will be dealt with in turn.

4.29 It has been firmly established that 'incidental to' is not synonymous with 'in connection with'. It has a much narrower meaning. Although it allows the authority to enter into activities which the court considers were not contemplated by the legislature the modern trend has been for a liberal interpretation. In *A-G v Smethwick Corpn*[1] the establishment of a department to carry out the council's printing operation was held to be intra vires. Further, in *Grainger v Liverpool Corpn*[2] it was lawful to employ a private consultant to advise on rating proposals. It could be suggested that this liberalisation may well be due to the phrase 'calculated to facilitate' which is also in this section.

1 [1932] 1 Ch 563.
2 [1954] 1 QB 351.

4.30 The question still remains as to what exactly constitutes a 'function' that may be facilitated. Woolf LJ in *Hazell v Hammersmith and Fulham London Borough Council*[1] gave a definition of what one may consider a function to be. His Lordship stated that –

> '... what is a function for the purposes of the subsection is not expressly defined but in our view there can be little doubt that in this context "function" refers to the multiplicity of specific statutory activities the council is expressly or impliedly under a duty to perform or has power to perform under the other provisions of the Act of 1972 or other relevant legislation. The subsection does not of itself, independently of any other provision, authorise the performance of any other activity. It only confers ... a subsidiary power. A subsidiary power which authorises an activity where some other statutory provision has vested a specific function or functions in the council and the performance of the activity will assist in some way in the discharge of that function or those functions.'

1 [1990] 2 QB 697 at 722–3 approved by the House of Lords: [1992] 2 AC 1.

4.31 There are a number of cases which apply these principles and serve as examples of whether or not an activity qualifies as a function. In *R v Greater London Council, ex p Westminster City Council*[1] the maintenance of good staff relations was held to be a proper function of a local authority and therefore the decision to release staff elsewhere was within LGA 1972, s 111. If, however, the purpose of that action was to conduct a political campaign against the Government, that was an irrelevant consideration and the decision was invalid.

In *R v Richmond upon Thames London Borough Council, ex p McCarthy & Stone (Developments) Limited*[2] Popplewell J held that s 111 gave local authorities the power to raise money by charging an individual company for pre-planning application discussions. He decided that the charges were there to facilitate the discharge of the authority's functions. Furthermore he held that LGA 1972, s 111(3) did not restrict the power to make charges. This decision was reversed by the House of Lords after it was affirmed by the Court of Appeal. Their Lordships held that the power to charge could not be implied into the statute and had to have express authority from another statute before it was a valid act by the local authority. They also held that the giving of pre-application advice was not of itself a function of the local authority. Although this advice was undoubtedly incidental to the planning process and therefore to a function of the council, charging for such advice was incidental to the incidental and therefore too remote. The council argued that there was a distinction between functions which they had a duty to perform and those which they had a power to perform. It was in regard to the latter, the council argued, that a charge could lawfully be made. This argument was rejected by the House of Lords[3].

Finally we return to the *Hazell v Hammersmith* case[4]. The Divisional Court held that interest rate swaps and similar transactions conducted by the local authority were not within the scope of s 111. In a nutshell they did not facilitate the management of a function, namely borrowing, but only the consequence of a function, that is the obligation to pay interest on borrowing.

1 (1985) Times, 22 January.
2 (1989) 58 P&CR 434.
3 [1992] 2 AC 48.
4 [1991] 2 AC 1.

4.32 LGA 1972, s 111(2) and (3) state respectively that transacting the business of a parish or community meeting or any other parish or community business shall be treated as a function of those authorities and that a local authority shall not under the section concerned raise money by rates, precepts or borrowing or lend money except in accordance with the enactments which relate specifically to those activities.

COMPANIES

4.33 This subject is dealt with fully in Chapter 16.

J The scope of Local Government Act 1972, s 137[1]

4.34 Under LGA 1972, s 137 a local authority may incur expenditure which is in the interest of their area and which brings direct benefit to that area. They are not allowed to spend on a purpose which they already have specific powers under pre-existing statute to spend on. Nor are they allowed to spend unless the expenditure is commensurate with the benefit to the area concerned. This is the main purpose of this long and much amended section of LGA 1972. The section is now contained in the Local Government and Housing Act 1989, Sch 2 as modified by LGA 2000, s 8 (not in force at the date of publication, 7 August 2000).

1 See generally C Crawford and V Moore *The Free Two Pence* (CIPFA, 1983).

4.35 The Secretary of State may limit the amount of expenditure by reference to any financial year. A local authority must decide at the beginning of each financial year whether they will take any action in that year to secure economic development in their area. If they decide to do so they must first consult the representatives of commerce and industry in their area. It is very important to note that as LGA 1972, s 137 prohibits expenditure on purposes which are already dealt with by statute it cannot be used to allow expenditure on economic development, as this is covered by the Local Government and Housing Act 1989.

The financial limit in s 137 is based on population and is calculated from a figure which is multiplied by the population of the area.

There have been a number of subsequent statutes affecting s 137 which deal with the giving of aid to industry.

4.36 As will be remembered from the previous section, a local authority may control companies and in that situation the controls that Parliament has laid down for local government should also apply to the company. The Local Government and Housing Act 1989, Pt V requires a controlling body to ensure that a controlled company does not make any payments by reference solely to LGA 1972, s 137 which when placed with the authority's own expenditure is above the financial limit set for s 137.

4.37 Having discussed the general effect of LGA 1972, s 137 some attention will now be paid to the individual subsections. This is a complex section with many subsections and amendments and needs this specific scrutiny.

1 SUBSECTION (1)

4.38 It has already been noted that the power conferred on the local authority by this section cannot be exercised for any purpose for which the authority has specific powers under another enactment. This only applies where the authority itself has the powers. Where other authorities have statutory functions the local authority may spend in those fields. This was established in *Manchester City Council v Greater Manchester Metropolitan County Council*[1].

1 (1980) 78 LGR 560.

4.39 This case also establishes a precedent on a different point. The power of the local authority to contribute financially to local bodies derives from this subsection. Contributions made to local bodies must be taken into account when the council calculates its total annual expenditure under this section. The *Manchester* case established the validity of payments by the county council, established under a trust, for the provision of free or assisted places at independent schools for the area. As education was not the concern of the county council, the metropolitan council argued that it was ultra vires. It was also argued the trust fund infringed the principle that local government finance should be conducted on an annual basis. It was held that provided the expenditure was properly incurred within the LGA 1972, s 137 budget for one year it did not matter that a large part of the money was to be spent in future years. The claim that the fact that the commitment could not be revoked infringed basic finance principles was also rejected.

4.40 The creation of a trust generally has been held to be incidental to the power of the local authority under LGA 1972, s 137(1). It does not represent an unlawful delegation of power to the trustees. However, a trust will not automatically be valid, as the case of *R v District Auditors No 3 Audit District of West Yorkshire Metropolitan County Council, ex p West Yorkshire Metropolitan County Council*[1] illustrates. In that case the setting up of a trust for, inter alia, the dissemination of information regarding the dissolution of the metropolitan county councils was held to be invalid. This was, however, decided on the basic principles of the law of trusts. The beneficiaries of the trust were too uncertain and it could not constitute a charitable trust.

1 [1986] RVR 24.

4.41 There are certain phrases which need some interpretation in the subsection. The expenditure must be in the interests of the local area. What is and is not in the interests of the area is decided by the council 'in their opinion'. It should be made clear that these words give the authority a wide discretion, although that discretion cannot be completely unfettered according to the principles of administrative law as decided in *Padfield v Minister of Agriculture Fisheries and Food*[1].

1 [1968] AC 997.

4.42 The 'interests' of the area is not restricted to financial interests. This was made clear by Pain J in *Lobenstein v Hackney London Borough Council*[1].

1 (1980) LGC 1292.

4.43 In *R v District Auditor for Leicester, ex p Leicester City Council*[1] the Court of Appeal held that apportioned expenditure on staffing accommodation and other overhead costs relating to projects which had been authorised under s 137 must be charged to the account of expenditure under the section and be counted against the rate limit.

1 [1986] RVR 191.

2 SUBSECTION (2)

4.44 Paragraphs (A) and (B) of this subsection have been repealed. Paragraphs (C) and (D) are in place to ensure that the section is not used for local authority publicity except where they are assisting a voluntary body or organisation and the publicity is incidental to the main purpose for which the assistance is given.

3 SUBSECTION (3)

4.45 This section specifies funds to which the local authority may contribute. This includes funds for charity, for public service and in connection with a particular event directly affecting persons resident in the United Kingdom. What is a charitable body is defined not in the statute but in the existing law on the subject. A 'particular event' must be an occurrence and not an ongoing state of affairs.

This removes the need for ministerial consent in incurring expenditure under this section. Under the Local Government Act 1948, s 136 ministerial consent was required before spending of this sort could be undertaken.

4 SUBSECTION (4) AS AMENDED BY 4AA AND 4AB

4.46 This section prescribes the annual limit on expenditure via a number of regulations. Under LGA 1972, s 4AA one multiplies the sum of £2.50 by the relevant population of the area. If the area in question is a metropolitan district council, a London borough or the Common Council of the City of London, then the figure to be multiplied is £5.00. If the area in question is a community or parish council, then the figure to be multiplied is £3.50. What is the relevant population is defined by regulations that are made under s 4(B).

4.47 The situation regarding the limit on expenditure was further clarified by the insertion of LGA 1972, s 4(A) and (B), which specify the sums which may be deducted from gross expenditure under the section.

5 SECTION 137A

4.48 This final amendment was made by the Local Government and Housing Act 1989. It states that local authorities must impose accounting conditions on the provision of any financial assistance given under LGA 1972, s 137(2) or (3). There must be a written statement to the authority within twelve months of the financial assistance. This requirement is necessary for the completion of an annual report.

CHAPTER 5

Financial responsibilities of officers

A Introduction

5.1 Every local authority must ensure that one of its officers has responsibility for the administration of its financial affairs[1]. That officer—the Chief Finance Officer—has a range of duties, including the issuing of reports under the Local Government Finance Act 1988, s 114 which may[2] limit the authority's powers pending their consideration. The Chief Finance Officer cannot be the authority's monitoring officer, appointed under the Local Government and Housing Act 1989, s 5(1), who has separate responsibilities to make similar reports (on which see later in this chapter).

1 Local Government Act 1972, s 151.
2 Local Government Finance Act 1988, s 115.

5.2 The LGA 1972, s 270 applies to:

(i) county councils;
(ii) district councils;
(iii) London borough councils;
(iv) parish or community councils;
(v) Isles of Scilly.

5.3 The Local Government Act 1985, ss 73 and 105(1) apply a similar regime to LGA 1972, s 151 to:

(i) metropolitan police authorities;
(ii) Northumbrian Police Authority;
(iii) metropolitan county fire and civil defence authorities;
(iv) London Fire and Civil Defence Authority;
(v) metropolitan county police authorities;
(vi) waste disposal authorities[1].

1 Waste Regulation and Disposal (Authorities) Order 1985, SI 1985/1884, reg 9.

5.4 The Local Government Finance Act 1988, s 112 applies a similar regime to:

(i) police authorities established under the Police Act 1996, s 3;
(ii) combined fire authorities.

5.5 Finally, the Local Government and Housing Act 1989, s 6(1) applies a similar regime to:

(i) the Common Council of the City of London (part functions only);
(ii) successor bodies created under the Local Government Act 1985, s 67(3).

5.6 LGFA 1988, Pt VIII (ss 111–116) applies to the same authorities (successor bodies and the Common Council)[1].

1 Local Government Finance Act 1988, s 111(1) and SI 1991/445.

B The statutory duty for proper administration

5.7 Every local authority shall 'make arrangements for the proper administration of their financial affairs and shall secure that one of their officers has responsibility for the administration of those affairs'[1].

'Proper administration' is not defined in the Act, but it is suggested that it must be broadly construed. It covers compliance with statutory requirements for accounting and internal audit, although obviously compliance with these requirements may not on their own amount to proper administration. It must also include consideration of authoritative non-statutory guidance from eg DETR and CIPFA.

1 Local Government Act 1972, s 151.

5.8 In *Hazell v Hammersmith and Fulham London Borough Council* [1992] 2 AC 1 the House of Lords held that the phrase is not wide enough to justify the use of financial techniques to manage the local authority's affairs that are not otherwise authorised by alternative statutory authority.

While an officer must be appointed with responsibility for the administration of the local authority's financial affairs, primary responsibility remains with the local authority, and ultimately the members for securing proper administration[1]. The appointment of an officer under LGA 1972, s 151 embraces wide delegation of powers to the officer without further formal delegation[2]. The financial decision-making functions lie with the local authority, although agents may be used.

1 *Lloyd v McMahon* [1987] AC 625, HL.
2 *Provident Mutual Life Assurance Association v Derby City Council* (1981) 79 LGR 297.

C Appointment of the Chief Finance Officer

5.9 A Chief Finance Officer[1] must be professionally qualified through membership of one of the professional accountancy bodies set out in LGFA 1988[2].

Every appointment to a paid office or employment in a local authority is to be made on merit[3]. In the case of the Chief Finance Officer, this requirement is subject to the provisions of the 1988 Act, s 113[4]. The Local Authorities (Standing Orders) Regulations 1993, SI 1993/202 make provision for standing orders in respect of the appointment of a Chief Officer. These require there to be a job specification, appropriate advertising, and interview[5].

As a statutory officer the Chief Finance Officer holds a politically restricted post. He is therefore disqualified from becoming or remaining a member of any local authority in Great Britain[6].

1 Appointed since 29 September 1988.
2 Local Government Finance Act 1988, s 113(3).

3 Local Government and Housing Act 1989, s 7(1).
4 Ibid, s 7(2)(e).
5 The Local Authorities (Standing Orders) Regulations 1993, SI 1993/202, reg 1(2)(c) and Sch 1.
6 Local Government and Housing Act 1989, s 1(1).

1 DUTIES OF THE CHIEF FINANCE OFFICER

5.10 Those have been summarised[1] as –

(1) provision of financial advice to the Authority and elected members to facilitate service delivery.
(2) provision of financial advice for strategic planning and policy making to ensure efficient and effective use of resources;
(3) provision of advice on the optimum use of available resources in and management of the capital and revenue budgets;
(4) provision of financial management information;
(5) preparation of statutory and other accounts, and associated grant claims;
(6) provision of an effective internal audit function and assistance to management in providing safe and efficient financial arrangements;
(7) provision of effective income collection and payment systems;
(8) advising on treasury management, pension and trust funds; and
(9) advice on the safeguarding of assets including risk management and insurance.

A Chief Finance Officer (or any other local authority officer) has no obligation to comply with an order that is illegal. The duties of the Chief Finance Officer are determined by the contract of employment, the duties imposed by statute as to reporting and accounting and audit. The Chief Finance Officer is personally liable for surcharge under the Audit Commission Act 1998, ss 17–18.

1 *The Role of the Chief Finance Officer in Financial Administration in Local Government*, CIPFA Statement 1993. See also the Audit Commission Report 'Worth more than money' of 1998. The Audit Commission questions whether there is a need for the post-holder to be a qualified accountant. It discusses the role of the Chief Finance Officer in the hierarchy of the council. Only 185 councils include the Chief Finance Officer on their management boards.

2 REPORTS

5.11 Where it appears to the Chief Finance Officer that his local authority –

(a) has made or is about to make a decision which involves or would involve the authority incurring expenditure which is unlawful;
(b) has taken or is about to take a course of action which, if pursued to its conclusion, would be unlawful and likely to cause a loss or deficiency on the part of the authority; or
(c) is about to enter an item of account the entry of which is unlawful;

he must make a report[1].

1 Local Government Finance Act 1988, s 114(2)(a)–(c).

5.12 The duty to report arises whether the unlawful conduct is being pursued by the local authority as a whole, or by a committee or by an officer of the local authority, a member of a police force maintained by the local authority or a joint committee on which the local authority is represented[1]. The Chief Finance Officer must also report where it appears to him that the expenditure incurred, or proposed in a year is likely to exceed the resources including sums borrowed available to meet that expenditure[2].

When preparing his report, the Chief Finance Officer must consult, where practicable, with the designated head of the local authority's paid service. Consultation should take place at an early stage, and also with the local authority's chief legal officer[3].

1 Local Government Finance Act 1988, s 114(2).
2 LGFA 1988, s 114(3).
3 LGFA 1988, s 114(3A).

5.13 The report must be sent to the local authority's auditor, and to all members of the local authority[1]. The duty to report cannot be delegated, except on account of absence or illness, in which case a deputy must be nominated by the Chief Finance Officer from amongst his staff, giving priority to a person who is a member of one of the professional accounting bodies identified in LGFA 1988, s 113(3)[2].

1 Local Government Finance Act 1988, s 114(4).
2 LGFA 1988, s 114(5),(6).

5.14 The local authority must consider the Chief Officer's report at a meeting, within 21 days of the report being sent[1]. At the meeting, the local authority must decide whether it agrees or disagrees with the contents of the report and decide what action, if any, to take upon it[2]. Until the first business day after those decisions have been made, the local authority is prohibited from entering into the course of conduct which led to the report, or from entering into any new agreement which may involve the incurring of expenditure[3].

During this period, the local authority does not have the legal power to make any payment which might arise from the conduct or to enter into any agreement[4]. Any such payment or agreement will be ultra vires and void.

If an LGFA 1988, s 115 meeting is proposed, a designated officer (which may or may not be the Chief Finance Officer) must, as soon as reasonably practicable, inform the local authority's auditor of its date, time and place[5]. After the meeting, that officer must, as soon as is reasonably practicable, notify the auditor of any decision made[6].

1 Local Government Finance Act 1988, s 115(2),(3).
2 LGFA 1988, s 115(2).
3 LGFA 1988, s 115(5),(6).
4 LGFA 1988, s 115(7),(8).
5 LGFA 1988, s 116(1).
6 LGFA 1988, s 116(2).

3 PREPARATION OF ACCOUNTS

5.15 The Chief Finance Officer also has to prepare the accounts of his/her local authority[1]. These regulations impose requirements relating to accounting control, the form of accounts and balance sheets, and gave the Chief Finance Officer powers to secure documents and information from officers.

1 Accounts and Audit Regulations 1996, SI 1996/590, reg 4.

4 SECURITY AND INFORMATION

5.16 A local authority is bound to take such security as it considers sufficient for the faithful execution of the office of and for the due accounting for all money or property which may be entrusted to any officer likely to be entrusted with the custody or control of money[1]. It has power to take like security for any other officer employed by them[2] or for any person not employed by them but who may yet be so entrusted[3]. Every officer employed by a local authority is bound, at such times as the local authority may direct or within three months of the cessation of his employment, to make out and deliver to that authority a true account in writing of all money and property committed to his charge, and of his receipts and payments, with vouchers and other supporting documents and records, and a list of persons from whom or to whom money is due in connection with his office, showing the amount due from or to each[4].

1 Local Government Act 1972, s 114(1).
2 LGA 1972, s 114(1).
3 LGA 1972, s 114(2).
4 LGA 1972, s 115.

5 DELEGATION

5.17 Although responsibility for the authority's financial affairs will be the responsibility of the Chief Finance Officer, he clearly cannot perform every task personally. Except for the duty to report under LGFA 1988, s 114, the duties may validly be delegated to other officers of the local authority[1]. Sub-delegation by officers is usually not possible: therefore the delegation scheme from a full council often provides explicitly for other officers to act.

1 *Provident Mutual Life Assurance Association v Derby City Council* (1981) 79 LGR 297, HL.

6 CIPFA GUIDANCE

5.18 CIPFA also publishes *Treasury Management in Local Authorities: A Code of Practice and A Guide for Chief Finance Officers* (1996 fully revised edn). This invaluable document is an essential tool for the Chief Finance Officer.

D The monitoring officer

5.19 Section 5 of the Local Government and Housing Act 1989 creates the post of monitoring officer, who *may* be the head of the paid service but shall not be the Chief Financial Officer[1]. It is important to note that the question of the sufficiency of the resources provided to execute the duties of monitoring officer is a question for the monitoring officer himself and not the local authority. Similar provisions are to be found in the Local Government Finance Act 1988, s 114(7) and the Local Government and Housing Act 1989, s 4(1)(b), in relation to the head of the paid service.

1 Local Government and Housing Act 1989, s 5(1).

5.20 The monitoring officer's duties are defined in s 5(2) of the 1989 Act as follows:

> '(2) It shall be the duty of a relevant authority's monitoring officer, if it at any time appears to him that any proposal, decision or omission by the authority, by any committee or sub-committee of the authority, by any person holding any office or employment under the authority or by any joint

committee on which the authority are represented constitutes, has given rise to or is likely to or would give rise to –

(a) a contravention by the authority, by any committee or sub-committee of the authority, by any person holding any office or employment under the authority or by any such joint committee of any enactment or rule of law or of any code of practice made or approved by or under any enactment; or

(b) any such maladministration or injustice as is mentioned in Part III of the Local Government Act 1974 (Local Commissioners) or Part II of the Local Government (Scotland) Act 1975 (which makes corresponding provision for Scotland),

to prepare a report to the authority with respect to that proposal, decision or omission.'

It will readily be seen that the monitoring officer's duty is very broad, but he does not have jurisdiction over appointments to local authority employment.[1] The monitoring officer is obliged to consult, in preparing his report, with the head of the paid service and the Chief Financial Officer 'so far as practicable'[2]. In practice the monitoring officer is often also the head of the paid service.

1 See the Local Government Act 1974, s 26(8) and Sch 5, para 4, and compare the reports of the head of the paid service under the Local Government and Housing Act 1989, s 4(3)(d).
2 Local Government and Housing Act 1989, s 5(3)(a).

5.21 The report must be sent 'as soon as practicable' to each member of the authority[1]. Where the matter under consideration relates to a committee or sub-committee then a copy of the report need only be sent to each member of the committee in question[2].

1 Local Government and Housing Act 1989, s 5(3)(d).
2 LGHA 1989, s 5(4).

5.22 If no report is presented despite the fact that there is evidence of breach of an enactment, then this is a breach of the duty imposed by LGHA 1989, s 5 and it may be challenged by judicial review. Any person affected by the breach of the enactment will have standing to challenge the monitoring officer's decision not to present a report. Indeed, the council tax payer or a non-domestic tax payer is also likely to have standing to bring proceedings.

5.23 The local authority or relevant committee must consider the monitoring officer's report at a meeting which is to be held not more 21 days after copies of the report are sent to members of the authority or the committee[1]. Consideration of the report may not be delegated. The effect of the issue of the report is to suspend any action upon the subject-matter of the report. The authority is required to ensure that no step is taken to give effect to any proposal or decision to which the report relates while the implementation of the proposal is suspended in consequence of the report.[2] The proposal or decision must be suspended until the first business day after the day upon which the monitoring officer's report is considered[3]. This power of suspension is, however, without prejudice to the similar duties which arise under the Local Government Finance Act 1988, s 115 in relation to the Chief Finance Officer of the local authority.

1 Local Government and Housing Act 1989, s 5(5)(a).
2 LGHA 1989, s 5(5)(b).
3 LGHA 1989, s 5(6).

E The head of the paid service

5.24 The Local Government and Housing Act 1989, s 4 requires a local authority to designate one of its officers as the head of the paid service. Usually this officer will be the Chief Executive of the local authority. However, a local authority is not obliged by the section to nominate its Chief Executive as the head of the paid service although it would obviously be useful to do so. He or she must be provided with such staff, accommodation and resources as are 'in his opinion' sufficient to allow the duties under the section to be performed[1].

1 Local Government and Housing Act 1989, s 4(1)(b).

5.25 The duties of the head of the paid service are set out in the Local Government and Housing Act 1989, s 4(2) and (3) which provide:

'(2) It shall be the duty of the head of a relevant authority's paid service, where he considers it appropriate to do so in respect of any proposals of his with respect to any of the matters specified in sub-section (3) below, to prepare a report to the authority setting out his proposals.

(3) Those matters are –

(a) the manner in which the discharge by the authority of their different functions is co-ordinated;
(b) the number and grades of staff required by the authority for the discharge of their functions;
(c) the organisation of the authority's staff; and
(d) the appointment and proper management of the authority's staff.'

5.26 A copy of any report must be sent to each member of the authority 'as soon as practicable'[1]. The local authority is obliged to consider the report at a meeting which is to be held not more than three months after copies of the report have been sent to members of the local authority. The local authority may not delegate consideration of the report[2]. Consideration must be given to the report at a meeting of the full council although obviously committees or sub-committees can consider relevant parts before that full council meeting.

1 Local Government and Housing Act 1989, s 4(4).
2 LGHA 1989, s 4(5).

F Code of conduct for local government employees

5.27 The Local Government Act 2000, s 82 gives the Secretary of State and the National Assembly for Wales power to issue a code of conduct for local government employees. The section requires each of them, in drawing up a code, to consult representatives of local government and also of local government employees. This code of conduct is to be incorporated into the terms and conditions of every local government employee. There must be little doubt that it will include requirements relating to financial matters to the protection of trade secrets in employment and business.

CHAPTER 6

Financial responsibilities of members

A Specific statutory duties

6.1 A member in his individual capacity has no executive power and can exercise no lawful authority. However, there are a number of conventions and practices which govern the rights and powers of members.

A member's principal legal rights relate to the inspection of documents and to the payment of allowances. The principal duty consists of an obligation to disclose any pecuniary interest a member may have in a matter before the local authority.

B Access to documents

6.2 The Local Government (Access to Information) Act 1985[1] created a statutory right of access to documents for members of 'principal councils' as defined for the purposes of Part VA of the Local Government Act 1972. Any document which is in the possession or under the control of a principal council and contains material relating to any business to be transacted at a meeting of the council or a committee or sub-committee of the council is to be open to inspection by any council member. However, there is no right of inspection where it appears to the proper officer that a document discloses certain classes of exempt information. Ten of the fifteen descriptions of exempt information specified in Part I of Sch 12A to LGA 1972 apply here. The Secretary of State may vary this list by order. This right of inspection is expressly stated to be in addition to any other rights that a member may have[2]. There is a common law right for a member to see such documents as are reasonably necessary to enable him/her to carry out his/her duties. Ultimately the council decides on such requests. The detailed law is outside the scope of this book[3]. The accounts[4] of a local authority or joint authority and of any proper officer may be inspected by any member and he may make a copy of them or take extracts from them[5].

1 Now Local Government Act 1972, s 100.
2 Local Government Act 1972, s 100F, added by the Local Government (Access to Information) Act 1985, s 1.
3 See Patrick Birkenshaw *Freedom of Information* (2nd edn, 1996) Butterworths.
4 See *Buckingham v Shackleton* (1981) 79 LGR 484.
5 Local Government Act 1972, s 228, as amended by the Local Government Act 1985, Sch 14, para 24.

C Monetary payments

6.3 The Local Government Act 1972[1] authorised the payment of allowances in respect of attendance, financial loss, special responsibilities, travelling and subsistence to members of local authorities, joint authorities and other bodies. For elected members of the major local authorities, attendance and special responsibility allowances have been replaced, as from 1 April 1991, by arrangements under the Local Government and Housing Act 1989, s 18. Otherwise, allowances continue to be paid under the provisions of LGA 1972.

1 Sections 173–178, as amended. The changes in the Local Government Act 2000, ss 99–100 should be noted. They are not in force at the time of writing.

1 ALLOWANCES UNDER LGHA 1989

6.4 The details of the arrangements are found in the Local Authorities (Members' Allowances) Regulations 1991[1]. Part II of the Regulations required each county, district and London borough council, and joint authority, and the Council of the Isles of Scilly to make a scheme, before 1 April 1991, for the payment of allowances to members. A scheme can be revoked, but must be replaced by another before the revocation takes effect. The scheme must provide for the payment of a 'basic allowance' of the same amount to each member. It may provide for 'special responsibility allowances,' which need not be the same, to such councillors as have such special responsibilities as are specified in the scheme, and fall into one or more categories specified in the Regulations[2]. It may provide for attendance allowances payable in respect of the performance of such duties as are specified in the scheme and fall into one of the categories set out in the Regulations[3]. An attendance allowance covers both the carrying out of the duty and the time spent travelling to and from the place where it is performed. The amount of the allowance may vary according to the time of day and duration of the duty, but must otherwise be the same for all members entitled to the allowance in respect of a duty of any description. A scheme may provide that a member shall not be entitled to payment of more than one attendance allowance in respect of any period of 24 hours. The amount of the various allowances must be set out in the scheme. There are now no restrictions on the amount paid by way of allowances. A scheme may be amended at any time but may only be revoked with effect from the beginning of the financial year on 1 April. A councillor may elect to forgo part of his entitlement to an allowance.

1 SI 1991/351, as amended.
2 SI 1991/351, reg 9(1): acting as leader or deputy leader of a political group; presiding at meetings; representing the authority at meetings of, or arranged by, any other body; membership of a committee or sub-committee that meets with exceptional frequency or for exceptionally long periods; acting as a spokesman for a political group on a committee or sub-committee; other activities requiring at least the same time and effort as any of the foregoing.
3 SI 1991/351, reg 10(3),(3A),(4); reg 10(3A) was inserted by SI 1995/553: attendance at meetings of the authority, or any of its committees or sub-committees, or any other body to which the authority makes appointment or nominations; at other meetings authorised by the authority, one of its committees or sub-committees, or a joint committee (but not private political group meetings); at meetings of local authority associations; duties undertaken on behalf of the authority in pursuance of any standing order requiring a member or members to be present while tender documents are opened; in connection with the discharge of any function of the authority involving the inspection of premises or arrangements for the attendance of pupils at special schools. A member who otherwise receives remuneration cannot claim under the scheme.

2 ALLOWANCES UNDER LGA 1972[1]

6.5 A member of a parish or community council who is a councillor[2] is entitled to receive an attendance allowance of such reasonable amount, not exceeding the prescribed amount, as the council may determine, for the performance of any approved duty[3]. Such a member may opt instead to receive a financial loss allowance[4], which is a payment not exceeding the prescribed amount in respect of any loss of earnings necessarily suffered, or any additional expenses (other than for travelling or subsistence) necessarily suffered or incurred in performance of the approved duty[5]. Payment may not be made under these provisions to parish or community councillors in respect of duties performed within the parish or community or grouped parish or grouped community[6]. A member of a local authority who is not a councillor is also entitled to a financial loss allowance[7].

1 LGA 1972, ss 173–178 (as amended by the Local Government, Planning and Land Act 1980, ss 24–26; the Miscellaneous Financial Provisions Act 1983, s 7; the Local Government Act 1985, Sch 14, paras 18–20, and Sch 17; and the Local Government and Housing Act 1989, Sch 11 and 12).
2 That is, a member of the council from which payment is claimed: *Hopson v Devon County Council* [1978] 1 WLR 553 (district councillor appointed to committee of the county council not entitled to claim attendance allowance from the county council).
3 Local Government Act 1972, s 173(1)–(3), as amended.
4 LGA 1972, s 173A, as amended.
5 LGA 1972, s 173(4), as amended.
6 LGA 1972, s 173(6).
7 LGA 1972, s 173(4), as amended, by virtue of the saving in the Schedule to the Local Government and Housing Act 1989 (Commencement No 11 and Savings) Order 1991, SI 1991/344. Members of a number of other prescribed bodies, other than councillors appointed to represent local authorities, may also claim financial loss allowance. These bodies include local valuation panels, joint committees, joint boards and the Cheshire Brine Subsidence Compensation Board: 1972 Act, s 177(1), as saved by the Schedule to SI 1991/344, and SI 1991/351, reg 19.

6.6 A member of a local authority is also entitled to travelling and subsidence allowances in respect of expenditure necessarily incurred in the performance of approved duties. Except in the case of parish and community councils travelling expenses are payable in respect of all approved duties, whether within or without the area of the authority, and with no minimum distance, and a subsistence allowance is payable to a member where the expenditure on subsistence is necessarily incurred by him. In the case of parish and community councillors, travelling expenses and subsistence allowances are not payable unless the duty lies outside the parish or community or grouped parish or grouped community[1]. A local authority may pay allowances to any member attending a conference or meeting held inside or outside the United Kingdom for the purposes of discussing matters which in its opinion relate to the interests of the area or its inhabitants; this does not however extend to conferences or meetings convened by a commercial or political organisation[2]. These allowances are payable to members of a number of other prescribed bodies[3]. Maximum rates of payments for certain allowances are specified or prescribed by the Secretary of State[4].

1 Local Government Act 1972, s 174, as amended by the Local Government, Planning and Land Act 1980, s 25(1),(2), Sch 34.
2 LGA 1972, s 175, as amended by the 1980 Act, s 25(3), and the Local Government and Housing Act 1989, Sch 11, para 27.
3 LGA 1972, s 177(1), as substituted by the 1989 Act, Sch 11, para 28(1)–(3); the Local Authorities (Members' Allowances) Regulations 1991, SI 1991/351, reg 2, as amended by SI 1996/469, reg 2, specifying the bodies listed in the Local Government and Housing Act 1989, s 21, except the Common Council of the City of London and successors to residuary bodies, and including National Park authorities; and prescribed bodies on which any of the former are represented. The prescribed bodies are a joint committee of two or more authorities, a joint education committee and the Cheshire Brine Subsidence Compensation Board.
4 Local Authorities (Members' Allowances) Regulations 1991, SI 1991/351, reg 17(2) (allowances under s 175 where there is no attendance scheme), and reg 18 (allowances under s 173(1) and (4)), as

amended by SI 1995/553 and SI 1996/469. Rates for travelling and subsistence are prescribed by circular: see eg DoE Circular 1/86.

6.7 A local authority also has power to defray travelling and other expenses reasonably incurred by or on behalf of any members in making official and courtesy visits, whether inside or outside the United Kingdom, on behalf of the council[1].

The term 'approved duty' is defined in regulations to cover the duties specified for the purposes of attendance allowance under LGHA 1989[2], and any other duty approved by the body for the purpose of or in connection with the discharge of the functions of the body or any of its committees or sub-committees[3].

1 Local Government Act 1972, s 176, as amended. The section also authorises expenditure on the reception and entertainment of distinguished persons visiting the area.
2 See para **6.3**, n 1.
3 The Local Authorities (Members' Allowances) Regulations 1991, SI 1991/351, reg 16.

D Pecuniary and non-pecuniary interests[1]

6.8 If a member has a pecuniary interest, direct or indirect, in any contract or proposed contract or other matter and is present at the meeting when it is discussed, he must disclose the fact and refrain from discussion and voting. An authority may, by standing orders, provide for the exclusion of such members, and this is commonly done, with a proviso that the member may remain if the majority of those present at the meeting so decides. A member has an indirect interest if:

(a) he or any nominee of his is a member of a company or other body with which the contract is made or is proposed to be made or which has a direct pecuniary interest in the matter under consideration; or

(b) he is a partner, or is in the employment, of a person with whom the contract is made or is proposed to be made or who has a direct pecuniary interest in the matter under consideration.

This does not apply to membership of or employment under a public body. In the case of married persons living together the interest of one is deemed to be the interest of the other if known to the other. Where the indirect pecuniary interest of a member arises from his beneficial interest in securities which he or his wife holds, and if the total nominal value of these shares does not exceed £5,000[2] (or one-hundredth part of the total nominal value of the issued share capital, whichever is the less), then whilst the member must declare his interest he is not precluded from speaking and voting. The Local Government Act 1972, s 97(5) provides that a member should not be treated as having a pecuniary interest in any contract, proposed contract or other matter by reason only of any interest (a) of that member, or (b) of any company, body or person connected with him, which was so remote or insignificant that it could not reasonably be regarded as likely to influence him in discussion and voting. The section also excludes an interest which a member has merely as a community charge or council tax-payer, a ratepayer, inhabitant of the area, or water consumer, or as a person entitled to participate in any service offered to the public.

1 Local Government Act 1972, ss 94–98. These provisions apply to local authorities, joint authorities and police authorities: s 98(1A), inserted by the Local Government Act 1985, Sch 14, para 13 and amended by the Police and Magistrates' Courts Act 1994, Sch 4, para 7; and to the Broads Authority: LGA 1972, s 265A, inserted by the Norfolk and Suffolk Broads Act 1988, Sch 6, para 10(1). See also the National Code of Local Government Conduct (DoE Circular 8/90) paras 8–12.

2 Local Government Act 1972, s 97(6), substituted by the Local Government and Housing Act 1989, Sch 11, para 23.

6.9 The phrase 'pecuniary interest' means more than pecuniary advantage, and voting in a matter which is to the financial detriment of a member is therefore illegal[1]. A member may disclose his interest in two ways. He may give a general notice of some interest to the proper officer of the authority or he may give particular notice as the occasion arises. A general or particular notice must be recorded, and the book in which the record is kept must be open for inspection by members of the authority[2].

The Secretary of State has made regulations under LGHA 1989, s 19 (the Local Authorities (Members' Interests) Regulations 1992)[3] with effect from 8 May 1992. These require each member to give the proper officer a notice about his direct and indirect pecuniary interests containing the information prescribed by the regulations. However, there is no provision under LGHA 1989, s 19(4)(a) that the giving of a notice under the regulations shall be deemed to be sufficient disclosure for the purposes of LGA 1972, s 94. The prescribed matters include information in respect of the councillor's employment, office, trade, profession or vocation; sponsorship; contracts; land; licences; corporate tenancies and interests in securities. Failure to comply with the regulations or knowingly or recklessly providing false information is a criminal offence punishable on summary conviction by a fine not exceeding level 4 on the standard scale. The regulations require records of the information contained in the notices to be maintained and open to public inspection.

Local authorities are not able to impose any obligations on their members to disclose any interests other than those required to be disclosed by virtue of LGA 1972, s 94 or regulations under LGHA 1989, s 19[4].

1 Local Government Act 1972, s 97(4), as amended by the Local Government Finance Act 1988 (Miscellaneous Amendments and Repeals) Order 1990, SI 1990/10 and the Local Government Finance Act 1992, Sch 13, para 32. See *Brown v DPP* [1956] 2 QB 369 and *Rands v Oldroyd* [1959] 1 QB 204.
2 Local Government Act 1972, ss 94(1), 96.
3 SI 1992/618, as amended by SI 1996/1215. The regulations apply to police authorities and National Park authorities.
4 LGHA 1989, s 19(5).

6.10 A member may commit one or more of three offences: (i) he may fail to disclose an interest; (ii) he may take part in consideration or discussion and (iii) he may vote at a meeting. There is no duty upon the proper officer to advise members who are in doubt as to their position, or to warn members who may be putting themselves in jeopardy of proceedings, but it is common enough to provide advice when requested to do so.

The Secretary of State is empowered by LGA 1972, s 97 to remove the disability imposed on members where the number of members disabled at any one time is so great as to impede the transaction of business or where it appears to him that it is in the interests of the inhabitants of the area that the disability be removed. General dispensations have been granted to enable council house tenants to speak and vote on matters of general housing policy (unless there are rent arrears of two months or more[1]), to enable parents of a child in full-time education to speak and vote on questions concerning school refreshments and transport[2], and to enable members to speak and vote on matters concerning the statutory sick pay scheme under the Social Security and Housing Benefits Act 1982[3]. In the case of parish or community councils it is the district council which may exercise this dispensing power.

The disability prevents a member from taking part in the consideration or discussion of the issue and prevents voting. The Secretary of State or district council granting a dispensation may choose to remove only the first disability, enabling a member to speak but not vote.

1 DoE Circular 25/92. See *Readman v DPP* (1991) Times, 4 March (general dispensation in previous circular).
2 DoE Circular 9/92.
3 DoE Circular 9/92.

6.11 A member may discuss, and vote on, an application for a dispensation even though he is one of the members concerned; and the chairman, vice-chairman or deputy chairman of a principal council is not to be regarded as having a pecuniary interest in the allowance paid to him, nor is a member to be so regarded in relation to travelling, subsistence or attending allowances[1].

A difficult situation arises where a member is clearly under a disability yet persists in speaking and voting. In our view if the member is manifestly interested the chairman should refuse to count his vote, for the 'vote' has been cast illegally and therefore can be said not to be a vote at all[2]. It would appear that where a council acts in a quasi-judicial capacity a vote cast by a member having an interest may render the decision void as contrary to natural justice on account of bias[3].

1 Local Government Act 1972, s 94(5), as amended.
2 *Nell v Longbottom* [1894] 1 QB 767.
3 *R v LCC* [1892] 1 QB 190; *R v Hendon RDC, ex p Chorley* [1933] 2 KB 696.

6.12 A member of a local authority, a committee of a local authority or a joint committee of two or more local authorities (or a sub-committee) who has not paid an amount due in respect of community charge or council tax for at least two months after it has become payable, may not vote on matters concerning the level of council tax or the administration of the community charge or council tax. If present at a meeting, he must disclose the fact that this provision applies to him. He may, however, speak. Non-compliance is a criminal offence[1]. It is possible to obtain a dispensation from the Secretary of State or (in the case of a parish council or community council) from the district council or Welsh principal council respectively[2].

1 There are separate offences in respect of (1) failing to disclose and (2) voting: *DPP v Burton* Times (1995) 8 June.
2 Local Government Finance Act 1992, s 106.

E The National Code of Local Government Conduct

6.13 LGHA 1989, s 31 enables the Secretary of State, for the guidance of members of local authorities, to issue a code of recommended practice as regards their conduct. He must consult such representatives of local government as appear to him appropriate, and the Code must be approved by both Houses of Parliament. The Code, a revised version of its non-statutory predecessor, came into operation in 1990[1].

The Code is a guide for all members of councils and their committees and sub-committees, whether elected or co-opted. It emphasises, inter alia, that compliance with the law, standing orders and the Code is the personal responsibility of each councillor. It is not enough to avoid actual impropriety; each councillor should at all times avoid any occasion for suspicion and any appearance of improper conduct. Although the law requires disclosure of pecuniary interests, non-pecuniary interests can be just as important[2].

1 The Code is set out as an Annex to DoE Circular 8/90.
2 National Code, para 9.

6.14 A private or personal non-pecuniary interest in a matter arising at a meeting should always be disclosed unless it is insignificant or shared with other members of the public generally as a ratepayer, chargepayer or inhabitant. If the interest is 'clear and substantial' then, subject to specified exceptions, the member should take no further part in the proceedings[1].

Interests should also be disclosed in dealings with council officers and at party group meetings. Where a councillor's business or personal interests are closely related to the work of one of the council's committees (or sub-committees), he should not seek or accept membership of that committee (or sub-committee) if that would involve him in disclosing an interest so often that he could be of little value to it or if it would weaken public confidence in the duty to work solely in the general public interest. A councillor should not seek or accept the leadership of the council, or chairmanship of a committee or sub-committee, if he, or an associated body, has a substantial financial interest in, or is closely related to, the business affairs of the council, committee or sub-committee. The Code emphasises that mutual respect between councillors and officers is essential to good local government, and that close personal familiarity between individual councillors and officers can damage this relationship. The Code also notes that it is a betrayal of trust to use confidential information for personal advantage or to the disadvantage of the council and that the receipt or offer of gifts should be reported to the appropriate senior officer.

The National Code may be incorporated into standing orders. Furthermore, a failure to comply with the Code may be regarded by the Commission for Local Administration as maladministration by the authority, whether or not the Code has been incorporated in standing orders[2].

1 National Code, para 12. Dispensations may be sought where the principles would require at least half the council or committee to withdraw or withdrawals would upset the electoral party balance to such an extent that the decision is likely to be affected: National Code, paras 15–19.
2 See Annual Reports of the English Commission for 1980–81, paras 27–32; 1981–82, paras 42–48; 1982–83, paras 29–40 and Appendix 5. In *R v Local Commissioner for Administration in the North and North East England, ex p Liverpool City Council* (2000) Times, 3 March, the Court of Appeal held that where the national code was more stringent than the law governing councillors' conduct, councillors should abide by it.

6.15 In *R v Local Comr for Administration in North and North East England, ex p Liverpool City Council*[1] the Court of Appeal held that the Local Commissioner had been correct in her application of the test envisaged by the National Code whereby 'a reasonable apprehension or suspicion of bias' had to be established when dealing with the councillors' duty to disclose their personal interest. Where the law was less restrictive than the National Code, the provisions of the Code were to prevail.

1 (2000) Times, 3 March, [2000] 3 CL 474.

F The Nolan Report

6.16 The Third Report of the Committee on Standards in Public Life (Chairman Lord Nolan) was published in July 1997[1]. The Report makes a number of substantial recommendations which, amongst others, recommend that the National Code should be replaced by a statement of the 'General Principles of Conduct for Local Councillors'. This should be a Great Britain document issued by the Secretaries of State for the Environment, for Scotland and for Wales, and approved by affirmative resolutions of both Houses of Parliament. The Secretaries of State should take powers to approve 'Model Codes of Conduct for Local Councils prepared by the Local Government Association and Ombudsman, provided that any Model Code which is approved incorporates and reflects the General Principles'. Each local authority should be required to adopt a Local Code of Conduct which incorporates and reflects the 'General Principles' and achieves at least the same effect as the approved Model Code. Every new councillor, and every councillor on re-election, should be required to state that they had read, understand and would observe their local code.

1 Cm 3702.

6.17 Among other proposals are that each council should have to maintain a public register of councillor's interests, listing their pecuniary interests, those non-pecuniary interests which relate closely to the activities of the council and its associated bodies, and which members of the public might reasonably think could influence a councillor's judgment; and pecuniary interests of close family members and people living in the same household as the councillor. It should no longer be a criminal offence to fail to register pecuniary interests. Unless they have a dispensation, councillors who have a direct pecuniary interest in a matter under consideration should have to declare that interest, withdraw from the meeting or discussion and take no further part in the business in question. Councillors should have to declare any interest which is not of a pecuniary kind, and which members of the public could reasonably think could influence their actions, speeches or votes. Unless they have a dispensation, councillors should withdraw from consideration of matters where they have an interest whose existence creates a real danger of bias, that is where they or their close family are likely to be affected more than the generality of those affected by the decision in question. All the existing primary legislation on conflicts of interest in local government should be repealed and replaced by a provision giving effect to the common law principles set out above.

6.18 The Government response to the Nolan Committee's Report was included in the consultation paper *Modernising Local Government: A New Ethical Framework*[1]. The paper set out possible arrangements for introducing such a new framework, subject to consultation. It broadly agreed with the Nolan Committee conclusions but went further in its emphasis on external independent investigation of discipline. A separate consultation paper, entitled *Modernising Local Government in Wales: A New Ethical Framework*[2], was published in Wales, setting out suggested arrangements for introducing a new framework tailored to Welsh requirements.

1 Published April 1998, DETR.
2 Published June 1998, Welsh Office.

6.19 The White Paper *Modern Local Government: In Touch with the People*[1] set out the Government's intention to provide for a new ethical framework for local authorities. It suggested three principal components of the new framework:

- (i) a requirement on every council to adopt a code of conduct, based on a national model, that all members will have to sign up to;
- (ii) a requirement for most authorities to set up a standards committee to oversee ethical issues and provide advice and guidance on the code of conduct and its implementation;
- (iii) the establishment of an independent body, the Standards Board, with responsibility for investigating alleged breaches of the council's code of conduct.

1 Cm 4014, July 1998.

6.20 A separate White Paper, *Modernising Local Government in Wales: Local Voices*[1], set out the intentions of the newly formed National Assembly for Wales to implement a new ethical framework for Welsh authorities, broadly comparable to the English framework. The Government Papers *Local Leadership, Local Choice*[2] in England and *A Stronger Voice for Local People*[3] in Wales provided further details of the framework and proposals which were included in the accompanying draft Local Government (Organisation of Standards) Bill which was submitted to the scrutiny of a Parliamentary Joint Committee of MPs and Peers in May 1999.

1 Cm 4028, July 1998.
2 Cm 4298, March 1999.
3 Published April 1998, Welsh Office.

6.21 Section 49(1)–(2) of the Local Government Act 2000 provides the Secretary of State in England and the National Assembly of Wales with a power to develop a set of general principles of conduct which will apply to all authorities covered by the new ethical framework. They are intended to provide a guide to councillors' behaviour in the execution of their duties and will underpin the model code of conduct referred to in LGA 2000, s 50 that these authorities will adopt for their members in England. The general principles will also be subject to approval by Parliament in respect of England, by affirmative resolution of both Houses, before the Secretary of State can introduce them[1]. In Wales, the general principles of conduct will be subject to approval by a resolution of the National Assembly of Wales.

1 As specified in LGA 2000, s 105(5).

6.22 LGA 2000, s 49(3)–(4) places a duty on the Secretary of State and the National Assembly of Wales to consult various bodies in developing the general principles of conduct. They include representatives of local government, the Audit Commission and the Commissioners for Local Administration in England and Wales (the local government ombudsmen).

6.23 LGA 2000, s 51(1) places a duty upon authorities listed in LGA 2000, s 49(6) to adopt a code of conduct within six months of the new model code coming into force. Where an authority already has a code of conduct in place, it will only be required to change if it is not consistent with the new model code. An authority's code of conduct must include any mandatory provisions of the model code that applies to the authority. However, the authority has discretion to incorporate in its code any optional or additional provisions it wishes to include, providing they are not contrary to any within the model code of conduct.

This section also makes provision that if an authority fails to adopt a code of conduct within the specified period, the mandatory provisions of the model code relevant to the authority will apply to it by default until it adopts its own code. Once an authority has adopted or revised its code of conduct, it must publish the fact, make the code of conduct available for public inspection, and send a copy to the Standards Board.

6.24 LGA 2000, s 52 places a duty upon each member of an authority listed in LGA 2000, s 49(6) to comply with any code of conduct adopted by the authority under these provisions. This is in contrast with the current system whereby, under the Local Government Act 1972, s 83, the declaration made by councillors includes an undertaking to be guided by the National Code of Local Government Conduct in the performance of their functions. Section 83 applies only to county, district, London borough and parish councils. However, the requirements in this section extend also to the other 'relevant' authorities listed in LGA 2000, s 49(6) which are required to develop codes of conduct (such as police and fire authorities).

Where an authority adopts a new code or revises an existing code of conduct, every member of the authority must make a written declaration that he or she will observe the code. Any member who does not make a declaration to this effect within two months of the code coming into effect will cease to be a member of the authority. Once a member has made the declaration to observe the code, the procedures set out in Part III of the Act may be followed in relation to any breaches of the code by that member.

6.25 LGA 2000, s 53 places a duty upon particular local authorities to establish a standards committee. In England, the duty applies to county councils and district councils, London borough councils, the Greater London Authority, the Common Council of the City of London and the Council of the Isles of Scilly. In Wales, all county councils and county borough councils are covered.

This section also specifies various details of the composition of an authority's standards committee. Whilst the authority has discretion over the overall number of members of the standards committee, it must have at least three members—two who are elected members of the authority and one of whom is an independent member (ie, not a member of that or any other authority). In an authority that operates under the executive arrangements set out in Part II of the Act, a standards committee must not include a directly-elected mayor or executive leader, and may not be chaired by a member of the executive.

6.26 LGA 2000, s 53 also gives each of the Secretary of State and the National Assembly of Wales power to make regulations on the appointment of the independent member, the size of standards committees, and the way in which standards committees conduct their business. It provides the independent members of the committee with voting rights, and requires the authority to provide the Standards Board with a copy of the standards committee's terms of reference.

6.27 LGA 2000, s 54 sets out the functions of a standards committee. The general functions are to promote and maintain high standards of conduct within the local authority and to assist members of the authority to observe the authority's code of conduct.

This section also outlines a range of specific functions. These are to:

- advise the authority on the adoption or revision of a local code of conduct;
- monitor the operation of the authority's code, for instance, making recommendations to the authority about changes to keep the code up to date;
- advise members of the authority on matters relating to their code of conduct. This might include providing or arranging for training of members;

LGA 2000, s 54(4)–(7) enables the Secretary of State and the National Assembly of Wales to issue further regulations in respect of the functions of the standards committee, although it is intended that these powers be held in reserve. It also allows the Standards Board to issue guidance on the matter. There may be further functions that individual standards committees might take on (for example, considering general staffing issues and disseminating good practice etc). It is likely that the Standards Board will want to lead on disseminating good practice on these issues.

6.28 LGA 2000, s 57 provides for the creation of a new independent body, the Standards Board for England[1]. The Secretary of State is given power to appoint members of the Standards Board for England. The Standards Board is to have at least three members.

The functions of the Standards Board are:

- to appoint employees known as ethical standards officers (ESOs);
- to issue guidance to local authorities in relation to the conduct of their members;
- such other functions as may be conferred on each Standards Board by order, made by the Secretary of State with regard to the Standards Board for England.

1 In Wales the Local Commissioner performs the same role: ss 68–74.

6.29 LGA 2000, Sch 4 covers the status and general powers of the Standards Board. It sets out the grounds for disqualification from being appointed as a member of the Standards Board. It requires the Secretary of State to appoint the chairman and deputy chairman of the Standards Board. It makes provision for the Secretary of State to determine and pay any remuneration and allowances for members of the Standards Board. This Schedule also enables the Standards Board to appoint (and pay) staff to carry out its functions and includes provision for the employment of staff to support the Adjudication Panel and case tribunals in the exercise of their functions. It provides that staff cannot support both the ethical standards officers and the Adjudication Panel or case tribunals.

6.30 LGA 2000, s 58 provides that a person may make a written allegation to either Standards Board that a member or members of a relevant authority has failed or may have failed to comply with the authority's code of conduct. If either Board considers that such an allegation should be investigated it must refer the case to its ethical standards officers.

6.31 LGA 2000, s 59 specifies the functions of ethical standards officers. Their main function will be to investigate allegations that a member (or members) of an authority has breached its code of conduct. Ethical standards officers may also investigate any associated cases that have come to their attention as a result of undertaking an investigation into a written allegation.

This section also states that the purpose of an investigation by an ethical standards officer is to find:

- that there is no evidence of a failure to comply with a code of conduct; or
- that there is no need to take action on the matter investigated (whether or not there was a breach of the code); or
- that the matter should be referred back to the standards committee of the authority to deal with; or
- that the matters which are subject of the investigation should be referred to the President of the Adjudication Panel.

6.32 LGA 2000, s 60 enables the ethical standards officers to investigate allegations even if the person concerned is no longer a member of the authority, thus preventing a councillor from evading an investigation by resigning. An investigation into a member of an authority may not be carried out by an ethical standards officer who has been a member of that authority (or any of its committees) at any time within the last five years. Ethical standards officers are also placed under a duty to declare to the Standards Board any direct or indirect interest in any matters referred to them and to take no further part in any investigation of such a matter.

6.33 LGA 2000, s 61 concerns the procedure for conducting an investigation. There is a specific provision that the person being investigated must have an opportunity to comment on the allegation. Other than that, the section gives wide scope for an ethical standards officer to conduct an investigation as he sees fit. There is specific provision allowing ethical standards officers to reimburse the costs of the people from whom they seek information. The section also provides that the conduct of an investigation should not affect the ability of the local authority to take action in respect of the matters being investigated.

6.34 LGA 2000, s 62 gives the ethical standards officer rights of access to the information or documents necessary to the investigation. These powers are also conferred upon any person the ethical standards officer authorises to assist with an investigation. Any person from whom the ethical standards officer makes enquiries or seeks information or explanations is obliged to co-operate. The duty to provide information extends to communications with government departments, including those that would ordinarily not be disclosed. The duty does not, however, extend to the Parliamentary Commissioner, a Local Commissioner, or the Health Service Commissioner. Ethical standards officers are to be able to obtain advice during an investigation and to pay for its provision.

Finally, LGA 2000, s 62(10) introduces a new offence of failing to provide the ethical standards officer with such information, documentation or other evidence he requires as part of his investigation. Any person convicted would be liable to a fine of level 3 on the standard scale (currently £1,000).

6.35 LGA 2000, s 63 provides that information may only be disclosed if at least one of the following conditions is met:

- the disclosure is for the purposes of any functions of the Standards Board, ethical standards officer or a case tribunal;

- the person to whom the information relates has consented to its disclosure;
- the information has previously been disclosed to the public with lawful authority;
- the disclosure is for the purposes of criminal proceedings in any part of the UK (note, however, that information and witness statements taken by the ethical standards officer may not be passed to the police: this is to comply with requirements under the Human Rights Act 1998);
- the disclosure is made to the Audit Commission for the purposes of any functions of the Commission or an auditor under the Audit Commission Act 1998.

6.36 LGA 2000, s 63(4) introduces a new offence of disclosing information in contravention of the restriction on disclosure. Any person on summary conviction would be liable to a term of imprisonment of up to six months. Any person on conviction on indictment would be liable to a term of imprisonment not exceeding two years, or to a fine, or both.

6.37 LGA 2000, s 64 provides that where an ethical standards officer concludes that there is no evidence of any failure to comply with the code of conduct of the relevant authority concerned or where no action needs to be taken in respect of the matters which are the subject of the investigation, he may produce a report and may provide a summary of the report to any newspapers circulating in the area. If a report is produced, a copy must be sent to the monitoring officer of the relevant authority. If the ethical standards officer does not produce a report, he must inform the monitoring officer of the relevant authority of the outcome of the investigation.

6.38 LGA 2000, s 64(2)–(3) places a duty on the ethical standards officer to produce a report when he concludes that the matters which are the subject of an investigation should be either referred to the standards committee of the relevant authority or referred to the President of the Adjudication Panel for adjudication. Copies of the reports must be sent to the monitoring officer of the authority concerned, to the standards committee of the relevant authority or, as the case may be, to the President of the Adjudication Panel. A report may cover more than one investigation.

The Standards Board must on the conclusion of all investigations give notice to any member of the relevant authority concerned who is the subject of the investigation and must take reasonable steps to inform the person who made the original allegation about the outcome of the investigation.

6.39 LGA 2000, ss 65 and 78 provide the ethical standards officer with the power to issue an interim report, if, during an investigation he considers that it would be in the public interest to do so (this is only likely to arise in the case of particularly serious allegations). Such reports can conclude that the person being investigated should be suspended from being a member of the authority or any of its committees or sub-committees. In such cases the local authority is under a duty to comply with the notice.

The maximum period of suspension is six months, though this can be extended by the ethical standards officer by issuing further notices. The period of suspension cannot last longer than the remainder of the member's term of office, nor can it extend beyond the date on which the case tribunal concludes its consideration of a full report. A copy of any interim report by the ethical standards officer must be sent to the person who is the subject of the report and the monitoring officer of that person's authority. The ethical standards officer must also take reasonable steps to inform the person who made the allegation. A person suspended following an interim report by the ethical standards officer can appeal to the High Court either against the suspension itself or the period of suspension.

6.40 LGA 2000, s 75 makes provision for two panels of persons known as the Adjudication Panel for England and the Adjudication Panel for Wales or Panel Dyfarnu Cymru.

The members of the Adjudication Panel for England are to be appointed by the Lord Chancellor and may identify a President and Deputy President from among those members. The National Assembly for Wales will appoint members of the Adjudication Panel for Wales and the Assembly may also identify a President and Deputy President from among them.

The President and Deputy President of each Panel are to be responsible for:

- training the members of their Adjudication Panel;
- issuing guidance on how case tribunals will reach decision.

6.41 LGA 2000, s 76 provides for adjudications to be conducted by case tribunals consisting of not less than three members of the Adjudication Panel appointed by the President or Deputy President, both of whom themselves can be case tribunal members. A case tribunal may conduct a single adjudication in relation to two or more matters which are referred to the President for adjudication. A member of the Adjudication Panel cannot be a member of a case tribunal constituted to look into a matter if he/she has been a member of the authority or a member of a committee of the authority concerned in the previous five years. Finally, this section makes provision for the Secretary of State and the National Assembly for Wales to issue guidance in respect of the composition of case tribunals.

6.42 LGA 2000, s 77 enables a person who is the subject of a tribunal hearing either to appear before the case tribunal in person or to be represented by a third party. This section also makes provision for the Secretary of State to make such further regulations covering the process of adjudication as is considered necessary. Such regulations might cover:

- requiring people to attend to give evidence to the case tribunal;
- requiring them to make relevant documents relating to the investigation available to the panel;
- prescribing the procedure to be followed by a case tribunal, for example, to ensure fairness in the proceedings;
- provision enabling the President or Deputy President to settle the procedure to be followed in relation to matters specified in the regulations;
- awarding or settling costs or expenses;
- the registration and proof of decision and awards of case tribunals.

LGA 2000, s 77(7) also introduces a new offence of failing to comply with any requirement imposed by the case tribunal in considering a case. It is similar to the offence introduced by LGA 2000, s 62(10) and also has the penalty of a level 3 fine (£1,000 at present).

6.43 LGA 2000, s 79 covers the outcome of the case tribunal's findings. It places a duty on the case tribunal to decide, on any case before it, whether or not there has been a breach of the code of conduct, and to notify the standards committee of the authority concerned. Where the case tribunal decides that a person has failed to comply with the code of conduct, this clause places the case tribunal under a duty to decide whether the nature of the failure is such that the person should be suspended from being a member of that or any other authority. Suspension can be for a period of up to one year, although this must not extend beyond the person's term of office. Disqualification may be for up to five years.

In any case where the case tribunal decides that a person has failed to comply with a code of conduct, this section requires the case tribunal to issue a notice to the standards committee of the authority concerned and specify the details of the failure. The case tribunal must also state whether it has decided that a member should be suspended or disqualified. This section also places a duty on the authority to comply with any notice from the case tribunal to its standards committee. The case tribunal is required to send a copy of any notice issued to the Standards Board and to anyone who is the subject of the notice and also to take reasonable steps to inform the person who made the initial allegation of the outcome of the tribunal's adjudication. Notices are to be published in the authority's local newspaper(s).

Finally, this section introduces a right of appeal to the High Court for a person that a case tribunal decides has failed to comply with the code of conduct.

CHAPTER 7

Best value

A Introduction

1 OVERVIEW

7.1 Improving the quality of local services and the efficiency and economy with which they are delivered were said to be a key objectives of the present government's plans to modernise local government[1]. The 'best value regime' created by the Local Government Act 1999 ('LGA 1999'), Pt I is intended to put these aims into effect by providing a framework for 'delivering local services to clear standards, covering both cost and quality'[2]. LGA 1999, Pt I might be viewed as a legislative framework to promote good management of, and continual improvement in, service delivery by local authorities and other bodies which provide local services. Rather than relying solely on a local authority's fiduciary duty to deploy the resources available to it to the best advantage, LGA 1999, Pt I, together with subordinate legislation and statutory guidance, spell out in considerable detail *how* local authorities should go about managing and improving their services and how their performance is to be judged, as well as providing the Secretary of State with extensive powers, should they fail to comply with their new 'best value duties'.

1 See the consultation paper issued by the DETR in March 1998 entitled *Modernising Local Government: Improving local services through best value*, at para 1.1.
2 See the White Paper: *Modern Local Government: In Touch with the People* Cm 4014, July 1998, ch 7.

7.2 The new regime appears to have been designed to take account of the views of a diverse range of interest groups, from local authorities themselves to service users, unions and private sector providers. The emphasis of the new regime is on a 'strategic approach' to the procurement/provision of local services, with continual reappraisal of the need for and manner of service provision.

7.3 Consistent with the pattern of much of the recent legislation concerning local government, the Local Government Act 1999 contains only a bare framework for the new best value regime, leaving the detailed controls to be dealt with in subordinate legislation or in guidance issued by the Secretary of State and giving the Secretary of State wide discretionary powers. Indeed, and again a recurrent feature of recent enactments, LGA 1999 confers on the Secretary of State certain regulation and order making powers (commonly referred to as 'Henry VIII provisions'), through which he is to be empowered (through secondary legislation) to modify or exclude both primary and secondary legislation, or to create new powers for best value authorities to facilitate compliance with the new duty.

7.4 Under the framework set by LGA 1999, Pt I, orders made and guidance issued by the Secretary of State are to provide a detailed system for best value authorities to monitor their own performance, assessed against externally prescribed national standards as well as the authority's own past performance and that of other authorities and bodies providing comparable services. Authorities are required to make public not only their proposals to comply with their duties concerning best value, but also their failures. Authorities' efforts at self-monitoring are backed up by mechanisms for external scrutiny of their compliance with the best value requirements through audit and inspection as well as the powers of the Secretary of State to prescribe *how* best value authorities should go about their new tasks and to tackle their failures to comply.

7.5 There is no explicit requirement in LGA 1999 itself for external as opposed to internal service provision (at least, so long as the authority complies with its new duties). However, comparison with private sector performance forms a key element of the statutory regime and the need for open competition in most instances is emphasised in the statutory guidance. Consultation and encouragement of innovation and a 'partnership approach' to the improvement of local services are further recurrent themes of the regime.

7.6 Government comment on the proposals in the consultation paper[1] and the White Paper[2] which preceded enactment of the Local Government Act 1999 and the guidance issued under LGA 1999, Pt I[3] all refer, in various contexts, to the importance of a 'partnership' approach to best value, whether with the private or voluntary sector, other public bodies in the area, or with central government.

1 *Modernising Local Government: Improving local services through best value*, DETR, March 1998.
2 *Modern Local Government: In Touch with the People* Cm 4014, July 1998.
3 Circular 10/99 issued by the DETR on 14 December 1999. Annex A to the Circular contains a brief description of the pilot projects and some of their achievements.

7.7 The main requirements under LGA 1999, Pt I are to apply to local authorities (and certain of the other specified bodies) in England and Wales as from 1 April 2000, although provisions concerning certain preparatory matters come into effect prior to that date[1]. LGA 1999, Pt I also provides for most of the statutory provisions concerning the compulsory competitive tendering ('CCT') regime[2] to cease to have effect on 2 January 2000. Unlike the CCT regime, which applied only to defined activities, the new duty of best value is to extend across the entirety of the services and other activities undertaken by a local authority or other best value authority.

1 See the Local Government Act 1999 (Commencement No 1) Order 1999, SI 1999/2169 and the Local Government Act 1999 (Commencement) (Wales) Order 1999, SI 1999/2815 and para **7.8** for a summary of the initial stages.
2 Under the Local Government, Planning and Land Act 1980, Pt III; the Local Government Act 1988, Pt I and the Local Government Act 1992, ss 8–11.

2 BEST VALUE TIMETABLE

7.8 Authorities were expected to have taken preparatory steps prior to the new regime coming into force. The timetable for the main initial stages for the new regime comprises:

July 1998	Informal encouragement to plan programme of fundamental performance reviews and prepare for performance plans (White Paper[1])
10 August 1999[2]	Definition of 'best value authority' Certain consultation requirements
27 Sept 1999[3]	Powers regarding orders, guidance and regulations Audit Commission code of practice under s 8(2) Duty to prepare performance plan under s 6
2 January 2000	Compulsory competitive tendering regime ends[4]
30 March 2000	First best value performance plan under s 6 published[5]
1 April 2000[6]	Best value duties under ss 3–5 come into force Five-year performance review cycle under s 5 begins Audit and inspection regime under ss 7–13 begins Secretary of State's enforcement powers under s 15
30 June 2000[7]	First audit report of performance plan issued under s 7 and to be published under s 9
31 March 2005[8]	First best value review of all functions complete.

1 *Modern Local Government: In Touch with the People* Cm 4014, July 1998, paras 7.16 and 7.52.
2 See SI 1999/2169, art 2(2) and Sch 1 for local authorities in England. For local authorities in Wales, the relevant date is 1 October 1999: see SI 1999/2815, art 2.
3 See SI 1999/2169, art 3 and Sch 2 for local authorities in England. For local authorities in Wales, the relevant date for certain of the relevant provisions is 1 October 1999: see SI 1999/2815, art 2.
4 The Local Government Act 1999, ss 21 and 34 and Sch 2.
5 See the 1999 Act, s 6(3). The plan must be published before 31 March in the financial year prior to that to which it applies. For Wales, 30 June has been specified by SI 2000/1271, art 5.
6 See SI 1999/2169, art 4 for local authorities in England. For local authorities in Wales, see SI 1999/2815, art 3.
7 See Local Government Act 1999, s 7(6). For Wales, 31 October has been specified by SI 2000/1271, art 6.
8 See SI 1999/3251, art 5(1).

3 BEST VALUE PILOT PROJECTS

7.9 To collate best practice and practical experience prior to the statutory regime coming into effect, in April 1998 the Government set up a scheme of 'best value pilot projects'. The scheme involved some 38 individual local authorities, two joint projects by local authorities and two police authorities, many of which were granted exemptions from the CCT regime. As a reflection of the 'partnership approach', six pilot 'Partnership Networks' were set up, experimenting with various forms of partnership, particularly with the private sector.

4 THE NATIONAL ASSEMBLY FOR WALES

7.10 In relation to local authorities in Wales, LGA 1999 is, in most cases, to be applied subject to the modification that the National Assembly for Wales is to be substituted for the Secretary of State[1]. However, the 'Henry VIII' power to make orders amending legislation under LGA 1999, ss 16 and 17 and to make orders under the Deregulation and Contracting Out Act 1994 in relation to the functions of best value authorities under LGA 1999, s 18[2] are exercisable only by the relevant

Secretary of State and not by the new Assembly[3]. Before making any order under LGA 1999, s 16[4] which has effect in relation to Wales, the Secretary of State must consult the National Assembly for Wales and must obtain its prior consent to any amendment, modification or exclusion of legislation which has been made by the Assembly[5].

1 Local Government Act 1999, s 29.
2 See para **7.64–7.72**.
3 Local Government Act 1999, s 29(2)(b).
4 See para **7.65**ff.
5 Local Government Act 1999, s 29(3).

7.11 In the following text, references to the Secretary of State should be read as being references to the National Assembly for Wales in relation to local authorities in Wales, save in respect of LGA 1999, ss 16–18[1]. However, for police authorities and fire authorities in Wales, the powers of the Secretary of State are not to be exercisable by the new Assembly[2]. The following text concentrates on the position which applies in England. Different provision has been made for best value authorities in Wales in certain circumstances.

1 See paras **7.64–7.72**.
2 Local Government Act 1999, s 29((2)(a).

B The duty to secure best value

1 BEST VALUE AUTHORITIES

7.12 LGA 1999, s 1 creates the classification of 'best value authorities' to whom the new duty under s 3 and other requirements under Part I are to apply. Best value authorities comprise local authorities in England and Wales[1] and most other bodies subject to the local government finance regime[2] and include certain new bodies, such as the Greater London Authority in so far as it exercises its functions through the Mayor, and the four functional bodies of the new Authority[3].

1 County, district, London borough, and parish councils (and parish meetings which have no separate parish council), the Council of the Isles of Scilly, the Common Council of the City of London in its capacity as a local authority, and the Greater London Authority in so far as it exercises its functions through the Mayor; and in Wales, a county, county borough or community council (see ss 1(1)(a), (2) and (3)).
2 National Park, police, fire, metropolitan county fire and civil defence, waste disposal and metropolitan county passenger authorities, the Broads Authority, the London Fire and Emergency Planning Authority, Transport for London and the London Development Agency (see s 1(1)(b)–(j)).
3 The four functional bodies of the Greater London Authority are: the Metropolitan Police Authority, the London Fire and Emergency Planning Authority, the London Development Agency and Transport for London. These four bodies, and the Greater London Authority, in so far as it exercises functions through the Mayor, become 'best value authorities' as from 3 July 2000, by virtue of SI 2000/1724. That Order also brought into force the powers of the Secretary of State under LGA 1999, s 2(4) to provide for the Greater London Authority to be a 'best value authority' in respect of other specified functions (see para **7.13**).

7.13 Under LGA 1999, s 2 the Secretary of State has discretion, by order, to provide for certain other bodies within the local government finance system to be 'best value authorities', and to modify certain of the provisions of the 1999 Act in their application to these additional authorities or bodies[1]. The specified bodies include local precepting authorities and levying bodies[2] and the Greater London

Authority[3] when it carries out functions otherwise than through the Mayor, or in respect of specified functions of another best value authority which are not functions of the new Authority itself. (An example of where this last option is intended to apply is where the Greater London Authority, through the Mayor, has a strategic role in relation to the operational functions of another body, such as one of its functional bodies[4].)

1 See LGA 1999, s 2(3) and (4).
2 See LGA 1999, s 2(2).
3 See LGA 1999, s 2(4).
4 See the Explanatory Notes to the Local Government Act 1999, para 17.

7.14 Under LGA 1999, s 2(5), the Secretary of State may, by order, exempt an individual best value authority, or a specified description of best value authority, from particular duties under LGA 1999, Pt I in relation to specified functions of that authority. Thus, smaller bodies, such as parish councils or community councils may be exempt from the full rigours of the new best value regime[1].

1 See SI 2000/339, concerning parish councils with a budgeted income for any of the financial years commencing in 1997, 1998 or 1999 of not more than £500,000. Such a parish council is not subject to any of the duties under the Local Government Act 1999, ss 3–6 in relation to any of its functions (the threshold for community councils in Wales is £1,000,000 based on budgeted gross revenue expenditure for either of the financial years commencing on 1 April 1998 or 1 April 1999, by virtue of SI 2000/1029).

2 THE CORE DUTY TO SECURE BEST VALUE

7.15 The prime duty is contained in the Local Government Act 1999, s 3. Under LGA 1999, s 3(1), a best value authority must:

> '... make arrangements to secure continuous improvement in the way in which its functions are exercised[1], having regard to a combination of economy, efficiency and effectiveness.'

1 LGA 1999, s 3(1) refers to the 'exercise' of functions, rather than the more usual expression of 'discharge' of functions. The language of the statute is adopted in this chapter.

7.16 It is to be noted that the heart of this main duty under LGA 1999, s 3(1) lies in 'making arrangements' to secure the required improvements. 'Functions' is not defined for the purpose of LGA 1999. Case law[1] indicates (albeit in relation to a different statutory provision where no definition is provided) that the expression embraces all the duties and powers of a local authority, the sum total of the activities Parliament has entrusted to it. It seems likely that a similarly wide interpretation of 'functions' would be applied for the purposes of LGA 1999, s 3(1)[2].

1 *Hazell v London Borough of Hammersmith and Fulham* [1990] 3 All ER 33 at 83, [1990] 2 QB 697 at 785, CA in connection with the definition of 'function' for the purposes of the Local Government Act 1972, s 111. This definition was subsequently approved by the House of Lords ([1991] 1 All ER 545 at 554).
2 The Explanatory Notes to the 1999 Act (at para 3) refer to the new duty of best value encompassing all functions undertaken by an authority 'whether statutory or not'. The suggestion that a function might not be statutory is clearly incompatible with the law relating to statutory bodies.

7.17 A best value authority must consult representatives of specified groups of people in deciding how to fulfil the best value duty in LGA 1999, s 3(1), including representatives of local tax payers, non-domestic rate payers, users of local services and those with an interest in any area within which the authority carries out functions[1]. In deciding whom to consult and the form, content and timing of consultation, the authority must have regard to any guidance issued by the Secretary of State[2]. The circular issued by the Department of the Environment, Transport and the Regions ('the DETR') on 14 December 1999: 10/99 (referred to in this chapter as 'Circular 10/99') which contains the statutory guidance from the Secretary of State to best value authorities in relation to other provisions of LGA 1999, Pt I, indicated that the Government had no current plans to issue guidance for the purpose of the consultation requirements under LGA 1999, s 3(4). It was being left to authorities to decide whom to consult and in what way, taking account of 'other statutory requirements and good practice[3]'.

1 Local Government Act 1999, s 3(2).
2 LGA 1999, s 3(4).
3 Circular 10/99, para 34.

3 BEST VALUE PERFORMANCE INDICATORS, STANDARDS AND TARGETS

7.18 The Local Government Act 1999, s 4 empowers the Secretary of State, by order, to specify 'performance indicators' against which a best value authority's performance is to be measured, and 'performance standards' to be met by authorities in relation to performance indicators. These national performance indicators and standards may be applied differently for different functions, for different authorities or at different times. Where a performance standard has been set, a best value authority is under an express duty to meet the applicable standard when exercising the function[1].

1 Local Government Act 1999, s 4(5).

7.19 In setting indicators and standards, the Secretary of State is under a comparable duty to best value authorities themselves: he must aim to promote improvement in the way in which their functions are exercised, having regard to a combination of economy, efficiency and effectiveness. He must also have regard to any recommendations made to him by the Audit Commission[1]. Under the Audit Commission Act 1998, s 44 the Commission is responsible for requiring local authorities and other bodies subject to audit to publish financial information about their activities to enable comparisons between their standards of performance to be made. (The Audit Commission has published performance indicators pursuant to its functions[2].) Before specifying performance indicators or standards, the Secretary of State must consult representatives of best value authorities and such other persons as he thinks fit[3].

1 Local Government Act 1999, s 4(4).
2 One of the factors to be addressed in an authority's best value performance plan under LGA 1999, s 6 is an assessment of its performance with regard to the relevant Audit Commission indicators, which are listed and defined in the 'Publication of Information Direction 1998' issued by the Commission in accordance with the provisions of the Audit Commission Act 1998, ss 44 and 46. See para **7.32**(f).
3 Local Government Act 1999, s 4(3).

7.20 On 23 December 1999 the DETR published combined best value and Audit Commission Indicators for 2000/2001. It was said that the document gave an indication, without prejudice to the order yet to be made, of the indicators the Government intended to set. As regards the relationship between the indicators specified by the Government and those set by the Commission, it was explained that they were intended to be complementary. The Government's best value performance indicators are to focus on key national interest issues, whilst the Commission's indicators are to reflect other areas of interest to the public, or information which provides a context for the Government's indicators. The Secretary of State has now made the Local Government (Best Value) Performance Indicators Order 2000, SI 2000/896, which includes schedules containing general indicators and specific indicators for individual functions, including education, housing, social services, environment, transport, planning and cultural and related services[1].

1 Performance indicators for authorities in Wales are prescribed in SI 2000/1030.

7.21 The Local Government (Best Value) Performance Plans and Reviews Order SI 1999/3251 ('the Plans and Reviews Order'), art 4(2)(d) requires best value authorities in England[1] to summarise their success in meeting any 'best value performance standard' which applied at any time in the previous financial year, in the best value performance plan which they are to prepare for the financial year 2001, and subsequent years[2]. For these purposes 'best value performance standard' is defined by the Plans and Reviews Order[3], art 1(2) as being the minimum acceptable level of service provision which must be met, measured by reference to a performance indicator specified for that function from time to time by an order made under the 1999 Act, s 4.

1 The following relates to the position in England. The position in relation to Wales differs in certain respects. The equivalent measure to the Plans and Review Order for Wales is the Local Government (Best Value) (Reviews and Performance Plans) (Wales) Order 2000, SI 2000/1271.
2 See para **7.33**.
3 SI 1999/3251.

7.22 Best value authorities are also required to specify and set 'best value performance targets'[1] against best value performance indicators. The Plans and Reviews Order[2], art 3(1)(e) requires authorities to specify these targets in all their annual best value performance plans. For the financial year 2001 onwards, art 4(2)(f)–(h) requires authorities to summarise their progress towards meeting any targets, any plan of action for meeting targets, and their basis for setting targets and plans of action in relation to functions reviewed in the previous financial year[3].

1 'Best value performance targets' are defined in the Plans and Reviews Order (SI 1999/3251), art 1(2) as meaning the level of performance in the exercise of a function that a best value authority is expected to attain, measured by reference to the performance indicator in relation to that function, as specified by the best value authority, in accordance with any guidance under LGA 1999, ss 5(6)(b) and (7).
2 SI 1999/3251.
3 See paras **7.33** and **7.34**.

4 BEST VALUE REVIEW

7.23 Reviews of functions undertaken by the best value authority itself are a key component of the best value regime. The purpose of reviews is said to be to ensure that continuous improvements to all services are made (and not just those with serious shortcomings). Under LGA 1999, s 5, best value authorities are required to conduct 'best value reviews' and to do so in accordance with the provisions of any order made under the section and having regard to any guidance issued by the Secretary of State. LGA 1999, s 5(3)(a) requires that in conducting a review, an authority shall aim to improve the way in which its functions are exercised, having regard to a combination of economy, efficiency and effectiveness.

7.24 The Plans and Reviews Order[1], art 5, requires best value authorities to conduct the first best value review of all their functions by 31 March 2005 and to conduct further reviews of all their function over successive five year periods ending on 31 March. More detailed arrangements regarding reviews of individual functions have been made for fire authorities. For other best value authorities, the Secretary of State has not used his powers (under LGA 1999, s 5(2)(c)) to prescribe a precise timetable for the review of individual functions within the five-year cycle. However, the guidance in Circular 10/99, para 19 suggests that poorly performing services should normally be reviewed early in the five-year period. Further, the annual best value performance plan[2] must include an indication of the timetable the authority proposes to follow in conducting its best value review (Plans and Reviews Order[3], arts 3(1)(d) and 4(1)). Whilst acknowledging that priorities may change during the review period, Circular 10/99, para 20 advises that authorities will need to justify any changes to the review programme as set out annually in their performance plan, particularly in relation to any postponement of a review of a poorly performing service.

1 SI 1999/3251. For Wales, the equivalent provision is contained in SI 2000/1271, art 2.
2 See para **7.32**ff.
3 SI 1999/3251.

7.25 The guidance recommends (Circular 10/99, para 21) that reviews should not merely centre on specific services, but should also include what are described as 'cross-cutting reviews', being those which affect several services and functions (for example, community safety or social exclusion, or other issues of particular importance to the authority's area).

7.26 LGA 1999, s 5(4), sets out matters which the Secretary of State may, 'in particular', specify in an order made to prescribe the matters which an authority must include in a best value review of any function. The Local Government (Best Value) Performance Plans and Reviews Order SI 1999/3251 ('the Plans and Reviews Order'), art 6(1)[1] follows almost verbatim the contents of LGA 1999, s 5(4), requiring an authority, in conducting a best value review, to:

(a) consider whether it should be exercising the function;
(b) consider the level at which, and the way in which, it should be exercising the function;
(c) consider its objectives in relation to the exercise of the function;
(d) assess its performance in exercising the function by reference to any performance indicator[2] specified for the function;
(e) assess the competitiveness of its performance in exercising the function by reference to the exercise of the same function, or similar functions, by other best value authorities and by commercial and other businesses, including organisations in the voluntary sector;
(f) consult other best value authorities, commercial and other businesses, including organisations in the voluntary sector, about the exercise of the function;
(g) assess its success in meeting any best value performance standard[3] which applies in relation to the function;
(h) assess its progress towards meeting any relevant best value performance

standard which has been specified but which does not yet apply; and

(i) assess its progress towards meeting any relevant best value performance target.

1 For Wales, see SI 2000/1271, art 3.
2 See para **7.18**ff.
3 See para **7.21** regarding the meaning of 'best value performance standard'.

7.27 Circular 10/99 at paras 15–50 then gives further, more detailed, guidance on the conduct of reviews, which is not repeated here, save to note three particular features. First, the encouragement to explore opportunities for innovation and 'genuine partnership' with others in the public, private and voluntary sectors (see para 36 of the Circular). Second, the often repeated summary of the requirements, known as the 'the 4Cs' (see para **7.28**) and finally, the advice on the role of competition and in-house provision (see para **7.29**).

7.28 The requirements for reviews, summarised as the 4Cs, comprise:

(a) **challenge**: why, how and by whom a service is being provided;
(b) **compare**: with the performance others across a range of relevant indicators, taking into account the views of both service users and potential suppliers;
(c) **consult**: local tax payers, service users, partners, and the wider business community in the setting of new performance targets; and
(d) **compete**: use fair and open competition wherever practicable as a means of securing effective services.

7.29 In relation to the role of competition and in-house provision, the guidance in Circular 10/99, para 36 notes that:

> 'The 1999 Act does not require authorities to subject their functions to competition in the way in which legislation on compulsory competitive tendering did. Even so, fair and open competition will, in the Government's view, most often be the best way of demonstrating that a function is being carried out competitively. Such competition is expected to play an essential and enduring role in ensuring best value, and reviews will need to consider how this can best be achieved.'

7.30 Under CCT legislation, in essence, a local authority had no power to undertake certain defined activities through its own staff unless the work had been 'won' following competition with private sector providers, having followed the specified tendering procedures. However, there was no requirement within the CCT legislation for competition between potential private sector providers in a situation where the authority had no intention to consider an in-house 'bid'. In contrast, the best value regime applies to all an authority's functions, does not spell out any special requirements for the tendering process (although many contracts will be subject to other requirements in this respect[1]) and would apply regardless of whether there is any prospect of providing services through directly employed staff.

1 For example, under the EC public procurement regime.

7.31 At para 46 the guidance in Circular 10/99 states:

> 'Services should not be delivered directly if other more efficient and effective means are available. Retaining work in-house will therefore only be justified where the authority can show it is competitive with the best alternative. The

way in which this is demonstrated is for an authority to determine in accordance with its procurement strategy and evaluation policy, but where there is a developed supply market this will most often be through fair and open competition.'

5 BEST VALUE PERFORMANCE PLAN

7.32 Best value authorities are required by LGA 1999, s 6 to prepare a 'best value performance plan' for each financial year, in accordance with any order made, or guidance issued, under s 6. The first such plan was to be prepared and published before 31 March 2000[1]. LGA 1999, s 6(2) sets out the matters which the Secretary of State may, in particular, specify for inclusion in the plan in any order made for the purpose of s 6. The Plans and Reviews Order[2], art 3(1) requires that the plan for the financial year 2000 should include:

(a) a summary of the authority's objectives in relation to the exercise of its functions;
(b) a summary of any assessment made by the authority of the level at which, and the way in which, it exercises its functions;
(c) a statement specifying any period within which the authority is required to reviews its functions under LGA 1999, s 5 and the Plans and Reviews Order, arts 5 and 6[3];
(d) a statement indicating the timetable the authority proposes to follow in conducting a best value review[4];
(e) a statement specifying any best value performance indicators, best value performance standards and best value performance targets specified or set in relation to the authority's functions[5];
(f) a summary of the authority's assessment of its performance in the previous financial year with regard to the relevant Audit Commission indicators[6], where applicable; and
(g) a comparison of that performance with the authority's performance in previous financial years.

1 See LGA 1999, s 6(3). For Wales, the equivalent date is 30 June: see SI 2000/1271, art 5.
2 SI 1999/3251. For Wales, see SI 2000/1271, art 4.
3 See para **7.24**.
4 The guidance in Circular 10/99, para 20 recognises that it will not be possible to set a review programme that anticipates all eventualities, and that priorities will change over any period; however, authorities will be expected to justify any changes in the review programme in their performance plan in subsequent years, in particular if a review of a poorly performing service is to be postponed.
5 See para **7.18**ff.
6 'Relevant Audit Commission indicators' means the indicators specified in Sch 1 to the Plans and Reviews Order (SI 1999/3251) which are listed and defined in the 'Publication of Information Direction 1998' issued by the Commission in December 1998 in accordance with the provisions of the Audit Commission Act 1998, ss 44 and 46.

7.33 For the financial year 2001 and subsequent years, the best value performance plan must include all the items (a)–(e) above and the further matters listed in the Plans and Reviews Order[1], art 4(2):

(a) a summary of the authority's assessment of its performance in the previous financial year with regard to best value performance indicators[2], where applicable;
(b) a comparison of that performance with the authority's performance in previous financial years;

(c) a comparison of the authority's performance as summarised in accordance with para (a) above, with the performance of other best value authorities in previous financial years;
(d) a summary of its assessment of its success in meeting any best value performance standard which applied at any time in the previous financial year;
(e) a summary of its assessment of its progress towards meeting any best value performance standard which has been specified but which does not yet apply;
(f) a summary of its assessment of its progress towards meeting any best value performance target[3];
(g) a summary of its plan of action to be taken in the financial year to which the plan relates for the purposes of meeting a best value performance target; and
(h) a summary of the basis on which any best value performance target was set, and any plan of action was determined, in relation to a function reviewed under the 1999 Act, s 5 and the Plans and Reviews Order[4], arts 5 and 6, in the previous financial year.

1 SI 1999/3251. For Wales, see SI 2000/1271, art 4.
2 See para **7.18**ff.
3 See para **7.22**.
4 SI 1999/3251.

7.34 The performance plan must include any statement the authority has been required to prepare in the preceding financial year under LGA 1999, s 9(3), in response to certain recommendations of the auditor made in a report under LGA 1999, s 7(4)[1]. The plan must also record any failure to comply with Part I which has been identified in an inspection report for the previous financial year and any action taken by the authority as a result of that report[2].

1 Local Government Act 1999, s 9(5); see para **7.40**.
2 LGA 1999, s 13(5); see para **7.51**.

7.35 The guidance in Circular 10/99 recommends that the performance plan should also include a 'statement of responsibility' regarding the authority's responsibility for preparation of the plan and the information it contains, including a statement of the authority's satisfaction as to the accuracy of the information and assessments contained in the plan and that the plan is realistic and achievable. Paragraph 63 of the Circular goes so far as to offer model wording for the statement.

C Securing compliance

1 AUDIT

7.36 External scrutiny of an authority's efforts to comply with new best value requirements is a further cornerstone of the new regime. The White Paper indicated that there would be a rigorous external check on the information provided by authorities in their best value performance plans and on the management systems that underpin them. The audit role is intended to fulfil this function.

7.37 The LGA 1999, s 7 concerns the auditor's role in relation to the best value performance plan prepared by a best value authority under LGA 1999, s 6. The performance plan must be audited by the authority's auditor[1], with a view to establishing whether the plan was prepared and published in accordance with s 6 and any order or guidance under that section[2]. The auditor's rights to documents and information under the Audit Commission Act 1998, s 6(1), (2) and (4)–(7) apply to the auditor's functions under the LGA 1999, Pt I[3]. In carrying out the audit of a performance plan, the auditor is to have regard to any code of practice issued by the Audit Commission[4].

1 Normally, the person or firm appointed by the Audit Commission to audit the authority's accounts pursuant to the Audit Commission Act 1998, s 3 in relation to the previous financial year. See the Local Government Act 1999, s 7(7)–(9).
2 LGA 1999, s 7(1) and (2).
3 LGA 1999, s 7(3).
4 LGA 1999, s 8.

7.38 Under LGA 1999, s 7(4) the auditor must issue a report:

(a) certifying that she or he has audited the performance plan;
(b) stating whether she or he believes that it was prepared and published in accordance with s 6 and any order or guidance under that section;
(c) if appropriate, recommending how it should be amended so as to accord with s 6 and any order or guidance under that section;
(d) if appropriate, recommending procedures to be followed by the authority in relation to the plan;
(e) recommending whether the Audit Commission should carry out a best value *inspection* of the authority under LGA 1999, s 10[1]; and
(f) recommending whether the Secretary of State should give a direction under LGA 1999, s 15[2].

1 See para **7.44**ff.
2 See para **7.57**ff.

7.39 The auditor's report must be copied to the authority, the Audit Commission and, if any direction under LGA 1999, s 15 is recommended, to the Secretary of State[1]. Copies of the report must be sent to these bodies no later than 30 June in the financial year to which the performance plan relates (or such other date as the Secretary of State may specify by order)[2]. The authority is then obliged to publish the auditor's report on its annual best value performance plan[3].

1 Local Government Act 1999, s 7(5).
2 LGA 1999, s 7(6). For Wales, the equivalent date is 31 October: see SI 2000/1271, art 6.
3 LGA 1999, s 9(1).

7.40 If the auditor has made any recommendation under paras (c)–(f) above, the authority must prepare a statement of the action which it proposes to take as a result of the report and its proposed timetable[1]. This statement must be prepared within 30 working days starting with the day on which the auditor's report is received (or any shorter period specified in the report for this purpose[2]). The authority must then incorporate this statement in its next annual best value performance plan which the authority is obliged to prepare[3]. If the report includes a recommendation that the Secretary of State should give a direction, then the authority must also copy its statement of the action it proposes to take to the Secretary of State within the 30 working day period (or any shorter period specified in the report[4]). Before giving any direction under LGA 1999, s 15 as a result of the auditor's recommendation, the Secretary of State must have regard to the statement the authority has made, provided that statement has been sent to him within one month of the day on which the authority received the auditor's report[5].

1 Local Government Act 1999, s 9(3).
2 LGA 1999, s 9(4).
3 LGA 1999, s 9(5). See paras **7.32–7.35** regarding the performance plan.
4 LGA 1999, s 9(6).
5 LGA 1999, s 15(10); see para **7.61**.

7.41 As noted in para **7.37**, auditors are required to have regard to any code of practice issued under LGA 1999, s 8. The Audit Commission is responsible for preparing a code of practice to prescribe the way in which auditors are to carry out their functions under LGA 1999, s 7[1]. That code of practice must embody best professional practice and must be approved by a resolution of each House of Parliament before it comes into force (and will only continue in force if so approved at intervals of no more than five years)[2]. Circular 10/99 specifies that auditors will consult with the relevant Inspectorates[3] before reaching a view on a performance plan and will 'adopt an open-minded and supportive approach to innovation; support well thought through risk-taking and experimentation and provide advice and encouragement to authorities by promoting good practice and shared experience'[4].

1 Local Government Act 1999, s 8(2).
2 The Audit Commission Act 1998, s 4(3)–(6) applies to the code prepared under the 1999 Act, s 8(2) by virtue of s 8(3).
3 See para **7.48**.
4 See Circular 10/99, paras 64 and 65.

7.42 The Audit Commission is responsible for prescribing a scale or scales of fees for the audit of the performance plan[1]. (These fees are payable by the authority concerned.) The Commission may charge a greater or smaller amount in an individual case, if the work involved in the audit is substantially more or less than that envisaged in the appropriate scale[2]. Before preparing or altering a code of practice under LGA 1999, s 8(2) or prescribing a scale of fees, under LGA 1999, s 8(4), the Audit Commission must consult the Secretary of State and persons who appear to the Commission to represent best value authorities[3].

1 Local Government Act 1999, s 8(4).
2 LGA 1999, s 8(4) and (5), which applies the Audit Commission Act 1998, s 7(3)–(8). The Secretary of State has a reserve power to prescribe a scale of fees in place of that set by the Audit Commission (see the Audit Commission Act 1998, s 7(8)).
3 LGA 1999, s 8(6).

7.43 To take account of the Commission's new functions in relation to best value, various amendments are made to the Audit Commission Act 1998 by LGA 1999, s 22. The Housing Associations Act 1985 is amended by LGA 1999, s 22(7) to enable the Housing Corporation to provide advice and assistance to the Audit Commission, on request, in relation to the Commission's functions regarding best value.

2 INSPECTION

7.44 To give still further rigour to external scrutiny of authorities' efforts to comply with the best value requirements, LGA 1999, s 10 provides for inspections to be undertaken by the Audit Commission. The aim of these inspections was described in the White Paper[1] as being to provide more in-depth scrutiny than the process of annual audit reporting could be expected to provide.

1 *Modern Local Government: In Touch with the People* Cm 4014, July 1998, at para 7.39ff.

7.45 Under LGA 1999, s 10(1) the Commission has a discretion, rather than a duty to carry out inspections, unless it receives a direction from the Secretary of State, under LGA 1999, s 10(2), requiring it to conduct an inspection. In the absence of such a direction, the frequency of inspections is left to the discretion of the Commission. Circular 10/99, para 76 indicates the Commission's expectation that inspections of each of an authority's functions will take place at least once within the five-year period and be aligned, so far as possible, with the review cycle. Ad hoc, unprogrammed inspections are also envisaged by the Government[1], particularly where an authority has no immediate plans to review a sub-standard service. It is recommended in the Circular (para 19) that at least during the first year of the regime, authorities may wish to align their reviews of services in advance of inspections where these are already planned.

1 See the Explanatory Notes to the Local Government Act 1999, para 37.

7.46 The Secretary of State is likely to direct the Commission to conduct a review where there is a particular concern about an authority's performance, but must consult the Commission before giving a direction[1]. In these circumstances, it is envisaged[2] that the inspection should take place *in advance* of the authority's own review, and would 'typically be more fundamental and searching in order to reach a proper diagnosis of the problems'.

1 Local Government Act 1999, s 10(3).
2 Circular 10/99, para 76.

7.47 By virtue of LGA 1999, s 10(4), in carrying out an inspection, and deciding whether to do so, the Commission must have regard to any recommendation made by the auditor in relation to the performance plan for a best value inspection to be undertaken[1] and to any guidance issued by the Secretary of State[2].

1 Under Local Government Act 1999, s 7(4)(e); see para **7.38**.
2 The Secretary of State must consult the Audit Commission, as well as best value authorities or their representatives, before issuing guidance for the purpose of s 10(4) (see s 26(3)).

7.48 Many local authority functions are already subject to scrutiny by specialist inspectorates such as the Benefit Fraud Inspectorate, HM Fire Services Inspectorate, HM Inspectorate of Constabulary, the Social Services Inspectorate and the Office for Standards in Education (OFSTED)[1]. Circular 10/99, para 72 indicates that the Audit Commission will 'work in partnership' with these existing specialist inspectorates where it is sensible to do so. Under LGA 1999, s 25(1), the Secretary of State is empowered to issue guidance aimed at securing co-ordination between the various kinds of external scrutiny of best value authorities undertaken by the persons and bodies listed in LGA 1999, s 25(2)[2].

1 See LGA 1999, s 25(2), which lists a variety of bodies with responsibilities for conducting inspection, inquiry or investigation in relation to bodies which are 'best value authorities'.
2 See further para **7.78**.

7.49 'Inspectors' for the purpose of the best value regime are officers, servants or agents of the Audit Commission who carry out an inspection under LGA 1999, s 10[1]. LGA 1999, s 11 gives inspectors rights of access at all reasonable times to documents and information and to require a person to attend before him or her to give information or explanation, or to produce a document. (These rights are comparable to the rights available to auditors in relation to accounts[2].) In addition, inspectors are given a right of access at all reasonable times to premises of the best value authority[3].

1 Local Government Act 1999, s 11(7).
2 Under the Audit Commission Act 1998, s 6.
3 Local Government Act 1999, s 11(1)(a).

7.50 The inspector must give three clear days' notice of any requirements under LGA 1999, s 11[1]. Best value authorities are under an express obligation to provide an inspector with every facility and all information she or he may reasonably require for the purposes of the inspection[2]. LGA 1999, s 11(5) creates an offence for failure to comply, without reasonable excuse, with a requirement of an inspector.

1 Local Government Act 1999, s 11(4).
2 LGA 1999, s 11(3).

7.51 Having undertaken an inspection under s 10, the Audit Commission must issue a report under s 13 mentioning any matter in respect of which the best value authority is failing to comply with the requirements of LGA 1999, Pt I. Where any such failure has been mentioned, the Commission has a discretion, under LGA 1999, s 13(2)(b), to recommend that the Secretary of State gives a direction to the authority under LGA 1999, s 15[1]. The Commission must send a copy of the report to the authority and may publish the report (and any information in respect of the report). If the report recommends that the Secretary of State give a direction under s 15, the Commission is under a duty, as soon as reasonably practicable, to arrange for the recommendation to published and send a copy of the report to the Secretary of State[2]. The authority must record any failure to comply with Part I identified in an inspector's report in its next best value performance plan, together with any action taken by the authority as a result of that report[3].

1 See para **7.57**.
2 Local Government Act 1999, s 13(4).
3 LGA 1999, s 13(5). See paras **7.32–7.35** regarding the performance plan.

7.52 The Audit Commission is required by LGA 1999, s 12 to set a scale of fees for inspections, and the authority is required to pay those fees. The Commission must consult the Secretary of State and persons appearing to the Commission to represent best value authorities before prescribing a scale of fees. As for fees in respect of best value audits, there is discretion for the Commission to depart from the scale rates, where substantially more or less work is involved in a particular inspection.

7.53 Amendments are made by LGA 1999, s 14 to the legislation concerning housing benefit and council tax benefit inspections[1], to allow the Secretary of State to request inspectors who undertake such inspections to consider and report to him on authorities' compliance with the best value requirements under LGA 1999, Pt I.

1 LGA 1999, s 139A(1) and (2) and part of s 139C(1) are substituted in the Social Security Administration Act 1992.

7.54 In relation to police authorities, LGA 1999, s 24(2)–(3) makes amendments to the Police Act 1996, ss 54 and 55 to provide for Her Majesty's Inspectorate of Constabulary to have power to inspect and report to the Secretary of State on police authorities' compliance with the requirements of LGA 1999, Pt I.

7.55 The Audit Commission and various other specified bodies who carry out inspections, inquiries or investigations in relation to best value authorities (such as Her Majesty's Inspector of Schools and persons appointed to carry out an inquiry under the Local Authority Social Services Act 1970[1]) must have regard to any guidance issued by the Secretary of State under LGA 1999, s 25(1) for the purposes of securing co-ordination of different kinds of inspection, inquiry and investigation into best value authorities.

1 See LGA 1999, s 25(2) for the full list of bodies to whom s 25 applies.

3 INTERVENTION BY THE SECRETARY OF STATE

7.56 In the event that the various requirements for plans and reviews under LGA 1999, Pt I, and in the Plans and Reviews Order[1], and in the statutory guidance, backed up by audit and inspection, should all prove inadequate to ensure compliance with the new requirements by best value authorities, the Secretary of State is given extensive powers of intervention under LGA 1999, s 15. A direction given under these powers is enforceable by an order of mandamus on the application of the Secretary of State[2]. Circular 10/99 notes[3] that the Government 'will not hesitate to act where necessary to protect the interest of local people and the users of services'.

1 SI 1999/3251.
2 Local Government Act 1999, s 15(13).
3 See Circular 19/99, para 79.

7.57 The powers of the Secretary of State under LGA 1999, s 15 comprise –

(a) powers to direct a best value authority to:
  (i) prepare or amend a performance plan,
  (ii) follow specified procedures in relation to a performance plan; and
  (iii) carry out a review of its exercise of specified functions[1];

(b) power to direct that a local inquiry be held into the exercise by an authority of specified functions[2];

(c) power to direct a best value authority to take any action which the Secretary of State considers necessary or expedient to secure the authority's compliance with the requirements of LGA 1999, Pt I[3];

(d) powers to direct that a specified function of a best value authority be exercised by:
  (i) the Secretary of State; or
  (ii) a person nominated by the Secretary of State;

  for a specified period, or for so long as the Secretary of State considers appropriate; and that the authority will comply with any instructions of the Secretary of State or his nominee in relation to the exercise of that function and will provide the Secretary of State or his nominee with such assistance as they may require for the purpose of exercising the function[4];

(e) power to make regulations to make provision in relation to an enactment which confers functions on the Secretary of State in respect of a function of a best value authority, where he considers this necessary or expedient for the purposes of a direction given under LGA 1999, s 15(6)(a) (ie where the Secretary of State has directed that he or his nominee should exercise a function of a best value authority); this includes the power to disapply or modify the enactment and may 'have an effect similar to the effect of an enactment of that kind[5]'.

1 Local Government Act 1999, s 15(2).
2 LGA 1999, s 15(3) and (4).
3 LGA 1999, s 15(5).
4 LGA 1999, s 15(6).
5 LGA 1999, s 15(7) and (8).

7.58 An example given in the Explanatory Notes[1] to LGA 1999 of the use of the power to disapply or modify enactments through regulations is local planning functions, which include various rights of appeal to the Secretary of State. In order to ensure that individual rights are properly protected, the Secretary of State would have power, through regulations, to make alternative arrangements in relation to appeals. (Although no indication is given of what these might be.)

1 See para 47 of the Explanatory Notes to LGA 1999.

7.59 In relation to local authorities in Wales, where the powers of the Secretary of State under LGA 1999, s 15[1] are exercisable by the National Assembly for Wales, the Assembly may not make regulations under LGA 1999, s 15(7) which relate to a function conferred on the Secretary of State without his approval[2].

1 And most other provisions of LGA 1999, Pt I: see paras **7.10–7.11**.
2 Local Government Act 1999, s 29(4).

7.60 Prior to giving a direction under LGA 1999, s 15, the Secretary of State must allow the authority an opportunity to make representations about:

(a) the report (if any) which has led to the direction being proposed (ie an audit report[1] or an inspection report[2]); and
(b) the direction the Secretary of State proposes to give.[3]

1 See Local Government Act 1999, s 7(4)(f) and para **7.38**.
2 LGA 1999, s 13(2)(b); and see para **7.51**.
3 LGA 1999, s 15(9).

7.61 By virtue of LGA 1999, s 15(10), where the proposed direction follows a recommendation made by the auditor under LGA 1999, s 7(4)(f)[1], the Secretary of State must have regard to any statement under LGA 1999, s 9 which the authority has sent to him within one month of the authority receiving the auditor's report[2].

1 See para **7.38**.
2 See para **7.40**.

7.62 In cases where the Secretary of State considers that there is sufficient urgency, he may give a direction without considering the authority's representations[1] or any statement from the authority[2]. He must, however, notify the authority concerned, and representatives of best value authorities, of the direction and of the reason why it was given without complying with these requirements[3].

1 Under Local Government Act 1999, s 15(9).
2 LGA 1999, s 15(10).
3 LGA 1999, s 15(11) and (12).

7.63 In November 1997, long before enactment of the Local Government Act 1999, the Secretary of State and the Local Government Association agreed a framework for the use of intervention powers by the Secretary of State which has now been incorporated as a 'Protocol on Intervention Powers' set out as Annex D to Circular 10/99. The basic principles of this Protocol reflect the Secretary of State's general legal responsibilities in the exercise of any such intervention powers, such as the principle that the Secretary of State will only act on the basis of clear evidence of failure and that the form and content of the intervention should reflect the type and seriousness of the authority's failure. A separate protocol has been agreed between the Home Office and the Association of Police Authorities and the Association of Chief Police Officers[1].

1 See Circular 10/99, para 83.

D Ancillary matters

1 THE SECRETARY OF STATE'S FURTHER 'HENRY VIII' AND CONTRACTING OUT POWERS

7.64 One of the most remarkable features of LGA 1999, Pt I is the extent of the powers it includes for the Secretary of State to amend legislation, including primary legislation, through subordinate legislation. An example of this has already been noted in relation to the powers of the Secretary of State under LGA 1999, s 15(7) and (8) to make, as it were, 'consequential amendments' to legislation through regulations, where the Secretary of State has given a direction to take over a function of a best value authority himself, or by a nominee[1]. LGA 1999, s 16 takes this legislative model still further.

1 See para **7.57**(e).

7.65 Under LGA 1999, s 16(1):

> 'If the Secretary of State thinks an enactment prevents or obstructs compliance by best value authorities with the requirements of [the 1999 Act, Pt I] he may by order make provision modifying or excluding the application of the enactment in relation to those authorities'

7.66 Under LGA 1999, s 16(2):

> 'The Secretary of State may by order make provision conferring on best value authorities any power which he considers necessary or expedient to permit or facilitate compliance with the requirements of [Pt I]'.

7.67 An order made under LGA 1999, s 16 may impose conditions on the exercise of any power conferred, amend an enactment, make consequential, incidental and transitional provisions and may make different provision for different cases[1]. In exercising any power which is conferred on a best value authority by an order made by the Secretary of State under LGA 1999, s 16(2), the authority must have regard to any guidance issued by the Secretary of State[2].

1 Local Government Act 1999, s 16(3).
2 LGA 1999, s 16(5).

7.68 Section 18 provides for an extension of the Secretary of State's pre-existing powers under the Deregulation and Contracting Out Act 1994, s 70, to enable the Secretary of State, by order, to authorise the contracting out of the functions of any best value authority. An example given in the Explanatory Notes to LGA 1999 of how this power might be used is to enable best value authorities to contract out housing benefits determination work[1]. Since most, but not all best value authorities are local authorities subject to the Deregulation and Contracting Out Act 1994, s 70 prior to its extension under LGA 1999, s 18, it would appear that the main significance of s 18 would be in relation to bodies which are best value authorities, but which are not local authorities.

1 See the Explanatory Notes to LGA 1999, para 51.

7.69 The report of the House of Lords Select Committee on Delegated Powers and Deregulation[1] contains a memorandum from the DETR which includes an outline of the Government's intentions, as at early 1999, for the use of the order making powers under what were then clauses 15–17 of the Bill, which preceded ss 16–18 of LGA 1999. Annex B to the Report listed the following possible uses for clauses 15–17:

(a) facilitating 'joined-up service delivery' including working across organisational boundaries to provide integrated services[2];
(b) the development of more service delivery models with an emphasis on partnerships[3];
(c) rationalisation of the circumstances where local authorities can provide goods and services to others[4]; and
(d) making better use of local authority assets[5].

1 12th Report, ordered to be printed 14 April 1999, HL Paper 51.
2 This appeared to contemplate a legislative model along the lines of the 'partnership' provisions of the Health Act 1999, s 31 which provides for the pooling of budgets, resources and delegation of functions as between local authorities and NHS bodies, in circumstances prescribed in regulations made by the Secretary of State.
3 This referred to the options of creating new powers for authorities to set up and participate in companies, joint committees and boards, and non-profit making entities including companies limited by guarantee; clarifying powers to participate in joint venture companies and powers for authorities to second or 'loan' staff to any other public, private or voluntary body.
4 Initially by 'streamlining' the operation of the Local Authorities (Goods and Services) Act 1970 (which would not require any new powers); and in the longer term, looking to enable authorities to provide goods and services to anyone in specified circumstances, such as social need.
5 Potentially involving commercial exploitation of local authority assets in order to generate additional resources for core objectives.

7.70 The Explanatory Notes to LGA 1999 (at para 48) suggest that the order-making powers under LGA 1999, s 16(2) might be used to confer on best value authorities a general power[1] to form companies through which to exercise their functions, subject to safeguards and limitations imposed by the Secretary of State. At the time of writing, Government consultation on a draft order under s 16 is awaited[2].

1 See Chapter 16 regarding the current uncertainties which surround local authority powers to form and participate in companies.
2 At the time of writing it is understood that consultation on a draft order under LGA 1999, s 16 may take place in the latter part of 2000. It is not known what, if any, relationship there might be between any order made under LGA 1999, s 16 in relation to companies and any order which might be made under the comparable (although less extensive) powers under the Local Government Act 2000, s 5 in connection with the new local authority function to promote economic, social or environmental well-being (for which no commencement date has been set at the time of writing). The White Paper, *Modern Local Government in Touch with the People*, Cm 4014, July 1998, para 8.24, suggested that the new 'well-being' powers might also be used to tackle the uncertainties surrounding local authority participation in companies and other external bodies (see paras **16.118–16.119** and para **17.51**). In principle, the order making powers under LGA 1999, s 16 appears to offer greater scope to tackle this issue than those under the Local Government Act 2000, s 5, as s 16(2) includes the power to

make provisions which confer *new* powers (but only if the Secretary of State considers it necessary or expedient to permit or facilitate compliance with the best value requirements of LGA 1999, Pt I).

7.71 LGA 1999, ss 16(4) and 17 deal with procedural matters in relation to orders made under LGA 1999, s 16. The Secretary of State must consult authorities or persons who appear to him to be representative of 'interests affected by his proposals'. He must lay before each House of Parliament a document explaining his proposals, including a draft of the order and giving details of the consultation he has conducted. A period of at least 60 days must elapse before a draft of the order to give effect to the proposals (with or without modification) is laid before Parliament. The Secretary of State must consider any representations which are made during this 60-day period. The draft of the order must be laid before, and approved by resolution of, each House. The draft order must be accompanied by a statement of any representations considered during the 60-day period and of any changes made to the proposals as outlined in the earlier explanatory document.

7.72 In relation to local authorities in Wales, the powers to amend legislation, or to authorise the contracting out of functions, by order made by the Secretary of State under LGA 1999, ss 16–18 are not (unlike other powers of the Secretary of State under LGA 1999, Part I) exercisable by the National Assembly for Wales[1], but must be exercised by the appropriate Secretary of State.

1 See Local Government Act 1999, s 29(2)(b) and paras **7.10–7.11**.

2 NON-COMMERCIAL MATTERS

7.73 LGA 1999, s 19 empowers the Secretary of State, by order, to amend the Local Government Act 1988, s 17 in its application to best value authorities. Section 17 of LGA 1988 concerns the 'non-commercial matters' which authorities are expressly prohibited from considering when they invite tenders and award contracts for the supply of goods, materials or services or for the execution of works. The Local Government Act 1988, s 19 already empowers the Secretary of State to *add to* the list of 'non-commercial matters' for the purpose of s 17 of that Act. An order under LGA 1999, s 19 would enable the Secretary of State to specify that a matter should *cease to be* a 'non-commercial matter' for the purpose of s 17 of LGA 1988. LGA 1999, s 19 follows on from a commitment in the White Paper[1] to modernise the procurement provisions of the Local Government Act 1988, Pt II by amending the list of factors which authorities are able to take into account in inviting tenders and awarding contracts. However, it is to be noted that many of the specified 'non-commercial matters' are matters which an authority would be debarred from considering under general principles of administrative law or the EC Treaty.

1 *Modern Local Government: In Touch with the People* Cm 4014, July 1998, para 7.26. The Government had also supported the failed private member's bill, the Local Authorities Tenders Bill, considered by Parliament in 1998, aimed at amending the Local Government Act 1988, s 17.

7.74 A government consultation paper[1] on a draft order under LGA 1999, s 19 was published on 11 April 2000. It proposed that 'workforce matters' should cease to be non-commercial matters 'to the extent that they are relevant to the achievement of best value and TUPE transfers'[2]. At the time of writing, no order has been made under LGA 1999, s 19.

1 *Best Value and Procurement: Handling of Workforce Matters in Contracting*, DETR, April 2000.

2 This is in part intended to enable local authorities to follow government advice on TUPE contained in *Staff Transfers in the Public Sector*: Statement of Practice, Cabinet Office, January 2000.

3 REPEAL OF THE COMPULSORY COMPETITIVE TENDERING REGIME

7.75 Sections 21 and 34 and Sch 2 to LGA 1999 provide for the compulsory competitive tendering ('CCT') regime to cease to have effect on 2 January 2000 and for the repeal of most of the statutory provisions relating to CCT[1]. The Secretary of State is empowered by LGA 1999, s 21(2) to issue guidance to authorities on the exercise of their functions in the period between 2 January 2000 and the date on which the best value regime comes into force (ie 1 April 2000 for local authorities in England and Wales[2]). No guidance has been issued for the purpose of s 21(2).

1 Isolated provisions, such as the Local Government Act 1988, s 33 on local authority companies undertaking defined activities appear to have survived the repeal of other CCT provisions, but, in the case of s 33 at least, it has been rendered redundant with the repeal of the connected definitions such as 'defined activity' under s 2 of the Act.
2 See paras **7.7** and **7.8**.

4 ACCOUNTING REGIME AND PUBLICATION OF INFORMATION

7.76 The Secretary of State is given power by LGA 1999, s 23 to make regulations regarding the accounting requirements which are to apply to best value authorities, covering the form and manner in which accounts are to be prepared, kept and certified, requiring that they be placed on deposit and information about them be published, and giving specified classes of person rights of inspection and to receive copies of specified documents.

7.77 LGA 1999, s 20 extends to all best value authorities the application of the provisions, under the Local Government, Planning and Land Act 1980, s 2, concerning the Secretary of State's powers to issue a code of recommended practice on the publication of information about the discharge of their functions. Prior to its amendment, s 2 applied to some, but not all, of the bodies designated as 'best value authorities' by LGA 1999, s 1(1). The intention is that bodies such as the functional bodies of the Greater London Authority, and the Mayor in exercising the functions of the new authority, should be brought within the ambit of LGPLA 1980, s 2.

5 GENERAL REQUIREMENTS CONCERNING GUIDANCE ISSUED BY THE SECRETARY OF STATE

7.78 LGA 1999, s 26 makes specific provision in relation to the guidance issued by the Secretary of State under Part I. Such guidance may apply to best value authorities generally, or to one or more particular authorities. Different guidance may be issued in respect of different authorities. Before guidance is issued, the Secretary of State must consult *either* best value authorities or persons who appear to the Secretary of State to represent them. He must consult the Audit Commission before issuing guidance under LGA 1999, s 10 (concerning inspections). Before issuing guidance under LGA 1999, s 25, on the co-ordination of inspections, inquiries and investigations by the various persons or bodies listed in LGA 1999, s 25(2), the Secretary of State is to consult the parties concerned[1].

1 Local Government Act 1999, s 26(4).

7.79 The Explanatory Note to LGA 1999 (para 66) indicates that it is intended that LGA 1999, s 26 should provide a general power of the Secretary of State to issue guidance in respect of Part I, to complement the many specific powers to issue guidance (for example, those in relation to the preparation of best value performance plans under LGA 1999, s 6(4), and in relation to inspections under LGA 1999, s 10(4)(b)).

E Conclusions

7.80 The LGA 1999, Pt I, together with the subordinate legislation and guidance issued by the Secretary of State constitute a detailed template for how best value authorities are to approach the task of 'making arrangements' to secure continuous improvement (having regard to a combination of economy, efficiency and effectiveness) in the way in which their various functions are exercised. As regards the procedural framework for achieving 'best value', little of substance is left to the discretion of the authority. In the initial years at least, administration of the best value regime is likely to have a significant impact on the resources, not only of best value authorities, but also of the Audit Commission, auditors and government departments.

7.81 From a legal perspective, the most interesting and challenging aspects of the new regime do not arise from the provisions of LGA 1999, Pt I (with the exception of those relating to the powers of the Secretary of State), but from the host of legal issues which will surround the methods of implementing 'best value arrangements' which best value authorities will seek to explore and pursue. These issues will include employment and industrial relations, procurement, competition, corporate, partnership, taxation and general commercial contractual issues as well as issues going to the heart of their statutory powers and duties, including delegation of functions, fetters on discretion, powers to provide services and staff to others and to establish separate entities or participate in outside bodies in the public, private and voluntary sectors, and powers to trade. Notwithstanding the abolition of CCT, the law relating to contracts and procurement by public bodies will be of continued, if not increasing, importance to best value authorities.

CHAPTER 8

Audit

A Introduction

8.1 This chapter deals with the requirements for audit of local authority accounts. Chapter 9 looks in more detail at some of an external auditor's specific duties and powers in relation to unlawful expenditure and losses and other unlawful action or proposed action by local authorities.

8.2 For a detailed history and explanation of the law relating to local government audit up to 1992 readers are referred to *Local Government Audit Law* by Reginald Jones[1].

1 Her Majesty's Stationary Office, 2nd edn, 1985 (with supplement, 1992). Unfortunately this excellent work has not been updated since that time.

8.3 Where section numbers appear in this chapter without details of any enactment they refer to the provisions of the Audit Commission Act 1998.

B Internal audit

8.4 In most contexts, references to local authority auditors are taken to be references to the external auditors appointed by the Audit Commission, to whom most of this and the following chapter are dedicated. However, local authorities are also required to maintain their own system of internal audit. Internal audit is often seen as one aspect of an authority's general obligation, under the Local Government Act 1972, s 151, to make proper arrangements for the administration of its financial affairs. More specifically, by virtue of the Accounts and Audit Regulations 1996[1], reg 5, local authorities[2] are required to maintain 'an adequate and efficient system of internal audit'.

1 SI 1996/590, made under the Local Government Finance Act 1982, s 23 (now repealed and replaced by the Audit Commission Act 1998, s 27).
2 And other bodies whose accounts are required to be audited under the Audit Commission Act 1998, Pt II: see para **8.21**.

8.5 Under the Accounts and Audit Regulations 1996, reg 5, the internal audit system must cover the local authority's accounting records and control systems. The local authority may require its officers and members to produce documents belonging to the authority which relate to its accounting and other records and which appear to it necessary for the purpose of the internal audit. Officers and members may also be required to supply such information and explanation as the authority considers necessary for the purpose of internal audit.

1 GUIDANCE ON INTERNAL AUDIT

8.6 Guidance for local authorities on internal audit is produced by the Chartered Institute of Public Finance and Accountancy (CIPFA). CIPFA issued guidance for local authorities in 1993[1] based on the 1990 Auditing Practices Board ('APB') internal auditing guideline. The CIPFA guidance is currently being updated to take account of developments in such areas as 'best value' (see Chapter 7), corporate governance and risk management, the modernisation of political arrangements in local government (see Chapter 1 on proposals for reform) and rapid changes in legislation. It is said that whilst the principles of the APB guidelines remain valid, the way in which they are to be interpreted has changed. At the time of writing, consultation on a draft *Code of Practice for Internal Audit in Local Government*[2] ('the draft Code') has been undertaken. CIPFA intends to publish the updated Code in October 2000, to be followed by a detailed audit manual for internal audit in local government[3]. The following is based on the contents of the *draft* Code (thus, the final version should be referred to, once available).

1 Entitled *Application of the APB's Guideline for Internal Auditors' in Local Government*, CIPFA (1993).
2 Consultative draft issued by CIPFA in April 2000.
3 Currently planned for publication during 2001.

2 DRAFT CODE OF PRACTICE

8.7 The draft Code recommends that the powers and responsibilities of internal audit should be based on the APB guideline, which emphasises two key attributes:

(a) independence; and
(b) a requirement to review and report upon the organisation's internal control mechanism.

8.8 The draft Code advises that the local authority's management should be responsible for agreeing the overall strategy and terms of reference of internal audit, whilst the head of audit should be responsible for agreeing the detail. The need for the objectives of internal audit to take account of the objectives of the organisation as a whole is highlighted. The 'organisational objectives' of internal audit are apparently wide, being said to include:

(a) developing and implementing the organisation's policies;
(b) meeting the organisation's objectives;
(c) complying with laws and regulations;
(d) that financial statements and other published information are accurate and reliable;
(e) managing human, financial and other resources efficiently and effectively;
(f) meeting social concerns, including environmental and community concerns; and
(g) that an anti-fraud and corruption environment exists.

8.9 As noted, it is emphasised that one essential prerequisite for an effective internal audit function is independence. In many local authorities, internal audit is treated as one of the functions of the chief finance officer[1]. The draft Code indicates that it is for the individual local authority to decide where internal audit fits best within its management structure, but the associated status must ensure that it can function effectively and independently; the head of internal audit should report directly to the responsible finance officer and 'the scrutiny function[2]' of the authority, and not at any lower level within the organisation. The head of internal audit should have freedom of access and reporting avenues to all officers and members, especially to the Chief Executive and the monitoring officer[3] (as well as to officials of 'partner organisations'). It is recommended that internal auditors should not have operational responsibilities outside audit.

1 The person appointed by a local authority to be responsible for its financial affairs under the Local Government Act 1972, s 151. Treating internal audit as part of this officer's functions is consistent with the concept of internal audit forming part of the proper administration of the authority's financial affairs: see para **8.4**.

2 This reference looks ahead to the new executive structures to be implemented under the Local Government Act 2000. Under Pt II of that Act, once in force, local authorities are to be required to establish special committees to scrutinise the discharge of the executive functions of the authority.

3 Designated under the Local Government and Housing Act 1989, s 5.

8.10 The head of internal audit is advised to present an annual report to senior management and to the 'scrutiny function' on the performance of the internal audit function, and expressing a view on the adequacy of the organisation's internal control systems.

C District audit; the Audit Commission; bodies subject to audit; the appointment of auditors

1 THE DISTRICT AUDIT SERVICE

8.11 The District Audit Service was founded following the Poor Law Amendment Act 1844, to examine the accounts of districts of the Poor Law 'unions' of parishes, predecessors of local government in England in Wales. Until the Local Government Act 1972 came into force[1], the District Audit Service was responsible for the audit of most[2] local authority accounts. Today, private sector auditors may also audit local authority accounts and District Audit operates as an arm's length agency of the Audit Commission.

1 On 1 April 1974.

2 Prior to April 1974, boroughs had the option to operate a system under which two 'elective auditors' were chosen annually by local government electors and one 'mayor's auditor' was appointed by the mayor from amongst the councillors. Elective auditors were not required to have any professional qualifications (although they had to be qualified for election as a councillor and could not be either a member or an officer of the council). The system of elective auditors was criticised by the High Court as being 'quite illusory' (see *A-G v De Winton* [1906] 2 Ch 106 at 119, per Farwell J). However, on the abolition of this system by the Local Government Act 1972 in 1974, some 21 boroughs still had elective auditors.

2 THE AUDIT COMMISSION

8.12 The origins of the Audit Commission lie in the recommendations of the *Layfield Committee of Inquiry into Local Government Finance*[1] in 1976, that the audit service should be made independent of both central and local government, and that it was wrong in principle that public bodies should be in a position to choose their own auditors. The Audit Commission was established on 21 January 1983 under the Local Government Finance Act 1982, s 11 and its existence is continued under the Audit Commission Act 1998, s 1. The proper title of the Commission is the Audit Commission for Local Authorities and the National Health Service in England and Wales, but in this and the next chapter we concentrate on its functions in relation to local authorities and refer to it as 'the Audit Commission', or simply 'the Commission'.

1 Cmnd 6453, 1976.

8.13 The Audit Commission is a statutory body corporate which consists of no less than 15, nor more than 20 members appointed by the Secretary of State following consultation with such bodies as appear to him to be appropriate[1]. Neither the Audit Commission, nor its members and officers, are to be regarded as having Crown status[2]. The Secretary of State may give directions to the Commission on the discharge of its functions and the Commission must give effect to any such directions[3]. The Audit Commission Act 1998, Sch 1 provides for constitutional matters relating to the Commission, its members and officers. The Commission operates on a self-financing basis, largely through its income from fees for audit work charged to local authorities and National Health Service bodies.

1 Audit Commission Act 1998, s 1 and Sch 1, para 1.
2 ACA 1998, Sch 1, para 2.
3 ACA 1998, Sch 1, para 3. Thus the recommendations of the Layfield Committee in relation to independence, at least in relation to the Commission itself, were not entirely fulfilled. See para **8.35**ff regarding the independence of auditors.

8.14 In 1990, the statutory functions of the Audit Commission were extended to apply to National Health Service authorities, trusts and other bodies[1]. In 1992, its functions were extended by the Local Government Act 1992 to include duties to direct local authorities to publish, annually, comparative indicators of their performance[2]. As outlined in Chapter 7, the role of the Commission has been still further expanded in relation to audit and inspection under the best value regime created by the Local Government Act 1999, Pt I. The functions of the Commission now extend to the Greater London Authority and its four functional bodies[3]. During 2000, the work of the Audit Commission was examined by the Environment, Transport and Regional Affairs Committee of the House of Commons, which made a number of recommendations for change and expressed concern about the new role of the Commission in relation to best value inspections[4].

1 By virtue of the National Health Service and Community Care Act 1990, s 20.
2 See Audit Commission Act 1998, ss 44–47.
3 By virtue of the Greater London Authority Act 1999, s 133 and Sch 8. In force in relation to the Greater London Authority: 8 May 2000, and in relation to the functional bodies (Transport for London, the London Development Agency, the Metropolitan Police Authority and the London Fire and Emergency Planning Authority): 3 July 2000 (see SI 1999/3434).
4 See the Tenth Report of the Committee, Parliamentary Session 1999–2000, HC 174-1, 14 June 2000.

(a) Codes of practice

8.15 The Commission is responsible for preparing and keeping under review a code of audit practice under the Audit Commission Act 1998, s 4. That code must be approved by resolution of each House of Parliament before it comes into force. At the time of writing, the most recent Code of Audit Practice came into force on 29 March 2000[1]. This code includes transitional provisions for audit work which relates to financial years ending on or before 31 March 2000, carried out before

31 December 2000[2]. Its remaining provisions apply to audit work which relates to financial years ending on or after 31 March 2001. ('The Code of Audit Practice'.)

1 Subject to transitional provisions, to replace that in effect from July 1995. The Code of Audit Practice March 2000 has (separately bound) Transitional Provisions, and a related document entitled Statement of Responsibilities of Auditors and Audited Bodies was issued at the same time as the Code.
2 Based on the code which came into effect on 21 July 1995. The transitional provisions lapse as from 1 January 2001.

8.16 Under the Local Government Act 1999, s 8 the Audit Commission is also required to prepare and keep under review a code of practice prescribing the way in which auditors are to carrying out their functions in relation to the audit of best value performance plans (see Chapter 7 and, in particular, para **7.41**).

(b) Maintaining proper standards in the audit of accounts

8.17 The Audit Commission has a role in maintaining proper standards in the auditing of accounts of bodies subject to the Audit Commission Act 1998 through its responsibilities under s 4 in relation to the preparation of the code of audit practice. In addition, the Commission has specific powers to require audited bodies to produce accounts and certain other documents to assist it in maintaining proper audit standards[1].

1 See Audit Commission Act 1998, s 48(3).

(c) Other functions of the Audit Commission

8.18 In addition to its functions regarding audits and the appointment of the auditors, the Audit Commission Act 1998, Pt III makes the Audit Commission responsible for promoting or undertaking a range of studies, reports and recommendations aimed at assessing or advising on economy, efficiency and effectiveness in local government[1] services, or on the financial or other management of the body concerned, including:

(a) undertaking comparative and other studies to enable the Commission to make recommendations on the improvement of economy, efficiency and effectiveness in the exercise of functions by best value authorities and in the provision of services by other bodies subject to audit, and improving the financial and other management of bodies subject to audit[2];
(b) undertaking studies and preparing reports in relation to the impact of the operation of particular statutory provisions, or of directions or guidance issued by a Minister of the Crown on economy, efficiency and effectiveness in the provision of local authority services or on their financial management[3];
(c) undertaking studies at the request of a local authority, certain educational and other bodies[4];
(d) undertaking studies at the request of the Secretary of State into the discharge of social services functions, or into housing benefit or council tax benefit administration[5];
(e) undertaking a programme of comparative studies, generally with the agreement of the Housing Corporation, to enable the Commission to make recommendations for improving the economy, efficiency and effectiveness of registered social landlords[6].

1 And in relation to other bodies subject to audit under the Audit Commission Act 1998.
2 Audit Commission Act 1998, s 33. For 'best value authorities' see Local Government Act 1999, s 1 (referred to at paras **7.12–7.14**).
3 ACA 1998, s 34.
4 ACA 1998, ss 35 and 36. Under s 35A, studies may be undertaken in relation to a functional body at the request of the Mayor of London. Magistrates' courts committees may also request the Commission to promote or undertake studies (under the Justices of the Peace Act 1997, s 39).
5 ACA 1998, ss 37 and 38.
6 ACA 1998, s 40. Or in agreement with the National Assembly for Wales, in relation to registered social landlords in Wales.

8.19 Over the years since 1982, the Commission has published a wealth of information on the activities and performance of local authorities. The Commission also publishes a series of Technical Releases for auditors which cover a wide range of legal matters and issues affecting audited bodies, many of which are of considerable practical assistance to local authorities. As noted above, by virtue of the Audit Commission Act 1998, ss 44–47 the Commission is empowered to direct local authorities to publish information annually on their activities and standards of performance.

8.20 The duties of the Commission in respect of confidentiality under the Audit Commission Act 1998, s 49 are referred to in para **8.39**ff, along with those of auditors.

3 BODIES SUBJECT TO AUDIT UNDER THE AUDIT COMMISSION ACT 1998

8.21 The bodies whose accounts are subject to audit under the Audit Commission Act 1998 are specified in ACA 1998, Sch 2 and include 'local authorities'[1], the Greater London Authority and its four 'functional bodies'[2], the Council of the Isles of Scilly, joint authorities, parish meetings[3], committees and joint committees of local authorities, police authorities established under the Police Act 1996, s 3, fire authorities constituted by a combination scheme, probation committees and bodies such as National Park authorities and the Broads Authority. The bodies listed in Sch 2 are referred to in ACA 1998 as 'bodies subject to audit'.

1 See para **8.22**.
2 Transport for London, the London Development Agency, the Metropolitan Police Authority and the London Fire and Emergency Planning Authority.
3 Where there is no separate parish council.

8.22 For the purposes of the Audit Commission Act 1998, 'local authority' is defined as in the Local Government Act 1972, s 270[1] to encompass county, district, London Borough and parish councils, and county borough and community councils in Wales.

1 The general interpretation provisions of the Local Government Act 1972, s 270 apply to the Audit Commission Act 1998 by virtue of ACA 1998, s 53(2) (subject to para 11(5) of Sch 1 of ACA 1998 regarding the definition of 'financial year' for the purpose of that Schedule).

8.23 Local authorities and other bodies subject to audit under the Audit Commission Act 1998 must make up their accounts to 31 March[1] each year. Those accounts must be audited, in accordance with the ACA 1998, by an auditor or auditors appointed by the Audit Commission[2].

1 Or such other date as the Secretary of State may generally, or in a special case, direct: see the Audit Commission Act 1998, s 2(1)(a).
2 Audit Commission Act 1998, s 2(1)(b).

8.24 In this and the following chapter, the text concentrates on the statutory and other provisions as they apply to local authorities (rather than other bodies subject to audit under the Audit Commission Act 1998).

4 APPOINTMENT OF AUDITORS

8.25 From 1974[1] until 1983[2] local authorities were entitled to choose whether their accounts should be audited by a district auditor[3], or by an 'approved auditor', ie a private auditor appointed by the audited body and approved by the Secretary of State.

1 When the Local Government Act 1972 came into force.
2 With the commencement of relevant provisions of the Local Government Finance Act 1982.
3 At this time, appointed by the Secretary of State with the consent of the Minister for the Civil Service.

8.26 The Audit Commission now exercises the choice in the appointment of an auditor to audit the accounts of a local authority. (Audit Commission Act 1998, s 3(1)). The appointee may be:

(a) an officer of the Commission (ie a district auditor[1]);
(b) an individual who is not an officer of the Commission; or
(c) a firm of individuals who are not officers of the Commission.

Before appointing an auditor, the Commission is required to consult the local authority concerned[2]. District auditors and private sector auditors are now referred to as 'appointed auditors'. In general, the following text applies to both types of external auditor.

1 Whilst the Act itself no longer refers to 'district auditors', the Commission continues to designate its officers by that title.
2 Audit Commission Act 1998, s 3(3).

8.27 The person to be appointed must be a member of one or more specified professional bodies[1], or have such other qualifications as may be approved for this purpose by the Secretary of State (or have been approved by the Secretary of State before 1 April 1996 under former legislation).

1 See the Audit Commission Act 1998, s 3(7); the specified bodies include CIPFA and the Institute of Chartered Accountants in England and Wales.

8.28 In practice, some 70% of local government audits are undertaken by district auditors as opposed to private firms of accountants. In recent years, on occasion, auditors have been appointed following a competitive process undertaken by the Commission.

D Functions, role and liabilities of external auditors

1 COMMON LAW FUNCTIONS

8.29 The role of the district auditor was described by Lord Denning in *Asher v Secretary of State for the Environment* [1974] Ch 208 at 219, in the following way:

'The district auditor holds a position of much responsibility. In some respects he is like a company auditor. He is a watchdog to see that the accounts are properly kept and that no one is making off with the funds. He is not bound to be of a suspicious turn of mind: see *In re Kingston Cotton Mill Co (No 2)* [1896] 2 Ch 279; but, if anything suspicious does turn up, it is his duty to take care to follow it up: see *In re Thomas Gerrard & Son Ltd* [1968] Ch 455. In other respects, however, the duties of a district auditor go far beyond those of a company auditor. He must see whether, on the financial side, the councillors and their officers have discharged their duties according to law. He must listen to any elector who makes objection to the accounts. He must make his own investigation also.'

8.30 Over the years since *Asher* was decided, the functions of local government auditors have been extended by statute. The position remains that an auditor's functions go far beyond those of a company auditor.

2 STATUTORY FUNCTIONS

8.31 The general statutory duties of auditors in auditing accounts are set out in the Audit Commission Act 1998, s 5. They include duties for the auditor to satisfy himself or herself:

(a) that the accounts are prepared in accordance with the Accounts and Audit Regulations 1996[1];
(b) that the accounts comply with the requirements of all other statutory provisions applicable to the accounts;
(c) that proper practices[2] have been observed in the compilation of the accounts;
(d) that the body whose accounts are being audited has made proper arrangements for securing economy, efficiency and effectiveness in its use of resources; and
(e) that the body, if required to publish information in pursuance of a direction under ACA 1998, s 44 (performance information), has made such arrangements for collecting and recording the information and for publishing it as are required for the performance of its duties under that section.

1 Or other regulations made under s 27.
2 For the meaning of 'proper practices', see the LGHA 1989, s 66(4) and (5). The Code of Practice on Local Authority Accounting in the United Kingdom, produced annually by CIPFA, currently constitutes a proper accounting practice for local authorities in England and Wales.

8.32 In carrying out his or her duties, the auditor is required to comply with the code of audit practice applicable to the accounts being audited, which is for the time being in force[1].

1 Audit Commission Act 1998, s 5(2). See para **8.15**.

8.33 Specific statutory functions of auditors in relation to expenditure and other matters involving actual or potential unlawfulness *currently* include:

(a) the duty to consider whether to make a report in the public interest on any matter which comes to his or her attention in the course of the audit[1];
(b) the discretion to apply to the court for a declaration that an item of account is contrary to law[2];
(c) the duty to 'surcharge' for failure to account or loss through wilful misconduct[3];

(d) the discretion to issue a prohibition order in respect of any decision or action of the audited body which would lead to unlawful expenditure or is likely to cause a loss or deficiency[4]; and
(e) the discretion to apply for judicial review of a decision or failure of a local authority which it is reasonable to believe would have an effect on its accounts[5].

1 Audit Commission Act 1998, s 8.
2 ACA 1998, s 17.
3 ACA 1998, s 18.
4 ACA 1998, s 20.
5 ACA 1998, s 24.

8.34 Items (b)–(e) are discussed in Chapter 9, together with prospective repeal of certain of these provisions under the Local Government Act 2000. Chapter 7 outlines the further functions of auditors in relation to the best value regime, including recommendations to the Commission on the need to carry out a best value inspection under the Local Government Act 1999, s 10, and recommendations to the Secretary of State in relation to his or her powers of intervention by way of direction under LGA 1999, s 15.

3 INDEPENDENCE OF AUDITORS

8.35 Case law and statements by ministers over the years have established the principle of the independence of district auditors from control by government departments and ministers of the Crown. In *R (Bridgeman) v Drury* [1894] 2 IR 489 the court firmly rejected any notion of departmental supremacy, or that the Local Government Board had any right to interfere with the auditor. The court asserted that 'the whole value of [the auditor's] office consists of his independence'. Thus, an appointed auditor may not lawfully be removed from office because the Audit Commission (or a government minister) disapproves of his or her decision in the discharge of his or her statutory functions.

8.36 As noted, auditors are required to comply with the code of practice produced by the Audit Commission[1] and the Commission is itself subject to direction by the Secretary of State[2]. However, the Code of Audit Practice emphasises the independence of auditors from the Commission and the need for auditors to maintain their independence and objectivity[3]. Once appointed under the Audit Commission Act 1998, s 3, the Commission would have no right to interfere in the exercise of the professional skill and judgment of an auditor carrying out his or her statutory functions in relation to the audit of accounts. The Commission endeavours to maintain the independent status of the District Audit Service by securing that it is operated on an arm's length basis from the Commission.

1 Audit Commission Act 1998, s 5(2).
2 ACA 1998, Sch 1, para 3.
3 See the foreword to the Code of Audit Practice, p 1 and para 13ff.

8.37 Auditors are required[1] not to undertake work for a body subject to audit which does not relate directly to the auditor's functions, if this would impair the auditor's independence or create a reasonable perception that his or her independence might be impaired.

1 Code of Audit Practice, para 15.

8.38 In practice, local government auditors are regularly asked to express a view on the legality, accounting treatment, or value for money aspects of a transaction which is under consideration by a local authority whose accounts they audit. Whilst auditors are encouraged to be as helpful as possible in these circumstances, they are precluded from giving any definite view if to do so would prejudice their independence, for example, by being involved in the local authority's decision-making processes, or by impairing the auditor's ability to deal with objections impartially, or by fettering the exercise of other powers and duties under the Audit Commission Act 1998 which arise regardless of whether any valid objection is made. The Statement of Responsibilities of Auditors and Audited Bodies (a separate document issued at the same time as the Code of Audit Practice) advises that in responding to ad hoc requests for their views, auditors can be expected to offer only an indication as to whether any information available to them at the time is likely to cause them to consider exercising specific powers conferred by statute[1]. Auditors are reminded[2] that they are not financial or legal advisers to the audited body (which must obtain its own professional advice).

1 See the Statement of Responsibilities of Auditors and Audited Bodies, para 48.
2 See the Statement of Responsibilities of Auditors and Audited Bodies, para 47.

4 CONFIDENTIALITY

8.39 No information relating to a particular body or person obtained by an auditor (or by the Commission) in the course of an audit or study or pursuant to any provision of the Audit Commission Act 1998 may be disclosed save in specified circumstances[1]. Criminal sanctions apply to a contravention of these requirements[2].

1 Audit Commission Act 1998, s 49(1).
2 ACA 1998, s 49(3).

8.40 The exceptional circumstances where disclosure is not prohibited by ACA 1998, s 49(1) include disclosure:

(a) with the consent of the body or person to whom the information relates[1];
(b) for the purposes of any functions of the auditor (or the Commission) under the Act;
(c) for the purposes of the functions of the Secretary of State relating to social security;
(d) in accordance with ACA 1998, s 37(6) (disclosure by the Commission to the Secretary of State of specified information for the purposes of his functions in connection with the local authority social services functions) or in accordance with ACA 1998, s 41(4) (disclosure by the Commission to the Relevant Authority[2] of information obtained in the course of a study under ACA 1998, s 40 relating to registered social landlords); and
(e) for the purposes of any criminal proceedings.

1 See para **8.42**, n 1.
2 The Housing Corporation or the National Assembly for Wales (see the Housing Act 1996, s 56 and SI 1999/672).

8.41 Thus, the auditor is not prohibited from disclosing information by way of a report in the public interest under ACA 1998, s 8, or in any other circumstance where disclosure is necessary in order to discharge any other statutory function under the Audit Commission Act 1998, or for the purposes of any criminal proceedings.

8.42 In *Bookbinder v Tebbit (No 2)* [1992] 1 WLR 217, the court set aside subpoenas duces tecum and ad testificandum served by a plaintiff in a libel action on employees of the Audit Commission in order to obtain evidence and documents from audit staff. Although the local authority had given its consent for the purpose of the statutory provision which preceded ACA 1998, s 49, the information also related to other people who had not given their consent[1]. Drake J found two further grounds for setting aside the subpoenas: (a) public interest immunity applied to investigations carried out by appointed auditors; and (b) the plaintiff had not shown that audit evidence was necessary to dispose fairly of the case.

1 Drake J also found that a person who provides information to an auditor is 'a person to whom the information relates' and whose consent is therefore required for the purposes of what is now s 49(1)(a).

8.43 In dealing with questions and objections from the public, the Code of Audit Practice reminds auditors that without the consent of the audited body, they should not disclose information about transactions which are not reflected in the accounts, nor should auditors disclose personal information about remuneration or other benefits paid to the body's staff[1]. However, where auditors are considering action under ss 8, 17 or 18, the Code states[2] that, at the appropriate time, they should make available to the parties (including any objector) any documents which they consider to be material to their decision, 'so far as is consistent with the good conduct of their enquiries and the principle of fairness[3]'.

1 Schedule 1 to the Code of Audit Practice, at para S1.7. See also the Audit Commission Act 1998, s 15(3) and (5) referred to in para **8.81**.
2 At Sch 1, para S1.11 of the Code (see para **9.39**).
3 As noted in para **8.40**, under ACA 1998, s 49(1)(b) there is an exception to the prohibition on disclosure of certain information, where disclosure is made for the purposes of the functions of an auditor.

5 NATURE OF AUDIT JURISDICTION

(a) General

8.44 Case law indicates that in exercising certain of their functions, auditors act in a judicial or quasi-judicial capacity, rather than in an administrative capacity (ie in a comparable position to a judge making decisions with legal effect subject to appeal, as opposed to exercising discretionary powers based on policy pursuant to statute). This applies particularly in relation to auditors' functions of 'surcharge', under what is now the Audit Commission Act 1998, s 18, but has also been suggested in relation to various other functions of an auditor.

8.45 As it is now established[1] that the duties to act fairly and in accordance with natural justice apply to administrative decisions which affect individual rights and interests, the question of whether audit proceedings have a judicial or an administrative nature is for many purposes of little practical significance, save in relation to such matters as the ability to take evidence on oath, privilege in respect of defamation and whether the auditor is bound to provide for an oral hearing[2].

1 *Ridge v Baldwin* [1964] AC 40.
2 In relation to the question of immunity from liability in tort, see the *Garland* case referred to in para **8.52**ff, which suggests that auditors would have no general immunity from such actions.

8.46 In *Lloyd v McMahon* [1987] AC 625, having described the auditor's function as 'quasi-judicial'[1] the court concluded that because the auditor's function in relation to what is now the Audit Commission Act 1998, s 17 (declaration) and s 18 ('surcharge') is in part inquisitorial, the role of the auditor was not identical to that of a judge. Whilst there was a clear duty to act fairly, there was no rigid requirement for an oral hearing[2].

1 [1987] AC 625 at 663E, per Woolf LJ.
2 [1987] AC 625 at 664F.

8.47 In *Porter v Magill* (1997) 96 LGR 157 (decided prior to the commencement of the Human Rights Act 1998), the Divisional Court (per Rose LJ at 168) observed that it appeared that the roles played by an auditor (investigator, prosecutor[1] and judge) would not meet the requirements of independence and impartiality demanded by the European Convention on Human Rights, art 6 (the right to a fair and public hearing to determine civil rights, by an independent and impartial tribunal). However, the roles of the auditor were laid down by Parliament in clear and unambiguous terms. Further, it was noted that art 6 was concerned with the procedure as a whole (*Bryan v United Kingdom* (1995) 21 EHRR 342). The audit procedure includes an appeal to the High Court, giving the appellants the right to an appeal to a judicial body that has full jurisdiction and does provide the guarantees of art 6(1). (The court had also recorded that, in accordance with RSC Ord 55, r 3, the appeal had been conducted by way of a re-hearing[2].) The specific issues referred to in this paragraph were not dealt with in the judgment of the Court of Appeal in *Porter v Magill* (1999) 97 LGR 375[3].)

1 It is submitted that the use of this word is misleading. An auditor has no function as a 'prosecutor'.
2 See para **9.78** regarding the position under the Civil Procedure Rules 1998 (CPR).
3 The points arose in the context of fairness. On appeal, Kennedy LJ did not consider it necessary to consider issues of fairness in view of his finding on the liability of the appellants. The judgment of Schiemann LJ regarding fairness does not address the question of the status of the auditor in relation to the requirements of the ECHR, art 6.

(b) Intervention by auditor in the exercise of discretion by a local authority

8.48 In deciding whether to intervene in the decision of a local authority involving its exercise of its statutory discretion, the auditor is required to apply the general administrative law principles enunciated in *Associated Provincial Picture Houses Ltd v Wednesbury Corpn* [1948] 1 KB 223; *Giddens v Harlow District Council* (1972) 70 LGR 485. The meaning of 'contrary to law', the ground on which an auditor may intervene by seeking a declaration from the court under s 17 in relation to an item of account, was described by the Court of Appeal in *Hazell v Hammersmith and Fulham London Borough Council* [1990] 2 QB 697 at 768 in short, as being where that item is for any reason unlawful or improper[1].

1 See the full passage cited at para **9.10**.

6 AVAILABILITY OF JUDICIAL REVIEW IN RELATION TO DECISIONS AND OTHER ACTION BY AUDITORS

8.49 The decisions made by an auditor appointed under the Audit Commission Act 1998, s 3 are amenable to challenge by way of judicial review, at least where there is no statutory right of appeal against the decision in question. One example of this was the Irish case of *State (Deane) v Moran* (1953) 88 ILTR 37, where an application for mandamus was made in relation to an auditor's decision that an objection was not valid.

8.50 Applications for judicial review have been made in relation to auditors' public interest reports under what is now the Audit Commission Act 1998, s 8. Whilst the court expressed doubt as to the availability of judicial review in this context[1], since the auditor makes no determination in such a report (any views expressed being only provisional), the parties and the court may agree to the court accepting limited jurisdiction in order to find a swift and convenient means of determining a legal issue[2].

1 See *R v District Auditor No 3 Audit District of West Yorkshire Metropolitan County Council, ex p West Yorkshire Metropolitan County Council* [1986] RVR 24.
2 *R v District Auditor for Leicester, ex p Leicester City Council* [1985] RVR 191 (affirmed on appeal [1989] 29 RVR 162).

8.51 More recently, two separate applications for permission to apply for judicial review were made by local government officers in respect of two public interest reports made by an auditor under the statutory provision which preceded ACA 1998, s 8[1] on grounds of irrationality and procedural impropriety. The reports were critical of officers and the council terminated the contract of employment of one officer and suspended another. However, in each case, leave to apply was refused, in part on grounds of delay in bringing the applications. In *R v District Auditor for Isle of Anglesey County Council, ex p Jones*, the Court of Appeal (23 July 1999, unreported)[2] found that such reports by an auditor were, in principle, susceptible to judicial review, but it would rarely be appropriate to give permission for proceedings to go ahead because the purpose of the report was to bring matters to the attention of the local authority to enable it to investigate. In *R v District Auditor for Isle of Anglesey County Council, ex p Owen* (13 December 1999, unreported), Tucker J found that the proper way for the officer to complain was in the disciplinary proceedings which ensued.

1 Local Government Finance Act 1982, s 15(3).
2 The decision of the Divisional Court was reported at (1999) 1 LGLR 626.

7 LIABILITIES OF AUDITORS

8.52 The liabilities of auditors appointed under the Local Government Finance Act 1982[1] to the bodies they audit and others was considered in *West Wiltshire District Council v Garland* [1995] Ch 297, CA, which concerned a striking out application in respect of parts of a claim made by former local government officers for a contribution from the council's auditor to any amounts for which they might be found liable in proceedings brought against them by the local authority for breach of contract and fiduciary duties.

1 The relevant provisions of which were replaced by the Audit Commission Act 1998.

8.53 The Court of Appeal affirmed the first instance decision that it was arguable that auditors appointed under LGFA 1982 owe the local authority a statutory duty of care and a breach of that duty would give the authority a right of action against an auditor. The court noted that the legislation made no explicit provision for securing the due performance of the auditor's duties and that an application for judicial review by a local authority would not be an appropriate remedy to secure damages. The court considered that auditors might also owe a common law duty of care to the body whose accounts they audit, the breach of which might give rise to an action in negligence. It was not so clear that remedies for negligence and in breach of statutory duty in tort could not co-exist so as to justify the striking out. No appeal was made in respect of the first instance decision that the auditor owed the officers themselves no duty, whether by statute or at common law, in relation to the audit. The case was eventually settled before the main hearing and the question of whether an auditor may be liable in tort remains for decision in another case.

E The audit process

1 CURRENT ACCOUNT AUDIT

8.54 External audit of local authority accounts is a continual process, although, as explained below, there are specific requirements for year end audits. Historically, local government accounts were only subject to audit under the relevant legislation[1] once the accounts had been closed, but this is no longer the case. Since the enactment of the Local Government Act 1972, the relevant legislation has made no express provision regarding the time at which the external audit was to be undertaken, and since 1982, the legislation has made clear that the auditor should have access to relevant documents at *all* reasonable times. The Audit Commission Act 1998, s 6(1) now provides:

> 'An auditor has a right of access at all reasonable times to every document relating to a body subject to audit which appears to him necessary for the purposes of his functions under this Act.'

1 Under the Local Government Act 1933 and earlier legislation.

8.55 There is no fixed date for the opening of the audit and the auditor is not constrained only to act during the course of an end of year or extraordinary audit. It would appear that his or her functions under ACA 1998 would come into play even where accounts have not been formally written up. Equally, there would appear to be nothing in the legislation which would prevent an auditor examining a matter arising from accounts which have been formally closed, although in practice it seems likely that this would occur only in exceptional circumstances, such as fraud.

2 YEAR END AUDIT

(a) Timing

8.56 Whilst there is no prescribed time at which the audit is to be undertaken, the Accounts and Audit Regulations 1996 do envisage that the local authority's accounts will be made up each year by a specified date, that there will then be an audit of those accounts, and that the public will be given notice to enable local electors to object to the accounts for each financial year (and that this opportunity will be afforded *before* the audit has been concluded). The Audit Commission Act 1998 specifies the duties of the auditor in relation to the audit without stipulating a time at which the audit itself must be undertaken. The Code of Audit Practice assumes that the financial audit will normally be complete within nine months after the end of the financial year in question[1].

1 See para **8.58**.

8.57 Under the ACA 1998 and the Accounts and Audit Regulations 1996, the broad sequence of events is as follows:

(a) the local authority must prepare, in accordance with 'proper practices[1]', a statement of accounts for each period up to 31 March each year[2]; that statement must include the information prescribed in reg 6 and the authority must ensure that the statement has been prepared in accordance with the Accounts and Audit Regulations[3];
(b) the statement of accounts must be signed and dated by the chief finance officer[4] and certified as presenting fairly the financial position of the authority at the end of the period to which it relates, and its income and expenditure for the period[5];
(c) the signed and certified statement must be approved by a resolution of a committee, or the full council, of the local authority as soon as reasonably practicable, and in any event within six months after the end of the period to which the statement relates (ie by 30 September immediately following the end of the relevant financial year[6]);
(d) the local authority must publish the statement of accounts, by whichever is the *earlier* of:
    (i) as soon as reasonably possible after the conclusion of an audit; or
    (ii) nine months from the day following the end of the period to which the accounts relate (ie by 1 January immediately following the end of the relevant financial year);

    together with either any certificate, opinion or report given or made by the auditor under ACA 1998, s 9, or a declaration and explanation of the fact that, as at the date of publication, no such opinion has been given by the auditor[7];
(e) the local authority must give notice by advertisement of public rights under ACA 1998, ss 15 and 16, at least 14 days before the beginning of the period during which the accounts and other documents are made available for public inspection under the next item[8];
(f) the local authority must make its accounts and the other documents referred to in ACA 1998, s 15(1) available for public inspection for 15 full working days before the day appointed by the auditor under the next item[9];
(g) the auditor must appoint a day on or after which local government electors may exercise their rights under ACA 1998, s 15(2) (to question the auditor about the accounts) or s 16(1) (to attend before the auditor)[10];
(h) as soon as reasonably possible after the conclusion of an audit, the local authority must give notice by advertisement that the audit has been concluded and that the statement of accounts is available for inspection by local government electors. The statement must be made available for inspection together with other specified items, including a statement of any amendments or alterations required as a result of an auditor's report and of the rights of local government electors under ACA 1998, s 14 to inspect the statement of accounts and any auditor's report[11].

1 'Proper practices' are defined by the Local Government and Housing Act 1989, s 66(4) as being accounting practices which the authority is required to follow by virtue of any enactment, or practices which are regarded as proper accounting practices by reference to any generally recognised code or otherwise. By virtue of LGHA 1989, s 66(5), this definition applies for the purposes of the Audit Commission Act 1998.
2 Or such other date as the Secretary of State may direct generally or in any special case: see the Audit Commission Act 1998, s 2(1).
3 Accounts and Audit Regulations 1996, regs 6(1) and 8(1).

4 That is, the person responsible for the authority's financial affairs for the purpose of the Local Government Act, 1972.
5 Accounts and Audit Regulations 1996, reg 8(3).
6 A&AR 1996, reg 8(2).
7 A&AR 1996, reg 9.
8 A&AR 1996, reg 14, which specifies the matters to be included in the advertisement.
9 A&AR 1996, reg 12.
10 A&AR 1996, reg 11.
11 A&AR 1996, reg 16.

8.58 Thus, the Accounts and Audit Regulations 1996 envisage that the financial audit may be completed by the 1 January following the financial year end, but there is no requirement that this should occur. However, the Code of Audit Practice (para 34) states that (other than in exceptional circumstances) the auditor's annual audit letter[1] issued at the conclusion of the audit, should be issued no later than 31 December following the end of the relevant financial year. Further, it is mandatory that the local authority should give local electors prior notice of the time at which they may make their objections to the auditor, and it is implicit that this right should be exercisable during the course of the audit.

1 See para **8.66**.

8.59 A contravention of the regulations referred to above, other than reg 11[1], constitutes an offence under the Accounts and Audit Regulations, reg 19.

1 See para **8.57**(a).

8.60 In practice, where there are no outstanding issues under ACA 1998, ss 8, 16, 17 or 18[1], auditors do complete the audit before the 31 December following the relevant financial year's end. Even where there are outstanding issues, the auditor's opinion, but not the certificate, may be issued[2].

1 See para **8.65**.
2 See paras **8.62** and **8.65**.

(b) Duties in relation to year end audit

8.61 The general duties of the auditor under the Audit Commission Act 1998, s 5 in undertaking the audit are referred to in para **8.31**. Detailed guidance on the conduct of local government audits is contained in the Code of Audit Practice which applies for the relevant financial year[1]. At each audit, the auditor must consider whether, in the public interest, he or she should prepare a report in the public interest in relation to any matter which comes to his or her notice in the course of the audit[2].

1 See para **8.32**.
2 See paras **8.68–8.71**.

(c) Conclusion of audit—certificate and opinion and other requirements

8.62 Once an audit of the accounts has been concluded, the auditor must enter on the statement of accounts: (a) a certificate to the effect that the audit has been completed in accordance with the Audit Commission Act 1998; and (b) his or her opinion on the statement of accounts[1]. This is referred to in the Act as a 'general report'. Where a report in the public interest is made under ACA 1998, s 8 at the *conclusion* of the audit[2], the auditor may include the certificate and opinion in that report, rather than by making an entry on the statement of accounts.

1 Audit Commission Act 1998, s 9.
2 See para **8.68**.

8.63 In giving an opinion on the accounts, auditors must consider whether the financial statements give a true and fair view of the financial position of the local authority and its expenditure and income for the year in question. Auditors must also consider whether the statements have been prepared properly in accordance with the relevant legislation and applicable accounting standards[1].

1 See the Code of Audit Practice, para 55.

8.64 The Code of Audit Practice[1] gives further guidance on the matters to be dealt with at the conclusion of the audit, including the statutory report on the audit of the local authority's best value performance plan under the Local Government Act 1999, s 7(4)[2] and an annual audit letter addressed to the audited body[3].

1 At para 27, and in the Statement of Responsibilities of Auditors and of Audited Bodies at para 52.
2 See Chapter 7.
3 See para **8.66**.

(d) Delay in the conclusion of the audit

8.65 The Code of Audit Practice acknowledges[1] that there will be occasions when although the audit work has been substantially completed, the audit cannot be concluded on account of action under ACA 1998, s 8 (public interest report); ACA 1998, s 16 (objection by a local elector); ACA 1998, s 17 (application to the court for a declaration in relation to an unlawful item of account); ACA 1998, s 18 ('surcharge' by an auditor); ACA 1998, s 20 (prohibition order); or ACA 1998, s 24 (application for judicial review by an auditor). The guidance recommends that in these cases, auditors should consider issuing an opinion as soon as the necessary audit work has been concluded, subject to whatever qualifications they consider appropriate.

1 At para 58.

(e) Annual audit letters

8.66 At the conclusion of the audit, auditors are required by the Code of Audit Practice[1] to issue an annual audit letter to the local authority concerned, and to ensure that it has copied it to all members of the authority. (This letter was formerly referred to as a 'management letter'.) The aim of an annual audit letter is to set out the scope, nature and extent of the audit work which has been undertaken and to summarise the auditor's opinions or conclusions, together with any matters of substance or significance arising from the audit[2].

1 At paras 27(f) and 33. As noted in para **8.58**, the audit letter is to be issued as soon as practicable, and normally no later than 31 December following the financial year end.
2 See the Code of Audit Practice, para 29ff.

8.67 The annual audit letter may include written recommendations which the auditor considers that the authority should consider publicly and respond to, pursuant to the Audit Commission Act 1998, s 11[1]. Where such recommendations are included in an annual audit letter, they should be specifically identified as being subject to ACA 1998, s 11[2].

1 See para **8.72**ff.
2 Audit Commission Act 1998, s 11(3).

3 PUBLIC INTEREST REPORTS

8.68 ACA 1998, s 8 requires an auditor, in carrying out an audit, to consider:

(a) whether, in the public interest, he or she should make a report on any matter coming to his or her notice in the course of the audit, in order for it to be considered by the body concerned or brought to the attention of the public; and
(b) whether the public interest requires any such matter to be made the subject of an immediate report, rather than of a report to be made at the conclusion of the audit.

8.69 Immediate reports must be sent 'forthwith' to the local authority. Other reports must be sent to the authority no later than 14 days after the conclusion of the audit[1]. The auditor must send a copy of the report to the Audit Commission within the same time limits[2].

1 Audit Commission Act 1998, s 10(1).
2 ACA 1998, s 10(2).

8.70 The Code of Audit Practice[1] recommends that a public interest report should only be made where an auditor considers a matter to be sufficiently important to be brought to the notice of the audited body or the public. However, auditors are not to be deflected from making a report because the subject matter is critical or unwelcome, if they consider it to be in the public interest to do so[2]. The emphasis of reports should be on the steps which are necessary to bring about improvement[3].

1 Schedule 1, para S1.24.
2 Schedule 1, para S1.25.
3 Schedule 1, para S1.26.

8.71 In practice, the subject matter of a report in the public interest is often one which is of specific concern primarily to the particular local authority, its officers and local people, rather than to local authorities in general. However, examples of matters of more widespread interest which have been the subject of public interest reports in recent years include members' expenses, gifts and hospitality, involvement in joint venture companies for the development of land, reliance on economic development powers under the Local Government and Housing Act 1989, Pt III[1] and severance payments to senior staff.

1 The public interest report concerning Doncaster Metropolitan Borough Council issued in January 1998 which referred to these issues is the subject of a Technical Release from the Audit Commission: TR 8/98: Doncaster Public Interest Report: Audit Considerations (dated 7 April 1998).

4 DUTY OF LOCAL AUTHORITY TO CONSIDER AUDITOR'S REPORT AND RECOMMENDATIONS

8.72 Within four months of the day on which the auditor has sent to a local authority:

(a) a public interest report under ACA 1998, s 8; or
(b) a written recommendation to which ACA 1998, s 11(3) applies;

the authority must consider the report or recommendation at a meeting of the full council[1]. The auditor may extend the four month time limit where he or she is satisfied it is reasonable to do so[2]. The general ability of local authorities to delegate functions to committees and officers under the Local Government Act 1972, s 101 does not apply to the consideration of an auditor's public interest report or recommendation to which ACA 1998, s 11(3) applies[3].The authority must decide at the meeting whether the report requires the authority to take any action or whether the recommendation should be accepted and what, if any, action it should take[4].

1 Audit Commission Act 1998, s 11(4).
2 ACA 1998, s 11(6).
3 ACA 1998, s 11(8).
4 ACA 1998, s 11(5).

8.73 The agenda supplied to members for a meeting at which a ACA 1998, s 8 report is to be considered must be accompanied by a copy of the report[1]. The report may not be excluded from the papers made available to the public under the Public Bodies (Admission to Meetings) Act 1960, or those made available for public inspection under the Local Government Act 1972[2].

1 Audit Commission Act 1998, s 10(4).
2 ACA 1998, s 10(5).

8.74 At least seven clear days notice must be given in a newspaper circulating in the local authority's area of a meeting at which either a public interest report under ACA 1998, s 8, or a written recommendation subject to ACA 1998, s 11(3), is to be considered. The notice must state the time and place of the meeting, indicate that the meeting is to consider an auditor's report or recommendation and describe the subject matter of the report or recommendation[1]. Additional requirements apply where the auditor has made an immediate report in the public interest under s 8 and ACA 1998, s 10(1)(a)[2].

1 Audit Commission Act 1998, s 12(1).
2 See para **8.77**.

8.75 As soon as practicable after the meeting, the local authority must ensure[1] that the auditor is notified of the decisions the authority has taken under ACA 1998, s 11(5) in relation to whether action is required or a recommendation is accepted and any action the authority proposes to take[2]. The authority must also publish in a newspaper circulating in its area a summary approved by the auditor of the decisions it has taken[3]. The provisions envisage that at least part of the consideration by the council of the auditor's report or recommendations may take place whilst the press and public are excluded from the meeting, as the authority is not obliged to summarise any decisions taken during such a session[4].

1 Audit Commission Act 1998, s 12(2)(a)).
2 See para **8.72**.
3 ACA 1998, s 12(2)(b).
4 ACA 1998, s 12(3).

8.76 The duty of an authority under the Audit Commission Act 1998, s 11 to give specific consideration to an auditor's report under s 8, or a written recommendation within ACA 1998, s 11(3), is in addition to and not in substitution for any responsibility the authority's chief finance officer or monitoring officer may have to prepare their own reports in relation to the subject matter of the auditor's report, or for the authority to consider those officer reports under the Local Government Finance Act 1988, s 114, or the Local Government and Housing Act 1989, s 5 respectively.

8.77 The Audit Commission Act 1998, s 13 imposes additional procedural requirements where an auditor has sent an authority an *immediate* report in the public interest under ACA 1998, s 8. Members of the public must be allowed to inspect and obtain a copy of the report 'from the time when [it] is received'. The authority must publish, forthwith on receipt of the report, a notice in a newspaper circulating in the area, identifying the subject matter of the report and stating that the public may inspect and make copies of it, and the time and place where they may do so. The authority must also supply, forthwith, copies of the report to all members of the authority. The auditor may notify, and supply copies of the report to, any person he or she thinks fit. There are criminal sanctions for obstruction or refusal to comply with the requirements for making the report available to the public by a person who has custody of an immediate report, and for failure to arrange for publication of the notice[1].

1 Audit Commission Act 1998, s 13(5)–(6).

5 INSPECTION OF DOCUMENTS AT EACH AUDIT BY ANY PERSONS INTERESTED

8.78 Under the Audit Commission Act 1998, s 15(1), at an annual audit (but not at an extraordinary audit[1]), any persons interested may inspect the accounts to be audited and all books, deeds, contracts, bills, vouchers, and receipts relating to them. Copies may also be taken of all or part of the accounts and those other documents. Regulation 12 of the Accounts and Audit Regulations 1996 requires that the accounts and other documents mentioned in ACA 1998, s 15(1) should have been made available for public inspection for 15 full working days before the day appointed by the auditor under reg 11 on or after which public rights are to be exercised[2].

1 See paras **8.110–8.115**.
2 See para **8.57**(f).

8.79 It is to be noted that the right of inspection of documents under ACA 1998, s 15(1) is available to a wider class of people than the rights under ACA 1998, s 14 (to inspect the statement of accounts and any auditor's report), those under ACA 1998, s 15(2) (to question the auditor), or those under ACA 1998, s 16 (to make objection at audit), each of which is only available to a local government elector for the area. 'Person interested' is considered to include a person with a financial or legal interest in the accounts, but in the context in which the expression appears (the protection of public rights), arguably it would not extend to commercial competitors seeking details of another party's contract for commercial purposes.

8.80 The extent of the documents which must be made available has been considered in a number of cases concerning the corresponding provisions of earlier legislation. Documents supplementary to a contract were considered to be open to inspection, but documents leading to an architect's certificate were not

(*Hillingdon London Borough Council v Paulssen* [1977] JPL 518). Application forms for educational bursaries were not 'vouchers' open to inspection (*R v Monmouthshire County Council, ex p Smith* 51 (1935) TLR 435).

8.81 By virtue of ACA 1998, s 15(3)–(5), the rights of persons interested under ACA 1998, s 15(1) do not extend to the inspection of personal information about a member of the council's staff, such as pay or other benefits.

6 RIGHTS OF LOCAL GOVERNMENT ELECTORS

8.82 The rights referred to in paras **8.84–8.101** are rights of 'local government electors' for the area to which the accounts relate. The expression is not defined within the Audit Commission Act 1998, save in respect of such bodies as the Broads Authority or a National Parks authority. By virtue of the Local Government Act 1972, s 270(1)[1] the expression is defined to mean a person registered as a local government elector in accordance with the provisions of Representation of the People Acts.

1 Which applies to the interpretation of the Audit Commission Act 1998 by virtue of s 53(2) thereof.

8.83 On the basis of the terms of the legislation itself, it would appear that a person wishing to exercise one of the following rights must be a local government elector for the area in question at the time the right is exercised.

(a) Inspection of statement of accounts and any auditor's report

8.84 By the Audit Commission Act 1998, s 14, local government electors for the area are given the right to inspect and take copies of the statement of accounts which the authority is required to prepare under the Accounts and Audit Regulations, reg 6[1] and to inspect and take copies of any report made to the body by the auditor (other than an immediate report in the public interest[2]). The elector may also require that copies of any statement or report be delivered to him or her on payment of a reasonable sum.

1 See para **8.57**(a).
2 Which is subject to separate provisions under s 13, as noted in para **8.77**, giving immediate rights of access to any member of the public.

8.85 Criminal sanctions are imposed on a person who has custody of any such document and obstructs the exercise of a local elector's rights, or refuses to give copies as required[1].

1 Audit Commission Act 1998, s 14(3).

8.86 The rights of local electors under ACA 1998, s 14 are in addition to those of 'persons interested' to inspect the accounts and other documents under ACA 1998, s 15(1)[1] and to those arising from the duty of the local authority to publish the statement of accounts following the conclusion of the audit under the Accounts and Audit Regulations, reg 9[2].

1 See para **8.78**ff.
2 Or by 1 January following the end of the relevant financial year, if earlier. See para **8.57**(d).

(b) Questions to the auditor

8.87 Under ACA 1998, s 15(2), local government electors for the area (or their representatives) must be afforded an opportunity to ask questions of the auditor about the local authority's accounts[1]. In common with the rights of 'interested persons' to inspect documents under ACA 1998, s 15(1), this right does not arise in respect of an extraordinary audit under ACA 1998, s 25[2].

1 Audit Commission Act 1998, s 15(2).
2 See paras **8.110–8.115**.

8.88 As noted in para **8.57**(g), the auditor must appoint a day on or after which this right may be exercised. No end date for the exercise of the right is specified; however, it would appear that the right must lapse at the conclusion of the audit for the year in question, when the auditor's duties for that audit are at an end.

8.89 The intention of the right given under ACA 1998, s 15(2) is to enable a local government elector to clarify any points of doubt or misunderstanding before considering further action. The Code of Audit Practice[1] advises that auditors should not admit questions which do not relate to the accounts for the financial year in question, such as general questions relating to the audited bodies' policies, finances or procedures. Nor, without the consent of the audited body, should the auditor disclose any information which is not disclosed in the accounts or other documents which are required to be made available under ACA 1998, s 15(1).

1 Schedule 1, para S1.7.

8.90 Neither the Audit Commission Act 1998 nor the Accounts and Audit Regulations 1996 prescribe a procedure for questions for the auditor. It is to be noted that the legislation does not impose any express obligation on the auditor to answer the questions put to him or her, or impose any sanction for failure to respond. However, in principle, a refusal by the auditor to answer a question put by a local government elector without proper cause would appear to be susceptible to judicial review, by way of an application for an order of mandamus.

(c) Objections to the accounts

8.91 By virtue of ACA 1998, s 16(1), at any audit (including an extraordinary audit under ACA 1998, s 25[1]), local government electors for the area (or their representatives) must be afforded an opportunity to 'attend before the auditor' and make objections:

(a) as to any matter in respect of which the auditor could take action under ACA 1998, s 17[2] (declaration that an item of account is unlawful) or ACA 1998, s 18[3] ('surcharge' by an auditor); or

(b) as to any other matter in respect of which the auditor could make a report under ACA 1998, s 8[4] (in the public interest).

1 See paras **8.110–8.115**.
2 See para **9.5**ff (and note the prospective amendment of ACA 1998, s 17 by the Local Government Act 2000, s 90(2), s 107 and Sch 6).
3 ACA 1998, s 18 is subject to prospective repeal by the Local Government Act 2000, s 90(3), s 107 and Sch 6 (and ACA 1998, s 16 is subject to consequential amendment). See para **9.41**ff.
4 See para **8.68**ff.

8.92 As noted, the auditor must appoint a day, on or after which the right of objection under ACA 1998, s 16(1) may be exercised[1]. Again, the legislation does not specify when the right to object ends, but it appears that the right must lapse once the audit for the relevant year has been concluded.

1 Under the Accounts and Audit Regulations, reg 11; see para **8.57**(g).

8.93 The objector must give the auditor written notice of the proposed objection and, at the same time, send a copy of the notice to the local authority concerned. The Accounts and Audit Regulations 1996, reg 15 prescribe the contents of any written notice of objection. The notice must include the facts on which the local elector proposes to rely and, so far as possible, contain particulars of:

(a) the item of account alleged to be contrary to law;
(b) any person from whom it is alleged the auditor should certify a sum or amount is due under ACA 1998, s 18 and the sum or amount in question; and
(c) any matter in respect of which it is proposed that the auditor could make a public interest report under ACA 1998, s 8.

8.94 The Code of Audit Practice requires auditors[1], on receipt of a notice of objection, to ensure that a copy has been supplied to the audited body and to verify that it relates to the relevant year of account and to a matter to which the auditor's powers are applicable, and that it is otherwise valid in law as an objection within the meaning of the Audit Commission Act 1998. An objection would not be valid if it did not relate to any matter which might lead to action by the auditor under ACA 1998, ss 8, 17 or 18.

1 Schedule 1, para S1.8.

8.95 The extent to which an objection may be rejected as invalid if it is vexatious, or has been heard previously in relation to the accounts of an earlier year, does not appear to have been tested by the courts[1].

1 See further, para **8.101** and notes thereto.

8.96 Whether or not auditors are acting judicially or quasi-judicially in discharging their functions in relation to objections from local electors[1], they are under a duty to act fairly and to observe the principles of natural justice, not only in respect of the objector, but in respect of the local authority and any person who might be directly affected by action the auditor decides to take. The auditor must hear both sides and decide the matter impartially.

1 See para **8.44**ff.

8.97 The Code of Audit Practice requires auditors to give notice of the objection to any person who might be adversely affected by a decision on the objection and to give them an opportunity to deal with any matter which is adverse to them[1].

1 Schedule 1, para S1.9.

8.98 The expression 'attend before the auditor' in ACA 1998, s 16(1) is based on early practice for the conduct of a local government audit which was held in public, but case law suggests that there is no obligation on the auditor to hold an oral hearing[1]. In practice many objections are dealt with by way of written representations. Whichever procedure is followed, the audited body and any individuals who are directly affected should be given an opportunity to answer allegations and to submit evidence. The Code of Audit Practice[2] requires auditors to consider whether justice or fairness would best be served by giving those affected by the exercise of the auditor's powers and duties the opportunity of an oral hearing and, if so, whether that hearing should be in public. If an oral hearing is arranged, then there should be an opportunity for cross examination of witnesses. If injustice might be caused by allegations made without due notice, the hearing should be adjourned or further time allowed for written representations[3].

1 *Lloyd v McMahon* [1987] AC 625. In relation to the early practice for the conduct of audits see p 662 of the report of the decision of the Court of Appeal in which Woolf LJ (as he then was) distinguishes the position under the nineteenth century legislation from that under more recent legislation and states that the reference to an objector having to attend (in the statutory provision which preceded ACA 1998, s 16(1)) was surprising and probably explicable because of the historical background to the legislation.
2 Schedule 1, para S1.12.
3 Schedule 1, para S1.14.

8.99 Before determining an objection, auditors are required to make whatever enquiries they consider necessary. Whilst there may be an onus on the objector to establish that grounds exist for the auditor to take action under the relevant statutory provisions, the auditor has an independent duty to investigate illegality etc regardless of any objection. Thus if an objector has established a prima facie case for concern, the auditor would be obliged to pursue his or her inquisitorial role.

8.100 If action under ACA 1998, ss 8, 17 or 18 is contemplated, auditors are required to make relevant documents available to the parties at the appropriate time[1]. In these circumstances auditors are also advised to consider issuing provisional views to the parties concerned. In practice, auditors normally invite representations on any provisional view or criticism which may adversely affect any person and take those representations into consideration before reaching a final view. Having reached their decision, auditors are required to notify the objector and others affected by it, and inform them of the rights of appeal and procedures for appeal[2].

1 Code of Audit Practice, Sch 1, para S1.11.
2 Code of Audit Practice, Sch 1, para S1.15.

8.101 The Government White Paper *Modern Local Government: In Touch with the People*[1] following recommendations in the Third Report of the Nolan Committee on Standards in Public Life[2] proposed that the right of a local government elector to challenge the accounts be amended to impose a time limit on objections and explicitly to allow the auditor to refuse to hear an objection, if it is vexatious, has been heard previously, or for other good reasons[3]. The Local Government Act 2000 does not implement these particular recommendations, and makes only a minor consequential amendment to ACA 1998, s 16, arising from the proposed repeal of ACA 1998, s 18 on 'surcharge' by the auditor[4].

1 Cm 4014, July 1998.
2 Cm 3702-1, July 1997.
3 One of the recommendations made in the report of the Environment, Transport and Regional Affairs Committee of the House of Commons (June 2000), referred to at para **8.14**, was that the Government should review the whole objection process, but in particular should consider whether objectors who persist in launching spurious or vexatious complaints could be debarred from doing so.
4 See further Chapter 9, regarding the extent of the repeals to the Audit Commission Act 1998, Pt II under the Local Government Act 2000.

7 APPEALS AGAINST AUDITOR'S DECISION ON AN OBJECTION BY LOCAL GOVERNMENT ELECTOR

8.102 A person who has made an objection under ACA 1998, s 16(1)(a) and is aggrieved by a decision of the auditor not to apply to the court under ACA 1998, s 17 for a declaration that an item of account is contrary to law may, not later than six weeks after being notified of the decision, require the auditor to state in writing the reasons for his or her decision and appeal to the court against the decision[1].

1 Audit Commission Act 1998, s 17(4).

8.103 Auditors are required by the Code of Audit Practice[1] to send statements of reasons by recorded delivery or by an equally reliable and recorded means, as the objector's time for appeal runs from the date of receipt[2]. Appeals are governed by CPR[3], Pt 52 (as supplemented by the *Practice Direction* on Pt 52) and CPR, Sch 1, Ord 98. The appellant's notice must be filed with the High Court within 28 days of the day on which the statement is received by the objector[4].

1 Schedule 1, para S1.15.
2 In practice, auditors send their statement of reasons to the objector with their decision letter. In *R v District Auditor for Gateshead, ex p Judge* (18 June 1996, unreported), QBD the court found that the statement of reasons which had been issued in this way was not invalid simply because it had been issued before the objector had made a specific request for it.
3 The Civil Procedure Rules 1998, SI 1998/3132 as amended. The procedure was formerly provided for in RSC Ords 55, 57 and 98; Ord 55 and Ord 98, r 3 were revoked by SI 2000/221. Order 57 is to be revoked by SI 2000/2092.
4 This is the current position but should be reconsidered at the relevant time. At the time of writing, para 17 of the *Practice Direction*, which supplements CPR, Pt 52, amends Pt 52 in its application to statutory appeals. As regards the time limits for an appellant's notice see CPR, r 52.4(2) and the *Practice Direction*, paras 17.3 and 17.4. The *Practice Direction*, para 5.6 provides for the documents which must be lodged with an appellant's notice. CPR, r 52.11 and the *Practice Direction*, para 9.1 deal with the manner of hearing of an appeal (see para **9.78**).

8.104 On an appeal under ACA 1998, s 17(4), the High Court has the same powers in relation to an item of account to which the objection relates as if the auditor had applied for the declaration. Those powers are referred to in para **9.27**ff (and are to be amended under the Local Government Act 2000, ss 90 and 107 and Sch 6, once the provisions are brought into force).

8.105 Under the law at the time of writing, an objector may also appeal to the court in respect of a decision by the auditor not to certify for recovery a sum due from any person for failure to bring into account or causing a loss or deficiency through wilful misconduct ('surcharge' by the auditor)[1]. However, as noted in para **9.42**, once the relevant provisions of the Local Government Act 2000 are brought into force, ACA 1998, s 18 on certification (or surcharge) by the auditor will be repealed in its entirety.

1 Audit Commission Act 1998, s 18(5).

8.106 There is no statutory right of appeal against the decision of an auditor not to issue a report in the public interest under the Audit Commission Act 1998, s 8. In principle, such a decision might be susceptible to judicial review[1], as would a failure by the auditor to give proper consideration to whether such a report should be issued.

1 Some doubt was cast on whether the converse decision (an auditor's decision to issue such a report) might be reviewed by the courts, since the report itself does not amount to a determination by the auditor: see *R v District Auditor No 3 Audit District of West Yorkshire Metropolitan County Council, ex p West Yorkshire Metropolitan County Council* [1986] RVR 24, referred to at para **8.50**. However, the two cases concerning the District Auditor for the Isle of Anglesey referred to in para **8.51** suggest that, in an appropriate case, judicial review might lie in respect of a decision to issue a report under s 8.

8.107 The rights of local government electors under the Audit Commission Act 1998 are not the only remedies available to a person who wishes to challenge the legality of local government expenditure. A person with 'sufficient interest' may apply for judicial review of the authority's decision or other action giving rise to the expenditure[1].

1 Historically, relator actions, brought by the Attorney General at the relation of an individual, have also been used to obtain a declaration and/or an injunction against a local authority (see, for example, *A-G v Crayford UDC* [1962] Ch 575).

8 APPEALS AGAINST AUDITOR'S DECISION ON OBJECTION BY PARTIES OTHER THAN THE OBJECTOR

8.108 The decision of an auditor on an objection may, of course, affect the local authority, its officers and members and conceivably other parties. The rights of appeal and other remedies available to certain of these parties are described in Chapter 9. The Code of Audit Practice states[1] that an auditor should communicate his or her decision to any persons who may be affected by it, and in respect of the auditor's functions under ACA 1998, ss 17 and 18, should inform them of their statutory rights of appeal (which are referred to in Chapter 9).

1 Schedule 1, para S1.15.

9 INFORMATION OBTAINED BY AUDITOR FROM PARTIES OTHER THAN LOCAL GOVERNMENT ELECTORS

8.109 As noted above, an auditor has a duty, independent of any valid objection being made to the accounts, to investigate illegality and other irregularities in relation to the accounts[1]. Consequently, an auditor may investigate information supplied by any person at any time (and not simply that supplied by a local government elector for the area), if the information is relevant to the auditor's functions under the Audit Commission Act 1998.

1 Audit Commission Act 1998, s 5(1), and see the common law duties of auditors described in para **8.29**.

10 EXTRAORDINARY AUDIT

8.110 In addition to the annual audit of accounts described in the preceding sections of this chapter, an extraordinary audit may be held at any time if an auditor is directed to do so by the Audit Commission, whether of its own initiative[1], or because the Commission has been required by the Secretary of State to direct that an extraordinary audit be held[2]. The Audit Commission may direct an auditor to hold an extraordinary audit where it appears to the Commission that it is desirable to do so, in consequence of a report made by the auditor under ACA 1998, or for any other reason. The Secretary of State may require the Commission to arrange an extraordinary audit where it appears to him that it is desirable to do so in the public interest.

1 Audit Commission Act 1998, s 25(1).
2 ACA 1998, s 25(2).

8.111 Prior to 1 April 1974 the power to direct an extraordinary audit was of greater significance than it is today. Until that time, auditors were unable to consider matters arising in the then current financial account, but were required to wait until the accounts had been completed. As described in para **8.54**, this is no longer the case and it is no longer necessary for an extraordinary audit to be held simply as a means of enabling the auditor to exercise his or her statutory functions at an earlier time.

8.112 However, directing an extraordinary audit might still provide a means of bringing the rights of local government electors into operation at an earlier time than would otherwise be the case, or to require the auditor to examine urgently one aspect of a local authority's affairs, for example in the case of suspected fraud.

8.113 On an extraordinary audit most, but not all, of the statutory provisions relating to year end audits apply. The following provisions of the Audit Commission Act 1998 do *not* apply to an extraordinary audit:

(a) the rights of local government electors to inspect the statement of accounts and reports from the auditor[1];
(b) the rights of 'interested persons' to inspect the accounts and other documents and of local government electors to question the auditor[2]; and
(c) regarding scale fees for audits[3]; instead special provision is made in respect of the expenditure incurred in holding an extraordinary audit, which is to be met in the first instance by the Audit Commission, who if it thinks fit, may recover the costs from the audit body[4].

1 Audit Commission Act 1998, s 14 (para **8.84**ff).
2 ACA 1998, s 15 (para **8.78**ff and para **8.87**ff).
3 ACA 1998, s 7 (para **8.124**).
4 ACA 1998, s 25(5).

8.114 Although an objector at an extraordinary audit will have no prior rights to inspect documents or question the auditor, *Colton v District Auditor for Wembley Borough Council* (1962) 60 LGR 247 at 253 suggests that an auditor has a common law duty to make available to an objector the documents put before him by the council during the inquiry and any document which the auditor had required the authority to produce, at least where these are material to his decision (and the Code of Audit Practice expressly requires this[1]).

1 See Sch 1, para S1.11, noted in paras **8.43** and **8.100**.

8.115 One example of the use of an extraordinary audit was in relation to Liverpool City Council, who had not made a valid rate (under former legislation) for the financial year 1985–1986 by June of 1985, at which time the Audit Commission directed that an extraordinary audit be carried out[1].

1 See *Lloyd v McMahon* [1987] AC 625. Although the issue in this case could not arise in precisely the same way now, the case illustrates the type of circumstances in which extraordinary audit has been considered to be appropriate. (Under the current law, a comparable situation might arise where a local authority had delayed setting the level of council tax beyond the time limits set by the Local Government Finance Act 1992, s 30.)

11 ACCESS TO DOCUMENTS BY THE AUDITOR

8.116 In order to carry out their functions under the Audit Commission Act 1998, auditors have extensive rights to obtain documents and other information.

8.117 ACA 1998, s 6(1), (2) and (4) provides:

> '(1) An auditor has a right of access at all reasonable times to every document relating to a body subject to audit which appears to him necessary for the purposes of his functions under this Act.
>
> (2) An auditor may –
>
> (a) require a person holding or accountable for any such document to give him such information and explanation as he thinks necessary for the purposes of his functions under this Act; and
>
> (b) if he thinks it necessary, require the person to attend before him in person to give the information or explanation or to produce the document.
>
> ...
>
> (4) Without prejudice to subsection (2) the auditor may –
>
> (a) require any officer or member of a body subject to audit to give him such information or explanation as he thinks necessary for the purposes of his functions under the Act; and
>
> (b) if he thinks necessary, require an officer or member to attend before him in person to give the information or explanation.'

8.118 Failure to comply with any requirement of an auditor under these sections without reasonable excuse carries criminal sanctions[1]. A mistaken view as to the effect of ACA 1998, s 6 would not constitute a 'reasonable excuse' for non-compliance with an auditor's requirement made pursuant to that section[2].

1 Audit Commission Act 1998, s 6(6).
2 *R v Reid* [1973] 3 All ER 1020.

8.119 Case law on earlier legislation in similar terms has established that the auditor's powers are not limited to documents of the authority. In *Re Hurle-Hobbs's Decision* [1944] 2 All ER 261 the Court of Appeal affirmed the right of the district auditor to call upon a contractor collecting and disposing of refuse for Lambeth Borough Council to produce documents and give him information. In *R v Hurle-Hobbs, ex p Simmons* [1945] KB 165, the court accepted that the district auditor was entitled to require a firm of accountants, who acted as auditor of the Council's contractor, to appear before him to produce documents belonging to the contractor.

8.120 In relation to the scope of the information an auditor may obtain, the fact that a document or other information is confidential or has been supplied to the person in confidence does not mean that the auditor would not be entitled to its production in an appropriate case[1]. As noted in para **8.39**ff, the auditor is bound to treat information obtained as confidential, save in specified circumstances.

1 See, for example, *R v Hurle-Hobbs, ex p Simmons* [1945] KB 165.

8.121 Case law in relation to other statutory provisions requiring the production of documents or the provision of information suggests that matters which might be protected from disclosure in court proceedings, on the basis of self-incrimination[1] or legal professional privilege, may be overridden by statutory powers to require disclosure. In *Customs and Excise Comrs v Harz* [1967] 1 AC 760 the court considered that self-incriminatory documents should be produced by a trader if a proper demand was made under statutory powers available to the Commissioners of Customs and Excise. In *Parry-Jones v Law Society* [1969] 1 Ch 1, the Law Society was entitled to obtain the production of documents under provisions of the Solicitors Act 1957, notwithstanding any privilege or confidentiality in respect of a solicitor's communication with his or her client. In *Bank of England v Riley* [1992] Ch 475, in proceedings under the Banking Act 1987, the Court of Appeal found that a person required to produce documents and information under the 1987 Act, s 42 could not rely on privilege against self-incrimination as 'reasonable excuse' for failure to comply. In *A v B Bank (Bank of England Intervening)* [1993] QB 311, disclosure of documents by a bank served with notice by the Bank of England under the Banking Act 1987, s 39 was required, notwithstanding the existence of an injunction restraining disclosure of the documents to third parties.

1 Self-incriminatory information obtained under a statutory power to require disclosure could not be used as evidence in a criminal prosecution, as this would be contrary to the European Convention for the Protection of Human Rights, art 6 (which includes the right to a fair hearing for a person charged with a criminal offence). Article 6 would not, however, entitle the person concerned to invoke the privilege against self-incrimination in order to refuse to respond to a statutory request, at least where that request is of a kind where failure to comply without reasonable excuse is itself a criminal offence: *R v Hertfordshire County Council, ex p Green Environmental Industries Ltd* [2000] 1 All ER 773, HL. Failure to comply with a notice served by an auditor under the Audit Commission Act 1998, s 6 is a request of this kind; see para **8.118** concerning s 6(6).

8.122 The documents 'relating to a body subject to audit' to which the auditor is entitled to access by virtue of ACA 1998, s 6 may include party political papers and will do so if they throw light on the evolution of council policy. This is particularly so if the papers have been prepared by council officers[1].

1 See *Porter v Magill* (1997) 96 LGR 157 at 168, QBD. This point was not overruled on appeal.

8.123 The auditor would be entitled to information held on computerised records. If not provided for otherwise, ACA 1998, s 6(5) requires the audited body to provide the auditor with every facility and all information he or she may reasonably require to discharge the statutory functions under the Act.

12 FEES AND FACILITIES FOR AUDITORS

8.124 Under the Audit Commission Act 1998, s 7 the Audit Commission is required to prescribe a scale of fees in respect of the audit of accounts under the Act and that fee is payable by the audited body. The same fees are payable whether the audit is undertaken by a district auditor or an appointed (private) auditor. Where it appears to the Commission that the work involved in a particular audit was substantially more or less than that envisaged in the appropriate scale, the Commission may charge a larger or smaller amount. As noted in para **8.113**, the scale fees do not apply to extraordinary audits.

8.125 Pursuant to the requirements of ACA 1998, s 6(5) for the body subject to audit to provide the auditor with 'every facility . . . which he may reasonably require for the purposes of his functions under this Act', local authorities often provide auditors with accommodation in which to undertake the audit.

CHAPTER 9

Specific powers of auditors to deal with financial irregularities

A Introduction

9.1 In this chapter we examine the duties and powers of external auditors[1] in relation to unlawful expenditure and other action and proposed action by local authorities. The chapter also considers the means by which the local authority, local electors and others may challenge an auditor's decisions and actions in relation to the accounts.

1 The auditors referred to throughout this chapter are auditors appointed by the Audit Commission under the Audit Commission Act 1998, Pt II to audit the accounts of a local authority.

9.2 The relevant statutory provisions are mainly contained in the Audit Commission Act 1998, and references to section numbers in this chapter without further details are references to the sections of that Act.

9.3 At the time of writing the functions of auditors under the Audit Commission Act 1998 are to be reformed by the repeal of their duties in relation to certification or 'surcharge'[1] and powers concerning prohibition orders[2]. The powers of the court to order repayment by a person responsible for incurring or authorising unlawful expenditure[3] and those of the Secretary of State to sanction unlawful expenditure[4] are also to be repealed. These repeals and the new regime of 'advisory notices' are provided for in the Local Government Act 2000 ('LGA 2000'), ss 90, 91 and 107 and Sch 6. At the time of writing, no date has been appointed by the Secretary of State for these provisions to come into force[5]. The current law relating to areas subject to prospective repeal are outlined only briefly, noting the proposed changes. The new powers of auditors under the LGA 2000, in the form of advisory notices, are described at paras **9.95–9.98**.

1 Under ACA 1998, s 18. See para **9.41**ff.
2 Under ACA 1998, s 20. See para **9.84**ff.
3 Under ACA 1998, s 17(2)(a) and (b). See para **9.28**.
4 See para **9.23**.
5 See the Local Government Act 2000, s 108(3)(a).

9.4 Notwithstanding the prospective repeals, the principles in many of the cases continue to be of relevance in relation to the legality of expenditure and accounting by local authorities, and/or the interpretation of the surviving provisions of the Audit Commission Act 1998 or other legislation, and have been included in the following text. Provisions of the Audit Commission Act 1998 which are quoted verbatim appear in italics if they are affected by prospective repeal.

B Declaration that an item of account is contrary to law

9.5 The Audit Commission Act 1998, s 17(1), currently provides:

'(1) Where –

(a) it appears to the auditor carrying out an audit under this Act, other than an audit of accounts of a health service body, that an item of account is contrary to law, *and*

(b) *the item is not sanctioned by the Secretary of State* [1],

the auditor may apply to the court for a declaration that the item is contrary to law.'

1 The words in italics are to be repealed by the Local Government Act 2000, ss 90, 107 and Sch 6 from a day to be appointed by the Secretary of State pursuant to s 108(3).

9.6 Where such an application is made, the court may make or refuse to make the order asked for[1]. Other than para (1)(b), the provisions of ACA 1998, s 17(1) are not subject to any current proposal for repeal[2].

1 Audit Commission Act 1998, s 17(2).
2 See para **9.29** regarding the prospective repeals affecting s 17(2) and (3).

1 ITEM OF ACCOUNT

9.7 ACA 1998, s 17(1) is concerned with 'items of account'. These are entries in an authority's accounts. They may record expenditure or income and they may also reflect balances and totals. The same transaction may give rise to a number of items of account, some of which may be credits and some of which may be debits and all or some of which may be 'contrary to law'.

(a) Heads, objects, entries

9.8 'Item of account' has a wide meaning. It is not restricted to a head of account, ie the object of expenditure (or income): it applies to all the accounting entries. Its meaning in relation to expenditure was examined by the House of Lords in *Roberts v Hopwood* [1925] AC 578, HL; Lord Wrenbury said at 616:

> 'Item of account is not the same as head of account. The wage bill is no doubt a head of account—but every item of weekly payment to each employee is an item of account.'

Lord Sumner stated (at 601) that the auditor was bound to examine the whole and every part of any expenditure. In the Irish case of *R (King-Kerr) v Newell* [1903] 2 IR 335 concerning equivalent statutory provisions, the court concluded that action might be taken in respect of part only of an item of account.

(b) Omissions

9.9 The exclusion of a transaction involving expenditure from the accounts can give rise to an item of account which is contrary to law: in *Wilkinson v Doncaster Metropolitan Borough Council* (1985) 84 LGR 257, CA, the costs of painting works undertaken by a direct labour organisation had been omitted from the statutory accounts. In *Taylor v Munrow* [1960] 1 All ER 455, QBD, the local authority omitted to review the rents payable by individual tenants of derequisitioned houses (and to get tenants to obtain certificates of disrepair which in some instances would have reduced rents payable to the owners of the houses). The auditor estimated the expenditure the authority had incurred through its obligation to make up the shortfall to the owners of the houses, and the court confirmed the auditor's decision that these payments were unlawful.

2 CONTRARY TO LAW

9.10 The court may grant relief if an item of account is for any reason unlawful or improper. The Court of Appeal stated in *Hazell v Hammersmith and Fulham London Borough Council* [1990] 2 QB 697 at 768:

> '... the expression "contrary to law" may be traced back at least to section 247(7) of the Public Health Act 1875. The decided cases since that date have clearly illustrated the grounds upon which items of account may be held to be contrary to law. Such a conclusion may be reached where the items of account relate to payments which were not authorised by the duty of the authority, or were contrary to the duty of the authority, or were beyond the powers of the authority, or were made in the exercise of a discretion vitiated by misdirection, consideration of irrelevant matters, failure to consider relevant matters or gross unreasonableness: *Thomas v Devonport Corpn* [1900] 1 QB 16; *R v Carson Roberts* [1908] 1 KB 407; *Roberts v Hopwood* [1925] AC 578. Breach of the fiduciary duty owed by a local authority to its ratepayers would found an application under s 19 of the Act of 1982[1]: *Roberts v Hopwood* [1925] AC 578; *Prescott v Birmingham Corpn* [1955] Ch 210 and *Bromley London Borough Council v Greater London Council* [1983] 1 AC 768. In short, the auditor is entitled to seek relief if he can show that an item of account is for any reason unlawful or improper.'

1 Local Government Finance Act 1982, s 19, the predecessor of the Audit Commission Act 1998, s 17.

9.11 Neither the courts nor an auditor are entitled to substitute their own view of what may be a desirable policy for that of a local authority. The courts can only intervene, on the application of an auditor or otherwise, if in exercising a discretion conferred on it by Parliament a local authority has acted unlawfully[1]. Despite the headnote in *Roberts v Hopwood*, there is no principle that expenditure which the auditor or the court considers to be 'excessive' is for that reason alone 'contrary to law'[2]. The issue at the heart of that and other cases was whether the local authority had taken into account all relevant considerations and left out of account irrelevant considerations in deciding to incur the expenditure. The test is essentially qualitative in relation to the decision and not quantitative in relation to the expenditure.

1 Per Diplock LJ in *Luby v Newcastle-under-Lyme Corpn* [1964] 2 QB 64 at 72.
2 A decision to incur expenditure of an exorbitant amount might, however, be construed as 'irrational' and unlawful on the basis of the *Wednesbury* principles.

9.12 Mere imprudence is not to be equated with 'contrary to law'[1]. But a payment which may not be made directly, cannot be made indirectly, or be legitimised by according it a false description: see *R (Jackson) v Newell* [1898] 2 IR 530, where interest on an overdraft which the local authority had no power to pay was described in the accounts as salary to the Bank of Ireland as treasurer[2].

1 *R (Inglis) v Drury* [1898] 2 IR 527.
2 See also *Rothnie v Dearne UDC* (1951) 50 LGR 123 and *Re Magrath* [1934] 2 KB 415 on retrospective remuneration, cited in para **9.16**.

9.13 An item of account recording expenditure is 'contrary to law' within the meaning of that phrase in ACA 1998, s 17(1), if:

(a) it records expenditure which a local authority has no power to incur or is otherwise 'ultra vires'[1];
(b) it records expenditure which was incurred without authority[2];
(c) it records expenditure which is debited to the wrong fund or account[3].

Another example would be improper capitalisation of revenue expenditure.

1 *Beecham v Metropolitan District Auditor* (1976) 75 LGR 79.
2 *Beecham v Metropolitan District Auditor* (1976) 75 LGR 79; *Murphy v Middleton* (1974, unreported).
3 *Stockdale v Haringey London Borough Council* (1989) 88 LGR 7; *Wilkinson v Doncaster Metropolitan Borough Council* (1985) 84 LGR 257.

9.14 Expenditure incurred or income received in consequence of an unlawful decision gives rise to an item of account which is 'contrary to law'. Some examples of items of account which have been found to be contrary to law on this basis include:

(a) *Roberts v Hopwood* [1925] AC 578: minimum wage of £4 per week unlawful[1];
(b) *A-G v Belfast Corpn* (1855) 4 IR Ch R 119: borrowing in excess of the statutory limit and monies borrowed for one purpose but applied for another;
(c) *R v Reed* (1880) 5 QBD 483: borrowing for purposes outside those specified in the statutory provisions on borrowing;
(d) *R (Bridgeman) v Drury* [1894] 2 IR 489: expenses of floral decorations, travelling expenses and a 'sumptuous' picnic in the Wicklow Hills;
(e) *R (John McEvoy) v Dublin Corpn* (1878) 2 LR Ir 371: no power to pay Mayor's gas bill;
(f) *Taylor v Munrow* [1960] 1 All ER 455: failure to exercise a discretion to recover sums may give rise to an item of account 'contrary to law' (and to a 'loss or deficiency').

1 Contrast *Pickwell v Camden London Borough Council* [1983] QB 962 (payment of 'cost of living increases' in settlement of strike action not unlawful) and *Newbold v Leicester City Council* [1999] ICR 1182 (scheme for 'buying out' of established and uneconomic working practices (stand-by payments for emergency work) was lawful and enforceable by the employees concerned).

(a) *Wednesbury* failings

9.15 The failings referred to in *Associated Provincial Picture Houses Ltd v Wednesbury Corpn* [1948] 1 KB 223 constitute unlawful action and are grounds upon which a purported decision is ultra vires and void[1]. The contrary view expressed by Ormrod LJ in *Pickwell v Camden London Borough Council* [1983] QB 962 at 1002 is inconsistent with authority and principle and has never been followed[2]. A court would be entitled to find that any item of account relating to expenditure arising from a decision or other action which is unlawful in the sense of the tests in *Wednesbury* is 'contrary to law'.

1 See, for example, *Roberts v Hopwood* [1925] AC 578; *Padfield v Ministry of Agriculture, Fisheries and Food* [1968] AC 997 at 1040–1; *Grunwick Processing Laboratories v Advisory Conciliation and Arbitration Service* [1978] AC 655 at 692b; and *R v Lord President of the Privy Council, ex p Page* [1993] AC 682 at 701.
2 It was not adopted by Forbes J, or any other member of the court in *Pickwell*.

(b) Gratuities, retrospective payments, and ex gratia payments

9.16 A general principle recurrent in audit cases is the 'rule' against gratuities, retrospective remuneration or ex gratia payments, particularly in relation to staff. In *Re Magrath* [1934] 2 KB 415 the court found that the auditor had been right to disallow as being 'contrary to law' additional salary paid to the County Accountant in 1931 in respect of additional duties carried out in the years 1921–1925. In *Rothnie v Dearne UDC* (1951) 50 LGR 123, the court refused 17 surcharged councillors relief from disqualification from office[1] for their decision to pay additional salary to staff in the current year equal to sums disallowed by the auditor in relation to the accounts of the previous year.

1 There was no appeal against the disallowance and surcharge in this case.

9.17 However, in *Re Hurle-Hobbs's Decision* [1944] 2 All ER 261, which concerned an ex gratia payment by a local authority to a contractor under a fixed sum contract in respect of additional costs due to the war, the court did not find the additional payment to be unlawful. The court emphasised that an authority should not merely consider the interests of the contractor to maintain its expected level of profit, but should address its mind to what was in the interest of ratepayers. Thus, payments made without legal liability may be permissible if authorised by statute and made in the interests of local taxpayers[1].

1 See also *R v Gloucester Corpn* (1859) 123 JP 709.

(c) Re-opening decisions in previous financial years

9.18 The issue involved in *Re Magrath* is also expressed in terms of the principle that decisions concerning financial transactions in earlier years should not be re-opened. A further example of this is *West Cheshire Water Board v Crowe* [1940] 1 KB 793, in which the Board purported to use its available powers to borrow for payment of interest during the initial years of a capital scheme, in order to meet (or reimburse) interest charges which had been paid in nine earlier financial years. The court found that the Board's power to borrow could not be used in respect of previous years' completed transactions.

(d) Redundancy and early retirement packages

9.19 In *Allsop v North Tyneside Metropolitan Borough Council* (1992) 90 LGR 462 the Court of Appeal found that an 'enhanced voluntary severance scheme' involving redundancy payments in excess of those permitted by the statutory scheme[1] was 'contrary to law'. Neither the Local Government Act, s 112, nor s 111 of that Act combined with s 112 or other powers, authorised the local authority to make payments under the voluntary scheme in excess of those permitted under the relevant regulations.

1 Under regulations made under the Superannuation Act 1972.

9.20 In *Hinckley and Bosworth Borough Council v Shaw* [2000] BLGR 9, following the intervention of the district auditor, the local authority sought recovery of an early retirement package which it had awarded to its former principal chief officer which included three months' pay in lieu of notice, a consultancy fee for five months and a pay increase (awarded during the course of his final year) in order to increase his redundancy and pension entitlements. The court found that the authority's agreement to make a payment in lieu of notice was void. Since the employee had received more than adequate notice, the payment amounted to an unlawful gift. The agreement to a salary increase in the final year was also void. The decision to make the increase had not been taken on the basis of power under the Local Government Act 1972, s 112 to fix rates of pay, but for the improper purpose of increasing the employee's redundancy and pension entitlements. However, the court found that the consultancy arrangement was probably a genuine arrangement or, at least, the fee for it was not a gift which no reasonable council could agree to pay. (The court also found that the solicitor who had advised the council on the arrangement had been negligent and was liable to pay the unlawful payments, concurrently with the recipient.)

9.21 Some examples of expenditure which is not, or is not necessarily, contrary to law include:

(1) compromise payments may be lawful[1]. However, as Lord Templeman noted in *Hazell v Hammersmith and Fulham London Borough Council* [1992] 2 AC 1 at 38, none of the cases on compromise provided authority for a statutory corporation to enter into a compromise agreement which involved the corporation performing an unlawful act. Thus, every element of a compromise agreement entered into by a local authority must itself be authorised by statute and otherwise lawful;
(2) a voluntary payment to a contractor in order to keep the contract alive may be lawful, if made with proper regard to the interests of local taxpayers and with reasonable business acumen[2];
(3) expenditure authorised by a court is not 'contrary to law'[3] (but expenditure which is lawful may give rise to a loss in the accounts amenable to the auditor's (current[4]) jurisdiction under ACA 1998, s 18[5]);
(4) breach of a collateral legal obligation does not of itself render expenditure 'contrary to law'[6];
(5) in general, a failure to comply with standing orders[7] would not, of itself, render expenditure incurred in breach thereof 'contrary to law'.

1 See for example *Page-Jones v District Auditor for No 6 Audit District* (1953, unreported).
2 *Re Hurle-Hobbs's Decision* [1944] 2 All ER 261.
3 *R (Duckett) v Calvert* [1898] 2 IR 511.
4 See para **9.42** regarding the prospective repeal of ACA 1998, s 18.
5 See *Davies v Cowperthwaite* [1938] 2 All ER 85.
6 See *Beecham v Metropolitan District Auditor* (1976) 75 LGR 79 in which it was found that demolition of houses by a local authority without planning permission (assuming such permission was required) did not amount to ultra vires action and consequently the expenditure on demolition was not 'contrary to law'.
7 Made under the Local Government Act 1972, s 135 (it is to be noted that LGA 1972, s 135(4) specifies that a contract is not invalidated in these circumstances). In contrast, a breach by a local authority of the requirements under the former compulsory competitive tendering regime ('CCT') (for example under the Local Government Act 1988, Pt I), was considered to give rise to items of account contrary to law. The CCT regime has now been replaced with the 'best value' regime under the Local Government Act 1999, Pt I (see Chapter 7). Whilst it is conceivable that a complete disregard by a local authority of the general statutory duty to make arrangements to secure 'best value' in the exercise of its functions (under the Local Government Act 1999, s 3) might give rise to an item of account which is contrary to law, the obligations of an authority under s 3 are far less specific as to the steps which must be taken by a local authority in relation to the award of an individual contract than those under the former CCT regime and consequently non-compliance is unlikely to be clear-cut. As far as the procedural requirements under the best value regime are concerned, the auditor is given separate obligations in relation to the required review of the best value performance plans (under LGA 1999, s 7) leading, potentially, to recommendations to the Audit Commission (to carry out an inspection under LGA 1999, s 10) and/or to the Secretary of State (to make a direction under s 15 of that Act).

(e) Items of account relating to income

9.22 There is no restriction contained in ACA 1998, s 17(1) which limits an auditor's power to apply to the court for a declaration that an item of account is 'contrary to law', or which constrains the court's power to grant such a declaration, to those cases in which there is some net expenditure incurred by, or loss caused to, the council as a consequence of a particular decision or course of action. Thus, for example, items of account reflecting income unlawfully obtained may be the subject of an application under s 17(1)[1].

1 See *Commission for Local Authority Accounts in Scotland v Stirling District Council* 1984 SLT 442; *Hazell v Hammersmith and Fulham London Borough Council* [1992] 2 AC 1.

3 SANCTION

9.23 At present, the auditor may not make application to the court under ACA 1998, s 17 in respect of an item of account sanctioned by the Secretary of State[1]. A failure to account may also be the subject of sanction[2].

1 See Audit Commission Act 1998, s 17(1)(b), subject to prospective repeal under the Local Government Act 2000.
2 ACA 1998, s 18(1)(a) quoted in para **9.41** and subject to prospective repeal.

9.24 Sanction by the Secretary of State does not make legal that which would otherwise be illegal[1]. It remains open to an objector to challenge the expenditure by other means. However, in *A-G v East Barnet Valley UDC* (1911) 9 LGR 913, in the exercise of its discretion, the court refused to issue an injunction to restrain expenditure which had been sanctioned under earlier comparable powers.

1 *R v Grain, ex p Wandsworth Guardians* [1927] 2 KB 205.

9.25 The policy originally adopted by the Local Government Board in issuing sanctions still appears substantially to be followed by the Secretary of State[1]. The Board said in its Annual Report for 1887–88:

> 'The power of sanction is intended to be used in those cases where the expenditure is incurred bona fide but in ignorance of the strict letter of the law, or inadvertently without the observance of requisite formalities, or under such circumstances as make it fair and equitable that the expenditure should not be disallowed by the auditor ... We do not regard the Act as intended to supply the want of legislative or other authority for particular expenditure or classes of expenditure and as justifying us in giving prospective sanction to recurring expenses'.

1 See the note by the Department of the Environment, Transport and the Regions on application for sanction under ACA 1998, ss 17 and 18, sent to local authorities with a letter dated 25 July 1997.

9.26 The power of the Secretary of State to sanction expenditure has, in practice, been used sparingly. This power is to be repealed by LGA 2000, s 90(2)(a) (and s 90(3) in relation to s 18), once in force. The explanatory notes to the LGA 2000[1] state that the repeal of the provisions on surcharge would remove the need for the Secretary of State to grant sanction.

1 Explanatory notes to the Local Government Act 2000, at para 231.

4 POWERS OF THE COURT

9.27 Under ACA 1998, s 17(2), on an application by an auditor the court may make or refuse the declaration sought. Even if the court is satisfied that an item of account is contrary to law, it still has a discretion to refuse to make a declaration.

9.28 Where the court makes the declaration sought by the auditor, currently, under ACA 1998, s 17(2), it may also:

'*(a) order that any person responsible for incurring or authorising the expenditure declared unlawful shall repay it in whole or in part to the body in question and, where there are two or more such persons, that they shall be jointly and severally liable to do so*[1]*;*

(b) if the expenditure declared unlawful exceeds £2,000 and the person responsible for incurring or authorising it is, or was at the time of his conduct in question, a member of a local authority, order him to be disqualified for being a member of a local authority for a specified period; and

(c) order rectification of the accounts.'

1 This is sometimes referred to as 'surcharge by the court', although the expression does not appear in the legislation.

9.29 The Local Government Act 2000, s 90(2)(b) and (c) provides for the repeal of the powers of the court under ACA 1998, s 17(2)(a) and (b), together with the related provisions of s 17(3) which restrict the powers of the court to order repayment in certain circumstances[1].

1 See para **9.35**.

5 PERSONS LIABLE TO MAKE REPAYMENT AND NATURE OF LIABILITY

9.30 ACA 1998, s 17(2)(a) refers to an order for repayment against 'any person'. The phrase as it appears in the legislation from which s 18 is derived was considered to apply, implicitly, to members and officers of a local authority, but not to a contractor who had submitted fraudulent claims[1]. To date, the position of the other people connected with the council, such as school governors or those running a voluntary organisation funded by a local authority, has not been considered by the courts.

1 *Re Dickson* [1948] 2 KB 95.

9.31 Where the court orders repayment by more than one person found to have been responsible for incurring or authorising expenditure declared to be unlawful, their liability is joint and several[1].

1 Audit Commission Act 1998, s 17(2)(a).

6 MEANING OF 'RESPONSIBLE FOR INCURRING OR AUTHORISING'

9.32 Where no vote is taken on a resolution to incur or authorise expenditure, those present are presumed to have assented[1]. But the presumption is rebuttable by evidence of opposition[2].

1 *R v Hendon RDC, ex p Chorley* [1933] 2 KB 696 at 703.
2 *A-G v Tottenham Local Board of Health* (1872) 27 LT 440; *R v Roberts, ex p Scurr* [1924] 1 KB 514 at 520; *Rothnie v Dearne UDC* (1951) 50 LGR 123.

9.33 Those abstaining or absenting themselves from a meeting may be held to share responsibility: there is a duty to oppose unlawful action[1].

1 Contrast *Joint Stock Discount Co v Brown* (1869) LR 8 Eq 381 at 402–4 and *A-G v Belfast Corpn* (1855) 4 Ir Ch R 119 at 159–161.

7 DISQUALIFICATION

9.34 Under ACA 1998, s 17(2)(b) the court has discretion as to whether to order disqualification of a member or former member (where the sum involved exceeds £2,000) and as to the period of disqualification. This is in contrast with disqualification under s 18(7) in connection with the duty of the auditor to certify under s 18(1)[1].

1 See para **9.73**.

8 RESTRICTIONS ON ORDERING REPAYMENT OR DISQUALIFICATION

9.35 No order for repayment or disqualification may be made if the person responsible for incurring or authorising the expenditure acted reasonably or in the belief that the expenditure was authorised by law. In any other case, the court is required to have regard to all the circumstances, including the person's means and ability to repay[1].

1 See ACA 1998, s 17(3) and cf s 18, referred to in para **9.41**ff, under which there is no parallel provision. It should be noted that both ACA 1998, s 17(3) and s 18 are to be repealed under the Local Government Act 2000, once the relevant provisions are brought into force.

9.36 The court cannot order repayment in a case where expenditure has been lawfully incurred but charged to the wrong account[1]. The same principle may apply where expenditure is charged to the wrong year[2].

1 *R v Dolby* [1892] 2 QB 301.
2 As noted in para **9.47** in relation to an auditor's duty to certify an amount in respect of a loss or deficiency caused by the wilful misconduct of any person under ACA 1998, s 18, no such duty arises if the loss or deficiency in one year's accounts has been made good by a payment recognised in those of a subsequent year: *Fleming v Lees* [1991] COD 50.

9 RECTIFICATION OF THE ACCOUNTS

9.37 Prior to the commencement of the Local Government Act 1972, there was no requirement for rectification of the accounts after an accounting entry had been disallowed. The Audit Commission Act 1998, s 17(2)(c) expressly empowers the court to order rectification of the accounts. This power is to survive the repeal of the remaining sub-paragraphs of ACA 1998, s 17(2). In practice, the court may order that rectification of the accounts be agreed between the audited body and the auditor, with liberty to apply if appropriate rectification cannot be agreed[1].

1 See *Hazell v Hammersmith and Fulham London Borough Council* [1992] 2 AC 1 and *Stockdale v Haringey London Borough Council* (1989) 88 LGR 7.

10 EXERCISE OF DISCRETION BY THE AUDITOR

9.38 The auditor has a *discretion* whether or not to apply to the court for a declaration under ACA 1998, s 17. The auditor must exercise this discretion in accordance with *Wednesbury* principles. Thus he or she might well decide not to apply for a declaration if no useful purpose would be served, for example, because the expenditure is not significant and is unlikely to recur, or if a local authority accepts that the items of account are 'contrary to law' and agrees to rectify its accounts. In such a case the authority and the auditor might agree to an alteration of the accounts pursuant to the Accounts and Audit Regulations 1996[1], reg 13.

1 SI 1996/590.

11 PROCEDURE TO BE FOLLOWED BY AUDITOR

9.39 The Code of Audit Practice[1] gives guidance to auditors on the steps they should take when considering action under ACA 1998, s 17, in consequence of an objection. These paragraphs emphasise the importance of the auditor acting fairly to all affected parties. Auditors are advised:

(a) to make available to the parties, at the appropriate time, any documents which auditors consider to be material to their decision, so far as it is consistent with the good conduct of their enquiries and the principle of fairness;
(b) if they believe fairness requires it, to make their provisional views known to the parties and to consider any further evidence with an open mind;
(c) to consider whether justice and fairness requires that an oral hearing should be arranged and, if so, whether that hearing should be in public, in either case giving all persons concerned due notice to enable them to be present or to be represented;
(d) to give the audited body and individuals directly affected an opportunity to answer relevant allegations and to submit evidence (and if an oral hearing is arranged, there should be an opportunity to cross-examine witnesses);
(e) to communicate their decisions to any persons affected by them and to inform them of the statutory right to appeal; and
(f) to send any statement of reasons by recorded delivery, or by an equally reliable and recorded means[2].

1 Schedule 1, para S1.5ff and in particular paras S1.11–S1.15. See para **8.15** regarding the Code of Audit Practice.
2 See para **8.103**.

12 APPEAL BY AGGRIEVED OBJECTOR

9.40 A person who has objected to the accounts under ACA 1998, s 16(1)(a) and is aggrieved by a decision of an auditor *not* to apply for a declaration under ACA 1998, s 17(1) may appeal to High Court against that decision[1]. On such an appeal the court has the same powers available to it as it would if an application for a declaration had been made by an auditor. At present this means the power to make a declaration, to order repayment by a person or persons responsible, to disqualify members if the expenditure declared unlawful exceeds £2,000 and to order rectification of the accounts. Once the repeals under LGA 2000, s 90(2)(b) are brought into effect, only a declaration and order for rectification could be made by the court.

1 ACA 1998, s 17(4). See para **8.102**ff.

C Duty to certify for failure to account or loss through wilful misconduct

9.41 The Audit Commission Act 1998, s 18(1) currently provides:

'*(1) Where it appears to the auditor carrying out an audit under this Act, other than an audit of accounts of a health service body –*

(a) that any person has failed to bring into account a sum which should have been brought into account and that the failure has not been sanctioned by the Secretary of State, or

(b) that a loss has been incurred or deficiency caused by the wilful misconduct of any person,

the auditor shall certify that the sum, or the amount of the loss or deficiency, is due from that person.'

9.42 The Local Government Act 2000, s 90(3) provides for the repeal of ACA 1998, s 18 in its entirety. The following paragraphs summarise the law prior to this repeal being brought into force.

9.43 Although the word no longer appears in the section, the power of the auditor under ACA 1998, s 18 continues to be referred to as the power to 'surcharge'.

9.44 In *Re Dickson* [1948] 2 KB 95 the Court of Appeal held that the expression 'any person' included officers and members of the body under audit, but excluded external parties such as contractors[1].

1 See further, para **9.30**.

9.45 There is a *duty* to issue a certificate once it appears to the auditor that there has been a failure to account or a loss or deficiency caused by wilful misconduct. (The auditor has a discretion as to recovery of the sum or amount certified as due[1].)

1 See para **9.74**.

9.46 Where a sum is certified as being due from more than one person, their liability is joint and several. Unlike the court considering an order for repayment under ACA 1998, s 17(2)(a), the auditor is not required nor empowered to consider whether the person from whom payment is certified as due has the means or ability to repay it.

9.47 If the failure to account, loss or deficiency is made good before a certificate is issued, the auditor has no duty to perform under ACA 1998, s 18[1].

1 *Fleming v Lees* [1991] COD 50.

1 FAILURE TO ACCOUNT

9.48 A decision not to collect (or a failure to collect) fees or charges as required by statute constitutes a failure to account[1]. This *may*[2] be confined to cases where a personal duty is imposed on the accounting officer by statute[3].

1 *R v Roberts* [1901] 2 KB 117.

2 There is limited case law on the meaning of 'failure to bring into account': *R v Roberts* (see n 1) and the Irish case of *R (O'Carroll) v King* (1910) 50 ILTR 193. Those cases both suggest that there must be

some personal responsibility of the individual to account for the sum. The historical background to this provision appears to be the 'writ of account', which was aimed at someone who had received money, but had not applied it correctly.

3 *R v Roberts* [1901] 2 KB 117.

9.49 It would also be a failure to account if sums collected were not paid over to the body under audit. Both the collector and the person(s) having responsibility for the collection would be liable[1].

1 *R (O'Carroll) v King* (1910) 50 ILTR 193.

9.50 A prima facie case of failure to account may be rebutted by the person responsible showing that the sums in question had been lost without negligence or default on his or her part.

9.51 Bribes and other sums received under colour of office by an individual by virtue of his or her office, or in breach of fiduciary duty, are liable to be paid over to the employer[1] and therefore may be the subject of a surcharge under this heading.

1 *Reading v A-G* [1951] AC 507.

9.52 Action by the auditor for failure to account is precluded, if the failure to bring into account is sanctioned by the Secretary of State[1].

1 ACA 1998, s 18(1)(a). See paras **9.24–9.26** regarding sanction by the Secretary of State.

2 LOSS CAUSED BY WILFUL MISCONDUCT

9.53 The expression 'wilful misconduct' was defined by Webster J in *Graham v Teesdale* (1981) 81 LGR 117 at 123 as follows:

> '"wilful misconduct" means deliberately doing something which is wrong knowing it to be wrong, or with reckless indifference as to whether it is wrong or not.'

9.54 This definition, which must be read so as to include wrongful omissions to act, was cited with approval by the Court of Appeal and accepted by the House of Lords in *Lloyd v McMahon* [1987] AC 625.

9.55 Although a ACA 1998, s 18 enquiry is not a criminal proceeding, it requires a high standard of proof to tip the balance in favour of a positive finding of wilful misconduct, because the accusation is serious and the consequences of such a finding are grave[1]. Of themselves, imprudence, error of judgment, negligence or misconduct, each falls short of wilful misconduct.

1 See per Lawton LJ in *Lloyd v McMahon* [1987] AC 625 at 647.

9.56 Intentional or reckless defiance of the law constitutes wilful misconduct whatever the motive. In the absence of some cogent reason to the contrary, if a member is advised or is otherwise conscious that action contemplated by him or her will amount to misconduct, he or she is guilty of wilful misconduct if he or she persists.

9.57 In *Asher v Lacey*, the case concerning the Clay Cross councillors who refused to raise rents of council housing, the court found[1] that:

> 'No matter how sincerely [the members] believed in the course they followed, no matter how strong their feelings of moral obligation and no matter whether this was a matter of policy or politics, the inescapable fact is that they quite deliberately broke the law.'

Accordingly, the court found that the auditor's decision to surcharge the councillors was correct.

1 [1973] 1 WLR 1412 at 1423, per James LJ.

9.58 In *Lloyd v McMahon* the House of Lords upheld certification by the auditor in respect of losses arising from the failure of Liverpool City councillors to make a rate at the appropriate time, where the councillors had disregarded advice from their officers and warnings from the auditor regarding the unlawfulness of the delay.

9.59 Expenditure which is lawful in itself may still constitute a loss due to wilful misconduct. In *Davies v Cowperthwaite* [1938] 2 All ER 685 it was held on appeal that a payment of costs awarded by a court against the council in connection with an injunction to prevent the authority incurring unlawful expenditure had been lawfully paid by the council to discharge a legally enforceable debt against it. Nonetheless, those who voted for the original resolution to incur the unlawful expenditure were liable to be surcharged with the amount of those costs, having been advised by the clerk as to the unlawfulness of the proposed expenditure.

3 MISCONDUCT

9.60 Withholding, by a member or officer, of information material to an authority's decision is misconduct: *Re Hurle-Hobbs, ex p Riley* (1944) unreported[1]. The case establishes that deliberate neglect amounts to misconduct and that excess of zeal, misplaced enthusiasm, error or lack of judgment is not misconduct.

1 Transcript in Hurle-Hobbs *The Law Relating to District Audit* (2nd edn, 1955), p 182.

9.61 Failure to institute proceedings to recover monies due to the council, without good reason, is misconduct[1].

1 See *Cardigan RDC* (Ministerial decision, 1930; an appeal to a minister from a decision of a district auditor under the law prior to the LGA 1972, not a binding authority).

9.62 Misconduct was found where there was a failure by a school caretaker to check that nothing was obviously wrong when fuel deliveries were made and there had been considerable deficiencies in the amount delivered[1].

1 *Pooley v District Auditor No 8 Audit District* (1964) 63 LGR 60, DC; on appeal (1965) 63 LGR 236, CA.

9.63 Failure to raise income as required by law, giving rise to a loss or deficiency, is surchargeable if caused by wilful misconduct[1].

1 *Asher v Lacey* [1973] 3 All ER 1008; *Smith v Skinner* [1986] RVR 45; on appeal sub nom *Lloyd v McMahon* [1987] AC 625.

4 MEMBERS (AND THEIR INDEPENDENT LIABILITY AT COMMON LAW)

9.64 In considering what conduct is required of a member of a local authority, it is necessary to have regard to his or her position.

9.65 Individual members have a duty to ensure that their authority complies with the law, so far as it is within their power to do so[1]. To the extent that a breach of statutory duty results from a deliberate or reckless failure by any member or officer to discharge his or her own duty, then such a person is guilty of wilful misconduct[2].

1 *Asher v Lacey* [1973] 3 All ER 1008.
2 *Smith v Skinner* [1986] RVR 45; on appeal sub nom *Lloyd v McMahon* [1987] 1 AC 625.

9.66 The members of a local authority hold the resources of the authority in trust to discharge the public purposes vested in them and they are trustees for that purpose[1].

1 See *A-G v Aspinall* (1837) 2 My & Cr 613 at 618, 623, 628–9; *Parr v A-G* (1842) 8 Cl & Fin 409, HL at 431–3; *A-G v De Winton* [1906] 2 Ch 106 at 115; *Barrs v Bethell* [1982] Ch 294 at 306d–h.

9.67 Thus, independently of the Audit Commission Act 1998 and absent of any statutory protection, members of a local authority may be liable to make good resources whose alienation they have wrongly procured[1]. As it was put in *A-G v Belfast Corpn* (1855) 4 Ir Ch R 119 at 161:

> 'As trustees of the corporate estate, nominated by the Legislature, and appointed by their fellow citizens, it is their duty to attend to the interests of the Corporation, conduct themselves honestly and uprightly, and to see that everyone acts for the interests of the trust over which he and they are placed.'

1 See for example *A-G v Wilson* (1840) Cr & Ph 1 at 23–8.

5 OFFICERS

9.68 Duress by threat of dismissal does not constitute a defence to a charge of wilful misconduct[1]. But in some cases duress might negative wilfulness and provide a defence.

1 *Re Hurle-Hobbs's Decision* [1944] 2 All ER 261.

9.69 Nor, in the case of an officer, is obedience to instructions or orders a defence[1].

1 *R v Saunders* (1854) 3 E & B 763; *A-G v De Winton* [1906] 2 Ch 106.

6 ASSESSMENT OF SUMS CERTIFIED DUE

9.70 The use of broad estimates by district auditors in making surcharges was approved in *Roberts v Hopwood* [1925] AC 578 and in *Asher v Secretary of State for the Environment* [1974] 1 Ch 208. In *Pooley v District Auditor No 8 Audit District*[1] the auditor calculated the deficiency of fuel at £6,000, but deducted £2,000 from the sum to be surcharged on the caretaker to allow for the possibility that the entirety of the loss might not have been caused by the caretaker's negligence or misconduct. In *R v Roberts* [1908] 1 KB 407 the auditor's role in assessing the amount to be surcharged was compared with that of a court in assessing damages. Just like a court, an auditor is not precluded from assessing an amount simply because it cannot be assessed with certainty.

1 (1964) 63 LGR 60, DC; on appeal (1965) 63 LGR 236, CA. See para **9.62**.

9.71 Interest must be added to a loss or deficiency[1].

1 *Smith v Skinner* [1986] 26 RVR 45; *Porter v Magill* (1997) 96 LGR 157 (not affected by the decision of the Court of Appeal (1999) 97 LGR 375).

9.72 'Loss or deficiency' is not limited to loss of money as such. Loss of a valuable asset, or even employees' time (involving wasted expenditure on salaries) may give rise to a loss or deficiency, even though the item may not be recorded in the accounts.

7 DISQUALIFICATION

9.73 In the case of wilful misconduct (but not failure to account), if the sum certified as due exceeds £2,000 and the person from whom it is certified as due is, or was at the time of the wilful misconduct, a local authority member, he or she is disqualified from being a member of a local authority for five years[1]. In contrast to the powers of the court where a declaration is made under ACA 1998, s 17[2], the period of disqualification is fixed by the statutory provision.

1 Audit Commission Act 1998, s 18(7).
2 See para **9.34**.

8 RECOVERY ACTION

9.74 The auditor has a power, but not a duty, to recover for the benefit of the body under audit sums certified as due. The body under audit has a concurrent power of recovery[1]. The sum or amount certified as due is payable within 14 days after issue of the certificate, or within 14 days of disposal of any appeal[2]. The usual remedies for the recovery and enforcement of debt apply.

1 Audit Commission Act 1998, s 18(2).
2 ACA 1998, s 18(8).

9.75 In any recovery proceedings, the auditor's certificate is conclusive evidence that the sum is due and a certificate purporting to be so signed is presumed authentic unless the contrary is proved[1].

1 Audit Commission Act 1998, s 18(9).

9 PROCEDURE TO BE FOLLOWED BY AUDITORS AND COSTS OF PARTICIPANTS IN AUDIT PROCEEDINGS

9.76 See para **9.39** regarding the guidance to auditors on procedure contained in Sch 1 to the Code of Audit Practice, which applies equally to consideration of action under ACA 1998, s 18. In relation to the legal costs of officers and members who take part in audit proceedings, the Divisional Court found that a local authority would be empowered to indemnify both officers and members for such costs under LGA 1972, s 111[1].

1 In *R v Westminster City Council, ex p Union of Managerial and Professional Officers* and *R v Westminster City Council, ex p Legg* (2000) Times, 13 June. The existence of such a power was not, however, disputed by any of the parties.

10 APPEAL AGAINST CERTIFICATION OR DECISION NOT TO CERTIFY

9.77 Under ACA 1998, s 18(3), a person aggrieved by a decision of an auditor to certify a sum due from him or her under this section may appeal to the High Court. Under ACA 1998, s 18(5), an objector aggrieved by a decision *not* to certify, may appeal to the High Court. On appeal, the court may confirm, vary or quash the decision and give any certificate which the auditor could have given.

9.78 Prior to the reform of the civil procedure rules it was clear that an appeal by a person aggrieved should be by way of a re-hearing under RSC Ord 55, r3[1]. In *Porter v Magill* (1997) 96 LGR 157 the Divisional Court considered that the appeal should be conducted as a re-hearing, even in circumstances where the auditor had arranged an oral hearing. The CPR[2] does not (as yet) deal specifically with appeals under the Audit Commission Act 1998. Rule 52.11, concerning appeal against a decision of a lower court[3], allows re-hearing as an exception to the rule that appeals should be limited to a review if the court considers that in the circumstances of an individual appeal it would be in the interest of justice to do so. The *Practice Direction* on Part 52 of the CPR[4] provides that an appeal from a minister, person or other body should be a re-hearing if no hearing was held by that party to come to the decision in question, or if the procedure for that hearing did not provide for the consideration of evidence. In *Boardman v Portman* (22 May 2000, unreported) Elias J considered that, at least in a case where no oral hearing had taken place, the position under the CPR was the same as that described in *Lloyd v McMahon*, ie a re-hearing should be conducted on appeal.

1 *Lloyd v McMahon* [1987] AC 625. The decision in *Re Baird* [1989] NI 56 to the contrary is inconsistent with the decision of the House of Lords in *Lloyd v McMahon*.
2 The Civil Procedure Rules 1998, SI 1998/3132 as amended.
3 'Lower court' is defined to include a person or body from whose decision an appeal is brought: CPR, r 52.1(3)(c).
4 Paragraph 9.1.

9.79 Both rights of appeal under ACA 1998, s 18 would be rendered redundant by the repeal of the auditor's power to surcharge and are included in the repeals to be implemented under the Local Government Act 2000.

11 THE NEW ETHICAL FRAMEWORK—LGA 2000, PT III

9.80 As noted at the outset of this section, the Local Government Act 2000, s 90(3), once in force, will repeal the Audit Commission Act 1998, s 18. This follows on from recommendations in the Third Report of the Nolan Committee on Standards in Public Life[1] ('the Nolan Report'), carried through into the White Paper, *Modern Local Government: In Touch with the People*[2] ('the White Paper').

1 Cm 3702-1, July 1997.
2 Cm 4014, July 1998.

9.81 Part III of the Local Government Act 2000[1] provides for the establishment of a new 'ethical framework' for local government, the features of which, for England[2], are to include:

(a) the introduction of statutory codes of conduct, with a requirement for every local authority to adopt a code covering the conduct of elected and co-opted members[3] and for such a code to be incorporated in contracts of employment of officers[4]; and

(b) the creation of a standards committee for each local authority to advise the authority on the adoption or revision of a code of conduct; monitor the operation of the authority's code; advise and train elected members on the code[5]; and if so provided for in regulations made by the Secretary of State[6], to take such action as may be prescribed against an elected or co-opted member (or former member), following consideration of a report from the authority's monitoring officer[7];

(c) the establishment of a new non-Departmental public body: 'the Standards Board for England' to provide an independent process for investigation of allegations that an elected or co-opted member has failed to comply with a code of conduct; to appoint 'ethical standards officers'; and to issue guidance to local authorities and other bodies within s 49(6)[8];

(d) the statutory functions of ethical standards officers are to include the investigation of allegations of misconduct by elected and co-opted members (and former members); the production of reports on investigations, and reference of matters of concern to the authority's monitoring officer or the president of the Adjudication Panel for England (see below); and powers to issue an interim report in the public interest in cases of serious concern, which may include a recommendation that a member be suspended, or partially suspended, for a period of up to six months[9];

(e) the establishment of the 'Adjudication Panel for England'[10] to conduct adjudications on findings of ethical standards officers and recommendations for suspension of members through 'case tribunals' and 'interim case tribunals' consisting of at least three members of the Panel appointed by the president or deputy president of the Panel[11] (with the case tribunals being placed under the supervision of the Council of Tribunals[12]);

(f) powers for a case tribunal to suspend, or partially suspend, a member for up to one year, or to disqualify a person from being a member of any relevant authority for up to five years, if the tribunal has found that the person has failed to comply with the code of conduct[13];

(g) rights for a member (or former member) to appeal to the High Court against suspension by an interim case tribunal, or a decision of a case tribunal[14].

1 See paras **6.19–6.43** for a fuller description of the new ethical framework under the Local Government Act 2000, Pt III, which is not in force at the time of writing. By virtue of s 108(4), this Part will come into force automatically on 28 July 2001, if no earlier date is appointed by the Secretary of State under s 108(5)(d) (in relation to England), or by the National Assembly for Wales under s 108(6)(b) (in relation to Wales). The current intention appears to be that Pt III should be brought into force from 1 April 2001.
2 Different provision is made for certain of the following matters in relation to Wales. See in particular the LGA 2000, ss 68–74 on investigations by a Local Commissioner.
3 LGA 2000, ss 49 and 50.
4 LGA 2000, s 82.
5 LGA 2000, s 54(2).
6 LGA 2000, s 66(2).
7 Designated by the authority under the LGHA 1989, s 5.
8 LGA 2000, ss 57 and 58 and Sch 4. See n 2 regarding investigations in Wales.
9 LGA 2000, ss 59, 64 and 65.

10 LGA 2000, s 75(1). The Adjudication Panel for Wales is to be established under s 75(2).
11 LGA 2000, s 76.
12 LGA 2000, Sch 5, para 28.
13 LGA 2000, s 79. An interim case tribunal can suspend, or partially suspend, a member for a maximum of six months (s 78(1)(b)) and the ethical standards officer may continue his or her investigation whether or not a decision to suspend is made (s 78(4)).
14 LGA 2000, ss 78(10) and 79(15).

9.82 Whilst the Local Government Act 2000 includes various criminal sanctions connected with the new ethical framework, including an offence of failure to provide information, explanation or certain documents to an ethical standards officer[1], and in respect of disclosure of information in contravention of a restriction[2], it does not deal with the creation of any new offence of 'misuse of public office', as was recommended in the Nolan Report. The White Paper indicated that this proposal was to be considered in the wider context of the Government's consideration of the criminal justice system[3].

1 LGA 2000, s 62(10).
2 LGA 2000, s 63(4).
3 See Cm 4014, para 6.30.

9.83 In relation to the financial consequences of the (then) proposed abolition of surcharge, the explanatory notes[1] to the Local Government Bill indicated that this should have minimal impact on public sector expenditure, suggesting that, as at present, local authorities would still be able to pursue losses arising through criminal misconduct through the courts. It is important to recognise that the repeal of the surcharge provisions will not remove liability in circumstances where surcharge would have been appropriate. What the repeal does is to remove a particular mechanism for recovery, with the result that local authorities may themselves have to assume responsibilities in this regard and/or, in some cases, recovery may be made by the making of compensation orders in criminal proceedings.

1 Explanatory notes to the Local Government Bill introduced in the House of Lords on 25 November 1999, at para 164.

D Prohibition orders

9.84 The Audit Commission Act 1998, s 20 currently provides:

> '*(1) The auditor for the time being of the accounts of a body subject to audit other than a health service body may issue an order under this section (a 'prohibition order') if he has reason to believe that the body or an officer of the body –*
>
> *(a) is about to make or has made a decision which involves or would involve the body incurring expenditure which is unlawful,*
>
> *(b) is about to take or has taken a course of action which, if pursued to its conclusion, would be unlawful and likely to cause a loss or deficiency; or*
>
> *(c) is about to enter an item of account, the entry of which is unlawful.*'

9.85 Once in force, the Local Government Act 2000, s 91(2) will repeal this, and the subsequent subsections of ACA 1998, s 20 and the related provisions of s 21 (restriction on powers to issue prohibition orders), s 22 (effect of orders and appeals) and s 23 (loss etc caused by prohibition orders).

9.86 The provisions on prohibition orders (and the provisions empowering auditors to apply for judicial review described at paras **9.99–9.105**) were originally introduced by the Local Government Act 1988, s 30 following recommendations made by the Widdecombe Committee of Inquiry into the Conduct of Local Authority Business[1], that the Audit Service should be empowered to apply legal remedies more quickly to stop a local authority incurring unlawful expenditure or loss or from entering an unlawful item of account. The intention was to give auditors the power to intervene at an early stage in order to reduce the risks of illegal spending and losses and, ultimately, the need for long and difficult cases on surcharge. The overall effect of a prohibition order is to *prevent* action by a local authority[2].

1 Report dated 19 June 1986, Cmnd 9797.
2 If the auditor seeks to compel action by a local authority he or she would need to consider resorting to an application for mandamus under the powers to apply for judicial review pursuant to ACA 1998, s 24.

9.87 In summary, the present provisions of ACA 1998, s 20:

(a) provide for the auditor to have discretion to serve a prohibition order where he or she has reason to believe that a decision or other action described in sub-paras (a)–(c) of ACA 1998, s 20(1)[1] is about to be (or in the case of (a) and (b), has been) taken by a local authority or one of its officers[2];
(b) specify that the actions of a committee or sub-committee of a local authority are to be treated as actions of the local authority itself[3];
(c) require that the prohibition order be addressed to the local authority or the officer concerned, and:
    (i) specify which para (a)–(c) of s 20(1) is relevant;
    (ii) specify the decision, course of action or item of account to which the order relates;
    (iii) require the body or officer to desist from making or implementing the decision, taking or continuing to take the course of action, or entering the item of account; and
    (iv) specify the date on which the order is to come into effect, being no earlier than the date on which it is served on the local authority and any officer to whom it is addressed[4] (but see (e) below);
(d) require that copies of the order be served on the local authority, any officer to whom it is addressed, and such other persons as the auditor considers appropriate[5];
(e) provide that the prohibition order will not have effect unless, within seven days of serving it, the auditor serves on the body and any officer to whom it is addressed, a statement of reasons for the auditor's belief referred to in s 20(1)[6];
(f) provide that the auditor may at any time revoke, but not vary, a prohibition order[7];
(g) specify that if more than one auditor is responsible for auditing the accounts of the local authority, they may either issue the prohibition order jointly or decide between them by whom it should be served[8].

1 See para **9.84**.
2 Audit Commission Act 1998, s 20(1).
3 ACA 1998, s 20(2).
4 ACA 1998, s 20(3).
5 ACA 1998, s 20(5).
6 ACA 1998, s 20(6). Section 22(2)(a) indicates that the order takes effect on the date specified within it subject to this requirement having been satisfied: thus there may be a period of a few days pending

service of the statement of reasons whilst it is unclear as to whether or not the prohibition will be fully effective.
7 ACA 1998, s 20(8).
8 ACA 1998, s 20(4).

9.88 The auditor is entitled to recover from the local authority concerned any expenses reasonably incurred in or in connection with the issue of a prohibition order[1].

1 Audit Commission Act 1998, s 22(5).

9.89 By virtue of ACA 1998, s 21, where the chief finance officer has made a report under the Local Government Finance Act 1988, s 114 in respect of a decision, course of action or item of account, no prohibition order can be issued by the auditor in respect of that matter during the period between issue of the finance officer's report and consideration by the local authority of that report[1]. A report from the chief finance officer has a similar effect to that of a prohibition order during this period in that until the local authority has considered the finance officer's report, it is prohibited from proceeding further with the course of conduct which is the subject of the report[2].

1 Compare the proposed provisions on 'advisory notices' referred to in para **9.95**ff.
2 See the Local Government Finance Act 1988, s 115(5) and (6).

9.90 Whilst a prohibition order has effect, it is unlawful for the local authority or any officer of the authority to make or implement the decision, to continue the course of action or to enter the item of account[1]. The order will continue to have effect, subject to any order or decision on appeal against it, until it is revoked by the auditor under ACA 1998, s 20(8)[2].

1 Audit Commission Act 1998, s 22(1).
2 ACA 1998, s 22(2).

9.91 Not later than 28 days after service of the statement of reasons under ACA 1998, s 20(6), the local authority (but not an officer of the authority) may appeal against the prohibition order to the High Court, in accordance with the rules of the court[1]. No statutory rights of appeal are given to any other party, whose means of challenge would be by way of an application for judicial review of the auditor's decision to issue the order (or indeed, revoke it).

1 Audit Commission Act 1998, s 22(3).

9.92 On an appeal under ACA 1998, s 22(3), the court may make such order as it thinks fit for the authority to pay the expenses incurred by the auditor in connection with the appeal[1]. It is envisaged that the court would have power to award costs against the auditor in an appropriate case[2].

1 Audit Commission Act 1998, s 22(4).
2 ACA 1998, s 23(2).

9.93 Where the effect of a prohibition order is to prevent the completion of a contract for the sale or acquisition of land by a local authority, the existence of the order is explicitly stated not to prejudice any entitlement to damages any third party might have by reason of the authority's failure to complete the contract[1].

1 Audit Commission Act 1998, s 23(1).

9.94 By virtue of ACA 1998, s 23(2), the auditor is protected from any action for loss or damage alleged to have been caused by a prohibition order issued in good faith.

E Advisory notices

9.95 In addition to the prospective repeal of the statutory provisions concerning surcharge, sanction by the Secretary of State, and the prohibition orders referred to in the previous section, the Local Government Act 2000 provides, in s 91(1), for the creation of a new discretionary power for an auditor to issue an 'advisory notice' on virtually identical grounds to those currently provided for in ACA 1998, s 20(1)[1]. Most of the procedural requirements for the service of an advisory notice and a statement of reasons are in comparable terms to those regarding prohibition orders, as are those concerning ancillary matters such as the effect on land transactions[2] and the protection from liability of the auditor[3]. However, there are some significant differences.

1 See LGA 2000, s 91(1), inserting new ss 19A, 19B, and 19C in the ACA 1998. In common with other amendments referred to in this chapter, at the time of writing no date has been appointed for these provisions to come into force (see LGA 2000, s 108(3)(a)). See para **9.84** regarding ACA 1998, s 20(1).
2 See para **9.93**. The equivalent provision in relation to advisory notices is s 19C(1).
3 See para **9.94**. The equivalent provision in relation to advisory notices is s 19C(2).

9.96 The main distinctions between the effect of an advisory note as opposed to the present prohibition order would be:

(1) An advisory notice would have effect on the day it is served and would cease to have effect if the statement of reasons is not served by the auditor within seven days or, if it is so served, when the notice is withdrawn by the auditor[1].
(2) Rather than prohibiting action until the matter has been disposed of by the court through an appeal, or until the auditor withdraws the order of his or her own volition, an advisory notice would require the local authority (or the officer) to give the auditor a specified period of prior notice (being no greater than 21 days) if the local authority (or officer) intends to make or implement the decision, take the course of action or enter the item of account, notwithstanding the service of the advisory notice[2].
(3) The effect of the notice would be such that it would only be unlawful for the local authority to proceed with the decision, course of action or entry of the item of account during any period whilst the local authority had not complied with specified conditions[3].
(4) The conditions are that the local authority:
    (i) has considered, in the light of the advisory notice and the statement of reasons, the consequences of doing the thing mentioned in the notice;
    (ii) has given the auditor the specified period of notice in writing of its intention to proceed; and
    (iii) the notice period (being a maximum of 21 days) has expired[4].

    In the absence of any effective action being taken by the auditor before the notice period expires[5], at the end of that period it would not be unlawful for the local authority to carry out its intentions.
(5) There would appear to be nothing in the advisory notice provisions which would prevent the auditor taking action concurrently with any which might be taken by way of report by the local authority's chief finance officer under the

Local Government Finance Act 1988, s 114[6] (or by its monitoring officer under the Local Government and Housing Act 1989, s 5).

1 ACA 1998, s 19B(3), to be inserted by LGA 2000, s 91(1).
2 ACA 1998, s 19A(3)(d).
3 ACA 1998, s 19B(1).
4 ACA 1998, s 19B(2).
5 See para **9.98**.
6 Contrast para **9.89** in relation to a prohibition order.

9.97 The explanatory notes to the Local Government Act 2000[1] indicate that the intention of the advisory notice procedure is to allow the auditor time to seek the opinion of the court on the legality of the local authority's intended decisions and action and suggests that the authority 'may then only proceed if the court decides that it is lawful or the auditor does not seek legal opinion within the notice period'. Thus, the intention of the proposals for advisory notices is to shift the onus from the authority to appeal to the court (as against a prohibition order), to the auditor to apply to the court for clarification in respect of a disputed matter arising from an advisory notice.

1 Explanatory notes to the Local Government Bill introduced in the House of Lords on 25 November 1999, at paras 233 and 234.

9.98 Where a local authority gives notice to the auditor of its intention to proceed, one course of action open to the auditor would be to apply for judicial review of that decision under the Audit Commission Act 1998, s 24[1]. In practice it is to be expected that the auditor would seek an undertaking from the authority not to implement its disputed course of action until the matter had been considered by the court. If no undertaking is given, the auditor might seek an interim order to preserve the position when making the application for permission to apply for judicial review.

1 See para **9.99**.

F Judicial review

9.99 The Audit Commission Act 1998, s 24 provides:

'(1) Subject to section 31(3) of the Supreme Court Act 1981 (no application for judicial review without leave) the auditor appointed in relation to the accounts of a body other than a health service body may make an application for judicial review with respect to –

(a) any decision of that body, or
(b) any failure by that body to act,

which it is reasonable to believe would have an effect on the accounts of that body.

(2) The existence of the powers conferred on an auditor under this Act is not a ground for refusing an application falling within subsection (1) (or an application for leave to make such an application).

(3) On an application for judicial review made as mentioned in subsection (1), the court may make such order as it thinks fit for the payment, by the body to whose decision the application relates, of expenses incurred by the auditor in connection with the application.'

9.100 ACA 1998, s 24 is not affected by any prospective repeal or amendment under the Local Government Act 2000.

9.101 Again, this is an example of a discretionary power and not a duty for the auditor to take action, in this instance by seeking permission to apply for judicial review of a decision taken by a local authority, or its failure to act.

9.102 The auditor may take action under this power in relation to matters even if they are not reflected in the accounts and/or do not involve expenditure, provided it is reasonable to believe that the matter would have an effect on the accounts. The time limit for action is that which relates to any application for judicial review under CPR[1], Pt 54, r 54.5, ie promptly and in any event not later than three months after the grounds to make the claim first arose.

1 The Civil Procedure Rules 1998, SI 1998/3132 as amended.

9.103 In appropriate cases, the court can order interim relief, for example prohibiting the authority from proceeding until the issues have been determined by the court.

9.104 In *R v Wirral Metropolitan Borough Council, ex p Milstead* (1989) 87 LGR 611, an application for judicial review was made by an auditor under the legislation which preceded ACA 1998, s 24. The court made an order of certiorari to quash an unlawful decision of a local authority to enter into a 'factoring agreement' to sell its anticipated receipts from future sales of land in order to increase the local authority's current year capital expenditure allocation by treating a proportion of the sums received under the factoring agreement as 'capital receipts' under the former system for control of local authority capital finance under the Local Government, Planning and Land Act 1980, Pt VIII.

9.105 Since the *Wirral* case, auditors have rarely relied on their powers under ACA 1998, s 24 (or on the earlier equivalent powers under the Local Government Finance Act 1982). It remains to be seen whether auditors will resort to the use of s 24 any more frequently once the relevant provisions of the Local Government Act 2000 are brought into force to repeal surcharge and prohibition orders and to create the system of 'advisory notices'.

PART III

Capital finance

CHAPTER 10

Introduction to capital finance

10.1 This chapter describes the context of the current capital finance system and introduces some of the underlying principles and concepts which are explored in greater depth in the subsequent chapters of this Part. The organisation of Part III is as follows:

Chapter 10	Introduction to Capital Finance
Chapter 11	Credit Approvals, Limits and Provision for Credit Liabilities
Chapter 12	Credit Arrangements
Chapter 13	Borrowing
Chapter 14	Capital Receipts and Notional Capital Receipts

10.2 Proposals for the reform of local government are summarised in Chapter 1. At the time of writing, there are indications that a Green Paper on Government proposals for reform of the current system of statutory controls on local authority capital finance may be issued during the late summer of 2000. The White Paper, *Modern Local Government: In Touch with the People*[1], stated that the Government would keep the capital finance system under review. During 1999 the Department of the Environment, Transport and the Regions ('DETR') commissioned consultants[2] to undertake research into options for an improved and simpler capital finance system. The consultants explored the possibility of a system which places less emphasis on statutory control mechanisms and gives greater dominance to professional standards and self-monitoring by local authorities. Their proposals envisage the replacement of some of the statutory controls on borrowing and other forms of credit with a framework of 'prudential indicators', and the possible replacement of mandatory debt redemption, with a non-statutory framework for prudent repayment of local authority debt.

1 Cm 4014, July 1998; see para **9.25**.
2 PriceWaterhouseCoopers, see the two papers on *Prudential Indicators* and *A Prudential Framework for Repaying Debt and Providing for the Replacement of Assets* published by the DETR Local Government Research Unit on 11 November 1999 and 7 December 1999 respectively.

10.3 It is unclear at the time of writing what will emerge from the Government's present deliberations, or what the impact on the current legislation would be if the consultants' proposals were to be adopted in whole or in part (their proposals retain many of the underlying features of the current system). This Part sets out the law as at August 2000, which seems set to apply (other than any minor changes) throughout the financial year 2000–2001.

A Background to the current system under the LGHA 1989, Pt IV

10.4 The enactment of Pt IV of the Local Government and Housing Act 1989 ('LGHA 1989') represented an attempt to overhaul and rationalise the legislation on local authority capital finance. The 1989 system was devised to provide the government with a more effective means of controlling local authority capital expenditure and borrowing than the previous legislation could provide. The immediate aims were to reduce the stock of capital assets owned by local authorities, to reduce the level of their debt and to redistribute spending power between authorities[1].

1 See the consultation paper issued by the Department of the Environment on 7 July 1988: 'Capital Expenditure and Finance'. These aims appear to go beyond the avoidance of 'dissipation by local authorities of the receipts from the disposal of their assets', which was how Judge LJ described the general purpose of LGHA 1989, Pt IV in *R v Brent London Borough Council, ex p O'Malley* (1997) 30 HLR 328 at 366.

10.5 LGHA 1989, Pt IV is a product of its time, tailor made to tackle the ingenuity local authorities had applied to minimising the impact of the previous systems under Pt VIII of the Local Government, Planning and Land Act 1980 ('LGPLA 1980'), which controlled 'prescribed expenditure' and the separate controls, in Sch 13 to the Local Government Act 1972, which dealt with borrowing. The approach used in Pt IV entailed a change in the technique for regulating local authority finance. Rather than imposing direct limits on capital spending as LGPLA 1980 had endeavoured to do, LGHA 1989 concentrates on regulating the *sources* from which local authorities finance capital expenditure. It stipulates the way in which receipts from the disposal of capital assets may be used and imposes mandatory requirements to make provision to meet 'credit liabilities[1]'.

1 Which includes liabilities in respect of borrowing and under credit arrangements.

10.6 The various approaches adopted by local authorities under the old legislation had resulted in manifold amendments to LGPLA 1980, but that Act was intrinsically ill-equipped to deal with the perceived problems. The replacement system under LGHA 1989, Pt IV was devised to address specifically the various methods used by local authorities to obtain capital assets which do not in law amount to borrowing, but which can nonetheless have a similar economic effect, such as deferred purchase, contractor credit and leasing schemes. Part IV also makes provision for other means by which local authorities might obtain capital assets such as barter, including land swaps. Through the process known as 'Receipts Taken Into Account'[1], used in setting authorities' annual credit approvals, the Secretary of State is provided with one means by which to achieve a redistribution of spending power between local authorities. Part IV applies, in an adapted form, to certain activities of companies (and industrial and provident societies) which are 'regulated' by local authorities[2].

1 See para **11.24**.
2 See Chapter 16.

B Importance of subordinate legislation

10.7 Part IV, like other Parts of LGHA 1989, contains the framework of the regulatory regime. Most importantly, it gives the Secretary of State extensive powers to create subordinate legislation and thereby a comparatively swift and flexible means through which to shift the effects of the legislation and to adjust it to prevailing circumstances. The changes introduced through the Local Authorities (Capital Finance) Regulations 1997 ('LA(CF)R 1997'[1]) and earlier regulations in relation to the Private Finance Initiative, which are described in Chapter 15 are a good example of this, created, paradoxically to facilitate some of the very types of scheme which the LGHA 1989 had been designed to curtail. A consistent theme of the use of subordinate legislation under Pt IV was to provide incentives to local authorities to dispose of capital assets, either through permanent concessions or during temporary periods, and often directed at particular categories of land or other assets. More recently, subordinate legislation[2] has been used to end set-aside on most capital receipts and notional capital receipts (other than those from the disposal of housing land), thus changing the effects of the present system simply but significantly[3]. In relation to Wales, subject to minor exceptions[4], the functions of the Secretary of State under LGHA 1989 have, since 1 July 1999, been exercisable by the National Assembly for Wales by virtue of the National Assembly for Wales (Transfer of Functions) Order 1999, SI 1999/672[5]. References to the Secretary of State in relation to LGHA 1989 as it applies to Wales should therefore be taken to be references to the National Assembly for Wales.

1 SI 1997/319 as amended by SI 1997/848, SI 1998/371, SI 1998/602, SI 1998/1937, SI 1999/501, SI 1999/1852, SI 1999/3423, SI 2000/992 (Wales), SI 2000/1033, SI 2000/1474, SI 2000/1553 and SI 2000/1773.
2 See the Local Authorities (Capital Finance) (Amendment No 3) Regulations 1998, SI 1998/1937.
3 See paras **10.26**(d), **10.34** and **14.26**.
4 The exceptions are LGHA 1989, s 43(3), and in so far as they relate to a fire authority: ss 43(2), 53(1) and 54(1).
5 See National Assembly for Wales (Transfer of Functions) Order 1999, SI 1999/672, art 2 and Sch 1.

C Introduction to controls under Pt IV of the LGHA 1989

10.8 The expression 'local authorities' for the purpose of Pt IV of the LGHA 1989[1], and as used in this Part of the book, encompasses not only county, borough county[2], district and London borough councils and the Common Council of the City of London, but also such bodies as police authorities[3], fire, civil defence and transport joint authorities, waste disposal authorities[4], National Park authorities, joint and special planning boards[5], and the Broads Authority . The Secretary of State may, by regulations[6], prescribe additional bodies to whom Part IV is to apply[7]. The LGHA 1989, s 39(1) lists the bodies which are subject to the revenue and capital finance regime under Pt IV of that Act. This list has been frequently amended, but includes:

(a) a county council;
(b) a county borough council (in Wales);
(c) a district council[8];
(d) the Greater London Authority;
(e) a functional body, within the meaning of the Greater London Authority Act 1999;
(f) a London borough council;
(g) the Common Council of the City of London, in the capacities specified in LGHA 1989, s 39(2);
(h) the Council of the Isles of Scilly;
(i) the Greater London Magistrates' Courts Authority;
(j) a waste disposal authority[9];
(k) a joint authority for fire services, civil defence or transport[10];

(l) a joint planning board for an area in Wales outside a National Park[11];
(m) the Broads Authority;
(n) a National Park authority;
(o) a fire authority constituted by a combination scheme[12];
(p) a police authority[13];
(q) the Service Authority for the National Crime Squad[14];
(r) any other body prescribed by regulations made by the Secretary of State under LGHA 1989, s 39(3)[15].

1 See Local Government and Housing Act 1989, s 39.
2 See Local Government (Wales) Act 1994.
3 See Police Act 1996.
4 See the Local Government Act 1985, s 10.
5 Created by orders under the Local Government Act 1972 or the Town and Country Planning Act 1990.
6 See Local Government and Housing Act 1989, s 39(3).
7 This power has been used to bring certain pension authorities within Pt IV of the 1989 Act: see SI 1990/404.
8 Unitary authorities created under local government reorganisation in England pursuant to the Local Government Finance Act 1992 have the status of district councils, except for the Isle of Wight, which has county status.
9 Established under LGA 1985, s 10.
10 Established under LGA 1985, Pt IV.
11 By an order made under the Town and Country Planning Act 1990, s 2(1B).
12 Made under the Fire Services Act 1947 in consequence of certain provisions for reorganisation in England and Wales.
13 Established under the Police Act 1996, s 3.
14 See the Police Act 1997, s 67.
15 See the Local Authorities (Capital Finance) (Prescribed Bodies) Regulations 1990, SI 1990/404. The London Pension Fund Authority and the South Yorkshire Pensions Authority have both been prescribed for these purposes.

10.9 LGHA 1989, Pt IV applies to the finances of local authorities for the financial years commencing on or after 1 April 1990, when most of the relevant subordinate legislation came into effect. The Act includes transitional provisions[1] to address the hand-over from the LGPLA 1980 system, which are now, in the main, of little practical consequence. Throughout Part III of this book the position is stated as it applies in England, although certain of the main provisions for Wales are referred to.

1 For example, in LGHA 1989, s 52 and Pt I of Sch 3.

10.10 The remainder of this chapter is dedicated to the basic principles on which LGHA 1989, Pt IV is built. It provides an introduction to the subsequent chapters, which cover the detailed controls in relation to credit arrangements, borrowing, capital receipts and the special reliefs and concessions from the basic regime, created by subordinate legislation.

D Expenditure to be charged to revenue account

10.11 Strange though it may at first appear, the starting point to describe the rules relating to capital finance is the fundamental principle, in LGHA 1989, s 41, that all local authority expenditure must be charged to a revenue account of the authority, *unless* one of the statutory exceptions applies[1]. An item of expenditure which must be charged to a revenue account should be so charged in the year in which it is incurred unless, in accordance with proper practices[2], it is appropriate for a particular item to be charged to an earlier or later year.

1 The 1988 consultation paper on capital finance (Cm 4014, July 1998) stated that the new system would adopt the accounting convention of presumption that all expenditure should be charged to a revenue account in the accounting period in which it is incurred unless all or a major part of the benefits would accrue in future accounting periods, in which case it could normally be capitalised.
2 Defined by LGHA 1989, s 66(4). Non-statutory 'proper practices' are listed in Circular 11/90, Annex D at para 4. They are currently contained in the Code of Practice on Local Authority Accounting in Great Britain published annually by CIPFA.

10.12 The requirement to charge expenditure to revenue, subject only to closely prescribed exceptions, forms an essential component of the controls on both revenue finance and borrowing.

E Exceptions to the obligation to charge to revenue account

10.13 LGHA 1989, s 42 prescribes the exceptions to the general obligation of local authorities to charge all expenditure to a revenue account. But even in these exceptional cases, authorities may choose to charge the expenditure to revenue, provided such treatment accords with proper practices.

10.14 The exceptions listed in LGHA 1989, s 42(2) mainly relate to expenditure which is, broadly speaking, connected with capital purposes[1]:

(a) expenditure arising from the discharge of any liability of the authority under a credit arrangement[2], other than an excluded credit arrangement[3];
(b) expenditure arising from the discharge of any liability of the authority in respect of money borrowed by the authority, other than a liability in respect of interest;
(c) expenditure which, in reliance on a credit approval[4], the authority have determined[5] is not to be chargeable to a revenue account of the authority;
(d) expenditure on making approved investments[6];
(e) expenditure consisting of the application or payment of capital receipts under LGHA 1989, s 59(7)–(9)[7];
(f) expenditure which is met out of the usable part of capital receipts[8];
(g) expenditure for capital purposes which the authority determine is, or is to be, reimbursed or met out of money provided, or to be provided, by any other person, (excluding grants from a Community institution, other than contributions from any of the Structural Funds[9]);
(h) expenditure in respect of payments out of a superannuation fund[10]; and
(i) expenditure in respect of payments out of a trust fund which is held for charitable purposes and of which the authority is a trustee.

1 Local Government and Housing Act 1989, s 40 and see para **10.15**ff.
2 LGHA 1989, s 48 (the categories of credit arrangement are summarised in para **12.4**).
3 Excluded by regulations made under para 11 of Sch 3 to the 1989 Act; see regs 122 and 123 of the 1997 Capital Finance Regulations and paras **12.45** and **12.46**.
4 Local Government and Housing Act 1989, ss 53 and 54 and see para **11.1**ff.
5 LGHA 1989, s 56(1)(a).
6 'Approved investments' is defined by LGHA 1989, s 66(1)(a) and a list of such investments is contained in the Local Authorities (Capital Finance) (Approved Investments) Regulations 1990, SI 1990/426.
7 Local Government and Housing Act 1989, ss 59(7)–(9) and see paras **14.32** and **14.34**.
8 LGHA 1989, s 60(2) and see para **14.42**ff.
9 See SI 2000/589.
10 Which the authority are required to keep by virtue of the Superannuation Act 1972.

F Expenditure for capital purposes: definition

1 BASIC DEFINITIONS OF CAPITAL EXPENDITURE

10.15 Under LGHA 1989, s 40(2), 'expenditure for capital purposes' is expenditure on:

(a) the acquisition, reclamation, enhancement or laying out of land, exclusive of roads, buildings and other structures;
(b) the acquisition, construction, preparation, enhancement or replacement of roads, buildings and other structures; and
(c) the acquisition, installation or replacement of movable or immovable plant, machinery and apparatus and vehicles and vessels.

10.16 Under LGHA 1989, s 40(4), the following expenditure, is also expenditure for capital purposes, unless it is expenditure on approved investments:

(a) the making of advances, grants or other financial assistance to any person towards expenditure on the matters mentioned in paras (a)–(c) of LGHA 1989, s 40(2) or on the acquisition of investments; and
(b) the acquisition of share capital or loan capital in any body corporate.

2 ENHANCEMENT

10.17 For these purposes, 'enhancement' in relation to any asset, means the carrying out of works which are intended:

(a) to lengthen substantially the useful life of the asset; or
(b) to increase substantially the open market value of the asset; or
(c) to increase substantially the extent to which the asset can or will be used for the purposes of or in connection with the functions of the local authority concerned;

provided, in each case, that it accords with proper practices to regard the expenditure as being for capital purposes[1].

1 Local Government and Housing Act 1989, s 40(3).

3 EXCEPTIONS CREATED BY REGULATIONS MADE BY THE SECRETARY OF STATE

10.18 Under LGHA 1989, s 40(5) the Secretary of State is empowered to make regulations which provide for other types of expenditure to be treated as being for capital purposes and, conversely, to specify that certain capital expenditure should not be treated in that way. Regulations 2–8 of LA(CF)R 1997 deal with expenditure which is to be for capital purposes, and regs 9 and 10 deal with that which is not.

10.19 In addition, under LGHA 1989, s 40(6), the Secretary of State may *direct* that expenditure may be treated by the authority concerned as expenditure for capital purposes which:

(a) is of a description, or for a purpose, specified in the direction; and
(b) has been or is to be incurred by a particular local authority; and

(c) does not exceed such amount as is specified in the direction; and
(d) was or will be incurred during a period specified in the direction.

10.20 An example of the use of the Secretary of State's power under LGHA 1989, s 40(5) has been to provide, by regulations, for expenditure incurred under a 'private finance transaction[1]' to be expenditure for capital purposes in so far as it would not otherwise be so[2]. An example of the use of the power of the Secretary of State to issue directions under LGHA 1989, s 40(6) is to authorise a local authority to 'capitalise' the costs of redundancy of staff in order to meet those costs from usable capital receipts.

1 Under LA(CF)R 1997, reg 16; see Chapter 15.
2 Ibid, reg 8, the intended effect of which is to ensure that the arrangement is within the authority's powers under s 50(1) of the LGHA 1989. (It has been suggested that an incidental effect of reg 8 is that it would enable a local authority to use, pursuant to LGHA 1989, s 60(2)(a), the usable part of capital receipts to meet its payment obligations under a private finance transaction, subject to proper accountancy considerations). Regulation 8A (introduced by SI 1998/1937) provides for expenditure by a 'participating authority' in making certain voluntary payments to a 'designated authority' in connection with local government reorganisation to be 'expenditure for capital purposes'.

G Approved investments

10.21 The purpose of approved investments is to enable a local authority to invest funds, which are not immediately required for the purposes for which they are held, in certain ways approved by the Secretary of State. Thus, balances, financial reserves and unapplied capital receipts, which are not held in the form of cash and which have not been lent internally within the authority, may be invested in approved investments. (It is to be noted that there is no all-embracing express power for a local authority to make investments, despite the apparent assumption behind several legislative provisions that such a general power does exist. There are, however, a number of specific investment powers[1].)

1 Examples of specific powers to make investments include those under the Local Government Finance Act 1988, s 89(5), which authorises an authority to invest (or otherwise use) sums held in the collection fund which are not immediately required in such manner as may be prescribed in regulations made by the Secretary of State. (The Local Authorities (Funds) (England) Regulations 1992, SI 1992/2428, reg 13 has been made under this provision.) Other examples of specific investment powers include the investment of superannuation funds under the Local Government Pension Scheme (Management and Investment of Funds Regulations 1998/1831, reg 9 and of the art fund under the Public Libraries and Museums Act 1964, Sch 2, para 4. In other cases investment might be authorised under the Local Government Act 1972, s 111 incidental to the function for which the money is held, and in view of the general obligations of the authority to make proper provision for financial administration (for example, under the Local Government Act 1972, s 151).

10.22 The normal controls on the use of capital receipts do not apply to approved investments, as expenditure on making them is not treated as being expenditure for capital purposes[1] (although they do not have to be charged to a revenue account[2]) and the receipts from their disposal are not capital receipts[3] and accordingly are not subject to the requirements on 'set-aside[4]'. In effect, approved investments are treated similarly to cash.

1 Local Government and Housing Act 1989, s 40(4).
2 LGHA 1989, s 42(2)(d).
3 LGHA 1989, s 58(1)(b).
4 See Chapter 14.

10.23 Approved investments are those specified by the Secretary of State in regulations made for the purpose of LGHA 1989, s 66(1)(a). The current regulations are the Local Authorities (Capital Finance) (Approved Investments) Regulations 1990 as amended[1] ('LAR 1990').

1 SI 1990/426, as amended or modified by SI 1991/501, SI 1992/1353, SI 1992/3218, SI 1994/2567, SI 1995/850, SI 1995/1041, SI 1995/1982, SI 1996/568, SI 1997/319, SI 1999/1852, SI 2000/968 and SI 2000/1033.

10.24 The list of approved investments encompasses[1]:

(a) certain investments made on or before 21 December 1989[2];
(b) any deposit with an 'authorised institution'[3], or the Bank of England;
(c) any deposit with, or shares in, a building society;
(d) shares in a successor of a building society, acquired by a local authority as a member of that society following a transfer of the society's business under the Building Societies Act 1986, s 97;
(e) any bill of exchange accepted by an authorised institution;
(f) Treasury bills;
(g) Gilt edged securities[4];
(h) listed securities issued by certain bodies specified in Pt I of the Schedule to the LAR 1990[5];
(i) listed securities issued by specified bodies or where repayment is guaranteed by the government;
(j) loans and advances made to other local authorities and the other bodies listed in Pt II of the Schedule to the LAR 1990.

1 See reg 2 of the LAR 1990.
2 Provided that expenditure on making the investment would not have been 'prescribed expenditure' under the LGPLA 1980 system if made on 21 December 1989, or the amount of prescribed expenditure would have been taken to be nil.
3 This expression has the same meaning as in the Banking Act 1987, but is taken to include a European deposit-taker; see reg 1(2) of SI 1990/426 and SI 1992/3218.
4 Any securities specified in an order made under para 1 of Pt I of Sch 2 to the Capital Gains Tax Act 1979 and the securities specified in Pt II of that Schedule.
5 The Schedule specifies such bodies as the European Investment Bank, the International Monetary Fund, the African, Asian, Caribbean and Inter-American Development Banks and the European Bank for Reconstruction and Development.

10.25 To qualify as an 'approved investment', the detailed arrangements must conform with LAR 1990, reg 3. For example, the investment and all other payments and repayments in respect of it must be made in sterling. All consideration received by the authority in respect of the investment must be wholly in money. Certain deposits, bills of exchange, loans and advances (other than those made with the Bank of England) under (a)–(e) and (j) above must (in brief) be:

(a) repayable or redeemable on less than 12 months' notice; or
(b) repayable or redeemable at less than five years' notice, provided that the authority has a nil or negative credit ceiling at the beginning of the year when the investment is made and, at the time the investment is made, has only limited forms of outstanding borrowings *and* the total amount invested in, or with, any one person does not exceed 25% of all their 'longer term investments[1]'.

1 As defined by reg 3(4) of the Local Authorities (Capital Finance) (Approved Investments) Regulations 1990, SI 1990/426 as amended.

H Overview of the controls under Pt IV of the LGHA 1989

10.26 Before looking in detail at individual aspects of the regime under LGHA 1989, Pt IV in subsequent chapters it may be helpful to provide an overview of the basic features of the current system, which illustrates how it is aimed at controlling the sources from which local authorities fund capital expenditure:

(a) The permitted sources of capital expenditure comprise:
  - (i) borrowing or credit arrangements;
  - (ii) government grants or contributions from third parties;
  - (iii) the local authority's own resources, either from revenue or usable capital receipts.

(b) Borrowing and credit arrangements are subject to common limits through the system of credit approvals and the aggregate credit limit. Credit arrangements are intended to cover leasing and all other forms of obtaining the use or benefit of capital assets on credit[1].

(c) The amount of the annual limits on borrowing and credit arrangements set by credit approvals are intended to take into account the extent to which the authority has available to it usable capital receipts with which to fund capital expenditure[2].

(d) When capital assets are sold, the basic rule under the scheme of the LGHA 1989 is that in most cases only a proportion of the capital receipt can be used for new capital projects. The remainder must be reserved (or 'set aside') for credit liabilities. Prior to September 1998, in the majority of cases, a specified proportion of 50% of the capital receipt had to be reserved, so that only 50% was usable. However, since September 1998[3], the obligation to set aside has been reduced to 0% for virtually all capital receipts, other than those from the disposal of housing land and certain shares[4].

(e) The receipt of non-monetary consideration by a local authority (a 'notional capital receipt') leads to a similar obligation to make provision for credit liabilities as if a cash payment had been received, which would often be met through the usable capital receipts generated from other transactions. Again, since 1 September 1998[5] the percentage to be set aside in respect of notional capital receipts has been reduced to 0% for most non-housing notional capital receipts[6].

(f) Although authorities are 'free' to use revenue to fund capital expenditure, their ability to raise revenue is constrained[7].

(g) Authorities are normally required to make minimum provision from revenue for their credit liabilities annually, both in respect of principal and notional interest on credit arrangements[8].

(h) The basic rules under LGHA 1989, Pt IV are subject to a number of variations and exceptions, mainly contained in the LA(CF)R 1997[9].

(i) Authorities which are debt-free can normally use 100% of most of their capital receipts, are not required to make minimum revenue provision annually, and are less restricted in the purposes for which provision they have made for credit liabilities can be applied.

1 See Chapters 11 and 12.
2 See Chapter 11.
3 See SI 1998/1937.
4 See Chapter 14.
5 See SI 1998/1937.

6 See Chapter 14.
7 Under the Local Government Finance Act 1992, Pt I as amended with effect from 1 April 2000 by the Local Government Act 1999, Pt II.
8 See Chapter 12.
9 See Chapters 12 and 14.

10.27 As noted in paras **10.2** and **10.3**, research is now under way into the possible replacement of the current arrangements for regulating local authority capital finance with a system based on 'prudential indicators' and greater self-regulation by local authorities, including the possible replacement of minimum revenue provision by a non-statutory scheme for debt provision.

I Special treatment of debt-free authorities

10.28 Throughout Part III of the Book, reference is made to exceptions made under the capital finance system for authorities who are 'debt-free'. This expression does not appear in the LGHA 1989 and the criteria under which an authority is to be eligible for special treatment are not identical in all cases. It may be helpful to summarise at the outset of this Part, the main ways in which authorities with debt-free status (as determined in different ways for different purposes) are accorded exceptional treatment.

1 Approved investments[1]

10.29 Under LAR 1990, reg 3(3)[2], a debt-free authority may make approved investments which are longer-term than those of other authorities, being repayable on up to five years' notice, rather than up to 12 months' (subject to a 25% limitation on the amount invested with a single body). This applies to authorities who have both a nil or negative credit ceiling at the beginning of the financial year in which the investment is made and at the time of the investment, have no borrowing outstanding other than short-term and certain hard to redeem debts.

1 See para **10.21**ff.
2 The Local Authorities (Capital Finance) (Approved Investments) Regulations 1990, SI 1990/426 as amended.

2 Minimum revenue provision[1]

10.30 By virtue of LGHA 1989, Sch 3, para 15(2), authorities who are debt-free are not required to make minimum revenue provision each year for their credit liabilities under LGHA 1989, s 63(1). This applies to local authorities who have a nil or negative credit ceiling on the last day of the previous financial year[2].

1 See para **11.46**ff.
2 In this case, there is no requirement that the authority should be free of long-term borrowing.

3 Application of provision for credit liabilities ('PCL')[1]

10.31 Under LA(CF)R 1997, reg 156[2] debt-free authorities can apply the provision they have made for credit liabilities to most expenditure for capital purposes (other than certain financial assistance for housing associations), or transfer PCL to certain other authorities under LGHA 1989, s 64(2)(b) and

LA(CF)R 1997, reg 158. This applies to authorities who not only have a *negative* credit ceiling at the beginning of the financial year but who also have no outstanding borrowing other than 'disregarded borrowing', which comprises short term borrowing and certain hard to redeem debts. The amount of PCL which can be applied in any financial year is restricted to the amount by which the credit ceiling was negative at the beginning of that year.

1 See para **11.61**ff.
2 Made under Local Government and Housing Act 1989, s 64(2).

10.32 If a debt-free authority (which meets the two criteria referred to in the previous paragraph) has balances which are even greater than the amount by which their credit ceiling is a negative figure and *if* it has any credit approvals, it will be able to spend those balances, pursuant to LGHA 1989, s 64(1)(c). LA(CF)R 1997, reg 119 ensures that the use of a credit approval in these circumstances will not increase the authority's credit ceiling, and thus the authority will not risk forfeiting the benefit of debt-free status.

4 Commutation loss[1]

10.33 Certain commuted payments made by the Secretary of State in the financial year 1992–1993 led, at least in the short term, to losses by local authorities. Adjustments were made to the provisions on minimum revenue provision to compensate for this loss. As debt-free authorities are not required to make minimum revenue provision, they cannot take the benefit of this adjustment. To compensate for this, under LA(CF)R 1997, reg 157 'debt-free authorities' are entitled to apply PCL for revenue purposes each year in a sum up to the amount of the commutation adjustment for the year in question. This applies to local authorities who have a negative credit ceiling on the last day of the preceding financial year.

1 See para **11.68**ff.

5 Reserved part of capital receipts and notional capital receipts[1]

10.34 Under LA(CF)R 1997, reg 65, the 'reserved part' of most capital receipts, and the equivalent provision to be made in respect of most notional capital receipts, of a debt-free authority is nil. Since the abolition in September 1998 of set-aside on most non-housing capital receipts and notional receipts for *all* local authorities, by the introduction of a set-aside percentage of 0% under LA(CF)R 1997, reg 64A[2], this distinction is of less practical significance. However, 'debt-free authorities' benefit from 0% set-aside in cases where other authorities continue to be required to make set-aside provision under –

reg 66 receipts from the disposal of share or loan capital;
reg 66A receipts from the disposal of non-approved investments other than share or loan capital;
reg 68A voluntary payments received as a 'designated authority' from a 'participating authority' in relation to local government reorganisation; and
reg 72 receipts from the disposal of hostels and lodging houses.

This beneficial treatment applies to local authorities who, at the beginning of the financial year, have a credit ceiling which is nil or a negative amount and, at the time the capital receipt is received, have no money outstanding by way of borrowing other than 'disregarded borrowing'. The most important exception to the 100% use of capital receipts by debt-free authorities concerns receipts from the sale of council houses *otherwise* than under the 'right to buy'. For example, where the receipt is derived from a large scale voluntary transfer of housing to a registered social landlord, the normal set-aside obligations in respect of the receipts from disposal of housing assets would apply. Further exceptions are made (ie where normal set-aside obligations apply) in respect of the repayment of certain housing association grants[3], contributions from other authorities in respect of transferred debt[4], and payments in respect of redemption of the landlord's share under the Housing Act 1985[5].

1 See para **14.24**ff.
2 Inserted in LA(CF)R 1997 by SI 1998/1937, reg 6.
3 LA(CF)R 1997, reg 67.
4 LA(CF)R 1997, reg 68.
5 LA(CF)R 1997, reg 69.

6 Private finance transactions[1]

10.35 Private finance transactions constitute a new category of credit arrangement created by the Secretary of State by regulations made under LGHA 1989, s 48(1)(c). Their nature and treatment within the capital finance system are described in subsequent chapters. Special administrative arrangements have been created to provide revenue support for such transactions. One method of providing this support has been through the issue of a supplementary credit approval (but given the title of a 'non scoring credit approval'). The use of a credit approval by a debt-free authority would normally have the effect of increasing the credit ceiling and putting the authority's debt-free status in jeopardy. However, in order to tackle this problem, use has been made of the concept of an 'excluded credit arrangement' under LGHA 1989, Sch 3, para 11(2)[2]. This is because one special feature of an excluded arrangement is that the use of a credit approval to provide credit cover for it has no effect on the credit ceiling[3]. Under LA(CF)R 1997, reg 123, if a debt-free authority makes a determination to use a supplementary credit approval (or 'non-scoring credit approval') which has been issued to it in relation to a private finance transaction[4], the credit arrangement is to be an 'excluded credit arrangement', and thus the use of the SCA will not result in an increase in the credit ceiling. This regulation applies to local authorities whose credit ceiling is either nil or a negative amount at the beginning of the financial year in which the credit arrangement is entered into and who have no money outstanding by way of borrowing, other than 'disregarded borrowing' within LA(CF)R 1997, reg 65.

1 See para **12.30**ff and Chapter 15.
2 See para **12.45**ff.
3 See Local Government and Housing Act 1989, Sch 3, para 11(2).
4 As defined by Local Authorities (Capital Finance) Regulations 1997, reg 16.

7 Regulated companies[1]

10.36 Under the Local Authorities (Companies) Order 1995[2], local authorities are required to provide credit cover for certain transactions of 'regulated companies'. This requirement applies equally to an authority which is debt-free. However, assuming that the authority continues to maintain its debt-free status, in subsequent years it will be entitled to rely on the concessions referred to in paras **10.31** and **10.32** to make use of any PCL it has made in respect of a regulated company's transaction[3]. If the authority provides 'credit cover' for a transaction of a regulated company by the means of treating a credit approval as reduced[4], this will not involve any increase in the credit ceiling[5]. Although debt-free authorities can use PCL for most capital purposes, this does not mean that they can use it to provide credit cover under the Order, as this would not constitute making 'expenditure for capital purposes'.

1 See para **16.50**.
2 SI 1995/849 as amended by SI 1996/621.
3 Under art 14(5)(a) of the Local Authorities (Companies) Order 1995, SI 1995/849 as amended by SI 1996/621.
4 SI 1995/849 as amended, art 14(5)(b).
5 This would be so regardless of whether the authority concerned was debt-free, because such action does not count as the 'use' of credit approval.

J Special treatment of European Community grants

10.37 Up to 31 March 2000 receipt of European Community grant of any kind was excluded from many of the basic capital finance provisions, such as those which authorise a local authority not to charge capital expenditure to a revenue account if it is to be reimbursed by a third party[1], or those which allow temporary borrowing for capital purposes in anticipation of reimbursement by an external body[2]. Further, if grant of any kind was received by an authority from a European Community institution, an amount equal to that grant was required to be set aside by the authority, immediately, for credit liabilities[3]. In practice, local authorities usually obtained supplementary credit approval from the Secretary of State under LGHA 1989, s 54 to enable them to spend such grants. The effect of this was to give the Secretary of State control over the potential for authorities to expand their spending power through obtaining European funds.

1 Local Government and Housing Act 1989, s 42(2)(g).
2 LGHA 1989, s 62(5).
3 LGHA 1989, s 63(4).

10.38 The policy behind this approach appeared to be that local authority expenditure financed by European Regional Development Fund and similar grants was considered to be public expenditure financed by UK taxpayers which should not provide authorities with additional spending power[1]. This corresponded with the previous capital finance system in treating the receipt of European grant assistance almost as a form of credit.

1 See para A.31 of the 1988 Consultation Paper referred to at para **10.2**.

10.39 However, as from 1 April 2000 the provisions of LGHA 1989, ss 42(2)(g), 62(5), 63(4) and 66(1) have been amended by SI 2000/589 so as to exclude references to grants from the Structural Funds[1], in order to ensure that they are consistent with the principle of 'additionality' in relation to Community structural funds as set out in art 11 of Council Regulation (EC) No 1260/1999.

1 'Structural Funds' means the European Regional Development Fund, the European Social Fund, the European Agricultural Guidance and Guarantee Fund and the Financial Instrument for Fisheries Guidance. See SI 2000/589.

CHAPTER 11

Credit approvals, limits and provision for credit liabilities

A Credit approvals

1 PURPOSE OF CREDIT APPROVALS

11.1 Credit approvals are a key component of central government control on local authority finance. As the name implies, the effect of a credit approval is to allow an authority to pay for capital expenditure through credit, either by means of conventional borrowing or by entering into a credit arrangement[1]. Under the LGHA 1989, s 56(1) a credit approval may be used either:

(a) as authority not to charge capital expenditure to a revenue account[2]; or
(b) as authority to enter into, or to agree to vary, a credit arrangement[3].

It will be noted that the LGHA 1989 does not, in explicit terms, state that a credit approval may be used to authorise borrowing, but this is the cumulative effect of the relevant provisions. Borrowing and credit arrangement, are two important methods by which local authorities finance capital expenditure, the remaining choices available to an authority to fund such expenditure would be from grants, usable capital receipts or revenue subject, of course, to the availability of these resources[4]).

1 See Chapter 12.
2 As a result of a determination by the authority under Local Government and Housing Act 1989, s 56(1)(a). See also s 42(2)(c).
3 See LGHA 1989, s 56(1)(b).
4 See Chapter 10.

11.2 Credit approvals take two forms: basic credit approval ('BCA') and supplementary credit approval ('SCA') and each is explained in more detail below. A credit approval is issued[1] in the form of a notice in writing to a local authority and is expressed as an amount in money[2].

1 BCAs are issued by the Secretary of State; SCAs may be issued by any minister of the Crown.
2 But in the case of a BCA, it may be nil.

11.3 The use of credit approval normally has the effect of increasing an authority's credit ceiling[1] by an equal amount, and in turn its aggregate credit limit ('ACL'[2]). In this way, the ACL 'expands', so that it is not exceeded because of the particular transaction for which the credit approval has been used.

1 See para **11.36**ff.
2 See para **11.29**ff.

11.4 The issue of credit approvals normally triggers an administrative mechanism for providing revenue support in successive years in respect of the financing cost of borrowing or expenditure under credit arrangements as described in para **11.27**.

11.5 Local authorities are given the opportunity to decide how best to use their credit approvals (if any) in terms of the choices under LGHA 1989, s 56(1)[1]. But an authority's determination as to whether to use a credit approval to authorise borrowing, or entry into or variation of a credit arrangement, must be made no later than 30 September in the financial year following that in which the authority defrays the expenditure, or enters into or varies the credit arrangement[2]. In the case of borrowing, the credit approval is 'used' when the cash is spent, rather than when a loan is taken out[3]. The use of a credit approval is the only means of ensuring that the expenditure of borrowed money is not charged to a revenue account. Reliance on a credit approval is one means of providing the 'credit cover' required[4] to enter into or vary a credit arrangement. The alternative method of providing credit cover is through the authority voluntarily setting aside usable capital receipts, or revenue, as provision to meet credit liabilities[5].

1 See para **11.1**.
2 See Local Government and Housing Act 1989, s 56(5).
3 LGHA 1989, s 56(3)(a).
4 LGHA 1989, s 50(2).
5 LGHA 1989, s 50(3). A determination under s 50(3)(c) to provide credit cover for a credit arrangement by making additional provision to meet credit liabilities from *revenue* must be made no later than 30 September in the financial year which follows that in which the particular credit arrangement requiring cover comes into being (LGHA 1989, s 50(5)).

11.6 Credit approvals are referred to as being 'used' if they are applied in one of the two ways envisaged in LGHA 1989, s 56(1) referred to in para **11.1**. Use of a credit approval will normally lead to an increase in the authority's credit ceiling[1]. Credit approvals are treated as 'reduced' or 'extinguished', with no effect on the credit ceiling if:

(a) they have been applied to an overspend arising in 1989–90 (as required under the provisions on transition from the previous capital finance system[2]); or
(b) they have been subject to a deduction as a consequence of the receipt of a specified capital grant[3]; or
(c) they are reduced to provide credit cover for a transaction of a regulated company[4].

1 See para **11.40**.
2 Local Government and Housing Act 1989, Sch 3, Pt 1, para 2.
3 LGHA 1989, s 57(2). See paras **11.9–11.11**.
4 Under Local Authorities (Companies) Order 1995 (SI 1995/849), art 14(5)(b).

11.7 In terms of the priority[1] of use or reduction of credit approvals, it seems that the 'first call' would be in respect of any 1989–90 overspend. The next in priority would be a deduction in respect of a specified capital grant, unless a credit approval relevant to that grant has been received *before* the grant itself is received and, by the time the grant is received, the approval has actually been 'used' in the terms of LGHA 1989, s 56(3). This means that not only has a determination been made to apply the approval to borrowing or to a credit arrangement, but that expenditure has by then actually *been defrayed*, or a credit arrangement *has been* entered into or varied.

1 See Circular 11/90, Annex A, para 42. This description appears to reflect the combined effect of various provisions of the 1989 Act: s 56(3) and s 57(4),(5),(6); Sch 3, para 2.

11.8 Any credit approval which has not been used, or reduced or extinguished by the authority to which it was originally issued, may be transferred to another local authority[1].

1 Local Government and Housing Act 1989, s 56(2).

2 SPECIFIED CAPITAL GRANTS

11.9 Specified capital grants (SCGs) merit a particular mention as they are given special treatment under the capital finance system. SCGs are defined in LGHA 1989, s 57(1) as being those which meet certain basic criteria, and are specified by the Secretary of State in regulations. The basic criteria in s 57 require that SCGs should constitute payments to authorities in aid of capital expenditure and exclude any 'commuted payments'. (Commuted payments are, in essence, single or other 'lump sum' payments made to a local authority by the Secretary of State or other minister in lieu of an annual or other periodic payment[1].) The current regulations made by the Secretary of State in respect of SCGs are contained in the LA(CF)R 1997, Pt V, regs 52–55.

1 See LGHA 1989, ss 63(2),(3) and 157.

11.10 SCGs currently relate to housing, and include disabled facilities grant. When a local authority receives an SCG it must treat such of its credit approvals as are 'relevant to that grant' as reduced or extinguished by the amount of the grant. If any balance remains after that reduction, it is a first call on any subsequent relevant credit approval. The rationale behind these special arrangements is that if a grant is given for a particular purpose, that should reduce or eliminate the authority's need to borrow (or enter into a credit arrangement) for that purpose.

11.11 A credit approval is 'relevant' to an SCG if it has effect when the grant is received, or at any subsequent time, and is an approval which can be used for the same purposes as the SCG. As BCAs can normally be used for *any* capital purpose they will usually be 'relevant', provided they have effect at the appropriate times. Whether an SCA is 'relevant' will depend upon the particular purpose for which it has been issued (which must be specified in the approval pursuant to LGHA 1989, s 54(2)[1]), as well as the period of time during which it has effect.

1 See para **11.14**.

3 BASIC CREDIT APPROVALS

11.12 BCAs are dealt with in LGHA 1989, s 53. They are issued to local authorities in England by the Secretary of State for the Environment, Transport and the Regions[1]. They have effect only in relation to a particular financial year and must be issued before the start of that year. The approval may be limited, by expressly excluding capital purposes of a particular description, but otherwise it may be used to authorise capital expenditure of any kind. A basic credit approval may be nil, but cannot be a negative amount.

1 Or for Welsh authorities, by the National Assembly for Wales, or the Secretary of State for Wales in relation to fire and police authorities: see the National Assembly for Wales (Transfer of Functions) Order, SI 1999/672, art 2 and Sch 1.

11.13 Under LGHA 1989, s 53(4), the Secretary of State has power to make regulations[1] to specify an 'amortisation period' during which the authority would be required to make provision to set aside money from a revenue account in order to discharge the credit liabilities authorised by the credit approval. Different amortisation periods may be specified by the Secretary of State for credit arrangements and capital expenditure of different descriptions[2]. The implications of an amortisation period being specified would be that the authority would have to make full provision for the liability (both principal and interest) out of revenue over the specified period through equal annual payments, rather than at the usual rate of 4% per annum, or 2% for housing.

1 As at 1 August 2000, no regulations had been made under these provisions.
2 Local Government and Housing Act 1989, s 53(5).

4 SUPPLEMENTARY CREDIT APPROVALS

11.14 SCAs, provided for under LGHA 1989, s 54, may be issued by *any* minister of the Crown and are issued for a particular transaction, project or programme. The approval will only apply to expenditure of the *description specified* in the approval and will have effect for the particular *period specified* in the approval (thus it might apply for a greater, or lesser, period than a single financial year). An SCA may be issued up to six months after the end of the financial year in which the specified period begins[1].

1 Notwithstanding this (limited) scope for retrospective approval, local authorities were advised against incurring expenditure, or entering into or varying a credit arrangement, on the assumption that an SCA would subsequently be issued, unless they had actually been informed (by the appropriate government department) that an SCA would be forthcoming and the basis on which it would be provided. See Circular 11/90, Annex A, para 37.

11.15 If the expenditure to which the SCA relates is only 'capital' expenditure on account of a *direction* given by the Secretary of State under LGHA 1989, s 40(6), then the Secretary of State has discretion to specify an amortisation period in issuing the approval[1]. The significance of an amortisation period being specified is mentioned in para **11.13**.

1 See LGHA 1989, s 54(5) as amended by s 2 of the Local Government Finance (Supplementary Credit Approvals) Act 1997, as from 6 November 1997 replacing the former obligation of the Secretary of State to specify an amortisation period of no more than seven years in such cases.

11.16 Under special administrative arrangements for private finance transactions[1], one aspect of which involves the issue of SCAs (formerly given the special title of 'non-scoring credit approvals'), a non-statutory system of 'promissory notes' has been devised with the intention of giving the local authority and other parties involved in the transaction sufficient certainty to enable them to complete the contractual arrangements before an approval is actually issued[2].

1 See Chapters 12 and 15.
2 Promissory notes are also issued in relation to 'notional credit approvals', the main form of 'PFI Credit'. See the Explanatory Note on the Private Finance Initiative and Local Authorities, updated by the DETR in September 1998, para 4.13 (and see Chapter 15). However, to date this particular form of support for PFI projects (an SCA) has not been used and, in general, revenue support for the initial years of PFI schemes is provided by way of Special Grant (paid by the Secretary of State with the consent of the Treasury under the Local Government Finance Act 1988, s 88B).

5 CRITERIA FOR ISSUING APPROVALS

11.17 The statutory criteria for issuing credit approvals are set out in LGHA 1989, s 55. Subject to the matters mentioned in the next two paragraphs, the Secretary of State or other minister may have regard to 'such factors as appear to him to be appropriate'.

11.18 In issuing BCAs or SCAs the Secretary of State *may*, in particular, have regard to the following:

(a) any grants or contributions from other persons received, or likely to be received, in respect of expenditure of the authority incurred before the expiry of the period for which the credit approval has effect[1];
(b) the amount of capital receipts which the authority has received, or might reasonably be expected to receive, before the expiry of the credit approval period, except those items referred to in sub-paras (a) and (b) of the next paragraph[2].

1 Local Government and Housing Act 1989, s 55(2)(a).
2 LGHA 1989, s 55(2)(b).

11.19 The Secretary of State may *not* have regard to the following:

(a) in determining the amount of a BCA (but not an SCA), the Secretary of State may not take account of *capital receipts* which the authority is *required*[1] to set aside for credit liabilities[2];
(b) in determining the amount of a BCA *or* an SCA, the Secretary of State may not take account[3] of capital receipts received by an authority as trustee of a charitable trust[4]; or receipts which are to be applied to fulfil 'clawback' or repayment provisions to a Minister of the Crown in respect of some earlier financial assistance[5]; or which have been applied to defray the administrative and incidental costs of disposals under the right to buy and certain other sales of housing land[6];
(c) in determining the amount of a BCA *or* an SCA the Secretary of State is prohibited from taking into account the extent to which the authority is, or is not, likely to be in a position to finance expenditure for capital purposes from a revenue account[7].

1 See the requirements under Local Government and Housing Act 1989, ss 59 and 61.
2 Local Government and Housing Act 1989, s 55(3) as amended by the Local Government Finance (Supplementary Credit Approvals) Act 1997, s 1. The significance of the amendment is that in determining the amount of any SCA the Secretary of State *may* take into consideration the amount of reserved capital receipts which a local authority has built up; see para **11.20**.
3 Local Government and Housing Act 1989, s 55(3) as amended.
4 LGHA 1989, s 59(7).
5 LGHA 1989, s 59(8).
6 LGHA 1989, s 59(9).
7 LGHA 1989, s 55(4).

11.20 The principle referred to in sub-para (a) above reflects an amendment made to LGHA 1989, s 55 by the Local Government Finance (Supplementary Credit Approvals) Act 1997, designed to facilitate the government's 'Capital Receipt Initiative'[1]. The Secretary of State is now able to take into account the extent to which a local authority has available to it set-aside capital receipts as one of the criteria for deciding the amount of any SCA. This was an impermissible factor prior to the amendment under the 1997 Act. (Consideration of set-aside receipts is still excluded in relation to the issue of BCAs). The broad aim of the Capital Receipts Initiative was to allow phased spending of built-up reserved capital receipts[2] on the improvement of local authority housing stock through the issue of SCAs. Under this Initiative the SCAs were distributed between authorities partly on the basis of the extent to which they had built up set-aside receipts since the introduction of the system under LGHA 1989, and partly in accordance with their assessed need to spend on housing[3]. No separate allocation of Capital Receipt Initiative resources was made for 2000–2001.

1 Described in a consultation paper issued to local authorities by the Department of the Environment, Transport and the Regions on 19 June 1997 and guidance issued by DETR to authorities on 1 October 1997.
2 Intended to be used particularly in relation to those reserved receipts which had been derived from the disposal of council dwellings.
3 This approach would enable the Secretary of State to redress the imbalance between authorities with a high need to spend on housing, but minimal levels of reserved capital receipts and those with less need to spend, but high levels of reserves. For 1999–2000, £570 million is to be made available to local authorities to fund investment in housing under the Capital Receipts Initiative in the form of SCAs and with revenue support provided through Housing Revenue Account Subsidy and Revenue Support Grant (announcement by Minister for Housing, 17 December 1998).

6 THE CURRENT PROCESS FOR ISSUING CREDIT APPROVALS

11.21 The national total available for allocation as BCAs among all local authorities derives from the Public Expenditure Survey and is determined by the Treasury. The Department of the Environment, Transport and the Regions notifies local authorities annually, usually in December, of how the total sum is to be allocated between individual authorities, when BCAs and Annual Capital Guidelines (ACGs) are announced.

11.22 ACGs are an assessment of a local authority's need for capital expenditure, calculated separately for individual 'service blocks': housing, social services, education, transport and 'all other services'.

11.23 In general terms, the calculation of an individual authority's share of the national total allocation of credit approvals depends upon:

(a) assessments made by government departments of that authority's need for capital expenditure relative to the needs of other local authorities (as reflected in the total of its ACG allocations for the 'service blocks' for which it is responsible); and
(b) at least in theory, an assessment of its relative ability to finance capital expenditure from its usable capital receipts (as reflected in the Receipts Taken into Account (RTIAs) deduction from its total ACG allocations).

11.24 RTIAs are notional amounts of usable capital receipts considered to be available to the local authority, based on a national figure. The RTIA system is intended to provide a mechanism through which support in the form of BCAs can be directed to those authorities who have fewer usable capital receipts available to them. For 2000–01 the national RTIA total was some £350 million[1].

1 DETR: *Local Government Finance Statistics—Key Facts*, December 1999.

11.25 An individual authority's BCA is determined by the Department as the sum of its ACGs for each service block, *less* its deemed share of the national total of RTIAs. It is said by the DETR that, in practice, between 25% and 30% of an authority's usable capital receipts are taken into account to reduce its ACG allocation and produce the figure for the amount of its BCA[1]. In 1998–99, 101 local authorities received no BCA at all because their usable capital receipts were considered sufficient to equal or exceed the amount of their ACGs[2].

1 DETR consultation paper *Modernising Local Government—Capital Finance*, 1998, Appendix A. For 2000–01, the proportion was 20.2%.
2 In 2000–01, 60 local authorities received no BCA.

11.26 At the time of writing the Government is pursuing proposals to reform the present system for allocating capital resources to local authorities through the introduction of what is termed the 'Single Capital Pot' covering most of the resources covered by ACGs, some resources now allocated through SCAs and certain grants and competitive funding regimes[1]. The Single Capital Pot would be allocated partly on the basis of a formula reflecting the government's perception of individual authorities' need to spend and partly on the basis of its competitive assessment of authorities' strategies and performance. The Single Capital Pot is to be introduced for the financial year 2002–2003[2].

1 See the White Paper, *Modern Local Government: In Touch with the People* Cm 4014 (July 1998), paras 9.6–9.16 and the letter to Chief Executives from the DETR of 23 June 1999, giving a progress report on the development of the Single Capital Pot.
2 With a 'dry run' of the required capital strategies and asset management plans during 2000.

7 REVENUE SUPPORT FOR CAPITAL FINANCING COSTS

11.27 Credit approvals fulfil another vital function, albeit not formally under the provisions of the LGHA 1989. Through administrative arrangements outside the legislation, the issue of credit approvals leads to an increase in the amount of the capital financing component of an authority's standard spending assessment (CFSSA), which in turn is reflected in the amount of the authority's Revenue Support Grant (RSG) received annually from central government in aid of the authority's services pursuant to the Local Government Finance Act 1988, s 78. CFSSAs allow for both minimum revenue provision of 4% and interest payable at a standard rate, based on the estimated average rate paid by all local authorities. Thus, for every £1 of credit approval an authority receives, its SSA and RSG are increased by a notional amount to allow for assumed debt charges[1].

1 See paras 22–26 of Circular 11/90 and the sections concerning the capital finance service block in the Local Government Finance Report (England) issued annually by the Secretary of State for the Environment under the Local Government Finance Act 1988, s 78A.

B Limits on credit

11.28 Under this heading we concentrate on the aggregate credit limit and the related provisions concerning the credit ceiling. However, the ACL is not the only limit relevant to borrowing by local authorities. Under LGHA 1989, s 44(3) a local authority may not borrow money at any time if to do so would cause the limits under LGHA 1989, s 45 to be exceeded. Under s 45, authorities are required to set their own limits on borrowing. But the obligation under s 45 is perhaps more directly related to ensuring proper management of an authority's financial affairs, and addressing gross amounts of borrowing and the balance between particular types of loans, rather than controlling the net indebtedness of the authority at any point in time. It is to be noted that an authority (acting by full council) is empowered to vary the limits it has set for itself under s 45, even during the course of the financial year to which they relate[1]. The duty under s 45 is discussed in Chapter 13 in connection with borrowing.

1 Local Government and Housing Act 1989, s 45(3).

I AGGREGATE CREDIT LIMIT

11.29 The ACL under the LGHA 1989, s 62 is perhaps the most significant feature of the system of control on credit under LGHA 1989, Pt IV. Although it is sometimes described as a borrowing limit, in effect an authority's ACL imposes a constant limit on the amount of its outstanding liabilities in respect of borrowing *and* credit arrangements. The amount of the ACL is unique to each authority. The limit is not static, but fluctuates with various factors as described in para **11.32**. The ACL is described in broad terms as being a control on the 'net indebtedness' of an authority, ie its credit liabilities less investments[1].

1 See para 40 of Circular 11/90.

11.30 Under LGHA 1989, s 44(1) an authority may not, at any time, borrow an amount of money if to do so would cause the total of:

(a) the amount outstanding at that time by way of principal of money borrowed; plus
(b) the aggregate cost of its credit arrangements[1] at that time (other than those excluded under Sch 3, para 11),

to exceed its ACL.

1 As determined under LGHA 1989, s 49 and the LA(CF)R 1997.

11.31 Under LGHA 1989, ss 50(4) and 51(3), a local authority is prohibited from entering into, or agreeing to vary any credit arrangement, if to do so would cause the total of the amounts under LGHA 1989, s 44(1) to exceed the ACL which applies at that time.

11.32 The method of calculating the ACL is set out in LGHA 1989, s 62. At any point in time, the ACL comprises the total, at that time, of the authority's:

(a) temporary revenue borrowing limit[1];
(b) temporary capital borrowing limit[2];
(c) credit ceiling[3]; and
(d) any excess of approved investments and cash[4] over (unapplied) usable capital receipts.

If usable capital receipts *exceed* investments and cash, this final item may be a negative amount[5] and therefore would count as a *deduction* from the other items.

1 As defined by Local Government and Housing Act 1989, s 62(3) and (4).
2 As defined by LGHA 1989, s 62(5).
3 See paras **11.37–11.42**.
4 'Approved investments and cash' does not include investments or cash held for the purposes of a superannuation fund or trust fund as referred to in s 42(2)(h) or (i).
5 Local Government and Housing Act 1989, s 62(6).

11.33 The temporary revenue and capital borrowing limits do not fulfil any independent function outside the calculation of the ACL[1]. They are described in

Chapter 13, but in essence the temporary *revenue* borrowing limit allows for borrowing for up to two years in anticipation of revenue payments due to the authority (eg housing rent or council tax arrears) without the need for credit cover. The temporary *capital* borrowing limit allows for borrowing for capital expenditure which is due to be reimbursed within the next eighteen months by an external party, including grant from central government (but not from an EC institution other than contributions from any of the Structural Funds).

1 See Circular 11/90, Annex A, para 66.

11.34 When the credit ceiling rises on account of the use of a credit approval, the ACL will rise by an equal amount. The ACL will also rise when cash, other than a usable capital receipt, is received or when approved investments are made (provided there is no counterbalancing adjustment in the other constituent elements of the limit).

11.35 The ACL allows for 'internal lending', in substitution for external borrowing, through the use of balances, revenue reserves and any other sums which might otherwise have been held in approved investments. When this occurs, the amount of the authority's approved investments (and its ACL) will be lower than it would otherwise have been, but so too will the external borrowing which counts against the ACL[1].

1 See Circular 11/90, para 40.

11.36 On application by a local authority, the Secretary of State has power to direct an increase in the authority's ACL for a specified period, subject to compliance with any terms and conditions he may stipulate[1]. It appears that this power might be used, for example, to allow for additional borrowings to cover arrears of income[2].

1 Local Government and Housing Act 1989, s 62(2).
2 See Circular 11/90, para 41.

2 CREDIT CEILING

11.37 The credit ceiling is an essential component of the ACL[1], and thus, of the controls on borrowing and other forms of credit. In essence, it is a measure of the authority's net credit liabilities, ie the difference between its gross liabilities in respect of borrowing and credit arrangements and the provision it has made to meet those liabilities. It may be a negative amount, if the authority has made more than sufficient provision to meet its credit liabilities. Each local authority's credit ceiling had to be fixed initially as at 1 April 1990 (the 'initial credit ceiling'). The formula for calculation of an authority's initial credit ceiling is set out in LGHA 1989, Sch 3, paras 8 and 9, subject to any prescribed modifications. In simplified terms it comprises:

(a) the amount of any outstanding advances made from the authority's loan fund established under LGA 1972, Sch 13, para 15;
(b) *plus* the total cost as at 1 April 1990 of the authority's transitional credit arrangements under LGHA 1989, s 52;
(c) *minus* the amount of the reserved part of LGPLA 1980 receipts;
(d) *minus* the amount (if any) which the authority determined to set aside as the provision for credit liabilities out of usable LGPLA 1980 receipts; and
(e) *subject to* certain modifications under the LAR 1990[2], reg 21(1) and Sch 3, Pt I

in respect of debt administration and deemed borrowing under the Local Government Act 1985, sums due in respect of transferred assets arising from local government reorganisation under the Local Government Act 1972 and housing transfers under the London Government Act 1963.

1 See para **11.32**.
2 LAR 1990, SI 1999/432 (now revoked).

11.38 From this base line, in broad terms, a local authority's credit ceiling rises whenever a credit approval is used and reduces when provision is made for credit liabilities. The detailed effects of various events and transactions are summarised in paras **11.39–11.42**.

11.39 The credit ceiling does not rise when a credit approval is used as authority to enter into an 'excluded credit arrangement[1]'. It will not *decrease* when the following amounts are set aside[2]:

(a) sums to provide credit cover for a credit arrangement (other than an excluded credit arrangement) under LGHA 1989, s 50(3)(b) or (c), because the reduction in credit liabilities is offset by the additional liabilities taken on in respect of the credit arrangement;
(b) usable LGPLA 1980 receipts which the authority determined to set aside voluntarily on or before 30 September 1990, because these were taken into account in calculating the initial credit ceiling[3]; and
(c) notional interest on credit arrangements[4], since the credit ceiling reflects only outstanding liabilities in respect of principal.

The detailed effects of various transactions on the credit ceiling are summarised in the next three paragraphs.

1 Under Local Government and Housing Act 1989, Sch 3, para 11(2), and see para **12.45**ff.
2 LGHA 1989, Sch 3, para 12(2).
3 LGHA 1989, Sch 3, para 9(1)(b).
4 LGHA 1989, Sch 3, para 15(1)(b).

(a) Transactions which lead to an increase in the credit ceiling

11.40

(a) Credit approval is used as authority not to charge expenditure to revenue under LGHA 1989, s 56(1)(a)[1].
(b) Credit approval is used as authority to enter into or vary a credit arrangement (other than an excluded credit arrangement) under LGHA 1989, s 56(1)(b)[2].
(c) Repayment or payment of a sum to the Secretary of State under LGHA 1989, s 157(7)(b) in respect of a commuted payment[3].
(d) Application or transfer of an amount set aside as provision for credit liabilities ('PCL') by a 'debt-free' authority pursuant to LGHA 1989, s 64(2)[4].
(e) Application of PCL by an authority which is *not* debt free pursuant to LGHA 1989, s 64(1)(c) to meet expenditure for which credit approval was used as authority not to charge the expenditure to revenue account[5].
(f) Provision for credit liabilities applied to meet the levy on large scale voluntary transfer under the Leasehold Reform, Housing and Urban Development Act 1993, s 136[6].
(g) Provision for credit liabilities applied to pay a premium payable to a lender by a local authority in England as a result of early repayment of a loan, other than an amount in respect of principal or interest[7].

1 Local Government and Housing Act 1989, Sch 3, para 11(1).
2 LGHA 1989, Sch 3, para 11(1).
3 LGHA 1989, Sch 3, para 14(2).
4 LGHA 1989, Sch 3, para 13. As regards the *application* of PCL by 'debt free' authorities pursuant to LGHA 1989, s 64(2)(a), see LA(CF)R 1997, regs 155–157. As regards *transfer* of PCL by such authorities, see reg 158.
5 LGHA 1989, Sch 3, para 11(1).
6 Local Authorities (Capital Finance) Regulations 1997, reg 118.
7 LA(CF)R 1997, reg 118A, inserted by SI 2000/1773 in relation to England.

(b) Transactions leading to a decrease in the credit ceiling

11.41

(a) Amount set aside as PCL to provide credit cover for an excluded credit arrangement under LGHA 1989, s 50(3)(b) and (c)[1].
(b) Amount set aside as PCL as the reserved part of a capital receipt under LGHA 1989, s 59(1)[2].
(c) Amount set aside as PCL voluntarily from usable capital receipts under LGHA 1989, s 60(2)(b)[3].
(d) Amount set aside as PCL in respect of the reserved part of a notional capital receipt under LGHA 1989, s 61(4)[4].
(e) Amount set aside as PCL as 'minimum revenue provision' ('MRP') in respect of *principal* under LGHA 1989, s 63(1)[5].
(f) Amount set aside as PCL voluntarily from revenue under LGHA 1989, s 63(1)[6].
(g) Amount set aside in respect of receipt of European grant under LGHA 1989, s 63(4)[7].
(h) Amount set aside as PCL in order to provide credit cover for a transaction of a 'regulated company' under art 14(5)(a) of the Local Authorities (Companies) Order 1995, as amended by SI 1996/621[8].
(i) Amount set aside in respect of a commuted payment from the Secretary of State under LGHA 1989, s 157 or a similar payment, pursuant to LGHA 1989, s 63(2) or (3)[9].
(j) Payment made by the Secretary of State to the Public Works Loans Commissioners to reduce or extinguish a local authority debt under LGHA 1989, s 157(1)(b)[10].

1 Local Government and Housing Act 1989, Sch 3, paras 12(1) and 12(2)(a).
2 LGHA 1989, Sch 3, para 12(1).
3 LGHA 1989, Sch 3, para 12(1).
4 LGHA 1989, Sch 3, para 12(1).
5 LGHA 1989, Sch 3, para 12(1); MRP in respect of notional interest on credit arrangements is excluded by para 12(2)(c).
6 LGHA 1989, Sch 3, para 12(1).
7 LGHA 1989, Sch 3, para 12(1); s 63(4) now excludes contributions from any of the Structural Funds.
8 LGHA 1989, Sch 3, para 12(1).
9 LGHA 1989, Sch 3, para 12(1).
10 LGHA 1989, Sch 3, para 14(1).

(c) Transactions with a neutral effect on the credit ceiling

11.42

(a) Use of a credit approval to enter into or vary an excluded credit arrangement under LGHA 1989, s 56(1)(b)[1].

(b) Setting aside an amount as PCL in order to provide credit cover for a credit arrangement under LGHA 1989, s 50(3)(b) or (c)[2].
(c) Amount set aside as PCL in order to make MRP in respect of notional *interest* under LGHA 1989, s 63(1)[3].
(d) Application of PCL in order to repay debt under LGHA 1989, s 64(1)(a).
(e) Application of PCL in order to meet the liabilities under a credit arrangement under LGHA 1989, s 64(1)(b).
(f) Application of PCL by a debt-free local authority pursuant to LGHA 1989, s 64(1)(c) to meet expenditure in respect of which credit approval is used as authority not to charge the expenditure to revenue account[4].
(g) Where a payment is made by the Secretary of State to the Public Works Loan Commissioners (other than a commuted payment under LGHA 1989, s 157) following a large-scale transfer of houses by the local authority[5].

1 Local Government and Housing Act 1989, Sch 3, para 11(2).
2 LGHA 1989, Sch 3, para 12(2)(a).
3 LGHA 1989, Sch 3, para 12(2)(c).
4 Local Authorities (Capital Finance) Regulations 1997, reg 119(3).
5 LA(CF)R 1997, reg 119A, inserted by SI 2000/1773 in relation to England.

3 ADJUSTED CREDIT CEILING

11.43 The only function of the adjusted credit ceiling ('ACC') is to form a basis for calculating the minimum revenue provision ('MRP') which authorities are required to make annually for their credit liabilities[1]. The ACC is calculated in the same way as the credit ceiling itself, but as modified by regulations made by the Secretary of State[2]. The current regulations are those contained in LA(CF)R 1997, Pt XI. Their general effect is to provide for the authority to disregard certain items from the normal calculation of a credit ceiling. The excluded items provided for in LA(CF)R 1997, regs 126–129 relate to amounts set aside in respect of transferred debt, advances to housing associations, credit cover for the transactions of a regulated company under the Local Authorities (Companies) Order 1995, art 14 (SI 1995/849 as amended by SI 1996/621) and by the Metropolitan Police Authority in respect of transferred liabilities. Special provision is made for each of these excepted items.

1 See para **11.46**ff.
2 By virtue of Local Government and Housing Act 1989, Sch 3, para 18.

11.44 Local authorities which are housing authorities are required to calculate a specific housing component of their ACC, which is used for the purposes of assessing the contribution made from the housing revenue account to an authority's overall minimum revenue provision[1].

1 Local Authorities (Capital Finance) Regulations 1997, regs 132(2) and 139–150 deal with the calculation of the housing and non-housing amounts and components. See para **11.52**.

C Provision for credit liabilities

11.45 Under various provisions of LGHA 1989, Pt IV, local authorities are required or empowered to make provision for credit liabilities ('PCL'). In this context, 'credit liabilities' broadly comprise liabilities in respect of the repayment of principal of borrowed money and any liability in respect of a credit arrangement, other than an 'excluded credit arrangement'[1]. The annual obligation to make 'minimum revenue provision' is described in para **11.46**ff. Other obligations or powers to make provision for credit liabilities are summarised in para **11.60**. In some cases the provision is to be made out of capital resources, and in others it is to be made from revenue. In some instances the authority is allowed to choose the sources from which PCL should be made. In this chapter we concentrate particularly on minimum revenue provision and the uses to which PCL can be put. As set out below, local authorities who are 'debt-free' are given special treatment. The obligations to set aside PCL in respect of capital receipts are mainly dealt with in Chapter 14.

1 'Excluded credit arrangements' are those described by the Secretary of State in regulations made under the 1989 Act, Sch 3, para 11(2). See para **12.45**ff.

1 MINIMUM REVENUE PROVISION

11.46 At the time of writing, the Government is considering the replacement of the statutory system for authorities to make annual provision for debt under the minimum revenue provision ('MRP') requirements outlined below, with the possible introduction of a mandatory accounting code[1]. The following refers to the position as at April 2000.

1 See the Government's Response to the Environment, Transport and the Regional Affairs Committee's Report on Local Government Finance Cm 4402 (July 1999) at para 58, referring to this and the separate research into a system reliant upon 'prudential indicators' of the amount of debt a local authority can afford. See also the two PriceWaterhouseCoopers' papers: *Prudential Indicators* and *A Prudential Framework for Repaying Debt and Providing for the Replacement of Assets* published by the DETR Local Government Research Unit on 11 November 1999 and 7 December 1999 respectively.

11.47 A local authority which is not 'debt-free' must normally set aside, in every financial year, amounts from *revenue* as provision for credit liabilities. These amounts are provided for in LGHA 1989, s 63(1). The amounts must be *not less than* the minimum revenue provision ('MRP') for that year referred to in LGHA 1989, Sch 3, Pt IV. These minimum amounts of PCL to be set aside from revenue are *additional* to those required in respect of capital receipts and notional capital receipts under LGHA 1989, ss 59(1) and 61(4) and the other obligations and powers to make PCL which are listed in para **11.60**.

11.48 Authorities who have a nil or negative credit ceiling on the last day of the immediately preceding financial year are not required to make MRP[1].

1 Local Government and Housing Act 1989, Sch 3, para 15(2).

11.49 Where this exemption for 'debt-free' authorities does not apply, there are broadly two types of MRP an authority must make: that in respect of principal and that in respect of notional interest on credit arrangements[1]. For every financial year beginning on 1 April 1991 onwards, an authority's MRP is the aggregate of:

(a) an amount in respect of *principal* which is the 'prescribed percentage' of the authority's *adjusted credit ceiling* on the last day of the immediately preceding financial year, subject to any exceptions contained in regulations made by the Secretary of State; and
(b) an amount in respect of *notional interest* on *each credit arrangement* entered into by the authority which came into being before the beginning of that year (other than an excluded credit arrangement under LGHA 1989, Sch 3, para 11[2]).

1 Interest on borrowing is charged direct to revenue.
2 See para **12.45**ff.

11.50 MRP must be set aside from a *revenue* account, but it may come from such revenue account or accounts as the authority thinks fit[1]. The amount calculated in accordance with LGHA 1989, Sch 3, Pt IV is the *minimum* provision the council must make: it may choose to make a greater provision.

1 Local Government and Housing Act 1989, s 63(1).

(a) Minimum revenue provision in respect of principal

11.51 Dealing first with MRP in respect of principal, this comprises the aggregate of various amounts determined under LA(CF)R 1997, regs 132–137[1], the main component of which is a prescribed percentage. Each of these various amounts is described in the following paragraphs.

1 Subject to an adjustment under LA(CF)R 1997, reg 138 in respect of certain effects of commutation referred to in paras **11.57** and **11.65**; and see paras **11.68–11.70**.

11.52 The main element of MRP in respect of principal is based on prescribed percentages of the ACC. In order to calculate this amount, the authority must first, if it is a housing authority, distinguish between the housing and non-housing components of its adjusted credit ceiling. In essence, the housing component comprises those elements of the authority's ACC which are attributable to the exercise of housing functions, whilst the non-housing component is the remainder of the ACC. The prescribed percentage in respect of the housing amount is 2%, and for the non-housing amount it is 4% of the ACC *as at the last day of the preceding financial year*[1]. If the authority is not required to keep a housing revenue account, the minimum revenue provision in respect of principal is 4%[2].

1 Local Authorities (Capital Finance) Regulations 1997, reg 132.
2 LA(CF)R 1997, reg 133.

11.53 The element of MRP which is based on these percentages is referred to as the 'reducing balance' method of calculation, because it continually reduces the housing and non-housing amounts used to calculate MRP.

11.54 Certain other items are added to the amount of MRP an authority must make in respect of *principal* each year, which are paid in equal instalments, rather than by the reducing balance method. These are:

(a) under LA(CF)R 1997, reg 134, an authority is required to set aside equal instalments in respect of certain borrowing under 'limited approvals' given under the previous capital finance system, which required that the borrowing should be repaid within 10 years;
(b) under LA(CF)R 1997, reg 136, an authority must set aside equal instalments in respect of any SCA which relates to expenditure which was treated as 'capital' expenditure only because of a direction given by the Secretary of State under LGHA 1989, s 40(6) and in respect of which the Secretary of State has used his discretion to specify an amortisation period[1].

1 Prior to the amendment of LGHA 1989, s 54(5) by s 2 of the Local Government Finance (Supplementary Credit Approvals) Act 1997 the Secretary of State was required to specify an amortisation period

of no more than seven years in such cases: he now has a *discretion* to specify an amortisation period, with no limitation on the period which may be set.

11.55 Special provision is made for authorities who have been exempt from the requirement to make MRP because their credit ceiling was nil or a negative amount at the end of the preceding financial year[1], but who again becomes liable for MRP. Under LA(CF)R 1997, regs 146 and 150, such an authority must increase its ACC by the amount of the previous year's 'missed' instalments of the items referred to in (a) and (b) of the preceding paragraph.

1 See para **11.48**.

11.56 The other additions to the amount of MRP an authority must make concern the following:

(a) under LA(CF)R 1997, reg 135, an authority which is a 'designated council' under an order made under the Local Government Act 1985 in respect of the loan debt of an abolished metropolitan county council, must set aside an amount equal to 'its share' of the transferred debt[1]; and
(b) under LA(CF)R 1997, reg 137, an authority must set aside an amount equal to any PCL which has been applied in the previous financial year to meet liabilities in respect of credit arrangements with an initial cost of nil (and which, at the time the amount was applied, had not been varied). The aim of this is to ensure that, in effect, liabilities in respect of any credit arrangement with a nil initial cost are met entirely out of revenue[2].

1 Other authorities in the area make regular payments to the 'designated council' of their contributions to the provision for repayment of the transferred debt. Under LA(CF)R 1997, regs 58 and 68, these contributions from other authorities are treated as capital receipts with a set-aside rate of 100% in the hands of the designated authority.
2 Circular 11/90, Annex A, para 76 explained that –

> 'In the Secretary of State's view, these payments [in respect of credit arrangements with a nil initial cost] should be charged directly to a revenue account. If, however, they are met from provision for credit liabilities, then an equivalent amount is added to minimum revenue provision for the following year.'

See para **15.61** in relation to the consequences of this for certain 'private finance transactions' and the need for additional revenue support.

11.57 Under LA(CF)R 1997, reg 138 and Sch 2, Pt II, the formula for calculating MRP is adjusted by a reduction to take account of the effects of certain commuted payments to authorities, and to the Public Works Loan Commissioners in respect of the authority's debt, by the Secretary of State in the financial year 1992–93[1].

1 See paras **11.68–11.70**.

(b) Minimum revenue provision in respect of notional interest on credit arrangements

11.58 The formula for calculation of minimum revenue provision in respect of notional interest is contained in LGHA 1989, Sch 3, para 19. Notional interest has to be set aside from revenue every year in relation to all the authority's credit arrangements other than excluded credit arrangements[1]. The formula for calculation of notional interest entails the use of the same percentage as is prescribed as the rate of discount for the purpose of LGHA 1989, s 49(2), used to calculate the initial cost of a credit arrangement[2]. (Interest on borrowing is charged direct to revenue: see LGHA 1989, s 40(2)(b).

1 See para **12.45**ff.
2 See para **12.65**; the Local Authorities (Capital Finance) (Rate of Discount for 2000/01) (England) Regulations SI 2000/259 prescribed a discount rate of 7.9% for the year beginning 1 April 2000. The equivalent provision for Wales in SI 2000/825 (W 31) specifies a discount rate of 7.5% for 2000–01.

11.59 The aim is that authorities should provide for notional interest on credit arrangements broadly as if they had been required to pay interest on borrowed money. Requiring authorities to provide for notional interest in this way is consistent with the general objectives of LGHA 1989, Pt IV: ensuring that there should be no incentive to choose a credit arrangement as opposed to borrowing, unless there are value for money grounds.

2 OTHER REASONS FOR MAKING PROVISION FOR CREDIT LIABILITIES

11.60 Whilst the preceding section has concentrated on MRP and PCL made from *revenue*, this is, of course, only one of the circumstances in which authorities are required, or may choose, to make provision for credit liabilities under LGHA 1989, Pt IV. As the rules on the application of amounts set aside in respect of PCL do not distinguish between the various reasons why the provision had been made, it may be helpful first to summarise what those various reasons comprise, before turning to the rules themselves. Provision for credit liabilities is *required* to be made in all the following cases:

(a) under LGHA 1989, s 63(1), in the form of MRP[1];
(b) under LGHA 1989, s 59(1), in respect of the reserved part of capital receipts[2];
(c) under LGHA 1989, s 61(4), in respect of notional capital receipts[3];
(d) under LGHA 1989, s 50(3)(b) and (c), in order to provide credit cover for a credit arrangement, rather using a credit approval[4];
(e) under LGHA 1989, s 51(4), in order to provide credit cover in respect of the variation of a credit arrangement[5];
(f) under art 14(5)(a) of the Local Authorities (Companies) Order 1995[6], in order to provide credit cover for a transaction of a regulated company, rather than treat a credit approval as reduced[7];
(g) under LGHA 1989, s 63(2) and (3) in respect of commuted and similar payments from the Secretary of State or other minister[8];
(h) under LGHA 1989, s 63(4) in respect of the receipt of a grant from an EC institution[9].

In addition to these express requirements to make PCL, an authority may *voluntarily* make further provision, either from revenue, under s 63(1), or from usable capital receipts under s 60(2).

1 See para **11.46**ff.
2 See para **14.24**.
3 See para **14.35**.
4 See para **12.9**.
5 See para **12.115**.
6 SI 1995/849 as amended by SI 1996/621.
7 See para **16.79**.
8 On receipt of a commuted payment from the Secretary of State under LGHA 1989, s 157, or a similar payment from any minister as referred to in LGHA 1989, s 63(3), an amount equal to that payment must be set aside for credit liabilities.
9 On receipt of a grant from a European institution, an equal amount must be set aside as provision for credit liabilities (see para **10.37**). LGHA 1989, s 63(4) is amended as from 1 April 2000 so as to exclude grants from the Structural Funds (SI 2000/589).

3 USE OF AMOUNTS SET ASIDE AS PROVISION FOR CREDIT LIABILITIES

11.61 It is important to note that the obligation, or discretion, of an authority under various provisions of LGHA 1989, Pt IV is *to make provision* for credit liabilities, but not necessarily *to apply* the amounts set aside to discharge those liabilities. Until PCL is applied in one of the ways described in this section, it is often invested in approved investments[1], or may be used as an alternative to short-term borrowing.

1 See para **10.21**.

11.62 For authorities who are not 'debt free', PCL may only be applied in the following ways:

(a) to meet any liability in respect of borrowing by the authority *other than* interest[1];
(b) to meet any liability of an authority in respect of a credit arrangement, *other than* an excluded credit arrangement[2];
(c) for capital expenditure which has been authorised by the use of a credit approval; in effect, in substitution for new borrowing[3].

1 Local Government and Housing Act 1989, s 64(1)(a). Interest on borrowing is charged direct to revenue.
2 LGHA 1989, s 64(1)(b). Excluded credit arrangements are described in para **12.45**ff. PCL cannot be used to meet liabilities under deferred purchase and similar agreements entered into prior to 7 July 1988, as such arrangements do not come within the definition of a 'credit arrangement' or 'transitional credit arrangement'.
3 Local Government and Housing Act 1989, s 64(1)(c).

11.63 Authorities who have 'debt free status' have far greater latitude in the use that can made of their PCL. LGHA 1989, s 64(2) enables the Secretary of State to make regulations which govern the use of PCL by authorities which have a *negative* credit ceiling as at the last day of the preceding financial year ('the relevant date'[1]). Eligible local authorities may either *apply*[2] PCL to the purposes specified in the regulations or *transfer*[3] it to another body specified in the regulations. The current regulations are contained in LA(CF)R 1997, Pt XIII. They apply to authorities which not only have a negative credit ceiling at the relevant time, but who are *also free of borrowing* (other than short term and other borrowing defined as 'disregarded borrowing' under LA(CF)R 1997, reg 65).

1 Local Government and Housing Act 1989, s 64(4).
2 LGHA 1989, s 64(2)(a).
3 LGHA 1989, s 64(2)(b).

11.64 Under LA(CF)R 1997, reg 156, authorities who meet both these criteria can apply PCL to virtually any expenditure for capital purposes. The exceptions are:

(a) spending on 'excluded expenditure', which comprises expenditure on grants, advances and other financial assistance to housing associations towards expenditure which is eligible for Housing Association Grant[1]; and
(b) the use of PCL which comprises an amount set aside in respect of a capital receipt to which reg 71 (now revoked[2]) applied, which concerned receipts from the disposal of of assets held for the purposes of the Central Criminal Court, the police, probation or magistrates' court services, and civil defence functions[3]. (Regulation 155 requires that PCL relating to capital receipts from

the disposal of assets within these categories should be re-applied to one of these purposes.)

1 Local Authorities (Capital Finance) Regulations 1997, reg 156(1).
2 By SI 1999/1937, reg 12.
3 LA(CF)R 1997, reg 156(2).

11.65 For authorities with a negative credit ceiling immediately before the start of the financial year and who are entitled to an adjustment in respect of the commutation of certain grants and subsidies for loan charges made by the Secretary of State in the financial year 1992–93, LA(CF)R 1997, reg 157 permits limited use of PCL for revenue purposes, up to the amount of the commutation adjustment for that year calculated in accordance with LA(CF)R 1997, Sch 2, Pt II.

11.66 As regards the transfer of PCL by a 'debt free' authority pursuant to LGHA 1989, s 64(2)(b), LA(CF)R 1997, reg 158 specifies the types of body to whom transfer may be made, which depends in part upon the type of local authority which is 'debt-free' and contemplating such a transfer. For example, an authority which is a combined fire authority may transfer PCL to a constituent council of the authority, or a non-metropolitan district council may transfer PCL to the county council. LA(CF)R 1997, reg 159 requires that the authority transferring PCL to another body should ensure that the expenditure which is to be met from it (by the transferee) meets certain conditions.

11.67 By virtue of LGHA 1989, s 64(3), the aggregate amount of PCL which 'debt-free' authorities may be permitted by the regulations to apply in any financial year may not exceed the extent to which their credit ceiling is negative as at the relevant date. If the authority wishes to ensure that its debt-free status is not forfeited through the use of its PCL in the manner permitted by the regulations, it will need to ensure that in each financial year it applies *a lesser amount* than the amount by which its credit ceiling was negative as at the relevant date. If the authority has balances which are greater than the negative amount of the credit ceiling, it will be able to spend them, pursuant to LGHA 1989, s 64(1)(c), but *only if* it has any credit approvals. *If* it does, then the use of a credit approval in these circumstances would not increase the authority's credit ceiling[1].

1 Local Authorities (Capital Finance) Regulations 1997, reg 119, and see para **11.42**(f).

4 IMPLICATIONS OF COMMUTATION ON 1 OCTOBER 1992

11.68 As a footnote to this chapter it will have been noted that reference has been made to the effects of certain commuted payments made by the Secretary of State to authorities and to the Public Works Loans Commissioners in the financial year 1992–93[1].

1 See paras **11.57** and **11.65**.

11.69 In October 1992, the Secretary of State made provision for a lump sum of £5.1 billion for repayment of local authority debt, in lieu of annual grant towards loan charges which had previously been paid. The intention was that over a 20 year period, this change should be cost neutral. However, in the short-term this commutation of annual grant led to losses by local authorities, which were not entirely offset by savings on interest and MRP.

11.70 Consequently various adjustments were made to the rules on MRP in order to mitigate this loss. The detailed mechanics for calculation of the commutation adjustment (intended to reflect the net loss to the authority in respect of this commutation) is contained in LA(CF)R 1997, Sch 2, Pt II and is applied in reg 138 in connection with the calculation of MRP and reg 157 for 'debt-free' authorities who do not make MRP. For authorities who still have a net loss having taken the benefit of these adjustments under the regulations, guidance suggests that they may apply to the Secretary of State for an SCA[1].

1 See the Department of the Environment 'A Guide to the Local Government Capital Finance System' (February 1997), Section 8, Technical Annex A3, para A3.3, item c.

CHAPTER 12

Credit arrangements

A Introduction

12.1 Chapter 10 (paras **10.2** and **10.3**) refers to the consideration which is being given by the Government at the time of writing to possible reform of the current system for control on local authority capital finance. The options for reform now under consideration envisage that credit arrangements (or arrangements with an analogous function) would continue to be subject to some form of regulation. The following sets out the position likely to apply at least until the end of the financial year 2000–2001.

1 BACKGROUND

12.2 'Credit arrangement' is a concept created by LGHA 1989, Pt IV intended to apply to a range of transactions entered into by local authorities which are considered to have a comparable economic effect to borrowing but which do not, in law, amount to borrowing. As described in Chapter 10, the aim of these provisions is to regulate the various methods by which local authorities might undertake capital schemes, which could not be controlled simply by imposing limits on conventional borrowing. Schemes involving leasing and other arrangements were explored extensively by local authorities during the 1980s to enable them to carry out projects outside the limits on borrowing and annual spending, usually by deferring the time at which payment was to be made by the local authority for capital works, land, or other assets. Certain of the more exotic schemes were of dubious legality and most were expensive in comparison with conventional borrowing.

12.3 The statutory provisions concerning credit arrangements do not expressly prohibit authorities from pursuing such transactions, nor render them ultra vires per se[1]; rather they are aimed at ensuring that if they are undertaken, they will count towards the authority's limits on credit. Borrowing and credit arrangements are subject to certain common limits and obligations under LGHA 1989, Pt IV. The intention is that there should be no incentive for an authority to pursue a credit arrangement unless it offers better value for money, or some other advantage over conventional borrowing[2] (or over one of the other permitted methods of funding capital expenditure).

1 But see Local Government and Housing Act 1989, s 50 discussed in paras **12.135**ff.
2 See Department of the Environment Circular 11/90, para 30.

12.4 LGHA 1989, s 48(1) creates three categories of credit arrangement, which in simplified terms comprise:

(a) leases of land and goods taken by local authorities;
(b) contracts under which local authorities obtain extended credit, in the sense that payment by the authority takes place more than a full financial year after receipt of value by the authority (for example, deferred purchase or contractor credit arrangements);
(c) any other type of transaction prescribed by the Secretary of State in regulations for the purpose of LGHA 1989, s 48(1)(c).

12.5 Each of these categories is examined in paras **12.12–12.41**. The LGHA 1989, Pt IV does not apply to any credit arrangement which came into being[1] before 1 April 1990, subject to the special provisions under LGHA 1989, s 52 on 'transitional credit arrangements'. These comprise certain arrangements which came into being on or after 7 July 1988 but before 1 April 1990 and they are described in paras **12.42–12.44**. There is one further category of credit arrangements known as 'excluded credit arrangements' which, despite their name, are nonetheless credit arrangements. These are explained in paras **12.45** and **12.46**.

1 Local Government and Housing Act 1989, s 48(3) specifies the times at which the various classes of credit arrangement are to be treated as coming into being for the purpose of Pt IV.

12.6 It should be noted that a contract is excluded from being a credit arrangement to the extent that it is a contract under which a local authority borrows money[1].

1 Local Government and Housing Act 1989, s 48(5).

2 CONSEQUENCES OF CREDIT ARRANGEMENTS AND THE NEED TO PROVIDE CREDIT COVER

12.7 The fact that a transaction constitutes a credit arrangement has several consequences. The arrangement must be for capital purposes. When it is entered into, the authority must have sufficient credit cover for the 'initial cost' of the arrangement[1].

1 Local Government and Housing Act 1989, s 50. See para **12.135** for a summary. An additional constraint is that the aggregate credit limit under LGHA 1989, s 62 must not be exceeded.

12.8 The initial cost is broadly the net present value of all the payments the authority is to make over the life of the arrangement, producing an indication of the amount of money the authority would have had to borrow if it had funded the transaction through borrowing[1].

1 See Department of the Environment Circular 11/90, para 30.

12.9 The requirement to provide credit cover equal to the initial cost has the effect of triggering financial limitations on the power to enter into credit arrangements. Under LGHA 1989, s 50(3) credit cover can be provided:

(a) by the use of a 'credit approval'[1];
(b) by setting aside usable capital receipts as provision for credit liabilities[2]; or
(c) by setting aside an additional amount from revenue for credit liabilities[3].

1 See Local Government and Housing Act 1989, ss 53, 54 and 56 and Chapter 11; basic and supplementary credit approvals give limited authority for borrowing and credit arrangements.

2 Through a determination under s 60(2)(b).
3 In accordance with a determination which specifically refers to the arrangement.

12.10 Hence, entering into a credit arrangement has a comparable financial effect to using borrowed money, or to applying usable capital receipts, or to funding capital expenditure from revenue. Entering into a credit arrangement will normally have the effect of reducing the authority's borrowing capacity, or will use up other permitted means of funding capital expenditure, to an extent equal to the initial cost[1].

1 See para **12.59**ff.

3 ORIENTATION TO PROVISIONS ON INITIAL COST, ETC

12.11 The statutory provisions on the calculation of the initial and subsequent cost of credit arrangements, and their adjusted cost on and following variation are, to say the least, a tangled maze. The chart over shows, at a glance, the main provisions of the LGHA 1989 and/or the Local Authorities (Capital Finance) Regulations 1997[1] ('LA(CF)R 1997') which deal with calculation of these costs in relation to the various kinds of credit arrangement, and the main sections of the text in which each is discussed.

1 SI 1997/319 as amended by SI 1997/848, SI 1998/371, SI 1998/602, SI 1998/1937, SI 1999/501, SI 1999/1852, SI 1999/3423, SI 2000/992 (Wales), SI 2000/1033, SI 2000/1474, SI 2000/1553 and SI 2000/1773.

B Categories of credit arrangement

1 LEASES OF LAND AND GOODS

12.12 LGHA 1989, s 48(1)(a) provides that a local authority shall be taken to have entered into a credit arrangement –

> '(a) in any case where they become the lessees of any property (whether land or goods) . . .'

(a) Analysis

12.13 It would appear that the 'credit arrangement' under LGHA 1989, s 48(1)(a) would normally be the lease itself[1].

1 LGHA 1989, s 48(1) specifies that 'the "credit arrangement" is the lease, the single contract or, as the case may be, the two or more contracts taken together'. The words after 'lease' reflect the drafting of s 48(1)(b) which creates the *second* category of credit arrangement (ie contracts *other* than leases).

12.14 The exemptions from this class of credit arrangement are referred to in paras **12.47–12.54**.

(b) Time of creation of credit arrangement under LGHA 1989, s 48(1)(a)

12.15 A credit arrangement under LGHA 1989, s 48(1)(a) comes into being when a local authority 'become' the lessees of land or goods[1]. In the ordinary case this should not present any problem, but in some instances it is less than clear whether the LGHA 1989 and subordinate legislation envisage that the normal

	Initial cost (IC)[1]	Cost at any subsequent time	Adjusted cost on variation[2]	Cost at any time following variation	Main references in text regarding IC[3]
Leases s 483(1)(a)					
General rules	reg 36	reg 39	regs 47 & 50	reg 51	**12.63–12.66**
Special cases/exceptions	regs 28–34 (*nil IC*) regs 35, 37 & 38	reg 27 reg 39	regs 47–50 regs 47–50	reg 51 reg 51	**12.89–12.102** **12.67–12.70** Chapter 15 **12.103–12.105**
Extended credit contracts s 48(1)(b)					
General rules	s 49(1) & (2)	s 49(4)	s 51(5)	s 51(8)	**12.73–12.78**
Special cases/exceptions	reg 45(2) (*heating & lighting contracts*)	reg 45(3)	reg 47	reg 51	**12.106–12.111**
Private finance transactions[4] s 48(1)(b) or s 48(1)(c)/reg 17					
If criteria for concessions met	reg 40 (*nil IC*) reg 41(4) reg 42(4)	reg 40 reg 41(6) reg 42(5)	reg 47 reg 47 reg 47	reg 51 reg 51 reg 51	Chapter 15 Chapter 15 Chapter 15
If criteria not met	s 49(1) & (2)	s 49(4)	s 51(5)	s 51(8)	**12.73–12.78**
Transitional credit arrangements s 52	s 52(3) & s 49(1) & (2)	s 52(3) & s 49(4)	s 52(3) & s 51(5)	s 52(3) & s 51(8)	**12.80–12.81**

1 For the amount of credit cover required, see Local Government and Housing Act 1989, s 50(2) (s52(3)(b) in relation to transitional credit arrangements).

2 For the amount of credit cover required, see s 51(4).

3 Adjusted cost on variation and the cost at any time following variation is dealt with generally at paras **12.112–12.134**.

4 Separate provision is made in relation to Wales for the application of regs 40–42 by SI 2000/992, reg 2.

principles of landlord and tenant law should apply in order to determine whether a particular transaction is to be treated as constituting the grant of a new lease (and a new credit arrangement)[2]. In general, each *new* lease would fall to be considered under LGHA 1989, s 48(1)(a) and LA(CF)R 1997, regs 27–39 concerning the calculation of its initial cost. The variation of an *existing* credit arrangement, which is a lease, would fall to be dealt with under LGHA 1989, s 51 and LA(CF)R 1997, regs 46–51 on the calculation of the 'adjusted cost' of leases which have been varied, normally requiring a recalculation of the amount of credit cover required. In addition, in certain instances, the LA(CF)R 1997 make special provision in cases where the local authority has held an earlier lease of all or part of the same land[3].

1 In contrast with credit arrangements under LGHA 1989, s 48(1)(b), which come into being when the contract or the later or latest of the contracts which constitute the contract for the credit arrangement is entered into: see LGHA 1989, s 48(3)(b).
2 See paras **12.125**ff on variation of leases.
3 See, for example, the criteria for nil initial cost treatment of certain leases referred to at paras **12.89–12.102**.

2 VARIOUS KINDS OF EXTENDED CREDIT

12.16 LGHA 1989, s 48(1)(b) provides that a local authority shall be taken to have entered into a credit arrangement –

> '(b) in any case (not falling within para (a) above) where, under a single contract or two or more contracts taken together, it is estimated by the authority that the value of the consideration which the authority have still to give at the end of the relevant financial year for or in connection with the provision to the authority of any land, goods or services or any other kind of benefit is greater than the value of the consideration (if any) which the authority were still to receive immediately before the beginning of that financial year . . .'

(a) Analysis

12.17 To break this complex provision into its constituent elements:

(a) leases granted to a local authority are expressly excluded from this category of credit arrangement;
(b) there may be one or more contracts which give rise to the credit arrangement;
(c) under the contract or contracts some land, goods or services[1] or 'other kind of benefit' (each of which, for brevity, is now referred to as 'the benefit') must be provided to the local authority;
(d) valuable consideration in some form must be provided by the local authority in connection with the benefit;
(e) an estimate must be made by the local authority when the contract is entered into (if a single contract) or at the time when the later or last of a series of contracts is entered into[2];
(f) a credit arrangement will arise if, based on that estimate, the value of the consideration the authority *has still to give* at the end of a relevant financial year for or in connection with the benefit is *greater* than the value of the consideration the authority was *still to receive* immediately before the beginning of that financial year; and
(g) a 'relevant financial year'[2] is defined as a financial year which begins *after* the contract or, as the case may be, the *first* of the contracts constituting the arrangement was entered into.

1 The reference to services is to be noted as, under LGHA 1989, s 50(1), local authorities are prohibited from entering into credit arrangements unless expenditure for the intended purpose would be expenditure for capital purposes. This suggests that contracts which include the deferral of payment for services so as to give rise to a credit arrangement, or simply credit arrangements which include a significant element of services, would be prohibited transactions. The special provisions on 'private finance transactions' in LA(CF)R 1997, regs 8(2) and 17 are intended to allay doubt about this defined class of arrangement by specifying that all expenditure under such a transaction is to be treated as expenditure for capital purposes and that all such arrangements are credit arrangements if they would not otherwise be so. See paras **12.30**ff and Chapter 15 regarding 'private finance transactions'.
2 LGHA 1989, s 48(2). Department of the Environment Circular 11/90, Annex A, para 14 advises that 'the estimates are to be made by the authority, using their professional staff where appropriate, on the basis of the best information available to them at the time the contract is entered into'.
3 Local Government and Housing Act 1989, s 48(2).

12.18 More detailed consideration is now given to the provisions regarding this category of credit arrangement.

(b) Multiple contracts and time of creation of credit arrangement

12.19 Even if an initial contract, considered in isolation, does not constitute a credit arrangement, the transaction may be 'converted into' a credit arrangement because of a subsequent contract (or, indeed, through some method of variation which does not in law amount to a contract, but which is to be regarded as a contract by virtue of LGHA 1989, s 48(8)[1]). If a subsequent contract (or deemed contract under s 48(8)) has this effect, the credit arrangement comes into being when the *later or latest* contract is entered into[2]. The estimate to be made under LGHA 1989, s 48(1)(b) is also to be made when the *later or last* of the contracts which constitute the credit arrangement is entered into[3]. In practice, it may be necessary to make an estimate on more than one occasion if there is a succession of contracts, in order to assess the effect of each contract and their cumulative effects in terms of s 48(1)(b), if the earlier contract or contracts did *not* constitute a credit arrangement.

1 LGHA 1989, s 48(8) appears to deal exclusively with the variation of an existing contract where that contract does *not*, in itself, amount to a credit arrangement, and where the variation is achieved through some method which does not in law amount to a contract (for example, because no consideration passes). See para **12.20**, n 1 regarding variation of *existing* credit arrangements.
2 Local Government and Housing Act 1989, s 48(3).
3 LGHA 1989, s 48(2).

12.20 Once a credit arrangement is found to exist, no account is taken *under LGHA 1989, s 48* of any later contract which has the effect of varying the arrangement[1]. The variation of an *existing* credit arrangement is dealt with separately under LGHA 1989, s 51.

1 See Local Government and Housing Act 1989, s 48(4) and note the distinction from s 48(8). LGHA 1989, s 48(4) refers to the variation of an existing credit arrangement by a subsequent contract (following which, the matter would be dealt with under s 51 concerning variation of credit arrangements). Section 48(8) applies where a contract which is not a credit arrangement is subsequently varied by some means other than a further contract. In such a case, further consideration would have to be given to whether the tests under s 48(1) would be satisfied.

12.21 It is to be noted that the first 'relevant financial year' to be *considered* for the purpose of estimating whether a credit arrangement under LGHA 1989, s 48(1)(b) exists is the financial year which begins after the *first* contract is entered into[1].

1 Local Government and Housing Act 1989, s 48(2).

12.22 Where more than one contact is involved, there is no express requirement that the contracting parties should be identical in order that the contracts should be considered together. The section stipulates that it is immaterial for the purpose of LGHA 1989, s 48 whether the consideration given or received by the local authority is given to or received from the person who provides the land, goods, services or other benefit to the authority[1].

1 Local Government and Housing Act 1989, s 48(6).

(c) Treatment of options and other assumptions for making estimates

12.23 Where all or part of the consideration under a contract consists of an option, then the estimate to be made under LGHA 1989, s 48(1)(b) has to be made on the basis of all the possible alternatives, namely on the assumption that the option is not exercised, or that it is exercised, and if it could be exercised in different ways, assumptions must be made based on each of the possible ways[1]. If the contract or contracts would be a credit arrangement on *any* of those assumptions, then it is to be regarded as a credit arrangement[2]. For the purpose of LGHA 1989, s 48(7), an option includes any right which is exercisable (or not) at the discretion of a party.

1 Local Government and Housing Act 1989, s 48(7).
2 LGHA 1989, s 49(5) (and see para **12.75** regarding the implications of assumptions made under s 48(7) about the exercise of an option when calculating the initial and subsequent costs of a credit arrangement).

12.24 When making the estimate or estimates, the local authority should include all consideration given by them and received by them under the contract or contracts, regardless of to whom it is given or from whom it is received. Where consideration consists of an undertaking or right to do something (or not to do something) at a future date, the consideration is be treated as given or received at the time the undertaking is *performed* or the right is *exercised*, rather than at the time when the undertaking or right is created[1].

1 Local Government and Housing Act 1989, s 48(6).

(d) Application of the test under LGHA 1989, s 48(1)(b)

12.25 In order to constitute a credit arrangement, as a minimum, the arrangements must span one entire financial year and at least a part of the immediately preceding and the immediately following financial years. No credit arrangement will arise if all 'payment' by the authority (in cash or non-monetary form) *precedes* the receipt of the benefit; if receipt of the benefit and payment for it is contemporaneous; or if full payment by the authority is completed during the financial year which follows the year in which the contract is entered into, or that when the benefit is received.

12.26 To take a simple example, using the case of an arrangement which comprises a single contract: if the local authority enter into the contract during 1994/95 (financial year 1), the first 'relevant financial year' will be 1995/96 (year 2). For the possibility of a credit arrangement to arise, there must be some consideration for the authority 'still to give' as at the end of 1995/96, ie during 1996/1997 (year 3) or a subsequent financial year. In this simple example, the credit arrangement test under LGHA 1989, s 48(1)(b) in respect of 1995/6 will only be satisfied if the value of the consideration the authority has still to give as at 31 March 1996 is greater than the value of the consideration it is still to receive as at 31 March 1995[1].

1 The use of the expression 'value of the consideration' in this provision and the fact that estimates must be made (subject to LGHA 1989, s 51 on variation) once and for all at the outset of the arrangement, suggests that amounts of consideration to be given or received by the authority in future years should all be discounted to present values as at the date the estimate is made, in order to enable comparison.

12.27 In the case of a straightforward contract, say for staged payments for building works, it will be a comparatively simple task to see whether a credit arrangement has come into being. But in more complex transactions, involving multiple contracts which span many years, perhaps with a number of elements of consideration passing between the parties during the life of the arrangements (for example, involving barter arrangements and the provision of services), it is necessary to analyse with care the precise nature of the benefit or benefits being provided to the council under the arrangements, and then to establish when each element of benefit is to be received (and its value) and when all 'payments' (in cash or non-monetary form) are to be made by the authority. The test in LGHA 1989, s 48(1)(b) will have to be considered in respect of each successive relevant financial year which begins after the contract, or first or several contracts, is entered into. (However, consideration given before the time the credit arrangement 'comes into being' will ultimately be disregarded: LGHA 1989, s 66(3)(a)[1].)

1 See paras **12.64** and **12.66** regarding the calculation of the initial cost/capital cost of leases and consideration given before the authority becomes the lessee.

12.28 The advice in Circular 11/90 suggests that LGHA 1989, s 48(1)(b) was intended to have a very wide application. Annex A, para 18 of the Circular describes its effects as follows:

> 'The category of credit arrangement in [LGHA 1989, s 48(1)(b)] is not confined to contracts for the supply of goods or services to the authority, the acquisition of land, or the carrying out of works. It also extends to arrangements (other than borrowing) under which money is provided to the authority (or to some other person for the benefit of the authority) in return for future monetary or non-monetary consideration to be provided by the authority and to arrangements under which capital assets are provided by or to some other person if the authority benefit by the provision and are giving consideration (which might take the form of a liability to make payments or the entering into of a guarantee or some other form of commitment which might result in future payments being made).'

More recent Departmental guidance in 'A Guide to Local Government Capital Finance System'[1] at para 7.8 is perhaps more constrained:

> 'Giving a guarantee could constitute a credit arrangement where it is probable that payments would be made under it'.

1 Issued by the Department of the Environment (as then called) in February 1997.

12.29 Whether or not contracts such as guarantees do, in fact, amount to credit arrangements is debatable and will turn on their precise terms. Since the introduction of these provisions there has been considerable doubt and confusion about the ambit of LGHA 1989, s 48(1)(b) and its application to a variety of contractual arrangements, certain of which may have been 'caught' unintentionally. The problems with this provision are well illustrated by the complex arrangements for 'private finance transactions' referred to in the following section and in Chapter 15, which entailed, inter alia, the need to create a new category of credit arrangement through regulations made under LGHA 1989, s 48(1)(c).

3 PRIVATE FINANCE TRANSACTIONS—PRESCRIBED TRANSACTIONS

12.30 The third main class of credit arrangement is that under LGHA 1989, s 48(1)(c), where a local authority enter into:

> '... a transaction of a description for the time being prescribed for the purposes of this section by regulations made by the Secretary of State.'

12.31 LA(CF)R 1997, reg 17 has been made by the Secretary of State under this subsection. It provides:

> 'A private finance transaction[1], which apart from this regulation, would not be a credit arrangement is prescribed for the purposes of section 48(1)(c).'

It should be noted that a private finance transaction ('PFT') which amounts to a credit arrangement by virtue of LGHA 1989, s 48(1)(b) (or, less likely, s 48(1)(a)) would not come within LGHA 1989, s 48(1)(c). In practice, most PFTs will be credit arrangements on account of s 48(1)(b) and not s 48(1)(c).

1 See the definition of 'private finance transaction' in the LA(CF)R 1997, reg 16, which is introduced in para **12.33** and explained more fully in Chapter 15.

(a) Background

12.32 The enactment of LA(CF)R 1997, reg 17 represented the first occasion on which the Secretary of State had used his powers under LGHA 1989, s 48(1)(c) to prescribe an additional class of credit arrangement. Whilst this provision first appeared in the LA(CF)R 1997, it is connected with arrangements which were originally introduced in March 1996[1] to create concessions for certain types of 'design, build, finance and operate' schemes ('DBFO schemes'). The original concessions have now been amended and elaborated upon in the LA(CF)R 1997 and subsequently amended on several occasions. These types of arrangement, sometimes described as being for the procurement of 'capital-intensive services' (as opposed to being for the procurement of the assets themselves), have been given positive encouragement by successive governments over recent years as part of Private Finance Initiative ('the PFI') for local government (see Chapter 15).

1 In the Local Authorities (Capital Finance and Approved Investments) (Amendment) Regulations 1996, SI 1996/568.

12.33 A 'private finance transaction' ('PFT') is defined in LA(CF)R 1997, reg 16[1]. In essence, it is a transaction under which a local authority receives from a contractor an asset (other than housing land) or works (other than those for the construction of a dwelling on housing land) which the authority requires for the discharge of its functions together with services for the discharge of the same function. In exchange, at least a part of the consideration provided by the authority under the transaction must comprise an annual or more regular fee. Originally that fee might only be varied for limited, specified, reasons. However, the elaborate restrictions on fee variation have been relaxed progressively over the years up to 1999. The requirements inherent in the definition of a PFT, and the additional criteria for eligibility for the special concessions created for them in the LA(CF)R 1997, are broadly intended to reflect the general principles of the PFI[2] as applied in other areas of the public sector, but adapted and standardised to fit within the local government financial regime.

1 As amended most recently by the Local Authorities (Capital Finance and Approved Investments) (Amendment) Regulations 1999, SI 1999/1852.
2 Normally summarised as involving the transfer of risk to the private sector, competition and value for money. DBFO schemes are thought to facilitate a 'whole-life approach' to procurement.

12.34 The provisions concerning 'private finance transactions' are explained in more detail in Chapter 15. An example of the type of arrangements envisaged would be those where a local authority wishes to procure a new school and enters into a contract with a private sector contractor (usually comprising a consortium of companies) under which the contractor would be required to design the building, fund and undertake any necessary land acquisition and works and then provide services for the building, such as heating, lighting, cleaning, security and general maintenance, throughout a period of say 25 to 30 years. In return, the authority would pay a regular fee throughout the life of the arrangement (with or without additional payment of capital sums, or the transfer of land or provision of other non-monetary consideration) to the contractor. The regulations which create the concessions for PFTs envisage that the arrangements might include a lease (or lease-back) of an asset to the authority[1].

1 Although this might pose difficulties in relation to the new 'off balance sheet' accounting test under LA(CF)R 1997, reg 40. See para **15.34**ff.

12.35 The need to prescribe this type of arrangement as a credit arrangement arose from a number of factors. The provisions in the subordinate legislation were originally devised on the assumption that all such arrangements would normally be credit arrangements under LGHA 1989, s 48(1)(b), as they entail receipt by an authority of valuable consideration in the form of the new or improved asset (or the benefit of that asset) in early years, with payment being made by the authority over a considerable number of subsequent financial years. Notwithstanding the underlying tenets of the PFI, the payment to be made by the council would in fact cover the contractor's capital costs of providing the new asset and not simply the on-going cost of providing services. Such a transaction might also entail a credit arrangement under LGHA 1989, s 48(1)(a), if the authority is to be granted a lease as part of the overall arrangements.

12.36 The need for an authority to provide significant credit cover for a PFI transaction (as constituting a credit arrangement) was considered to be a major constraint on authorities entering into such transactions[1]. Hence the concessions under the capital finance system first introduced in March 1996 were based on alleviating the adverse effects of such transactions as *credit arrangements*, by reducing the amount of credit cover required to enter into them. Additional administrative arrangements to provide special revenue assistance for authorities who engage in certain of these schemes were also introduced, in order to make these schemes attractive to local authorities. These special arrangements for revenue assistance were first devised in October 1996 and were based (indirectly) on the assumption that these kinds of DBFO schemes would normally amount to credit arrangements.

1 See for example the Department of the Environment publication 'The Private Finance Initiative and Local Authorities—An explanatory note on PFI and Public/Private Partnerships in local government' (updated September 1998) at para 2.7.

12.37 In the majority of cases, where a contractor is to provide the authority with a new or improved building or other significant capital asset under the transaction in return for long-term payments from the authority (particularly where there is to be a lease or lease-back to the authority of the completed asset), it is highly likely that a credit arrangement under LGHA 1989, s 48(1)(b) and/or (a) would come into being. However, DBFO contracts under 'PFI arrangements' normally involve a significant service element and, as noted above, are often presented as being contracts for the purchase of 'capital-intensive services'. Consequently, concern was expressed by those involved in transactions that certain PFI arrangements (particularly those where the authority's regular fees predominantly relate to services and any capital costs are minimal) would not be credit arrangements at all, or would be outside the authority's powers under LGHA 1989, s 50(1), if the purposes of the contract(s) were not ones which would involve expenditure for capital purposes.

12.38 The consequence, if such transactions were not credit arrangements, would be that they would not be eligible for the special arrangements for additional revenue support. If they were not 'for capital purposes' and were beyond LGHA 1989, s 50(1), they would risk being treated as void.

12.39 LA(CF)R 1997, reg 17 deals with the first of these concerns. In so far as a PFT as defined by LA(CF)R 1997, reg 16 is not already a credit arrangement by virtue of LGHA 1989, s 48(1)(a) or (b), it has now been prescribed as being a credit arrangement under s 48(1)(c). The intention of the provision is to put the position beyond doubt. But, as noted, in practice most PFTs will be credit arrangements by virtue of s 48(1)(b) and not on account of s 48(1)(c) and reg 17.

12.40 LA(CF)R 1997, reg 8[1] is aimed at the second concern, that the arrangement might be beyond the authority's powers under LGHA 1989, s 50(1). It provides that expenditure incurred by a local authority under a PFT (as defined in the LA(CF)R 1997) is to be expenditure for capital purposes if it would not otherwise be so[2].

1 Made by the Secretary of State by exercise of his powers under LGHA 1989, s 40(5).
2 It is said that one incidental effect of reg 8 is that usable capital receipts could be used to meet payments under a PFT (see LGHA 1989, s 60(2)(a)).

(b) Time of creation of credit arrangement under LGHA 1989, s 48(1)(c)

12.41 A credit arrangement under LGHA 1989, s 48(1)(c) comes into being 'at the time the authority enter into the transaction concerned or such other time as may be specified in the regulations concerned'[1]. As the LA(CF)R 1997 do not stipulate a time at which a credit arrangement constituted by a PFT under reg 17 is to come into being, the relevant time will be when the authority 'enter into the transaction concerned'.

1 Local Government and Housing Act 1989, s 48(3)(c).

4 TRANSITIONAL CREDIT ARRANGEMENTS

(a) Practical significance

12.42 The provisions on transitional credit arrangements are now of limited practical significance, but they are referred to here for the sake of completeness. The main issue which could still arise is the variation[1] of a contract which constitutes (or forms part of) a transitional credit arrangement based on LGHA 1989, s 48(1)(b). A lease[2] cannot be a *transitional* credit arrangement[3], and the category of 'PFT' of a kind under LGHA 1989, s 48(1)(c) did not exist at the relevant time.

1 For the purposes of variation, a transitional credit arrangement would be treated in the same way as any other credit arrangement, save that it is to be taken to have come into being on 1 April 1990 and the authority is to be taken to have provided credit cover for it of an amount equal to its cost as at that date: see Local Government and Housing Act 1989, s 52(3) and para **12.80**.
2 Local Government and Housing Act 1989, s 48(1)(a).
3 See para **12.44**.

12.43 A local authority is to be taken to have entered into a transitional credit arrangement if, applying the rules in LGHA 1989, s 48(3)[1], the arrangement 'came into being' on or after 7 July 1988[2] and before 1 April 1990[3]. References to a 'credit arrangement' in LGHA 1989, Pt IV are to be taken to include references to a transitional credit arrangement, unless specifically stated otherwise[4].

1 And see para **12.19**.
2 The date on which the Department of the Environment issued the Consultation Paper 'Capital Expenditure and Finance', which outlined the proposals for LGHA 1989, Pt IV.
3 See Local Government and Housing Act 1989, s 52(1).
4 LGHA 1989.

(b) Exclusion from transitional credit arrangement provisions

12.44 There are a number of exclusions from the class of transitional credit arrangement under LGHA 1989, s 52. The most important being arrangements under which local authorities become lessees of land and goods (provided they would *only* be credit arrangements within LGHA 1989, s 48(1)(a)). The remaining exemptions relate to arrangements which benefited from some special exemption under the previous capital finance regime of the Local Government, Planning and Land Act 1980 ('LGPLA 1980') to the effect that they were not treated as involving 'prescribed expenditure'. By virtue of LGHA 1989, s 52(2) none of the following are treated as transitional credit arrangements even though the arrangement came into being on or after 7 July 1988 and before 1 April 1990:

(a) arrangements under which the local authority became the lessees of any property (whether land or goods) and the arrangement was a credit arrangement by reason *only* of s 48(1)(a) (concerning leases);
(b) cases where the amount of 'prescribed expenditure' under the LGPLA 1980 system which the local authority was taken to have paid on entering into the arrangement was nil by virtue of LGPLA 1980, s 80(11) or (12)[1];

(c) cases where by virtue of regulations made under certain provisions[2] of the LGPLA 1980, any expenditure of the local authority under the arrangement was not 'prescribed expenditure'; or
(d) arrangements which related only to works, which in whole or part were carried out before 1 April 1990, and which, by reason only of regulations made under certain provisions[3] of the LGPLA 1980, were specially exempt from LGPLA 1980, s 80A(1).

1 Under the valuation provisions of the LGPLA 1980, s 80(11) and (12) the acquisition of property by gift, or the acquisition of a right or interest in property for a period not exceeding one year, was treated as involving prescribed expenditure of nil.
2 Regulations made under the LGPLA 1980, Sch 12, para 4. The relevant regulations were SI 1987/2186, as amended (temporarily) by SI 1988/434 and by SI 1988/1534.
3 Regulations made under LGPLA 1980, s 80A(7) (being the regulations referred to in the previous footnote). These regulations made special provision to exclude certain deferred or advance purchase schemes costing not more than £3,000,000.

5 EXCLUDED CREDIT ARRANGEMENTS

12.45 The LGHA 1989 creates a special class of credit arrangements known as 'excluded credit arrangements'. These are credit arrangements described in regulations made by the Secretary of State under the LGHA 1989, Sch 3, para 11(2), as being excluded from the normal requirement that the authority's credit ceiling is to increase when an authority enters into or agrees to vary a credit arrangement. Two categories of excluded credit arrangement currently exist:

(a) under LA(CF)R 1997, reg 122, a lease of land at a full open market rent; and
(b) under LA(CF)R 1997, reg 123, certain PFTs entered into by a 'debt-free' authority if the authority uses a supplementary credit approval to provide credit cover.

12.46 The consequences of entering into an *excluded* credit arrangement are as follows:

(a) credit cover is required to enter into the arrangement, but if the arrangement is a lease, any consideration given by the authority during the first three months is to be disregarded[1];
(b) reliance on a credit approval to provide credit cover does not increase the authority's credit ceiling[2];
(c) the cost of an excluded credit arrangement does not count against the authority's aggregate credit limit for the purpose of LGHA 1989, s 44(1)[3];
(d) expenditure on the discharge of any liability in connection with an excluded credit arrangement must be charged to a revenue account and may not be met out of amounts set aside as provision for credit liabilities[4];
(e) setting aside amounts of usable capital receipts or revenue as credit cover for an excluded credit arrangement decreases the credit ceiling[5]; and
(f) there is no requirement to make minimum revenue provision in respect of principal because an authority's credit ceiling does not rise when credit approval is used to authorise entering into or variation of an excluded credit arrangement, and MRP in respect of notional interest on an excluded credit arrangement is expressly excluded[6].

1 Local Authorities (Capital Finance) Regulations 1997, reg 15(3).
2 Local Government and Housing Act 1989, Sch 3, para 11(2).
3 LGHA 1989, s 44(1)(b).
4 LGHA 1989, s 64(1)(b).

5 LGHA 1989, Sch 3, para 12(2)(a).
6 LGHA 1989, para 15(1)(b).

C Exceptions—arrangements which are not credit arrangements

1 ARRANGEMENTS NOT CREDIT ARRANGEMENTS BY VIRTUE OF LGHA 1989, S 48(5)

12.47 LGHA 1989, s 48(5) provides that a contract is not a credit arrangement to the extent that it is a contract under which a local authority borrows money.

12.48 LGHA 1989, s 48(5) also provides that a lease or contract which is excluded from s 48 by regulations made by the Secretary of State is not a credit arrangement.

2 ARRANGEMENTS NOT CREDIT ARRANGEMENTS BY VIRTUE OF THE LA(CF)R 1997

12.49 LA(CF)R 1997, regs 18–25 deal with leases and contracts which are *not* credit arrangements. These regulations make the following special provisions.

(a) Regulation 18—de minimis provision—under £12,000

12.50 Leases and contracts of a small value, being those where the authority estimates, when it enters into the lease or contract, that the total value of the consideration which will fall to be given by the authority will not exceed £12,000, are not credit arrangements. In making this estimate, the authority must include consideration given under any *other* arrangements entered into with the same person in the same financial year, or with any 'associate' of the same person. Two persons are treated as associates if one is a subsidiary of the other, or they are both subsidiaries of the same person, for the purposes of the Companies Act 1985[1]. Two or more leases entered into in the same financial year, with the same lessor or lessors who are associated persons, would fall to be considered together when estimating the £12,000 threshold[2].

1 Local Authorities (Capital Finance) Regulations 1997, reg 18(2)(b).
2 LA(CF)R 1997, reg 18(2)(a).

(b) Regulation 19—leases with a significant premium

12.51 Leases where most of the consideration is given by the end of the first year are not credit arrangements (ie leases with a substantial premium and only a minimal rent). More specifically, where the authority estimate, on the date when they become lessees, that the value of the consideration which they will have given in respect of the lease by the end of the first year following that date will be at least 90% of the 'capital cost of the lease'[1] will not amount to a credit arrangement[2].

1 'The capital cost of a lease' is defined by LA(CF)R 1997, reg 14: in essence it amounts to the total of all consideration to be given before or during the first financial year in which they become the lessees, added to the total value of the consideration given in all subsequent years, (discounted in accordance with a prescribed formula): see para **12.64**.
2 LA(CF)R 1997, reg 15(2), which provides for consideration given before the authority became the lessee to be disregarded, does not appear to apply for the purposes of LA(CF)R 1997, reg 19. (However, it is to be noted that LGHA 1989, s 66(3)(a) provides for all consideration given by an authority before a credit arrangement comes into existence to be disregarded for the purpose of Pt IV of the Act.)

(c) Regulation 20—operating leases

12.52 An 'operating lease' which meets specified conditions, and any arrangement entered into in connection with such a lease, are not credit arrangements. An operating lease is a lease taken by a local authority of any vehicle, vessel, plant, machinery or apparatus ('the asset'[1]). The estimated residual value of the asset on termination must be at least 10% of its value at the commencement of the arrangement. More specifically:

(a) the local authority must make an estimate, on the date they become the lessees or, if earlier, on the date when the connected arrangement is entered into, of the value of the asset on termination (the 'termination value');
(b) the 'termination value' is the authority's estimate of the value of the asset when the lease expires or when the arrangement terminates. If the authority has any right to renew or continue the lease or the arrangement, it must base its estimate on the latest date on which the lease or arrangement could expire;
(c) the lease, taken together with any connected arrangement, must not provide for[2]:
   (i) the transfer of the property in the asset to the local authority;
   (ii) renewal or continuation of the lease or arrangement on terms which provide for transfer of the property in the asset to the local authority;
   (iii) for renewal or continuation for a consideration which is materially less than the amount which would reasonably be regarded as the open market rent for the period (assessed as at the commencement date);
   (iv) receipt by the authority of any consideration which is equivalent to, or determined by reference to, the termination value of the asset.

1 See Local Authorities (Capital Finance) Regulations 1997, reg 20(1).
2 LA(CF)R 1997, reg 20(2).

(d) Regulations 21 and 24—property transactions arising from local government reorganisation and similar matters

12.53 Contracts for the transfer of land from a residuary body[1] to a local authority are not credit arrangements[2]. Nor are leases assigned to the authority from a new town corporation[3], or granted in accordance with regulations made under the Housing Act 1988, s 100[4].

1 The Local Government Residuary Body (England) established under SI 1995/401, or the Residuary Body for Wales or Corff Gweddilliol Cymru established by the Local Government (Wales) Act 1994, s 39, pursuant to SI 1995/103.
2 Local Authorities (Capital Finance) Regulations 1997, reg 21(1)(a) and (b).
3 LA(CF)R 1997, reg 24(1)(a).
4 To facilitate the continuity of a secure tenancy, where individual tenants opt out of a 'change of landlord' scheme under which a body approved by the Housing Corporation has acquired the freehold of council dwellings: see LA(CF)R 1997, reg 24(1)(b).

12.54 Other local authority leases of property excluded from constituting credit arrangements are cases where the authority becomes the lessee by virtue of specified legislation made in connection with:

(a) local government reorganisation[1];
(b) the establishment of new police authorities[2];
(c) the establishment of new fire authorities[3];
(d) the establishment of National Park authorities[4].
(e) the establishment of the National Criminal Intelligence Service and the National Crime Squad[5]; and
(f) the creation of the Greater London Authority and the Regional Development Agencies[6].

1 Local Authorities (Capital Finance) Regulations 1997, reg 24(2)(a) and (d). See SI 1995/402 (regulations made under the Local Government Act 1992), and SI 1996/532 (a property transfer order made under the Local Government (Wales) Act 1994).
2 LA(CF)R 1997, reg 24(2)(b). See art 9 of SI 1994/3262 (an order made under the Police and Magistrates' Court Act 1994 (now consolidated in the Police Act 1996)).
3 LA(CF)R 1997, reg 24(2)(c). A combination scheme under the Fire Services Act 1947.
4 LA(CF)R 1997, reg 24(2)(e). See art 15 of SI 1996/1243 (an order made under various statutory provisions in connection with National Parks). Leases taken by a local authority by virtue of an agreement under the Environment Act 1995, s 76 are also excluded from LGHA 1989, s 48.
5 LA(CF)R 1997, reg 24(2)(f) (inserted by SI 1998/602). See art 5 of SI 1998/354 (c 8) made under the Police Act 1997.
6 LA(CF)R 1997, reg 24(2)(g) (inserted by SI 2000/1033).

(e) Regulation 22—licensing contracts

12.55 'Licensing contracts' are not credit arrangements. In simple terms, licensing contracts are contracts for the provision or improvement of housing by the private sector on local authority land under which the authority is required, on completion of the works, to dispose of the dwelling to the public. In the absence of this exemption, such an arrangement might well give rise to a credit arrangement, if payment by the local authority in respect of the works is deferred until the authority disposes of the new or improved dwellings[1].

1 Further concessions for capital receipts and notional capital receipts generated from certain types of housing scheme are provided for in LA(CF)R 1997, reg 97.

12.56 The contract with the authority must provide for the construction or enhancement of a dwelling, or the provision of a dwelling through conversion, of all or part of a building. The works must be undertaken *for*[1] the local authority on land in which the local authority owns the freehold or has a leasehold interest. On completion of the works, the authority must be required to sell the freehold, grant a long lease[2], or grant a shared ownership lease[3] of the dwelling to a body *other than* another local authority, a new town corporation, an urban development corporation, or to a 'regulated company'[4].

1 If the works are not undertaken for the local authority it seems doubtful that a credit arrangement would arise. (In a case where a developer undertakes works under an agreement for lease or development agreement relating to local authority land and on completion of the works is granted an interest in the land, it is submitted that the works are generally carried out on the developer's behalf and for its own benefit (and not 'for' the local authority), so that such arrangements should not, of themselves, give rise to any credit arrangement under LGHA 1989, s 48(1)(b).)
2 Local Authorities (Capital Finance) Regulations 1997, reg 22(1): 'long lease' means a lease which is a long tenancy for the purposes of the Housing Act 1985, Pt IV (secure tenancies and rights of secure tenants), eg a term exceeding 21 years.

3 'Shared ownership lease' is a lease of a dwelling granted on payment of a premium which is calculated by reference to a percentage of the value of the dwelling or the cost of providing it, and is not less than 25% of that value or cost (LA(CF)R 1997, reg 22(1)).
4 Under the Local Authorities (Companies) Order 1995, SI 1995/849 amended by SI 1996/621. See Chapter 16.

(f) Regulation 23—superannuation investments

12.57 A lease or contract entered into by a local authority as an investment for the purposes of a superannuation fund which an authority are required to keep by virtue of the Superannuation Act 1972, is excluded from LGHA 1989, s 48 and is not a credit arrangement.

(g) Regulation 25—three per cent disregard

12.58 This regulation is intended to deal with contracts which would not otherwise be credit arrangements, but for provisions which allow the authority to retain part of its payment for a period of time, for example in relation to defects under a building contract. The retained payments must not exceed three per cent of the total value of the consideration to be given by the authority under the arrangement. The intention[1] is that such a minor deferred payment is to be disregarded when establishing whether a credit arrangements exists, provided that the retained sum is paid by the end of the second financial year which follows the financial year in which the authority receive the last element of consideration. To use the building contract example, the retention must be paid within two financial years after the year in which the building works are completed and be no greater than three per cent.

1 See Circular 11/90, Annex A, para 13(ix) which refers to the corresponding provision under the Local Authorities (Capital Finance) Regulations 1990 (SI 1990/732 as amended).

D Initial and subsequent cost of credit arrangements

12.59 The 'initial cost' of a credit arrangement is a measure of the amount of credit which an authority has obtained by entering into a credit arrangement and 'the cost at any subsequent time' is a measure of the amount of credit which has not yet been repaid[1]. Initial cost, together with the prohibition[2] on the authority entering into the arrangement unless it can provide credit cover of an amount equal to that cost, are key components of the limits on an authority's capacity to enter into credit arrangements. Special rules contained in the LA(CF)R 1997, Pt IV, which apply a reduced or nil initial cost to credit arrangements which meet specified criteria, provide a means of creating concessions to facilitate certain types of credit arrangement.

1 Circular 11/90, Annex A, para 20.
2 Local Government and Housing Act 1989, s 50(2).

12.60 The basic provisions on the calculation of initial and subsequent cost of credit arrangements are contained in LGHA 1989, s 49. However, there are extensive exceptions to those general rules. The Secretary of State is empowered under s 49(3) to make regulations which exclude credit arrangements of a particular description from s 49(2) and to make special provision for the calculation of their initial and subsequent costs:

(a) all leases are excluded from LGHA 1989, s 49(2) by LA(CF)R 1997, reg 26[1] and their initial cost and cost at any time after they have come into being are calculated in accordance with regs 27 to 39[2];
(b) certain PFTs are excluded from LGHA 1989, s 49(2) by LA(CF)R 1997, regs 40–42, each of which regulations contains provisions for the calculation of their initial cost and cost at any time[3]; and
(c) certain heating and lighting contracts are excluded from LGHA 1989, s 49(2) by LA(CF)R 1997, regs 43 and 44 and their initial cost and cost at any time are calculated in accordance with reg 45[4].

1 Made in exercise of the Secretary of State's powers under LGHA 1989, s 49(3).
2 See paras **12.62–12.72** and **12.89–12.101**.
3 See Chapter 15.
4 See paras **12.107–12.111**.

12.61 This section deals first with the 'general rules' for calculating initial and subsequent costs of leases contained in the LA(CF)R 1997, before turning to the 'general rules' for extended credit and PFT arrangements under LGHA 1989, s 49. The numerous exceptions to these general rules are explained at paras **12.84–12.111**, which deal with the concessions created by the LA(CF)R 1997, and in Chapter 15, which deals specifically with the major concessions for PFTs. However, in the case of leases and PFTs, the exceptions are so considerable that it would be misleading to consider what we have called 'the general rules' in paras **12.62–12.79** as providing any norm. The concessions created under the LA(CF)R 1997 are essential to an understanding of the treatment of credit arrangements constituted by leases or PFTs. The chart opposite para **12.3** summarises the location of the main provisions in the LGHA 1989 and the LA(CF)R 1997 which apply to the calculation of initial, subsequent and adjusted cost.

I CALCULATING INITIAL AND SUBSEQUENT COST—GENERAL RULES FOR LEASES—CAPITAL COST

12.62 All leases (of land and goods) are excluded from LGHA 1989, s 49(2) by LA(CF)R 1997, reg 26 of the 1997 Regulations. Calculation of their initial cost and cost at any time are therefore provided for in regs 27–39, rather than in s 49 itself. Many of these regulations create special 'concessions'. Those under regs 27–34 concerning leases of land which have an initial cost of nil are described at paras **12.89**ff.

(a) Initial cost of leases of land and goods

12.63 The 'general rule' for calculating the initial cost of a lease of land or goods is that it is the 'capital cost of the lease'. But this general rule under LA(CF)R 1997, reg 36 does not apply if the lease comes within one of the special concessions (and related provisions) under regs 28–35[1]. Regulation 36 is subject to modification in further special cases under regs 37[2] and 38[3].

1 See paras **12.89**ff.
2 For leases forming part of a private finance transaction under LA(CF)R 1997, reg 41 or 42 (see para **12.103** and para **15.54**).
3 Concerning the ability to off-set 'unused' credit cover against a subsequent lease, if a lease which required credit cover ends before its expiry date (see para **12.104**).

12.64 The 'capital cost of a lease' is defined by LA(CF)R 1997, reg 14 as being the amount which, at the time they become the lessees, the authority estimate will be the aggregate of –

(a) the value of the consideration given, or failing (sic[1]) to be given by them in respect of the lease before[2] or during the financial year in which they become the lessees; and
(b) the value of the consideration falling to be given by them in respect of the lease in any subsequent financial year.

1 Presumably, 'falling'.
2 See para **12.66**.

12.65 For each subsequent financial year referred to in (b) above the value of the consideration is to be determined by the daunting formula:

$$\frac{x}{\left(1 + \frac{r}{100}\right)^{n}}$$

where –

'x' is the value of the consideration which the authority estimate will be given by them under the lease in that financial year;
'r' is the percentage rate of discount prescribed for the financial year in which the authority became the lessees by regulations made by the Secretary of State for the purposes of LGHA 1989, s 49[1]; and
'n' is the financial year concerned, expressed as a year subsequent to the financial year in which the authority became the lessees (so that the first of the subsequent financial years is 1, and the next financial year is 2, and so on).

1 The current regulations made under LGHA 1989, s 49(2) are the Local Authorities (Capital Finance) (Rate of Discount for 2000–01) (England) Regulations, SI 2000/259 which, under reg 2, prescribe a discount rate of 7.9% for the year beginning on 1 April 2000. The equivalent regulations for Wales (SI 2000/825) prescribe a discount rate of 7.5% for that year.

12.66 In determining the 'capital cost' of a lease for the purposes of LA(CF)R 1997, reg 36, a local authority is to disregard any consideration given by it *before* it became the lessee[1]. The formula is essentially the same as that for other types of credit arrangement under LGHA 1989, s 49. In simple terms, the 'initial cost' of a lease under the 'general rules' for leases is the total of any premium paid by the local authority after they become the lessee[2], plus the value of all rental payments and other consideration given by the local authority over the life of the lease, discounted to present day values.

1 Local Authorities (Capital Finance) Regulations 1997, reg 15(2). This is consistent with the provisions of LGHA 1989, s 66(3)(a), which excludes any consideration given before the credit arrangement came into being for the purposes of LGHA 1989, Pt IV.
2 Whilst not beyond argument, it would appear that the normal type of premium, paid on the grant of a lease, should be taken into account as it is not paid 'before' the authority becomes the lessee.

(b) Initial cost of leases–special cases under LA(CF)R 1997, regs 35–39 and 50[1]

12.67 LA(CF)R 1997, reg 35 deals with the situation where an authority takes consecutive leases of the whole or any part of the same land. Where there has been a preceding interest, which was acquired on or after 1 April 1990, under a lease which had an initial cost of nil (either by virtue of the LA(CF)R 1997[2] or by virtue of the Local Authorities (Capital Finance) Regulations 1990 (now revoked)[3]), the initial cost of the new lease is the aggregate of the capital cost of the new lease and the value of the consideration given by the authority in respect of the preceding interest. In this way, the LA(CF)R 1997 prevent the time limits in the special concessions being circumvented by an authority taking consecutive leases of the same land. LA(CF)R 1997, reg 35 does not apply if the new lease is itself eligible for the concessions under regs 28–34[4].

1 Further special cases on the calculation of the initial cost of leases are described in paras **12.89–12.105** in the context of the concessions under the LA(CF)R 1997.
2 See Local Authorities (Capital Finance) Regulations 1997, regs 28–34 and paras **12.89**ff.
3 Regulation 7 of the Local Authorities (Capital Finance) Regulations 1990, SI 1990/432 (now revoked).
4 Each of which regulations would give the new lease a nil initial cost. However, under LA(CF)R 1997, regs 29, 31 and 32, the existence (or terms) of the earlier leasehold interest *may* represent a bar to eligibility for nil initial cost treatment.

12.68 LA(CF)R 1997, reg 35 is subject to reg 37.

12.69 LA(CF)R 1997, reg 37 provides for a reduction in the initial cost of a lease of land which forms part of a private finance transaction under regs 41 and 42 and is referred to in para **15.54**ff.

12.70 LA(CF)R 1997, reg 38 applies where an authority's lease of land which initially required credit cover under regs 35, 36 or 37 comes to an end early, for some reason *other* than the expiry of its term (for example, through surrender or assignment). Under reg 38, the authority can 'transfer' the 'unused' credit cover to a subsequent lease which itself requires credit cover under regs 35, 36 or 37. In this way, the amount of credit cover needed for the new lease can be treated as reduced by the 'unused' credit cover[1].

1 See para **12.104**.

12.71 LA(CF)R 1997, reg 50 makes special provision for the *continuation* of tenancies under the Landlord and Tenant Act 1954, s 24 (ie where no notice is served by the lessor or the lessee which would entail the grant of a new lease). Such a continuation is to be treated as a 'variation' of the credit arrangement, requiring the calculation of the adjusted cost of the lease in accordance with regs 47 or 49[1].

1 See variation and adjusted cost of leases in paras **12.125**ff and in particular para **12.128**.

(c) Cost at any subsequent time of leases under regs 35–37

12.72 By virtue of LA(CF)R 1997, reg 39, the 'cost at any time' of a lease which is subject to:

(a) reg 36 ('general rules' for leases of land or goods);
(b) reg 35 (subsequent leases of the same land); or
(c) reg 37 (leases of land forming part of certain PFTs),

is the amount which would be the 'capital cost of the lease', if it had been entered into at the time in question, on the basis of an estimate made at that time, but disregarding any consideration given by the authority in respect of the lease *before* that time.

2 CALCULATING INITIAL AND SUBSEQUENT COST—GENERAL RULES FOR EXTENDED CREDIT AND CERTAIN PFT ARRANGEMENTS

12.73 For most practical purposes, LGHA 1989, s 49 deals only with the calculation of the initial and subsequent costs of credit arrangements under LGHA 1989, s 48(1)(b) (extended credit). It applies to PFTs under s 48(1)(b) or (c) (and LA(CF)R 1997, reg 17) only where these are *not eligible* for any of the special concessions under the LA(CF)R 1997, Pt IV[1]. The special concessions and other provisions of LA(CF)R 1997, Pt IV for certain classes of transaction within s 48(1)(a) and (b) are set out at paras **12.89–12.111** and in Chapter 15 concerning PFTs under s 48(1)(c). For the vast majority of PFTs, it will be the rules under the LA(CF)R 1997, as described in those other parts of this work, which will apply and *not* the following 'general rules'. In practice, a PFT will usually be carefully structured so as to ensure that the criteria under LA(CF)R 1997, reg 40 (or 41 or 42) are met, bringing them outside the calculations stipulated in LGHA 1989, s 49, which are described at para **12.74**ff.

1 All leases and certain private finance transactions are excluded from LGHA 1989, s 49(2) by regulations made by the Secretary of State under s 49(3): see regs 26 and 40–44. For local authorities in Wales, in effect, all PFTs within LA(CF)R 1997, reg 16 are excluded from s 49(2) and have an initial cost of nil by virtue of amendments made to LA(CF)R 1997, regs 40–42 for Wales by SI 2000/992.

(a) Initial cost of extended credit and PFT arrangements

12.74 To calculate the initial cost of an arrangement under LGHA 1989, s 48(1)(b) (or s 48(1)(c)) under the 'general rules', s 49(1) requires the local authority to make an estimate, at the time the arrangement comes into being[1], of the aggregate of:

(a) any consideration which falls to be given by the authority under the arrangement in the financial year in which it comes into being; and
(b) the value of the consideration falling to be given by the authority under the arrangement in any subsequent financial year determined in accordance with LGHA 1989, s 49(2).

1 See Local Government and Housing Act 1989, s 48(3) for the time at which a credit arrangement is treated as coming into being, and paras **12.19** and **12.41**.

12.75 Where the arrangement constituted a credit arrangement on account of an assumption made about the exercise of an option under LGHA 1989, s 48(7)[1], the authority must make the same assumption when calculating the initial and subsequent cost of the arrangement under LGHA 1989, s 49. If the arrangement constituted a credit arrangement on the basis of *more than one* assumption about the exercise (or non-exercise) of the option, the local authority is to apply whichever of those assumptions seems most likely[2].

1 See para **12.23**.
2 Local Government and Housing Act 1989, s 49(5)(b).

12.76 LGHA 1989, s 49(2) sets out the formula for the determination of the value of the consideration in subsequent financial years:

$$\frac{x}{\left(1 + \frac{r}{100}\right)^{n}}$$

where –

'x' is the amount of consideration which the authority estimate will be given by them under the arrangement in that financial year;

'r' is the percentage rate of discount prescribed for the financial year in which the arrangement came into being[1]. (A discount rate to be used for this calculation is prescribed annually by the Secretary of State by regulations); and

'n' is the financial year in which the consideration falls to be given, expressed as a year subsequent to the financial year in which the arrangement came into being (so that the first of the subsequent financial years is 1, the next financial year is 2, and so on.)

1 See Local Government and Housing Act 1989, s 49(3) for the time at which a credit arrangement is treated as coming into being, referred to in para **12.19** (in relation to credit arrangements under LGHA 1989, s 48(1)(b)) and in para **12.41** (PFT under s 48(1)(c)).

12.77 The formula incorporates (in item 'r') a rate of discount (current for the year in which the arrangement came into being). The discount rate to be used for this calculation is prescribed annually by the Secretary of State by regulations[1].

1 The current regulations made under Local Government and Housing Act 1989, s 49(2) are the Local Authorities (Capital Finance) (Rate of Discount for 2000–01) (England) Regulations, SI 2000/259 which prescribe a discount rate of 7.9% for the year beginning on 1 April 2000. The equivalent regulations for Wales (SI 2000/825) prescribe a discount rate of 7.5% for that year.

12.78 In basic terms, the initial cost is the net present value of all payments due under the arrangement. Any consideration given *before* the credit arrangement 'comes into being[1]' is disregarded[2].

1 As defined in Local Government and Housing Act 1989, s 48(3).
2 See LGHA 1989, s 66(3)(a): any references to 'consideration given or to be given by the local authority' in LGHA 1989, Pt IV does not include a reference to any consideration which is given before the time the arrangement comes into being (as defined in LGHA 1989, s 48(3)).

(b) Cost at any time of extended credit and PFT arrangements

12.79 Under the general rules[1], the 'cost at any time' of a credit arrangement in these two categories is, by virtue of LGHA 1989, s 49(4), calculated on the basis of the factors set out in paras **12.74** and **12.76**, but leaving out of account any consideration which has been given by the authority *before* the time in question. The cost of a credit arrangement at a subsequent point in time is relevant, for example, in relation to calculation of the borrowing limit under LGHA 1989, s 44[2].

1 But note that these are unlikely to apply to PFTs for the reasons explained in para **12.73**.
2 Where one of the factors to be taken into account is the aggregate cost at the given time of the authority's credit arrangements.

3 INITIAL AND SUBSEQUENT COSTS OF TRANSITIONAL CREDIT ARRANGEMENTS AND MINIMUM REVENUE PROVISION

12.80 For the purposes of calculating the initial and subsequent costs of a transitional credit arrangement under LGHA 1989, s 49[1] the arrangement is deemed to have come into being on 1 April 1990. Any consideration given under the arrangement *before* that date is therefore disregarded[2]. No credit cover under LGHA 1989, s 50 was required to be provided in respect of a transitional credit arrangement, as this was *deemed* to have been made available on 1 April 1990 in an amount equal to its cost on that date[3].

1 Or the costs on or following variation of a transitional credit arrangement under LGHA 1989, s 51.
2 Local Government and Housing Act 1989, s 52(3)(a).
3 LGHA 1989, s 52(3)(b). These 'deeming provisions' also apply to the calculation of the costs arising on variation of a transitional credit arrangement under s 51.

12.81 During the first five years of the present system (ie the financial years starting on 1 April 1990 and ending on 31 March 1995), local authorities were required to make additional minimum revenue provision[1] in respect of the total cost of their transitional credit arrangements as at 1 April 1990. The additional provision required to be made in each of those years equated to 20% of their total cost, thus amortising them by equal instalments over the five year period[2].

1 See para **11.47**ff.
2 Under reg 26(1)(a) and (2)(c) of the Local Authorities (Capital Finance) Regulations 1990, SI 1990/432 (now revoked by SI 1997/319).

4 EXCEPTIONS TO THE GENERAL RULES FOR CALCULATING INITIAL AND SUBSEQUENT COST

(a) Leases and PFTs

12.82 As emphasised in para **12.61**, the LA(CF)R 1997 create a number of exceptions to the 'general rules' for calculating initial and subsequent cost described at paras **12.62–12.79**, provided specified criteria are met. Exceptions are made in relation to all three categories of credit arrangement, but they are most extensive in relation to leases and PFTs. These exceptions are set out at paras **12.84–12.111**, and those concerning the most important kinds of PFT are expanded on in Chapter 15. In many instances the concessions provide for the initial cost of the arrangement to be nil (and thus, the amount of credit cover required under LGHA 1989, s 50(2)) will be nil). In others, they provide for the initial cost to be reduced below that which would apply under the 'general rules'.

(b) Important exceptions for two common types of lease

12.83 When considering the financial implications of leases taken by local authorities two commonly encountered rules should be born in mind:

(a) *Leases at a premium* As noted in para **12.51**, by virtue of LA(CF)R 1997, reg 19, all leases (of land or goods) where at least 90% of the capital cost of the lease is paid by the end of the first year are not credit arrangements at all.
(b) *Leases of land at a full commercial rent* Leases of land taken by a local authority, at a rent which is no less than the amount which would be payable on the

assumptions that there is no premium and that the only consideration given by the local authority comprises an open market annual rent, fall within the special category 'excluded credit arrangements' under LA(CF)R 1997, reg 122, described in paras **12.45** and **12.46**. As noted there, 'excluded credit arrangements' are credit arrangements for which credit cover is required, but they are subject to special treatment in a number of respects. In calculating their 'capital cost', any consideration which falls to be given by the local authority during the first three months after the lease is entered into is to be disregarded[1] and expenditure on them (other than any initial premium) is charged directly to revenue account.

1 Local Authorities (Capital Finance) Regulations 1997, reg 15(3).

E Special rules for certain credit arrangements under the LA(CF)R 1997

12.84 To recap, the three categories of credit arrangement are in summary:

(a) leases of land and goods taken by authorities under LGHA 1989, s 48(1)(a);
(b) arrangements which provide an authority with extended credit under LGHA 1989, s 48(1)(b); and
(c) private finance transactions[1] ('PFTs') not within (a) or (b), prescribed by regulations under LGHA 1989, s 48(1)(c).

1 As defined in Local Authorities (Capital Finance) Regulations 1997, reg 16.

12.85 Earlier parts of this chapter explain the need for local authorities to provide credit cover equal to the initial cost of their credit arrangements, as part of the mechanism for limiting the extent to which authorities can enter into them. The aim of most of the special rules in LA(CF)R 1997, Pt IV concerning credit arrangements is to provide exceptions from a strict application of the 'general rules' for calculation of initial cost under the LGHA 1989, and the 'general rules' under the LA(CF)R 1997 concerning leases[1], in order to allow certain transactions to occur, or to occur with less onerous implications for the local authority[2]. Under these special rules, certain arrangements are entirely exempt from being credit arrangements. Others remain as 'credit arrangements', but their initial cost (and therefore the amount of credit cover required) is either treated as reduced, or as a nil amount.

1 Local Authorities (Capital Finance) Regulations 1997, reg 36; see paras **12.63**ff.
2 However, some of the exceptional rules in the LA(CF)R 1997 are not truly 'concessions', but are aimed at addressing technical issues and/or correcting anomalies.

1 ARRANGEMENTS WHICH DO NOT CONSTITUTE CREDIT ARRANGEMENTS UNDER LGHA 1989, S 48

12.86 Certain leases and contracts have been excluded from LGHA 1989, s 48 by regulations made by the Secretary of State under s 48(5)[1], and hence are not credit arrangements at all. LA(CF)R 1997, regs 18–25 have been made by the Secretary of State under these powers. These provisions are covered in paras **12.49**ff. In brief, the arrangements which *do not amount to credit arrangements at all*, by virtue of the LA(CF)R 1997 comprise those under:

Regulation 18 De minimis provisions for leases and contracts below £12,000.

Regulation 19	Leases under which most of the consideration is given by the authority in the first year.
Regulation 20	'Operating leases' of vehicles, vessels, plant and machinery and connected arrangements which meet specified conditions.
Regulation 21	Certain contracts with residuary bodies.
Regulation 22	Licensing contracts for certain housing schemes.
Regulation 23	Superannuation fund investments.
Regulation 24	Property transferred by new town corporations and under local government reorganisation and leases taken in connection with certain housing transfers in order to preserve secure tenants' rights.
Regulation 25	Retained payments of no more than three percent.

1 Under Local Government and Housing Act 1989, s 48(5) a contract is also excluded from being a credit arrangement to the extent that it is a contract under which a local authority borrows money.

2 CREDIT ARRANGEMENTS WHERE SPECIAL PROVISION IS MADE FOR THE CALCULATION OF THEIR INITIAL COST

(a) Leases

12.87 By virtue of LA(CF)R 1997, reg 26, all leases are excluded from the 'general rules' for calculating the initial and subsequent costs of credit arrangements under LGHA 1989, s 49(2)[1]. Paragraphs **12.62–12.72** describe the 'general rules' for calculating the initial cost of a lease of land or goods under reg 36[2], and the cost at any time of such a lease under reg 39[3]. Paragraphs **12.89–12.101** summarise the *exceptions* created in the LA(CF)R 1997 which are in the nature of concessions or relaxations of the general provisions on leases of land taken by local authorities, but under which the leases are, nonetheless treated as credit arrangements[4]. Since the LGHA 1989 was first enacted, these particular concessions, most of which have their origins in the Local Authorities (Capital Finance) Regulations 1990 (now revoked), have been amended on innumerable occasions. The overall effect has been to extend the circumstances in which a lease of land will have an initial cost of nil, but the various amendments have resulted in provisions which are complex and cumbersome, notwithstanding their rationalisation within the LA(CF)R 1997. Indeed, since 1997, they have been subject to still further revision.

1 The 'general rules' for calculating initial cost under LGHA 1989, s 49 are described in para **12.74**ff.
2 Being the 'capital cost of the lease' as defined in LA(CF)R 1997, reg 14: see paras **12.63**ff. See also paras **12.45**ff concerning leases of land at a full commercial rent which constitute the special category of credit arrangement under reg 122 of 'excluded credit arrangements'.
3 See para **12.72**.
4 See para **12.49**ff summarised in para **12.86** regarding various kinds of leases which are treated as *not* being credit arrangements at all.

(b) Contracts

12.88 Paragraphs **12.106**ff. refer to contracts (as opposed to leases) which have an initial cost of nil or a reduced initial cost.

3 LEASES OF LAND WITH AN INITIAL COST OF NIL

12.89 Leases which have an initial cost of nil (and any other credit arrangement treated in this way) do not require credit cover to authorise the local authority to enter into them. Thus, the authority is not concerned about the effects of the various limits on credit referred to in Chapter 11. To a degree, a credit arrangement with an initial cost of nil is a mixed blessing, as the ongoing liabilities in respect of such an arrangement fall entirely on revenue account[1]. Further, because credit approvals are used as the basis for calculating the capital finance component of revenue support for credit arrangements[2] (and no credit approval is required for a nil initial cost lease), no allowance will be made in the amount of Revenue Support Grant provided by central government towards their costs over subsequent years[3]. Nonetheless, the fact that the authority will not be constrained[4] by any lack of available credit cover when it enters into 'a nil initial cost lease' is an important practical consideration. The following describes the main categories of leases of land which have an initial cost of nil.

1 Although PCL may be used to meet liabilities under such a credit arrangement with a nil initial cost, LA(CF)R 1997, reg 137 requires that applications of PCL made for this particular purpose must be made up from revenue in the following year.
2 See para **11.27**.
3 In the case of private finance transactions under LA(CF)R 1997, reg 40 which have an initial cost of nil, special administrative arrangements have been made to tackle this issue, as described in para **15.61**, to provide an additional incentive to pursue such schemes, but these do not apply outside the special PFT arrangements.
4 See Local Government and Housing Act 1989, s 50(2).

(a) Leases of land under certain private finance transactions—reg 28

12.90 Where an authority enters into a lease of land under the provisions of a PFT and that transaction benefits from LA(CF)R 1997, reg 40 (giving it a nil initial cost[1]), the lease will also have an initial cost of nil[2].

1 See para **15.27**ff.
2 LA(CF)R 1997, reg 37 provides an equivalent concession for a lease of land entered into in connection with a PFT under reg 41 or 42, but in this case, providing for the initial cost to be reduced by at least 30% in line with the reduction applying to the main PFT contract: see para **15.54**.

(b) Leases of land for a term not exceeding three years—reg 29

12.91 The initial cost of a lease of land for a term of no more than three years is nil, provided that:

(a) the authority has not, at any time during the five years before it became the lessee, had a freehold interest in any part of the land; and
(b) neither that authority, *nor any other local authority*, has held an earlier leasehold interest in any part of the land during that five year period for a term which, when combined with the new lease, would exceed the three year limit.

(c) Leases of dwelling houses for use as accommodation for homeless persons—reg 30

12.92 A lease taken by a local authority of a 'dwelling-house'[1] has an initial cost of nil, provided the term of the lease does not exceed 10 years and the authority decided, before it became the lessee, to use or to continue to use the dwelling-house to provide accommodation for homeless people[2].

1 As defined in Pt IV of the Housing Act 1985 regarding secure tenancies.
2 In the exercise of their functions under Pt VII of the Housing Act 1996 on homelessness.

(d) Leases of land for non-housing purposes—reg 31

12.93 In three cases, leases of land taken by a local authority have a nil initial cost, even though they are for a term of up to 10, rather than three years[1]. The initial conditions for eligibility which apply in all three cases are that:

(a) the lease is of 'non-housing land'[2];
(b) the term of the lease does not exceed 10 years;
(c) the lease does not confer any option to purchase the lessor's interest in the land; and
(d) the capital cost does not exceed 70% of the 'relevant value' of the land[3].

1 Contrast reg 29 referred to in para **12.91**.
2 This means any land *other than* land, houses, or other property which would fall to be accounted for under the Housing Revenue Account under LGHA 1989, s 74(1): see LA(CF)R 1997, reg 13(1).
3 The capital cost of a lease is defined in LA(CF)R 1997, reg 14: see para **12.64**. The 'relevant value' means the value of the lessor's interest in the land, as estimated by the authority before it became the lessee, on the basis of certain assumptions specified in LA(CF)R 1997, reg 13(1). The intention is that the risks of ownership should remain with the lessor (see 'Local Government and the Private Finance Initiative—an Explanatory Note on PFI and Public/Private Partnerships in Local Government', DETR, updated September 1998 at para 8.9).

12.94 Provided these initial conditions are met, the lease will have a nil initial cost in three distinct cases, each involving additional criteria:

(a) *no previous interest of specified kinds*, ie where:
  (i) the authority has not previously had a leasehold interest in the whole or any part of the demised land;
  (ii) the authority has not, at any time after 31 March 1989[1], had a freehold interest in the whole or any part of the land; and
  (iii) no *other* authority has had an earlier 'nil initial cost' lease of the land (whether by virtue of this, or any other concession);
(b) *renewal of old lease*, ie where the authority had a leasehold interest under an earlier lease acquired *before 1 April 1989* and that lease is being renewed upon its expiry date; and
(c) *leaseback*, ie where the authority has disposed of the freehold or a leasehold interest in the land and the new lease is a leaseback of either:
  (i) the whole or any part of a *new building constructed on the land* after the disposal; or
  (ii) part of a building which was occupied *before* the disposal for the purposes of, or in connection with, the exercise of the council's functions and the capital cost of the new lease is less than 50% of the amount which would be the capital cost of a lease on identical terms of the whole building.

1 This reflects an amendment, introduced by SI 1999/1852 as from 23 July 1999. It represents a relaxation of the former requirement, that the authority should have had no previous freehold interest at all. The restriction is aimed at inhibiting sale and leaseback arrangements benefiting from nil initial cost treatment other than those specifically envisaged under the third case.

(e) Consecutive leases of non-housing land for a total term not exceeding 10 years—reg 32

12.95 This applies where a local authority has taken a lease of land for a term of no more than three years, which had an initial cost of nil by virtue of LA(CF)R 1997, reg 29[1], or under the equivalent provision in the Local Authorities (Capital Finance)

Regulations 1990 (now revoked)[2] ('the preceding interest'). The authority may take a new lease of that land for non-housing[3] purposes with an initial cost of nil, provided that the term of the new lease, added to the term of the preceding interest, produces a combined term of no more than ten years and provided that the only reason the new lease cannot benefit under LA(CF)R 1997, reg 31 is the preceding (up to three year) interest.

1 See para **12.91**.
2 Regulation 7(3) of the Local Authorities (Capital Finance) Regulations 1990 (now revoked) as amended by SI 1995/850.
3 'Non-housing land' is defined in LA(CF)R 1997, reg 13(1). It is implicit that the use of the land must be for 'non-housing' purposes through the link to reg 31.

(f) Leases re-acquired by a local authority—reg 32A

12.96 This concession was introduced in July 1999[1]. It applies in the limited circumstances where a local authority became the lessees of land before 1 April 1989 and then assigned the lease. If the lease is then assigned back to the authority, at a time when the unexpired portion does not exceed ten years, the initial cost is nil.

1 By SI 1999/1852.

(g) Fire authority leases of land for up to 10 years—reg 33

12.97 This provides a concession for 'new fire authorities' constituted under combination schemes[1] following local government reorganisation, allowing them to take leases for up to 10 years of land previously occupied by the old fire authority, with an initial cost of nil, provided that:

(a) the old fire authority occupied the land immediately before the combination scheme came into full operation('the relevant date');
(b) the new fire authority took up the lease within 12 months of the relevant date;
(c) another local authority held the freehold or a leasehold interest in the land immediately before the new lease is taken;
(d) the new lease does confer an option to acquire the lessor's interest; and
(e) if the new lease is for more than three years, the capital cost does not exceed 70% of the relevant value[2].

1 Under the Fire Services Act 1947 made in consequence of an order under Pt II of the Local Government Act 1992 to give effect to a structural change, or in consequence of the provisions of the Local Government (Wales) Act 1994.
2 See Local Authorities (Capital Finance) Regulations 1997, reg 13(1) for the meaning of 'relevant value'.

12.98 An equivalent concession applies to leases of up to 10 years taken by the old fire authority from the new fire authority within the first year after it comes into operation, giving them an initial cost of nil. This applies where the old authority had a freehold or earlier leasehold interest in the land immediately before the relevant date and that interest has been transferred to the new fire authority under the combination scheme. The restrictions referred to in subparas (d) and (e) of para **12.97** also apply.

(h) National Park authority leases of land for up to 10 years—reg 34

12.99 Leases of land for up to 10 years taken by National Park authorities[1] ('NPAs') have an initial cost of nil if the 'relevant council' which appointed the

National Park Committee occupied the land on 31 March 1997 and the NPA became the lessee within the period of 12 months beginning on 1 April 1997, other than by virtue of a 'relevant agreement or award'[2]. Immediately before the NPA became the lessee, another local authority must have held a freehold or leasehold interest in the land. The conditions mentioned in subparas (d) and (e) of **12.97** also apply.

1 As defined in art 2 of the National Park Authorities (England) Order 1996 SI 1996/1243: see LA(CF)R 1997, reg 34(1).
2 Being an agreement under s 76 of the Environment Act 1995 or an award under s 76(3) of that Act: see LA(CF)R 1997, reg 34(1).

12.100 An equivalent concession applies to a 'relevant council' who become a lessee of the NPA in the period of 12 months beginning on 1 April 1997, if they had a freehold or earlier leasehold interest in land on 31 March 1997 which has since vested in the NPA[1].

1 By virtue of art 15 of the National Park Authorities (England) Order 1996, or a relevant agreement or award: see LA(CF)R 1997, reg 34(3) for the detailed conditions.

4 SUBSEQUENT COST OF A LEASE WITH AN INITIAL COST OF NIL

12.101 If the initial cost of a lease is nil, the cost at any time of that lease is also nil (LA(CF)R 1997, reg 27[1]). The cost at any time of a credit arrangement is relevant to the calculation of the limit on borrowing under LGHA 1989, s 44(1)[2].

1 LA(CF)R 1997, reg 27 is subject to reg 46, which makes provision for the calculation of adjusted cost on the variation of leases (and other credit arrangements which are excluded from LGHA 1989, s 49(2)).
2 See Chapter 13.

5 LEASES SUBSEQUENT TO, OR VARIATION OF, A NIL INITIAL COST LEASE

12.102 The benefits of the lease having an initial cost of nil *may* eventually be forfeited if the authority takes a new lease of the same land, or varies the lease. The complex provisions on the effect of subsequent leases are contained in LA(CF)R 1997, reg 35[1] and those concerning variation in LA(CF)R 1997, regs 47–50[2]. In *some*[3] cases where the special regulations concerning subsequent leases or variation of leases apply, the effect will be that the value of the consideration given under the earlier lease which benefited from nil initial cost treatment has to be aggregated with the capital cost of the new lease, or taken into account when accessing the adjusted cost of the lease as varied. It should be borne in mind that if the term of years of a lease of land is 'varied' by agreement, this normally takes effect in law as a surrender of the original lease and the re-grant of a new lease (rather than as a variation of the original lease). However, LA(CF)R 1997, reg 48 envisages that the grant of a new lease of the same land could amount to a 'variation'. Further, LA(CF)R 1997, reg 50 expressly provides for the continuation of a lease under the Landlord and Tenant Act 1954, s 24 to be treated as a variation of the original lease[4].

1 See para **12.67**.
2 See para **12.125**ff.
3 Note, for example, LA(CF)R 1997, reg 35 on subsequent leases would *not* apply if the initial cost of the *new lease* falls to be determined under regs 28 to 34 (although certain of these regulations, in themselves, exclude cases where the authority has held a previous interest in the land) and reg 48

allows for nil initial cost treatment to be preserved on variation in specified circumstances.
4 Although not in a case where a notice served under the Landlord and Tenant Act 1954 leads to the grant of a new lease: see paras **12.128** and **12.133**.

6 REDUCTIONS IN THE INITIAL COST OF CERTAIN LEASES OF LAND

12.103 LA(CF)R 1997, regs 37 and 38 deal with two separate instances where deductions are to be made from the normal calculation of the initial cost of a lease of land. Regulation 37 is mentioned para **15.54** in conjunction with the special concessions for PFTs. In essence, it provides for the initial cost of the PFT to be reduced by at least 30%.

(a) Transfer of 'released credit cover' on unexpired leases of land—reg 38

12.104 In simplified terms, LA(CF)R 1997, reg 38 allows for the 'transfer' of credit cover from one lease to another, if the first lease ends early and it required credit cover at the outset. This concession applies where the authority's interest under a lease of a specified kind[1] (the 'old lease'), ends for a reason *other* than that the term has expired: for example where the authority surrenders or assigns the old lease. The authority can then reduce the initial cost of a new lease (or leases) taken under LA(CF)R 1997, reg 35, 36, or 37[2] (a 'relevant lease') by an amount up to the 'balance of the released credit cover' which arises from the termination of the old lease.

1 Being a lease of which the initial cost fell to be determined under reg 35 (subsequent lease of the same land), reg 36 ('general rules' for leases of land or goods), or reg 37 (leases of land forming part certain PFTs), or under corresponding provisions of LAR 1990 (SI 1990/432).
2 See previous footnote.

12.105 Under LA(CF)R 1997, reg 38(3)(a) 'released credit cover' is to be calculated by the authority by making an estimate of the initial cost of a hypothetical new lease of the old land as at the early termination date, using various assumptions listed in para (4) of the regulation. (This estimate gives an indication of the amount of credit cover which was 'over-provided for' by the authority at the outset, because the old lease has ended sooner than was originally expected[1].) The initial cost of this hypothetical new lease is the amount of the 'released credit cover'. To establish the '*balance* of the released credit cover', the authority must then deduct any amount of released credit cover which has already been applied to any other relevant lease[2]. Thus, the concession envisages that released credit cover arising from the termination of one old lease might be applied to reduce the credit cover needed for two or more (new) relevant leases (provided the aggregate amount deducted from all new leases does not exceed the total amount of cover released).

1 Absent a provision such as that under LA(CF)R 1997, reg 38, no subsequent adjustment in respect of credit cover is to be made if the estimates made by the authority at the outset of the credit arrangement of its initial cost and of the required amount of credit cover prove to be excessive (for example, because a credit arrangement ends earlier than anticipated). See LGHA 1989, s 51(1) and LA(CF)R 1997, reg 46, which provide for adjustments only in respect of *increased* requirements for credit cover. However, in certain circumstances, LGHA 1989, s 51(10) could provide for the 'cost at any subsequent time' of a credit arrangement to be adjusted downwards, if the credit arrangement had been varied in such a way as to reduce the amount of consideration actually payable by the local authority in any year.
2 See LA(CF)R 1997, reg 38(3)(b).

7 CREDIT ARRANGEMENTS OTHER THAN LEASES HAVING AN INITIAL COST OF NIL, OR A REDUCED INITIAL COST

12.106 These concessions are described para **15.27**ff, together with other special arrangements for PFTs. A contract which meets the various criteria under LA(CF)R 1997, reg 40 has an initial cost of nil. Those which satisfy reg 41 or 42, have an initial cost which is reduced by at least 30%. As noted in Chapter 15, separate provision has now been made for Wales in relation to the application regs 40–42 (by SI 2000/992, reg 2).

8 HEATING, LIGHTING AND STREET LIGHTING CONTRACTS —THE 'EQUIPMENT REPLACEMENT SCHEME'

12.107 These concessions are intended to give some relaxation of the normal requirements[1] to provide credit cover for credit arrangements for contracts for the improvement, and subsequent maintenance and repair of systems for:

(a) heating and/or lighting buildings (LA(CF)R 1997, reg 43); and
(b) street lighting (LA(CF)R 1997, reg 44).

1 Under Local Government and Housing Act 1989, s 49(2) (see para **12.74**ff).

12.108 The type of contracts envisaged under these concessions will normally constitute credit arrangements within LGHA 1989, s 48(1)(b) if the contractor is to make significant capital investment in improving or replacing the system at the outset of the arrangement and then recover this outlay from the authority over a number of subsequent years. If the relevant criteria in LA(CF)R 1997, regs 43 or 44 are met, then through a complex formula provided for in reg 45, the initial cost of the credit arrangement is treated as reduced by an amount equal to the authority's average annual expenditure on operating, maintaining and repairing the system over the five years preceding the commencement of the improvement and maintenance contract(s).

12.109 The concessions are designed to give some incentive to authorities to contract-out both the initial improvement of these types of systems, and their ongoing repair and maintenance. Although authorities were given informal encouragement[1] to consider negotiating a contract which resembles a private finance transaction (under LA(CF)R 1997, reg 16), with performance related payments to the contractor, there is no requirement under the relevant regulations that they should do so in order to take the benefit of the concessions.

1 See para 13.5 on p 21 of 'A Guide to the Local Government Capital Finance System', published by the Department of the Environment (as it then was) in February 1997.

12.110 For contracts relating to the heating or lighting of a building, the criteria under LA(CF)R 1997, reg 43 comprise:

(a) the arrangement must either be for the improvement of an *existing* system in a building in which the authority has a freehold or a leasehold interest, or be for the installation of a *new* system; and
(b) the same contractor as that undertaking the works in (a) above must be required to maintain and repair the heating or lighting system (either under the same arrangement, or a separate contract entered into no later than that under (a)).

12.111 For street lighting contracts the criteria for eligibility under LA(CF)R 1997, reg 44 comprise:

(a) the arrangement must be for works to improve a system of lamps, lamp posts and other materials and apparatus which supplies the means of lighting of streets, markets and public buildings in the authority's area ('the lighting system');
(b) the works must consist of the installation of new lamps, lamp posts and other materials and apparatus;
(c) the same contractor as that undertaking the works must be required to maintain and repair the lighting system *in whole or in part* (either under the same arrangement, or under a separate contract entered into no later than that under (a)); and
(d) the lighting system must have been provided by the authority[1] or have been vested in it[2] by virtue of specified statutory provisions.

1 In exercise of powers under the Public Health Act 1875, s 161 or the Highways Act 1980, s 97.
2 By virtue of the Highways Act 1980, s 270.

F Variation of credit arrangements

1 GENERAL RULES ON VARIATION AND CALCULATION OF ADJUSTED COST

12.112 LGHA 1989, s 51 provides for the situation where a credit arrangement which has been entered into by a local authority is subsequently varied. A variation for the purpose of s 51(1) may occur 'by the making of a new contract or otherwise'. The provisions of s 51 (other than subs (10)), only apply if the effect of the variation is such that if the variation had been part of the credit arrangement at the outset, the arrangement would have had a *greater* initial cost.

12.113 It should be noted that LGHA 1989, s 51 does not apply to the situation where a contract which is *not* a credit arrangement is varied in such a way as to *create* a credit arrangement. This would be dealt with under the main provisions of LGHA 1989, ss 48 and 49[1].

1 See paras **12.19** and **12.20** regarding the distinction between the variation of a contract which *does not* constitute a credit arrangement in such away as to *create* a credit arrangement (to be dealt with under s 48) and the variation of a credit arrangement (to be dealt with under s 51 and not under s 48; see s 48(4)).

12.114 If the whole, or part, of the consideration under the contract (or a contract forming part of the credit arrangement) consists of an option, then LGHA 1989, s 51(2)[1] may apply. This provides for the exercise of (or failure to exercise) an option to be treated as a variation for the purpose of s 51 if:

(a) the option is exercised in a different way from that which was assumed for the purposes of LGHA 1989, s 49(5) when the initial cost of the credit arrangement was originally calculated; or
(b) it had originally been assumed that the option would not be exercised, but in fact it is exercised; or
(c) it had originally been assumed that the option would be exercised, but it subsequently appears to the authority that it will not be exercised.

1 See also Local Government and Housing Act 1989, ss 49(5) and 48(7).

12.115 If the credit arrangement is varied (or, on account of an option, is deemed to have been varied as described in para **12.114**) and the effect is such as to increase the amount which would have been its initial cost at the outset, then by virtue of LGHA 1989, s 51(4) the authority must ensure that it has sufficient credit cover equal to the lesser of the following two amounts:

(a) the *difference* between the total amount of consideration paid and payable[1] under the arrangement disregarding the variation, and as varied; and
(b) the *difference* between the 'adjusted cost' of the arrangement and the credit cover already made available for it[2].

1 No discount formula is to be applied in assessing amounts payable in the future.
2 Under Local Government and Housing Act 1989, s 50.

12.116 The general rules for calculation of the 'adjusted cost' of the credit arrangement following variation are contained in LGHA 1989, s 51(5) and (6). However, it should be noted that these rules do not apply to leases and certain other arrangements which are referred to separately in para **12.125**ff[1].

1 By virtue of LGHA 1989, s 51(7), s 51(5) and (6) do not apply to those credit arrangements for which the method of calculating initial cost is provided for by regulations made under s 49(3) which exclude the application of s 49(3). LA(CF)R 1997, reg 26 made under LGHA 1989, s 49(3) specifies that any credit arrangement which is a lease is to be excluded from s 49(2). Other types of credit arrangement are excluded from LGHA 1989, s 49(2) by LA(CF)R 1997, regs 40–44. Variation, adjusted cost and cost at any time of leases and other arrangements to which LGHA 1989, s 49(2) does not apply is provided for in LA(CF)R 1997, regs 46–51.

12.117 Under LGHA 1989, s 51(5), the adjusted cost of a credit arrangement (other than a lease or other exceptional case) following variation is the aggregate of:

(a) the consideration which, in the financial year in which the arrangement is varied and in any earlier financial year, has been or falls to be given by the local authority; and
(b) the amount which, at the time of the variation, the authority estimates will be the cost of the arrangement, as varied, in each subsequent financial year determined in accordance with the following formula.

12.118 For any subsequent financial year, by virtue of LGHA 1989, s 51(6), the cost of the credit arrangement as varied is determined using the formula in LGHA 1989, s 49(2) for a new credit arrangement (see paras **12.76**ff) but where:

'x' is the amount of consideration which the authority estimate will be given by them in that financial year under the arrangement as varied;
'r' is the percentage rate of discount for the financial year in which the arrangement is varied, as prescribed by regulations made by the Secretary of State for the purposes of LGHA 1989, s 49[1]; and
'n' is the financial year in which the consideration falls to be given, expressed as the year subsequent to the financial year in which the arrangement is varied (so that the first of the subsequent financial years is 1, the next is 2 and so on).

1 The current regulations made under Local Government and Housing Act 1989, s 49(2) are the Local Authorities (Capital Finance) (Rate of Discount for 2000–01) (England) Regulations, SI 2000/259 which prescribe a discount rate of 7.9% for the year beginning on 1 April 2000. The equivalent regulations for Wales (SI 2000/825) prescribe a discount rate of 7.5% for that year.

12.119 The cost of the arrangement at any time *after* variation is to be determined under LGHA 1989, s 51(8), in the same way as the 'adjusted cost', but on the basis of an estimate made at the time in question and leaving out of account any consideration given by the authority prior to that time.

12.120 Credit cover in relation to a variation can be provided from the same sources as those prescribed in LGHA 1989, s 50(3) for the original credit arrangement, namely through the use of a credit approval, a determination to set aside usable capital receipts under LGHA 1989, s 60(2), or a determination to set aside revenue as a provision to meet credit liabilities. In this last case, the determination must be made no later than 30 September in the financial year following that in which the variation takes place[1].

1 See Local Government and Housing Act 1989, s 51(4) which applies s 50(3) and (5), with modification.

12.121 A local authority may not agree to the variation of a credit arrangement in such a way as to increase the amount which would have been its initial cost[1], if to do so would cause the authority to exceed its ACL[2] for the time being[3].

1 As envisaged in s 51(1).
2 Under Local Government and Housing Act 1989, s 62: see para **11.29**.
3 LGHA 1989, s 51(3).

12.122 It is to be noted that a deemed variation of a credit arrangement in relation to an option under LGHA 1989, s 51(2) might occur without the concurrence of the local authority concerned, for example if the other contracting party does not exercise an option as had been expected at the outset of the arrangement. If this leads to an increase in the initial cost, there would be a need for the authority to provide credit cover in respect of the variation[1].

1 See the wording of LGHA 1989, s 51(4), imposing an absolute requirement to provide credit cover in such a case and cf the restriction in s 51(3) (concerning the limitation imposed by the ACL) which would only apply where the authority has *agreed* to the variation.

12.123 LGHA 1989, s 51(9) covers the position where, following a variation of a credit arrangement in such a way as to increase the amount which would have been its initial cost, there is then a *subsequent* variation. Where this occurs, a further review must be undertaken under the provisions of s 51. Broadly the position is as for the first variation, but adapted by using the time of the *last variation* (rather than the time the arrangement came into being) and the *adjusted cost* as last varied (rather than the initial cost) as the 'baseline' for making the assessments. In making the calculation required under s 51(4)(b)[2], the credit cover made available for the previous variation (or variations) is taken into account.

1 See para **12.115**.

12.124 Under LGHA 1989, s 51(10), if the terms of a credit arrangement are varied at any time in a way which does *not* fall within s 51(1), for example if the variation would have resulted in a *lower* initial cost if it had been included in the arrangement at the outset, then for most purposes the variation is to be disregarded. However, as an exception to this, in so far as the variation affects the consideration falling to be paid by the local authority in any year, its affects *are* to be taken into account when determining the cost of the arrangement at any *subsequent time*. This applies for the purposes of assessing the costs at any subsequent time under:

(a) s 49(4) in relation to the 'cost at any time' of extended credit (and PFT arrangements) which are *not* excluded from s 49(2) by regulations;

(b) s 49(3) in relation to leases, PFTs and other contracts excluded from s 49(2) by regulations; and
(c) s 51(8) in relation to the 'cost at any time' following variation.

2 VARIATION OF LEASES AND ADJUSTED COST OF LEASES

12.125 Most of the basic rules concerning variation of credit arrangements under LGHA 1989, s 51 apply to leases as to other credit arrangements. In particular, those concerning the amount of credit cover needed in respect of the variation under s 51(4) would apply[1]. However, the provisions regarding the calculation of adjusted cost under s 51(5) and (6) arising from a variation, do not apply to leases or other credit arrangements excluded from LGHA 1989, s 49(2), for which, by virtue of regulations made under s 49(3), special provision is made for the calculation of their initial cost and cost at any time[2].

1 See para **12.115**. The amount of credit cover needed will, in most cases, be a lower amount than that calculated as being the 'adjusted cost' in accordance with the appropriate rules.
2 Local Government and Housing Act 1989, s 51(7).

12.126 Before turning to the special rules concerning the adjusted cost of leases and certain other arrangements, it is worth considering the question of what amounts to the variation of a lease as opposed to the grant of a new lease for the purpose of s 51 or s 48(1)(a). The general principles of landlord and tenant law would suggest that a purported variation of the terms of a lease which extends the premises demised, or the length of the term of years, would alter the legal estate and would therefore take effect as the surrender of the old lease and a re-grant of a new lease. Thus an agreement to extend either the term of years or the property comprised within a lease would entail a local authority becoming the lessees under a new lease. However, a mere increase in rent would not normally lead to any inferred surrender and re-grant, but would amount to a variation of the existing lease[1].

1 See for example *Woodfall on Landlord and Tenant*, para 17.026 (January 1997 re-issue).

12.127 LA(CF)R 1997, reg 50 of the 1997 Regulations deals specifically with the continuation of a business tenancy under the Landlord and Tenant Act 1954, s 24 treating it as a variation. LA(CF)R 1997, reg 48 refers to the variation of a credit arrangement which is a lease of land 'by the grant to the authority of a new lease of the same land for a term of years which extends beyond the expiry date of the arrangement'. It is not clear how reg 48 fits within the general principles of landlord and tenant referred to in the preceding paragraph.

12.128 DOE Circular 11/90, Annex A, para 27, which was written when the relevant provisions were contained in reg 8 of the Local Authorities (Capital Finance) Regulations 1990[1], advised authorities:

> 'A s 51 variation of a credit arrangement which is a lease may also occur where the local authority's tenancy continues after expiration of a lease under rights under the Landlord and Tenant Act 1954, Pt II and no statutory notice is served by the authority or by the lessor. Where a new tenancy is created by the service of a statutory notice under Part II a new credit arrangement would come into being. The operation of a rent review does not involve a variation of a lease and hence of the credit arrangement. The exercise of an option to renew a lease or an agreement as to a new term of the lease or that the lease

should apply to new land would involve the grant of a new lease and accordingly a new credit arrangement.'

1 SI 1990/432 (now revoked).

12.129 LA(CF)R 1997, regs 46–50 provide for the variation and adjusted cost of leases and certain other credit arrangements which are excluded from LGHA 1989, s 49(2)[1] regarding the calculation of initial and subsequent costs. Regulation 51 deals with the cost at any time after variation[2].

1 As previously noted, reg 26 excludes all leases from LGHA 1989, s 49(2) and LA(CF)R 1997, regs 40–44 exclude certain categories of PFT and certain lighting and heating contracts from that subsection so that calculation of initial cost and related matters are dealt with under the LA(CF)R 1997 and not under LGHA 1989, s 49.
2 Regulation 51 is in broadly analogous terms to LGHA 1989, s 51(8): see para **12.119**.

12.130 LA(CF)R 1997, reg 47 sets out the general rules for calculation of adjusted cost in relation to the variation of credit arrangements which are excluded from LGHA 1989, s 49(2), and is subject to the provisions of three further regulations described below. Under the general rules for these cases, the adjusted cost is the aggregate of the amounts the authority estimates, at the time of variation, will be:

(a) the value of the consideration falling to be given by them in respect of the arrangement before or during the financial year in which the arrangement is varied; and
(b) the value of the consideration falling to be given by them in respect of the arrangement, as varied, in any subsequent financial year.

The cost in each subsequent year is calculated in accordance with LA(CF)R 1997, reg 47(2), which applies an adapted form of the formula for the calculation of the 'capital cost of a lease' under LA(CF)R 1997, reg 14(2).

12.131 LA(CF)R 1997, reg 48 creates an exception to reg 47 for a subsequent lease to the authority of the *same* land, for a term of years which extends beyond the original term[1]. Provided that, if the new lease had been granted on the *expiry* of the earlier lease, it would fall to be determined under regs 29, 30, or 32[2], then the adjusted cost is to be nil. The apparent intention of reg 48 is that, provided the detailed requirements of one of the three concessions can still be met notwithstanding the 'variation' envisaged, the benefits of nil initial cost treatment should not be forfeited.

1 As noted in para **12.126**, it is difficult to see why this should be treated as a variation.
2 LA(CF)R 1997, reg 29 (lease for less than three years), reg 30 (lease of a dwelling in connection with homelessness, for less than 10 years), reg 32 (consecutive leases for non-housing purposes for less than 10 years) each provide, subject to the satisfaction of their detailed terms, for a lease of land to have an initial cost of nil.

12.132 LA(CF)R 1997, reg 49 creates an exception from LA(CF)R 1997, reg 47 for the variation of a lease within reg 35 (or within the previous provisions of reg 7(6) of the Local Authorities (Capital Finance) Regulations 1990 (now revoked)[1]). LA(CF)R 1997, reg 35 (and the earlier provisions) deal with the situation where a local authority, having taken the benefit of certain concessions for leases of land granted on or after 1 April 1990 giving them an initial cost of nil then takes a further lease of the same land. Regulation 35 (like the Local Authorities (Capital Finance) Regulations 1990 (now revoked), reg 7(6)) requires the authority to add in the consideration given under the former lease (originally given a nil initial cost) when calculating the initial cost of the new lease[2]. Where such an aggregation of costs of successive leases has occurred and the lease is then varied, its adjusted cost is the adjusted cost calculated in accordance with the normal rules of reg 47[3], *plus* the value of the consideration given in respect of the previous interest. This complex provision appears to be aimed at ensuring that the consideration for the previous interest is not left out of account in the event of 'revaluation' arising from a variation.

1 The Local Authorities (Capital Finance) Regulations 1990, SI 1990/432. Regulation 7(6) was amended by SI 1992/3257, SI 1995/850, SI 1996/ 568 and SI 1996/2539.
2 So that in the long term, there is no overall benefit in taking successive short leases as opposed to a single lease for the full term envisaged.
3 See para **12.130**.

12.133 LA(CF)R 1997, reg 50 is the final special case for calculation of the adjusted cost of credit arrangements excluded from LGHA 1989, s 49(2). It deals with statutory continuation of business tenancies under the Landlord and Tenant Act 1954, s 24 treating this as a variation. It would not apply in a case where a *new* lease is granted pursuant to the Landlord and Tenant Act 1954. This has already been referred to in paras **12.71** and **12.127**. If a business lease is to continue under the Landlord and Tenant Act 1954, s 24, the adjusted cost is to be calculated under the general rules of LA(CF)R 1997, reg 47, or the special provisions of reg 49, if there has been a previous lease with a nil initial cost and the current lease was therefore subject to reg 35 (or reg 7(6) of the Local Authorities (Capital Finance) Regulations 1990 (now revoked)).

3 VARIATION AND ADJUSTED COST OF TRANSITIONAL CREDIT ARRANGEMENTS

12.134 If a transitional credit arrangement under LGHA 1989, s 52 is varied, then its 'adjusted cost' would be calculated in the same way as that arising on a variation of any other credit arrangement under LGHA 1989, s 51[1], save that:

(a) the arrangement is to be taken to have come into being on 1 April 1990, in the form in which it was on that date (and, accordingly, any consideration given under the arrangement *before* that date should be disregarded); and
(b) the local authority is to be taken to have made available in connection with the arrangement (and in accordance with s 50) an amount of credit cover equal to the cost of the arrangement on 1 April 1990[2].

1 See para **12.112**ff.
2 Local Government and Housing Act 1989, s 52(3).

G Limits on powers to enter into credit arrangements

12.135 LGHA 1989, s 50 includes a number of limits on the powers of a local authority to enter into credit arrangements. These have been described as both 'qualitative and quantitative limits'[1]. The limits comprise:

(a) under s 50(1), a local authority may not enter into a credit arrangement for any purpose unless, if they incurred expenditure for that purpose, it would be expenditure for capital purposes[2];
(b) under s 50(2), a local authority may not enter into a credit arrangement unless, at the time the arrangement comes into being[3], there is available to the authority an amount of credit cover[4] equal to the initial cost[5] of the arrangement;
(c) under s 50(4), a local authority may not enter into a credit arrangement at any

time if to do so would at that time cause the total referred to in s 44(1)[6] to exceed the aggregate credit limit for the time being applicable to the authority by virtue of s 62 ('the ACL'[7]);

(d) under s 51(3), a local authority may not agree[8] to vary a credit arrangement in such a way as to increase the amount which would have been its initial cost, if to do so would cause the ACL which applies at the time to be exceeded.

1 See Circular 11/90, Annex A, para 25.
2 See Local Government and Housing Act 1989, s 40 and para **10.15**ff.
3 LGHA 1989, s 48(3) specifies when each of the three types of credit arrangement comes into being. An arrangement under s 48(1)(a) comes into being when the authority becomes the lessee; under s 48(1)(b), when the later or latest contract constituting the arrangement is entered into; and under s 48(1)(c), when the transaction is entered into, or such other time as may be specified in regulations concerned.
4 LGHA 1989, s 50(3) and see para **12.9**.
5 LGHA 1989, s 49 and see regs 26–45. In the case of a transitional credit arrangement, credit cover is deemed to have been provided in an amount equal to its initial cost as at 1 April 1990 (see s 52(3)).
6 See para **11.30**.
7 See paras **11.29–11.36**.
8 As noted in para **12.122**, certain deemed variations could occur without the agreement of the local authority; however, this restriction appears to apply only if the authority has agreed to the variation.

12.136 In relation to the requirement under LGHA 1989, s 50(2) that an authority must have sufficient credit cover available when the credit arrangement comes into existence, it should be noted that the three permissible options for providing such cover allow a degree of flexibility, albeit subject to the extent to which the authority can afford each of the alternatives. The three alternative sources for credit cover under LGHA 1989, s 50(3) comprise the use of a credit approval, setting aside usable capital receipts specifically 'earmarked' for the arrangement in question in a determination to make PCL under LGHA 1989, s 60(2)(b), or voluntarily setting aside additional revenue as PCL, again earmarked for the particular arrangement. Despite the fact that the authority must know, at the time the arrangement comes into existence, that sufficient credit cover can be provided, it has until 30 September in the next financial year to decide whether to use the third option of providing cover from revenue[1], which might perhaps be viewed as the last resort (and is subject, of course, to the constraints on revenue).

1 Local Government and Housing Act 1989, s 50(5).

12.137 It is to be noted that in contrast to borrowing and the protection for lenders under LGHA 1989, s 44(6), there is no express 'safe harbour' provision for a person who enters into, or agrees to vary a credit arrangement with a local authority which contravenes the various restrictions summarised in para **12.135**[1].

1 Although the three different of ways of providing the necessary 'credit cover' under LGHA 1989, s 50(3) to meet the requirement under s 50(2), as referred to in para **12.136**, should reduce the risks that this particular limitation would be contravened by the authority.

12.138 The limits on powers in LGHA 1989, s 50 do not apply to a transitional credit arrangement[1]. Credit cover is deemed to have been made available for such transactions as at 1 April 1990 under LGHA 1989, s 52(3)(b). However, if a transitional credit arrangement is varied, then the requirements of LGHA 1989, s 51(3), to keep within the current ACL, would apply[2].

1 Local Government and Housing Act 1989, s 50(6); absent this provision, a transitional credit arrangement would be treated in the same way as any other credit arrangement: s 52(1).
2 LGHA 1989, s 52(1) and (3).

CHAPTER 13

Borrowing

A General borrowing powers

13.1 Paragraphs **10.2** and **10.3** refer to the consideration which is being given by the Government at the time of writing to the possible replacement of the current statutory controls on local authority capital finance, including those on borrowing, with a system based on 'prudential indicators' and self-monitoring by authorities. The following sets out the position likely to apply at least until the financial year 2000–2001.

13.2 Local authorities are empowered by LGHA 1989, s 43(1), as part of the proper management of their affairs, to borrow money for any purpose relevant to their functions under any enactment. Subsequent provisions of s 43 detail the manner in which borrowing may be undertaken[1].

1 See para **13.7**ff.

13.3 Borrowing is permitted to fulfil statutory functions, but it would not be permitted, for example, for the purpose of speculation nor solely in order to invest the borrowed funds[1]. Borrowing in order to replace an earlier external loan, as part of the prudent management of the authority's portfolio of debts, would be permissible[2].

1 Speculation is not a function of a local authority. There is no 'all-embracing' power to invest: rather investment is authorised in specified circumstances (for example, under the Local Government Finance Act 1988, s 89(5) sums in the collection fund not immediately required to make payments may be invested in the manner prescribed by regulations made by the Secretary of State; or under LGHA 1989, s 33(3)(e) which authorises an authority to invest in an undertaking as a means of providing financial assistance in order to promote economic development provided certain pre-conditions are met).
2 See the passage cited in para **13.39** regarding debt management, which would appear to apply equally in respect of the current legislation. New borrowing simply in order to replace an earlier loan would *not* require the use of a credit approval (as no expenditure is involved which, absent credit approval, would be charged to revenue—expenditure on the redemption of the old debt is excluded from the obligation to charge to a revenue account: see LGHA 1989, s 42(2)(b)).

13.4 The legislation does not specify any maximum period between the date of borrowing and actual expenditure, but as a 'rule of thumb', the Audit Commission recommends a period of 12–18 months[1]. This advice was given in the light of apparent concern about some of the reasons for which borrowing was being undertaken by local authorities.

1 In Audit Commission Technical Release 13/95, p 43, para 18. See also TR 37/95, p 51, paras 19 and 20.

13.5 Although the legislation does not, in explicit terms, prohibit borrowing for revenue purposes[1], in practice, all long term-borrowing will be for capital purposes. The very reason for borrowing will normally be a lack of immediately available resources and the need to ensure that the expenditure is not charged to a revenue account. The only practical means of achieving this is through reliance on a credit approval[2]. Such an approval may only be used if the expenditure is for capital purposes[3]. Some short-term borrowing for revenue purposes without the need for credit approval is, however, envisaged[4].

1 Contrast credit arrangements, which, by virtue of LGHA 1989, s 50(1), may only be entered into for capital purposes.
2 Local Government and Housing Act 1989, s 42(2)(c).
3 LGHA 1989, s 56(1)(b).
4 See paras **13.32–13.35**.

13.6 There are no statutory provisions which govern the rate of interest which a local authority may pay in respect of its borrowings. However, the terms on which an authority agrees to borrow money would be subject to the normal administrative law principles of 'reasonableness' and the authority's quasi-fiduciary duty to its local tax payers not to act 'thriftlessly' referred to in Chapter 5. The provisions of LGHA 1989, s 45(1)(c) which require local authorities to set an annual limit on the proportion of fixed and variable loans may influence an authority's decision in an individual case[1]. Under LGHA 1989, s 44(2), the Secretary of State is empowered to make provision to regulate borrowing by local authorities 'in the interests of prudent financial management' through regulations, but to date this power has not been utilised.

1 See para **13.26**(c).

B Permitted means of borrowing

13.7 By virtue of LGHA 1989, s 43(2) the only means by which local authorities may borrow are:

(a) by overdraft or short-term loan from the Bank of England or from a body or partnership which at the time the borrowing is undertaken, is an 'authorised institution' within the meaning of the Banking Act 1987;
(b) from the National Debt Commissioners or from the Public Works Loan Commissioners;
(c) by means of a loan instrument (see below); or
(d) in any other manner approved by the Secretary of State given with the consent of the Treasury.

13.8 'Short term' means that the sum borrowed is repayable without notice, on less than twelve months' notice, or within twelve months of the date of the borrowing[1].

1 Local Government and Housing Act 1989, ss 43(2) and 45(6).

13.9 Approvals issued by the Secretary of State with the consent of the Treasury under item (d) in para **13.7** allow borrowing from the European Investment Bank, or in sterling from any authorised European Union credit institution, or by the issue of stocks[1].

1 Letters from the Department of the Environment to all local authorities dated 28 July 1992; 27 May 1993 and 15 December 1993 respectively.

13.10 Except with the consent of the Treasury, local authorities may not borrow from a lender outside the United Kingdom, or otherwise than in sterling[1].

1 Local Government and Housing Act 1989, s 43(3).

13.11 The restrictions on borrowing by local authorities under LGHA 1989, s 43(2)–(6) apply to all borrowing powers, whenever enacted[1].

1 Local Government and Housing Act 1989, s 43(7).

13.12 As an alternative to new external borrowing, amounts set aside by an authority as provision for credit liabilities ('PCL'[1]) may be used for capital expenditure where a credit approval has been used 'as authority not to charge particular expenditure to a revenue account'[2]. This will have the same effect as external borrowing in terms of a reduction in credit approvals and an increase in the credit ceiling. A degree of 'internal borrowing' is also envisaged. Until PCL is actually applied to one or more of the uses authorised under LGHA 1989, s 64, one of the permissible means of dealing with the cash amounts involved would be to use them temporarily as an alternative to short-term borrowing[3].

1 See para **11.45**ff.
2 Local Government and Housing Act 1989, s 64(1)(c).
3 See 'A Guide to the Local Government Capital Finance System', issued by the Department of the Environment (as then called) in February 1997 at para 21.6.

C Loan instruments and register of loan instruments and loans

13.13 In straightforward terms, 'loan instruments' under LGHA 1989, Pt IV will comprise all the various legal documents under which authorities borrow money, including bills, bonds, debentures, annuities and mortgages (subject to the prohibition which now exists on charging assets, referred to in para **13.18**).

13.14 To be more specific, loan instruments are documents which contain the information and an acknowledgement as prescribed in the LGHA 1989, s 43(4) (subject to the provisions of any regulations made by the Secretary of State with the consent of the Treasury under LGHA 1989, s 43(5)[1]). All loan instruments must contain an acknowledgment that the loan has been made to the local authority concerned (or at least that payment or repayment in respect of funds provided is due), a statement of the due dates and amounts of all payments or repayments (or a method for their calculation), the person to whom payments and repayments are due, and they must specify provisions about transferability of the instrument. If more than one authority is party to the loan instrument, the document must stipulate the proportion of payments due from, and the responsibilities of, each authority.

1 Such regulations may regulate the terms, restrict the issue of certain instruments, regulate the manner of payment and provide for the custody of loan instruments. See the Local Authorities (Borrowing) Regulations 1990, SI 1990/767.

13.15 The Local Authorities (Borrowing) Regulations 1990, SI 1990/767 as amended[1] made by the Secretary of State under LGHA 1989, s 43(5), regulate the terms of loan instruments and restrict the issue of loan instruments which are transferable by delivery. The regulations also make detailed provision for the register of loans which must be maintained by all authorities under LGHA 1989, s 46(1).

1 By SI 1990/1091, SI 1991/551, SI 1991/2000, SI 1998/1129 and the Audit Commission Act 1998.

13.16 Under s 46, every local authority is to maintain a register which gives particulars of all loan instruments issued by or to the authority, on or after 1 April 1990. The authority may, if it thinks appropriate, appoint an external registrar, someone who is neither an officer nor an employee of the authority concerned, for some or all of the purposes of the register. The register must include details of certain loans already in existence as at 1 April 1990, which had not been repaid by that date. These registrable pre-April 1990 loans are loans of any kind other than those resulting from borrowing by overdraft or short-term from the Bank of England or an authorised institution (under s 43(2)(a)), or from the National Debt Commissioners or from the Public Works Loan Commissioners (under s 43(2)(b)). The obligation to enter particulars of these types of outstanding loan had to be discharged by 30 September 1990. No date is stipulated in relation to the continuing obligation to register loan instruments, although unnecessary delay in making a required entry in the register would provide grounds for a person aggrieved to apply to the High Court or a county court for rectification of the register under LGHA 1989, s 46(9). The register must be in a form which is legible, or in a form which is capable of being reproduced in a legible form[1]. So, for example, the register might be maintained on computer, provided that a 'print-out' can be produced.

1 Local Government and Housing Act 1989, s 46(3).

13.17 Under LGHA 1989, s 46(9), a person aggrieved by certain omissions or defaults in relation to the register may apply to the High Court or to a county court for rectification of the register.

D Security for money borrowed, remedies and protection for creditors

13.18 LGHA 1989, s 47(7) prohibits a local authority from mortgaging or charging any of its property as security for money borrowed or otherwise owned by them. Any security purporting to be given in contravention of this prohibition is unenforceable. Thus, there is no power, for example, for an authority to offer a charge over a particular freehold title to land as security for a loan. Local authorities may not pledge or dispose of interests in their assets in order to provide security for borrowing.

13.19 The provisions of LGHA 1989, s 47(1)–(3) largely re-enact the previous legislation under Sch 13, paras 11(1)–(3) of the Local Government Act 1972. LGHA 1989, s 47(1) provides that all money borrowed by a local authority, together with any interest thereon, is to be 'charged indifferently' on all the revenues of the authority (ie as opposed to being a charge on any of its property). This applies to borrowing taken out before or after s 47 came into force[1]. All securities created by a local authority rank equally, subject to an exception for any priority accorded to a security created before 1 June 1934[2].

1 Local Government and Housing Act 1989, s 47(1). The previous legislation, under the Local Government Act 1972, Sch 13, made exception for mortgages created under the Public Health Act 1936, s 310 and earlier legislation to create mortgages, but that exception has not been preserved in the LGHA 1989, s 47; see Local Government Act 1972, Sch 13, para 21.
2 Local Government and Housing Act 1989, s 47(2) and (3).

13.20 If principal or interest in respect of money borrowed by a local authority remains unpaid for two months after a written demand, and the amount involved is at least £5,000, the creditor can apply to the court for the appointment of a receiver. A court can confer on the receiver the powers of collecting, receiving and recovering the authority's revenues and issuing levies and precepts and setting, collecting and recovering community charges as are possessed by the local authority itself[1]. This was said to be intended to provide powers of the court, equivalent to those which existed prior to 1990, in respect of local authority mortgages and bonds[2].

1 In Local Government and Housing Act 1989, s 47(4)–(6).
2 See para A49 of the Consultation Paper issued by the Department of the Environment in July 1988 on Capital Expenditure and Finance.

13.21 LGHA 1989, s 44(6) includes an important 'safe harbour provision' for lenders to local authorities. It provides that:

> 'A person lending money to a local authority shall not be bound to enquire whether the authority have power to borrow the money and shall not be prejudiced by the absence of any such power.'

It is to be noted that there is no comparable 'safe harbour' provision in relation to credit arrangements[1].

1 See para **12.137**.

E Limits on borrowing

13.22 In summary, there are currently two forms of limitation on borrowing by local authorities:

(a) LGHA 1989, s 44(1)—the aggregate credit limit;
(b) LGHA 1989, s 44(3)—the authority's own limits under s 45.

Whilst the Secretary of State has power to impose further limitations through regulations made under LGHA 1989, s 44(2), see para **13.25**.

13.23 Borrowing and credit arrangements are subject to a common limit under LGHA 1989, s 44[1]. Under s 44(1), at no time may an authority borrow any amount of money, if the result would be that the total of all principal of borrowed money, plus the aggregate cost of all its credit arrangements at that time (other than excluded credit arrangements), would exceed the 'aggregate credit limit' ('ACL'). Paragraphs **11.29**ff explain the method of calculating the ACL and its functions.

1 See Chapter 11.

13.24 The limit imposed by LGHA 1989, s 44 applies not only to borrowing under LGHA 1989, s 43, but also to borrowing under any other power available to the authority under any enactment, whenever passed[1]. Temporary use of money in a superannuation fund (established under the Superannuation Act 1972), or money in a trust fund held for charitable purposes (of which the authority is a trustee) for a purpose other than that of the fund in question, is treated as borrowing for the purposes of s 44(1)[2].

1 Local Government and Housing Act 1989, s 44(4).
2 LGHA 1989, s 44(5), but temporary use of money forming part of any *other* kind of fund for a purpose other than that for which the fund was established is not treated as borrowing for the purposes of LGHA 1989, Pt IV (s 66(7)).

13.25 LGHA 1989, s 44(2) empowers the Secretary of State to make regulations 'in the interests of prudent financial management' to regulate borrowing by local authorities. A local authority may not borrow to any extent or in any manner which would contravene any provision of those regulations. Thus, the Secretary of State has further means of regulating the amount of borrowing local authorities may undertake. However, to date, no regulations have been made under s 44(2).

13.26 In addition to the limit imposed by the ACL, by virtue of LGHA 1989, s 45, for every financial year a local authority must determine its own limits for:

(a) the amount of money which is for the time being the maximum amount which the authority may have outstanding by way of borrowing (referred to as 'the overall borrowing limit');
(b) the amount of money, being a part of the overall borrowing limit, which is for the time being the maximum amount which the authority may have outstanding by way of short-term borrowing (referred to as 'the short-term borrowing limit'); and
(c) the proportion of the total amount of interest payable by the authority which is payable at a rate or rates which can be varied by the person to whom it is payable or which vary by reference to any external factors.

13.27 'Short-term borrowing' for the purpose of item (b) above comprises borrowed money which is repayable without notice, at less than 12 months' notice, or within 12 months of the date of the borrowing[1].

1 Local Government and Housing Act 1989, s 45(6).

13.28 By virtue of LGHA 1989, s 44(3), an authority is prohibited from borrowing any amount of money, if to do so would cause any of the limits set by the council under LGHA 1989, s 45 to be exceeded. However, as noted below, it is possible for the limits under s 45 to be varied by the authority, even during the course of the financial year to which they relate.

13.29 The duty to determine the limits under LGHA 1989, s 45 must be performed before the beginning of the financial year to which they relate. However, once the limits have been set, the authority can subsequently vary them, before or after the beginning of the financial year in question by making a new determination[1].

1 Local Government and Housing Act 1989, s 45(3).

13.30 The duty to determine the limits under LGHA 1989, s 45(1), and the power to vary them under s 45(3), must be discharged by full council; the decision cannot be delegated to a committee or officer (as would be the case in relation to the discharge of most local government functions, pursuant to Local Government

Act 1972, s 101[1]). Once the limits have been set or varied by full council, it is submitted that they can be implemented by a committee or by officers. The former wording of Local Government Act 1972, s 101(6), which suggested that even incidental matters connected with borrowing might not be delegated, has been amended in relation to bodies subject to LGHA 1989, Pt IV, as from 1 April 1990, by LGHA 1989, s 45(5).

1 See Local Government and Housing Act 1989, s 45(4).

13.31 Circular 11/90, Annex A, para 89 advised local authorities that the Department of the Environment would expect them to have regard to the following factors when determining their overall borrowing limit:

(a) their existing external capital debt;
(b) the level of capital expenditure for the forthcoming year expected to be financed by borrowing;
(c) net repayments of principal expected to be made during the year;
(d) the level of temporary borrowing during the year expected on revenue or capital account; and
(e) a margin for contingencies.

F Short-term borrowing

1 SHORT-TERM BORROWING WITHIN THE ACL UNDER LGHA 1989, S 62 TO COVER TIMING DIFFERENCES

13.32 Through the mechanism of the aggregate credit limit ('ACL') described in Chapter 11, local authorities are permitted to borrow short-term for revenue and for certain capital purposes, to cover timing differences between making payments and receiving income, or obtaining reimbursement of capital expenditure from external bodies, without the need for credit approval.

13.33 Temporary borrowing for revenue purposes within the ACL may be for a period of no more than two years. In simplified terms, the amount of permitted short-term borrowing for revenue purposes is constantly limited[1] at any point in time by reference to the lesser of (a) the amount of revenue still due to be received for the current financial year and (b) the amount of revenue disbursements made (in the current or a previous financial year) which falls to be charged to the current year (plus certain arrears for which provision is to be made in the current year). An addition to this limit is permitted[2] in respect of revenue still owed to the authority in respect of the immediately preceding financial year. The aim is to enable authorities to borrow short-term in anticipation of revenue receipts, for example arrears of council tax or housing rents.

1 Under Local Government and Housing Act 1989, s 62(3).
2 LGHA 1989, s 62(4).

13.34 Temporary borrowing which is permitted within the ACL for capital purposes may be for a period of no more than 18 months. Such borrowing is restricted at any time by reference to the amount of capital expenditure actually defrayed by the authority in the preceding 18 months which is due to be reimbursed by any external party (whether a public or private body) but which has not, in fact, been reimbursed[1]. Temporary borrowing in anticipation of grants due from a European Community institution, other than contributions from any of the Structural Funds, is excluded from this provision[2].

1 See Local Government and Housing Act 1989, s 62(5).
2 See para **10.39**, which explains that the exceptional treatment for EC grants is revised with effect from 1 April 2000, in so far as it relates to grants from the Structural Funds by SI 2000/589.

13.35 These temporary borrowing limits are not applied independently of the ACL. They are components of that limit[1]. No credit approval is needed for temporary borrowing within the ACL.

1 See Local Government and Housing Act 1989, s 62(1)(a) and (b) and Circular 11/90, Annex A, para 66.

2 SHORT-TERM BORROWING LIMITS

13.36 The responsibility of local authorities to determine the proportion of their overall borrowing in any financial year which is to be short-term, under LGHA 1989, s 45(1)(b) has been described in para **13.26**. The obligation under LGHA 1989, s 44(3) to remain within that limit is referred to in para **13.28**. The short-term borrowing limit under LGHA 1989, s 45(1)(b) should not be confused with the temporary revenue borrowing limit and temporary capital borrowing under LGHA 1989, s 62(1)(a) and (b) referred to above.

G Debt management powers

13.37 The provisions concerning determination of an authority's own borrowing limits under LGHA 1989, s 45 clearly envisage that authorities (acting by full council) should give positive consideration to the management of their loan portfolio, and the balance between their fixed and variable interest rate loans.

13.38 In relation to borrowing under the LGA 1972, the question of whether local authorities had any more extensive implied or incidental powers of debt management was considered by the House of Lords in *Hazell v London Borough of Hammersmith and Fulham*[1]. The House of Lords concluded that the local authority had no power to enter into an interest rate swap as a means of managing a portfolio of loans (or, indeed, for any other reason).

1 [1992] 2 AC 1, [1991] 1 All ER 545.

13.39 Lord Templeman made the following observations[1]:

> 'Debt management is not a function. Debt management is a phrase which has been coined in this case to describe the activities of a person who enters into the swap market for the purpose of making profits which can be employed in the payment of interest on borrowings. The expression 'debt management' could be employed to describe the duty of a local authority to consider from time to time whether it should change a variable PWLB loan into a fixed interest loan, whether it should redeem one loan and take out another, whether when a new borrowing is contemplated the borrowing should be at a variable or fixed rate taking into account all other borrowings of the local authority. Debt management is a phrase which describes prudent and lawful

activities on the part of the local authority. If swap transactions were lawful a local authority would be under a duty to consider entering into swap transactions as part of its duty of debt management. If a swap transaction is not lawful then it cannot be lawful for a local authority to carry out a swap transaction under the guise of debt management.'

Lord Templeman went on to conclude that a local authority had no power to enter into a swap transaction under the Local Government Act 1972, s 111 (or otherwise).

1 [1992] 2 AC 1 at 34, [1991] 1 All ER 545 at 558.

13.40 An important principle in the decision in *Hazell* was that because the then current legislation contained a comprehensive code which defined and limited the powers of a local authority with regard to its borrowing, that was inconsistent with any incidental power to engage in swap transactions. The case was decided at a time when local government borrowing was governed by the Local Government Act 1972, Sch 13. However, the principles in relation to debt management activities and the unlawfulness of swap transactions appear to hold good in relation to the powers under LGHA 1989, Pt IV.

H The Public Works Loan Board

13.41 At the end of the financial year 1999–2000, total local authority longer term debt stood at some £68,846.2 million. Debt to the Public Works Loan Board (PWLB) accounted for some 66.9% of that debt[1].

1 Appendix A to the Public Works Loan Board 125th Annual Report 1999–2000.

13.42 The origins of the PWLB date back to legislation in 1793. The Board consists of 12 Loan Commissioners whose functions now mainly derive from the Public Works Loans Act 1875 and the National Loans Act 1968.

13.43 The functions of the Commissioners are to consider loan applications from local authorities and other prescribed bodies and, where loans are made, to collect the repayments. At present, nearly all borrowers from the PWLB are local authorities. The security for the money borrowed (with interest) is provided in the normal way referred to in para **13.19**; it is charged indifferently on all the revenues of the authority concerned. The Commissioners are under an obligation, before making a loan, to satisfy themselves that the authority is able to service and repay the loan[1]. Their powers are to make loans to local authorities for any purpose for which an authority has power to borrow[2].

1 Public Works Loans Act 1875, s 9 requires the Commissioners to have regard to the sufficiency of the security for the repayment of the loan when considering the propriety of granting it.
2 See the National Loans Act 1968, Sch 4, para 1.

13.44 The National Loans Act 1968, s 4 imposes a limit on the aggregate amount of loans the PWLB may make. The moneys are provided by Act of Parliament, drawn from the National Loans Fund at rates of interest determined by the Treasury. The Board makes an Annual Report to Parliament and its accounts are audited by a Comptroller and Auditor General, whose reports on the Board are laid before Parliament.

13.45 Loans to authorities by the PWLB comprise:

(a) a quota entitlement (including an additional quota entitlement);
(b) 'non-quota A loans', which apply where an authority needs to borrow immediately and cannot raise money by other means, in which case the PWLB acts as 'the lender of last resort' to make loans in excess of the quota;
(c) 'non-quota B loans', in excess of the quota (and at a higher rate of interest than the two previous categories), where the authority can demonstrate that additional capital finance is needed in the relatively near future (but without the requirement to demonstrate that money is not available on the open market).

13.46 As no applications for the non-quota loans have been made since 1976[1], the most important category is the loan quota itself. For 1999–2000, the quota entitlement was an amount equivalent to the authority's basic and supplementary credit approvals used in 1999–2000, plus repayments of principal due in that year on loans from the PWLB. Authorities who do not use their entire quota in the financial year in question can normally carry forward a proportion to the following year. Conversely, some authorities overdraw their quotas, for example because estimates of the amounts of credit approvals to be used are not fulfilled.

1 According to the PWLB Annual Report for 1999–2000.

13.47 Quota loans for 1999–2000 were made available at two sets of rates of interest: the Higher Rates and the Lower Rates, with the Lower Rates set close to the cost of government borrowing and the Higher Rates close to, but just below, market rates. The Lower Rates are available for that part of the quota which represents the excess over the amount of the authority's unapplied PCL[1]. Both fixed and variable rate loans are made available. Options are available for the conversion of loans from fixed to variable or variable to fixed rates. Such an option can be exercised on more than one occasion, provided that there is an interval of at least two years (formerly four years) between successive loans made on the exercise of an option. (Replacement loans do not count against the authority's quota entitlement.) Details of quotas and lending arrangements are contained in circulars issued annually by the PWLB[2].

1 (Provision for credit liabilities: see para **11.45**ff.) As PCL could be used in substitution for new external borrowing under Local Government and Housing Act 1989, s 64(1)(c).
2 See Circular No 121 in force during 2000–2001.

13.48 The Commissioners are prepared to consider applications for amounts in excess of the quota 'on an additional quota basis' in cases of exceptional difficulty or hardship and in certain other circumstances. These include efficient management by the authority of its debt portfolio. The Higher and Lower Rates apply to any such borrowing as if it formed part of the quota.

13.49 Loans from the Board are primarily intended to be used to finance capital payments which have either been made or which will be made within a short time of the loan being advanced. The PWLB's Annual Report for 1999–2000 illustrates the extent to which authorities also used loans from the Board as part of the management of their portfolio of debts. Applications were approved for such purposes as the refinancing of maturing long-term market debt, to replace short term borrowing from market lenders and to restructure their portfolio of loans from the PWLB.

13.50 As a result of Treasury concern about interest rates, the Loan Commissioners have agreed that, as from 22 February 2000, they will not normally make loans for periods greater than 25 years. The arrangements for loans from the PWLB in years subsequent to 1999–2000 may change from those described in this section. The arrangements for a particular financial year are usually set out in a circular from the Board issued before the beginning of the year in question.

CHAPTER 14

Capital receipts and notional capital receipts

A Capital receipts

14.1 When the Local Government and Housing Act 1989 ('LGHA 1989') was first enacted, the requirements concerning capital receipts and notional capital receipts had far greater impact on local authority transactions, and particularly those concerning the sale of local authority land, than they do today. Through amendments to the Local Government (Capital Finance) Regulations 1997, SI 1997/319[1] ('LA(CF)R 1997') introduced on 1 September 1998 by SI 1998/1937, the rules on 'set-aside' described in this chapter were, in effect, abolished for the vast majority of capital receipts and notional capital receipts by reducing the proportion required to be set aside to 0%. The main exception to this extensive relaxation is where the receipts are derived from the disposal of 'housing land' which fall to be dealt with within the Housing Revenue Account which an authority is required to maintain under LGHA 1989, Pt VI.

1 As amended by SI 1997/848, SI 1998/371, SI 1998/602, SI 1998/1937, SI 1999/501, SI 1999/1852, SI 1999/3423, SI 2000/992 (Wales), SI 2000/1033, SI 2000/1474, SI 2000/1553 and SI 2000/1773.

14.2 Nonetheless, the rules concerning capital receipts and notional capital receipts continue to be essential to an understanding of the regime of controls under LGHA 1989, Pt IV and are of practical importance in housing schemes and other instances where the relaxations introduced in 1998 do not apply.

14.3 The general significance of whether a sum of money received by a local authority amounts to a 'capital receipt' under LGHA 1989, Pt IV is that it will dictate the use which can be made of that receipt. If none of the exceptions apply, the authority will be required to 'reserve' or 'set aside'[1] a proportion of any capital receipt as provision for credit liabilities under s 59[2]. Where 'set-aside obligations' (greater than 0%) apply, only a proportion of any capital receipt can be used to fund capital expenditure on a new project. The purposes for which the part reserved for credit liabilities can be used are described in para **11.61**ff. The permitted uses of the usable part are described in paras **14.42** and **14.43**. Expenditure which is met from the usable part of capital receipts need not be charged to a revenue account (LGHA 1989, s 42(2)(f)[3]).

1 In this and subsequent chapters the expressions 'to reserve' or 'to set aside' a proportion of capital receipts are used synonymously. (LGHA 1989, s 59(1) refers to the part of the receipt which is set aside for credit liabilities as being 'the reserved part'). The expression 'set-aside obligation' is also used as an abbreviated reference to the obligation under LGHA 1989, s 59(1), although it does not appear in the legislation itself.

2 See paras **14.24ff.**
3 See paras **10.13** and **10.14**.

14.4 Capital receipts for the purposes of Pt IV are defined in LGHA 1989, s 58 and in regulations made under s 58(9). The relevant regulations currently comprise LA(CF)R 1997, Pt VI. References in this chapter to section numbers, without more, are references to the sections of the LGHA 1989; numbered regulations, without more, are references to the LA(CF)R 1997.

1 SUMS WHICH ARE CAPITAL RECEIPTS UNDER LGHA 1989, S 58

14.5 By virtue of LGHA 1989, s 58(1), the capital receipts of a local authority are sums (ie money) received by the authority in respect of the four classes of transaction described in paras **14.6–14.9**.

(a) 'Sums'

(i) Sums received in respect of the disposal of any interest in an asset if, at the time of disposal, expenditure on the acquisition of the asset would be expenditure for capital purposes[1]

14.6 This category covers the receipts from the disposal by the authority of any interest in land. This encompasses the receipts from the sale of a freehold interest, or from the grant or assignment of a lease (subject to an important exception in respect of rents[2]), and from the disposal of any other type of interest in land. In addition to land, this category covers receipts from the disposal of an interest in any other kind of asset which, if the council concerned had been buying rather than selling the asset, would have involved 'expenditure for capital purposes'[3]. Thus, receipts from the sale, or lease by an authority of vehicles, vessels, plant, machinery, apparatus or most computer programs[4] are also capital receipts (but again subject to the exception for rents referred to in para **14.19**).

1 Local Government and Housing Act 1989, s 58(1)(a).
2 See para **14.19**.
3 Which is defined in LGHA 1989, s 40 and LA(CF)R 1997, regs 2–8, to cover expenditure on various tangible assets, computer programmes and under 'private finance transactions' as defined in reg 16.
4 See Local Authorities (Capital Finance) Regulations 1997, reg 7 making expenditure on the acquisition or preparation of a computer program expenditure for capital purposes, in so far as it is not already capital expenditure for the purpose of LGHA 1989, s 40.

(ii) Sums received in respect of the disposal of any investment other than an investment which, at the time of disposal, is an approved investment[1]

14.7 This category covers receipts from the sale of share or loan capital, or any other investments which are not 'approved investments' at the time of the disposal. (Approved investments are defined in LGHA 1989, s 66(1)(a) and are considered to be less speculative forms of investment in which authorities are encouraged to hold their cash resources until they are used. They are given special treatment under the capital finance system as described in para **10.21ff.**)

1 Local Government and Housing Act 1989, s 58(1)(b).

(iii) Sums received in respect of the repayment of, or a payment in respect of, any grants or other financial assistance of such a description that, if the expenditure on the grant or assistance had been incurred at the time of the repayment or payment, it would have constituted expenditure for capital purposes[1]

14.8 This category would cover the repayment of a grant to the authority by a third party, if the authority had given the grant for, say, the enhancement of a building (or for any other capital purpose within LGHA 1989, s 40, or under the relevant regulations). However, the payment or repayment to the authority will only constitute a capital receipt if it is made by the person to whom the authority gave the grant or other financial assistance[2].

1 Local Government and Housing Act 1989, s 58(1)(c).
2 See Local Authorities (Capital Finance) Regulations 1997, reg 63.

(iv) Sums received in respect of the repayment of the principal of an advance (not being an approved investment) made by the authority for such a purpose that, if the advance had been made at the time of the repayment, expenditure incurred on it would have constituted expenditure for capital purposes[1]

14.9 This category of capital receipt relates to the principal component of loan repayments to the authority (other than approved investments). It is similar to that for repayment of grants and other financial assistance, save that in this case it is irrelevant if the repayment is made by someone other than the original borrower.

1 Local Government and Housing Act 1989, s 58(1)(d).

(b) 'Received'

14.10 Sums received by a local authority within these four categories become 'capital receipts' at the time they are 'in fact received'[1]. Subject to the exceptions mentioned in para **14.11**, the provisions on capital receipts only apply to sums received on or after 1 April 1990. However, it is irrelevant when the disposal or advance was made, or when the financial assistance was given. Disposals of assets and investments under LGHA 1989, s 58(1)(a) and (b), described in paras **14.6** and **14.7**, which took place prior to 1 April 1990 (which give rise to payments on or after that date) are deemed to have taken place on 1 April 1990 for the purpose of interpreting these provisions[2].

1 Local Government and Housing Act 1989, s 58(1).
2 LGHA 1989, s 58(3).

14.11 Under s 58(4)–(6), at the outset of the system under LGHA 1989, Pt IV, local authorities were required to identify certain sums in their accounts which had been received prior to 1 April 1990 which were (mainly) 'capital receipts' under the LGPLA 1980 system and which were shown, as at the end of the financial year 1989–90, as unapplied, or as a balance in a special fund[1]. These sums were treated as being 'capital receipts' for the purposes of Pt IV (unless they were invested *otherwise* than in approved investments) and were treated as having been received on 1 April 1990. Consequently they were subject to an immediate obligation to set aside the reserved part under LGHA 1989, s 59 on that date[2].

1 Established under Sch 13, para 16 of the Local Government Act 1972.
2 See paras **14.24ff**.

2 SUMS TREATED AS CAPITAL RECEIPTS BY VIRTUE OF THE LA(CF)R 1997

14.12 Through the exercise of the Secretary of State's powers under LGHA 1989, s 58(9)(a) the following sums received by local authorities have been designated as 'capital receipts' by virtue of the LA(CF)R 1997:

(a) *Regulations 56 and 57* Payments received in respect of principal of notional debt created in favour of the authority concerned by virtue of certain orders made in respect of the transfer of housing land[1]; under certain orders, regulations or agreements connected with local government reorganisation[2]; and under certain orders concerning the transfer of assets to regional water authorities[3];
(b) *Regulation 58* Payments made by other authorities to the lead authority administering the debt of an abolished metropolitan county council, in respect of repayment of principal of money deemed to have been borrowed from the lead authority[4];
(c) *Regulation 58A*[5] Voluntary additional payments made by a 'participant authority' to a 'designated authority' to assist the designated authority in meeting its increased obligations to make revenue provision for credit liabilities arising from local government reorganisation[6];
(d) *Regulation 58B*[7] Payments made to the Metropolitan Police Authority in respect of a repayment of principal to be made by it in relation to financial liabilities transferred to it by virtue of a scheme made under the Greater London Authority Act 1999, s 409(2); and
(e) *Regulation 59* Interim or final payments made to a local authority in accordance with Sch 6A of the Housing Act 1985 in respect of redemption of the landlord's share (in so far as they are not already capital receipts by virtue of LGHA 1989, s 58(1)(a)).

1 Under the London Government Act 1963, s 23(3) or s 84.
2 Under the Local Government Act 1972, s 51(2), s 58(2), s 67(4), s 67(1) or (2) or s 68.
3 LGA 1972, s 254 as extended by the Water Act 1973 s 34 and Sch 6.
4 By virtue of an order under the Local Government Act 1985, s 66(1) or s 67(3).
5 Inserted by SI 1998/1937, reg 4, to supersede SI 1995/2895, reg 9, which was revoked.
6 Under the Local Government Changes for England (Payments to Designated Authorities) (Minimum Revenue Provision) Regulations 1995, SI 1995/2895, reg 8.
7 Inserted by SI 2000/1474.

B Notional capital receipts

14.13 LGHA 1989, s 61 includes special provisions concerning barter transactions and other arrangements under which an authority enters into a transaction of a kind which would normally give rise to a capital receipt, but where instead of receiving payment entirely in money, the authority either receives non-monetary consideration or directs that payment be made to a third party. The intention of these provisions was to ensure that authorities did not evade the obligations to set aside a proportion of their (money) capital receipts. Where a set-aside rate greater than 0% applies (for example, in a housing scheme), the effect of s 61 may be quite onerous for the authority. In a complex transaction, the application and/or the effects of s 61 may be difficult to identify. However, the abolition of set aside on most non-housing capital receipts by virtue of LA(CF)R 1997, reg 64A[1] benefits equally the treatment of notional capital receipts, so that the 0% set-aside rate would apply in respect of any notional receipt generated in a case which benefits under reg 64A.

1 Inserted in the 1997 Regulations by SI 1998/1937, reg 6.

14.14 LGHA 1989, s 61 applies where:

(a) the whole or part of the consideration received by a local authority on or after 1 April 1990 for a disposal falling within LGHA 1989, s 58(1) either is not in money or consists of money which, at the request or with the agreement of the local authority concerned, is paid otherwise than to the authority[1]; or
(b) the right of a local authority to receive such a repayment or payment as is referred to in s 58(1) is assigned or waived for a consideration which is received on or after 1 April 1990 and which, in whole or part, is not in money or which, at the request or with the agreement of the local authority, is paid otherwise and to the authority[2]; or
(c) on a disposal falling within s 58(8) (of a lease of land or goods), any consideration which is received on or after 1 April 1990 and, if it had been in money paid to the authority, it would have been a capital receipt[3].

1 Local Government and Housing Act 1989, s 61(1)(a).
2 LGHA 1989, s 61(1)(b).
3 LGHA 1989, s 61(1)(c).

14.15 If a transaction within LGHA 1989, s 61(1) occurs, the authority must determine the amount which 'would have been the capital receipt' if the consideration had been wholly in money paid to the authority. From this amount, the council must then deduct any payment which has been made in money to the authority (and in respect of which s 59 regarding set aside applies directly). The resulting figure is the 'notional capital receipt'[1], to which a 'set aside obligation' under s 61(4) applies in an amount equal to that which would have applied to a cash receipt of that amount under s 59 (see para **14.35ff**). This formulation raises the question whether, in determining what the consideration 'would have been', the authority is required to value the asset that it has disposed of, or the consideration which it is to receive. Although, in general, it would be expected that the two valuations should produce a similar figure this is, of course, not necessarily so (for example, where a local authority disposes of land at less than full value, with the benefit of any necessary ministerial consent). In *R v Brent London Borough Council, ex p O'Malley*[2] the Court of Appeal (approving the findings of Schiemann LJ at first instance) concluded that in order to calculate a notional capital receipt, what had to be valued was the total contribution made by or on behalf of the dispondee, whether in cash or in kind or in promises.

1 See Local Government and Housing Act 1989, s 61(2) and (3).
2 (1997) 30 HLR 328 at 367–8.

14.16 There is an apparent overlap between LGHA 1989, sub-s 61(1)(a) and (c) in relation to cases where the nature of the disposal is the grant, assignment or surrender of a lease of land or goods. It is not entirely clear whether any non-monetary consideration given to a local authority in lieu of rent, or rent paid otherwise than to the authority, should count as a notional capital receipt within s 61(1)(a), or whether it is intended that the position should be dealt with entirely under s 61(1)(c) (in which case, any form of consideration in respect of rent would be disregarded[1]). As s 61(1)(c) is specifically directed at leasehold disposals, arguably it should apply in such cases, to the exclusion of the more general provisions of s 61(1)(a).

1 See para **14.19**. The legislation may, perhaps, be based on the assumption that rent, by its nature, is a monetary payment which can only be made to the local authority as lessor.

14.17 The obligation to make special set-aside provision for credit liabilities in respect of notional capital receipts is referred to in para **14.35**. The concessions for notional capital receipts generated under certain classes of transaction are referred to at para **14.57**ff.

C Exceptions: items which are not capital receipts

14.18 LGHA 1989, s 58 and the regulations made by the Secretary of State under s 58(9)(b), exclude certain kinds of payments to a local authority amounting to capital receipts. Where such an exemption applies, the receipts will not be subject to the obligation to set aside a proportion for credit liabilities under LGHA 1989, s 59. The provisions on non-monetary consideration and other special arrangements within LGHA 1989, s 61 will not apply. Expenditure of the receipts will *not* be exempt from being charged to a revenue account by virtue of LGHA 1989, s 42(2)(f), although it is possible that one of the other exemptions under s 42(2) may apply, dependent upon the nature of the expenditure (see, for example, s 42(2)(g) for capital expenditure reimbursed by third parties).

1 SUMS WHICH ARE NOT CAPITAL RECEIPTS BY VIRTUE OF THE LGHA 1989

(a) Leases

14.19 Perhaps the most significant exception to the definition of 'capital receipts' is that in respect of 'normal' rents. Under LGHA 1989, s 58(8), where a local authority grants, assigns or surrenders a leasehold interest in any land or the lease of any other asset, only the following are capital receipts:

(a) any premium paid on the grant or assignment;
(b) any consideration received in respect of the surrender;
(c) any sum paid by way of rent more than three months before the beginning of the rental period to which it relates;
(d) any sum paid by way of rent in respect of a rental period which exceeds one year; or
(e) so much of any other sum paid by way of rent as, in accordance with directions given by the Secretary of State, falls to be treated as a capital receipt.

(b) Approved investments

14.20 Receipts from the disposal of investments, which are 'approved investments' at the time they are disposed of, are not capital receipts[1]. 'Approved investments' are various kinds of investment specified by the Secretary of State in regulations made for the purpose of LGHA 1989, s 66(1)(a) considered to be less speculative than other forms of investment[2].

1 Local Government and Housing Act 1989, s 58(1)(b).
2 See paras **14.7** and **10.21**ff regarding approved investments.

(c) Superannuation fund receipts

14.21 Sums received by a local authority in respect of:

(a) the disposal of assets or investments of a superannuation fund which the authority is required to keep by virtue of the Superannuation Act 1972; and
(b) any repayment or payments made to such a superannuation fund in respect of grants, financial assistance or advances within LGHA 1989, s 58(1)(c) or (d),

are excluded from being capital receipts by virtue of LGHA 1989, s 58(2).

(d) Interest for late payment

14.22 Under LGHA 1989, s 58(7), if a payment to the authority of the purchase price for the disposal of an asset or investment is deferred, then any interest payable on the price is not a capital receipt.

2 SUMS WHICH ARE NOT CAPITAL RECEIPTS BY VIRTUE OF THE LA(CF)R 1997

14.23 Through regulations[1] made under LGHA 1989, s 58(9)(b), the Secretary of State has excluded the following items from amounting to capital receipts:

(a) *Regulation 61* Sums received by a local authority for the disposal of an interest in an asset under LGHA 1989, s 58(1)(a) are not capital receipts if the aggregate amount received for the disposal does not exceed £6,000.
(b) *Regulation 62* Receipts from the disposal of certain limited kinds of investments are excluded from being capital receipts (even though they are not approved investments[2]). It applies to the disposal of investments made with certain bodies who have ceased to be 'authorised institutions' for the purposes of the Local Authorities (Capital Finance) (Approved Investments) Regulations 1990[3] and receipts from the disposal of certain investments to which reg 10[4] applies.
(c) *Regulation 63* Any payment to a local authority in respect of a grant or other financial assistance under s 58(1)(c) is not a capital receipt if it is paid to the authority by someone *other* than the person to whom the authority gave the grant or other financial assistance[5].

In each of these cases the sums received are not subject to the set-aside obligations under LGHA 1989, s 59. In each case if, instead of money, the council receives non-monetary consideration, or directs that payment be made to a third party, s 61 on notional capital receipts would not apply[6].

1 Currently the LA(CF)R 1997, Pt VI.
2 See paras **14.20** and **10.21**ff regarding 'approved investments'. Receipts from the disposal of approved investments are excluded from the definition of 'capital receipt' under s 58(1)(b).
3 SI 1990/426 as amended.
4 Concerning the reinvestment of funds paid to an authority in respect of a default or breach of

covenant by certain institutions or building societies.

5 See para **14.8**. Local Authorities (Capital Finance) Regulations 1990 (now revoked), reg 13(1) (SI 1990/432 as amended), from which LA(CF)R 1997, reg 63 derives, was in slightly different terms. Regulation 13(1) was seen as helpful in clarifying that payments made by a developer pursuant to a planning obligation under s 106 of the Town and Country Planning Act 1990, or similar arrangement, would not amount to capital receipts subject to set-aside obligations by virtue of LGHA 1989, s 58(1)(c).

6 LGHA 1989, s 61(2) provides that the authority has to determine the amount 'which would have been the capital receipt' in respect of any consideration subject to s 61. In the cases covered by LA(CF)R 1997, regs 61–63 there would be no capital receipt.

D Reserved part

1 RESERVED PART OF CAPITAL RECEIPTS

14.24 At the time when a local authority receives a capital receipt it must set aside[1] a proportion to meet credit liabilities[2].

1 But see the exceptions or modifications to this general requirement in s 59(7)–(9) mentioned in para **14.32–14.34**.

2 Local Government and Housing Act 1989, s 59(1). In relation to the reserved part of notional capital receipts, see para **14.35**ff.

14.25 LGHA 1989, s 59(2) specifies the percentages of the reserved part of capital receipts which apply *unless* the Secretary of State has altered the required percentage for the particular description of receipt (or description of authority) through regulations made under s 59(3), or through a direction under s 59(6). The 'basic rules' as prescribed by s 59(2) are:

(a) 75% for receipts in respect of the disposal of dwelling houses held for the purposes of Pt II of the Housing Act 1985;

(b) 50% for any other receipt.

These basic percentages still apply to all housing revenue account receipts of local authorities in England if they are not 'debt free'[1].

1 See para **14.27**.

(a) Special percentages and abolition of set aside on most non-housing receipts

14.26 Under LGHA 1989, s 59(3) the Secretary of State has the power to alter these basic percentages to anything from nil up to 100%, either in relation to different descriptions of capital receipts, or in relation to different descriptions of local authorities. LA(CF)R 1997, Pt VII deals with special 'set-aside percentages' for particular classes of capital receipt (and for certain housing receipts of local authorities in Wales). The altered percentages prescribed under the regulations are now extensive, and are summarised in para **14.30**. It was through this power to make subordinate legislation under s 59(3) that the rate of set aside for most capital receipts was reduced to 0% by the Secretary of State in September 1998, under the Local Authorities (Capital Finance) (Amendment No 3) Regulations 1998, SI 1998/1937 and, in particular, through the introduction of the new reg 64A. Some of the most important remaining set-aside requirements now concern receipts from the disposal of housing assets.

(b) Housing assets

14.27 The treatment of receipts from the disposal of housing assets requires particular attention. For a local authority in England which is not 'debt free', the percentages which must be set aside are:

(a) 75% in respect of receipts from the disposal of dwelling houses held for the purposes of the Housing Act 1985, Pt II (which must be accounted for within the Housing Revenue Account which the authority is required to maintain under LGHA 1989, s 74 (the 'HRA'))[1];

(b) 75% in respect of receipts from the disposal of hostels[2] or lodging houses[3] held for the purposes of the Housing Act 1985, Pt II[4]; or

(c) 50% in respect of receipts from the disposal of *all other* housing assets which fall to be accounted for within the HRA[5].

1 Local Government and Housing Act 1989, s 59(2)(a) (and see the LA(CF)R 1997, reg 64A regarding the general exception of receipts from the disposal of HRA land from nil per cent set-aside treatment).
2 As defined in the Housing Act 1985, s 622.
3 As defined in the Housing Act 1985, s 56.
4 Local Authorities (Capital Finance) Regulations 1997, reg 72.
5 Local Government and Housing Act 1989, s 59(2)(b).

14.28 LA(CF)R 1997, regs 76–78 make special provision for receipts from disposals by local authorities in Wales of certain housing land (excluding dwellings), dwellings on shared ownership leases or on conditions requiring improvements or significant works and certain other dwellings (which have never been occupied under secure tenancies or introductory tenancies, unless they are reacquired right to buy properties). In each case where these special provisions apply, the reserved part is nil.

14.29 If the authority is 'debt-free' for the purposes of LA(CF)R 1997, reg 65(2)(a) and (b) set-aside requirements (greater than 0%) in respect of the disposal of housing assets[1] *only arise* in a case where a local authority sells a Pt II dwelling *otherwise* than under the right to buy provisions of the Housing Act 1985, Pt V. Receipts from the 'non-right to buy' sale of HRA dwellings by debt-free authorities are subject to 75% set aside as for other authorities.

1 For debt-free authorities virtually all capital receipts and notional capital receipts are subject to nil set-aside: see reg 65. The exceptions (in addition to sale of dwellings otherwise than under the right to buy) are receipts subject to reg 67 (payments in respect of grants to housing associations), reg 68 (payments in respect of transferred property and deemed borrowing) and reg 69 (redemption of landlord's share under the Housing Act 1985, Sch 6A).

(c) Set-aside percentages under the LA(CF)R 1997, Pt VII

14.30 In summary, the 'altered percentages' from those stipulated in LGHA 1989, s 59(2) in relation to the reserved part of various categories of capital receipt as prescribed by the Secretary of State for the purpose of s 59(3), which are contained in LA(CF)R 1997, Pt VII, are as set out in the following chart. By virtue of LGHA 1989, s 61(4), these percentages apply equally to notional capital receipts. They also apply to the obligations analogous to set aside which local authorities are required to make in respect of the capital receipts and notional capital receipts of 'regulated companies' under Pt V of the Local Authorities (Companies) Order 1995[1].

Regulation	Type or source of capital receipt	Set aside rate
64A	All capital receipts *other than* those from the disposal of housing land[2], *or where special provision is made in one of the following regulations.*	Nil
65	All receipts of debt-free[3] authorities other than those from non-right to buy disposal of dwellings and cases where regs 67, 68 or 69 apply.	Nil[4]
66(2)	Receipts from the disposal of share or loan capital in a company *other than* in a company of a kind listed in reg 66, paras (2)(a)–(g).	75%[5]
66(2)(a)–(g)	Receipts from the disposal of share or loan capital in: (a) a bus company; (b) a public airport company; (c) a company which has issued the share or loan capital to the authority in exchange for the transfer of non-housing local authority assets to the company; (cc) certain companies which operate airports other than public airport companies; (d) an education or training company; (e) a non-housing company where the share or loan capital was acquired: (i) before 10 March 1988; or (ii) on or after 1 April 1990 to provide financial assistance to promote economic development under LGHA 1989, s 33; (f) a company formed for a purpose within s 145 of the Local Government Act 1972 (provision of entertainments); or (g) a local authority waste disposal company formed pursuant to s 32 of the Environmental Protection Act 1990.	Nil
66A	Receipts from the disposal of 'non-approved' investments[6] other than share or loan capital.	50%[7]
67	Payment and repayments in respect of grants and advances to housing associations (social housing grant).	100%
68	Sums received in respect of transferred property and deemed borrowing in connection with local government reorganisation (which are capital receipts by virtue of regs 56–58[8]).	100%
68A	Sums received by a local authority as 'designated authority' in connection with local government reorganisation (which are capital receipts by virtue of reg 58A[9]).	100%[10]

Regulation	Type or source of capital receipt	Set aside rate
68B	Sums received by the Metropolitan Police Authority in connection with financial liabilities transferred to it by a scheme under the Greater London Authority Act 1999, s 409(2) (which are capital receipts by virtue of reg 58A[11]).	100%
69	Payments for redemption of landlord's share in accordance with Sch 6A to the Housing Act 1985 (under reg 59[12]).	75%
72	Receipts from the disposal of hostels or lodging houses.	75%[13]

1 SI 1995/849; see art 14(2)(a) concerning the requirement to provide credit cover in respect of capital receipts and notional capital receipts of a regulated company in an amount equal to that which a local authority would be required to set aside under LGHA 1989, s 59 or s 61(4) if it had received such a receipt.
2 'Housing land' is defined in LA(CF)R 1997, reg 64 as being any land, house or other building in respect of which sums fall to be credited or debited in accordance with LGHA 1989, s 74 (duty to keep Housing Revenue Account) (see paras **14.27**ff for the percentages which apply to receipts from disposal of housing land).
3 'Debt free' within the terms of paras (2)(a) and (b) of reg 65, ie the authority has a nil or negative credit ceiling at the beginning of the financial year of receipt, and no outstanding borrowing (other than disregarded borrowing as defined in reg 65(1)) at the time the receipt is received.
4 Subject to exceptions for receipts within regs 67–70 (see below in this table) and receipts from the disposal of dwellings held for the purposes of Pt II of the Housing Act 1985 otherwise than pursuant to the right to buy under the Housing Act 1985, Pt V (see reg 65(2)(c) and (d)).
5 Or nil if reg 65 applies because the authority is 'debt free'.
6 See para **10.21**ff regarding 'approved investments'. The disposal of an *approved* investment does not give rise to set-aside obligations, as the receipts from their disposal are excluded from the definition of 'capital receipt' under LGHA 1989, s 58(1)(b).
7 Or nil if reg 65 applies because the authority is 'debt free'.
8 See para **14.12**.
9 See para **14.12**.
10 Or nil if reg 65 applies because the authority is 'debt free'.
11 See para **14.12**.
12 See para **14.12**.
13 Or nil if reg 65 applies because the authority is 'debt free'.

14.31 All the special percentages summarised above were created through regulations made by the Secretary of State for the purpose of LGHA 1989, s 59(3). There is a further means by which the Secretary of State can specify a different set-aside percentage for a particular capital receipt than that which would normally apply under s 59(2). This is through a direction made in an individual case under s 59(6). However, the power to make such a direction only arises in a case where the disposal (of a dwelling or other property) requires the consent of the Secretary of State, for example under the Housing Act 1985, s 32 or 43, or the Local Government Act 1972, s 123. In practice, the power to issue directions to create a special set-aside rate for an individual disposal has been used sparingly, and it is yet to be seen whether it will be used any more frequently in relation to the disposal of housing land.

14.32 The obligation to set aside a proportion of capital receipts under LGHA 1989, s 59(1) does not apply if the receipts are received by the authority as trustee of a fund held for charitable purposes[1].

1 See Local Government and Housing Act 1989, s 59(7).

14.33 Special provision is also made, in LGHA 1989, s 59(8), for capital receipts which arise from the disposal of an asset or investment, or the repayment of a grant or other financial assistance, which was originally acquired or made by the authority wholly or partly out of moneys provided by Parliament on terms which enable or require a Minister of the Crown to seek repayment. In such a case, the capital receipt is treated as reduced by the amount which appears to the authority to be payable to the Minister, before the obligation to set aside part is calculated under s 59. (See also the chart at para **14.56** which notes the treatment of repayment obligations in respect of certain land improvement grants under LA(CF)R 1997, regs 94 and 95).

14.34 In the case of capital receipts from the disposal of land held for the purpose of the Housing Act 1985, Pt II, or any other disposal made under the right to buy provisions in the Housing Act 1985, Pt V, the capital receipt is treated as reduced by so much of the receipt as is applied in defraying the administrative costs 'of and incidental to' the disposal, before set-aside is calculated[1].

1 See Local Government and Housing Act 1989, s 59(9).

2 RESERVED PART OF NOTIONAL CAPITAL RECEIPTS

14.35 The obligation to make provision to meet credit liabilities in respect of notional capital receipts arises at the time of the disposal, or the assignment or waiver of the repayment or payment[1] rather than, as in the case of a (money) capital receipt, at the time the consideration is actually received[2].

1 See Local Government and Housing Act 1989, s 61(4).

2 In *R v Brent London Borough Council, ex p O'Malley* (1997) 30 HLR 328 at 367, CA, Judge LJ found that notional capital receipts arise when they are 'received' (and considered that this view was reinforced by LGHA 1989, s 61(4)) such that the obligation to set aside could not arise *before* the non-monetary consideration was received. However, regardless of when a notional capital receipt 'arises', the clear words of s 61(4) stipulate that the time at which a local authority is to *set aside* an amount as provision to meet credit liabilities is 'at the time of the disposal or the assignment or waiver of the repayment or payment'.

14.36 As described in para **14.15**, if a local authority has entered into an arrangement which gives rise to a notional capital under s 61 it has to set aside an amount equal to that which, under LGHA 1989, s 59, would have been the reserved part of the receipt (having made an allowance for any sum paid in money in respect of which set aside under s 59 actually applies). Excepted from this is the case where through regulations or a direction[1], the Secretary of State has stipulated an exceptional set-aside rate for the particular type of receipt. Thus the percentage of set aside on a notional capital receipt is normally the same as that which would have applied to a (money) capital receipt generated in the same circumstances. In the majority of cases (other than those concerning the disposal of housing land or certain shares and other investments) that percentage will now be nil, by virtue of LA(CF)R 1997, reg 64A. Therefore notional capital receipts benefit equally from the abolition of set aside on most capital receipts.

1 The Secretary of State's power to give directions in an individual case in relation to *notional* capital receipts is wider than that under LGHA 1989, s 59(6) in relation to capital receipts (see para **14.31**). LGHA 1989, s 61(4) makes no reference to the direction being linked to a consent to the disposal of the land in question.

14.37 Where a percentage greater than 0% does apply, the sources from which set-aside provision may be made comprise[1]:

(a) the usable part of the authority's capital receipts; or
(b) a revenue account of the authority.

1 Under Local Government and Housing Act 1989, s 61(5).

14.38 Set-aside obligations on notional capital receipts of significant value can have onerous implications for the authority, particularly if the transaction in question involves exclusively notional receipts. Where no money is received, the effect of the rules is to require the authority to identify either usable capital receipts or revenue generated from *outside* the transaction, in order to meet the set-aside obligation.

3 LAND DISPOSALS

14.39 Section 123 of the Local Government Act 1972 and other statutory provisions concerning the disposal of local authority land generally require an authority to obtain the best consideration reasonably obtainable for its land, unless the consent of the Secretary of State is obtained. Case law on s 123 acknowledges that non-monetary consideration can be taken into account when establishing whether this obligation has been fulfilled, provided that the consideration is capable of being ascribed with a commercial or monetary value[1].

1 See *R v Middlesbrough Borough Council, ex p Frostree Ltd* (16 December 1988, unreported).

14.40 There is no explicit statutory relationship between the obligations to obtain best price and the provisions of LGHA 1989, s 61 on notional capital receipts as they apply to land disposals. Indeed, in *R v Brent London Borough Council, ex p O'Malley*[1] the court noted that LGHA 1989, Pt IV and LGA 1972, s 123 have distinct purposes. Nonetheless, in the case of a disposal of local authority land involving non-monetary consideration it seems inevitable that, in practice, there should be some (albeit informal) relationship between the exercise which is undertaken by a local authority to ensure that all the monetary and non-monetary consideration it receives constitutes the 'best consideration reasonably obtainable' for the purpose of LGA 1972, s 123 and the determination it is required to make of what the money receipt to it 'would have been' for the purposes of s 61(2) in order to establish the amount of the notional capital receipt (where a percentage greater than 0% applies). Whilst acknowledging that these are two distinct exercises, it would seem difficult for an authority to form a wholly inconsistent view on the valuation of non-monetary consideration for the purpose of LGA 1972, s 123, as opposed to that formed in respect of a notional receipt for the purpose of LGHA 1989, s 61.

1 (1997) 30 HLR 328, CA.

14.41 If the disposal is to be made at less than best consideration (for example, where the consent of the Secretary of State is available for the purpose of LGA 1972, s 123(2)), again, it seems likely that the valuation of the consideration offered to the authority which led to the need for consent should arise again in answering the question what the money receipt 'would have been' (so that it will be that lesser figure). This, of course, assumes that the exercise under LGHA 1989, s 61 requires the authority to value what it receives and not what it sells: see the *O'Malley* case referred to in para **14.15**.

E Usable part of capital receipts

14.42 Under LGHA 1989, s 60(2) the part of any capital receipt which remains after the set-aside obligation has been met may only be used for the following prescribed purposes:

(a) to meet expenditure incurred for capital purposes; or
(b) as provision to meet credit liabilities.

14.43 The usable part of a capital receipt can, however, be applied for the permitted purposes at any time, whether in the financial year in which it is received or at any subsequent time[1]. It is to be noted that a capital receipt cannot be used for revenue purposes (although revenue may be used to fund capital expenditure).

1 See Local Government and Housing Act 1989, s 60(2).

F Reliefs in respect of capital receipts under the LA(CF)R 1997

1 BACKGROUND

14.44 Before looking briefly at the concessions themselves, it is helpful to understand the original need for these complex arrangements. When the LGHA 1989 first came into force, a strict application of the rules on set aside of capital receipts and in respect of notional capital receipts under LGHA 1989, ss 59 and 61 would have meant that many transactions which were not intended to be discouraged, particularly those involving the disposal of local authority land, would lead to onerous consequences for the authority concerned in terms of set aside, making them difficult if not impossible for the authority to undertake. To provide for cases where there was an acknowledged need to allow the particular type of transaction to take place without 'penalties' for the authority's capital (or revenue) budget, or where, on policy grounds, it was considered desirable to give positive encouragement to certain types of transaction, particularly those involving the disposal of certain local authority assets[1], the LA(CF)R 1997 have always provided for a number of concessions from, or relaxations of, the usual rules on set aside.

1 For example the 13 month 'capital receipts holiday', giving a set-aside rate of nil on most capital receipts received during the period 13 November 1992 to 31 December 1993 inclusive introduced under SI 1992/2819, or under LA(CF)R 1997, reg 66(3) and (4) as originally enacted, which allowed for a reduced set-aside rate of 25% on receipts from the disposal of share or loan capital in a bus company and certain public and other airport companies received between 1 April 1997 and 31 March 1998.

14.45 Under the LGHA 1989, there are various methods by which exceptions can be made from the usual rules on capital receipts and notional capital receipts through regulations made by the Secretary of State:

(a) by specifying that certain receipts are not to be capital receipts at all (so that the set-aside obligations do not arise on cash or notional receipts)[1];
(b) by reducing the normal percentage of set aside that applies to the particular type of capital receipt or notional capital receipt[2];
(c) by allowing deductions to be made from the total capital receipt (or notional receipt) before the set-aside obligation is calculated (usually in respect of

related expenditure or credit arrangements[3]);or

(d) by specifying a special set-aside rate on certain notional capital receipts[4].

1 Local Government and Housing Act 1989, s 58(9)(b) (and see LGHA 1989, s 61(2) for the implications for notional capital receipts as referred to at para **14.23**, n 5).
2 LGHA 1989, s 59(3) (regulations) and s 59(6) (directions).
3 LGHA 1989, s 59(4).
4 LGHA 1989, s 61(4).

14.46 The categories of receipt which are given special treatment under method (a) have already been described in para **14.23** (LA(CF)R 1997, regs 61–63) and are perhaps not truly 'concessions' in all cases. As described in para **14.26**, method (b) was used to sweeping effect to abolish set aside on the vast majority of capital receipts as from 1 September 1998 by SI 1998/1937. The extensive and complex concession in LA(CF)R 1997, Pts VIII and IX, which adopt methods (c) and (d), were then rendered redundant as from 1 September 1998 in all cases where a set-aside rate of nil has been prescribed for the capital receipt concerned by virtue of LA(CF)R 1997, reg 64A (which benefits both capital receipts and notional capital receipts generated in the eligible circumstances, as well as the obligations analogous to set aside, which authorities must make in respect of the receipts of 'regulated companies'[1]). However, LA(CF)R 1997, Pts VIII and IX were not repealed at that time, and indeed have since been slightly updated. Their remaining relevance is primarily in relation to the disposal of housing land particularly for an authority which is not debt free. LA(CF)R 1997, Pt VIII deals with capital receipts which are to be treated as reduced by certain costs or expenditure (and in most cases the concessions apply equally to a notional capital receipt which is generated in eligible circumstances, by virtue of reg 106). LA(CF)R 1997, Pt IX deals with various circumstances in which a notional capital receipt is to be treated as having a set aside requirement of nil[2].

1 Under the Local Authorities (Companies) Order 1995, SI 1995/849, Pt V.
2 See paras **14.57–14.62**.

14.47 In view of the their limited practical application since 1 September 1998, the complex rules under LA(CF)R 1997, Pts XIII and IX are not described in detail in this work, but as they have a residual relevance, particularly in relation to housing transactions, they are summarised in the charts at paras **14.56** and **14.62**.

14.48 In order to understand and apply these regulations in those cases where they continue to be of relevance, it helps to consider their development. Several of the main concessions in LA(CF)R 1997, Pt VIII have their origins in the special 'in-and-out rules' devised as administrative arrangements in connection with the previous capital finance system under the Local Government, Planning and Land Act 1980[1]. These administrative 'rules' were replicated by analogous concessions under the LGHA 1989 system by provisions contained in the Local Authorities (Capital Finance) Regulations 1990 (now revoked) made by the Secretary of State under LGHA 1989, s 59(4). These concessions were then amended over the years and have survived, with further revisions, in the LA(CF)R 1997[2].

1 Which were mainly dependent on a successful individual application to a government department.
2 See in particular LA(CF)R 1997, regs 96 and 99, based on regs 15 and 18 of the Local Authorities (Capital Finance) Regulations 1990 (now revoked).

14.49 As noted earlier, one of the original aims of the LGHA 1989 system was to bring about a reduction in the overall stock of capital assets held by authorities, as well as a reduction in their borrowing[1]. Thus, many of the provisions are constructed so as to ensure that where an authority disposes of land, it can only benefit under the concession if it divests itself of a substantial property interest (ie the freehold or a long lease with only a minimal rent), rather than where it retains a valuable land interest. (If the council receives consideration exclusively in the form of rent for the grant of a lease, the concessions will be irrelevant, as no capital receipt will arise[2]). In many cases, the intention is to facilitate a transaction only if the overall effects will be broadly neutral in terms of the level of assets the authority holds before and after the transaction (eg where certain kinds of facilities are replaced, or where land is sold not long after it is purchased). Other concessions have been more blatantly aimed at encouraging authorities to divest themselves of land or other assets, but in some cases they allow authorities to increase the value of the asset before sale[3].

1 See para **10.4**ff.
2 Local Government and Housing Act 1989, s 58(8).
3 See, for example, Local Authorities (Capital Finance) Regulations 1997, reg 103.

14.50 It is necessary to dispose of one common misconception. The provisions of LA(CF)R 1997, Pts VI–IX which concern capital receipts and notional capital receipts are not directed at the question whether the authority concerned has the legal capacity to enter into a particular transaction. They simply tackle the *consequences* of transactions in terms of (the existence of and) treatment of any capital receipts or notional capital receipts which are generated.

2 CAPITAL RECEIPTS TO BE TREATED AS REDUCED DERIVED FROM THE DISPOSAL OF LAND

14.51 LA(CF)R 1997, Pt VIII includes concessions which, prior to the abolition of set aside on receipts from the disposal of non-HRA assets in September 1998, were frequently relied upon in connection with local authority land transactions. The need to conform with the criteria for eligibility for these concessions often affected the structure of land transactions undertaken by local authorities prior to that time. All these concessions work by allowing the authority to treat capital receipts from a disposal of land as reduced by certain costs or expenditure, before the set-aside obligation under LGHA 1989, s 59 is calculated, provided the detailed requirements of the individual regulations are met. These regulations were made by the Secretary of State in exercise of his powers under s 59(4). In some cases the effect will be that the receipt becomes 100% usable. Take as an example a case where a local authority sells land and obtains a capital receipt of £1,000,000. If a reserved part of 50% applies (for example, where a local authority sells HRA land with no dwellings), the amount to be set aside would normally be £500,000. If a deduction can be made for the purpose of s 59 under an appropriate regulation of, say, £1,000,000, no set aside at all will be required. If the permitted deduction under the regulation is £600,000, there will be a set-aside obligation of £200,000 (50% x £400,000).

14.52 Many of the concessions in LA(CF)R 1997, Pt VIII incorporate reg 84, which concerns the nature of the interest disposed of by the council and creates a standard 'disposal condition' for eligibility in those cases where it applies. Regulation 84 requires that the nature of the disposal made by the local authority should conform with the following:

(a) the authority makes the disposal by conveying the freehold interest in the land, granting a lease for a term of not less than 125 years, or assigning their entire leasehold interest in the land; and
(b) where the interest disposed of is a lease, the authority estimate that not less than 90% of the capital value of the lease[1] has been, or is to be, received by the authority within one year after the date of the disposal.

1 'Capital value of a lease' is defined in LA(CF)R 1997, reg 80. In simple terms it is the authority's estimate of the aggregate of all the sums it is to receive from the grant of a lease, before and during the financial year in which the disposal is made and in all subsequent financial years. A discount formula is applied to payments in subsequent years, to give an indication of their net present value.

14.53 Wherever this standard disposal condition under reg 84 applies, it means that the authority can only benefit from the concession if it is to dispose of a significant land interest (the freehold, a lease of at least 125 years, or the entirety of its leasehold interest). If the disposal takes the form of the grant or assignment of a lease, the major part of the consideration received by the council must be in the form of a premium (or some other payment received within the first year) rather than a significant rental stream. In part, this is because the way these concessions work is to treat a capital receipt as reduced, and as a rental stream would not amount to such a receipt[1], no relief in respect of that element of consideration is needed. However, the fact that only a minimal allowance is made under LA(CF)R 1997, reg 84 for the percentage of rent, as opposed to that of any premium, is consistent with one of the original intentions of the legislation, namely encouragement to dispose of local authority assets. The majority of the following concessions would not apply if the authority is to retain a significant property interest in the land which it sells.

1 Local Government and Housing Act 1989, s 58(8).

14.54 By virtue of LA(CF)R 1997, reg 106, the concessions shown in the following chart apply equally to notional capital receipts which arise from the particular land transactions covered in the same way as they do to (money) capital receipts[1]. LA(CF)R 1997, regs 83 and 106(2) make special provision to ensure that authorities cannot benefit more than once, if the consideration is partly 'notional' and partly in money. LA(CF)R 1997, reg 82 makes special provision in cases where an authority receives more than one capital receipt in respect of their interest in a single asset. The following concessions would, in theory, benefit the treatment by a local authority of capital receipts obtained by a regulated company for the purpose of the Local Authorities (Companies) Order 1995, Pt V[2], although this is unlikely to be of any practical significance now that set aside on most non-HRA receipts has been reduced to nil.

1 See para **14.60**.
2 SI 1995/849.

14.55 Several of the following concessions entail a formal decision of the local authority concerned to pursue a particular course of action. In most of the following cases, the 'costs' which can be taken into account as a deduction from the capital receipt before calculating the set-aside obligation include not only actual expenditure, but the initial cost of a credit arrangement entered into for the relevant purposes. Where a deduction is permitted in respect of 'associated' or 'connected' costs, the precise terms of the allowance vary between individual concessions. In relation to the disposal of housing assets, the separate requirements for consent of the Secretary of State in relation to certain disposals (for example, under the Housing Act 1985, s 32 or s 43) must be observed.

3 CONCESSIONS IN LA(CF)R 1997, PT VIII OF POTENTIAL RELEVANCE TO THE DISPOSAL OF HOUSING ASSETS

14.56

Reg no	Assets disposed of and comments	Disposal condition	Reduction in receipt for the purpose of s 59
85–87 & 93	Unoccupied dwellings or hostels[1], where receipts applied to assist a 'regeneration project', provided the private sector meets at least 50% of the costs	reg 84	'qualifying receipts' treated as reduced by contribution to regeneration project
94 & 95	Land improved with the benefit of grant or other financial assistance from central government, the Urban Regeneration Agency (English Partnerships), or the Welsh Development Agency on terms which require the repayment of grant etc if the land is sold	–	the amount repayable to central government or the Agency concerned
96[2]	Land acquired (freehold or leasehold) no more than five years before the disposal takes place *other than* dwellings and hostels where receipts dealt with under reg 97(3) (ie reg 96 could apply to disposal of dwellings which have formerly been let on secure tenancies)	reg 84	costs of acquisition + administrative costs
97	Dwellings and certain hostels[3] disposed of by a local authority in England which have never been occupied under secure or introductory tenancies (unless reacquired following a right to buy sale)	reg 84 or shared ownership lease under reg 22(1)	costs of acquisition, or construction or conversion and land acquisition (if within three years preceding disposal) + costs of enhancement + administrative costs
98	Recently improved land. Applies to dwellings *other than those* where the receipts are subject to reg 97(3) (ie reg 98 could apply to dwellings which have formerly been let on secure tenancies). Expenditure on enhancement of land must have been incurred in the financial year of sale or two immediately preceding years. Does not cover major works such as construction, reclamation or laying out of land	reg 84 or shared ownership lease under reg 22(1)	costs of enhancement

Reg no	Assets disposed of and comments	Disposal condition	Reduction in receipt for the purpose of s 59
99	Disposal and replacement of specified types of land and buildings for specified categories of purposes (Sch 1 and reg 99(5)(b) and (c)), now mainly redundant, but available for disposal of housing land pursuant to a compulsory purchase order, hostels for the homeless and any instances where HRA land includes either tied accommodation or defective dwellings	reg 84	costs of acquiring new land and/or carrying out works + connected costs
100 & 101	Former new town dwellings and former residuary body assets, in cases where all or part of the consideration received from the disposal is due to be paid in respect of the original acquisition costs	–	amount payable out of receipts from sale
102	Compulsorily acquired land, where a planning decision or permission (made within 10 years of acquisition) has made the land more valuable, and the former owner makes a claim for compensation under the Land Compensation Act 1961, s 23 or s 25. The amount realised by the authority on sale is treated as reduced by the compensation payable	–	the amount of compensation payable, or estimated to be payable
103	Land which a local authority has prepared for development prior to sale by obtaining planning permission, preparing the land for development, acquiring interest or rights over the land or adjoining land, or by obtaining the release of a restrictive covenant, and has thereby increased the value of the land on sale	–	expenditure on preparing the land prior to sale excluding any which has been met out of central government or EC grants or subsidies + administrative costs
104	Dwelling disposed of by a local authority in Wales[4] to a former tenant in exchange for a flat[5] which the former tenant had acquired under the right to buy within the previous three years, where the former tenant would have difficulties in selling the flat due to the unlikelihood of any purchaser obtaining a mortgage on the property	reg 104(3) (c)–(e)	the price paid on the original right to buy sale of the flat + connected costs

Reg no	Assets disposed of and comments	Disposal condition	Reduction in receipt for the purpose of s 59
104A[6]	Sale by a local authority in England of a dwelling-house[7] which has been reacquired by the authority from an individual owner (not a corporate body), if the dwelling was formerly owned by a local authority, new town corporation, housing action trust or urban development corporation and the receipts from sale would otherwise be subject to s 59(2)(a) (75% set aside)	reg 84 or shared ownership lease under reg 22(1)	a proportion of the costs incurred by authority in the preceding financial year on reacquiring the dwelling-house

1 This regulation adopts the extended meaning of 'dwelling' in LA(CF)R 1997, reg 22(1) which includes certain hostels.
2 As amended by SI 1999/1852.
3 This regulation adopts the extended meaning of 'dwelling' in LA(CF)R 1997, reg 22(1) which includes certain hostels.
4 As a result of an amendment under SI 1999/501, this regulation now applies only to local authorities in Wales.
5 As defined in the Housing Act 1985, s 183.
6 Inserted by SI 1999/501.
7 As defined for the purpose of the Housing Act 1985, Part V.

G Reliefs in respect of notional capital receipts

1 INTRODUCTION TO PART IX OF THE LA(CF)R 1997

14.57 Paragraphs **14.13**ff explain the circumstances in which notional capital receipts under LGHA 1989, s 61 arise. In essence, the provisions of s 61 apply to barter transactions and cases where an authority foregoes payment of a capital receipt in favour of a payment directed to a third party. The various forms of consideration under s 61 which can lead to a notional capital receipt are referred to in LA(CF)R 1997, Pt IX as 'non-monetary consideration' and that expression is used here. (In certain cases the consideration may be in money, but paid to a third party at the authority's direction, rather than to the authority itself.)

14.58 In practice, the requirements concerning notional capital receipts can be of even greater concern to a local authority than those regarding the reserved part of money capital receipts; first because the transaction itself may not have led to any money payment to the authority with which the set-aside obligation can be satisfied and second, because notional receipts are not always immediately recognisable. The following concessions (other than LA(CF)R 1997, reg 106) specify that the amount to be set aside under LGHA 1989, s 61(4) in respect of the particular notional capital receipt covered is to be nil if the conditions for entitlement are met. Any money consideration would be subject to the normal rules under LGHA 1989, s 59, unless some other concession applies to it. The relief under reg 106 is calculated by reference to the amount of the reduction which would have been permitted if the consideration had been in money.

14.59 Transactions involving the disposal of land in return for non-monetary consideration are, of course, subject to the normal requirements in relation to 'best consideration reasonably obtainable' for the disposal of local authority land[1]. Provided any such non-monetary consideration has a commercial or monetary value, capable of being assessed by an appropriate expert, it is generally accepted[2] that the value of the non-monetary consideration can be taken into account in establishing whether the statutory requirements on land disposals would be fulfilled.

1 For example, under the Local Government Act 1972, s 123 or the Town and Country Planning Act 1990, s 233.
2 See, for example, *R v Middlesbrough Borough Council, ex p Frostree Ltd* (16 December 1988, unreported).

2 GENERAL APPLICATION OF CONCESSIONS UNDER LA(CF)R 1997, PT VIII TO NOTIONAL CAPITAL RECEIPTS

14.60 By virtue of LA(CF)R 1997, reg 106, all the concessions for the reduction of (money) capital receipts under LA(CF)R 1997, Pt VIII summarised in the chart at para **14.56** apply to cases where a local authority disposes of land for non-monetary consideration, giving rise to a notional capital receipt under LGHA 1989, s 61. If the consideration for a land disposal, had it been in money, would have benefited from a reduction before calculation of the set-aside requirements under LGHA 1989, s 59 by virtue of regulations:

reg 86	regeneration;
reg 94	repayment of money provided by Parliament;
reg 95	repayment of money provided by the Urban Regeneration Agency or Welsh Development Agency;
reg 96	disposal of recently acquired land;
reg 97	disposal of certain dwellings in England;
reg 98	disposal of recently improved land;
reg 99	disposal and replacement of land or buildings;
reg 100	disposal of former new town assets;
reg 101	disposal of former residuary body assets;
reg 102	compensation for former owners;
reg 103	preparation of land for sale;
reg 104	in Wales, dwellings in exchange for flats[1]; or
reg 104A	in England, certain reacquired dwelling-houses,

then reg 106 would allow an equal deduction to be made from any notional capital receipt received instead of payment in money.

1 Under which it appears to be envisaged that the consideration received by the authority would mainly be non-monetary in any event, being in the form of the surrender or assignment of the former tenant's flat.

14.61 LA(CF)R 1997, regs 83 and 106(2) make special provision to ensure that if the consideration received by the authority is partly in money and is partly non-monetary, there is no 'double benefit'.

3 CONCESSIONS IN LA(CF)R 1997, PT IX OF POTENTIAL RELEVANCE TO THE DISPOSAL OF HOUSING ASSETS

14.62

Reg no	Application
107	Disposal of land which has not been used for the purposes for which it is held for at least two years in exchange for land on which there are no buildings or other structures
108	Exchange of land with another local authority where the use of the land disposed of and intended use of that to be acquired fall within specified categories (which include defective dwellings, hostels and the purposes of the Housing Act 1985, Part II)
109	Disposal of land in exchange for housing nomination rights[1]
110	Disposal of land in exchange for works on land (known as 'dual use' with the private sector), unlikely to be relevant to housing land save in exceptional circumstances
111	Disposal of land in exchange for right to use land after enhancement (known as 'dual use' with the private sector), unlikely to be relevant to housing land save in exceptional circumstances
112	Disposal of land[2] under a private finance transaction for the purposes of reg 16, which is either eligible under regs 40, 41 or 42 or benefits from a supplementary credit approval (the PFT itself could not be for the provision of HRA housing[3])
113	Assignment or surrender of a lease in consideration of the lessor's promise not to sue for breach of a repairing covenant under that lease, unlikely to be relevant to housing land save in the exceptional circumstance where the authority held housing land on lease.

1 Since amendment of this regulation by SI 1999/1852 there is no longer any stipulation as to the location of the land on which the nomination rights are granted.

2 Regulation 112 also applies where an investment (for example, the types of company shares or other non-approved investments which continue to attract set-aside obligations) are disposed of by a local authority under a 'private finance transaction' of the specified kinds.

3 See paras **12.33** and **15.22**ff.

PART IV

Selected aspects of local government finance

CHAPTER 15

Private finance transactions and the Local Government (Contracts) Act 1997

A Background to the Private Finance Initiative

15.1 The Private Finance Initiative[1] was launched in the Chancellor's Autumn Statement in November 1992. The background to the Initiative was the Government's desire to encourage private sector investment in public sector projects whilst reducing the amounts which would count against the public sector borrowing requirement ('PSBR'). These broad aims appeared to carry cross-party support: indeed the drive to promote the PFI has gained further momentum since the change of government in 1997. The Initiative involved changes to rules known as the 'Ryrie Rules', created in 1981, under which nationalised industries had access to private finance. In essence, the Ryrie Rules normally resulted in private finance for nationalised industries and other public undertakings counting towards public expenditure limits and external financing limits. These rules had been elaborated by the Treasury and, by 1989, they had been publicly criticised as being incomprehensible and hampering private finance by the imposition of impossible hurdles. The changes announced in the Autumn Statement in 1992 entailed a relaxation of the Ryrie Rules which, in effect, redefined the expenditure which would count against the PSBR.

1 For a comprehensive consideration of the topic, see *Butterworths PFI Manual*.

15.2 The PFI was promoted as providing a means of reducing inefficiencies and cost overruns associated with public sector procurement. Part of the rationale entailed an assumption that greater efficiency and economy would result from introducing private sector management and innovative skills into the public sector and through an expansion of competition in certain areas.

15.3 The basic criteria for the PFI were said to be:

(a) value for money;
(b) transfer of risk to the private sector (subsequently modified to an appropriate allocation of risks between the public and private sectors); and
(c) open competition.

15.4 Whilst the PFI is said to take many forms, a hallmark of the Initiative has been an effort to encourage the private sector to accept combined responsibility for the provision of a capital asset needed by a public sector body (including its initial design) and the provision services[1] related to that asset, often over the useful life of the asset. This is said to create an internal commercial incentive for the private sector to manage risks effectively and to design the asset with the costs of running and maintaining it in mind. The approach is said to be based on the public sector procuring a 'capital intensive service' rather than the asset itself. The philosophy of the PFI entailed encouragement to the parties to move away from conventional property structures. The theory, at least, is that the public sector should not underwrite the costs of the arrangements, nor give any guarantee of the PFI contractor's liabilities.

1 Usually 'non-core' services, such as building maintenance, heating, lighting, cleaning and security, rather than medical or teaching services.

15.5 The Government dedicated considerable effort to promoting the Initiative. Led by HM Treasury, a non-governmental body known as the Private Finance Panel was established to promote the PFI and special units were set up within government departments. A wide body of largely administrative rather than statutory rules and guidance for PFI projects evolved and the Initiative was given further impetus following the general election in 1997. The Private Finance Panel was disbanded in 1997, following recommendations made by Malcolm Bates to the Paymaster General on 23 June 1997 (the 'Bates Review'). From 1 July 1997 the PFI was led, administratively, by a team in HM Treasury known as 'the Treasury Taskforce'[1].

1 Which was set up to have limited life span and was disbanded during 2000. Its policy responsibilities have now been transferred to a new office of HM Treasury known as the Office of Government Commerce ('OCG'), and its project advice function has been moved to a new public-private body known as Partnerships UK.

15.6 From 1992 onwards, with varying degrees of 'purity' in the application of its principles, the PFI was adopted in such areas as roads, prisons, government accommodation and hospitals. The 'PFI contractor' in these schemes is rarely a single entity. Consortia of companies have been formed to bid for most major PFI projects, typically comprising a facilities management company, specialist service providers, an information technology company and a builder or developer.

15.7 The contractual model used in most PFI schemes is that known as 'Design, Build, Finance and Operate' ('DBFO'), or a variant of this model. As the name suggests, a DBFO scheme entails the contractor designing, building, arranging finance for and then operating the asset concerned. In return, the procurer will normally pay regular fees to the contractor over the life of the arrangement. Those fees will cover not only the operating costs, but the costs of financing the scheme. DBFO arrangements had been in use by both the public and the private sector, long before the PFI was launched, but this type of contractual arrangement was considered to be particularly appropriate to delivering the PFI philosophy.

15.8 In a PFI project, the detailed contractual arrangements normally reflect the results of an analysis of the various risks which will arise throughout the life of a project (and on its termination) and of negotiations as to which party is best placed to accept and manage them or, in some cases, as to how those risks are to be shared[1]. In the 'non-local government' sectors, generally, there has always been a requirement that the assets which are provided or enhanced under the PFI arrangement can properly be regarded as 'off balance sheet' by the procuring body in accordance with accounting practice. (Similar requirements have been introduced for the main concession for local government projects as from April 2000[2].) There is usually a single payment stream made by the public body (or 'unitary charge') in which any element equivalent to 'rent' or other occupational charge cannot be separately identified (nonetheless, there is often an element of the payment known as an 'availability payment', which might be viewed as an equivalent of rent).

1 For example, the risk of additional costs arising from legislative changes which affect the PFI project may be divided between the parties on the basis of the kind of legislative change involved, or the risk of additional cost from a change in legislation of a particular type may be accepted up to a capped figure by one party, with the other party at risk for the whole or a percentage of the costs in excess of the cap. One function of the contract standardisation exercise undertaken by the Treasury Taskforce referred to in para **15.10** has been to endeavour to create some consistency in the allocation of risks in PFI projects undertaken in all areas of the public sector.
2 See para **15.34**.

15.9 Emphasis is placed on the need to avoid over-specifying the procurer's requirements, to concentrate on 'outputs' and results rather than the precise methods by which they are to be achieved. A major DBFO contract will typically last for at least 20–30 years. Commonly, there is a 'direct agreement' between the PFI contractor's funder and the procurer, which may give the funder 'step-in rights' to take over the contract(s) and/or the assets and/or to appoint another contractor in certain circumstances, such as the insolvency of the original contractor.

15.10 Most major PFI schemes in areas other than local government have always been subject to individual approval by the appropriate government department and/or the Treasury. Since the introduction of the arrangements for special revenue support for certain local government PFI schemes in 1996 a local authority wishing to benefit under these administrative arrangements must now make an application to central government. There was originally scope in other sectors to create unique structures designed to accommodate the particular nature and agreed allocation of the risks and other circumstances which apply in the individual case, whilst maintaining conformity with PFI principles. The form of local authority PFI projects, on the other hand, has always been more closely prescribed, due to the need to meet the requirements of the capital finance concessions described in this chapter. In recent years, the arrangements for local government PFI projects have been moving closer to those for other sectors. Government policy on the PFI has been to bring the application of the Initiative in all sectors, including local government, more closely into line. One aspect of this is the 'contract standardisation exercise' completed by the Treasury Taskforce[1] in 1999, which involved the production of 'generic' contract information and 'templates' for PFI schemes in all sectors. For local authorities, some unique features will inevitably persist on account of their legal nature, the means by which they obtain funding and their financial affairs are controlled, and the nature of the PFI schemes they are encouraged to pursue.

1 Now disbanded: see para **15.5**, n 1.

15.11 A special body was formed in 1996 to promote the PFI (and other types of public-private partnerships) in local government. The Public Private Partnerships Programme Limited, known as 'the 4Ps', was initiated by the local authority associations in England and Wales (the forerunners of the Local Government Association). The 4Ps was launched on 11 April 1996 with all-party support. Its express aim was to bring about increased investment in local services through PFI and other private-public sector partnerships. The intention was that such partnerships would enable capital-intensive services to be delivered to local communities in an enhanced and cost effective way. Unlike the Private Finance Panel, the 4Ps survived the reorganisation of PFI arrangements which followed the first Bates Review in 1997. 4Ps was intended to have an initial life of three years, but this has now been extended.

B Evolution of the PFI for local government and initial capital finance measures

15.12 The introduction of the PFI for local government was slower than that in other sectors. The local government financial system and the statutory framework governing local authority powers are quite distinct from those which apply to other parts of the public sector and did not lend themselves easily to PFI arrangements. Two particular reasons for the later introduction of the PFI into the local government sector were:

(a) concerns about the inadequacy of local government powers and the consequences for the private sector of involvement in a 'contract' which was found to be ultra vires the authority concerned, particularly in the wake of the decision of the Court of Appeal in *Crédit Suisse v Allerdale Borough Council*[1]; and
(b) the way in which most PFI schemes would fall to be treated under the local government capital finance regime: the DBFO arrangement, so heavily relied on in other sectors, would normally fall to be categorised as a 'credit arrangement' and bore striking similarities to the very type of scheme that LGHA 1989, Pt IV was designed to restrict.

Added to these legal factors, local government PFI schemes, whilst no less complex than those undertaken in other sectors, taken individually, tend to be of a lower value, such that the high transaction costs may be difficult to justify.

1 [1997] QB 306, [1996] 4 All ER 129, CA (see para **15.75**ff).

15.13 The government sought to deal with the second of these legal issues first, by introducing successive amendments to the subordinate legislation which provides the detailed workings of LGHA 1989, Pt IV described in earlier chapters, in order, eventually, to facilitate a modified form of the PFI as applied in other sectors. However, the first tentative steps to introduce the PFI into local government which are summarised below were barely recognisable as manifestations of the Initiative by those more familiar with the PFI in other sectors. Paragraphs **15.73–15.116** on the Local Government (Contracts) Act 1997 return to the question of how the concerns about local government vires have been addressed. In order to deal with the issue of whether local government PFI schemes can be a commercially attractive proposition, there has been a continual drive over the life of the Initiative, particularly by the Treasury Taskforce[1] and the 4Ps, to find ways of 'standardising' local authority PFI projects in order to reduce transaction costs and make them more easily replicable, and to find ways of 'bundling' together a number of small projects for broadly the same purposes.

1 Now disbanded: see para **15.5**, n 1.

1 INITIAL MEASURES

15.14 On 31 October 1994 the Department of the Environment announced an initial package of measures for local government said to be introduced under the Government's Private Finance Initiative. At this stage, the proposals were of a markedly different nature to those adopted in other parts of the public sector and appeared to amount to very little more than an extension of the then prevailing trends in central government's intentions for local government. The stated objective of the initial measures was to give authorities greater incentive to enter into joint ventures with the private sector and to dispose of assets. The proposals were described as including:

(a) fewer controls on local authority participation in private sector led companies;
(b) incentives for councils to dispose of assets that would be better managed and utilised by the private sector;
(c) more relaxed rules on leasing of commercial properties by local authorities.

15.15 The first of these proposals eventually led to the full implementation of Pt V of the Local Government & Housing 1989 concerning local authorities' participation in companies and industrial and provident societies, which by that time had been delayed for many years[1]. This first tranche of 'PFI measures' for local government was implemented on 1 April 1995 through the full commencement of LGHA 1989, Pt V[2] and the introduction of the LACO 1995[3] and on 1 April 1995 and 24 August 1995 through amendments to Local Authorities (Capital Finance) Regulations 1990 (now revoked)[4]. The LACO 1995 created the concept of 'regulated companies' and imposed propriety and financial controls on authorities' participation in them. The changes to Local Authorities (Capital Finance) Regulations 1990 (now revoked) involved measures to relax, but further complicate, some of the rules in relation to leases taken by local authorities; to encourage the disposal of certain company shares through reductions in the reserved part of the capital receipt; and to create a special concession for exchanges of non-housing land for company shares. The changes introduced in August 1995 included time-limited incentives to dispose of certain local authority assets such as car parks, crematoria and shops, by providing for a reduction in the then normal set-aside percentage on the receipts from their disposal.

1 See Chapter 16.
2 See the Local Government and Housing Act 1989 (Commencement No 17) Order 1995, SI 1995/841.
3 See the LACO 1995, SI 1995/849 as amended by SI 1996/621; see also Chapter 16, which deals with local authorities' interests in companies.
4 The Local Authorities (Capital Finance) Regulations 1990, SI 1990/432 (now revoked). The amendments referred to were made by the Local Authorities (Capital Finance and Approved Investments) (Amendment) Regulations 1995, SI 1995/850 and the Local Authorities (Capital Finance and Approved Investments) (Amendment No 2) Regulations 1995, SI 1995/1982.

2 ADDITIONAL MEASURES

15.16 On 30 March 1996[1] a second tranche of measures was introduced, which this time came a little closer to the PFI in other sectors. In particular, encouragement was given to authorities to enter into DBFO projects for the replacement or upgrading of existing local authority facilities through the introduction of special concessions in the Local Authorities (Capital Finance) Regulations 1990 (now revoked). Other changes introduced in March 1996 included various relaxations of the capital finance concessions then in force under the Local Authorities (Capital Finance) Regulations 1990 (now revoked) to:

(a) relax the 'in-and-out' concessions for certain land transactions, then contained in Local Authorities (Capital Finance) Regulations 1990 (now revoked), regs 15 and 18[2];
(b) relax the specified percentage for set aside on capital receipts from the disposal of certain local authority assets (farms and education assets);

(c) relax the rules on property leases; and
(d) encourage the dual use of facilities with the private sector[3].

1 See the Local Authorities (Capital Finance and Approved Investments) (Amendment) Regulations 1996, SI 1996/568 and further amendments under SI 1996/2121 with effect from 4 September 1996.
2 Now contained in LA(CF)R 1997, regs 96 and 99, subject to further revisions (see the chart at para **14.56**).
3 Dual use schemes were seen at the time as being an important feature of PFI for local government. See para **15.19**(a).

3 FURTHER MEASURES

15.17 On 31 October 1996[1] still further measures were introduced to extend DBFO arrangements to cover all local authority services, other than the provision of housing within the Housing Revenue Account. It is from these provisions that the current arrangements for 'private finance transactions', now contained in the LA(CF)R 1997, have evolved. It was also in October 1996 that the special arrangements for revenue support for certain DBFO schemes and equipment replacement schemes were first announced and described in a Guide issued by the Department of the Environment entitled 'The Private Finance Initiative for Local Authorities—an Explanatory Note'. This publication has subsequently been reissued and updated on several occasions and is referred to in this chapter as 'the PFI Guide' (the most recent edition at the time of writing was issued by the Department of the Environment, Transport and the Regions ('DETR') in September 1998). The Guide is important as a statement of the Government's policy on the provision of special revenue support, which is dealt with at para **15.61**ff.

1 See the Local Authorities (Capital Finance) (Amendment No 3) Regulations 1996, SI 1996/2539.

15.18 The following sections of this chapter concentrate on the concessions for DBFO schemes in the form of 'private finance transactions' as defined in LA(CF)R 1997, reg 16 ('PFTs'). However, it is to be noted that the original PFI Guide classified all of the following measures as being part of the PFI arrangements for local government:

(a) *Companies* The provisions for local authority interests in companies and other bodies as implemented under the Local Authorities (Companies) Order 1995[1], the capital finance concessions for exchanges of local authority non-housing assets for company shares[2] and the reduced rates of set aside on the receipts from the disposal of shares[3] (these last two items have largely been superseded by the abolition of set aside on most non-housing capital receipts under SI 1998/1937[4]).
(b) *Leases* The changes to the rules on leases taken by local authorities (under various statutory instruments which were made to amend the Local Authorities (Capital Finance) Regulations 1990 (now revoked)[5] from 1995 onwards).
(c) *Capital receipt concessions* Relaxations of the 'in-and-out' rules concerning receipts from certain land disposals[6], now largely redundant in view of the abolition of set aside on most non-housing receipts.
(d) *Notional capital receipt concessions* These concern dual use of facilities, now provided for in LA(CF)R 1997, regs 110 and 111[7], again largely superseded by the abolition of set aside on most non-housing receipts.
(e) *Incentives to dispose of local authority assets* The reductions in the rate of set aside on certain capital receipts for limited periods of time (for example, in relation to local authority farms, education assets, airport and bus company shares) were, again, superseded by the abolition of set aside on most non-housing receipts.

1 SI 1995/849 as amended by SI 1996/621 (see Chapter 16).
2 Currently contained in LA(CF)R 1997, reg 114, but apparently redundant as from 1 September 1998 when set aside was abolished on most categories of non-housing capital receipt (see para **14.26**) as it is inapplicable in those cases where set-aside obligations continue to apply: reg 114 explicitly excludes the disposal of housing land, and does not appear to be intended to apply to the *disposal* by a local authority of shares or other investments, in exchange for shares in a company.
3 See LA(CF)R 1997, reg 66(2)(a)–(g) (the percentages have since been reduced further to nil in these special cases by SI 1998/1937: see the table in para **14.30**).
4 See Chapter 14 and, in particular, para **14.26**.
5 SI 1990/432 (now revoked).
6 See para **15.16**(a) and the current provisions under LA(CF)R 1997, regs 96 and 99 referred to in Chapter 14.
7 See the chart at para **14.62**, and para **15.19**(a).

15.19 Two particular sets of concessions introduced under the banner of the PFI for local government, which need not amount to PFTs, warrant explanation here:

(a) *Dual uses schemes under LA(CF)R 1997, regs 110 and 111* As one facet of the PFI for local government, it was seen as important to remove obstacles created by the capital finance rules to the dual use of facilities by the public and private sectors. An example given in the original PFI Guide[1] was a case where the private sector would either improve an existing local authority facility such as a school sports hall and take over its management and operation, or build a new facility on local authority land. With the abolition of set aside on most non-housing capital receipts and notional capital receipts these arrangements are now of little practical significance.

(b) *The equipment replacement scheme under LA(CF)R 1997, regs 43–45* These concessions apply to certain credit arrangements arising from contracts for the repair and maintenance of heating or lighting systems, giving them a reduced initial cost, as described in para **12.107**ff. The original PFI Guide categorised such schemes as forming part of what was called 'Route 3', along with the schemes for certain buildings under LA(CF)R 1997, regs 41 and 42 (referred to in para **15.43**ff). These arrangements offer only limited assistance in the form of a reduction in the initial cost of the credit arrangement, and no special revenue support. It does not appear that they have been widely used by local authorities.

1 October 1996.

15.20 The following sections of this chapter set out the arrangements for PFTs, covering both the capital finance provisions and the administrative arrangements for revenue support for certain PFTs. Before looking at the technical provisions, it may be helpful to mention the types of schemes being pursued by authorities under these arrangements. Examples include: schools, libraries, museums, roads, leisure facilities, office accommodation, magistrates' courts, police stations, social services residential care homes, heating schemes, information technology and waste management and disposal facilities. In each case, the special arrangements apply to schemes under which the private sector contractor is responsible for both providing (or improving) capital assets and 'non-core' services[1] in relation to that asset.

1 For example, heating, lighting, repair and maintenance, cleaning and security.

15.21 The background to the special provisions for PFTs, in terms of the general controls on credit arrangements and the significance of 'initial cost', are described in Chapter 12, and the general provisions concerning credit approvals are described in Chapter 11. The following describes the position as it applies to England, noting the changes implemented as from April 2000. The legislative and administrative arrangements for local authorities in Wales differ in certain instances. Some of the distinctions are highlighted (see in particular the notes to paras **15.34**, **15.43** and **15.49** concerning regs 40–42.

C Definition of private finance transaction

15.22 LA(CF)R 1997, reg 16 contains the important basic definition of the expression 'private finance transaction'. Transactions which fit this basic definition *and* meet specified additional criteria, may take the benefit of LA(CF)R 1997, regs 40, 41 or 42, concerning three types of DBFO scheme. Certain PFTs also benefit from related concessions concerning leases and notional capital receipts. The definition of a PFT has been amended, substantially, on two occasions since the LA(CF)R 1997 were first introduced, making it considerably less restrictive, particularly as regards the scope for variation of the regular fees payable by the authority.

1 REQUIREMENTS

15.23 Under LA(CF)R 1997, reg 16 (as amended by SI 1998/371 and SI 1999/1852) a PFT is a transaction which fulfils all the following requirements:

(a) the consideration received by the authority under the transaction includes –
  (i) the provision or making available of a relevant asset[1] or the carrying out of works[2] for the purposes of, or in connection with, the discharge of a function of the authority; and
  (ii) the provision of services for the purposes of, or in connection with, the discharge of the same function;

(b) the authority do not give to any other person any indemnity or guarantee in respect of any liabilities of the person with whom they enter into the transaction (whether those liabilities are incurred in respect of the transaction or otherwise);

(c) the consideration given by the authority under the transaction includes the payment of fees by instalments at annual or more frequent intervals;

(d) the fees are determined in accordance with factors which in every case include –
  (i) standards attained in the performance of the services; or
  (ii) the extent, rate or intensity of use of the relevant asset, or, as the case may be, of the asset which is constructed, enhanced, replaced or installed under the transaction; and

(e) the first instalment of fees falls to be paid after the services have started to be provided.

1 'Asset' means any tangible asset, including (in particular) any land, house or other building, plant, machinery, vehicle, vessel, apparatus or equipment; or any computer software. 'Relevant asset' means any asset *apart from 'housing land'* (LA(CF)R 1997, reg 16(1)). Housing land is defined by reg 13 as being any land, house or other building in respect of which sums fall to be credited or debited in accordance with LGHA 1989, s 74 (duty to keep Housing Revenue Account).

2 'Works' means any works consisting of the construction, enhancement, replacement or installation of an asset, *apart from* works consisting of the construction of a house or other dwelling on housing land (reg 16(1)).

15.24 Through the definition of 'relevant assets' and 'works' (and 'housing land'), a significant exclusion from LA(CF)R 1997, reg 16 definition of a PFT is a scheme for the provision of dwellings on land held for the purposes of the Housing Revenue Account ('HRA') which an authority is required to maintain under LGHA 1989, s 74[1]. A PFI scheme for works *other than* the construction of a house or other dwelling on HRA land would be permissible (eg a PFI scheme for the improvement of council dwellings), as would a scheme involving the construction of houses on land which is not held for the purposes of the HRA (eg a housing project for non-HRA homes).

1 See Local Authorities (Capital Finance) Regulations 1997, regs 16(1) and 13.

2 TECHNICAL MEASURES ASSOCIATED WITH PRIVATE FINANCE TRANSACTIONS

15.25 Two important technical changes were made in connection with PFTs. First, under LA(CF)R 1997, reg 17, a PFT within reg 16 has been prescribed by the Secretary of State as a new category of credit arrangement under LGHA 1989, s 48(1)(c), if it would not otherwise amount to a credit arrangement under s 48(1)(a) or (b) of that Act (concerning leases and extended credit respectively[1]). This measure was included to remove any doubt that all PFTs *are* credit arrangements and are subject to the new provisions, so that, in eligible cases, they can benefit from the separate administrative arrangements for revenue support described at paras **15.61–15.72**.

1 See further Chapter 12 on credit arrangements. Most PFTs will, in fact, be credit arrangements within the LGHA 1989, s 48(1)(b) and not s 48(1)(c).

15.26 The second technical measure is that in reg 8. This provides that expenditure under a PFT within LA(CF)R 1997, reg 16 is to be treated as expenditure for capital purposes (if it would not otherwise be treated in this way). This is to ensure that a PFT is not beyond an authority's powers under LGHA 1989, s 50(1), which prohibits a local authority from entering into a credit arrangement for any purpose unless, if it incurred expenditure for that purpose, that expenditure would be expenditure for capital purposes. This measure was considered necessary in the light of the emphasis placed in PFI arrangements on the authority's payment relating to the provision of services rather than simply to the provision of capital assets. Regulation 8 is considered to have the incidental effect of enabling a local authority to make payments in respect of a PFT out of usable capital receipts under LGHA 1989, s 60(2)(a)[1].

1 Subject to this being acceptable in accordance with proper accounting practices.

D Reduced or nil initial cost for private finance transactions

1 LA(CF)R 1997, REG 40: TRANSACTIONS INVOLVING THE PROCUREMENT OF CAPITAL ASSETS AND SERVICES

15.27 The most important of the capital finance concessions for DBFO schemes entered into by a local authority is that under LA(CF)R 1997, reg 40. Most (if not all) of the local government PFI projects pursued to date which have sought special revenue support have followed this concession. In order to be eligible, the initial requirement is that the arrangements must fit the criteria for a PFT[1].

1 See para **15.22**ff.

(a) Regulation 40 prior to 1 April 2000

(i) Criteria

15.28 For projects entered into prior to 1 April 2000, the further criteria under LA(CF)R 1997, reg 40 comprise:

(a) the services provided by the contractor in relation to the asset provided under the transaction must be more comprehensive than those needed to fulfil the basic requirements for a PFT. They must consist of, or include:

> '... maintaining and repairing the asset and doing everything necessary to ensure that the asset can be used in safety and comfort and in accordance with any requirements specified by the authority';

and

(b) the 'contract structure test' must be met immediately before the date on which the authority enters into the transaction.

(ii) The contract structure test

15.29 For projects entered into prior to 1 April 2000, the contract structure test has been an important feature of local government PFI. It has been described as a measure of the risk transferred to the private sector through the mechanism of the variable fee (as supposedly offering an assessment of the scope for that fee to be reduced on account of poor performance by the contractor, and/or on account of the use of the assets not reaching expected levels). To be eligible under LA(CF)R 1997, reg 40 in its form up to 31 March 2000, the payment structure has to pass a test[1] which entails a comparison between:

(1) *Amount A* the 'initial cost' of the credit arrangement (assuming no exemption under reg 40) and on the assumption that the expected level of performance and/or usage is achieved; and

(2) *Amount B* the 'initial cost' (again assuming no exemption under reg 40) but on the assumption that the performance and/or use fall below the expected level and that, without there being a breach of any term of the agreement[2], the fee payable by the authority is reduced to the minimum provided for under the terms of the contract and assuming that the minimum extent, rate, or intensity of use of the asset is 80% of the expected level.

1 Based on estimates made by the local authority itself, immediately before the date on which they enter into the transaction.

2 It is intended that Amount B should be calculated on the assumption of the poorest level of performance possible, but without there being a breach of the agreement *of a kind or degree which would warrant termination of the contract*, ie on the assumption that the contract continues to run despite unsatisfactory contractor performance. The DETR's guidance on this is set out in the PFI Booklet, Appendix 1, para 37.

15.30 In order to pass the contract structure test, Amount B, the 'worst case payment', must be no greater than 80% of Amount A, the expected level of payment. To put this another way, at least 20% of the total payments (in cash and in kind) which the authority is to make to the contractor must be variable, dependent upon the contractor's performance and/or the usage factors. The set assumed level of 80% for minimum usage was stipulated in order to prevent the test being satisfied through applying improbably low assumptions about the level of use.

15.31 Capital assets transferred to the contractor (for example, in order to diminish the regular charges made to the authority), or any lump sum payments by the authority, would be taken into account in estimating both Amount A and Amount B so that, in principle at least, it would be far more difficult to demonstrate that the contract structure test is satisfied if a significant part of the consideration to be paid or given by the authority either includes non-variable payments, or is in a non-monetary form.

15.32 The contract structure test is based on estimates made by the local authority itself, immediately before the date on which the transaction is entered into[1].

1 See LA(CF)R 1997, reg 40(2)(b). The LGHA 1989, s 49 contains the general rules on the calculation of initial cost of credit arrangements to be used in assessing Amounts A and B; s 49(1) requires that the calculation be based on an estimate made by the authority 'at the time the credit arrangement comes into being'. Once it is established that a PFT conforms with LA(CF)R 1997, reg 40, LGHA 1989, s 49(2) would not apply to it.

15.33 It is to be noted that prior to 1 April 2000 a scheme might meet the tests under reg 40 in its then current form and qualify for nil initial cost treatment (and the special revenue support referred to at paras **15.61–15.72**) notwithstanding the fact that, in terms of the relevant accounting standards, the assets would clearly fall to be regarded as being 'on' the authority's balance sheet. As from April 2000 this will no longer be the case, at least as regards eligibility for nil initial cost treatment under reg 40[1].

1 Although the authority may instead apply for a supplementary credit approval to provide the necessary credit approval (as the contract would have a significant 'initial cost'), and to trigger special revenue support in respect of a scheme which fails the new 'off balance sheet' test under reg 40: see para **15.72**.

(b) Regulation 40 as from 1 April 2000

15.34 As from 1 April 2000[1] for local authorities in England[2] LA(CF)R 1997, reg 40 has been replaced in its entirety to introduce new provisions more closely in line with the accounting standards tests for 'off balance sheet treatment' which have been used in relation to PFI schemes undertaken in other parts of the public sector since the inception of the PFI.

1 See letter from the DETR to Chief Executives and others in local government dated 23 December 1999 and the enclosed note on the amendments to be introduced under SI 1999/3423.
2 Separate provision is made for Wales by SI 2000/992, under which LA(CF)R 1997, regs 40–42 are substituted by a new reg 40, the effect of which is that all PFTs within reg 16 are eligible for nil initial cost treatment.

15.35 By virtue of amendments to the LA(CF)R 1997 introduced by SI 1999/3423 for local authorities in England, as from 1 April 2000 reg 40 provides:

(1) A credit arrangement which is a private finance transaction shall be excluded from LGHA 1989, s 49(2), and the initial cost and the cost at any time of the arrangement shall be nil, if the authority determine that in accordance with proper practices no item, other than an item specified in para (2), is required to be recognised as an asset in any balance sheet they are required to prepare in accordance with such practices for the financial year in which the credit arrangement comes into being with respect to property which is either:

(a) provided or made available under the transaction, or

(b) constructed, enhanced, replaced or installed under the transaction.

(2) The following items are specified for the purposes of paragraph (1):

(a) any item relating to a contribution by the authority of an asset to any person with whom they enter into the private finance transaction in return for a reduction in the consideration payable by the authority to that person under the transaction; or

(b) any item relating to an asset to be provided or made available under the private finance transaction by any person which is transferred into the ownership of the authority, whether or not upon payment of any consideration by the authority, at the end of the contract term relating to the transaction.

15.36 Thus, for local authorities in England, eligibility for nil initial cost treatment for a PFT under LA(CF)R 1997, reg 40, as from April 2000, depends on accounting practices for the treatment of assets as being on, or off, the authority's balance sheet[1]. 'Proper practices' are defined in LGHA 1989, s 66(4) and are currently contained in the Code of Practice on Local Authority Accounting in Great Britain—A Statement of Recommended Practice, issued annually by the Chartered Institute of Public Finance and Accountancy ('CIPFA'). The 2000 edition, at Appendix E, incorporates a summary of the issues raised in Application Note F 'Private Finance Initiative and similar contacts as an amendment to FRS5—Reporting the substance of transactions', issued by the Accounting Standards Board on 10 September 1998. This sets out the approach to accounting for PFI contracts which is now, in effect, adopted for local authority accounting purposes by virtue of the new reg 40, as from 1 April 2000.

1 That is, whether an asset of any property is to be 'recognised' in a balance sheet of the authority for accounting purposes.

(i) Consequences if the criteria under reg 40 are met

15.37 Provided the criteria for LA(CF)R 1997, reg 40 are met (whether in their pre- or post- April 2000 form dependent upon when the contracts are executed), the initial cost of the credit arrangement created by the PFT will be nil. Thus, the authority need not provide credit cover in order to enter into the arrangement.

(ii) Consequences of variation of a PFT under reg 40

15.38 If the PFT is subsequently varied (whether by the making of a new contract or otherwise[1]), it would be necessary to reapply the tests in LA(CF)R 1997, regs 16 and 40 to establish whether or not nil initial cost treatment under reg 40 continues to apply.

1 See LGHA 1989, s 51(1) and (2) regarding the meaning of variation for the purpose of these requirements, and para **12.112**ff.

15.39 LGHA 1989, s 51 deals with the variation of credit arrangements. If the effect of the variation is such that, had the revision been part of the arrangement at the outset, the initial cost would have greater than it was, then it is necessary to calculate the 'adjusted cost' of the credit arrangement. This would apply if, following the variation, any one of the criteria in LA(CF)R 1997, reg 16 or 40 is no longer satisfied, so that the arrangement would no longer benefit from a nil initial cost.

15.40 The detailed rules for calculating the adjusted cost of a PFT following variation are contained in LA(CF)R 1997, regs 46–50[1], of which the provisions of most general relevance are likely to be those of reg 47[2]. In effect, 'adjusted cost' under reg 47 requires a recalculation of the amount of consideration given by the authority under the arrangement going back to its inception (based on the amounts actually paid by the authority up to the year of variation), combined with the discounted value of all payments to be made in future years under the terms as varied.

1 The general rules for calculation of adjusted cost contained in the LGHA 1989, s 51(5) and (6) do not apply to credit arrangements which are excluded from the 'initial cost' formula in LGHA 1989, s 49(2) by regulations made under s 49(3): see the LGHA 1989, s 51(7) (and see para **12.125**ff). LA(CF)R 1997, reg 51 deals with the cost at any time following variation of a credit arrangement which is excluded from s 49(2).
2 See para **12.130**.

15.41 LGHA, s 51(4) deals with the amount of credit cover needed if a credit arrangement is varied under s 51(1), which would often produce a lower figure than the 'adjusted cost'[1]. Section 51(3) prohibits a local authority from agreeing to a variation (which increases the initial cost as provided for in s 51(1)) if to do so would lead the combined value of (a) the authority's outstanding borrowing, and (b) the aggregate cost of all its credit arrangements to exceed its 'aggregate credit limit' for the time being under LGHA, s 62[2].

1 See para **12.115**ff. The amount of credit cover needed in this instance would often be equal to the difference between the total amount of the consideration paid and payable with and without variation under LGHA, s 51(4)(a): s 51(4) provides for the required amount of credit cover to equate to the *lower* of the two figures produced under paras (a) and (b) of that subsection.
2 See paras **11.29** and **12.121**.

(iii) Importance of reg 40

15.42 The concession created by LA(CF)R 1997, reg 40, together with the special administrative arrangements for revenue support set out in the PFI Guide[1] summarised below, were described in the original PFI Guide[2] as 'Route 1'. This Route constitutes the main concession pursued in most local government PFI schemes.

1 September 1998.
2 October 1996.

2 LA(CF)R 1997, REG 41: TRANSACTIONS INVOLVING THE REPLACEMENT OR ENHANCEMENT OF BUILDINGS AND PROCUREMENT OF HEATING SERVICES

(a) Spend to save schemes

15.43 LA(CF)R 1997, reg 41, and the concession under LA(CF)R 1997, reg 42 are often considered together. For local authorities in England[1], these regulations provide less extensive concessions for DBFO arrangements than that under LA(CF)R 1997, reg 40 and were described by the DETR as 'spend to save schemes'. Regulation 41 concerns replacement or enhancement of certain buildings. Replacement may be undertaken on the original site or elsewhere. The transaction must satisfy all the criteria for a private finance transaction[2].

1 For local authorities in Wales, as from 1 April 2000, LA(CF)R 1997, regs 41 and 42 have been superseded by a new reg 40, by virtue of SI 2000/992. See para **15.34**, n 2.
2 See para **15.22**ff.

(b) Qualifying purposes

15.44 LA(CF)R 1997, reg 41 applies to buildings only within defined categories of use, described as 'qualifying purposes'. These comprise categories 1 to 6 and 8 and 9 of LA(CF)R 1997, Sch 1, and encompass a wide range of uses of land relevant to the discharge of local government functions:

(1) the fire service or police service, the magistrates' courts services, the probation service, or the functions conferred on the authority under the Civil Defence Act 1948, s 2;
(2) a hostel for the homeless, or the social services functions of a local authority within the meaning given to that expression in the Local Authority Social Services Act 1970;
(3) a school, or an institution providing further education, or training, or education for adults;
(4) an archive, a library, a museum or an art gallery;
(5) a community hall, a conference centre, a theatre, a concert hall, a leisure centre or other indoor recreation, a swimming pool, or a pier;
(6) a bus station, a vehicle depot, a garage, or a public park for cars, caravans, lorries or other vehicles;
(7) ...[1]
(8) an industrial unit, a dog compound, a market, a public convenience, or the disposal of waste, or (except so far as falling within any other category) a workshop, a kitchen, a warehouse, or the storage of goods or equipment;
(9) a town hall, or local authority offices (other than offices which fall within any other category);
(10) ...[2]

1 This paragraph in Sch 1 is not a 'qualifying purpose' under reg 41.
2 This paragraph in Sch 1 is not a 'qualifying purpose' under reg 41.

15.45 The services to be provided by the contractor under LA(CF)R 1997, reg 41 need not be as extensive as those required to qualify under LA(CF)R 1997, reg 40 in its form prior to amendment in April 2000, but they must include heating services, which consist of or include:

> '... maintaining and repairing the system for heating the new building and providing for the supply of gas, electricity and fuel required for such heating.'

15.46 Further conditions for eligibility under LA(CF)R 1997, reg 41 are that:

(a) LA(CF)R 1997, reg 40 does not apply;
(b) the building which the authority wishes to replace or improve ('the relevant building') must be in use by the authority for a qualifying purpose at the time of the decision referred to in (e) below[1];
(c) the relevant building cannot be situated on housing revenue account land[2];
(d) the authority must hold the freehold interest in the relevant building, or a leasehold interest granted for a term of not less than 99 years[3];
(e) the local authority must have made a single decision, within five years preceding the date on which they enter into the PFT either to:

(i) *replace* the relevant building, ie to cease to use the relevant building and to use a different building for a 'corresponding purpose' (which means the same qualifying purpose[4] as the relevant building or a different qualifying purpose within the same category); or

(ii) *improve* the relevant building, ie to carry out works for the enhancement of the relevant building and to continue to use that building after completion of the works for a corresponding purpose.

1 This is implicit from the definition in LA(CF)R 1997, reg 41(1) of 'relevant building' and the terms of reg 41(3)(b).
2 See the definition of 'relevant building' in LA(CF)R 1997, reg 41(1).
3 See the definition of 'relevant building' in LA(CF)R 1997, reg 41(1).
4 That is, a purpose within paras 1–6, 8 or 9 of LA(CF)R 1997, Sch 1.

15.47 If the conditions for eligibility are met, the benefits of LA(CF)R 1997, reg 41 are that the initial cost of the credit arrangement is reduced by the greater of:

(a) 30%; and
(b) the capitalised value of the average annual running costs of the same services[1] in respect of the original building over the preceding five years[2].

1 That is, the same services as those which are to be provided by the contractor under the PFT.
2 See LA(CF)R 1997, reg 41(5) for the detailed calculation of the permitted deduction.

15.48 By virtue of LA(CF)R 1997, reg 41(7), in calculating the 'initial costs', non-monetary consideration given by the authority, eg land transferred to a contractor in order to reduce the authority's regular fees, is to be disregarded. In the absence of this exclusion, the value of any land transfers to the contractor (which authorities were encouraged to make under these arrangements) would have the effect of increasing the initial cost.

3 LA(CF)R 1997, REG 42: TRANSACTIONS INVOLVING THE PROCUREMENT OF A BUILDING AND HEATING SERVICES

15.49 The second of the concessions for 'spend to save' DBFO schemes for local authorities in England[1] under LA(CF)R 1997, reg 42 again offers a less extensive concession than reg 40. Regulation 42 concerns the provision of *new* buildings (rather than the replacement or improvement of an existing building). Buildings to be used for the same categories of 'qualifying purposes'[2] as those eligible under LA(CF)R 1997, reg 41 are covered. The arrangements must fulfil the basic criteria for a PFT[3]. Again, the services required to be provided by the contractor under the PFT are not as extensive as those under reg 40, but they must *include* the heating services described in connection with reg 41[4]. It is a requirement of eligibility under reg 42 that neither reg 40 nor reg 41 apply to the arrangement.

1 See para **15.43**, n 1 regarding Wales.
2 Categories 1–6 and 8 and 9 of LA(CF)R 1997, Sch 1: see para **15.44**.
3 See para **15.22**ff.
4 See para **15.43**.

15.50 If the criteria are met, the consequence of eligibility under LA(CF)R 1997, reg 42 is that the initial cost of the credit arrangement is reduced by 30%. Again, non-monetary consideration is disregarded in calculating the initial cost[1].

1 See Local Authorities (Capital Finance) Regulations 1997, reg 42(6).

15.51 LA(CF)R 1997, regs 41 and 42 (together with the 'equipment replacement scheme' under LA(CF)R 1997, regs 43–45[1]) were described as 'Route 3' in the original (October 1996) PFI Guide. In all these cases, there are no special administrative arrangements for revenue support. It is, however, conceivable that a PFT which conforms with reg 41 or 42 might qualify for assistance by way of a 'non-scoring credit approval' ('NSCA') under the wholly discretionary arrangements (described in the original PFI Guide as 'Route 2') or under new arrangements to issue supplementary credit approvals (under the general discretion of the Secretary of State under LGHA 1989, s 54[2]), although at the time of writing there is no practical experience of this[3].

1 See para **12.107**ff (to be eligible under LA(CF)R 1997, regs 43–45 the arrangements need not meet the criteria for a PFT under LA(CF)R 1997, reg 16).
2 See para **11.14**ff.
3 See paras **15.61–15.72** on administrative arrangements for revenue support.

E Leases as part of a private finance transaction

15.52 LA(CF)R 1997, regs 28 and 37 make special provision for cases where, as part of a private finance transaction within LA(CF)R 1997, reg 16, the local authority takes a lease of land. This might occur where the local authority transfers to the PFI contractor its interest in the land on which a new facility is to be constructed, or where a building is constructed on a new site, and the authority either takes a lease back, or a lease of the asset, after construction.

15.53 LA(CF)R 1997, reg 28 deals with leases under PFTs of which the initial cost falls to be determined under LA(CF)R 1997, reg 40. In this case, the lease will also have an initial cost of nil.

15.54 LA(CF)R 1997, reg 37 deals with leases taken as part of a PFT where the initial cost falls to be determined under reg 41 or 42. For a lease taken as part of an arrangement which benefits under reg 41, the initial cost of the lease is reduced by the *greater* of 30% or any amount by which the 'relevant deduction' in respect of annual running costs of the old buildings exceeded the full (undiscounted) initial costs of the PFT under reg 41. For leases taken under a PFT which falls within reg 42, the initial cost is reduced by 30%.

15.55 It is unclear how such a lease would relate to the requirements of LA(CF)R 1997, reg 16, but it would appear that any rent paid by the authority in respect of the lease might be quite distinct from the regular fees envisaged under reg 16(2)(c). The requirement under reg 16(2)(c) is that the authority's consideration should 'include' the regular fees, not that fees must be the *only* consideration given by the authority under the arrangement. Nor is it entirely clear how the existence of a rental stream would fall to be treated under the contract structure test in LA(CF)R 1997, reg 40 in its form prior to 1 April 2000, although the apparent intention would be that such a rent should be brought into account (as part of the overall consideration given by the authority under the arrangement) when assessing whether the required level of variation could occur, otherwise the intended effect of reg 40 would be undermined.

15.56 Of more significance, perhaps, is what the effects of such a lease might be on the new 'off balance sheet' accounting test under LA(CF)R 1997, reg 40 as from

1 April 2000. Whilst legal title to property, for example under a lease, is not necessarily determinative of the balance sheet treatment of the asset concerned, the terms of any lease to the local authority, taken together with other factors, might give rise to an inference that the asset should be regarded for accounting purposes as being 'on balance sheet' for the authority. Whilst reg 40 in its amended form as from April 2000 excludes the effects of assets which are transferred into the ownership of the authority on the *expiry* of the PFT in establishing the proper accounting treatment under reg 40(2)(b), there is no such exclusion in relation to assets transferred to the authority *during the life of* the arrangement. This is an issue which would need to be considered in the light of all the circumstances of an individual case, but the accounting implications may constitute a disincentive to the authority taking a lease (or lease back).

F Notional capital receipts in connection with private finance transactions

15.57 The guidance to local authorities on PFI transactions contained in the PFI Guide gives encouragement to local authorities to transfer assets to the contractor in exchange for a reduction in the regular charges payable by the authority[1]. Prior to the abolition of set-aside on most non-housing receipts in September 1998[2], this would normally have given rise to a notional capital receipt under the LGHA 1989, s 61[3] leading to an obligation to make set-aside provision (and, in general, continues to do so, if housing land within the HRA or certain kinds of investment are transferred to the contractor).

1 See, for example, the PFI Guide, Appendix 3, para 7(b) concerning the value for money criteria for eligibility for PFI credits in the form of 'notional credit approvals' and 'non-scoring credit approvals'.
2 By SI 1998/1937: see para **14.26**.
3 See para **14.13**ff.

15.58 To deal with this, LA(CF)R 1997, reg 112 (as amended by SI 1997/848) provides for there to be nil set-aside under LGHA 1989, s 61(4) in respect of notional capital receipts which arise where a local authority disposes of any asset, investment or other property in connection with a PFT of which the initial cost falls to be determined under LA(CF)R 1997, regs 40, 41 or 42[1]. Regulation 112 also applies where the PFT is entered into in reliance on a supplementary credit approval which applies for the purposes of the PFI and for no other purposes. This is to accommodate notional capital receipts which might arise in connection with a scheme under the wholly discretionary arrangements to provide revenue support (originally known as 'Route 2') which is not, strictly, dependent on eligibility under the capital finance regulations[2].

1 In calculating the initial cost of credit arrangements under regs 41 and 42 the value of this non-monetary consideration is disregarded (see regs 41(7) and 42(6) and paras **15.48** and **15.50**.
2 See para **15.69**. In relation to the new LA(CF)R 1997, reg 40 in force as from April 2000 (by virtue of SI 1999/3423), the revised administrative arrangements for revenue support continue to envisage that in certain exceptional cases, supplementary credit approval might be given for schemes which do not meet the accounting tests under the new reg 40. See note enclosed with letter from the DETR to Chief Executives and others in local government dated 23 December 1999 regarding changes to the revenue support arrangements in the light of the amendments to reg 40.

15.59 Since 1 September 1998, most notional capital receipts should not present a difficulty such that LA(CF)R 1997, reg 112 would need to be relied up. However, it is available to assist in a case where a notional capital receipt subject to set-aside at a rate greater than nil would arise under a PFT, because the authority is to transfer housing land, certain company shares or other non-approved investments to the contractor, and in return receives non-monetary consideration (for example, a reduction in the regular fees).

G Special arrangements for 'debt-free' authorities

15.60 As described in the next section, one method of providing revenue support (under what was formerly known as 'Route 2', and under the new arrangements implemented in April 2000) is through the issue of a supplementary credit approval under the LGHA 1989, s 54[1]. The use of a supplementary credit approval by a debt-free authority[2] would normally have the effect of increasing the credit ceiling and putting the authority's debt-free status in jeopardy. In order to prevent any unintentional penalty for authorities who are 'debt free', use has been made of the concept of an 'excluded credit arrangement' under the LGHA 1989, Sch 3, para 11(2). One special feature of an 'excluded credit arrangement' is that the use of a credit approval to provide credit cover for it has no effect on the credit ceiling[3]. Under LA(CF)R 1997, reg 123, if a debt-free authority (as defined in reg 123(3)) makes a determination to use a supplementary credit approval which has been issued to it specifically in relation to a PFT, the credit arrangement is to be an 'excluded credit arrangement', and thus the use of the supplementary credit approval (formerly NSCA) will not result in any increase in the authority's credit ceiling, or pose a threat to its debt-free status.

1 Originally given the special title of a 'non scoring credit approval' (or 'NSCA') but as from April 2000 simply referred to as a supplementary credit approval.
2 'Debt-free authorities' (defined in different ways for different purposes) benefit from special treatment in a number of respects under the capital finance system; for example, most of their capital receipts have always been 100% usable: see para **10.28**ff. For the purpose of LA(CF)R 1997, reg 123, the term 'debt-free' would apply to local authorities whose credit ceiling is either nil or a negative amount at the beginning of the financial year in which the credit arrangement (ie the PFT) is entered into and who have no money outstanding by way of borrowing, other than 'disregarded borrowing' within the meaning of SI 1997/319, reg 65 (see reg 123(3)).
3 See Local Government and Housing Act 1989, Sch 3, para 11(2).

H Administration of revenue support for local government PFI schemes

15.61 As further encouragement to authorities to pursue PFI transactions, in October 1996 the Government announced special administrative arrangements for revenue support for certain PFTs. Treating selected kinds of PFTs as having a nil initial cost overcame one disincentive to their use, in the form of the limits on credit arrangements, but it shifted the burden of the on-going costs of the arrangement onto authorities' revenue resources. It also meant that the normal administrative arrangements for giving revenue support towards the financing costs of capital schemes over successive years did not apply. As no credit cover is needed for a credit arrangement with a nil initial cost (as under LA(CF)R 1997, reg 40), normally there would be no question of any credit approval being issued, so that the usual mechanism to trigger revenue support through Revenue Support Grant[1] would be absent. The means by which special revenue support for certain local government

PFI schemes is triggered, in the form of notional credit approval (or supplementary credit approval) and non-scoring credit approval, are collectively known as 'PFI credits'. The following summarises the administrative arrangements for local authorities in England. Separate administrative arrangements have been made to provide revenue support for PFI schemes undertaken by local authorities in Wales.

1 See para **11.27**.

15.62 In all cases, a PFI credit is only made available to an authority if a successful application is made to a government department. Publications (such as the PFI Guide) and letters circulated by the DETR provide important information on the administrative arrangements and policy for the issue of PFI credits which are primarily based on the exercise of discretion by the Secretary of State, rather than any statutory code. These documents describe the overall prioritisation criteria used by individual government departments (the DETR, the Department for Education and Employment, the Department of Health, the Home Office and the Lord Chancellor's Department) for local government PFI schemes within their sphere of responsibility[1]. The PFI Guide[2] gives details of the criteria for the issue of PFI credits for individual projects and the means by which the amount of credit is calculated. The basic criteria for the issue of all PFI credits include checks on the proportion of capital investment to total costs and value for money assessments.

1 At the time of writing, the guidance on prioritisation of schemes by individual government departments was most recently set out in a letter from the DETR to Chief Executives and Chief Finance Officers in local authorities dated 21 December 1998 headed 'Revised Criteria for Allocation of PFI Credits'.

2 See the 'Local Government and the Private Finance Initiative—an explanatory note on PFI and Public/Private Partnerships in local government' dated September 1998 ('the PFI Guide' current at the time of writing) at Section 4 and Appendix 3.

15.63 An administrative framework has grown up within central government to deal with PFI projects in local government. As a result of recommendations made under the Bates Review[1], the administrative arrangements for local government PFI projects were 'streamlined'. In November 1997 arrangements were announced under which an early indication would be given of those schemes which would, in principle, attract funding from central government in the form of revenue support, with the aim of enabling private sector parties contemplating bidding for local government PFI projects to concentrate their efforts on those schemes with a good prospect of success. Local authorities are now required to submit an outline business case concerning their proposal to the appropriate government department before advertising it and inviting interest in the Official Journal of the European Community[2]. Projects are reviewed by a group chaired by the Office of Government Commerce[3] known as the 'Project Review Group' and involving the sponsoring government department and attended by representatives of the 4Ps[4], which meets at regular intervals to consider schemes for which applications for revenue support have been made by authorities. Following these meetings, lists are published to inform the private sector of those schemes which can be expected to receive revenue support, if the proposals proceed to signed contracts.

1 Malcolm Bates's review of the PFI which reported to the Paymaster General on 23 June 1997.

2 Most local government PFI projects meet the financial thresholds and other criteria under the EC public procurement directives and UK regulations (SI 1991/2680 (works contracts), SI 1993/3228 (services contracts) and 1995/201 (supply contracts)), which impose requirements for advertisement in the Official Journal.

3 A new office of HM Treasury which has taken over this role from the Treasury Taskforce (see para **15.5**).

4 See para **15.11**.

15.64 As PFI credits are not actually issued until *after* PFI contracts are signed, the administrative arrangements outlined in the PFI Guide indicate that local authorities will receive 'promissory notes' for eligible schemes once cost estimates can be provided, in order to give them sufficient certainty to execute the PFI contracts. In practice, to date this support has been provided in the form of Special Grant (under the Local Government Finance Act 1988, s 88B) as this offers a far more flexible means of catering for the costs in the initial years of a scheme than the Revenue Support Grant system (and in view of the prospect of wider changes being made to the revenue support system).

15.65 A total of £3 billion in PFI credits for local government schemes has been made available by central government over the financial years 1997/98 to 2001/02, of which over two billion had been allocated by the end of 1999. On 1 August 2000, as part of the Spending Review 2000, the Government announced a further £4 billion of funding for local government PFI schemes for the years 2001/02–2003/04. The existence of special revenue support for local government PFI schemes has provided a considerable incentive to authorities to pursue capital schemes by means of a PFI proposal, rather than under less complex arrangements such as borrowing.

I NOTIONAL CREDIT APPROVAL (ROUTE 1)

15.66 The special administrative arrangements for revenue support for PFTs under LA(CF)R 1997, reg 40 (described by the Department of the Environment in the original PFI Guide[1] as 'Route 1') tackle the issues described in para **15.61** by creating the concept of 'notional credit approvals' ('NCAs') which reflect the *capital* component of the authority's payments under the PFT arrangements. NCAs trigger an increase in the capital finance component of authorities' standard spending assessment, in turn increasing Revenue Support Grant, in a similar way to 'conventional' credit approvals under LGHA 1989, ss 53 and 54.

1 October 1996.

15.67 The criteria for obtaining NCA for a PFT which satisfies LA(CF)R 1997, reg 40 are set out in Appendix 3 of the current PFI Guide[1], as well as the means by which the amount of the NCA is to be calculated. This generally involves an abatement in respect of the revenue costs of the scheme, or disregarding that element by considering only the capital value of the project. This is intended to ensure that there is no 'double counting' in the amount offered by way of an NCA, as the revenue costs are considered to be provided for within the relevant service element of standard spending assessments.

1 September 1998. Revisions to these criteria were set out in a letter from the DETR to the local authorities dated 21 December 1998.

15.68 With the replacement of LA(CF)R 1997, reg 40 in April 2000, the basic arrangements for the issue of the NCAs remain broadly as set out in Section 4 and Appendix 3 to the current PFI Guide (September 1998), subject to minor modifications and additional administrative requirements[1].

1 See note enclosed with letter from the DETR to Chief Executives and others in local government dated 23 December 1999 regarding changes to the revenue support arrangements in the light of the amendments to LA(CF)R 1997, reg 40.

2 NON-SCORING CREDIT APPROVAL (ROUTE 2) OR SUPPLEMENTARY CREDIT APPROVAL

15.69 The PFI Guide describes an alternative method of obtaining revenue support for schemes which do not fully satisfy the criteria for reg 40, but are nonetheless considered to be good PFI projects which merit special support. In the original PFI Guide this was described as 'Route 2'. This route is not available if the scheme does satisfy reg 40. Rather than being specifically linked to the provisions of LA(CF)R 1997, this concession is entirely based on the exercise of discretion by the Secretary of State, in effect to issue a supplementary credit approval under LGHA 1989, s 54[1], but formerly given the special title of a 'non-scoring credit approval' ('NSCA').

1 See para **11.14**.

15.70 A scheme following this route is likely to involve a credit arrangement with a substantial initial cost (as the nil initial cost treatment under LA(CF)R 1997, reg 40 will *not* be available). As well as triggering revenue support, the PFI credit in the form of an NSCA fulfils the necessary function of providing credit cover for the arrangement. The amount of that credit cover may, however, differ from the amount of revenue support awarded[1]. Again, a revenue abatement would apply to the calculation of any NSCA, to reflect the fact that part of the costs to the authority will be for services rather than capital assets or works.

1 The necessary credit cover would relate to the initial cost calculated in accordance with LGHA 1989, s 49, whilst the revenue support may be subject to a reduction in respect of the revenue component of the costs to the authority.

15.71 The criteria for eligibility for an NSCA are set out in Appendix 3 of the PFI Guide and are particularly obscure. It is said that the intention is to avoid rigid rules in order to allow flexibility and discretion for government departments. In addition to general criteria which apply to all PFI credits, authorities are required to answer various questions, aimed at establishing why the contract structure test[1] under LA(CF)R 1997, reg 40 was not satisfied and whether there was other evidence of satisfactory transfer of risk to the contractor. One of the questions to be addressed was whether the assets involved in the PFI contract could be regarded as 'off balance sheet' under the accounting standards adopted in other parts of the public sector (and now provided for in local government schemes in the revised reg 40[2]). In theory at least, Route 2 might have accommodated a wide variety of schemes, but to date it does not appear that it has been widely used (if at all). Again, assistance is dependent upon the successful outcome of an application to the appropriate government department.

1 See para **15.29**ff.
2 See para **15.34**ff.

15.72 As from 1 April 2000, there continue to be special administrative arrangements for providing support for schemes which do not satisfy the new LA(CF)R 1997, reg 40[1] (and therefore have a positive initial cost), but new criteria are to be applied. The expression 'non-scoring credit approval' has been abandoned and authorities would simply apply for supplementary credit approval ('SCA') for the scheme. In applying for an SCA, authorities are required to confirm that the scheme satisfies the basic test for a PFT under LA(CF)R 1997, reg 16[2], to explain any departures from the contract structure as recommended in the Treasury Taskforce contract standardisation guidance[3] and provide information on the accounting analysis and the value for money case[4].

1 See para **15.34**ff.
2 See para **15.22**ff.
3 See para **15.10**.
4 See note enclosed with letter from the DETR to Chief Executives and others in local government dated 23 December 1999 regarding changes to the revenue support arrangements in the light of the amendments to LA(CF)R 1997, reg 40.

I Local Government (Contracts) Act 1997

I BACKGROUND TO THE INTRODUCTION OF THE LOCAL GOVERNMENT (CONTRACTS) ACT 1997

15.73 The measures implemented to encourage PFI schemes for local government in the form of changes to the capital finance regulations addressed one aspect of the obstacles to the development of the Initiative in local government. The arrangements for additional revenue support offered authorities a positive incentive to pursue PFTs as defined[1]. However, these changes did nothing to address what was possibly an even greater difficulty, namely the widely held doubts about the adequacy of local government powers to accommodate the comparatively complex and often wide ranging contractual arrangements normally required in such transactions. Nor did they deal with the concerns of the private sector about the lack of protection, or effective remedies, if a PFT did entail an excess, or improper exercise of an authority's statutory powers.

1 See para **15.22**ff.

15.74 When the PFI Guide was first published in October 1996, it asserted (at para 2.2):

> 'The Government can see no reason to doubt the legal capacity of a local authority to enter into a DBFO contract ... for a project relevant to the exercise of their functions. Such contracts bear no resemblance to the sort of arrangements made by local authorities which have been the subject of recent court judgments.'

15.75 The reference to 'recent judgments' was to the decisions of the Court of Appeal in *Crédit Suisse v Allerdale Borough Council*[1] and *Crédit Suisse v Waltham Forest London Borough Council*[2] in May of 1996, which were then followed by the court's decision in *Sutton London Borough Council v Morgan Grenfell & Co Ltd*[3] in October of that year, around the time the PFI Guide was first published.

1 [1997] QB 306, [1996] 4 All ER 129.
2 [1997] QB 362, [1996] 4 All ER 176.
3 (1996) 29 HLR 608, CA.

15.76 In each of these cases the bank involved lost a significant sum of money lent to a company whose borrowing had been guaranteed by a local authority. In each case, the guarantee was found to be ultra vires and unenforceable when the bank sought to rely upon it because the company concerned had run into financial difficulties. Apart from the amounts of money involved, these cases drew the attention of banks and other potential PFI financiers to the risks of transactions with local authorities:

(a) In each case, the local authority itself had successfully asserted that its act was ultra vires[1]. As Peter Gibson LJ concluded in *Sutton London Borough Council v Morgan Grenfell & Co Ltd*[2]:

> 'Again as in the *Allerdale* and *Waltham Forest* cases this is a case where the local authority is now asserting that it was beyond its powers to do what it warranted it had the power to do and the innocent Bank is left to suffer the consequences.'

(b) The cases illustrated that as regards the enforceability of the arrangements, it made no difference whether the ultra vires finding was based on a lack of power in the 'absolute' sense of an absence of any statutory authority, or a case where a statutory power existed, but there had been some defect in the manner in which that power had been exercised (eg improper motive, irrationality or unlawful delegation). Identifying an appropriate local government power is sometimes less than straightforward, but checking on the *proper exercise* of a power could present a greater difficulty for the private sector party, as any defect may not be readily apparent.

(c) Each of the cases involved a claim in private law proceedings. They illustrated that, in certain respects, the position in private law could be even harsher for the private sector party than a case where a contract might be found to be ultra vires following an application for judicial review, where any challenge must be brought expeditiously and there is judicial discretion to refuse a remedy (albeit on limited grounds).

1 The authority's external auditor may well have been concerned that it should do so.
2 (1996) 29 HLR 608, CA.

15.77 These factors combined suggested that a party 'contracting' with a local authority could be vulnerable to the authority defending a private law claim on the ground that the 'contract' was ultra vires the authority, possibly many years after the 'contract' had been entered into and on the basis of factors which that party may have had little or no means of discovering. If the authority established its own lack of power, the court would have no choice but to treat the arrangement as void[1].

1 See Neill LJ in *Crédit Suisse v Allerdale Borough Council* [1996] 4 All ER 129 at 158–9 describing the absence of judicial discretion in private law proceedings where a local authority decision is found to be ultra vires.

15.78 Added to this was the practical experience of parties involved in litigation following the decision of the House of Lords in *Hazell v Hammersmith and Fulham London Borough Council*[1] who were endeavouring to 'unwind' the interest rate swap arrangements which had been found to be beyond the powers of local authorities. Whilst these follow-up cases raised interesting questions in the law of restitution[2] from the perspective of the parties involved, they represented a complex, costly and unpredictable means of dealing with the after-effects of an ultra vires finding.

1 [1992] 2 AC 1, [1991] 1 All ER 545.
2 See, for example, *Kleinwort Benson Ltd v Lincoln City Council* [1999] 2 AC 349, [1998] 4 All ER 513.

15.79 Notwithstanding the comments on behalf of the government in the PFI Guide referred to in para **15.74** and similar assurances, parties contemplating

PFI proposals and, in particular, banks and other financial institutions, made it clear that they would be reluctant to pursue PFI projects involving local authorities until new legislation had been enacted to tackle their concerns about the risks and consequences of ultra vires local government 'contracts'.

15.80 Following the general election in 1997, the Bates Review of the PFI recommended, in June of that year:

> 'As well as the proposed legislation concerning the vires of NHS Trusts, the Government should, if necessary, bring forward similar legislation in respect of other public sector bodies, certainly including local authorities.'

15.81 Similar, but less extensive concerns had arisen in relation to the powers of NHS Trusts in connection with the application of the PFI to projects being promoted by Trusts. The National Health Service (Private Finance) Act 1997 received Royal Assent on 15 July 1997. As a model of simplicity[1] it seeks to render intra vires any 'externally financed development agreement' which the Secretary of State has certified under s 1, and gives the Secretary of State fairly wide discretion as to the type of contracts eligible for certification. The equivalent measure for local government, the Local Government (Contracts) Act 1997 (the LGCA 1997), received Royal Assent on 27 November 1997. In comparison with the National Health legislation it is a far more complex measure. Although particularly aimed at PFI projects, the LGCA 1997, s 1 has implications for other areas of local government activity. Certain aspects of the LGCA 1997 entail important changes in public law, at least in relation to contracts which have been certified[2] under the Act.

1 The NHS legislation is silent on the complex issue of the potential distinction between the treatment of an ultra vires act in private law as opposed to public law proceedings, and on the consequences in terms of remedies for the private sector if, notwithstanding the legislation, a contract is found to be ultra vires, in effect leaving it to the courts to interpret the effects of certification in each case. In contrast, the Local Government (Contracts) Act 1997 endeavours to address these issues explicitly. The former has been described as a 'quick and dirty solution'. It is yet to be seen which approach will be more effective in practice.
2 Only certain types of local authority contract are intended to be eligible for certification. See para **15.88**.

2 OVERVIEW OF THE LOCAL GOVERNMENT (CONTRACTS) ACT 1997 (LGCA 1997)

15.82 The LGCA 1997 applies[1] to all authorities whose finances are subject to the Local Government and Housing Act 1989 (LGHA 1989), Pt IV (eg county councils, district councils, London borough councils, unitary authorities and special purpose authorities or joint authorities for police, fire, civil defence, transport, waste disposal, the Residuary Body for Wales, National Parks authorities and the Broads Authority). It also applies to probation committees. In Scotland, the Act applies to local authorities and joint boards as defined by the Local Government (Scotland) Act 1973, s 235(1). The Act will apply to the new Greater London Authority and its four functional bodies, as all are bodies subject to LGHA 1989, Pt IV[2]. Most of the provisions of the LGCA 1997 came into force on 30 December 1997, but can apply to contracts entered into after 12 June 1997[3]. The functions of the Secretary of State to make regulations under the LGCA 1997 (s 11), so far as exercisable in relation to Wales, were transferred to the National Assembly for Wales by virtue of SI 1999/672, art 2, Sch 1.

1 See Local Government (Contracts) Act 1997, s 1(3) as amended by the Greater London Authority Act 1999, s 325, Sch 27, para 116; s 423, Sch 34, Pt VII.
2 See the Greater London Authority Act 1999, s 111.
3 See Local Government (Contracts) Act 1997, s 12(2) and (3) and the Local Government (Contracts) Act 1997 (Commencement No 1) Order 1997, SI 1997/2843, under which 30 December 1997 is the 'appointed day' for the commencement of ss 2–9, other than the regulation making powers of the Secretary of State under s 3, which came into force on 1 December 1997. In the case of a contract entered into after 12 June 1997 and before 30 December 1997, the certification period of six weeks ran from 30 December 1997.

15.83 The LGCA 1997 has two main strands. The first, under LGCA 1997, s 1 'clarifies' local authorities' powers to enter into certain contracts. The second, under LGCA 1997, ss 2–9, accords special treatment to 'certified contracts', which comprise a narrower class of contract than that covered by s 1. The Act creates a procedure for a local authority to certify certain contracts for services and then affords special treatment to certified contracts in private law, and (to a lesser degree) in public law proceedings. The LGCA 1997 creates a means of compensating the private sector parties if a certified contract is found to be ultra vires by a court with public law jurisdiction. It also extends the powers of ministers to authorise delegation of local authority functions in connection with a certified contract through subordinate legislation made under the Deregulation and Contracting Out Act 1994, for a period to match the length of most PFI contracts. Each of these points is expanded upon in paras **15.84–15.116**.

3 THE FIRST STRAND: LOCAL GOVERNMENT (CONTRACTS) ACT 1997, S 1

15.84 The Local Government (Contracts) Act 1997 (LGCA 1997), s 1 'clarifies' that local authorities have power to enter into contracts:

> '*... for the provision or making available of assets or services, or both, (whether or not together with goods) for the purposes of, or in connection with, the discharge of* ... [their statutory functions].'[1]

Section 1(1) makes this power an integral part of every local authority statutory function: '[e]very statutory provision conferring or imposing a function on a local authority confers power' on the authority to enter into such a contract. The contracts covered by s 1(1) are referred to as 'provision contracts'.

1 This is to be compared with the wording of the Local Government Act 1972, s 111(1) conferring on authorities the power to do anything (subject to certain express limitations) 'which is calculated to facilitate, or is conducive or incidental to, the discharge of any of their functions'. 'Function' is not defined in either context, but in relation to s 111 it has been considered to mean all powers and duties of the local authority concerned (see Lord Templeman in *Hazell v Hammersmith and Fulham London Borough Council* [1992] 2 AC 1, [1991] 1 All ER 545 at 554).

15.85 'Assets' are widely defined by the LGCA 1997, s 1(4), to include assets of any description (whether tangible or intangible), including (in particular) land, buildings, roads, works, plant, machinery, vehicles, vessels, apparatus, equipment and computer software. This definition may be amended by regulations made by the Secretary of State under s 1(5).

15.86 Importantly, the LGCA 1997, s 1(2) expressly authorises a local authority, in connection with a provision contract, to enter into a contract with any person who makes a loan to, or provides any other form of finance for, a party to the provision contract other than the local authority ('the financier'), or to contract with the financier's insurer or trustee. Again, this power is made an integral part of the statutory provision with which the provision contract is concerned. Section 1(2) is particularly aimed at expressly authorising what are known as 'direct agreements'[1] between the local authority and the main contractor's financiers. The debates on the Bill indicated that this subsection was intended to make provision for arrangements which would give the financier 'step-in' rights to appoint a new contractor, or would deal with rights and liabilities in respect of assets on termination of the PFI arrangements. However, there is no explicit limitation on the subject matter of the local authority's contract with the financier, simply that it should be entered into 'in connection with' a provision contract.

1 See para **15.9**.

15.87 In information published by the DETR about the Bill and during the course of the Parliamentary debates, considerable emphasis was placed on the proposition that the provisions now included in LGCA 1997, s 1 were intended only to 'clarify' local government powers, rather than to create new powers. Whether this was to minimise the risk of casting doubt on the legitimacy of contracts entered into prior to the enactment of LGCA 1997 (or those which fall outside the definition of a 'provision contract'), or simply to avoid opening floodgates in relation to s 1(2) concerning contracts with financiers, is unclear. However, for the particular types of contract covered by s 1(1), the drafting of the new provisions suggests that some effort has been made to avoid some of the complexities identified in recent cases in relation to the Local Government Act 1972 (LGA 1972), s 111, particularly in connection with certain activities being characterised as 'incidental to the incidental' (rather than directly incidental to discharging a function) and hence not authorised under s 111[1].

1 See Chapter 4.

4 THE SECOND STRAND: LOCAL GOVERNMENT (CONTRACTS) ACT 1997, SS 2–9

15.88 The LGCA 1997, ss 2–9 concern 'certified contracts'. These provisions are intended to apply to a smaller class of contract than that covered by LGCA 1997, s 1. Not every 'provision contract', or connected agreement with a financier, is intended to be capable of certification. The types of contract which are intended[1] to be eligible for certification are those:

(a) for the provision or making available of services (whether or not together with assets or goods) for the purposes of, or in connection with, the discharge by a local authority of any of its functions, provided that the contract operates, or is intended to operate, for a period of at least five years[2]; and
(b) a contract entered into in connection with a contract under (a) above with a person who, in connection with that contract, makes a loan to, or provides any other form of finance for, a party to that contract (other than the local authority), or any insurer of or trustee for such a person[3].

The certificate issued by the authority must state within which of these two subsections the contract falls. These two categories of contract (implicitly) eligible for certification can be amended by regulations made by the Secretary of State under the LGCA 1997, s 4(5).

1 It is to be noted that care has been taken in drafting the legislation to avoid stipulating explicitly that a contract must fall within one of these categories in order to be eligible for certification; however the certification requirements include (under LGCA 1997, s 3(1)(c)) a requirement to specify within which of LGCA 1997, s 4(3) or (4) the contract falls.
2 Local Government (Contracts) Act 1997, s 4(3).
3 LGCA 1997, s 4(4).

15.89 With the emphasis on contracts for services, the sections of the Act which deal with certified contracts are more specifically aimed at the PFI type of contract than LGCA 1997, s 1. The provisions of the LGCA 1997, ss 2–9 create special treatment for certified contracts:

(a) in *private law* 'certified contracts' are to be treated, for most purposes, as being intra vires; thus the parties to the contract are prevented from contending that the authority lacked the necessary power or 'had exercised a power improperly'[1];
(b) the *public law* position is broadly preserved, so that a certified contract may still be challenged by way of judicial review or 'audit review', but:
    (i) the private sector parties are provided with a more predictable mechanism than restitution to tackle the consequences if a certified contract is, ultimately, found to be ultra vires in public law proceedings; and
    (ii) a court in judicial or audit review proceedings is given a new discretion, in view of specified factors, to determine that a 'certified contract' has and always has had effect, notwithstanding a finding that the local authority lacked the necessary power to enter into the contract, or had exercised a power improperly.

1 This expression (and its converse, 'to exercise a power properly') is used throughout the Local Government (Contracts) Act 1997. It is intended to encompass all the ways in which there might be a defect in the exercise of a local government power which might lead to a finding of invalidity, for example 'irrationality', improper purpose, unlawful fetter on the exercise of discretion or unlawful delegation of a function (see Chapter 4).

15.90 An 'application for judicial review', for the purposes of LGCA 1997, ss 5–7, is defined to include any appeal (or further appeal) against a determination or order made on such an application[1]. The LGCA 1997, s 8[2] defines 'audit review' as encompassing an application or appeal to the court by the auditor[3] or by a local government elector who has objected to an authority's accounts under the Audit Commission Act 1998, s 17, or an appeal by a local authority in relation to a 'prohibition order' under ACA 1998, s 22, as well as consideration by the auditor of certain matters under the ACA 1998, ss 18 and 20. For Scotland, the expression covers comparable audit provisions under the Local Government (Scotland) Act 1973. As noted in Chapter 9, certain of the relevant provisions of the Audit Commission Act 1998 are subject to prospective repeal, by virtue of the Local Government Act 2000, ss 90 and 91.

1 Local Government (Contracts) Act 1997, s 5(4).
2 As amended by the Audit Commission Act 1998, s 54(1) and Sch 3, as from 11 September 1998.
3 See the Audit Commission Act 1998, ss 3 and 53(1).

15.91 The following sections examine the certification procedure under the LGCA 1997, the extent of the protection of certified contracts in private law proceedings, the concept of 'relevant discharge terms' and the new discretion of the court in judicial review or audit proceedings.

5 CERTIFICATION PROCEDURE—LOCAL GOVERNMENT (CONTRACTS) ACT 1997, SS 2–4

15.92 As certification is a vital feature of the new procedure, the drafting of the LGCA 1997, ss 2–4 has been designed to minimise the possibility of challenge to the validity of the certificate itself[1]. Provided that the 'certification requirements'[2] have been satisfied, a certificate is not invalidated 'by reason that anything in the certificate is inaccurate or untrue'[3]. This should be read together with the certification requirements in LGCA 1997, s 3(2)–(4); many of those under s 3(2) simply amount to 'statements' about, or 'confirmation' of, certain factors. The local authority itself is responsible for issuing the certificate. Under the Act there is no compulsion on any party to the contract to pursue certification (although there will usually be strong commercial incentives to do so). If certification is to be effective, all the non-local authority parties to the contract must consent to the issue of the certificate.

1 See para **15.100**.
2 Local Government (Contracts) Act 1997, s 3(1).
3 Local Government (Contracts) Act 1997, s 4(1).

15.93 The certification requirements must be satisfied within a period of six weeks beginning with the day on which the authority entered into the contract[1] ('the certification period'[2]). The certificate may be issued before, or within six weeks of, the contract being entered into. If the contract provides that the certification requirements are intended to be satisfied by the local authority with respect to the contract before the end of the certification period, the contract is to be treated as a 'certified contract' throughout that period[3].

1 Or within six weeks from 30 December 1997, for contracts entered into after 12 June 1997 and before 30 December of that year (see Local Government (Contracts) Act 1997, s 12(3)).
2 See Local Government (Contracts) Act 1997, s 2(5).
3 LGCA 1997, s 2(3).

15.94 The certification requirements under LGCA 1997, s 3 and as further provided for in the Local Authorities (Contracts) Regulations 1997[1] ('LACR 1997'), relate to the contents of the certificate, the signatory of the certificate, the necessary consents to the issue of the certificate and the people to whom it must be copied.

1 SI 1997/2862, made under the Local Government (Contracts) Act 1997, s 3(2)(e),(f) and (3).

15.95 The LGCA 1997, s 3(2) deals with the contents of the certificate and stipulates that it must:

(a) include details of the period for which the contract operates, or is intended to operate;
(b) describe the purpose of the contract;
(c) state that the contract is, or is to be, a contract falling within LGCA 1997, s 4(3) or (4) (a contract for services which is to operate for at least five years, or a connected agreement with the contractor's financier[1]);
(d) state that the authority had or has power to enter into the contract and specify the statutory provision, or each of the statutory provisions, conferring the power[2] (by virtue of the Local Authorities (Contracts) Regulations 1997, reg 6, if the provision, or one of the provisions, relied on is the Local Government Act 1972, s 111 the authority must also specify each statutory provision conferring a relevant function, or, where there are two or more relevant functions,

the provisions which confer the *main* relevant functions[3];

(e) state that a copy of the certificate has been, or is to be given to each of the persons to whom a copy is required to be given by the regulations[4] (all authorities must provide a copy of the certificate to the other parties to the contract; for most types of local authority[5], copies of the certificate must also be given to the authority's monitoring officer and auditor[6];

(f) deal in the manner prescribed by regulations with any matters required by regulations to be dealt with in certificates under LGCA 1997, s 3;

(g) confirm that the authority has complied, or is to comply, with any requirement imposed by regulations with respect to the issue of certificates under 'this section'[7].

1 See para **15.88**.

2 In the case of an agreement with a financier, it would seem that Local Government (Contracts) Act 1997, s 1(2) might be an appropriate power to cite, in addition to the underlying function involved.

3 See SI 1997/2862, reg 6. This has been stipulated because the Local Government Act 1972, s 111, in isolation, will not authorise any activity; it must be used in conjunction with another statutory provision which does confer a function. Analogous requirements now apply to certificates issued under LGCA 1997 by the Greater London Authority and Transport for London, if the power under the Greater London Authority Act 1999, s 34, or Sch 10, para 1(3) respectively are relied on.

4 See SI 1997/2862, regs 3–5.

5 SI 1997/2862, reg 4 applies to most local authorities; reg 5 makes special provision for authorities which are not required to appoint a monitoring officer under the Local Government and Housing Act 1989, s 5(1).

6 Appointed under the Audit Commission Act 1998, s 3.

7 It is unclear whether 'this section' in the Local Government (Contracts) Act 1997, s 3(2)(g) refers to the whole of s 3 or to s 3(2)(g) alone, or precisely what requirements with respect to 'the issue' of certificates it is intended to encompass. On first reading, s 3(2)(g) appears to require the authority to provide general confirmation of compliance with the requirements of the Contracts Regulations (SI 1997/2862) made under LGCA 1997, s 3(2)(e),(f) and (3). However, the model certificates issued by the DETR in 1998 (at Appendix 2, Annexes 1–3 to the PFI Guide) indicate that no regulations have been made under s 3(2)(g), implying that, in the Department's view, currently, nothing need be stipulated in the certificate in respect of this requirement.

15.96 The PFI Guide[1] includes three model certificates (at Appendix 2, Annex 1–3) and a table summarising the requirements concerning the persons to whom copies of the certificates should be provided (Appendix 2, Annex 4). The model certificates are issued by way of guidance; they are not prescribed forms.

1 September 1998.

15.97 Under the LGCA 1997, s 3(3), the certificate must be signed by a person required by the regulations to sign it. The Local Authorities (Contracts) Regulations 1997, SI 1997/2862, regs 7 and 8 deal with signatories. The precise requirements depend on the type of authority concerned:

(a) in the majority of cases (where the authority is of a kind required to appoint a chief finance officer[1] and is obliged to appoint one of its officers as head of its paid service[2]) the certificate must be signed by a statutory[3] or non-statutory chief officer[4] or a deputy chief officer[5];

(b) if the authority is required to appoint a chief finance officer, but there is no obligation to appoint a head of paid service (as applies, for example, to joint fire, civil defence and transport authorities, combined fire authorities, police authorities, waste regulation and pension authorities), the certificate must be signed by the chief finance officer, or a person who mainly reports directly to, or is directly accountable to, the chief finance officer[6];

(c) special arrangements for signatories are made under LACR 1997, reg 8 in relation to certificates issued by probation committees, the Residuary Body for Wales, the Broads Authority, Lee Valley Regional Park Authority and the Receiver for the Metropolitan Police[7].

1 Under the Local Government Act 1972, s 151; the Local Government Act 1985, s 73; the Local Government Finance Act 1988, s 112; or the Local Government and Housing Act 1989, s 6, or the Greater London Authority Act 1999, s 127.
2 By virtue of the Local Government and Housing Act 1989, s 4(1).
3 See Local Government and Housing Act 1989, s 2(6).
4 LGHA 1989, s 2(7).
5 See SI 1997/2862, reg 7(2).
6 SI 1997/2862, reg 7(3).
7 SI 1997/2862, reg 8.

15.98 The PFI Guide (Appendix 2, Annex 5) contains a helpful table which summarises the requirements concerning signatories of certificates.

15.99 The final certification requirement, under the LGCA 1997, s 3(4), is that the local authority must have obtained the consent of every party with whom the authority has entered into the contract, to the issue of the certificate. This is because one effect of the certificate is to restrict their rights to contend that the contract is ultra vires the authority in private law proceedings.

15.100 The efforts to minimise the risk of challenge to the certificate itself are emphasised in the LGCA 1997, s 4(1), which provides that where the certification requirements have been satisfied in relation to a contract, the certificate which has been issued:

> '... shall have effect (and be deemed always to have had effect) as if the local authority had power to issue it (and had exercised that power properly in issuing it).'

15.101 Whilst inaccuracy or untruth in the certificate will not invalidate it[1], it would appear that the validity of the certificate may, potentially, be in question (and the contract may not benefit from the special treatment for certified contracts under the LGCA 1997) if the certificate has not been signed by the correct officer, or one of the contractual parties has not consented to its issue. Further, by virtue of LGCA 1997, s 2(2), the contract cannot *be* a 'certified contract' unless the 'certification requirements', as defined in LGCA 1997, s 3(1) have been satisfied by the authority within the certification period[2]. Under s 3(1), the certification requirements are those specified in s 3(2) and (3), which incorporate the additional provisions of the LACR 1997[3].

1 Local Government (Contracts) Act 1997, s 4(1).
2 Normally the period of six weeks beginning with the day on which the authority entered into the contract. See the Local Government (Contracts) Act 1997, s 2(5) (and s 12(3) for contracts prior to commencement of the provisions) referred to in para **15.93**.
3 SI 1997/2862.

6 IMPLICATIONS FOR PROHIBITION ORDERS ISSUED UNDER THE AUDIT COMMISSION ACT 1998, S 20

15.102 A 'prohibition order' under the Audit Commission Act 1998, s 20 may be issued by an auditor[1] to a local authority when the auditor has reason to believe that the authority, or one of its officers, has made or is about to make a decision, or to take a course of action, or to enter an item of account which entails unlawfulness. In general, as from the date specified in the prohibition order, it becomes unlawful for the authority or any officer to make or implement the decision, to continue the course of action, or to enter the item of account to which the order relates. (Chapter 9 describes prohibition orders and the prospective repeal of the relevant provisions of the Audit Commission Act 1999 by the Local Government Act 2000, s 91(2).)

1 Appointed under the Audit Commission Act 1998, s 3.

15.103 The Local Government (Contracts) Act 1997, s 8(2) suspends these restrictions if a prohibition order is issued in relation to a certified contract. At least until an appeal against the order under the Audit Commission Act 1998, s 22(3) has been determined, or the period for such an appeal has expired, or any appeal has been withdrawn, the prohibition order does not make it unlawful for the authority (or its officers) to pursue the specified activities in relation to a certified contract.

7 NOVATION OF CERTIFIED CONTRACTS

15.104 The LGCA 1997, s 2(4) makes special provision for cases where a certified contract is novated through a new contract. This is to cover the possibility which is commonly catered for in PFI arrangements (often in the context of 'step in rights'[1]), of a new contractor taking over the rights and liabilities of one of the private sector parties to the contract. The subsection provides that where a local authority has entered into a certified contract ('the existing contract') and the existing contract is replaced by a contract between the authority and a person or persons not identical with those with whom the authority entered into the existing contract, the replacement contract will also be a certified contract provided that:

(a) the period for which the replacement contract operates, or is intended to operate, ends at the same time as that for which the existing contract was to operate; and
(b) apart from that, the provisions of the replacement contract are the same as those of the existing contract.

1 For example, where the original contractor fails to achieve the required level of performance, or becomes insolvent.

8 PUBLIC INSPECTION OF CERTIFICATES

15.105 Under the LGCA 1997, s 4(2), local authorities in England and Scotland (which in this case excludes probation committees) who have certified a contract under the LGCA 1997 are required to secure that throughout the period for which the certified contract operates, a copy of the certificate is open to inspection by members of the public at all reasonable times without payment. The public must be afforded facilities for obtaining copies of the certificate on payment of a reasonable fee.

9 EXTENT OF PROTECTION IN PRIVATE LAW PROCEEDINGS FOR CERTIFIED CONTRACTS

15.106 The LGCA 1997, s 2(1) specifies:

> '... [w]here a local authority has entered into a contract, the contract shall, if it is a certified contract, have effect (and be deemed always to have had effect)

as if the local authority had power to enter into it (and had exercised the power properly in entering into it).'

The clear intention is that the parties to the certified contract should be unable, at least in private law proceedings, to claim that the contract is ultra vires the local authority.

15.107 This sweeping provision is subject to three important exceptions; the LGCA 1997, s 2(1):

(a) does not apply for the purpose of determining any question arising on an application for judicial review or audit review[1];
(b) is subject to any determination or order made in relation to a certified contract on such an application[2]; and
(c) does not affect any claim for damages made by a person who is not (and never has been) a party to the certified contract in respect of a breach by the local authority of any duty to do, or not to do, something *before* entering into the contract (this refers, in particular, to any duty imposed by a statutory provision for giving effect to any European Community obligation relating to public procurement, or by the Local Government Act 1988, s 17(1)[3]).

1 See Local Government (Contracts) Act 1997, ss 2(6) and 5(1).
2 LGCA 1997, s 5(2).
3 LGCA 1997, s 2(7).

15.108 The intention of the exception for claims for damages referred to in item (c) above is to make clear the relationship between the new provisions and the remedies conferred on an aggrieved party where a contract is concluded in breach of the EC public procurement legislation, or the implementing domestic procurement regulations. It also deals with the relationship between the new provisions and an authority's duties under the Local Government Act 1988, s 17[1] to disregard 'non-commercial matters' when it lets a 'public supply or works contract' as defined in those provisions.

1 At the time of writing the 1988 Act, s 17 is proposed to be amended by an order to be made by the Secretary of State under the Local Government Act 1999, s 19.

10 RELEVANT DISCHARGE TERMS

15.109 The purpose of 'relevant discharge terms' is to enable the parties to agree what should happen if a certified contract (either with the service provider, or with the service provider's financier) is found to be unenforceable in judicial review or audit review proceedings. By virtue of the LGCA 1997, s 6(3), relevant discharge terms can cover either or both of the following:

(a) the payment of compensatory damages (measured by reference to loss incurred or loss of profits, or to any other circumstances) by one of the parties to the other;
(b) the adjustment between the parties of rights and liabilities relating to any assets or goods provided or made available under the contract.

15.110 The relevant discharge terms may either be contained within the certified contract or in a separate contract entered into no later than the date on which the certified contract was entered into[1]. Either type of certified contract (ie the main service contract, or a connected contract between the authority and the service provider's financier) can make provision for relevant discharge terms. It seems that the relevant discharge terms may be entered into with one (or more) of the individual parties to the certified contract[2].

1 Local Government (Contracts) Act 1997, s 6(2)(b).
2 LGCA 1997, s 6(2)(a).

15.111 By virtue of LGCA 1997, s 6(1), no determination or order made in relation to a certified contract on an application for judicial review or an audit review is to affect the enforceability of any relevant discharge term relating to the contract. However, this does not appear to mean that the court is entirely excluded from considering the validity of relevant discharge terms. Debates on the Bill in the Lords suggest that it was envisaged that (albeit in exceptional circumstances) the relevant discharge terms might themselves be found to be invalid in public law proceedings. This is substantiated by the provisions of LGCA 1997, s 7(3) referred to below.

11 ABSENCE OR INVALIDITY OF RELEVANT DISCHARGE TERMS

15.112 The LGCA 1997, s 7(1) contemplates the possibility of the absence or invalidity of relevant discharge terms, in a case where a court has found that a certified contract does not have effect. It deals not only with the situation where the parties have failed to agree any relevant discharge terms, but also those where 'despite section 6(4)' such terms 'do not have effect' as a result of a determination or order made on an application for judicial review or an audit review[1].

1 See Local Government (Contracts) Act 1997, s 7(3).

15.113 In both these cases, the LGCA 1997 provides for a statutory 'fall back position', to compensate the private sector parties. In order to assess the amount of compensation payable, the contract is to be treated as having had effect, but as having been terminated on the date of the court's determination or order, by a repudiatory breach by the local authority which has been accepted by the other party. The contracting party would then be entitled to be paid such sums as would normally be payable in common law in respect of such a breach. The debates on the Bill indicated that it was envisaged that this might include an element in respect of actual or anticipated loss of profit. Where the parties are entirely satisfied with the statutory 'fall back position' of damages as for repudiatory breach, there would appear to be little incentive for them to dedicate any considerable time to negotiating 'relevant discharge terms'. In practice, it seems that the private sector may see advantages in concluding relevant discharge terms, as this is considered to offer a greater degree of certainty. Local authorities may wish to make express provision for payment of any compensation over time, rather than in a lump sum. Both parties may wish to take the opportunity to make express provision in relation to rights and liabilities relating to assets.

12 COURTS' DISCRETION IN PUBLIC LAW PROCEEDINGS IN RELATION TO CERTIFIED CONTRACTS

15.114 The LGCA 1997, s 5(3) includes an important new discretion for a court in judicial review or audit review. Where the court is of the opinion that the local authority did not have power to enter into the contract, or had exercised a power improperly in entering into the contract, then in certain circumstances it may, nonetheless, determine that the contract has (and always has had) effect as if the authority had power to enter into it and had exercised that power properly. This discretion arises where the court considers that the certified contract should have effect, having regard, in particular, to the likely consequences of a finding of invalidity for the financial position of the local authority and for the provision of services to the public: ie 'the balance of harm'. The effect of a determination being made by a court under s 5(3) appears to go some way beyond the general position which would apply in a case where, on an application for judicial review, the court exercises its inherent discretion not to make any order. If the discretion is exercised by the court under s 5(3), there is a positive finding that the 'contract' should be given effect.

13 CONTRACTING OUT OF FUNCTIONS IN CONNECTION WITH A CERTIFIED CONTRACT

15.115 The powers to contract under the LGCA 1997, s 1 (and the remaining provisions of the Act) are not intended to authorise the delegation of local government functions otherwise than as already permitted by other legislation. Delegation is generally dealt with under the Local Government Act 1972, s 101 (although certain individual statutes contain special provisions which affect the extent to which lawful delegation is possible). Under the Deregulation and Contracting Out Act 1994, s 70 a minister may, by order, enable a local authority to contract out functions specified in the order for a period of up to ten years. In relation to a certified contract, the LGCA 1997, s 9 now enables authorisation for contracting out to the PFI contractor under such an order to be for a term equal to that of the certified contract, subject to a maximum of 40 years. This applies where the authorisation is given to enable the contractor 'to perform or better perform his obligations under the [certified] contract[1]'.

1 Local Government (Contracts) Act 1997, s 9(3)(c).

14 CONCLUSIONS ON THE LOCAL GOVERNMENT (CONTRACTS) ACT 1997

15.116 The LGCA 1997 is, without doubt, an interesting measure. The extent to which it will be effective in protecting certified contracts will only be seen in the light of experience. Some two and a half years after its enactment there are no reported cases on the provisions of the LGCA 1997. There is a temptation to conclude that the care which has been taken to limit the possibility of challenges to certified contracts and to the certificates themselves might be matched by the ingenuity of lawyers endeavouring to find ways around the exclusions, if there is ever a practical incentive to do so.

CHAPTER 16

Local authorities' interests in companies

A Background

16.1 The role played by companies and other external bodies in the conduct of local authority affairs was examined as long ago as 1986 by the Widdecombe Committee of Inquiry into the Conduct of Local Authority Business[1]. At the time of writing, the law relating to this area continues to be unsatisfactory, but the present Government has indicated its intention to 'clear up the current uncertainties about councils' powers to establish and participate in companies'[2]. Notwithstanding the recent enactment of the Local Government Act 2000 at the time of writing, the means by which this is to be achieved is not yet clear. Proposals for change and recent developments are referred to at the end of this chapter[3].

1 Report dated 19 June 1986, Cmnd 9797.
2 See the White Paper 'Modern Local Government—In Touch with the People' (July 1998, Cm 4014), para 8.24.
3 See para **16.116**ff.

16.2 The Widdecombe Committee recommended[1] that the law should be amended, first to make it clear that local authority controlled companies should only be set up where specific enabling legislation exists, and second to incorporate safeguards concerning their articles of association, membership, audit and reporting arrangements. In response to the Committee's recommendations, the Department of the Environment issued a consultation paper, 'Local Authorities' Interests in Companies' (13 June 1988). This consultation paper set out the basis of proposals which eventually led to the enactment of Pt V of the Local Government and Housing Act 1989 (LGHA 1989). But it was not until 1 April 1995 that most of the provisions of Pt V were brought into full effect[2].

1 Paragraph 8.117.
2 Or 1 July 1995, in respect of certain provisions, particularly in relation to companies formed on or before 31 March 1995. Certain provisions of LGHA 1989, Pt V are still not in force: s 71(2),(3),(5)(b) and (7). See SI 1989/2445 and SI 1993/2410 regarding the commencement of ss 67–70 and s 72; SI 1993/2410 regarding the commencement of s 73; and SI 1989/2445 and SI 1995/841 regarding the commencement of s 71. (The relevant parts of SI 1990/1274 which would have commenced LGHA 1989, ss 67–73 in July 1990 were omitted by SI 1990/1335.) It was not until the Local Authorities (Companies) Order 1995, SI 1995/849, as subsequently amended by SI 1996/621, came into force that the provisions of LGHA 1989, Pt V (excluding the subsections of s 71 referred to above) were given full effect.

16.3 The 1988 consultation paper on companies included the findings of the Department of the Environment's own survey into local authorities' interests in companies, intended to test the accuracy of the Committee's assumptions that most local authority companies were wholly owned by authorities and were concerned with economic development. The survey revealed that by far the most common purpose of local authority companies was economic development[1], but there was no clear preference for local authority control, as opposed to the authority holding only a minority interest in a company.

1 127 of 372 companies disclosed by respondents to the questionnaire.

16.4 The consultation paper rejected the Committee's recommendation that the law should be amended to make it clear that companies should only be set up by authorities where specific enabling legislation exists (although important express powers concerning company involvement were created shortly thereafter by LGHA 1989, Pt III, in connection with the promotion of economic development[1]). The consultation paper did not explore or question in any depth the extent of a local authority's powers to acquire shares or otherwise participate in a company incorporated under the Companies Acts, nor indeed in an unincorporated trust. Whilst referring to a variety of specific enabling provisions[2], only the most cursory consideration was given to these powers and to cases which fall outside these tightly prescribed areas. It was asserted that some 'discretionary powers' of local authorities, eg under Local Government Act 1972, s 145 (relating to the provision of entertainments), enable a local authority to form or control a company. The paper expressed the view that Local Government Act 1972, s 111 'is widely drawn' and can authorise the formation, or the acquisition of, or control over, a company by a local authority.

1 See Chapter 17.
2 For example, the Housing Associations Act 1985, s 58 (see now the Housing Act 1996, s 22) and the Further Education Act 1985, s 2 (see para **16.9ff**).

16.5 These comments, of course, predate the House of Lord's decision in *Hazell v Hammersmith and Fulham London Borough Council*[1] which adopted a narrow interpretation of the ambit of LGA 1972, s 111 (albeit not specifically in the context of companies) and the decision of the Court of Appeal in *Crédit Suisse v Borough Council of Allerdale*[2] (in which the question of companies was addressed[3]). As far as funding companies was concerned, the consultation paper simply observed that authorities 'have a number of powers which enable them to put a company in funds for various broad purposes', referring in particular to the power under LGA 1972, s 137[4] (which is available only in the absence of some express statutory authorisation and is subject to strict annual limits on expenditure[5]). We return to the question of local authority powers to participate in companies, and developments in case law at para **16.20**.

1 [1992] 2 AC 1, [1991] 1 All ER 545; see Chapter 4.
2 [1997] QB 306, [1996] 4 All ER 129; see also *Crédit Suisse v London Borough of Waltham Forest* [1997] QB 362, [1996] 4 All ER 176.
3 In which the court did not discount the possibility that statutory provisions which create what were described as 'secondary functions', such as the Local Government Act 1972, s 144 or s 145, might form the basis of powers to authorise company formation, but found that powers such as those under the Local Government (Miscellaneous Provisions) Act 1976, s 19 which require the authority itself to discharge a function, could not alone or in conjunction with LGA 1972, s 111, authorise the formation of a company to discharge a local government function. See further para **16.20**.
4 See Chapters 4 and 17. (Local Government Act 1972, s 137 is no longer available in relation to economic development expenditure; further, its ambit is to be substantially curtailed in relation to local authorities subject to the LGA 2000, Pt I, once in force (see LGA 2000, s 8).)
5 Local Government Act 1972, s 137(4)–(4c), and see SI 1984/197, SI 1993/40, SI 1993/41, SI 1995/651 and SI 1995/3304.

16.6 The 1988 consultation paper stated that the Government saw important operational advantages in a local authority using a company and that it did not wish to interfere with the flexibility of local authority companies, which had 'a particular usefulness in joint ventures with the private sector'. (The potential benefits of local authority involvement in companies have been asserted repeatedly in various papers produced on behalf of central government over the years up to the present time.)

16.7 It was against this background that the general statutory controls on local authority involvement in companies, now contained in LGHA 1989, Pt V, were devised. The provisions as brought into force in April 1995, are aimed at dictating the consequences of local authority involvement in companies (and certain other bodies) and not at whether a local authority is empowered to participate in an external body in the first place. Although LGHA 1989, Pt V does contain a mechanism through which it could be placed beyond an authority's powers to participate in specified ways in any company which it does not 'control'[1] unless the company is of a description expressly authorised by the Secretary of State, at the time of writing the relevant provisions have not been brought into force[2].

1 See para **16.35ff.**

2 Local Government and Housing Act 1989, s 71(2). The Department of the Environment Guide to Local Authorities' Interests in Companies issued in March 1995 stated that there was 'no current intention' to commence s 71(2). So far, that position does not appear to have changed.

B Provisions expressly authorising local authority participation in companies

16.8 Before turning to the system for regulating local authority participation in companies, it is worth considering some examples of statutory provisions which expressly require, authorise or envisage local authority participation in, or the setting up of, a company or other external body.

1 LOCAL GOVERNMENT AND HOUSING ACT 1989, PT III—ECONOMIC DEVELOPMENT

16.9 Provisions of potentially wide application are those contained in LGHA 1989, Pt III concerning the promotion of economic development by a local authority. The powers under this Part of LGHA 1989 are dealt with in detail in the next chapter (together with their prospective repeal under the LGA 2000) and are subject to certain preconditions and restrictions. Under Pt III, the steps which a local authority is expressly authorised to take to promote the economic development of its area include participation in, and the encouragement of, and the provision of financial and other assistance for, the setting up and expansion of commercial, industrial or public undertakings to be situated in the authority's area or likely to increase opportunities for the employment of people in the authority's area[1]. For these purposes, an authority is treated as providing 'financial assistance' to a person if, inter alia, 'it invests in that person's undertaking, in the case of a body corporate, by acquiring share or loan capital in that body or otherwise'[2]. Thus, LGHA 1989, Pt III specifically envisages that a local authority may participate in setting up a company, or provide financial assistance to a company through investing in it by acquiring shares, provided the authority considers that any such action would be an appropriate step to take to promote the economic development of its area[3].

1 Local Government and Housing Act 1989, s 33(2).
2 LGHA 1989, s 33(3)(e).
3 And the pre-conditions for the exercise of powers under LGHA 1989, s 33 are met; see, in particular, the consultation requirements under LGHA 1989, s 35.

16.10 The remaining statutory provisions listed below are of more limited application. Certain of them entail obligations on authorities to form companies, potentially as a preparatory step towards the eventual disposal of the particular undertaking to the private sector.

2 HOUSING ASSOCIATIONS ACT 1985, S 58 AND HOUSING ACT 1996, S 22

16.11 These provisions expressly empower a local authority to promote the formation or extension of a housing association[1] or other registered social landlord. In order to assist a housing association or other registered social landlord, an authority may also subscribe for its share or loan capital.

1 Housing associations which are registered social landlords are now the subject of the Housing Act 1996 and not the Housing Associations Act 1995 powers (see Housing Associations Act 1985, s 58(4), as substituted by SI 1996/2325.

3 ENVIRONMENTAL PROTECTION ACT 1990, S 32

16.12 These provisions required local authorities which were waste disposal authorities, on receiving a direction from the Secretary of State, to form or to participate in forming, separate waste disposal companies (known as 'LAWDCs') and to transfer certain functions to them. The provisions include express authority for councils to hold securities[1] in a company so established (Environmental Protection Act 1990, s 32(2)). For so long as a LAWDC is controlled by a local authority, the authority must so exercise its control as to secure that the company is an 'arm's length controlled company'[2] under LGHA 1989, s 68(6)[3].

1 'Securities' includes shares, debentures, bonds or other securities (Environmental Protection Act 1990, Sch 2, para 1).
2 See paras **16.37** and **16.38**.
3 Environmental Protection Act 1990, s 32(9).

4 TRANSPORT ACT 1985, S 67

16.13 This Act imposed a duty on non-metropolitan district councils to form one or more companies to take over council bus undertakings when directed to do so by the Secretary of State. Such companies are required to be limited by shares and registered under the Companies Act 1985. The LGHA 1989 imposes a code for regulation of such companies.

5 AIRPORTS ACT 1986, S 13

16.14 This Act imposed a duty on principal councils which control certain airports[1] to form companies to take over the commercial undertaking when directed to do so by the Secretary of State. Such companies must be limited by shares and registered under the Companies Act 1985. The 1986 Act includes provisions which regulate airport companies' activities and personnel[2].

1 If the annual turnover of the business carried on at the airport by the airport operator exceeded £1,000,000 in at least two of the last three financial years ending before the 'relevant date' of any direction given by the Secretary of State under s 13 (see Airports Act 1986, s 14).
2 See also para **16.30**.

6 FURTHER EDUCATION ACT 1985, S 2

16.15 Whilst this Act does not include any express authorisation for a local authority to set up or hold shares in a company, it specifically authorises an authority to lend money to a body corporate which is involved in the supply of goods or services to higher or further education establishments, provided that the authority participates in the company by holding not less than 20% of the issued shares which carry full voting rights at general meetings[1].

1 Further Education Act 1982, s 2(2)(c) and (8).

C Assumptions regarding local authority participation in companies

16.16 The Further Education Act provision referred to above is based on the premise that a local authority would have the power to hold shares in such a company, but without expressly authorising such participation. A number of other statutory provisions, especially those concerning capital finance under LGHA 1989, Pt IV, and indeed the whole of LGHA 1989, Pt V, have been drafted on the assumption that local authorities do participate in companies, particularly by way of shareholding, but without actually authorising any such involvement.

16.17 As an example of the assumptions as to company shareholding made in relation to capital finance, local authority receipts from the sale of shares are given individual treatment in LGHA 1989, Pt IV and in the regulations made under that Part (the Local Authorities (Capital Finance) Regulations 1997[1] (LA(CF)R 1997). As described in Chapter 14, such receipts are treated as capital receipts arising from the disposal of 'non-approved' investments and are normally subject to a requirement to reserve 75% as provision to meet credit liabilities[2]. The exceptions from these general requirements[3], which specify a nil 'reserved part' for receipts from the sale of particular kinds of shares, illustrate the range of local authority shareholding assumed to exist by the legislators. These exceptions apply, for example, to shares or loan capital in a company:

(a) involved in the activities of providing, constructing, improving, repairing and maintaining land and any other assets for the purposes of a maintained school within the meaning of the Education Act 1993, s 305[4];
(b) involved in the provision of the services which the Secretary of State is under a duty to secure under the Employment and Training Act 1973, s 8 (careers services for school and college students), or has a power to secure under s 9 of that Act (careers services for others[5]);
(c) formed by, or with the participation of, the authority for any of the purposes of the Local Government Act 1972, s 145 (provision of entertainments[6]).

1 SI 1997/319, as amended by SI 1997/848, SI 1998/371, SI 1998/602, SI 1998/1937, SI 1999/501, SI 1999/1852, SI 1999/3423, SI 2000/992 (Wales), SI 2000/1033, SI 2000/1474, SI 2000/1553 and SI 2000/1773.
2 See Local Government and Housing Act 1989, s 58(1)(b) and s 59(3) and Local Authorities (Capital Finance) Regulations 1997, reg 66.
3 See paras **14.7** and the chart in para **14.30**.
4 Local Authorities (Capital Finance) Regulations 1997, reg 66(2)(d) and the definition of 'education or training company' in reg 66(1).
5 LA(CF)R 1997, reg 66(2)(d) and the definition of 'education or training company' in reg 66(1).
6 LA(CF)R 1997, reg 66(2)(f).

16.18 Yet a further example of the type of company in which a local authority is presumed to be able to participate is a development company which trades in land, for which special provision has been made in the drafting of financial provisions under the Local Authorities (Companies) Order 1995[1], reg 16(1)(a)[2]. As an illustration of company participation envisaged in a different statutory context, the Local Government Act 1988, s 33 makes special provision in connection with the former compulsory competitive tendering ('CCT') regime, in cases where a local authority participates in a company involved in the provision of a 'defined activity' for the purpose of LGA 1988, Pt I[3].

1 SI 1995/849.
2 See para **16.87**.
3 Unlike other provisions of LGA 1988 concerning CCT, s 33 has not been repealed by the Local Government Act 1999.

D Case law on powers to set up and participate in external bodies

16.19 LGHA 1989, Pt V is the prime example of legislation based on the premise that local authorities have power to participate in (if not to set up) companies. The consultation paper on local authorities' interests in companies issued by the Department of the Environment in June 1988 which preceded the enactment of LGHA 1989, Pt V, considered the specific enabling legislation for local authority involvement in companies and included the statements:

> '6. Most importantly, however, local authorities' subsidiary powers under section 111 of the 1972 Act are widely drawn. They authorise the doing of "anything ... which is calculated to facilitate, or is conducive or incidental to" the discharge of a function of the local authority. The judgment of the House of Lords in the case of *Manchester City Council v Greater Manchester Metropolitan County Council*[1] makes it clear that this can cover the formation of a trust. By parity of reasoning, the section would also appear to authorise the formation, or the acquisition of control over, a company under the Companies Acts.
>
> 7. A local authority may not delegate to a company discretion conferred by statute on the authority. But it can enter into a contract with a company with which it is involved to do things on its behalf, in the same way as it contracts with an independent contractor.'

1 (1979) 78 LGR 71, CA; affd (1980) 78 LGR 560, HL.

16.20 The following summarises the decision in the *Manchester* case and the case law as it has developed since 1988 when these views were written.

Manchester City Council v Greater Manchester County Council (1980) 78 LGR 560, HL

In 1978, Greater Manchester County Council ('GMC') established a trust for the advancement of education of young persons resident in the authority's area as part of a scheme to secure free or assisted places at independent schools throughout a seven year period for a particular intake of children. Relying on powers under s 137 of the Local Government Act 1972, GMC transferred some £1.12 million to the trust to enable the trustees to pay bursaries. Manchester City Council attacked the scheme, inter alia, on the ground that the creation of the trust was an end or object in itself, outside the powers of s 137(1) and also involving a delegation of GMC's powers.

Held: On this point Lord Keith of Kinkel found (affirming the decision of the Court of Appeal):

> 'I am of the opinion that ... the creation of the trust was purely incidental to the exercise of GMC's power to expend the £1.12 million as they desired to do. I am of the further opinion that there is no substance in the point about delegation. GMC exercised their own powers exhaustively when they paid the money over to the trustees. In carrying out the purposes of the trust, the trustees, for their part, were exercising their own powers and not those of GMC.'

R v Tameside Metropolitan Borough Council, ex p Governors of Audenshaw High School and Education Asset Board (1990) Times, 27 June

The council purchased an 'off-the-shelf' £100 company and transferred the freehold of school playing fields to it in anticipation that the school would vote to become grant-maintained. The council then took a leaseback of the playing fields at a rack-rent. The council had borrowed money to lend to the company to pay for the freehold. When the school became grant-maintained, only the council's leasehold interest and not the freehold would have been available for transfer to the school under s 74 of the Education Reform Act 1988.

Held: A failure to consult and to consider the educational implications vitiated the decisions. However, the Divisional Court considered that all the steps involved in the scheme, 'albeit unorthodox', formed part of the fulfilment of the proper function of the council in managing its property to the best advantage of ratepayers and that all the steps fell within s 111(1) of the Local Government Act 1972. The formation of the company was a convenient vehicle and fell within LGA 1972, ss 111 and 123.

The reasoning adopted by the Divisional Court in *Thameside* was consistent with that of the Court of Appeal in *Hazell v Hammersmith and Fulham London Borough Council*[1] a few months earlier; however, that reasoning was subsequently rejected by the House of Lords in *Hazell*[2].

Crédit Suisse v Borough Council of Allerdale [1995] 1 Lloyd's Rep 315 (Commercial Court); affd [1997] QB 306, [1996] 4 All ER 129, CA

The Borough Council engaged in a scheme to provide a new leisure facility and time-share accommodation, intending that rental income from the time-share units would assist with the costs of the leisure facility. As part of the scheme, the council purchased a '£100 company' and changed the company's name and memorandum and articles of association, to enable it to promote and undertake the development. Shares were issued to two council officers as nominees for the council. The directors of the company were all members or officers of the council. The company arranged a loan facility of up to £6,000,000 from the bank. The council provided a guarantee of sums due from the company to the bank. Leading counsel's opinion obtained by the authority indicated that reliance might be placed on a number of statutory powers, including s 19 of the Local Government (Miscellaneous Provisions) Act 1976, and that the giving of the guarantee was within LGA 1972, s 111. The company purchased land and commenced the timeshare development and completed the pool. Sale of the time-share units did not proceed as projected. The district auditor advised the council of his provisional view that the establishment of the company and the giving of the guarantee were both ultra vires. The bank demanded repayment of principal and interest due from the company. The company was unable to pay and went into liquidation. The bank demand repayment of the whole amount (some £5.2 million) and called on the council's guarantee. The council did not pay and the bank issued proceedings against the council which were heard by the Commercial Court in 1993 and 1994. The council contended that both the giving of the guarantee and the interposition of the company were ultra vires. Colman J found that the council had no statutory power to give the guarantee, and that, even if it had, the decision to give it was based on irrelevant and impermissible considerations (namely to circumvent the financial controls on local authorities and to engage in the trade of time-share accommodation for profit). In relation to the council's powers to engage in the scheme, Colman J said[3]:

> 'I have already held that the use of a company and the guarantee of its borrowings may, in some circumstances, be a permissible means of accomplishment of a local authority's objective, that is to say that such a means is not intrinsically incapable of being permissible.'

The bank appealed against the dismissal of its claim under the guarantee.

Held: The Court of Appeal affirmed that the guarantee was ultra vires the council and unenforceable. In relation to the use of a company, Neill LJ did not consider it necessary to decide whether, in the absence of some statutory power, there might be cases where a council can lawfully use a wholly owned subsidiary as a means of carrying out its functions as 'the point [did] not arise in this case'[4]; the company acted independently of the council and was not its agent. Peter Gibson LJ considered that on the facts of this case Colman J had been wrong to consider that the use of the company was not necessarily an impermissible means of discharging the council's functions of providing recreational facilities, or any other statutory function. Section 111 cannot be utilised to procure a company (or any other person) to discharge the authority's statutory functions in contravention of LGA 1972, s 101. The judge had also been wrong to consider that s 101 applied only to the decision-taking (as opposed to the ministerial) part of an authority's functions. Hobhouse LJ agreed that s 111 referred to the discharge by the council of functions, which it was unable to delegate even to individual council members, still less to the directors of a company. Whilst he acknowledged that certain local authority functions are 'secondary', in the sense that they consist of encouraging, assisting or arranging for others to do something[5], that did not assist the bank here.

Crédit Suisse v Waltham Forest London Borough Council [1997] QB 362, [1996] 4 All ER 176

The council owned 50% of the shares and nominated two of the four directors of a company involved in a scheme to purchase houses to be made available on short lease to the authority in order to provide housing for homeless people. The company drew down over £9 million of a loan facility from the bank. The council had provided a guarantee for the loan and an indemnity for the company against 'all losses arising out of the scheme'. Following a slump in the property market, the company was unable to pay its debt to the bank, who called on the council's guarantee. The district auditor took the view that the guarantee was ultra vires. The council made no payment and the bank issued a writ against the council, claiming in excess of £4.3 million. The company claimed the same amount under the indemnity agreement. Gatehouse J in the Commercial Court found that the council had implied power under LGA 1972, s 111 to guarantee the company's loan from the bank and to indemnify the company itself. The council appealed.

Held: An identically constituted Court of Appeal to that in the *Allerdale* case reversed the decision of the Commercial Court. Whilst local authorities have express powers to assist registered housing associations by providing guarantees for their borrowing (under Housing Associations Act 1985, s 58), the company was not a registered housing association, nor even a housing association. LGA 1972, s 111 did not give the authority implied power to give the company assistance in the form of the guarantee or the indemnity. Where Parliament has made detailed provision as to how certain functions are to be carried out there is no scope for implying additional powers which lie wholly outside the statutory code. LGA 1972, s 101 contains provisions relating to the arrangements which can be made for the discharge of functions by local authorities. Those powers are limited and do not entitle a local housing authority to discharge any of their functions by means of a partly owned company. Peter Gibson LJ concluded that the scheme involved an impermissible delegation of the function of providing housing under s 9 of the Housing Act 1985. It is inconsistent with the statutory scheme that a local authority should set up a company and give a guarantee of the company's liabilities and an indemnity. Hobhouse LJ saw a parallel with the position considered by the House of Lords in *Hazell*[6] (in relation to interest rate swaps and borrowing functions). The transactions were remote from the actual function of housing the homeless or the acquisition of housing for the purpose of providing accommodation; they related to an exercise in property speculation on borrowed money and the needs of a trading company, not to the needs of the council and the discharge of its functions.

1 [1990] 2 QB 697 at 781 per Sir Stephen Brown P.
2 [1992] 2 AC 1, [1991] 1 All ER 545.
3 [1995] 1 Lloyd's Rep 315 at 334.
4 [1996] 4 All ER 129 at 145.
5 In relation to 'secondary functions', Hobhouse LJ relied on *Ebbw Vale UDC v South Wales Traffic Area Licensing Authority* [1951] 2 KB 366. He gave as examples of secondary functions the Local Government Act 1972, s 144 (encouragement of visitors) and, possibly, the Local Government Act 1972, s 145 (provision of entertainments).
6 *Hazell v Hammersmith and Fulham London Borough Council* [1992] 2 AC 1, [1991] 1 All ER 545.

16.21 Thus, the case law since the 1988 consultation paper was written indicates that considerable caution should be exercised before an authority endeavours to rely on s 111 of the LGA 1972 to authorise the setting up of a company in the absence of specific enabling legislation. Particular thought should be given to the question of whether the arrangements might be construed as entailing unlawful delegation of a function. The *Allerdale* and *Waltham Forest* decisions indicate that such a conclusion would, almost inevitably, be drawn if the main statutory provision in question creates a function that only a local authority can, itself, discharge such as that under the Local Government (Miscellaneous Provisions) Act 1976, s 19.

Whilst Hobhouse LJ in *Allerdale* acknowledged the distinction between such a power and a power such as that under the Local Government Act 1972, s 144 (power to encourage visitors) which includes the power (alone or jointly with others) to encourage or assist others to do something, or to arrange for others to do something, the judgment is not determinative on the question of whether such secondary functions (alone or in conjunction with the Local Government Act 1972, s 111) would authorise a local authority to establish a company, as that question was not before the court.

E Local Government and Housing Act 1989, Pt V

16.22 LGHA 1989, Part V contains the framework of a system for regulating local authorities' involvement in companies. Like other Parts of this Act, the effectual controls are contained in subordinate legislation made by the Secretary of State, in this case by orders[1].

1 Made under Local Government and Housing Act 1989, ss 39(5)–(7), 67(4), 70(1),(5) and 71(1)(b).

16.23 The current order made under these provisions is the Local Authorities (Companies) Order 1995[1] (LACO 1995). The order came into force, for most purposes, on 1 April 1995 although for companies formed on or before 30 March 1995, certain provisions took effect on 1 July 1995.

1 SI 1995/849 as amended by SI 1996/621.

1 LOCAL AUTHORITIES SUBJECT TO LOCAL GOVERNMENT AND HOUSING ACT 1989, PT V

16.24 LGHA 1989, Pt V and LACO 1995 apply to all county, district, London borough, parish and community councils, county borough councils in Wales, the Common Council of the City of London (in various of its capacities), the Council of the Isles of Scilly and to fire, police and waste disposal authorities and certain joint authorities and boards. They also apply to Passenger Transport Executives[1]. In the following paragraphs of this chapter the expression 'local authority' (and consequently, 'relevant authority'[2]) refers to each of these types of statutory body.

1 Local Government and Housing Act 1989, s 67(3).
2 See para **16.65**.

2 BODIES SUBJECT TO PART V

16.25 The provisions of LGHA 1989, Pt V and LACO 1995 apply to participation by a local authority in the following types of body corporate[1]:

(a) a company limited by shares;
(b) a company limited by guarantee which does not have a share capital;
(c) a company limited by guarantee which has a share capital;
(d) an unlimited company;
(e) a society registered or deemed to be registered under the Industrial and Provident Societies Act 1965 or the Industrial and Provident Societies Act (Northern Ireland) 1969.

In the remainder of this chapter the word 'company' is used to mean all these types of body.

1 Local Government and Housing Act 1989, s 67(1).

16.26 Since 22 December 1980[1], no further companies limited by guarantee and having a share capital can be formed. Thus there are four types of body which can now be formed which might be subject to LGHA 1989, Pt V.

1 The 'appointed day' under s 1 of the Companies Act 1980.

16.27 LGHA 1989, s 72 empowers the Secretary of State, by order, to adapt the provisions of the Act relating to influenced companies[1] to make them applicable to non-charitable trusts. To date, no such order has been made.

1 See para **16.39**.

3 EXCLUSIONS

16.28 In addition to limited exceptions contained in the LGHA 1989 itself[1], there are two principal means by which a company may be wholly or partially exempt from the regulatory regime.

1 See Local Government and Housing Act 1989, s 69(1) regarding the exclusion of banking and insurance companies and members of banking and insurance groups from the category of influence.

16.29 The first is by a direction made by the Secretary of State under LGHA 1989, s 68(1) or s 69(1) excluding a particular company, or a specified description of companies, from the category of 'control' or 'influence' respectively, or from both those categories. Such directions may be limited in time and may be conditional. If a direction is made under both provisions, the only controls which apply are those concerning 'authorised companies'[1]. A number of directions have been made by the Secretary of State under these powers[2], in most cases applying both LGHA 1989, ss 68(1) and 69(1), to exclude several classes of company (mainly permanently) and a range of individual companies (mainly for a limited period of time) from the categories of control and influence.

1 See para **16.47**ff. Although guidance issued by the Department of the Environment in March 1995 suggested that the effect is to entirely exempt the company from the regulatory regime ('A Guide to Local Authorities' Interests in Companies', Department of the Environment and Welsh Office, March 1995, para 6).
2 On 21 March 1995 and subsequently.

16.30 The second means of exclusion is through the Schedule to LACO 1995. The types of company listed in the Schedule are the various kinds of transport and airport companies which are not subject to regulation under the Companies Order as each is subject to a regulatory regime within the particular legislation which created them. The excluded bodies comprise statutory transport[1] and airport companies[2], companies controlled or influenced by Passenger Transport Executives, and companies which are themselves 'controlled' by any of these types of company. (Local authority airport companies are subject to a separate order which imposes capital finance controls, although many such airport companies have now been freed from controls arising from their borrowing: see the Public Airport Companies (Capital Finance) Order 1996[3]).

1 Within the meaning of Transport Act 1985, s 72.
2 Within the meaning of Airports Act 1986, Pt II.
3 SI 1996/604 as amended by SI 1999/554 and SI 1999/2125. See also DETR Press Notice 476, 11 June 1998.

4 CLASSIFICATION OF COMPANIES

16.31 LGHA 1989, Pt V and the LACO 1995 create various categories of company, and the Secretary of State has power to apply different regulatory controls in respect of each of the categories created under the Act[1]. The relationship between the various categories of company under LGHA 1989 and the LACO 1995 and the various forms of control which apply to them are shown in the diagram which is appended to this chapter.

1 See Local Government and Housing Act 1989, s 70(1) regarding the Secretary of State's order-making powers in relation to controlled, arm's length controlled, and influenced companies; and s 71 (so far as it is in force) regarding authorised companies.

16.32 The categories of company created under LGHA 1989 comprise:
(a) under LGHA 1989, s 68: companies under the control of a local authority (referred to below as 'controlled companies') and a subclass of 'arm's length companies[1]';
(b) under LGHA 1989, s 69: companies subject to the influence of a local authority (referred to below as 'influenced companies');
(c) under LGHA 1989, s 71(1): 'authorised companies', which are now further defined by LACO 1995, art 11.

1 Local Government and Housing Act 1989, s 68(6).

16.33 The LACO 1995 created the now vital concept of 'regulated companies', which comprises controlled companies under LGHA 1989, s 68 and certain influenced companies under LGHA 1989, s 69[1]. In doing so, the Order added yet another layer of complexity to legislation which was already abstruse.

1 Assuming, in each case, that the company is not subject to any exemption: see para **16.28**ff.

16.34 In considering each of the following classes of company it is important to bear in mind the provisions of LGHA 1989, s 73, which apply where more than one local authority participates in the company. These provisions are described under a separate heading at para **16.94**ff.

(a) Controlled companies under LGHA 1989, s 68

16.35 Subject to the exceptions in respect of companies which benefit from a direction made by the Secretary of State described at para **16.28**ff, a company is treated as being under the control of a local authority at any time when:
(a) the company is a subsidiary of the local authority for the purpose of s 736 of the Companies Act 1985[1]; or
(b) the local authority has power to control a majority of the votes at a general meeting[2]; or
(c) the local authority has power to appoint or remove the majority of the board of directors; or

(d) the company is under the control of another company which is itself under the 'control' of the local authority.

1 That is:
(a) the local authority is a member of the company and controls the composition of the board of directors; or
(b) the authority holds more than half the nominal value of the company's equity share capital; or
(c) the company is itself a subsidiary of a company which is a subsidiary of the authority.
2 Whether through its own shares and voting rights or through those of nominees and others acting under its control: see Local Government and Housing Act 1989, s 68(3).

16.36 Detailed provision is made in LGHA 1989, s 69(3)–(5) regarding means of exerting control. In simple terms, control relates to cases where the council's interest (direct or indirect) enables it to control more than 50% of the voting rights or composition of the board of directors of the company. As explained at para **16.51**, controlled companies are also regulated companies[1], so that the main propriety and financial controls under the Companies Order apply to them and arise from their financial activities.

1 Local Authorities (Companies) Order 1995, art 1(4)(a).

(b) Arm's length controlled companies under LGHA 1989, s 68(6)

16.37 These are controlled companies which, throughout the entire financial year in question, satisfy eight criteria specified in LGHA 1989, s 68(6) which are intended to establish the company's arm's length status. In addition, in advance of each financial year during which arm's length status is sought for a company, the authority must have passed a resolution to the effect that the company should be 'an arm's length company'.

16.38 Whilst LGHA 1989, s 70(1)(a) empowers the Secretary of State to make different provision in relation to arm's length companies as opposed to other companies, the present Companies Order differs only slightly in its treatment of them[1]. Their treatment in terms of the financial controls under Pt V of the LACO 1995 is identical to that of all other regulated companies (the legislation concerning local authority waste disposal companies requires that a company established by a local authority should have arm's length status whilst the authority controls it[2]).

1 See Local Authorities (Companies) Order 1995, art 10. Arm's length companies are relieved of the obligation which applies to other controlled (and therefore regulated) companies to make minutes of their general meetings available for public inspection for a period of four years (see para **16.68**).
2 See the Environmental Protection Act 1990, s 32(9).

(c) Influenced companies under LGHA 1989, s 69

16.39 A company which is not exempt[1] and which is not a controlled company, is to be treated as subject to the influence of a local authority at any time when at least 20% of certain voting rights or directorships are held by 'persons who are associated with the local authority' *if* at that time there is also a 'business relationship' between the authority and the company. This two-fold test appears to be aimed at indirect methods by which a local authority might exert influence over a company, albeit that there is no direct local authority control within the tests under LGHA 1989, s 68.

1 See para **16.29**ff regarding directions made by the Secretary of State under the 1989 Act ss 68(1) and 69(1); and s 69(1) itself, regarding the exclusion of banking and insurance companies and members of banking and insurance groups.

(i) The associated persons test

16.40 Under LGHA 1989, s 69(5) a person is 'associated with' a local authority whilst that person is:

(a) a member of that local authority;
(b) an officer of that local authority;
(c) both an employee of and either a director, manager, secretary or other similar officer of a company which is under the control of the local authority;

or if, *at any time in the preceding four years*, that person:

(d) has been a member of the local authority.

16.41 The Secretary of State has power to provide, by order, that certain other specified categories of people should be treated as associated with a local authority, but to date these powers have not been used[1].

1 Local Government and Housing Act 1989, s 69(6).

16.42 Under LGHA 1989, s 69(1), the '20% associated persons test' may be satisfied, at any time, in one or more of three ways, namely where:

(a) at least 20% of the total voting rights of all the members having the right to vote at a general meeting of the company are held by persons who are associated as mentioned in LGHA 1989, s 69(5);
(b) at least 20% of the directors of the company are persons who are so associated;
(c) at least 20% of the voting rights at a meeting of the directors of the company are held by persons who are so associated.

16.43 It is to be noted that LGHA 1989, s 69(1)(a) refers to voting rights at general meetings which are *held* by associated persons (and not to voting rights *exercised* by such persons). Where the shares are owned by a local authority so that the voting rights are held by the authority itself, arguably it is not relevant under this subsection that a person who is associated with the local authority might attend a general meeting in order to vote on the council's behalf[1].

1 In practice, where a local authority which wishes to ensure that a company limited by shares in which it is involved is not treated as regulated under the Companies Order, it may wish to arrange matters so as to ensure that the company would not be treated either as controlled (under LGHA 1989, s 68) or influenced (under LGHA 1989, s 69) so that the company would not be eligible, or potentially eligible, under the Companies Order tests for regulated status (see para **16.50**ff). In relation to the influenced company tests, where the business relationship test (see para **16.44**ff) is or might be met, local authorities often arrange for the percentage of *the council's voting rights* at general meetings (and its shares carrying such rights) to be kept below the 20% level. However, strictly, it is the voting rights/shareholding of associated persons which is the decisive test for 'influence' under s 69(1)(a). (The council's voting rights/ shareholding would need to be maintained below the majority interest tests for control under s 68, if it is intended that the company should not be treated as regulated.) The number of, and voting rights of, directors who are associated must be kept below the 20% level if it is intended that the company should not come within the category of influence (where the business relationship test is, or is likely to be, met).

(ii) The business relationship test

16.44 Under LGHA 1989, s 69(3) the 'business relationship test' may be fulfilled, at any time, in one or more of the following ways:

(a) *Local authority payments—company turnover* Within a period of twelve months which includes that time the aggregate of the payments to the company by the authority or by another company which is under the control of the authority represents more than one-half of the company's turnover, as shown in its profit and loss account for the most recent financial year for which the company's auditors have made a report on the accounts or, if there is no such account, as estimated by the authority for the period of twelve months preceding the date of the estimate or for such part of that period as follows the formation of the company;

(b) *Exploitation of local authority assets—company turnover* More than one-half of the company's turnover referred to in para (a) above is derived from the exploitation of assets of any description in which the local authority or a company under the control of the authority has an interest (disregarding an interest in land which is in reversion on a lease granted for more than seven years);

(c) *Local authority grants and shares—company net assets* The aggregate of –

  (i) grants made either by the authority and being expenditure for capital purposes or by a company under the control of the authority, and

  (ii) the nominal value of shares or stock in the company which is owned by the authority or by a company under the control of the authority,

  exceeds one-half of the net assets of the company[1];

(d) *Local authority grants, loans and shares—company fixed and current assets* The aggregate of –

  (i) grants falling within para (c)(i) above,

  (ii) loans or other advances made or guaranteed by the authority or by a company under the control of the authority, and

  (iii) the nominal value referred to in para (c)(ii) above,

  exceeds one-half of the fixed and current assets of the company[2];

(e) *Company occupation of local authority land obtained at undervalue* The company at that time occupies land by virtue of an interest which it obtained from the local authority or a company under the control of the authority and which it so obtained at less than the best consideration reasonably obtainable; and

(f) *Intention to enter into a business relationship* The company intends at that time to enter into (or complete) a transaction and, when that is done, there will then be a business relationship between the company and the authority by virtue of any of paras (a) to (e) above.

1 The reference in para (c) to 'the net assets of the company' is to be construed in accordance with s 152(2) of the Companies Act 1985 (and as being a reference to those assets as shown in the most recent balance sheet of the company on which, at the time in question, the auditors have made a report or, if there is no such balance sheet, as estimated by the local authority for the time in question): Local Government and Housing Act 1989, s 69(4)(a).

2 The reference in para (d) to 'the fixed and current assets of the company' is to be construed in accordance with the Companies Act 1985, Sch 4, para 77 (and as being a reference to those assets as shown in the most recent balance sheet of the company on which, at the time in question, the auditors have made a report or, if there is no such balance sheet, as estimated by the local authority for the time in question): Local Government and Housing Act 1989, s 69(4)(b).

16.45 Thus, a 'business relationship' between a local authority and a company may arise through payments, capital grants, loans or guarantees of borrowing made by the council to or for the company, as well as through the exploitation of assets in which the council has an interest, or through a transfer of land to the company at less than best consideration. However, the company will only be treated as subject to the influence of the local authority at any time if a 'business relationship' as defined in LGHA 1989, s 69(3) exists contemporaneously with one of the '20% associated persons tests' under s 69(1) being fulfilled.

16.46 As described at para **16.51**ff, some, but not all, influenced companies are treated as regulated under the LACO 1995[1].

1 Local Authorities (Companies) Order 1995, art 1(4)(b).

(d) Authorised companies under LGHA 1989, s 71(1) and Local Authorities (Companies) Order 1995, art 11

16.47 LGHA 1989, s 71(1) provides that an authorised company is a 'company of a description specified for the purposes of this section by an order made by the Secretary of State'. The drafting of s 71(1) suggests that the main relevance of this category would be for companies which are not controlled by a local authority[1]. (It should be noted that, to date, certain of the provisions of s 71 on authorised companies have not been brought into force[2], so that the section has somewhat different effects from those originally envisaged when LGHA 1989 was first enacted[3].)

1 LGHA 1989, s 71(1) is linked to LGHA 1989, s 71(2), under which local authorities were to have been prohibited from participating in certain companies in specified ways unless the company was either to be treated as controlled within LGHA 1989, s 68 or an authorised company. However, s 71(2) has not been commenced. The implications of whether or not a company is to be treated as 'authorised' are perhaps less significant than appeared when LGHA 1989, Pt V was first enacted.
2 Local Government and Housing Act 1989, s 71(2),(3),(5)(b) and (7).
3 For the provisions of s 71 which are in force see SI 1989/2445 (commencing the order-making powers of the Secretary of State) and SI 1995/841 commencing LGHA 1989, s 71(1) (for the purposes only of s 71(4)–(6)) and s 71(4),(5)(a),(6) and (8). (The whole of LGHA 1989, s 71 (and certain other provision of LGHA 1989, Pt V) were to have been brought into force during 1990, but the relevant part of the commencement order (SI 1990/ 1274) was amended before it came into effect (see SI 1990/1335).)

16.48 Under art 11 of the Companies Order, the Secretary of State has specified that the category of 'authorised company' is to comprise any company which is not regulated (or listed in the Schedule to the Order), but in which any person associated with a local authority (within the meaning of LGHA 1989, s 69(5))[1] has a right to vote at a general meeting or is a director. In theory at least, this category is very wide. There is nothing in the definition of associated person under s 69(5) or elsewhere which requires the local authority to concur in (or even have knowledge of) the involvement of the member, former member, or officer in the company.

1 See paras **16.40–16.41**.

16.49 Authorised companies are sometimes referred to as 'minority interest companies'[1]. The category would include the following:

(a) companies in which the local authority's interest through voting rights and directorships held by associated persons is below the 20% threshold in s 69(1) (so that the company is not influenced (nor controlled));
(b) companies where the authority's interest is at any level up to 50%, but where

no 'business relationship' under s 69(3) exists (so that the company is not influenced (nor controlled));

(c) influenced companies within s 69 which are *not* regulated under the Companies Order;

(d) companies excluded from the categories of control and influence by a direction of the Secretary of State under s 68(1) and s 69(1).

1 See headings to Local Government and Housing Act 1989, s 71 and LACO 1995, Pt 11.

(e) Regulated companies under Local Authorities (Companies) Order 1995, art 1(4)

16.50 Of all the classifications, the category of regulated company is the most complex and of the greatest significance. It is complex because it is dependent upon first establishing whether the categories of control or influence under LGHA 1989 apply to a particular company and then upon considering the effect of the convoluted terms of the LACO 1995, which in turn rely heavily upon accounting standards in certain instances. The 'regulated' classification is important because, if the company is to be treated as regulated, financial consequences for the local authority may arise from certain of the company's financial transactions and activities[1]; in addition, the company will be required to comply with the main 'propriety controls' contained in the Order.

1 These financial consequences for the local authority have been less extensive since 1 September 1998, when set aside on most non-housing capital receipts and notional capital receipts was abolished (see para **14.26**). However, they continue to apply where a regulated company borrows money, otherwise increases its relevant liabilities or enters into a transaction which, for a local authority, would amount to a credit arrangement. See para **16.69**ff.

16.51 Under LACO 1995, art 1(4) a regulated company is one which is for the time being:

(a) a controlled company (under LGHA 1989, s 68), or

(b) an influenced company (under LGHA 1989, s 69) and which—
   - (i) is an unlimited company or an industrial and provident society[1]; or
   - (ii) satisfies either or both of the first and second conditions set out in LACO 1995, art 1(5) and (7).

1 A society registered or deemed to be registered under the Industrial and Provident Societies Act 1965 or under the Industrial and Provident Societies Act (Northern Ireland) 1969.

16.52 Thus, in the absence of any special exception[1], all controlled companies are also to be treated as regulated companies under the Companies Order. Companies which are influenced and are either unlimited or an industrial and provident society are also treated as regulated companies, without any further tests applying. But if the company is influenced and it is limited by shares and/or guarantee, it will only be regulated if either or both of two further tests in LACO 1995, art 1(5) and (7) are satisfied. The conditions in these paragraphs are complex and merit consideration.

1 See para **16.28**ff.

16.53 The *first condition* under LACO 1995, art 1(5) is that:

'... the relevant authority would, if it were a company registered under the 1985 Act[1], be treated by virtue of section 258 of that Act as having the right to exercise, or as having during the relevant period[2], actually exercised, a dominant influence over the company in question.'

1 Companies Act 1985.
2 'Relevant period' is defined for the purpose of LACO 1995, art 1(5) by art 1(6). In relation to any duty or any action referred to in Pt II of the Order (which deals with the various propriety controls on regulated companies), it means the financial year of the relevant authority which ended immediately before the financial year in which, if the company in question were a regulated company, that duty would fall to be fulfilled, or in which that action is performed.

16.54 The first condition turns on whether, if the authority were a registered company, the company law tests for dominant influence would apply to the council's relationship with the company. Under the Companies Act 1985, s 258 'dominant influence' is used in the context of two distinct tests concerning parent and subsidiary undertakings for the purposes of the law relating to company accounts[1].

1 The provisions derive from the requirements of the European Community Seventh Company Law Directive.

16.55 The expression 'a right to exercise a dominant influence' is used in the Companies Act 1985, s 258(2)(c) and is defined by CA 1985, Sch 10A. Such a right can only exist if there is a right (created in one of two specified ways) to give directions with respect to the operating and financial policies of another undertaking which its directors are obliged to comply with, whether or not they are for the benefit of that other undertaking. In view of the fiduciary duties of directors under English company law, it is unclear how much practical significance this test has.

16.56 The expression 'actually exercises a dominant influence', although used in CA 1985, s 258(4)(a), is not defined in the Act itself. Financial Reporting Standard 2[1] ('FRS 2'), produced by the Accounting Standards Board, gives guidance on its meaning, describing it in these terms:

> 'The actual exercise of dominant influence is the exercise of an influence which achieves the result that the operating and financial policies of the undertaking influenced are set in accordance with the wishes of the holder of the influence and for the holder's benefit whether or not those wishes are explicit. The actual exercise of dominant influence is identified by its effect in practice rather than by the way in which it is exercised.'[2]

1 Issued June 1992 (amended November 1997, July 1998 and December 1998).
2 FRS 2, para 7(b).

16.57 Further advice in FRS 2[1] suggests that the full circumstances of each case must be considered, including the effect of any formal or informal agreements between undertakings. Commercial arrangements such as that of supplier, customer or lender do not, of themselves, constitute dominant influence. A rare intervention on a critical matter might constitute evidence of such influence. A power of veto which has the necessary effect in practice can form the basis whereby one undertaking actually exercises a dominant influence over another.

1 FRS 2, paras 71–73.

16.58 The test in LACO 1995, art 1(5) is potentially of wide ranging effect and is one which, in practice, may be applied initially by accountants, looking retrospectively at the relationship between the company and the local authority. In the company law context there is a dearth of judicial guidance on its ambit. Guidance from the Department of the Environment[1] suggests that 'dominant influence' might arise in circumstances where there is a spread in share ownership:

> 'In particular, if an authority owns a substantial minority of the shares, with the remaining shares spread across a range of shareholdings, and with other partners not operating in concert, then this will need close scrutiny and there will need to be clear evidence that the local authority does not exercise effective control.'[2]

1 'A Guide to Local Authorities' Interests in Companies', Department of the Environment and Welsh Office, March 1995.
2 Ibid, para 13.

16.59 The *second condition* under art 1(7) of the Companies Order is that:

> '... if the authority were a company registered under the [Companies Act 1985] it would be required, by virtue of s 227 of that Act, or of accounting standards such as would, by virtue of that Act, be applicable in the circumstances, to prepare group accounts in respect of the company in question.'[1]

1 Under Local Authorities (Companies) Order 1995, art 1(8), in applying the assumptions in art 1(7) all the exemptions and exclusions from the Companies Act 1985, s 227 (eg those which apply to small and medium sized groups under s 248) must be disregarded, other than those in the Companies Act 1985, s 229(3)(a) and (c). These exclusions concern severe long term restrictions substantially hindering the parent undertaking's rights over the assets or management of the undertaking, and cases where the parent company's interest is held exclusively with a view to resale and the undertaking has not previously been included in the parent's consolidated group accounts.

16.60 In applying the second test, the situation must again be assessed by reference to the situation which would apply if the local authority were itself a registered company. The authority must then consider whether, in this situation, it would be required to prepare group accounts in respect of the company concerned.

16.61 CA 1985, s 227 relates to the duty to prepare group accounts and the consolidation of parent and subsidiary undertakings' accounts. These provisions include what is sometimes described as the 'true and fair override'. If, in special circumstances, compliance with the provisions of CA 1985 regarding group accounts would not be sufficient to give a true and fair view, directors are required to depart from that statutory provision to the extent necessary to give a true and fair view[1].

1 Companies Act 1985, s 227(6).

16.62 The Department of the Environment Guide[1] (at para 20) indicates that the provisions of both FRS 2 and FRS 5[2] are relevant to this second test under art 1(7). FRS 5 provides guidance on reporting the substance of transactions. It creates the concept of 'quasi-subsidiaries'. These are bodies which do not meet the legal definition of a subsidiary, but their commercial effect is considered to be no different. They have a particular significance in the context of company law where the 'parent' does not hold a 'participating interest' in the other company. Such a 'participating interest' is required before the provisions under s 258(4)(a) on actual exercise of a dominant influence apply under CA 1985. However, as this test of 'participating interest' has not been transposed into the local government companies provisions, it seems doubtful that the concept of 'quasi-subsidiary' in FRS 5, or indeed LACO 1995, art 1(7) as a whole, extends significantly the tests contained in art 1(5). In practice, it seems likely that most companies within art 1(7) would in any event be treated as regulated on account of one of the grounds mentioned in art 1(5), of which the most important appears to be that regarding having 'actually exercised a dominant influence' over the company in question.

1 See para **16.56**, n 1.
2 Issued April 1994 (amended December 1994, November 1997, September 1998 and December 1998).

16.63 Accounting standards play a vital part in the application of the tests in LACO 1995, art 1(5) and (7). It is to be noted that accounting standards are not static and may change with time. In the context of corporate accounting, consideration has been given to the status of accounting standards under law in the United Kingdom. In relation to the question of whether accounts satisfy the 'true and fair view' requirement, it has been said that whilst this is a question of law for the court, this task cannot be performed by the court without evidence as to the practices and views of accountants[1].

1 See the Opinion of Mary Arden QC (now Mrs Justice Arden) published as an Appendix to the Accounting Standards Board's 'Foreword to Accounting Standards' (June 1993) on the status of accounting standards under United Kingdom legislation.

5 CONTROLS ON REGULATED COMPANIES

16.64 The regime of controls on regulated companies created under the Companies Order falls into two broad categories:

(a) propriety controls, which are mainly expressed in terms of obligations imposed on the company itself; and
(b) financial controls, which are expressed in terms of obligations on the part of the relevant authority.

16.65 The sanctions for non-compliance, such as they are, are referred to in para **16.99**ff. For the purposes of the LACO 1995, the 'relevant authority' in relation to a regulated company is any local authority having control of that company, or to whose influence the company is subject, or which is, by virtue of LGHA 1989, s 73[1], treated as having control or influence[2]. The expression 'relevant authority' is used in same way in the following paragraphs.

1 See para **16.94**ff regarding authorities acting jointly.
2 Local Authorities (Companies) Order 1995, art 1(4).

(a) Propriety controls on regulated companies under Local Authorities (Companies) Order 1995, Pts II and III

16.66 Under LACO 1995, arts 4–8, all regulated companies are:

(a) required to mention on all relevant company documents that the company is controlled or influenced by a local authority within the meaning of Pt V (and to name the relevant authority or authorities);
(b) prohibited from paying to directors, who are also members of the relevant

authority, remuneration or travelling and subsistence allowances in excess of the maximum prescribed amounts payable for comparable local authority duties;

(c) prohibited from publishing material which a local authority would be prohibited from publishing by s 2 of the Local Government Act 1986 (material which appears to be designed to affect public support for a political party);

(d) required to arrange for a resolution to be moved for the removal of any director who becomes disqualified for membership of a local authority[1] for any reason other than being employed by a local authority);

(e) required to provide (and authorise or instruct its auditors to provide) information and explanation about the company's affairs to the auditor of the authority's accounts[2] and information to any person authorised by the Audit Commission[3];

(f) required to provide to a member of the relevant authority such information about the affairs of the company as the member may reasonably require for the proper discharge of duties;

(g) required to provide the relevant authority with such information about the affairs of the company as the authority may reasonably require for the purposes of any order for the time being in force under LGHA 1989, s 39 (for example, for the purpose of the capital finance provisions of LACO 1995, Pt V).

1 See Local Government Act 1972, ss 80 and 81.
2 For the purposes of auditing the local authority's accounts.
3 Such information as that person may require for the discharge of any function under Pt III of the Local Government Finance Act 1982 (now superseded by the Audit Commission Act 1998, Pt II).

16.67 Under LACO 1995, art 9, *controlled companies* must obtain the consent of the Audit Commission prior to first appointing any auditor.

16.68 Controlled companies which are not arm's length companies under LGHA 1989, s 68(6), are required by LACO 1995, art 10 to make copies of minutes of their general meetings available for public inspection for a period of four years following the date of the meeting, save where disclosure would be in breach of any enactment or of an obligation owed to any person.

(b) Financial controls arising from activities of regulated companies under Local Authorities (Companies) Order 1995, Pt V

16.69 The capital finance provisions of the Order are complex and were amended not long after their enactment[1]. Only a summary of the main provisions is given in this section. In essence, the controls under the Order work by requiring the relevant authority to make special provision under the capital finance system of LGHA 1989, Pt IV in respect of certain activities of a regulated company. Only a modified form of Pt IV applies in respect of selected regulated company activities; its provisions are not adopted 'wholesale'. The overall intention of the financial provisions is that, so far as the capital finance regime is concerned, a local authority should be in no better (nor worse) position on account of a transaction of a regulated company, than if it had undertaken that transaction itself. Through the effects of several separate provisions, dealings within a 'local authority group'[2] are generally disregarded. Unlike the propriety controls, the financial requirements are expressed as being obligations of the local authority and not of the company. As described at para **16.66**(g), under the LACO 1995, art 8(1), the company is required to provide the authority with the necessary information about the company's affairs to enable the authority to comply with its obligations under Pt V of the Order.

1 By SI 1996/621.
2 A local authority and any regulated companies for which it is the 'relevant authority' constitute a 'local authority group': Companies Order, art 12(1); arts 12(1)(a) and (b), 13(2)(a) and 17 concern dealings within such a group.

(i) Abolition of set aside on capital receipts

16.70 The abolition of set aside on most non-housing capital receipts (and notional capital receipts) from 1 September 1998, through the introduction of reg 64A into LA(CF)R 1997[1] is of equal benefit to the treatment of the receipts of regulated companies. The most important remaining effects of LACO 1995, Pt V are those which arise from borrowing by a regulated company (and other transactions leading to an increase in the company's 'relevant liabilities') and cases where such a company enters into a transaction which is analogous to a 'credit arrangement'[2], eg where the company takes a lease or enters into a deferred purchase arrangement.

1 And other amendments made to the LA(CF)R 1997 by SI 1998/1937: see paras **14.26** and **14.30**.
2 Credit arrangements arise under LGHA 1989, s 48 (and regulations made under the Act) and comprise various means by which a local authority may obtain credit, which do not amount to borrowing; they are dealt with in Chapter 12.

(ii) Article 13—receipts, contracts and liabilities of regulated companies

16.71 Subject to the exceptions mentioned below, the controls under the Order arise when (on or after 1 April 1995) a regulated company:

(a) receives a sum which, if it were a local authority, would be a capital receipt;
(b) receives consideration to which, if it were a local authority, LGHA 1989, s 61 would apply (ie a 'notional capital receipt');
(c) receives a sum by way of grant from a Community institution to which, if it were a local authority, LGHA 1989, s 63(4) would apply[1];
(d) enters into a credit transaction[2];
(e) with respect to a credit transaction, agrees to a variation of terms which, if it were a local authority, would be a variation within the meaning of LGHA 1989, s 51(1);
(f) incurs additional liabilities within the meaning of LACO 1995, art 16(3); or
(g) reduces its liabilities within the meaning of LACO 1995, art 16(4).

1 That is, a grant from a Community institution towards expenditure on capital purposes. LGHA 1989, s 63(4) has been amended by SI 2000/589 so as to exclude contributions from any of the Structural Funds.
2 'Credit transaction' is defined in art 12(2) to encompass leases and other contracts which, if entered into by a local authority, would constitute credit arrangements (under LGHA 1989, s 48 and regulations made under that Act), subject to exceptions for transactions between 'members of a local authority group' as defined in LACO 1995, art 12(1) (see para **16.69**, n 2) (see also art 17 regarding dealings between members of a local authority group, in relation to leases etc *taken* by a local authority from a company within such a group).

16.72 In the above circumstances, the sum, consideration, credit transaction, variation, liability or reduction in question is to be treated for the purposes of the application of LGHA 1989, Pt IV as having been received, entered into, agreed, incurred or, as the case may be, made by the relevant authority[1]. However, modifications to the basic system under LGHA 1989, Pt IV are then incorporated into the subsequent provisions of LACO 1995, Pt V.

1 Local Authorities (Companies) Order 1995, art 13(1).

16.73 Exceptions[1] from art 13 apply to any sum or consideration which is received by a regulated company –

(a) from a person who is a member of the same local authority group[2]; and
(b) in respect of the disposal of assets held for charitable purposes.

1 Local Authorities (Companies) Order 1995, art 13(2).
2 See para **16.69**, n 2.

16.74 It is to be noted that the definition of 'credit transaction' excludes leases granted or assigned to the regulated company by another member of the same local authority group[1] and other contracts entered into between members of the same group[2].

1 Local Authorities (Companies) Order 1995, art 12(2).
2 See para **16.69**, n 2.

16.75 The transactions of companies which were regulated on 1 April 1995 but which were no longer regulated on 31 March 1996 (and which did not again become regulated on or before 31 March 1997) are disregarded[1].

1 Local Authorities (Companies) Order 1995, art 13(3) and (4).

(iii) Article 14—requirement for relevant authority to provide credit cover

16.76 LACO 1995, art 14 deals with the action which a relevant authority is required to take where, in any financial year[1] (the 'current year') it is to be treated, by virtue of LACO 1995, art 13, as having received a capital receipt, notional capital receipt, entered into or agreed to vary a credit transaction or incurred additional liabilities, on account of the activities of a regulated company. (The effect of a *reduction* in a regulated company's liabilities is dealt with separately in LACO 1995, art 15.) With respect to each regulated company in the local authority group, LGHA 1989, Pt IV applies with modifications. Subject to the de minimis exemption referred to below, the relevant authority is required to make available, in the financial year following the current year, an amount of 'credit cover' which is equal to the aggregate of –

(a) *if the company receives sums or consideration which are to be treated as capital receipts or notional capital receipts:* the amount which, if the company were a local authority[2], the company would have been required to set aside as provision for credit liabilities in accordance with LGHA 1989, s 59 or s 61(4);
(b) *if the company receives grant from a Community institution:* an amount equal to the total receipts by the company which would be subject to LGHA 1989, s 63(4)[3], if received by a local authority;
(c) *if the company enters into a credit transaction:* the amount which, if the company were a local authority, would be the 'initial cost' of that transaction;
(d) *if the company varies the terms of a credit transaction:* the amount of credit cover which, if the company were a local authority, would be required to be made available to it in accordance with LGHA 1989, s 51(4) with respect to such a variation; and

(e) *if, in the current year, the company incurs 'additional liabilities' within the meaning of art 16:* the amount of the excess referred to in LACO 1995, art 16(3).

1 Local Government and Housing Act 1989, s 66(1)(b) defines 'financial year' as meaning the period of 12 months beginning on 1 April.
2 And on the assumption that it is not a 'debt-free' authority: see Local Authorities (Companies) Order 1995, arts 14(2)(a) and (3). See para **10.28**ff regarding debt-free authorities generally.
3 LGHA 1989, s 63(4) has been amended by SI 2000/589 so as to exclude contributions from any of the Structural Funds.

16.77 By virtue of LACO 1995, art 14(4), it is only where the aggregate amount of (c), (d) and (e) above exceeds £10,000, that credit cover in respect of those particular amounts need be provided by the relevant authority.

16.78 Capital receipts in respect of the disposal of an interest in a capital asset which, in aggregate, do not exceed £6,000 are disregarded by virtue of a general exemption under LGHA 1989, Pt IV[1]. In calculating the amount of credit cover to be made available in respect of capital receipts and notional capital receipts received by a regulated company, the special provisions of the LA(CF)R 1997 which allow for a reduction of a receipt prior to calculating set aside in specified circumstances would apply[2]. This is because LACO 1995, art 14(1)(a) requires the calculation to be made in exactly the same way as if the company were a local authority[3] receiving a capital receipt. It is because of this, that the abolition of set aside on most non-housing capital receipts is of equal benefit in respect of company receipts[4]. Consequently, since 1 September 1998, item (a) in para **16.76** (the need to make special provision in respect of company capital receipts and notional receipts) has been largely redundant.

1 Amounts less than £6,000 in aggregate in respect of the disposal of an interest in an asset are not capital receipts: see Local Authorities (Capital Finance) Regulations 1997, reg 61 and para **14.23**(a).
2 This was confirmed in para 36 of the Department of the Environment Guide to the Companies Order (March 1995).
3 And on the assumption that the local authority is not 'debt-free'. See LACO 1995, arts 14(2)(a) and 14(3) and para **10.28**ff regarding debt-free authorities generally.
4 See para **16.70**.

(iv) Article 14(5)—sources of credit cover

16.79 LACO 1995, art 14(5) specifies the means by which the authority may make available the credit cover required under these provisions, being either or both in any combination of the following:

(a) an amount which the authority determine to set aside from the usable part of the authority's capital receipts or from a revenue account as provision to meet credit liabilities (being an amount over and above the amounts required to be set aside by virtue of any other provision in LGHA 1989, Pt IV); or
(b) an amount by which the authority determine to treat as reduced the balance of a credit approval[1].

1 That is, a basic credit approval under Local Government and Housing Act 1989, s 53 or a supplementary credit approval under s 54. See para **11.12**ff regarding basic and supplementary credit approvals generally.

(v) Article 15—increase in basic credit approval

16.80 Where in any financial year (the 'current year') a regulated company reduces its liabilities within the meaning of LACO 1995, art 16, then in the financial year *following* the current year, the relevant authority is entitled to treat a basic credit approval[1] as increased by the amount of the excess referred to in art 16(4). Thus, the relevant authority may reap some benefit if a regulated company reduces its liabilities (as defined), eg where the company has reduced the level of its borrowing or other liabilities, but has not reduced its 'current assets' (eg cash) by an equivalent amount.

1 Under Local Government and Housing Act 1989, s 53.

(vi) Article 16—liabilities of regulated companies

16.81 The method of calculating the 'relevant liabilities' of a regulated company is prescribed in detailed terms in LACO 1995, art 16 and is only summarised here. These calculations are used to establish whether the company has incurred any additional liabilities (leading to a requirement for the authority to provide credit cover in the following year under LACO 1995, art 14), or alternatively, whether there has been a reduction in liabilities (entitling the authority to treat a basic credit approval as increased in the following year under LACO 1995, art 15).

16.82 A regulated company is to be treated as has having 'incurred additional liabilities'[1] where, in any financial year ('year two'), its relevant liabilities exceed those in the previous year ('year one'). Such an increase will usually lead to an obligation of the relevant authority to provide credit cover under LACO 1995, art 14, as described in paras **16.76**(e) and **16.79**.

1 LACO 1995, art 16(3).

16.83 A regulated company is to be treated as having made a *reduction* in its relevant liabilities[1], if those in year one exceed those in year two. Such a reduction will usually entitle the relevant authority to treat a basic credit approval as increased by an appropriate amount in the following financial year under LACO 1995, art 15, as described in para **16.80**.

1 LACO 1995, art 16(4).

16.84 Special rules apply in the years in which the company becomes and ceases to be a regulated company of the relevant authority[1] and in respect of expenditure by the company of any revenue reserves which the company had built up for specific purposes before becoming regulated[2].

1 See Local Authorities (Companies) Order 1995, art 16(5A),(6)–(7).
2 See para **16.89**.

16.85 'Relevant liabilities'[1] means the total of a regulated company's liabilities less its current assets (and may be a negative amount).

1 LACO 1995, art 16(1).

16.86 'Liabilities'[1] is largely defined by reference to exclusions, but it is clearly intended that the expression should include a regulated company's liabilities in relation to borrowing. For these purposes 'liabilities' does not include a regulated company's liabilities under a credit transaction (otherwise there would be a double penalty for the relevant authority, as these are catered for separately under LACO 1995, arts 13 and 14). Nor does the expression include liabilities owed to another member of the same local authority group, unless those liabilities were incurred before the date on which the company became regulated ('the relevant date'). However, the amount of the company's called-up share capital and any premium paid for those shares is treated as a liability of the company, unless the shares are held by other members of the local authority group.

1 LACO 1995, art 16(1)(c).

16.87 'Current assets' is to be construed in accordance with the Companies Act 1985, s 262(1) (ie assets of a company which are not intended for use on a continuing basis in the company's activities) and includes, in particular, cash. Land in which the company has an interest would not normally be considered to be a current asset, but has been explicitly excluded from the definition in the Companies Order[1] in order to provide for the case of a company which deals in land[2]. Liabilities which are owed to the company by another member of the same local authority group are also excluded, unless the liability was incurred before the 'relevant date'.

1 By Local Authorities (Companies) Order 1995, art 16(1)(a)(i).
2 A Guide to Local Authorities' Interests in Companies, Department of the Environment and the Welsh Office, March 1995, para 43. (This constitutes an indication of the extent of the powers a local authority is *assumed* to have for the purpose of the regulatory regime, ie the ability to participate in a development company which is trading land).

16.88 Generally, a regulated company's relevant liabilities for any financial year are determined by reference to amounts shown as assets and liabilities in the company's balance sheet prepared during that year (or if more than one balance sheet, the last within that financial year), combined with the amounts which the authority determines to be assets and liabilities of the company on the last day of that financial year[1]. Where a company ceases to be a regulated company, or becomes the regulated company of another local authority, the relevant authority is to determine relevant liabilities by reference to amounts which the authority determines to be assets and liabilities on the day immediately before the day on which the company ceases to be a member of the local authority group[2].

1 Local Authorities (Companies) Order 1995, art 16(5).
2 Ibid, art 16(5A) and (5B).

16.89 A special allowance is made[1] for companies which have built up revenue reserves for capital expenditure prior to becoming regulated. Expenditure by the company of such reserves for capital purposes is not to be treated as reducing its current assets (and accordingly will not affect the calculation of the company's relevant liabilities).

1 Through an amendment to art 16 made by 1996 SI 1996/621, inserting art 16(1)(bb).

(vii) Debt-free authorities and Local Authorities (Companies) Order 1995, Pt V

16.90 Where an authority which is debt-free[1] provides credit cover in respect of the activities of a regulated company by setting aside sums as provision for credit liabilities, generally that amount can be used again by the authority for most kinds of capital expenditure in the financial year following that in which the set-aside provision has been made. The debts of a regulated company do not count as being the debts of the relevant authority (whether or not that authority is debt free).

Consequently the debts of a regulated company do not, in themselves, jeopardise an authority's debt-free status.

1 See para **10.28**ff.

6 CONTROLS ON AUTHORISED COMPANIES

16.91 There are no special financial requirements in relation to authorised companies[1], either under LGHA 1989 or the LACO 1995.

1 See para **16.47**ff for a description of the companies which amount to 'authorised companies'.

16.92 The propriety controls for authorised companies contained in LGHA 1989, s 71(4),(5)(a) and (6)[1] are minimal. They comprise:

(a) a prohibition on the local authority taking any action, or refraining from exercising a right, which would have the result that a person disqualified from membership of a local authority[2] (otherwise than through being employed by a local authority or by a controlled company):
   (i) becomes a member or director of an authorised company, or
   (ii) acts as the local authority's representative at a general meeting of the company (having been authorised so to do under the Companies Act 1985, s 375[3]); and

(b) if any member or officer is authorised to act as the authority's representative under s 375, to make arrangements to enable members of the local authority to put questions to that person about the company's activities, at a council, committee or sub-committee meeting[4].

1 Which apply by virtue of Local Authorities (Companies) Order 1995, art 11 and the partial commencement of Local Government and Housing Act 1989, s 71.
2 See Local Government Act 1972, ss 80 and 81.
3 Local Government and Housing Act 1989, s 71(4).
4 LGHA 1989, s 71(5)(a).

16.93 The obligation referred to in (b) above does not require the member or officer concerned to disclose any information about the company which has been communicated to that person in confidence[1].

1 Local Government and Housing Act 1989, s 71(6).

7 COMPANIES SUBJECT TO THE CONTROL OR INFLUENCE OF MORE THAN ONE LOCAL AUTHORITY

16.94 LGHA 1989, s 73 makes special provision for the situation where two or more local authorities participate in a company in connection with the classifications of 'control' and 'influence'. LACO 1995, art 18 deals with the financial implications for those authorities under Pt V of the Order.

16.95 Under LGHA 1989, s 73(1), where, considering the interests of one local authority alone, the company would not be controlled, but if the combined actions, powers and interests of two or more local authorities are such that if held by one authority, the company would be treated as controlled, then the company is to be treated as under the control of *each* of the local authorities for the purpose of LACO 1995, Pt V.

16.96 LGHA 1989, s 73(2) and (3) apply where the company is not treated as influenced looking at the interests of each participating authority in isolation. The company will nonetheless be treated as influenced by each of two or more authorities if all the following conditions apply:

(a) one of the 'business relationship' tests in paras (a)–(e) of LGHA 1989, s 69(3) would be fulfilled[1] if the interests of the participating authorities were to be combined; and
(b) one of the '20% associated persons tests' in s 69(1)[2] would be satisfied if those interests were combined; and
(c) if the 20% test is satisfied on account of members' voting rights under s 69(1)(a), that at least one person associated[3] with each authority in the group has the right to vote at a general meeting; and, if that does not apply, that each of the authorities in the group has at least one person associated with it who acts as a director (so there must be some personnel link with each of the local authorities concerned).

1 See para **16.44**.
2 See para **16.42**.
3 See paras **16.40–16.41**.

16.97 By virtue of LACO 1995, art 18, if a regulated company is treated as under the control or subject to the influence of each of two or more local authorities, the provisions of Pt V of the Order under which certain things done by or to a regulated company are treated as having been done by or to a relevant authority, are treated as having been done by or to *each* of the authorities involved to the extent of their involvement in the company. The obligations (eg to provide credit cover) and the entitlements (eg to treat a basic credit approval as increased) of the 'relevant authority' under Pt V of the Order are treated as having been imposed or conferred on each authority 'to the extent of their involvement' in the company.

16.98 The authorities themselves must determine by agreement the extent of each authority's involvement in the company concerned. If they cannot agree, they are to nominate a person to determine the issue. In default of agreement regarding such a nomination, the Secretary of State may appoint a person to determine the issue[1].

1 Local Authorities (Companies) Order 1995, art 18(4).

8 SANCTIONS FOR NON-COMPLIANCE

16.99 The propriety controls on regulated companies contained in the LACO 1995 are expressed as being obligations of the company itself. However, the Order includes no specific sanctions against the company for non-compliance.

16.100 As far as local authorities are concerned, LGHA 1989, s 70(2) imposes a duty to ensure, so far as practicable, that any company under the *control* of a local authority complies with the provisions of the LACO 1995[1] which regulate controlled (or influenced) companies. Failure to discharge the duty in relation to a controlled company will lead to any payment made to the company, or other expenditure incurred by the authority in contravention of such provisions, being deemed to be unlawful expenditure for the purpose of the Audit Commission Act 1998.

1 Or of any such order for the time being made under Local Government and Housing Act 1989, s 70(1).

16.101 It is implicit that if the local authority fails to make any financial provision required of it under LACO 1995, Pt V, the usual sanctions for defects in a local authority's accounts would apply (including the powers of the auditor under the Audit Commission Act 1998: see Chapter 9).

9 LOCAL AUTHORITY EXPENDITURE ON REGULATED COMPANIES

16.102 In general, any payment made by a relevant authority to a regulated company, for example a grant for capital purposes or a loan, would fall to be accounted for by the authority in the usual way under LGHA 1989, Pt IV. There must be an appropriate statutory power to authorise the expenditure.

F Council members and officers as company directors

1 DUTIES OF MEMBERS AND OFFICERS WHO ACT AS DIRECTORS VIS À VIS THE COMPANY

16.103 Local authority appointed directors of a company will owe duties to the company itself. The general requirements of company law will apply to them and to their relationship with the company. Their duties to the company fall into two broad categories: (a) fiduciary duties of good faith and honesty; and (b) duties of skill and care. As their primary fiduciary duty, directors are bound to exercise the powers they have, bona fide (in what they consider, not what a court might consider) in the interests of the company[1].

1 *Re Smith and Fawcett Ltd* [1942] Ch 304, CA.

16.104 General company law[1] suggests that a nominee director will owe distinct duties:

(a) to the company;
(b) to those with whom, in the capacity as a director of a company, they have entered into contracts; and
(c) in the case of nominee directors who are employees of the body which has nominated them, to exercise reasonable diligence and skill in the performance of their duties as a director of a company.

1 *Kuwait Asia Bank EC v National Mutual Life Nominees Ltd* [1991] 1 AC 187, PC.

16.105 In a commercial context, it is not unusual for a director, with the consent of the company, to represent the interests of a body which is external to the company and the constitution of the company may explicitly permit this. The nominee director would still have to preserve a substantial degree of independent discretion in the exercise of his powers as a director and should not subordinate the interests of the company to those of the body which has nominated him or her.

16.106 For nominee directors who are local authority members or officers, difficult issues may arise. In *Crédit Suisse v Borough Council of Allerdale*[1] Peter

Gibson LJ observed in relation to a specially formed company whose directors were all associated with the authority:

> 'It is not difficult to conceive of circumstances in which the Company's interests and the Council's interests might conflict. For example, if the Company fell into financial difficulty, its interests, which the directors would be obliged to further, might dictate the disposal of the swimming pool to the purchaser who offered the best price and who might want to develop the site, whereas the Council's interests would lie in the continued availability of the pool as such.'

1 [1997] QB 306, [1996] 4 All ER 129, CA.

16.107 If a conflict of interest arises which cannot be resolved, a nominee director may consider that they have no option but to resign. However, if such a conflict were to arise in the course of company insolvency, the directors may find themselves in an even more parlous position, as resignation may conflict with a director's implicit obligation to take every step, as he or she ought to take, with a view to minimising the potential loss to the company's creditors[1].

1 Under Insolvency Act 1986, s 214(3) concerning an application for a declaration of personal liability of a director in respect of wrongful trading, a court may not make a declaration if satisfied that once the director knew (or ought to have concluded) that there was no reasonable prospect that the company would avoid going into insolvent liquidation, that person took every step he or she ought to have taken with a view to minimising the potential loss to the company's creditors.

2 DUTIES OF MEMBERS AND OFFICERS WHO ACT AS DIRECTORS VIS À VIS THE COUNCIL

16.108 Further complications may arise for elected members of a local authority who act as directors of a company if any contract or other matter between the council and the company is to be considered at a meeting of the council. In view of the general law and guidance on 'non-pecuniary interests' in the National Code of Local Government Conduct[1], councillors who are directors of the company may consider that they should disclose a non-pecuniary interest and not take part in consideration or discussion of the contract or other matter, or take part in any vote.

1 Department of the Environment Circular 8/90.

3 INDEMNITIES FOR OFFICERS AND DIRECTORS WHO ACT AS DIRECTORS OF A COMPANY

16.109 Council officers and members may well seek some special protection in respect of their potential personal liabilities if asked to act as a director of a company.

16.110 The extent to which local authority officers are able to rely on a contractual indemnity given by a local authority, or on the provisions of s 265 of the Public Health Act 1875[1] when they act as directors of a company at a local authority's behest, was considered by the court in *Burgoine v London Borough of Waltham Forest*[2]. The liquidators of a company brought proceedings against two directors who were council officers, claiming substantial amounts in respect of wrongful trading under the Insolvency Act 1986, s 214. Half the shares in the company were owned by the local authority. In separate proceedings, the scheme and joint venture in which the company played an integral role had been found to be ultra vires the council and void. The officers sought a declaration against the local authority (and its auditor) that they had an enforceable indemnity from the council in relation to any liability they might incur in the insolvency proceedings.

1 As amended by the Local Government (Miscellaneous Provisions) Act 1976, s 39.
2 (1996) 95 LGR 520. (For consideration by the court of indemnities for officers and members in the context of the costs of taking part in audit hearing proceedings, see *R v Westminster City Council, ex p Union of Managerial and Professional Officers* and *R v Westminster City Council, ex p Legg* (2000) Times, 13 June, QBD.

16.111 In *Burgoine*, Neuberger J concluded that, as a matter of construction of the particular contractual indemnity, it was capable of extending to the activities of council officers who had been validly appointed by the council as directors of a company (at least where no conflict of interest between the council and the company could arise). However, as the whole of the council's involvement with the project was ultra vires and the authority had no capacity to appoint the officers as directors, as a matter of ordinary language, the terms of the contractual indemnity (which referred to officers' 'duties on behalf of the council' and 'acting within the scope of their authority') could not apply. The court concluded that the Public Health Act 1875, s 265 did not assist the officers. The purpose of s 265 was to confer immunity from suit and to cover officers' expenses, but not to provide for substantive sums or damages which might be claimed. As to whether the giving of the contractual indemnity was itself ultra vires the council, Neuberger J found that the Local Government Act 1972, s 112 did not preclude the giving of such an indemnity. As regards the effects of the prohibition on indemnities for company officers in the Companies Act 1985, s 310(1), despite its wide wording it only applies to indemnities given by the company itself and consequently it did not render void a contractual indemnity given by a local authority to company directors[1].

1 Companies Act 1985, s 310(3) would permit a company to purchase and maintain insurance for directors against liabilities they incur and may offer a practical solution to this problem.

16.112 In practice, council members and officers who are nominated to act as directors of a company are often advised to ensure that the company arranges insurance for them in respect of their personal liabilities. Whilst the Companies Act 1985, s 310(1) prohibits the company exempting any director (or other company officer, or auditor employed by the company) from liability for breach of duty to the company or indemnifying such a person, s 310(3) expressly provides that this does not prevent the company purchasing or maintaining insurance for directors etc against such liabilities.

G The concept of shadow director

16.113 A general issue for consideration in connection with a local authority's relationship with any company is the concept of 'shadow director'. For the purpose of many company law provisions, shadow directors are subject to the same duties and liabilities as the company's appointed directors. The provisions concerning shadow directors are of particular significance in the context of insolvency. If the council were to be considered to be a shadow director of a company found to have engaged in wrongful trading it is conceivable that the liquidator of the company might seek a declaration from the court under the provisions of the Insolvency Act 1986, s 214[1] to make the authority liable to contribute to the company's assets.

1 See s 214(7); 'director' includes a shadow director for the purpose of s 214.

16.114 For the purposes of the Insolvency Act 1986, a shadow director as defined by s 251:

> '. . . in relation to a company, means a person in accordance with whose directions or instructions the directors of the company are accustomed to act (but so that a person is not deemed a shadow director by reason only that the directors act on advice given by him in a professional capacity).'

16.115 Cases on this section suggest that it is the whole of the board of directors, or at least a governing majority, who should act as so directed or instructed. The test adopted in many cases in recent years was that the board would need to be the 'cats paw'[1], puppet or dancer to the shadow director's tune, before the test for a shadow director would come into play. However, the Court of Appeal in *Secretary of State for Trade and Industry v Deverell*[2] rejected any such embellishment on the plain words of the statute. What is needed to satisfy the test is that the board is accustomed to act on the directions or instructions of the shadow director. The purpose of the legislation is to identify those, other than professional advisers, with real influence over company affairs. It is not necessary that such influence should be exercised over the whole field of the company's corporate activities.

1 See, for example, *Re Unisoft Group Ltd (No 3)* [1994] 1 BCLC 609, [1994] BCC 766.
2 (2000) 2 All ER 365 at 372–6.

H Proposals for change and recent developments

16.116 The law in relation to local authorities' involvement in companies is complex and unclear. Despite the sophisticated regime for dealing with the financial and other consequences of local authority participation in companies, their legal powers to set up and participate in companies are utterly opaque. The full enactment of LGHA 1989, Pt V and the introduction of the Companies Order have done nothing to dispel the uncertainties. The current trend of encouraging local authorities to explore flexible methods of working with the private sector, whether as part of the Private Finance Initiative, in relation to 'best value' or otherwise, might have been expected to accelerate developments in this area.

16.117 The consultation paper published by the DETR in February 1998, *Modernising local government—Local democracy and community leadership* raised the possibility of replacing the Local Government Act 1972, s 111 with a broader power, in part to deal with doubts in relation to its use for participation in companies[1]. This particular possibility was not pursued in the White Paper, *Modern Local Government—In Touch with the People* (July 1998, Cm 4014), although it was said that the Government intended to provide councils with clear discretionary power to engage in partnership arrangements with other bodies for purposes which support their functions and that this proposed new power would help to clear up the uncertainties about local authorities' powers to establish and participate in companies[2].

1 See paras 6.13 and 6.14 of the consultation paper.
2 See paras 8.23 and 8.24 of the White Paper.

16.118 The Local Government Act 1999 includes a mechanism through which, it has been said, the Government could act to resolve the present uncertainties about local authority participation in companies and other external bodies, at least in relation to authorities' new obligations concerning 'best value' under the LGA 1999, s 3. LGA 1999, s 16 contains what is known as a 'Henry VIII' provision. It empowers the Secretary of State, by order, to make provision conferring on best value authorities any power which he considers necessary or expedient to permit or facilitate compliance with the requirements of LGA 1999, Pt I regarding 'best value' (or to modify or exclude the application of an enactment to a best value authority if he considers that the enactment prevents or obstructs their compliance with that Part). During consideration of the clause in the Bill which preceded s 16 by the House of Lords Select Committee on Delegated Powers and Deregulation, it was reported that one possible option for the use of this order-making power of the Secretary of State might be the creation of powers for authorities to establish and participate in companies and non-profit making organisations such as companies limited by guarantee[1]. The explanatory notes to the LGA 1999 (at para 48) also indicate that the order-making power under s 16 might be used to confer on best value authorities a general power to form companies through which to exercise their functions. At the time of writing, consultation by the DETR on a draft order under the Local Government Act 1999, s 16 is awaited.

1 See the 12th Report of the Select Committee, HL Paper 51, ordered to be printed 14 April 1999, at Annex B.

16.119 The Local Government Act 2000[1] also includes a 'Henry VIII' provision which would enable the Secretary of State to make an order to amend, repeal, revoke or disapply any enactment which prevents or obstructs authorities exercising their proposed new powers to promote the economic, social or environmental well-being of their areas. Again, it has been suggested that this order making power might assist in the context of companies, although the scope for this is not immediately obvious (see para **17.51**).

1 LGA 2000, s 5.

16.120 At the time of writing it is yet to be seen how the Government intends to tackle the issue of local government powers to set up and participate in companies.

Classification of local authorities' interests in companies under Local Government and Housing Act 1989, Pt V and the Local Authorities (Companies) Order 1995, SI 1995/849[1]

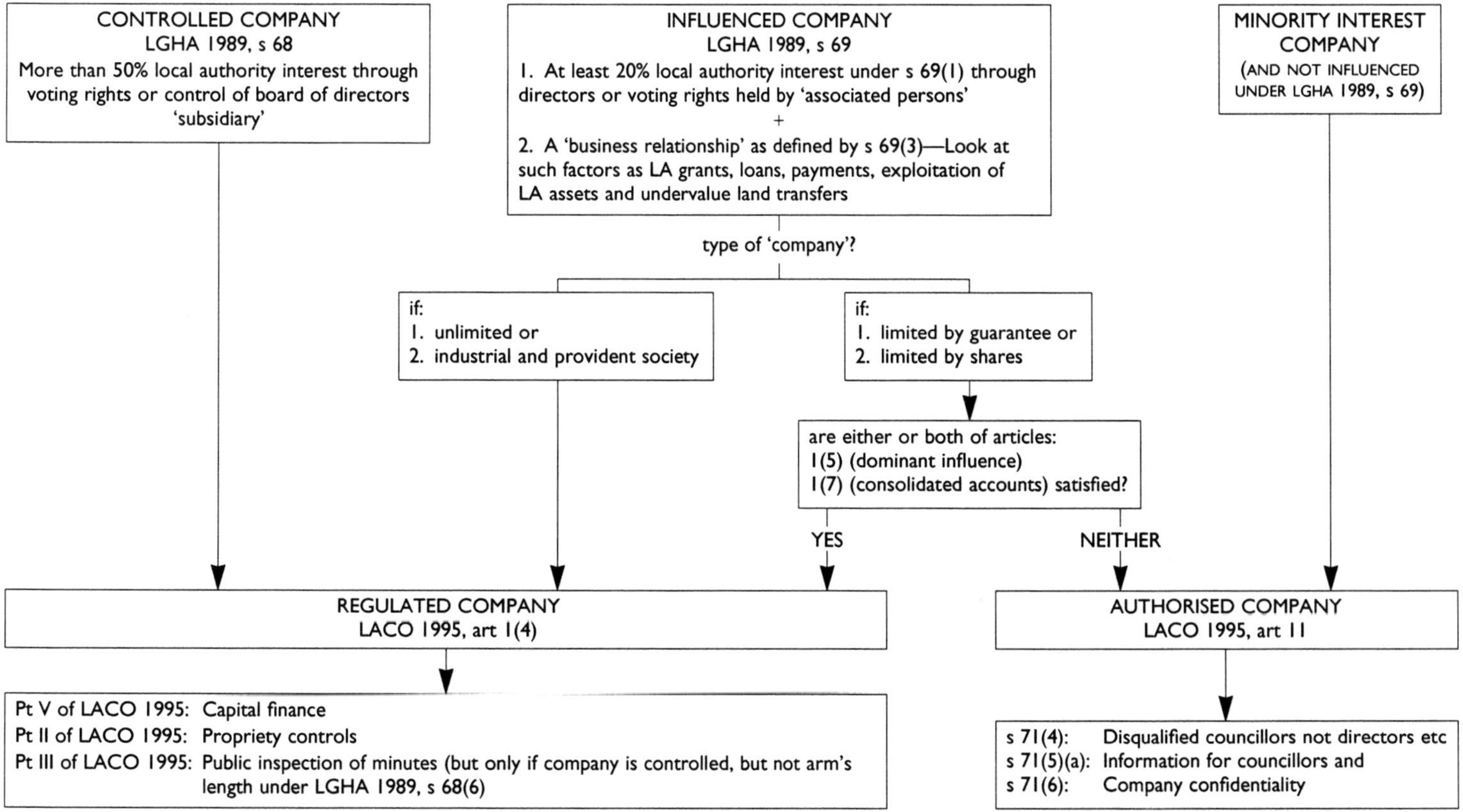

1 Subject to exceptions through directions made by the Secretary of State under LGHA 1989, ss 68(1) and 69(1) or the Schedule to LACO 1995.

CHAPTER 17

Local economic development

A Context

17.1 Local authorities have always played a part in the economic well-being of their areas. The exercise of many of their statutory functions, eg in relation to planning, highways, housing, education, and the encouragement of tourism, and as an employer of staff, often has a direct or indirect impact on the local economy. Local authority economic initiatives have been described as an important element in the success of central government policies[1]. When local authorities obtain funding for local regeneration from central government or European sources they must, of course have an appropriate statutory power to enable them to spend the money.

1 The Conduct of Local Authority Business—the Government response to the Widdecombe Committee of Inquiry (July 1998, Cm 433), para 7.7.

17.2 However, it was not until 1989 that local authorities were given a 'tailor-made' power to promote the economic development of their areas. Prior to that date, the Local Government Act 1972, s 137 (the discretionary power to incur a limited amount of expenditure for purposes not otherwise authorised by statute, but for the benefit of the area[1]) was possibly the single statutory authority most often relied on for 'purely' local economic development purposes, such as the provision of grants or other support to promote the growth of local business.

1 See Chapter 4.

17.3 The role of local authorities in relation to economic development was addressed in the report of the Widdecombe Committee[1] in 1986 and has been revisited more recently in the Government consultation paper on modernising local government: *Local Democracy and Community Leadership* (February 1998) and the White Paper *Modern Local Government—In Touch with the People* (July 1998, Cm 4014). The 1998 papers expanded on the present government's manifesto commitment to place council's under a duty to promote the economic social and environmental well-being of their areas. That proposed new duty has now evolved into a new *discretionary power*, in Pt I of the Local Government Act 2000 which is not yet in force at the time of writing and is referred to in the final section of the this chapter. When the relevant provisions of the Local Government Act 2000 are brought into force they will lead to the repeal of LGHA 1989, ss 33–35, the main provisions of Pt III which concern economic development.

1 The Widdecombe Committee of Inquiry into the Conduct of Local Authority Business, June 1986, Cmnd 9797.

B Background to the Local Government and Housing Act 1989, Pt III

17.4 The research commissioned by the Widdecombe Committee indicated that in 1984/1985 economic development activities had accounted for more than two-thirds of all spending by local authorities under s 137 of the Local Government Act 1972[1] and the equivalent powers in Scotland[2]. Although the use of LGA 1972, s 137 to further economic development was clearly significant, the Government's response to Widdecombe suggested that it represented only 38% of total spending by local authorities on economic development objectives in that financial year. Local authorities were said to be relying on a range of explicit statutory powers to authorise their economic development activities[3].

1 See Chapter 4 and note the prospective modification of this provision by the Local Government Act 2000, s 8, as referred to in para **17.53**.
2 Local Government (Scotland) Act 1973, s 83.
3 Other powers relied on by authorities included Local Authorities (Land) Act 1963, ss 2 and 3; Local Government Act 1972, ss 144 and 145; and Weights and Measures Act 1985, s 95.

17.5 The Widdecombe Committee recommended that the Government should initiate a review of the proper role of local authorities in economic development, taking account of the part played by other government agencies, with a view to identifying areas in which additional local government powers should be introduced. The Government's response[1] was to propose new legislation, which eventually emerged as the Local Government and Housing Act 1989, Pt III.

1 See the Government Response to the Report of the Widdecombe Committee of Inquiry Cm 433, Chapter VII and the Annex to the Response, at para 58.

17.6 With the creation of express powers to promote economic development under LGHA 1989, Pt III, the power to incur expenditure for economic development purposes under LGA 1972, s 137 was repealed[1]. The restrictions on powers to promote economic development created under LGHA 1989, s 34 apply not only to the exercise of such powers under LGHA 1989, s 33, but also to economic development activities undertaken by relevant authorities[2] under other enactments.

1 Local Government Act 1972, s 137 specifically excludes expenditure for purposes authorised or required under other legislation, whether unconditionally or subject to limitation or satisfaction of condition. The section was substantially revised by Local Government and Housing Act 1989, s 36. See para **17.53** regarding the modification of s 137 by the Local Government Act 2000, s 8, so as to remove most of the powers under s 137 from authorities to whom the LGA 2000, s 2 applies.
2 See para **17.11**.

17.7 A criticism levelled at local authorities' ability to spend on economic development in the Government's response to the Widdecombe Committee in 1988 was that it was not governed by an objective assessment of what was needed and what was likely to be cost effective (the reason for this was said to be the nature of the powers then available to authorities[1]). Whilst local authorities have used LGHA 1989, Pt III to great effect in a number of different contexts over the years since 1990, criticisms about objective justification for spending, poor analysis of need and targeting of expenditure have, on occasion, continued to be made about their reliance on LGHA 1989, s 33[2].

1 The Government's response to the Widdecombe Committee of Inquiry (Cm 433), para 7.12.
2 See, for example, the Technical Release published by the Audit Commission on 7 April 1998: TR 8/98

concerning the Doncaster Public Interest Report regarding objective justification, and the paper published by the Audit Commission in September 1999 entitled 'A Life's Work' (ISBN 1 86240 183 7), which includes criticism of way in which local authorities target their spending on economic regeneration.

C Local Government and Housing Act 1989, Pt III

17.8 LGHA 1989, s 33 gave local authorities specific power 'to take such steps as they may from time to time consider appropriate for promoting the economic development of their area'. These apparently wide powers are subject to a number of restrictions and conditions contained in the Act itself and in Regulations made by the Secretary of State[1].

1 Under Local Government and Housing Act 1989, s 33(3)(f),(4), s 34(1),(2),(5), s 190 and s 191(1).

17.9 The exercise of powers under LGHA 1989, s 33 is expressed to be subject to:

(a) LGHA 1989, s 34, which provides the Secretary of State with power to specify, in regulations, steps which a local authority may not take in order to promote economic development under s 33; and
(b) LGHA 1989, s 35, the duties of an authority:
    (i) to have regard to any guidance issued by the Secretary of State in determining whether and in what manner to incur expenditure for economic development purposes (no such guidance has, in fact, been issued); and
    (ii) more importantly, to consult specified parties on the authority's proposals to incur expenditure in advance of the financial year in which the spending is to take place[1].

1 See para **17. 29**ff.

17.10 The current regulations made by the Secretary of State for purposes of various provisions of Pt III are the Local Government (Promotion of Economic Development) Regulations 1990[1] (LG(PED)R 1990).

1 SI 1990/763 as amended by SI 1990/789, SI 1991/473, SI 1992/2242 and SI 1995/556.

17.11 The local authorities which are 'relevant authorities' to whom LGHA 1989, Pt III applies are the council of any county, county borough in Wales, district or London borough, the Common Council of the City of London in its capacity as a local authority and the Council of the Isles of Scilly.

D Extent of powers envisaged by LGHA 1989, Pt III

17.12 LGHA 1989, s 33 describes what the economic development powers include, but it does not contain an exhaustive definition. Under s 33(2), the steps relevant authorities[1] are empowered to take include participation in, and the encouragement of and provision of financial and other assistance for –

(a) the setting up or expansion of any commercial or industrial or public undertaking –
    (i) which is to be situated in the authority's area; or

(ii) the setting up or expansion of which appears likely to increase the opportunities for employment of persons living in that area; and

(b) the creation or protection of opportunities for employment with any such undertaking or with any commercial, industrial or public undertaking opportunities for employment with which have been or appear likely to be made available to persons living in that area.

1 See para **17.11**.

17.13 Of these 'steps', only financial assistance is further defined. The provisions envisage assistance for both new and existing undertakings, as well as local authority participation in setting up undertakings, provided that the authority considers, in each case, that these would be appropriate steps to take to promote economic development. An authority's powers to promote economic development extend to activities involving assistance to bodies located *outside* the authority's area, if it appears likely that employment opportunities for its local residents would be increased, created or preserved.

17.14 Under LGHA 1989, s 33(3), if a relevant authority does or agrees to do any of the following, it is to be treated as providing 'financial assistance' to a person:

(a) make a grant to that person;
(b) make a loan to that person or provide him with any other form of credit;
(c) guarantee the performance of any of that person's obligations;
(d) indemnify that person in respect of any liability, loss or damage;
(e) invest in that person's undertaking, in the case of a body corporate, by acquiring share or loan capital in that body or otherwise;
(f) provide that person with any property, services or other financial benefit (including the remission in whole or in part of any liability or obligation) for no consideration or for a consideration which does not satisfy such conditions as may be specified in regulations made by the Secretary of State[1];
(g) join with any other person in doing anything falling within paras (a) to (f) above;
(h) enter into such other transaction, in the nature of anything falling within paras (a) to (g) above, as may be specified in regulations made by the Secretary of State.

1 Regulation 4 of the LG(PED)R 1990 (as amended) specifies the following condition for the purpose of s 33(3)(f) of the LGHA 1989: 'that the property, services or other financial benefit is provided for a consideration that is the best that can reasonably be obtained.' Regulation 5 and Sch 2, para 2 of the Regulations then, in effect, prohibit an authority from disposing of land at less than best consideration as a form of financial assistance to promote economic development, unless the disposal is pursuant to a consent given by the Secretary of State for the purposes of the Local Government Act 1972, s 123 (or by way of a short tenancy) (see para **17.20**).

17.15 These provisions are important, both as examples of the extent of the powers created under LGHA 1989, s 33, and because certain of them are then made subject to limitations or conditions under the subsequent provisions of LGHA 1989, Pt III and under the LG(PED)R 1990. Despite the various restrictions, the provisions of s 33 have gained in significance in the context of economic development, in view of the line of cases[1] since *Hazell v Hammersmith and Fulham London Borough Council*[2], which have made clear that the subsidiary powers under Local Government Act 1972, s 111 would not authorise the giving of a guarantee or an indemnity by a local authority, nor, generally, authorise all forms of involvement in companies, in cases where no explicit statutory power exists.

1 See in particular *Crédit Suisse v Allerdale Borough Council* [1997] QB 306, [1996] 4 All ER 129; *Crédit Suisse v London Borough of Waltham Forest* [1997] QB 362, [1996] 4 All ER 176; and *Sutton London Borough Council v Morgan Grenfell & Co Ltd* (1997) 29 HLR 608, CA.
2 [1992] 2 AC 1.

E Restrictions on powers to promote economic development

17.16 LGHA 1989, s 34(1) enables the Secretary of State to exclude from all relevant authorities' economic development powers[1] such steps as may be specified or described in regulations. Thus the powers are limited by reference to exclusions, rather than by prescribing the precise ambit of what may constitute the promotion of economic development.

1 Whether created under Local Government and Housing Act 1989, s 33 or under any other enactment.

17.17 When the LG(PED)R 1990 were first brought into force, they contained more onerous restrictions on the economic development activities of certain relevant authorities which were *not* 'scheduled authorities' as listed in LG(PED)R 1990, Sch 1. The aim was to impose fewer restrictions on those authorities (ie the scheduled authorities) considered to be in the greatest need to spend on economic development. Since 1 April 1995 the special restrictions and Sch 1 have both been revoked[1]. All relevant authorities are now subject to identical provisions.

1 SI 1995/556.

1 EXCLUDED ACTIVITIES—LG(PED)R 1990, REG 5

17.18 Under LG(PED)R 1990, reg 5(1)(a), the steps listed in Sch 2, para 1 of the Regulations are 'excluded activities' for the purpose of s 34(1), which no relevant authority may undertake in pursuance of its economic development powers. The prohibited steps include such activities as investment business, estate agency work, valuation of land for reward, the publication of a newspaper[1], the purchase of goods for resale or hiring and the employment of persons for the purpose of manufacture of goods[2]. These prohibitions are interesting as illustrating the breadth of the powers to promote economic development assumed to exist in the absence of the exclusions.

1 As defined in Newspaper Libel and Registration Act 1881, s 1.
2 See full list in Local Government (Promotion of Economic Development) Regulations 1990, Sch 2, para 1.

17.19 LG(PED)R 1990, reg 5(2) then provides for certain activities to be exempt from the exclusions in Sch 2, para 1 (ie they may be permitted), eg carrying out estate agency work which consists solely of publication of information about land, or publishing a newspaper where the sole or main purpose of publication is the promotion of economic development of the authority's area.

17.20 Under LG(PED)R 1990, reg 5(1)(b) and Sch 2, para 2, all relevant authorities other than the Common Council of the City of London, are prohibited from disposing of land for a consideration which is less than the best which can reasonably be obtained, otherwise than by way of a short tenancy[1], or, if the disposal is pursuant to a consent given by the Secretary of State under Local Government Act 1972, s 123, otherwise than in accordance with the terms of that consent[2].

1 That is, one which is for a term no longer than seven years (Local Government Act 1972, s 123(7)).
2 There appears to be no reason why a general consent, such as those under the Local Government Act 1972 General Disposal Consents 1998, should not be relevant here.

2 EXCLUDED FORMS OF FINANCIAL ASSISTANCE—LG(PED)R 1990, REG 6

17.21 LG(PED)R 1990, reg 6 deals with the prohibited forms of financial assistance which have been specified by the Secretary of State for the purpose of LGHA 1989, s 34(1).

17.22 The restrictions in LG(PED)R 1990, reg 6(1) and (2) relate to the powers of relevant authorities to provide financial assistance in the particular forms of grants[1], loans or other forms of credit[2], and guarantees of the performance of any person's obligations[3].

1 Under Local Government and Housing Act 1989, s 33(3)(a).
2 LGHA 1989, s 33(3)(b).
3 LGHA 1989, s 33(3)(c).

17.23 In cases where the party proposed to be assisted is a person who conducts a business or undertaking with a view to profit, relevant authorities may not provide any of these three forms of 'financial assistance' in order to promote economic development where[1]:

(a) the amount of assistance is determinable solely by reference to the financial results of that business or undertaking over a period which, at the date on which the authority considers the provision of the assistance, is not wholly in the past; or
(b) it is intended that the assistance should be applied, either wholly or in part, in or towards the payment of wages or salary of any employee of that person.

1 Local Government (Promotion of Economic Development) Regulations 1990, reg 6(2).

17.24 The first of these restrictions appears to be aimed at cases where the amount of assistance is calculated exclusively on the basis of the financial results of the proposed recipient which includes any future projection of financial performance. (Assistance calculated exclusively on the basis of the recipient's *past financial results* does not appear to be expressly prohibited[1]).

1 Grants to meet existing deficits of a business may be objectionable on other grounds, eg efficacy in promoting economic development, financial prudence and 'reasonableness' (or 'irrationality').

17.25 Again these exclusions are subject to exceptions. LG(PED)R 1990, reg 6(3) specifies that (notwithstanding the provisions of reg 6(1) and (2)), a relevant authority may give grant assistance to a body for economic development purposes to enable the recipient to employ someone who has been unemployed for at least seven days, or during a training period, or to employ a maximum of three people qualified to provide some knowledge or skill needed by the business or undertaking.

3 EXCLUDED STEPS IN THE ABSENCE OF CONSULTATION— LG(PED)R 1990, REG 8

17.26 LG(PED)R 1990, reg 8 deals with specified steps for the purpose of LGHA 1989, s 34(1) which are excluded unless undertaken after consultation with specified bodies. (This is in addition to the general requirements to consult on economic development proposals in advance of the financial year of spending under LGHA 1989, s 35(3), referred to in para **17.30**ff.)

17.27 A relevant authority which is not a 'local education authority' under the (Education Act 1944) has no power to provide a person[1] with training or education services in order to promote economic development, unless it has first consulted the local education authority for the area.

1 Other than a member, officer or other employee of the relevant authority.

17.28 A relevant authority has no power to acquire land outside its area, nor to provide financial assistance for the acquisition or improvement of any such land, or plant or machinery on or under such land, unless it has first consulted the appropriate authority listed in the Table contained in LG(PED)R 1990, reg 8.

4 GUIDANCE, ECONOMIC DEVELOPMENT PLANS AND CONSULTATION

17.29 LGHA 1989, s 35(1) imposes a duty on relevant authorities to have regard to any guidance issued by the Secretary of State in determining whether (and in what manner) to incur expenditure for the purpose of promoting economic development, but to date no such guidance has been issued.

17.30 In advance of each financial year, a relevant authority is required[1] to determine the steps it proposes to take to promote the economic development of its area in the forthcoming year. If any such steps are to be taken, the relevant authority must draw up a document (sometimes called an 'economic development plan') setting out the matters specified in LGHA 1989, s 35(4) concerning its expenditure proposals. That document must include details of the proposed expenditure and the extent to which it is to be capital or revenue expenditure and is attributable to different proposals; the authority's estimate of any income likely to accrue and what the authority intends to achieve through the implementation of the proposals.

1 Under Local Government and Housing Act 1989, s 35(2).

17.31 The document must be made available to bodies which represent commercial and industrial undertakings in the area; to such of the persons carrying on commercial, industrial or public undertakings in the area as the authority considers appropriate; and to such other persons whom the authority thinks it desirable to consult about the proposals. The bodies to whom the plan has been made available must all be consulted[1].

1 The statutory requirements under LGHA 1989, s 35(2)–(4), prescribe what must be consulted upon and when. The common law tests for proper consultation entail a four stage process: (a) consultation must be undertaken at a time when the proposals are still at a formative stage; (b) sufficient reasons for proposals should be given to allow intelligent consideration and an intelligent response; (c) adequate time should be given for this purpose; and (d) the product of consultation must be conscientiously taken into account when the ultimate decision is taken (*R v Brent London Borough Council, ex p Gunning* (1985) 84 LGR 168).

17.32 As LGHA 1989, s 33 is expressed to be subject to LGHA 1989, s 35, local authorities have sometimes run into difficulties in wishing to rely on the economic development powers where proposals, although known about in advance of the financial year in question, were not included in a document which was consulted upon at the proper time.

F Accounting requirements and conditions of assistance

17.33 LG(PED)R 1990, reg 9 requires a relevant authority to maintain (within its accounts) a separate account of any loans it has provided in order to give financial assistance under economic development powers, in cases where the form of the loan and the rate of interest applied is more favourable than that reasonably obtainable on the open market. A statement of this account must be deposited with the 'proper officer' when the authority's accounts are published under the requirements of regulations[1] made under s 23 of the Local Government Finance Act 1982.

1 Accounts and Audit Regulations 1996, SI 1996/590.

17.34 LGA 1972, s 137A contains explicit requirements for the conditions on which certain financial assistance may be given to any 'voluntary organisation' as defined in LGA 1972, s 137(2D)[1] or to a body or fund within s 137(B). Where an authority provides financial assistance in the form of a grant, loan or guarantee of borrowing, of an amount above that specified by the Secretary of State (currently £2,000), the authority must require the recipient to provide a written statement of the use to which the money has been put, within a period of 12 months from the date on which the assistance is provided. The requirement for conditions to be imposed on assistance to voluntary and other bodies and funds under LGA 1972, s 137A does not appear to be limited to expenditure under LGA 1972, s 137[2], and could therefore apply where the power to provide assistance to such a body arises under LGHA 1989, s 33.

1 A body which is not a public body, but whose activities are carried on otherwise than for profit.
2 The former powers to incur expenditure for economic development purposes under LGA 1972, s 137(2A)–(2C) were repealed by LGHA 1989, s 36(4). In general, LGA 1972, s 137 is not available if the expenditure is authorised by virtue of any other enactment (eg the economic development powers under LGHA 1989, Pt III).

17.35 Whilst the LGHA 1989 itself contains no explicit requirements for conditions to be imposed on the financial assistance given by an authority to any organisation (voluntary or profit-making) in reliance on Pt III powers, it will often be necessary for an authority to do so in order to ensure proper and prudent use of the assistance, or compliance with any relevant restrictions under the Economic Development Regulations or other legislation.

G Relationship with the financial provisions of Local Government and Housing Act 1989, Pt IV

1 REPAYMENT OF FINANCIAL ASSISTANCE

17.36 Any sum received by a local authority in respect of the repayment of, or a payment in respect of, any grants or 'other financial assistance'[1] which was given for capital purposes[2] is a 'capital receipt' by virtue of LGHA 1989, s 58(1)(c), if the payment or repayment to the authority is made by the person to whom the grant or other assistance was given[3]. Sums received in respect of the repayment of the principal of an advance made by a local authority are also capital receipts by virtue of LGHA 1989, s 58(1)(d). Prior to the abolition of 'set-aside obligations' in relation to most non-housing receipts in September 1998[4], receipt by a relevant authority of repayment of a capital grant or other assistance given under economic development powers would normally have been subject to a requirement to set aside a proportion to meet credit liabilities under LGHA 1989, s 59. The percentage required to be set aside would now be nil by virtue of Local Government (Capital Finance) Regulations 1997, reg 64A[5].

1 Not defined for the purpose of these provisions.
2 See Local Government and Housing Act 1989, s 40.
3 If the payment or repayment is made by anyone *other than* the recipient of the grant etc, it will not be a capital receipt (Local Authorities (Capital Finance) Regulations 1997, SI 1997/319, reg 63). See further paras **14.8** and **14.23**(c).
4 See para **14. 26**.
5 SI 1997/319 as amended by SI 1998/1937.

2 GUARANTEES

17.37 In the Circular issued on LGHA 1989, Pt IV[1], the Department of the Environment expressed the view that the giving of a guarantee by a local authority might give rise to a credit arrangement under LGHA 1989, s 48(1)(b). This view was repeated in the Guide to the Local Authority Capital Finance System issued by the Department in February 1997, at least in cases where it 'is probable that payments will be made under [the guarantee[2]]'. However, the position is far from clear and will turn on the precise terms of the particular contract which creates the guarantee.

1 Circular 11/90, Annex A, para 18.
2 At para 7.8.

3 SALE OF SHARES IN ECONOMIC DEVELOPMENT COMPANIES

17.38 As from 1 September 1998 a nil 'set-aside rate' applies to the receipts from the sale of share or loan capital in non-housing companies which was acquired by the authority on or after 1 April, 1990 for the purpose of providing financial assistance for economic development under LGHA 1989, s 33[1]. (The 'usual' rate for receipts from the disposal of share and loan capital is 75%.)

1 See the Local Authorities (Capital Finance) Regulations 1997, SI 1997/319, reg 64A (introduced from 1 September 1998 by SI 1998/1937) and reg 66(2)(e)(ii).

17.39 The wider considerations concerning local authority participation in companies are addressed in Chapter 16.

H Notification of state aids

17.40 Assistance to industry and commerce given by local authorities under economic development (or other available powers) is potentially a state aid which might conflict with art 87 (formerly art 92) of the Treaty of Rome[1]. The notification procedures are subject to a number of de minimis thresholds and accelerated procedures for small and medium sized enterprises ('SMEs'[2]).

1 Which applies to state aid 'in whatever form which distorts or threatens to distort competition by favouring certain undertakings or the production of certain goods . . . insofar as it affects trade between Member States'.
2 SMEs are defined by the Commission as being companies with 250 or fewer employees; and an annual turnover of less than 20 million ECU, or a balance sheet total of less than 10 million ECU, of which less than 25% is owned by one or more companies which do not fall within these criteria.

17.41 Prior to the enactment of LGHA 1989, Pt III, the Department of the Environment advised local authorities that it was proposed that regulations should be made, to provide a machinery through which the duties in connection with the state aids might be discharged. To date, no such regulations have been made. Nonetheless, the requirements of the Treaty of Rome apply directly in the United Kingdom without any domestic legislation being made.

17.42 'Block approval systems' for aid to SMEs were put in place by the United Kingdom Government in 1995, covering certain of the aid given by local authorities to such enterprises. As a condition of the block approval, the UK government is required to submit an annual report showing the value of all aid given by local authorities to SMEs and the number of enterprises who have benefited. In October 1995 the Department of the Environment wrote to all local authority chief executives[1] notifying them that their authorities would be required to supply the Department with this information. Aid by authorities which falls outside the block approval system should be notified to the Commission, normally via the Department of Trade and Industry. A new European Council General Regulation on state aid in structural fund programmes is to be introduced for the period 2000–2006 to ensure conformity with state aid rules in the operation of these programmes[2].

1 Letter from P Rowsell, Local Government Sponsorship Division, 31 October 1995.
2 A helpful overview of the rules concerning state aid is contained in a vade-mecum published by the European Commission: *Community rules on State aid* (1 June 1999) ISBN 92 828 8058 3.

I The Local Government Act 2000

17.43 In February 1998 the Department of the Environment, Transport and the Regions published a consultation paper entitled *Modernising local government—Local democracy and community leadership*. Among the proposal outlined in that paper[1] was the creation of a new duty on authorities to promote 'the economic, social and environmental well-being of their areas'. The consultation paper indicated that any such new duty would not be intended to extend significantly the scope of local authorities' powers, but would help to remove uncertainty about the extent of their powers. The proposed responsibility would 'require local councils to take a holistic view of their local communities and take steps to promote their well-being'. Authorities would be expected to act on their new duty from within their existing financial powers and resources, but should have 'complete discretion in how they discharge the duty'.

1 See paras **6.10–6.12** thereof.

17.44 The White Paper *Modern Local Government—In touch with the people*, published in July 1998 (Cm 4014), reiterated the Government's intention to introduce legislation placing local authorities under a duty to promote the economic, social and environmental well-being of their areas (and to strengthen councils' powers to enter into 'partnerships')[1]. This proposed new duty was to be underpinned by a new discretionary power enabling local authorities to take steps which, in their view, would promote the well-being of their areas and those who live, work and visit there, provided that this power would not be used in ways which prejudice other council functions or the functions of other statutory bodies. The White Paper indicated that the Government would retain a reserve power to exclude particular activities or to set a financial limit 'where national interests might need to be protected'.

1 See Chapter 8 of the White Paper.

17.45 Following the Queen's Speech in November 1999 a Local Government Bill was introduced in the Lords, Pt I of which included the Government's proposals for the role of local authorities in promoting the economic, social or environmental well-being of their areas or its inhabitants. The Bill received Royal Assent on 28 July 2000. Under the Local Government Act 2000, Pt I, which contains the new 'well-being provisions', the concept of an all embracing duty has been abandoned: LGA 2000, s 2 creates a *discretionary power* rather than a duty. This power would apply to the same categories of local authority as the 'relevant authorities' covered by the current provisions of LGHA 1989, Pt III[1]. It is intended that the new provisions would broaden the scope for action by local authorities and reduce the scope for challenge on the basis that authorities lack specific powers[2]. The following outlines the new provisions under the Local Government Act 2000, Pt I. At the time of writing the commencement date for the relevant provisions is not known, but can be no later than 28 July 2001[3].

1 See para **17.11**.
2 See the Explanatory Notes to the Local Government Act 2000, para 15.
3 See the Local Government Act 2000, s 108(4), which specifies that provisions of the Act for which no specific provision is made under s 108(1)–(3) are to come into force at the end of 12 months beginning with the day on which the Act was passed, save where (in the present case) an earlier date is appointed for the provisions to come into force in England under s 108(5)(d) by order made by the Secretary of State, or for Wales under s 108(6)(b) by order made the National Assembly for Wales. In terms of simplicity of transition from the present arrangements under LGHA 1989, Pt III, a commencement date of 1 April 2001 would appear to offer advantages, but at the time of writing no firm proposals for commencement are known and an earlier date (or later date up to 28 July 2001) could be appointed.

17.46 Authorities are to be given the power to do anything which they consider 'is likely to achieve' the promotion or improvement of (the three distinct objectives of) the economic, the social, or the environmental well-being of their areas[1]. This power could be exercised in relation to the whole or any part of the authority's area or all or any persons resident or present in the area[2] and could include steps to assist a person located outside the authority's area if the authority considers this likely to achieve one or more of the primary objectives in s 2(1)[3]. In deciding whether and how to use this power, authorities will be required to have regard to their 'community strategy' under s 4[4].

1 LGA 2000, s 2(1)(a)–(c).
2 LGA 2000, s 2(2).
3 LGA 2000, s 2(5).
4 LGA 2000, s 2(3), and para **17.50** regarding the 'community strategy'.

17.47 The new power would *include* (but without prejudice to the generality of the primary power under s 2(1))[1] power not only to incur expenditure, give financial assistance and enter into 'arrangements or agreements' with any person, but also[2] power to:

(d) co-operate with, or facilitate or co-ordinate the activities of, any person;
(e) exercise on behalf of any person *any functions of that person*; and
(f) provide staff, goods, services or accommodation to any person.

1 LGA 2000, s 2(4) and (6).
2 Local Government Bill 1999, s 2(4)(d)–(e).

17.48 Items (d) and (e) are potentially extremely wide and it is yet to be seen whether any limitations are intended to be imposed on such activities through subordinate legislation which may be made by the Secretary of State under s 3(3) (see below). It is to be noted that, in contrast with the current provisions of LGHA 1989, s 33(3), no express reference is made to any power to provide a guarantee or indemnity, or to invest by acquiring share or loan capital in a company[1].

1 See para **17.51** regarding the scope for the Secretary of State to address uncertainties about these matters through his powers to make orders.

17.49 There are to be a number of limits on the new power under s 2(1). By virtue of LGA 2000, s 3:

(a) section 2(1) would not enable a local authority to do anything which they are unable to do by virtue of any prohibition, restriction or limitation on their powers contained in any enactment whenever passed or made[1];
(b) section 2(1) would not enable an authority to raise money (whether by borrowing, precept or otherwise);
(c) the Secretary of State may by order make provision to prevent an authority from doing anything under s 2(1) which is specified, or is of a description specified, in the order;
(d) before exercising the power under s 2(1) the authority would be required to have regard to any guidance issued by the Secretary of State[2] about the exercise of the power.

1 LGA 2000, s 3(1). This provision looks set to give rise to difficulties of interpretation as to the extent of this limitation, akin to those which currently exist in relation to similar provisions, for example under LGA 1972, s 137(1)(a).
2 In relation to Wales, the National Assembly for Wales is substituted for the Secretary of State (s 3(7)).

17.50 Under the Local Government Act 2000, s 4, local authorities are to have a duty to prepare a strategy for promoting or improving the economic, social and environmental well-being of their area and contributing to the achievement of sustainable development in the United Kingdom. This strategy is referred to as a 'community strategy' and may be modified from time to time. In preparing or modifying their community strategy, authorities must consult and seek the participation of such persons as they consider appropriate. They must also have regard to any guidance which has for the time being been issued by the Secretary of State[1]. It is to be noted that in contrast with the current provisions of LGHA 1989, ss 33 and 35, the primary power under s 2 of the new Act is not expressed to be subject to compliance with the consultation requirements (see para **17.9**), nor is there a requirement in the Act itself to prepare or modify the community strategy at specified intervals. Before issuing guidance under s 4, the Secretary of State[2] must consult representatives of local government and such other persons (if any) as he considers appropriate.

1 In relation to Wales, the relevant guidance is to be issued by the National Assembly for Wales, rather than by the Secretary of State. See LGA 2000, s 4(5).
2 See n 1 above.

17.51 Part I of the Local Government Act 2000, following the theme of a number of recent enactments (such as the Local Government Act 1999, s 16 and the Greater London Authority Act 1999, s 405) incorporates 'Henry VIII clauses' intended to empower the Secretary of State to amend, repeal, revoke or disapply other legislation (primary or secondary) by order made by statutory instrument if the Secretary of State thinks that the enactment prevents or obstructs local authorities from exercising their proposed new power under s 2(1)[1]. The Secretary of State is also given the power to amend, repeal or disapply any enactment which requires a local authority to prepare, produce or publish any plan or strategy relating to any particular matter[2]. It is to be noted that the order making powers of the Secretary of State under LGA 2000, s 5, unlike those under LGA 1999, s 16 concerning best value (referred to in para **7.64ff**), do not include the power to make orders which confer new powers on local authorities. The order making powers under s 5 appear to offer limited scope to address issues involving a complete absence of statutory authority and thus to tackle *all* the uncertainties which surround such matters as local authority participation in and formation of companies, or the giving of guarantees or indemnities. In respect of the exercise of the Secretary of State's order making powers under ss 5 and 6 in relation to Wales, the National Assembly of Wales may submit proposals for such orders (see ss 5(5) and 6(6)).

1 LGA 2000, s 5.
2 LGA 2000, s 6.

17.52 Section 107 and Sch 5 to the new Act provide for the repeal of ss 33–35 of the LGHA 1989 on the promotion of economic development. It is to be assumed that the commencement of these provisions will be scheduled to coincide with the commencement of Pt I (see para **17.45**, n 3).

17.53 At the time of writing it is not apparent how the intended affects of the new provisions of the LGA 2000, Pt 1, 'to broaden the scope for local authority action while reducing the scope for challenge on the grounds that local authorities lack specific powers'[1], are to be achieved. The commencement of Pt I is to lead to the repeal of express economic development powers in relation to setting up and participation in companies, and in respect of indemnities and guarantees[2]. The general powers to incur expenditure for certain purposes not otherwise authorised, under LGA 1972, s 137, are to be modified so as to remove most of these powers from authorities to whom LGA 2000, s 2 applies[3]. Further, the relationship between the new power under LGA 2000, s 2(1) and functions under other pre-existing local government legislation is open to different interpretations, particularly in view of the provisions of s 3(1)[4]. However, the Government's fuller intentions may be revealed if orders are to made by the Secretary of State, whether under powers under LGA 2000, s 5 or under the best value provisions of LGA 1999, s 16[5].

1 See the Explanatory Notes to the LGA 2000, para 15.
2 Under LGHA 1989, s 33(2) and s 33(3)(c)–(e).
3 See LGA 2000, s 8.
4 See para **17.49** and n 1 to that para.
5 See para **17 51** and para **7.64ff** (regarding LGA 1999, s 16).

CHAPTER 18

Value Added Tax

A The basis of VAT and its administration

18.1 Value added tax ('VAT') derives from European Community law, primarily from the EC 6th Council Directive on VAT[1]. VAT was introduced in the United Kingdom in 1973. The main statutory provisions concerning the tax are now contained in the Value Added Tax Act 1994 (VATA 1994) and subordinate legislation made under that Act and under earlier legislation.

1 EC Directive 77/388.

18.2 VAT is administered by Her Majesty's Customs and Excise ('C&E'), and is under the 'care and management' of the Commissioners of C&E[1]. C&E operates local offices and VAT Business Advice Centres throughout the country. As part of the Commissioners' general management powers, C&E issues 'VAT Notices', 'VAT Leaflets', 'VAT Information Sheets' and 'VAT Notes', which give detailed explanations of C&E's interpretation of the VAT rules and changes in policies and procedures. C&E Notice 700 (The VAT Guide, March 2000) provides a general explanation of the tax. C&E Notice 749 (Local authorities and similar bodies, April 2000) is of specific relevance to local authorities[2].

1 Value Added Tax Act 1994, s 58 and Sch 11, para 1(1).
2 C&E Notice 749A (Local authorities and similar bodies—VAT status of activities), which was also relevant to local authorities as it contained guidance on the VAT status of their various activities for VAT purposes, was withdrawn with effect from 30 June 1999 (see para **18.19**). A range of VAT Information Sheets and other guidance is issued by C&E on specific activities and issues of relevance to local authorities and other public bodies, such as schools, supplies between local authorities, pension funds, local authority land, capital items and charities.

18.3 The Chartered Institute of Public Finance and Accountancy ('CIPFA') produces The VAT Reference Manual, which includes a wealth of detailed information on the tax for local authorities and similar bodies. The Manual contains the various news sheets produced by the Financial Information Service[1], at the request of C&E, which contain advice on selected VAT issues of relevance to local authorities and other public bodies.

1 Produced by the Institute of Public Finance Limited.

18.4 This chapter provides a brief outline of VAT and its application to local authorities. A detailed analysis of the tax is contained in De Voil *Indirect Tax Service*[1].

1 Butterworths.

B Basic outline of the tax

18.5 VAT is a tax charged on the supply of most goods and services made in the course of a business. The current VAT standard rate is 17.5%.

18.6 *Output tax*: a person who is required to register for VAT (X), must account to C&E for VAT in addition to the contract price[1] for taxable supplies[2] of goods and services made in the course or furtherance of any business carried on by him or her. That VAT is known as output tax.

1 Unless the contract price is quoted to be inclusive of VAT, or the contract is silent about VAT. See Value Added Tax Act 1994, s 19(2).
2 Taxable supplies are supplies of goods and services made in the United Kingdom other than exempt supplies: Value Added Tax Act 1994, s 4(2).

18.7 *Input tax*: is the VAT X incurs when buying in goods and services for the purpose of his or her business.

18.8 X must make periodic returns[1] to C&E showing:

(a) the output tax for which X is accountable; and
(b) the input tax which X has incurred in making those taxable supplies.

1 Returns are generally made at quarterly intervals (not necessarily calendar quarters), but local authorities are permitted to submit monthly returns. Local authorities may apply to C&E for permission to make estimated returns (as an acknowledgment that, in view of the wide range of their activities, it is not always possible to process all purchase invoices in time for the appropriate VAT return). If permission is given, the local authority's input tax and VATA 1994, s 33 refunds due (see paras **18.21–18.34**) may be estimated.

18.9 If the output tax for the period exceeds the input tax, X must pay the surplus to C&E. If the input tax exceeds the output tax, C&E refunds the difference to X.

18.10 All VAT registered bodies in the supply chain repeat this process of accounting for and recovering VAT until a supply is made to someone (usually a member of the general public) who is not required or permitted to register for VAT (or who is registered, but does not obtain the supply in order to make a taxable supply). That person, in effect, bears the VAT.

18.11 Not all supplies made in the course of a business attract VAT at 17.5%:

(a) some supplies are zero-rated (eg the first sale[1] of a dwelling by the person who constructed it);
(b) some supplies are exempt supplies (eg most sales or lettings of non-residential property[2]);
(c) some supplies are subject to a reduced rate of VAT, currently 5% (eg supplies of fuel and power for domestic use).

1 Provided it is the sale of the freehold or the grant of a lease for a term exceeding 21 years.
2 Unless the person making the supply has elected to waive the exemption from VAT (for which, see paras **18.45–18.50**).

18.12 The difference between zero-rated and exempt supplies is as follows:

(a) *zero-rated:* the supply is technically subject to VAT, but the appropriate VAT rate is nil (or 0 per cent); thus, no VAT is added to the price charged to the customer by X, nor is any accounted for to C&E by X. However, X is entitled to recover its input tax incurred in respect of that supply;

(b) *exempt supply:* again, no VAT is charged or accounted for by X. However, *normally* X cannot recover any input tax in respect of that supply.

18.13 In general, businesses registered for VAT are unable to recover input tax paid on supplies used for non-business activities. However, local authorities are given special treatment in respect of their non-business activities[1].

1 See para **18.21**ff.

18.14 Further, subject to limitations, local authorities[1] are able to recover input tax they have paid in respect of exempt (business) supplies[2].

1 Other VAT-registered persons who make both exempt and taxable supplies are eligible for a comparable entitlement to reclaim 'insignificant' input tax in respect of their exempt supplies (see C&E Notice 706 (Partial exemption), para 6 which prescribes the level of 'insignificance'). The distinct recovery arrangements for local authorities and other bodies subject to Value Added Tax Act 1994, s 33 are referred to at paras **18.26–18.34**.
2 See para **18.26**ff.

C Local authorities and VAT

18.15 The fact that a tax on business supplies should have any application to local authorities is a difficult concept for those familiar with the fundamental principles of local government law, in view of authorities' lack of any general power to trade. The division of their activities into the categories of 'business' and 'non-business' appears somewhat perverse.

18.16 'Business' is defined by VATA 1994, s 94(1) to include any trade, profession or vocation. For VAT purposes, it is considered to have a very wide meaning to include any continuing activity which is mainly concerned with making supplies to other persons for any form of payment or consideration, whether in money or otherwise[1]. A profit motive is not relevant, for example.

1 See further C&E Notice 749, para 3; and C&E Notice 700, para 2.6.

18.17 EC law[1] requires that bodies which make supplies in the course or furtherance of a business, including local authorities and other public bodies, must normally register for VAT. By virtue of VATA 1994, s 42, every local authority[2] which makes *any* taxable supplies must register for VAT, regardless of the value of those supplies[3].

1 EC 6th Directive on VAT (77/388), art 4.
2 For these purposes, 'local authority' is defined by Value Added Tax Act 1994, s 96(4) to include the council of a county, district, London borough, parish or group of parishes (or, in Wales, a community or group of communities), the Common Council of the City of London, the Council of the Isles of Scilly, and any joint committee or joint board established by two or more of the foregoing authorities. VATA 1994 also applies to local authorities in Scotland.
3 This is in contrast to other public bodies eligible to claim a refund of tax on non-business supplies under Value Added Tax Act 1994, s 33 (see para **18.21**ff), who need only register if the value of their taxable supplies exceeds the normal registration threshold.

18.18 The underlying aim of the provisions which apply VAT to local authority 'business activities' is that a public body should not be at any competitive advantage compared to the private sector. With the outsourcing of more and more local authority services over recent years, the risk of 'significant distortion of competition' (the test under the EC 6th VAT Directive) is considered to apply in relation to a wider range of local authority activities than was formerly the case. Consequently, the list of local authority activities categorised as 'business' has grown over the years. The fact that local authority activities are derived from statute does not, in itself, determine whether a 'business' activity is involved for VAT purposes. However, in practice, if the nature of the activity is such that the authority is in the position of being the only or virtually the only supplier, then generally that activity is likely to be categorised as 'non-business'[1].

1 See, for example, *Rhondda Cynon Taff County Borough Council v Customs and Excise Comrs* LON/99/670 regarding the provision and maintenance of cemeteries (non-business), as opposed to the view expressed by C&E in Customs & Excise Business Brief 4B/2000 (17 March 2000) regarding the treatment of crematoria (business), because of the higher incidence of privately owned crematoria. The tribunal in *Rhondda* concluded that in providing and maintaining cemeteries, the Council was acting under the special legal regime applicable to it and was not acting under the same legal conditions as those which apply to traders.

18.19 Detailed guidance on the categorisation of various local government activities into business and non-business was formerly contained in C&E Notice 749A (Local authorities and similar bodies—VAT status of activities) which was withdrawn as from 30 June 1999, following changes in legislation and the growth of contracting-out of services to the private sector. C&E Notice 749 now contains general guidance[1] on the distinction between 'business' and 'non-business' activities of local authorities and other public bodies. Appendix B to the Notice contains a 'decision chart' to assist in establishing the correct treatment of activities, and some examples of each category are given in Appendix C.

1 See C&E Notice 749, Section 3.

18.20 In relation to local authority activities, most of the VAT rules apply in the same way as they might to any other body which is registered for VAT. However, there are a number of factors which distinguish the VAT position of local authorities from that of the private sector:

(a) a significant proportion of their 'business' supplies involve making exempt supplies;
(b) a significant proportion of their activities are categorised as 'non-business';
(c) there are special rules which allow local authorities to claim a refund of the VAT which they pay in connection with their non-business activities; and
(d) subject to limitations, they can obtain a refund on 'insignificant' input tax which they pay on making exempt (business) supplies, which would otherwise be irrecoverable.

D VATA 1994, s 33 refunds and the de minimis threshold

1 NON-BUSINESS SUPPLIES

18.21 As noted in para **18.20**, in comparison with many private sector traders, a significant proportion of the activities of a local authority are categorised as being non-business. In the absence of some specific concession, a local authority would bear a disproportionate amount of the tax, through being unable to recover the VAT which it had paid on items needed for the purpose of 'non-business' activities. Ultimately, this cost would fall on local tax payers.

18.22 VATA 1994, s 33(1) makes special provision to ameliorate the effects of this by enabling local authorities[1] and other bodies listed in s 33(3)[2] to obtain a refund of tax paid on items acquired for the purpose of non-business activities. Under VATA, the recoverable tax is not strictly input tax. Rather, recovery under s 33 is a form of exemption from VAT on goods the authority has acquired or services it has received (or on certain importations from an EC member state it has made) for the purposes of making non-business supplies.

1 See para **18.17**, n 2 for the definition of 'local authorities' in Value Added Tax Act 1994, s 96(4).
2 The list includes such bodies as passenger transport authorities and executives and police authorities. Metropolitan authorities for fire and civil defence, police, passenger transport and residuary bodies were also specified for this purpose by SI 1985/1101. Probation committees and magistrates' courts committees were specified by SI 1986/336. Joint waste disposal authorities were specified by SI 1986/532. National Parks authorities and fire authorities (constituted under a combination scheme under the Fire Services Act 1947) were specified by SI 1995/2999.

18.23 Paragraph 5.1 of C&E Notice 749 sets out the criteria for entitlement to refunds of tax paid by local authorities on non-business activities. In summary:

(a) the supplies, acquisitions or items imported must not be for the purpose of any business activity;
(b) the tax must not have been incurred on the purchase of a motor car or on certain other specified 'blocked purchases'[1];
(c) the refund must relate to goods or services which have been *supplied directly* to the local authority; this means that the authority must:
    (i) place the order;
    (ii) receive the supply;
    (iii) receive a VAT invoice addressed to it; and
    (iv) make payment from its own funds[2] (or from a trust fund for which the authority acts as the sole trustee, subject to certain additional conditions[3]).

1 See C&E Notice 700, para 4.1.
2 This includes funds awarded to the local authority, such as lottery funds.
3 See C&E Notice 749, para 5.4.

18.24 One effect of the concession made under VATA 1994, s 33(1) is that, provided the above conditions are met, a local authority may provide goods or services to a voluntary organisation[1], in lieu of a cash grant, and recover any VAT it has incurred.

1 This assumes that the authority has power to do so, eg under the Local Authorities (Goods and Services) Act 1970.

18.25 Local authorities may also claim VATA 1994, s 33(1) refunds of the VAT they incur on purchases made out of funds which have been donated to them for specified purposes, provided that the authority (rather than the donor or any third party) benefits from the items purchased. To be eligible for a refund in respect of such a purchase, the authority must make the purchase itself, retain ownership of the purchased item, use it for its own non-business purposes and keep sufficient records of the purchase so that it can be easily identified. The money given to the authority must be a gift, rather than consideration for any supply the authority has made[1].

1 C&E Notice 749, paras 5.2 and 5.3.

2 EXEMPT (BUSINESS) SUPPLIES AND THE 5% DE MINIMIS THRESHOLD

18.26 As noted in para **18.12**(b), input tax incurred for the purposes of making exempt (business) supplies is not normally recoverable. However, local authorities and other bodies subject to VATA 1994, s 33 benefit from a special exemption[1] from the VAT they pay in order to make such supplies, subject to satisfaction of certain conditions.

1 VAT-registered persons who fall outside Value Added Tax Act 1994, s 33 who make some exempt supplies are also entitled to reclaim input tax relating to exempt supplies subject to de minimis limits. However, the thresholds for eligibility in these other cases are such that this entitlement is generally of less significance (see C&E Notice 706 (Partial exemption), para 6).

18.27 Under VATA 1994, s 33(2) where goods or services acquired by a local authority[1] for the purposes of making their non-business, as opposed to their business, supplies cannot be 'conveniently distinguished', the authority may claim a refund not only in respect of input tax incurred for the purpose of making non-business supplies, but also that incurred in respect of exempt (business) supplies. However, this additional element of refund under s 33(2) is subject to an important limitation. In the opinion of the C&E Commissioners, the tax attributable to the exempt (business) supplies must be 'an insignificant proportion of [all] tax so chargeable'.

1 Or other body to which Value Added Tax Act 1994, s 33 applies: see s 33(3).

18.28 The interpretation which C&E have applied to 'insignificance'[1] is a limit which amounts to the *greater* of:

(a) not more than £625 a month on average (ie not more than £7,500 per annum); or
(b) less than 5% of the total tax incurred on all goods and services purchased over the year.

If the exempt input tax exceeds both these figures, *none* of it can be recovered.

1 See C&E Notice 749, para 5.5. See also *Haringey London Borough Council v Customs and Excise Comrs* [1995] STC 830 (QBD), in which the court found it was for the Commissioners to decide what should be taken into account in assessing the limit of insignificance.

18.29 For the purpose of calculating the de minimis threshold for claiming refunds in respect of input tax on exempt (business) supplies, generally the comparison must be made between:

(a) input tax which is attributable to the making of exempt (business) supplies, whether that input tax relates to a supply which is *exclusively* an exempt supply, or relates to *part* of a supply for mixed purposes, only part of which is exempt[1]; and
(b) input tax which is attributable to *all* the supplies made by the local authority, whether non-business or business (and including exempt (business) supplies[2]).

1 In the *Haringey* case (supra), the court found that the Commissioners would not be entitled to disregard input tax paid on the exempt element of a mixed supply if to do so would render the level of input tax on exempt supplies to be, in the opinion of the Commissioners, a significant proportion of all tax paid. Thus, local authorities are generally advised to take any exempt elements of their mixed supplies into account when calculating the thresholds, subject to the transitional arrangements for capital projects referred to at para **18.30**, n 2 in relation to 'mixed supplies'. Unfortunately, the legislation itself offers no assistance as how an attribution of the input tax incurred as between business and non-business supplies is to be made.

2 But excluding goods and services listed in C&E Notice 700, para 4.1 on which VAT is irrecoverable (eg on motor cars and business entertainment expenses).

18.30 In calculating the amount of input tax attributable to exempt (business) activities:

(a) the local authority must include an appropriate proportion of input tax incurred on general expenditure, including overheads;

(b) a local authority can ignore VAT incurred on purchases related to exempt supplies which partly-exempt businesses outside the financial sector would be entitled to ignore when working out whether they can be treated as fully taxable[1]; and

(c) in general, a local authority must include capital projects in its VATA 1994, s 33 recovery calculations[2].

1 See De Voil *Indirect Tax Service* at p 6227. Examples of such VAT which may be disregarded are included in C&E Notice 706 at para 4.3.

2 However, C&E operated a period of transitional relief for capital projects involving mixed supplies (eg both non-business and exempt) subject to certain financial thresholds, which expired on 31 March 2000. See C&E Notice 749, para 6.2.

18.31 If the local authority remains below the 5% threshold[1], then all input tax on exempt (business) supplies is refundable except where this is specifically excluded by legislation (eg in relation to motor cars and business entertaining[2]).

1 Or below the £625 monthly average, if greater.

2 See the other excluded purchases listed in C&E Notice 700, para 4.1.

18.32 If the amount of input tax paid by the local authority in respect of making exempt (business) supplies exceeds the de minimis threshold, then *none* of the tax on such supplies is recoverable. It is not just the excess over the threshold which is forfeited, but the right to a refund on *all* input tax paid by the authority in respect of exempt (business) supplies over the year in question. In practice this may be a very significant amount, such that most authorities would normally wish to ensure that, where practicable, this threshold is not exceeded inadvertently[1].

1 See further para **18.42**ff in relation to property transactions.

18.33 C&E has developed a special method of calculating the partial exemption in respect of exempt (business) activities of local authorities and other bodies subject to VATA 1994, s 33, which is set out as Appendix F to C&E Notice 749. If authorities wish to adopt this method of calculation, they are required to obtain agreement from their local VAT office or VAT Business Advice Centre at the start of the financial year in which the method is to be used[1].

1 C&E Notice 749, para 6.1. See also VAT Information Sheet 2/99, paras 1 and 2.

18.34 Appendix G to C&E Notice 749 contains further advice of relevance to local authorities in planning and administering their refunds under VATA 1994, s 33.

This Appendix deals with such situations as those where an authority, having incurred some input tax, changes its intentions about the supplies it is to make or the activities it is to undertake using the acquired items (eg where those supplies are to be taxable, rather than exempt as originally intended) and in relation to adjustments in respect of capital goods items.

E VAT and local authority land transactions and construction

1 GENERAL TREATMENT OF LAND, PROPERTY AND CONSTRUCTION SUPPLIES FOR VAT PURPOSES

18.35 VAT on land and property is one of the most complex areas of VAT law. There are two sets of VAT rules, one for residential and the other for non-residential (mainly commercial) property These rules are mainly contained in VATA, Sch 8 (Zero-rating), Group 5 (Construction of Buildings, Etc); Sch 9 (Exemptions), Group 1 (Land); and Sch 10 (Buildings and Land[1]).

1 See also C&E Notice 742 (Land and property) and C&E Notice 708 (Buildings and construction).

18.36 Until 1989, the sale of new buildings was either VAT-exempt or zero-rated. Repairs, refurbishments, etc were and are normally subject to VAT at the standard rate.

18.37 Zero-rating offers two advantages. As noted above[1], the supply attracts VAT at a rate of 0 per cent. As the supply is regarded as taxable, input VAT incurred by the VAT-registered person making the supply and attributable to that supply can be recovered through the VAT system. By contrast, a VAT-exempt supply means that input tax incurred by the person making the supply and attributable to that supply is normally[2] irrecoverable through the VAT system.

1 See para **18.12**.
2 Subject to partial exemption referred to at paras **18.26–18.34**.

18.38 The UK was forced to abandon its zero-rating of new commercial property from 1 April 1989, because this was regarded as being in breach of a permitted derogation which allows zero-rating only for 'clearly defined social reasons and for the benefit of the final consumer'.

18.39 In general[1], the VAT rules for land transactions and construction apply to local authorities as to any other person who is registered for VAT, although the overall effect of those rules will be influenced by the particular uses to which properties owned by local authorities are put.

1 But see paras **18.21–18.34** regarding s 33 refunds on non-business activities and 'insignificant' input tax on exempt (business) supplies.

18.40 As a general rule, most supplies of land and/or buildings are VAT-exempt. A supply can include the transfer, grant, assignment or surrender of any interest in, right over, or licence to occupy land. However, where a supply involves the use or occupation of land and/or buildings, the supply is not automatically VAT-exempt[1].

1 See para **18.41**(c) and n 8 thereof, for example.

18.41 Exceptions to the VAT-exempt rule for land and buildings include:

(a) zero-rating of certain major interests[1] in 'qualifying buildings'. These are new and certain newly-converted dwellings, and new and certain newly-converted relevant residential buildings[2], charitable buildings[3] and certain listed buildings;

(b) standard-rating of supplies of non-qualifying buildings[4] or civil engineering works which are:

  (i) the freehold interest in a 'new' building[5]; or

  (ii) subject to an election to waive exemption (also described as 'an option to tax', or 'a VAT election'[6]); or

  (iii) specifically excluded from exemption[7];

(c) standard-rating of supplies which are *not* the grant or assignment of 'an interest in, a right over, or a licence to occupy' land. Standard-rating under this head may apply to supplies of certain (limited) forms of licence to *use* land or the grant of admission to the public to premises or events[8]; and

(d) the transfer of a business (or part of a business) as a going concern, which is treated as 'outside the scope of tax' (or 'OST'), provided that certain conditions are met[9]. This could include a situation where a tenanted property is acquired by a person who intends to use the property to carry on a property-letting business.

1 The grant by the developer of a major interest is the sale of a freehold or the grant of a lease for a term in excess of 21 years.

2 A building is a 'relevant residential building' if it is a residential building, or a residential part of a building, which the person to whom the supply is made has certified will be used as:

1. a children's home;
2. an old people's home;
3. a home for the rehabilitation of persons who suffer or have suffered from alcohol dependency, drug dependency or mental disorder;
4. a hospice;
5. living accommodation for students or school children;
6. living accommodation for members of religious communities; or
7. any communal living accommodation which at least 90% of the residents use as their sole or main residence.

The expression 'relevant residential building' does not include a hospital, prison or other penal institution, or an hotel, inn or similar establishment.

3 A 'relevant charitable building' is a building used by a charity solely in one of two ways: either as part of its non-business activities; or as a village or similar hall, providing social or recreational facilities for a local community.

4 'Non-qualifying buildings' include offices, retail premises, industrial buildings such as factories and warehouses. These uses are generally 'commercial'. See para 3.1 of C&E Notice 742 (Land and property).

5 A building is 'new' for three years from the date that it is completed. All freehold sales which take place within this three year period are standard-rated unless the 'going concern transfer' provision applies (for which, see para **18.41**(d)).

6 See paras **18.45–18.50**.

7 C&E Notice 742 (Land and property) sets out a list in para 2.8.

8 Caution is necessary in relation this narrow category. See, for example, para 2.7 of C&E Notice 742 (Land and property) which contains examples of exempt and non-exempt (standard-rated) licences and permissions. C&E are currently reviewing the VAT treatment of licences.

9 See C&E Notice 700/9 (Transfer of a business as a going concern).

2 PRACTICAL CONSEQUENCES OF MAKING EXEMPT (BUSINESS) SUPPLIES OF LAND AND/OR BUILDINGS

18.42 For most VAT-registered businesses, the danger of making supplies of land/buildings which are exempt from VAT is that (if it is not already) the business will become a VAT partially-exempt trader as a consequence. As the supplier, not only will it be unable to recover input VAT which it incurs in buying in goods and services which it uses to make exempt supplies of land/buildings, but it will be able to recover a smaller proportion of the input VAT which it incurs on goods and services which are attributable to its overheads (rather than to any specific supplies it may make).

18.43 There is a further consequence of engaging in any high value exempt transaction involving significant amounts of input tax (such as those concerning construction, or acquisition and sale, of land/buildings) beyond simply the risk of a reduced rate of recovery on VAT attributable to overheads. Where the local authority is to incur significant amounts of input tax in connection with the making of such supplies, there is likely to be a risk that its de minimis threshold for the recovery of input tax on exempt supplies will be exceeded[1]. The authority may thereby forfeit its entitlement to recover input VAT on *all* its exempt supplies for the year[2].

1 For VAT-registered persons outside s 33, their de minimis threshold for recovery of input tax on exempt supplies might also be forfeited in these circumstances. However, the financial consequences of this may be less significant (see para **18.26**, n 1).
2 And not simply (a) that in respect of the transaction in question, or (b) that in respect of the authority's overheads, or (c) the excess over the de minimis threshold: see para **18.32**.

18.44 In some situations, the authority may be able to overcome the difficulties this might otherwise cause by making an option to tax as described at paras **18.45–18.50**. In relation to VAT-exempt supplies of land and commercial buildings, a supplier can[1] 'convert' what would otherwise be a VAT-exempt supply into a standard-rated supply through such an election. For any supplier, this improves the proportion of input VAT which that person can recover. For a local authority concerned about the de minimis threshold for VATA 1994, s 33 recovery referred to at paras **18.26–18.34**, such an election would also reduce the amount of input tax on exempt supplies to be brought into the calculation of the de minimis threshold percentage (or average value). The opportunity to make such an election is not, however, available to a local authority in relation to all the types of transaction concerning land/buildings in which the authority might be involved. For example, normally no election can be made in respect of the sale of dwellings or residential buildings.

1 Subject to the prior permission of C&E in specified cases: see para **18.50**.

3 ELECTION TO WAIVE THE VAT EXEMPTION (OR 'OPTION TO TAX')

18.45 Supplies of non-qualifying (commercial) buildings[1] which would be exempt from VAT will normally be standard-rated if an election to waive exemption[2] is made in relation to that property[3].

1 See para **18.41**, n 4 for the definition of 'non-qualifying building'.
2 An election to waive exemption is sometimes known as 'the option to tax' or a 'VAT election'.
3 'Property' here means land, buildings and civil engineering work.

18.46 The consequence of making an election is that future transactions made in respect of the 'elected' property, by the person who has made the election, normally become standard-rated. This enables the recovery of input VAT on goods and services acquired, and which are attributable to the standard-rated supply. For a local authority, it also means a lower proportion/value of input tax will be incurred in relation to making exempt supplies[1].

1 See para **18.44**.

18.47 Once made, VAT must be accounted for on all future supplies of the 'elected' property made by the person who made the election . An election cannot be made retrospectively. If VAT is charged on rents due on a tenanted property, then it must also be charged on a subsequent disposal of the building (whether freehold or leasehold)[2]. An election can be revoked only in very limited circumstances.

1 Certain exceptions are set out in C&E Notice 742 (Land and property), para 8.4.
2 Unless the 'going concern transfer' provision applies. See para **18.41**(d).

18.48 An election has effect in relation to the whole of the building and all the land in its curtilage, howsoever the election is expressed. Buildings linked internally or by a covered walkway are treated as parts of a single building, as are buildings making up a complex, such as a purpose-built shopping centre, if they are grouped around a fully-enclosed concourse.

18.49 To have legal effect, an election must be notified in writing to C&E[1] within 30 days of the election being made. There are requirements as to the contents of the notification of the election. The VAT registration number of the person making the election, the property the subject of the election and the effective date of the election must all be stated in the notification[2].

1 The local office dealing with the person's VAT affairs.
2 There is no required format for notification; a suggested format is set out in Appendix H to C&E Notice 742 (Land and property).

18.50 If the property has been used by the person seeking to make the election to make any exempt supply (sale, leasing or letting), however trivial, between 1 August 1989 and the intended effective date of the election, C&E's permission is first required. This permission may be conditional on complying with input VAT recovery conditions. Without prior permission, an election cannot be effective in this situation.

4 ('REVERSE') SURRENDERS, ('REVERSE') ASSIGNMENTS, 'REVERSE PREMIUMS' AND RENT-FREE PERIODS

18.51 Supplies between landlords and tenants raise many VAT issues[1]. The following summarises the treatment for VAT purposes of surrenders, 'reverse surrenders', assignments, 'reverse assignments', 'reverse premiums' and rent-free periods. In addition to case law, the main rules are contained in VATA 1994, Sch 9 (Exemptions), Group 1 (Land).

1 See C&E Notice 742 (Land and property), Chapter 4.

(a) Surrender

18.52 The surrender of a lease to a landlord, in the course or furtherance of the tenant's business, is generally VAT-exempt. Where a tenant has elected to waive exemption in respect of the property the subject of the lease, the surrender is covered by the election and is standard-rated (where the landlord is paying).

(b) Reverse surrender

18.53 Where a landlord accepts the surrender of a lease, with the tenant paying (known by C&E as a 'reverse surrender'), the supply (by the landlord) is VAT-exempt, except where the landlord has elected, in which case it is standard-rated.

(c) Assignment

18.54 An assignment of a lease by a tenant, with the assignee paying, is exempt unless the tenant (the assignor) has made an election.

(d) Reverse assignment

18.55 C&E regard an inducement paid by a tenant to a third party to accept the assignment of a lease (known by C&E as a 'reverse assignment') as consideration for a standard-rated supply of services made by the assignee. The VAT status is irrespective of any election made.

(e) Reverse premium

18.56 Similarly, C&E regard an inducement paid by a landlord (known by C&E as a 'reverse premium') to a prospective tenant for the latter to enter into a lease as consideration for a standard-rated supply of services (made by the tenant); again, the VAT status is irrespective of any election being made.

18.57 The status of reverse assignments and reverse premiums is to be considered by the European Court of Justice[1]. Pending resolution of these cases, C&E has indicated that businesses receiving payments in these circumstances may choose not to account for VAT on the transaction, in which case C&E may raise a protective assessment. If the final decision is in C&E's favour, businesses will be required to pay the VAT and interest. Alternatively, businesses may continue to account for VAT on such payments and submit claims for repayment and statutory interest if the final decision goes against C&E (subject to the three year capping limit[2]).

1 Following references to the ECJ made in respect of *Mirror Group plc v Customs and Excise Comrs* [1998] BVC 2180, VAT and Duties Tribunal—regarding a reverse premium; and *Customs and Excise Comrs v Cantor Fitzgerald International* [1998] STC 948, QBD—regarding a reverse assignment. Earlier decisions in each of these cases had indicated that the supplies were VAT-exempt (subject to being standard-rated as a result of an election).

2 Customs & Excise Business Brief 28/97, 12 December 1997; Customs & Excise Business Brief 17/98, 10 August 1998.

(f) Rent-free periods

18.58 The grant by a landlord of a rent-free period is not a supply for VAT purposes except where the rent-free period is given in exchange for something which the tenant agrees to do, such as carrying out works for the benefit of the landlord. In the example given, VAT would be due on the amount of the rent foregone by the landlord.

5 COMPULSORY PURCHASE[1]

18.59 The transfer of land under a compulsory purchase order is a VAT-exempt supply unless:

(a) it is a 'new' freehold building[2] or 'new' civil engineering works; or
(b) the option to tax has been made by the owner; or
(c) it is the sale of the freehold in holiday accommodation which is less than three years old.

In each case ((a) to (c)), the supply will be standard-rated.

1 See C&E Notice 742 (Land and property), para 7.4, which specifies that the transfer of bare land or non-qualifying buildings (see para **18.41**, n 4) which are not 'new', pursuant to a compulsory purchase order, will be treated as exempt.
2 See para **18.41**, n 5.

18.60 If the amount of compensation is not known at the tax point (the date of transfer of the property, or (if earlier) the date of payment), there is a tax point each time any element of the compensation is received by the owner[1].

1 C&E's advice to that effect in para 7.4 of C&E Notice 742 (Land and property) has been criticised by the VAT Tribunal in *L Landau* (13644), where the tribunal chairman suggested that in a case where the compensation was not quantified, there was no reason why VAT should not be accounted for on an estimated amount.

6 LOCAL AUTHORITY PLANNING AND RELATED FUNCTIONS[1]

18.61 The dedication or vesting of a new road by a developer under an agreement under the Highways Act 1980 for no monetary consideration is not a supply made by the developer to the local authority. No VAT is therefore chargeable to the local authority.

1 See C&E Notice 742 (Land and property), paras 7.11, 7.12 and 7.13.

18.62 Agreements under the Town and Country Planning Act 1990, s 106 and similar agreements under which goods and services are provided to the authority free, or for a purely nominal charge, do not constitute a supply by the developer. Again, no VAT is chargeable to the local authority. Similarly, sums of money (whether alone or in addition to buildings or works) paid by the developer to the authority are not consideration for a supply made by the authority.

F Appeals concerning VAT

18.63 In practice, a person who objects to a decision made by C&E is generally advised to ask the relevant local VAT office to review its decision before any appeal is initiated[1].

1 See 'VAT: Appeals and Applications to the Tribunals—explanatory leaflet' (revised 1 August 1995).

18.64 The statutory provisions regarding appeals are contained in VATA 1994, Pt V. VATA 1994, s 82 and Sch 12 provide for the constitution of VAT and duties tribunals. These tribunals have jurisdiction to hear those matters relating to VAT which are specified in VATA 1994, s 83. Normally, an appeal will only be entertained by a tribunal where various pre-conditions specified in VATA 1994, s 84 have been satisfied by the appellant (such as payment of sums due in respect of all returns), although in limited circumstances the Commissioners are empowered to waive these requirements. An appeal to a VAT and duties tribunal must be made within 30 days of the date of the decision complained of. The appeal can be made on a form provided by the local VAT office, or may simply be set out in a letter containing specified information. A tribunal is empowered to make orders for costs[1].

1 In practice, C&E do not normally seek costs in the tribunal against the losing taxpayer.

18.65 An appeal from a VAT and duties tribunal may be made on a point of law to the High Court, or a party may require the tribunal to state and sign a case for the opinion of the High Court[1]. Under VATA 1994, s 86 certain appeals may be made direct to the Court of Appeal. Such an appeal may be made where the tribunal has certified that its decision involves a point of law relating (wholly or mainly) to statutory construction, the parties' consent and the permission of a single judge of the Court of Appeal has been obtained[2].

1 Tribunals and Inquiries Act 1992, s 11. The *Practice Direction* to Part 52 of the Civil Procedure Rules 1998 (SI 1998/3132 as amended) ('the CPR'), para 23.8, makes specific provision for the procedure on an appeal to the High Court.
2 The *Practice Direction* to Part 52 of the CPR, para 21.6, makes specific provision for the procedure on an appeal to the Court of Appeal.

18.66 Where a question as to the validity or interpretation of Community law is raised before any court or tribunal, the court or tribunal may, if it considers that a decision on the question is necessary to enable it to give judgment, request the European Court of Justice to give a ruling on it (under the EC Treaty, art 177).

CHAPTER 19

Housing finance

A Introduction

19.1 Local housing authorities are now regulated by Part VI, ss 74–80 and Sch 4 of the Local Government and Housing Act 1989 (LGHA 1989). Other sections within Part XIII of the Housing Act 1985, which formerly applied to all public housing authorities, including local authorities, now apply only to new town corporations and the Development Board for Rural Wales.

19.2 LGHA 1989, Pt VI contains two sets of provisions: one sets out the rules on housing accounts; the other sets out the provisions about housing subsidies. See also the Housing Revenue Manual 1994[1] (henceforth 'Manual') and DoE Circular 8/95. Both are essential reading.

1 DETR, April 1994 with updates (2 volumes).

B The housing revenue account[1]

19.3 Section 74 requires every local housing authority[2] to keep a housing revenue account ('HRA'), setting out the sums to be debited and credited to that account[3]. The HRA is a landlord account, showing income and expenditure arising out of the exercise of powers conferred on local housing authorities by the Housing Act 1985, Pt II. It is not a separate fund, but a ring-fenced account within the general fund of the housing authority. It is based on accruals rather than cash accounting[4]. The main items of expenditure are loan charges, management and maintenance costs, and rent rebates and items of income are rent and subsidy from central government[5].

1 See Manual, ch 7.
2 Housing Act 1985, ss 1-2: applied by the Local Government and Housing Act 1989, s 88(1).
3 Local Government and Housing Act 1989, s 74(1).
4 See *R v Secretary of State for the Environment, ex p Camden London Borough Council* [1998] 1 All ER 937.
5 Manual, ch 7.4.

19.4 The HRA is to be kept in respect of the following categories of property[1]:

(i) houses and other buildings provided under Part II of the Housing Act 1985;
(ii) land acquired or appropriated for the purposes of Part II;
(iii) houses purchased under s 192 of the Housing Act 1985 (now repealed);
(iv) dwellings in relation to which a housing authority has received assistance under the Housing (Rural Workers) Act 1926;

(v) property brought within the former housing revenue account for years before 1 April 1990;
(vi) such other land or other property as the Secretary of State may direct[2].

1 Manual, ch 8.
2 Local Government and Housing Act 1989, s 74(1); references to the Housing Act 1985 include references to earlier legislation replaced by that Act: LGHA 1989, s 74(2). The power to make directions has been exercised in the Housing Revenue (Dwellings in the Account) Direction 1990.

19.5 The above rules (save the last) do not apply to the following categories of property:

(i) land, houses or other buildings disposed of by a housing authority;
(ii) land acquired by a housing authority for the purpose of disposing of houses provided or to be provided on the land, or of disposing of the land to a person who intends to provide housing accommodation on it[1];
(iii) houses provided by a housing authority on the land so acquired; or
(iv) such land or other buildings as the Secretary of State may direct.

Dwellings provided on or before 9 February 1919 are not to be brought into the HRA, unless they were charged to the HRA in the year beginning 1 April 1989[2].

1 Under the terms of the Housing Revenue Account (Dwellings in the Account) Direction 1990, dwellings built on land so acquired may be brought into the account if they are in fact rented or let under a shared ownership lease, rather than sold outright.
2 LGHA 1989, s 74(3) and the Housing Revenue (Dwellings in the Account) Direction 1990.

19.6 The word 'disposal' includes not only a conveyance of the freehold, but also includes any grant or assignment of a lease (other than a shared ownership lease[1]) which is a long tenancy as defined by the Housing Act 1985, s 115. Dwellings disposed of under the 'right to buy' provisions, whether by outright conveyance of the freehold, or by the grant of a long lease, accordingly fall outside the scope of the HRA.

If a housing authority has no dwellings or other property falling within any of the categories listed above, it must still keep an HRA unless the Secretary of State consents to their not so doing[2].

1 Local Government and Housing Act 1989, s 74(5)(b).
2 LGHA 1989, s 74(4). Conditions may be attached to any such consent.

C The housing repairs account[1]

19.7 In addition to the HRA, which is mandatory, housing authorities have power to maintain a housing repairs account[2]. If used, the account must cover the whole of an authority's HRA stock of housing.

The housing repairs account must show, on the credit side, sums paid into it from the HRA plus any other sums received from tenants for repair or maintenance (eg charges for services rendered) or other sums (eg from the sale of scrapped or salvaged materials)[3].

Debit items are sums expended on the repair or maintenance of houses or other property in the HRA, or expenditure on the improvement or replacement of property in the HRA as determined by the Secretary of State, together with any balances transferred at the end of the financial year to the HRA from the housing repairs account[4]. Costs of supervision and management are not to be included in the housing repairs account.

The housing repairs account must not show a debit balance at the end of the year[5]. This account is within the HRA 'ring-fence', so there is no power to transfer sums between the housing repairs account and any other account of a housing authority, except the HRA[6].

1 Manual, ch 10.
2 Local Government and Housing Act 1989, s 77(1).
3 LGHA 1989, s 77(2).
4 LGHA 1989, s 77(3),(5).
5 LGHA 1989, s 77(4).
6 Manual, ch 10.2.

D Practice and procedure

19.8 The Secretary of State has power to give directions as to the proper accounting practices to be followed by housing authorities in keeping the HRA and housing repairs account[1].

1 LGHA 1989, s 78. See also s 78A–B added by the Housing Act 1996, Sch 18, para 4(1).

19.9 Two basic principles are imposed by the LGHA 1989 in relation to the HRA. The first is that only those matters prescribed by law can be brought into the HRA[1]. The second is that housing authorities must endeavour to secure that, in any financial year, the HRA does not show a debit balance. Thus the HRA is self-supporting—the HRA cannot be subsidised by funds other than those that are prescribed, and rents must be set at levels which reflect the value of the dwelling.

1 Local Government and Housing Act 1989, s 75 and Sch 4 as amended by s 127 of the Leasehold Reform, Housing and Urban Development Act 1993, s 127.

1 HRA CREDITS

(1) Rent

19.10 All rents and charges, including rent remitted by way of rent rebate, are to be included as a credit in the account. Provision for bad or wrongful debts is accounted as a debit item. Rent foregone on empty property is not to be included as rent[1]. The rent is to be shown on an accruals basis, ie as a sum that is due, rather than one actually received as cash.

1 Local Government and Housing Act 1989, Sch 4, Pt I.

(2) Charges for services and facilities

19.11 There is a general power to charge, eg for facilities provided under the Housing Act 1985, ss 10–11 (provision of furniture and laundry facilities). Other charges might include those for communal central heating systems or community alarm systems[1]. Also included are charges for expenditure on works on the common parts of blocks of flats, in which individual flats have been bought under the right to buy, or rent to mortgage provisions. (This requirement ceases once all flats in the block have been disposed of on a lease for 21 or more years). Charges for the purchase of furniture are not to be included[2].

1 Manual, ch 11.1.
2 Manual, ch 11.2.

(3) HRA subsidy

19.12 This is self-explanatory.

(4) Contributions towards expenditure

19.13 This relates to contributions payable by a housing authority for items of housing expenditure. The Manual[1] gives, as examples, payments under the 'Bellwin' scheme, relating to compensation for damage caused by natural or other disasters; sums received from social services authorities to contribute to the provision of special facilities for the elderly; contributions from tenants by way of refund of the costs of house repairs which are the tenants' liability; and annual payments from displacing authorities under Land Compensation Act 1973, s 42.

1 Manual, ch 11.2.7.

(5) Housing benefit transfers

19.14 This covers so much of any rent rebates as are granted at the discretion of the housing authority or by virtue of any modifications to the national scheme made by the housing authority. It may also include the additional cost of any disregard of war pensions over and above that provided for under the national scheme[1].

1 Housing Act 1996, s 140D(2); Manual, ch 11.5.

(6) Transfers from the housing repairs account

19.15 This is self-explanatory.

(7) Reduced provision for bad or doubtful debts

19.16 Any arrears recovered from a tenant are to be credited to the HRA. If the provision for bad debt in any year has been over-conservative, then any subsequent revision downwards of that provision is also to be accounted as a credit[1].

1 Manual, ch 11.7 and 12.7.

(8) Sums calculated as determined by the Secretary of State

19.17 This refers to interest which it is assessed has been earned by a housing authority. The sum is determined by a formula. The current determination is set out in the Determination of Item 8 Credit and Item 8 Debit (General) Determination 2000–2001[1]. On the credit side, broadly speaking, the determination provides for the HRA to be credited with an amount by way of interest earned by

HRA capital resources, to the extent that such sum exceeds the costs of HRA debt[2].

1 Changed and amended annually and sent direct by DETR to the Chief Finance Officer of housing authorities.
2 Manual, ch 11.8.

(9) Sums directed by the Secretary of State

19.18 The Secretary of State retains a residual power to direct that a sum from another account in the control of a housing authority should be paid into the HRA under this head. The power is to be used only very exceptionally. The Manual states that even if a serious deficit in the HRA has arisen, for example in circumstances beyond a housing authority's control, and which were uncontrollable, a direction would not normally be made, but the authority would be expected to carry forward the deficit to the next year[1].

1 Manual, ch 11.9. Special rules allow housing authorities to apply for a direction that surpluses from any Direct Service Organisation in the authority can be brought into the HRA under this item. This is being limited to profits on housing maintenance work.

(10) Credit balance from previous year

19.19 In cases where no housing revenue account subsidy is payable at all, the housing authority has power to pay the whole or part of any credit balance in the HRA into any other revenue account of the authority[1].

1 1989 Act, Sch 4, Pt III, para 2.

2 HRA DEBITS[1]

(1) Expenditure on repairs, maintenance and management

19.20 These include, repairs, maintenance, management and supervision of houses and other property in the account. The Manual indicates that the precise scope of this item may need some further definition[2]. Three categories of expenditure fall under this head:

(i) the cost of repairs and maintenance, other than that which is the responsibility of tenants, or which is charged to a housing repairs account, or which falls under item 2 or which has been capitalised;
(ii) the costs of general management including policy and management, tenancy applications and selection procedures[3], and rent collection and accounting but excluding the administration of rent rebates which falls under the General Fund;
(iii) the costs of special services, often shared, to tenants for eg caretaking, cleaning, communal lighting and lifts[4].

Where repair work involves an 'enhancement'[5] of the property, it is possible to 'capitalise' the value of the expenditure, in which case the revenue consequences for the HRA will appear as an item 8 debit rather than under this head[6].

Compensation paid to tenants for the cost of improvements they have made to their properties and paid for can fall under this item. Such costs may arise under the discretionary power to pay compensation for improvements under the Housing

Act 1985, s 100; or under the more recent mandatory power to pay compensation when a tenancy ends[7].

1 Local Government and Housing Act 1989, Sch 4, Pt II; Manual, ch 12.
2 See *R v London Borough of Ealing, ex p Lewis* (1992) 24 HLR 484, CA, which was overruled the Leasehold Reform, Housing and Urban Development Act 1993, s 127.
3 *Shelley v LCC* [1949] 1 AC 56, CA.
4 Where services benefit the wider community, there must be an apportionment as between the debit to the HRA and a debit to the housing authority's General Fund: Manual, ch 6.12.
5 As defined in LGHA 1989, s 40(3). It means work intended to lengthen substantially the useful life of an asset, or substantially to increase its open market value, or to increase substantially the extent to which an asset can be used: see Manual, ch 4.17.
6 Manual, ch 12.8.3 and 12.8.4.
7 Housing Act 1985, ss 99A and 99B, inserted by 1993 Act, s 122, and the Secure Tenants of Local Authorities (Compensation for Improvements) Regulations, 1994, SI 1994/613.

(2) Expenditure for capital purposes

19.21 While the costs of capital expenditure (ie interest charges) will usually be chargeable under item 8 below, housing authorities do have a discretion to charge capital expenditure to revenue under this head should they so determine. If capital expenditure is incurred which is neither undertaken in reliance on a credit approval[1] nor met from capital receipts, then it must be charged under this item.

1 This is the mechanism by which the Secretary of State seeks to influence the overall level of local authority capital expenditure: Manual, ch 4.2.

(3) Rents, rates, taxes and other charges

19.22 These are charges which a housing authority is liable to pay. Council tax collected from tenants by the authority for convenience' sake does not have to be entered, as it is not a liability of the authority[1].

1 Manual, ch 12.3. Other examples are rents on leases, and guarantee arrangements to those providing water and sewerage services.

(4) Rent rebates

19.23 All rent remitted by way of rebate to tenants of dwellings in the HRA[1] has to be entered as a debit item[2]. The inclusion of rent rebates in the HRA means that there will be some housing authorities who are able to cover a proportion of their expenditure on rent rebates not from special government subsidy, but by surpluses on the income side of the HRA. Administration charges, which are funded partly by a separate administration subsidy from the Department of Social Security, and partly by the Revenue Support Grant, are not included.

1 This includes dwellings managed by a body other than the housing authority, but still owned by the Authority: Manual, ch 12.4.4(i).
2 All other forms of housing benefit, whether rent rebates for non-HRA dwellings, or rent allowances for private sector tenants (including housing associations) fall into the authority's General Fund. See also Manual, ch 12.4.

(5) Sums transformed under LGHA 1989, s 80(2)

19.24 LGHA 1989, s 80(2) provides that in defined circumstances, the amount payable by way of HRA subsidy may be a negative account. In such cases, that sum must be entered as a debit item.

(6) Contributions to the housing repairs account

19.25 This is self-explanatory.

(7) Provision for bad or doubtful debts

19.26 Actual arrears, or anticipated defaults in payment must be shown as a debit to the HRA[1]. Transitional limits to the amounts to be shown under this head were set down in the Housing Revenue Account (Arrears of Rent and Charges) Directions 1990[2].

1 Advice on the control of rent arrears is given in DoE Circular 18/87 and an Audit Commission report published in 1989.
2 Manual, ch 5.6.

(8) Sums calculated as determined by the Secretary of State

19.27 Where the amount of loan charges on HRA debt exceeds the amounts of interest earned by HRA capital resources, the difference must be shown under item 8 on the debit side of the account[1].

1 See the annual Item 8 Credit and Item 8 Debit (General) Determination 1995–1996 at para 4; Manual, ch 12.8.

(9) Debit balances from the previous year

19.28 Although housing authorities are under a duty to ensure that the HRA is in balance, this will not always prove possible. In such a case the debit balance must be carried forward.

E Special rules

19.29 LGHA 1989, Sch 4, Pt III provides for a number of special situations. Apart from a special provision relating to balances for the year 1989–1990 and the special rule where no HRA subsidy is payable, these rules are as follows:

(1) *Amenities shared by the whole community*
Where the community can share in benefits or amenities provided for persons housed by an authority, the authority should make a contribution to the HRA from other revenue accounts of such sums and for such periods as will properly reflect the community's share of the benefits or amenities. Although the Secretary of State has power to make a general direction under these provisions, he has not done so[1].

(2) *Provision of welfare services*
Where a housing authority provides welfare services, it may carry to the credit of the HRA any charges received from tenants by way of payment for those services, or any sum from some other revenue account representing the whole or part of that income. Amounts by way of expenditure on such services are attributed to the debit side of the account[2].

(3) *Land disposed of at less than market value*
If the Secretary of State gives permission for disposal of land at less than market

value, he may make it a condition that the authority make a contribution to the HRA[3].

(4) *Adjustment of account on appropriation of land*
These are as the Secretary of State directs[4].

There are also special rules relating to transfers of housing stock between housing authorities in London, and contributions in respect of land on general improvement areas or renewal areas[5].

1 LGHA 1989, Sch 4, Pt III, para 3; Manual, ch 7, Annex C.
2 LGHA 1989, Sch 4, Pt III, para 3A, added by Leasehold Reform, Housing and Urban Development Act 1993, s 127. This amendment overrules the decision in *R v London Borough of Ealing, ex p Lewis* (1992) 24 HLR 484, CA.
3 LGHA 1989, Sch 4, Pt III, para 4.
4 LGHA 1989, Sch 4, Pt III, para 5.
5 LGHA 1989, Sch 4, Pt III, paras 6 and 7.

F The budget

19.30 LGHA 1989, s 76 lays down detailed provisions for ensuring that housing authorities not only set a budget that will satisfy that statutory objective, but also do so within a defined timescale before the beginning of the financial year in April each year[1].

In the January–February preceding the relevant financial year, the housing authority must formulate proposals which, if implemented would secure that the HRA will not show a debit account at the end of the year. In making the proposals, such authority must take into account the income from rents and other charges, the expenditure in respect of repairs, maintenance, management and supervision of their property, and such other matters as the Secretary of State may direct[2].

The Secretary of State's decision on the subsidy should ideally be determined in advance of the setting of the HRA budget[3].

1 LGHA 1989, s 76; Manual, ch 9.2.
2 LGHA 1989, s 76(2).
3 In practice, the information is provided by the Department of the Environment at around the end of the calendar year preceding the new financial year.

19.31 A housing authority is entitled to take into account the best assumptions it is able to make as regards the amounts to be debited or credited to the HRA (eg in relation to the level of council house sales, or new accommodation coming available for letting), and the best estimates derived from those assumptions[1]. In so far as assumptions depend on information from the Secretary of State, it is expressly provided that a housing authority can only rely on information already communicated to it, not information it hopes to hear[2]. Once published, the proposals must be put into practice[3]. A statement of the proposals must be published within a month of being settled, which must be open for inspection by the public[4].

1 Local Government and Housing Act 1989, s 76(3); Manual, ch 9, para 2.5.
2 LGHA 1989, s 76(4). The Manual gives an example that an authority cannot apply for a special subsidy determination and then set its budget on the assumption that the application will be successful. It must wait until a decision is reached, and then may if desired alter the budget already set: ch 9, para 2.6.
3 LGHA 1989, s 76(5). There is power to revise the proposals during the year and implement the proposals as amended: LGHA 1989, s 76(6) and (7).
4 LGHA 1989, s 76(8) and (9).

G Housing subsidies

19.32 LGHA 1989, ss 79–88 deal with the main source of subsidy to housing authorities for their housing costs. The principal form of subsidy is now the housing revenue account subsidy[1].

1 LGHA 1989, s 79. The subsidy may be paid by the Secretary of State at times, in the manner and subject to conditions as to audit, record-keeping and provision of certificates, as he may with the agreement of the Treasury determine: LGHA 1989, s 79(2). In practice, payments are made throughout the year at monthly intervals. There is a power for the Secretary of State to recoup subsidy that it transpires has been overpaid: see Recoupment of Housing Revenue Account Subsidy Rules 1993.

19.33 The HRA subsidy is calculated in accordance with formulae determined by the Secretary of State[1]. Unlike previous schemes where such formulae were laid down in the body of the legislation, the present scheme relies on determinations, made in accordance with s 88 of the Act[2].

The basic principle is that HRA subsidy is an amount calculated to make up the deficit on a notional account comprising the following seven items, which are calculated in accordance with rules set out in the determination[3]. Thus, the level of subsidy equals the housing authority's assumed expenditure minus its assumed income[4].

1 1989 Act, s 80. The bases of these formulae were unsuccessfully challenged in *R v Secretary of State for the Environment, ex p London Borough of Greenwich* (1990) 22 HLR 543 (QBD).
2 1989 Act, s 87.
3 The amounts involved are notional, and are calculated differently from the items recorded in the actual HRA: Manual, ch 14.2.
4 Subsidy Determination, art 3.

19.34 The subsidy is the sum of the following items:

(1) management and maintenance;
(2) charges for capital;
(3) rent rebates;
(4) other items of reckonable expenditure less the sum of the following items –
  (a) rent;
  (b) interest on receipts;
  (c) other items of reckonable income.

19.35 The details of each of the items of expenditure are set out in the Subsidy Determination[1]. Some comment is necessary. Management and maintenance are based on the principle of 'targeted allowances', reflecting a housing authority's relative need to incur expenditure under this head[2].

1 Manual, ch 15–20.
2 Subsidy Determination, art 4; Manual, ch 15, Annex A.

19.36 Charges for capital are set out in detail in art 5 of the Subsidy Determination[1]. Housing authorities have to include 100% of the costs of their borrowing for housing purposes[2] under this item[3]. The item for the rent rebates[4] is the total expenditure by way of rent rebates (ie that component of housing benefit that goes to subsidise the tenants of a housing authority) for housing within the HRA. There is no separate subsidy to housing authorities for the rent rebate element of housing benefit[5]. The precise amount of subsidy for rent rebates is the sum of qualifying expenditure on rent rebates plus a sum determined in relation to each housing authority by the Secretary of State and set out in Sch 2 of the Determination[6], less the cost of 'overruns'[7].

1 The details have changed since the new housing finance regime was introduced in April 1990.
2 It is only borrowing for housing purposes that can be included here: *R v Secretary of State for the Environment, ex p Enfield London Borough Council* (1994) 26 HLR 51, CA.
3 This is a very substantial component of HRA subsidy—about £2.5 billion a year; Manual, ch 17.
4 Manual, ch 16.
5 One practical consequence of including rent rebate expenditure in the formula for the determination of HRA subsidy is that if a housing authority receives a very low level of HRA subsidy, or even a negative sum, as can happen, the costs of the rent rebates are thus met, not from grants paid by central government, but through the rents paid by other tenants.
6 This is known as the 'cash limited' sum and is designed to offset in part deductions made from qualifying expenditure in respect of backdated claims and overpayments.
7 Which may occur where an award of rent rebate has been made, entitlement has expired, but the authority goes on making the rebate without making a further award of benefit.

19.37 Items of actual expenditure excluded from the definition of 'qualifying expenditure'[1] include: expenditure on backdated claims to housing benefit[2], expenditure as a result of overpayments[3], expenditure on rebates to cover charges attributable to the provision of extra or enhanced services, facilities or rights at the discretion of the tenant[4], payment of rent rebate for a rent-free period not taken into account in the housing benefit calculation, cash awards to tenants credited to their rent account, or expenditure resulting from a decision by an authority to modify the statutory housing benefit scheme[5].

1 Determination, para 6.3.
2 Housing Benefit (General) Regulations, 1987, reg 72(15), SI 1989/1971.
3 Other than those caused by error in the Department of Social Security, or by fraud.
4 Determination, para 6.3.3.1. These are known generically as 'modular improvement schemes': Manual, ch 16.6. This does not apply where the sole purpose for which such services or facilities are provided is to meet the needs of the tenant, or to improve the physical condition of the dwelling; the services/facilities are available to all tenants, whether or not they get rent rebates; the letting policy of the authority has not been deliberately to put tenants likely to be entitled to rebates in the properties in question; and charges for the services/facilities are reasonable: Determination, para 6.3.3.2.
5 Under the Social Security Administration Act 1992, s 134(8).

19.38 The category 'other items of reckonable expenditure' includes the rents payable by the authority on leasehold property, guarantee payments to a water or sewerage undertaker, costs of the leasing of equipment, miscellaneous other interest charges, and the costs of tenants' choice leasebacks[1].

1 Determination, para 7 and Table B; Manual, ch 19.

19.39 The key element in the equation is the cost of the notional rents charged by a housing authority. Paragraph 8 of the Subsidy Determination lays down the detail of the formula to be used in determining the notional rents to be charged by housing authorities for dwellings in their HRA[1].

Notional rents are now determined by reference to the current value of the dwelling being provided. Movements in the level of rents from year to year must reflect general trends of incomes, costs and prices in the wider economy.

1 Manual, ch 18.

19.40 A formula-driven figure representing the average gross rent per dwelling is determined for each housing authority. Each such authority retains freedom to set rent of varying levels in relation to different estates, or different types of dwelling. An authority's average must match the centrally determined figure. The Subsidy Determination makes provision for 'damping': damping the extremes of change in rent levels that might otherwise occur through the strict application of the new approach. There are also provisions to take account of voids and inflation.

19.41 Article 3 of the Annual Determination deals with interest and other items of reckonable income. The 'other items' refers to any grant, contribution or compensation—other than a loan—which may be received by a local housing authority.

19.42 Housing subsidies for new town corporations and the Development Board for Rural Wales continue to be provided under the Housing Act 1985, ss 421–427A on an annual basis[1]. This sum is calculated as the sum total[2] of the 'base amount'[3] and the 'housing costs differential'[4] less the 'local costs differential'[5]. There is power to recoup subsidy that appears not to have been used either wholly or in part for the purpose for which it was given, where the case falls within the scope of rules published by the Secretary of State[6]. Subsidy is still payable where the body has entered into a management agreement with agents[7].

1 Housing Act 1985, s 421(1).
2 Housing Act 1985, s 422 applied to the Development Board for Rural Wales by s 426.
3 Housing Act 1985, s 423 as the amount of the housing subsidy for the previous year, though the Secretary of State has power to adjust the amount.
4 Housing Act 1985, s 424. This is the amount by which the body's reckonable expenditure exceeds the amount of reckonable expenditure for the previous year; what is 'reckonable', however, is effectively determined by the Secretary of State, as he determines what is or is not reckonable.
5 Housing Act 1985, s 425 This is the amount by which the body's reckonable income for the current year exceeds the reckonable income for the previous year. Again, what is reckonable is determined by the Secretary of State.
6 Housing Act 1985, s 427.
7 Housing Act 1985, s 427.

H Capital finance for public sector housing[1]

19.43 LGHA 1989, s 42 regulates the provision of capital finance to housing authorities. Housing authorities must charge all expenditure to a revenue account[2], except for such expenditure as is expressly exempt from that requirement under s 42. LGHA 1989, s 41 provides that expenditure for capital purposes[3] which is undertaken in reliance upon a credit approval or is met out of the useable part of capital receipts does not need to be charged to revenue. These rules apply to local authority capital expenditure as a whole, and are not specific to housing capital expenditure.

1 Manual, ch 4 and 5. See also DoE Circular 11/90.
2 LGHA 1989, s 41
3 Defined as expenditure on the acquisition, reclamation, enhancement or laying out of land, the acquisition, construction, preparation, enhancement or replacement of roads, buildings or other structures, and the acquisition, installation or replacement of moveable or immoveable plant, machinery and apparatus and vehicles and vessels: LGHA 1989, s 40(2). 'Enhancement' means work to substantially extend the useful life of an asset; or to increase substantially its open market value; or to increase substantially the extent to which an asset may be used: LGHA 1989, s 40(3).

19.44 Credit approvals come in two forms: a basic credit approval (BCA) given by the Secretary of State each year[1], and a supplementary credit approval (SCA) given from time to time in relation to specific projects. This is the Secretary of State's mechanism for controlling overall levels of capital expenditure on housing purposes. Where money is borrowed under the terms of a credit approval and spent on housing purposes, the costs of such borrowing will usually attract housing subsidy.

1 1989 Act, s 53.

19.45 Capital receipts are to be treated in two ways: reserved and useable. The ratio between the two depends on the nature of the receipt. In the context of housing finance, receipts from council house sales are 25% usable and 75% reserved. 'Usable' means that they can either be used by a housing authority for capital purposes or to meet credit liabilities; 'reserved' means they can only be used to meet credit liabilities.

Expenditure based on BCAs must be made in the year to which the BCA relates: usable capital receipts may be rolled forward from year to year. There is no 'ring-fence' on capital expenditure. Housing authorities are able to spend the usable part of their capital receipts and to use their BCAs on whatever capital programmes they wish.

In determining that element of the BCA which might be attributable to investment in housing, government also takes into account the plans of a housing authority as set out in its Housing Investment Programme (HIP). Decisions on housing investment are affected by current government policy. Capital approvals tend to be limited to bids for the renovation of existing stock and support for the private sector through renovation grants and the financing of housing association developments, rather than new build[1].

1 Manual, ch 5.2.

I Proposals for reform

I THE SINGLE CAPITAL POT

19.46 Following extensive consultation by the DETR with local authorities and others the DETR wrote to the chief executives of housing authorities setting out the revised arrangements for the commencement of the single capital pot system. What the Government proposes is a 'dry run' according to a prescribed timetable. The purpose of the dry run is to:

(a) enable local authorities and central government to assess progress on developing asset management and to begin establishing minimum standards and milestones for measuring progress in future;
(b) identify any actual likely problems in moving forward, so that these can be addressed for next year's round; and
(c) give feedback to authorities on their capital strategies and asset management plans.

The aim is that each authority should 'own its capital strategy and asset management plan and use them routinely as corporate management tools. The structure and content must therefore suit the authority's guidance. Prescriptive central guidance is not appropriate.'

The capital strategy will set out the corporate aims and principles that will underpin the production of the capital programme. Guidance on capital strategies and the information to be provided to the Government by July 2000 is the subject of written guidance. The Government together with central departments will assess the strategies and supply feedback during Autumn 2000. The 'dry run' timetable has been set to allow the capital strategies to be considered alongside the service-based information being provided for the 2001/02 Allocation. A similar timetable is expected to apply for the single pot in Summer 2001.

19.47 Information on an authority's corporate asset management plan (AMP) for the dry run should be provided to the appropriate Government Office by the end of November 2000. The information will then be assessed by the Government Office and feedback will be supplied as soon as possible—probably early in the New Year. The 'dry run' timetable has been set to allow rather more time for authorities to develop and report on their corporate AMP systems during 2000. It is broadly in line with DfEE's timetables for schools' AMP. For the single pot proper, authorities will be asked to provide AMP information alongside the capital strategy in Summer 2001. The capital strategy provides the policy framework for the operational work of asset management. The AMP should cover all the council's capital assets and result in a realistic cost in a 3–5 year programme linked to output. In some areas the authority will need to look much further forward at the revenue consequences of capital decisions and consider whole-life costs in project appraisal. The underlying purpose of both strategies and AMPs is to achieve better use of public assets. The corporate AMP needs to take account of, and join up with the capital consequences of, all the council's other plans.

19.48 To assist authorities the DETR has issued various guidance:

(a) single capital pot 'dry run' requirements and timetable;
(b) capital strategies;
(c) asset management of local authority land and buildings—good practice guidelines;
(d) property performance indicators,

all dated March 2000. The 'dry run' timetable is as follows:

Date	Topic	Action required
31 March 2000	Capital Strategy and Asset Management	Guidance issued and disseminated to appropriate officers
May 2000	Regional Seminars in each Government Office area	Date to be arranged; DETR to provide further information
31 July 2000	Last date for receipt of Capital Strategy by relevant Government Office	Strategy document passed to Government Offices
30 November 2000	Last date for receipt of AMPs by relevant Government Offices	AMP to be passed to Government Offices
January 2001	Department consults on single capital pot guidance for 2002/03	DETR to disseminate information to Chief Executive

2 RESOURCE ACCOUNTING

19.49 The DETR has also issued a consultation paper entitled 'A New Financial Framework for Local Authority Housing: Resource Accounting in the Housing Revenue Account'. The consultation paper was issued in November 1999 and the deadline for comments was 31 March 2000. It is unlikely that any action will be taken at least until Autumn 2000. Ministers have confirmed that the Government is to go ahead with its plans to introduce Resource Accounting to the Housing Revenue Account. A part of this process will remove rent rebates from the Housing Revenue Account, making it into a pure landlord account. It will go ahead, subject to Parliamentary approval of the necessary legislation. The consultation paper seeks views on the detailed arrangements for removing rent rebates from the Housing Revenue Account.

19.50 The proposals are that:

(1) The calculation of the entitlement to HRA subsidy for individual authorities should continue on broadly the same basis as at present, but that account should also be taken of the Major Repairs Allowance (MRA). The MRA is being introduced as part of the move to Resource Accounting.

(2) Subsidy for local authority housing should continue to be regarded as a national programme, and assumed surpluses in the subsidy calculation should be pooled and redistributed to authorities in assumed deficit. Local responsibility for decisions on rent levels and spending will remain unchanged.

(3) Rent rebate subsidy will be paid in the General Fund. Rent Rebate limitation will continue, although the mechanism by which it is applied will be different. There will be arrangements to ensure that any shortfall in income as a result of limitation will show as a deficit on an authority's HRA, not on its General Fund. Ministers have not come to a view on how best to pay subsidy in the future.

(4) The present arrangements, whereby authorities in 'Negative Subsidy' transfer resources from their HRA to their General Fund, will end. Subject to the views expressed in relation to this consultation paper, transitional measures will be provided to ease the transfer. But these will mainly benefit those authorities where the transfer represents a significant proportion of the General Fund expenditure, and is longstanding.

CHAPTER 20

Local education finance

A Before the School Standards and Framework Act 1998

20.1 Prior to the implementation of the School Standards and Framework Act 1998 (SSFA 1998) on 1 September 1999 the provision of schools was governed by the Education Act 1996, Parts II and III (EA 1996). These provisions have been repealed.

1 CLASSIFICATION OF SCHOOLS

20.2 Under the EA 1996, schools fell into one of the following categories:

(1) county schools[1];
(2) voluntary schools[2]:
 (i) controlled schools;
 (ii) aided schools; or
 (iii) special agreement schools;
(3) maintained nursery and special schools[3];
(4) grant maintained schools[4].

County schools were primary or secondary schools established and maintained by the LEA. Voluntary schools were not established by the LEA (they were often church schools), but maintained by them, subject to limited exceptions in relation to some expenses incurred by aided and special agreement schools. Grant-maintained schools were independent of the LEA, being run by a governing body and maintained by the Secretary of State. County and voluntary schools could opt to become grant maintained schools by balloting the parents of children at the school.

1 Education Act 1996, s 31.
2 EA 1996, ss 31 and 32.
3 EA 1996, s 33.
4 EA 1996, s 183.

2 FUNDING OF SCHOOLS

(a) County and maintained nursery and special schools

20.3 The LEA had to defray all the expenses of maintaining county and maintained nursery and special schools. This included providing a site and buildings.

(b) Voluntary schools

(i) Controlled schools

20.4 The LEA had to defray all expenses of controlled schools as well as providing any new site or buildings which were to form part of their premises, except where it had been part of the proposals for the establishment of the school, or the special agreement, that they should be provided by a third party[1].

1 Education Act 1996, ss 34 and 60.

(ii) Aided and special agreement schools

20.5 The governing bodies of these schools had to fund many of their expenses themselves[1], including any expenses incurred in connection with the provision of premises or equipment for the purposes of the school and any repairs other than internal repairs or those attributable to use of the school buildings by the LEA for purposes other than those of the school. Any other expenses were to be paid by the LEA. In addition, the LEA had to provide any new site (but not buildings) required in addition to or instead of the school's existing site, except where it had been part of the proposals for the establishment of the school, or the special agreement, that it should be provided by a third party[2]. Where a site was provided by the LEA, its interest in the site had to be conveyed to the trustees of the school for the purposes of the school.

1 Although the Secretary of State had power to make grants of up to 85% of these costs.
2 In such a case, the Secretary of State had power to make a grant not exceeding 85% of the cost of providing a site and buildings for the school.

(c) Grant maintained schools

20.6 Grant maintained schools in England were funded by grants from the Funding Agency for Schools, in accordance with regulations. Those in Wales were funded by grants from the Secretary of State. The grants covered maintenance, capital expenditure and other special purposes.

B Under the School Standards and Framework Act 1998

1 CLASSIFICATION OF SCHOOLS

20.7 The SSFA 1998 establishes five main categories of maintained schools which came into effect from 1 September 1999:

(1) community schools;
(2) foundation schools;
(3) voluntary schools, comprising –
    (i) voluntary aided schools;
    (ii) voluntary controlled schools;
(4) community special schools; and
(5) foundation special schools.

All existing schools will become one of the new categories of school as follows[1]:

Category of School under EA 1996	Category of School under SSFA 1998
County school	Community school
Controlled school	Voluntary controlled school
Aided school	Voluntary aided school
Special agreement school	
Maintained special school	Community special school
Grant maintained school, formerly a county controlled school	Foundation school
Grant maintained school, formerly an aided or special school or grant maintained school established by promoters under Part III of the Education Act 1996	Voluntary aided school
Grant maintained special school	Foundation special school

The main change is the abolition of grant maintained schools, whose governing body can choose whether to accept the statutory allocation or to become a different category of school.

1 School Standards and Framework Act 1998, Sch 2. For Wales see the Education (Change of Category of Maintained Schools) (Wales) Regulations 1999, SI 1999/2633. The functions of the Secretary of State in Wales have been transferred to the National Assembly for Wales by the National Assembly for Wales (Transfer of Functions) Order 1999, SI 1999/672 and the National Assembly for Wales (Transfer of Functions) Order 2000, SI 2000/253.

2 DUTIES AND ROLE OF LEA

20.8 The LEA remains under the duty set out in EA 1996, s 14 to secure that sufficient[1] schools for providing primary and secondary education are available for their area. By SSFA 1998, s 20, LEAs will remain liable for maintaining any schools for which they were previously liable. In addition they will be liable for former grant maintained schools within their area unless, prior to their grant-maintained status, they were maintained by another LEA, in which case the Secretary of State may order that other LEA to maintain them. The substance of this duty to maintain varies between categories of school. Essentially, it is a question of funding, which is dealt with in detail below.

1 This requires them to be sufficient in number, character and equipment: Education Act 1996, s 14(2).

20.9 LEAs are required by the Department for Education and Employment (DfEE) to prepare an Asset Management Plan[1], which records information on the educational building stock and provides a basis for assessing needs for capital expenditure in all categories of school. This is intended to enable the LEAs, amongst other things, to identify where capital needs are appropriate for a PFI solution. All capital funding decisions should be in line with the Asset Management Plan.

In the context of the PFI, projects have normally been initiated by the LEA and it is normally the LEA which seeks approval from the DfEE and the Treasury

Taskforce. Where the LEA is providing the site or contributing towards the costs of any capital elements of the scheme, it will receive any PFI credits and the consequent revenue funding.

1 See guidance at www.dfee.gov.uk/amps/index.htm

3 GOVERNING AND FOUNDATION BODIES

20.10 Every school is required to have a governing body, which is a body corporate[1], and the governors are, therefore, able to enter into agreements which will bind their successors. The governors are drawn from parents, the LEA, teachers, staff other than teachers, co-opted governors and, in the case of foundation, voluntary controlled or voluntary aided schools, foundation governors. The balance of the governors is prescribed in relation to each category of school[2]. There is to be an instrument of government determining the constitution of the governing body and other matters relating to the school, which must comply with any trust deed relating to the school[3]. The governing body is responsible for the conduct of a maintained school and must act with a view to promoting high standards of educational achievement at the school.

1 Established under Sch 9 of the School Standards and Framework Act 1998.
2 SSFA 1998, Sch 9.
3 SSFA 1998, s 37, Sch 12.

20.11 Foundation schools, voluntary controlled and voluntary aided schools may also have a 'foundation' which is either a body of persons holding land on trust for the purposes of the school or a 'foundation body', which is a body corporate established in relation to three or more schools to hold the property of those schools for the purposes of the schools and to appoint foundation governors[1]. Accordingly, former voluntary and ex-voluntary grant maintained schools that become foundation or aided schools will retain their existing trustees and trust deeds and their trustees will retain all their existing rights, responsibilities and assets.

The governing bodies of foundation, voluntary or foundation special schools and any foundation body established under SSFA 1998, s 21 are exempt charities for the purposes of the Charities Act 1993. A foundation established otherwise than under the SSFA 1998 with no property other than the premises of such a school will be a charity, but not an exempt charity.

1 School Standards and Framework Act 1998, s 21.

20.12 Maintained schools are funded, to varying degrees, by the LEA in accordance with a financial scheme approved by the Secretary of State. Any funds applied by the LEA will be subject to general local authority financial controls. In the case of voluntary aided schools, LEA financial support is more limited, with further funds being provided by the Secretary of State.

4 COMMUNITY SCHOOLS, COMMUNITY SPECIAL SCHOOLS AND MAINTAINED NURSERY SCHOOLS

20.13 The LEA must defray all the expenses of maintaining these schools and have a duty to make premises available to be used for the purposes of the school[1]. Such premises will usually be owned by the LEA.

1 School Standards and Framework Act 1998, s 22(3).

5 FOUNDATION, VOLUNTARY CONTROLLED AND FOUNDATION SPECIAL SCHOOLS

20.14 The LEA must defray all the expenses of maintaining these schools. In general, the LEA must provide any new site and buildings which are to form part of the school premises[1]. Importantly, for the purposes of the PFI, the LEA is not required to finance the acquisition by the governing body of any site or buildings provided otherwise than by the authority. This may impact on any provisions in a private finance transaction for the transfer of assets to the school at the end of the contract period.

1 Except that it need not provide any site or buildings which are required to be provided by a third party under proposals for the establishment or alteration of a school, under ss 28, 29 and 31 and Sch 6 of the School Standards and Framework Act 1998.

20.15 Where the LEA provides a site for a school under this paragraph, it must transfer its interest in the site and any buildings to the trustees of the school, the school's foundation body or the governing body, as appropriate. In general, no payment will be made by the school. Where, however, the trustees, foundation body or governing body have or are entitled to the proceeds of sale of any other premises used by the school, they may have to pay a just proportion of those amounts to the local authority[1]. The proceeds of sale include consideration for the creation or disposition of any kind of interest in the premises, including any sums received by way of rent and accrued interest[2]. This could impact on private finance transactions which involve disposals to the private sector.

1 School Standards and Framework Act 1998, Sch 3, para 2(6).
2 SSFA 1998, Sch 3, para 2(7).

6 VOLUNTARY AIDED SCHOOLS

20.16 The governing body of a voluntary aided school[1] is responsible for much of its expenditure. This includes any liability incurred by the governing body, any former governors or any trustees in connection with the provision of premises or specified equipment for the purposes of the school and of repairs to the school buildings, but not the cost of internal repairs nor of any repairs necessary in consequence of the use of school premises, when required by the LEA, for purposes other than those of the school. Where the school is a church school, diocesan authorities will often underwrite the commitments entered into by the governing body and keep its financial position under regular review. The LEA must meet any expenses for which the governing body is not liable, including general maintenance, and has power to give such assistance to the governing body as it thinks fit.

1 See generally School Standards and Framework Act 1998, Sch 3, Pt II.

20.17 The LEA must provide any new site (but not buildings) which is to form part of the school premises[1]. As with foundation schools, the LEA is not required to finance the acquisition of any site or buildings provided otherwise than by the authority. Where the LEA provides a site, it must transfer its interest in it to the trustees or foundation body of the school, as appropriate. The same provisions for payment apply as for foundation schools.

1 Except where the site is to be provided by third parties under a proposal for the establishment or alteration of a school.

20.18 The Secretary of State has power to give grants to the governing body of up to 85% of any expenditure in respect of the provision, alteration or repair of premises or equipment for the school. In addition the Secretary of State may pay grants in respect of up to 85% of preliminary expenditure incurred by the governing body for the purposes of any scheme for the transfer of the school to a new site or the enlargement or alteration of the school premises. Thus, the governing body will have to find at least 15% of the preliminary and capital costs of any PFI. Funders of PFI schemes with voluntary aided schools will want assurance that the governing body can afford its contributions and that it has access to grants from the DfEE.

20.19 If, at any time, the governing body of a voluntary aided school is unable or unwilling to carry out its financial obligations (including any PFI liabilities), it must publish proposals to change its status to a voluntary controlled school[1] under SSFA 1998, Sch 8. The LEA would then become liable for all of the maintenance costs of the school and take over outstanding liabilities on PFI contracts.

1 After a date to be prescribed, they may become foundation schools.

7 DELEGATED BUDGETS

20.20 The SSFA 1998 operates so as to devolve to all maintained schools the greater part of their budgets. The LEA may retain amounts to cover prescribed items of expenditure, but must delegate to the school its 'budget share', which for England is calculated in accordance with the Financing of Maintained Schools (England) Regulations 2000, SI 2000/478 and the Financing of Maintained Schools (England) (No 2) Regulations 2000, SI 2000/1090.

The sums to be delegated to individual schools are principally revenue funds, as capital funds are currently excluded from the definition of the LEA's 'local schools budget', which forms the basis for calculating each school's budget share[1]. There are proposals to devolve to schools some elements of capital expenditure[2], but detailed provisions are awaited[3]. The LEA must calculate a school's budget share in accordance with a formula developed under the Financing of Maintained Schools Regulations 2000, reg 10. This may take into account payments in relation to a PFI transaction which falls within the definition in the LA(CF)R 1997[4].

1 The Financing of Maintained Schools (England) Regulations 2000, SI 2000/478, regs 3(1) and 4(d).
2 Announced by the Schools Minister, Charles Clarke, on 22 July 1997.
3 At the time of writing, it has not been decided whether this devolution is to be achieved through the delegated budget, or by some other means.
4 The Financing of Maintained Schools (England) Regulations 2000, SI 2000/478, reg 14 and Sch 2, para 17.

20.21 The governing body will be responsible for ensuring that its share of the PFI operating fees is available from its delegated budget. It should be noted that monies delegated to the school through the delegated budget remain the property of the LEA until they are spent; when the governing body or head teacher spends those sums, they are to be treated as acting as the LEA's agent[1].

Where the LEA is of the view that the governing body of a school has persistently failed to comply with any restriction or requirement of the delegation or to manage the budget properly, it can suspend the governing body's right to a delegated budget[2] and control of the budget would revert to the LEA.

1 School Standards and Framework Act 1998, s 49(5); see also *R v Yorkshire Purchasing Organisation, ex p British Educational Suppliers Ltd* [1998] ELR 195, CA.
2 SSFA 1998, s 51, Sch 15.

8 OWNERSHIP OF ASSETS

20.22 The LEA will own all the assets of community schools, community special schools and nursery schools. It is required, however, to transfer its interest in any sites or buildings provided for foundation, voluntary controlled, voluntary aided or foundation special schools to the school's governing body, trustees or foundation body, as appropriate.

The assets of voluntary aided schools are usually held by trustees, who will hold them under the terms of the trust deed and must operate accordingly.

9 RESTRICTIONS ON DISPOSAL OF ASSETS

20.23 The SSFA 1998 contains certain restrictions on disposals of land by the governing bodies of foundation, voluntary and foundation special schools or by foundation bodies[1]. The Secretary of State's written consent is required to dispose of land acquired or enhanced by public money or of any land acquired from a foundation body, a governing body, or the Funding Agency for Schools. The Secretary of State may impose conditions requiring the school to make payments to himself or the LEA or requiring the school to transfer the land to the LEA outright.

An LEA, governing body or foundation body may not dispose of any playing fields used by a school within the ten years preceding the disposal without the consent of the Secretary of State[2]. Playing fields are defined as 'land in the open air which is provided for the purpose of physical education or recreation, other than any prescribed description of such land'. The Secretary of State has issued a general consent[3] to the grant of various interests, including easements, leases for a term not exceeding five years and not protected by Part II of the Landlord and Tenant Act 1954 which have certain restrictions on building on the land, disposals where the playing fields remain as playing fields and disposals where the authority previously had the Secretary of State's consent which has not been implemented.

Where trustees of a school which is not an exempt charity propose to dispose of an asset (including by way of lease), they must comply with the requirements of the Charities Act 1993.

1 School Standards and Framework Act 1998, s 76, Sch 22.
2 SSFA 1998, s 77.
3 The School Playing Fields General Disposal and Change of Use Consent 1999; see also DfEE Circular 3/99.

10 CLOSURE OF SCHOOLS

20.24 Schools may be discontinued at the instance of the LEA or the governing body. The procedural requirements are set out in SSFA 1998, ss 29–31 and Sch 6. Proposals must be published and objections considered and communicated to the Secretary of State. The consent of the Secretary of State may be required.

The Secretary of State has power to direct the discontinuance or closure of a school. Under SSFA 1998, s 32, he may direct the LEA to discontinue a community or foundation special school in the interests of health, safety or welfare of pupils. He may direct the closure of any maintained school which has been identified in an inspection report as needing special measures under SSFA 1998, s 19.

11 DISPOSAL OF ASSETS

20.25 When a school is discontinued, the disposal of its assets is governed by SSFA 1998, s 76 and Sch 22 and is usually subject to the consent of the Secretary of State.

12 DISCHARGE OF LIABILITIES

20.26 There is no specific provision for the transfer of liabilities. This means that the question of school closure must always be specifically dealt with in the terms of a PFI contract. In the case of a community school, that contract will be with the LEA, which will remain liable according to its terms on closure of the school.

In the case of a voluntary aided school, where the governing body becomes unwilling or unable to meet its financial commitments, it must apply to become a voluntary controlled or foundation school[1] and the Secretary of State may make regulations providing for the transfer of the assets and liabilities. The LEA will then become liable to maintain the school. Unless the LEA was party to the original agreement, a new agreement will be required whereby the LEA agrees to take over the liabilities of the governing body. If, however, a school publishes proposals under SSFA 1998, s 30 for its discontinuance, there is no guarantee of continuity. Specific provision will have to be made in the PFI contract for discharge of liabilities in such a case. The impact of relevant provisions in any trust deed will also have to be considered.

1 School Standards and Framework Act 1998, s 35, Sch 8, para 3.

13 PRACTICAL ISSUES FOR INDIVIDUAL SERVICES

20.27 In progressing PFI transactions in different fields of local government activity, various issues arise which are specific to the service concerned. The following are but a few examples of some of the major areas.

The promotion of the PFI for local government has been particularly important in the context of the Government's policy objectives for the improvement of schools. There are around 23,000 maintained schools in England. As at April 1999, seven schools PFI projects in England had reached the stage of contractual completion. A further 28 schools PFI projects had received endorsement from the Project Review Group, giving them an initial indication that revenue support would be made available. The signed projects include five new or rebuilt schools, a networked IT service for a group of over 100 schools, and a catering service being run from 66 school kitchens (which also provides for social services and town hall catering). Many of the proposals which have received endorsement from the PRG involve refurbishment and services to large groups of schools in the area of a local education authority (LEA), others entail the provision or replacement of individual schools or small groups of schools, or the rationalisation of schools. At the time of writing it is understood that demand from local education authorities for revenue support for schools PFI projects considerably exceeds the allocated resources. Against a sum of £350 million allocated for schools PFI projects for the financial year 2001–2002, the Department for Education and Employment (DfEE) has received applications estimated to be worth in excess of £1.3 billion.

20.28 Under the Education Act 1996, s 12 local education authorities comprise the councils of counties, metropolitan districts, London boroughs and the City of

London. Under EA 1996, s 14, they have a duty to ensure that there are sufficient schools in their areas for providing primary and secondary education. For the purposes of the School Standards and Framework Act 1998, 'school' means a primary, secondary or special school (and includes a nursery if it is a special school). The classification of maintained schools and the arrangements for their funding are currently undergoing a number of changes as a result of the School Standards and Framework Act 1998. As from 1 April 1999 schemes for local management of schools have been replaced by more extensive 'devolved funding' arrangements. The School Standards and Framework Act 1998, provides for the dissolution of the Funding Agency for Schools, which formerly provided funding for grant-maintained schools. On 1 September 1999 all maintained schools will have entered into new legal categories which will entail changes in the composition of their governing bodies and will require a new instrument of government. The categories of maintained schools, as from September 1999 under the School Standards and Framework Act 1998, s 20 and Sch 2 (and their counterparts under the Education Act 1996, current at the time of writing) comprise:

(a) community schools (county schools);
(b) foundation schools (grant-maintained schools which were formerly county or controlled schools and which have not opted for another category);
(c) voluntary controlled schools (controlled schools) and voluntary aided schools (aided and special agreement schools, and grant-maintained schools which were formerly aided or special agreement schools and which have not opted for another category); and
(d) community special schools (maintained special schools) and foundation special schools (grant-maintained special schools which have not opted for another category).

20.29 The rules governing the ownership of assets, management responsibilities and funding arrangements for the various categories of maintained school all differ. In the most basic terms:

(a) for community schools the LEA will own the land, the governing body cannot propose its own organisational changes, such as opening, closure, enlarging or changing;
(b) for foundation schools, the governing body will own the land (although where there is a separate charitable foundation, the trustees will hold the land and buildings); the consent of the Secretary of State is required for disposal of their assets (including the grant of leases and barter arrangements); the authority and the governing body can propose organisational changes to a foundation school;
(c) for voluntary controlled schools, the trustees are usually the land owner; local education authorities are responsible for all maintenance costs; the authority cannot propose alteration of a voluntary controlled school, but may propose its closure;
(d) for voluntary aided schools, trustees, often a church body, will own the land; the governing body is responsible for the provision of school buildings, exterior repairs and alterations and must contribute 15% to capital costs. Local education authorities are responsible for almost all the recurrent costs of maintaining voluntary aided schools; the authority cannot propose alteration of a voluntary school, but may propose its closure.

The governing body of each of the classes of maintained school is a body corporate, constituted in accordance with Sch 9 to the School Standards and Framework Act

1998. Securing the consensus of the governing body of each school and the trustees where relevant, is a key factor in schools projects, especially where a high number of schools is needed to make a proposal viable. The relevant consultation requirements (for example, in relation to proposals for organisational changes) under the education legislation must be properly complied with. For each type of maintained school, the LEA will normally be involved in seeking revenue support in the form of a PFI credit from the DfEE. The LEA will usually be a party to the contractual arrangements—in most cases, to the main PFI contract, in view of their ownership of assets and/or responsibilities for providing funding. In the case of a foundation school, where assets are vested in the governing body, that body would normally be a party to the main PFI contract. In some cases, trustees will also participate as contractual parties. In the case of a voluntary aided school, the governing body would normally be a party to the main PFI contract (on account of their responsibilities for premises and equipment) as well as the trustees (in view of their interests in school land[1]. Where land is vested in a charitable trust, the consent of the Charities Commissioners will be required for proposals which entail the disposal of that land.

1 One method devised to deal with the complex funding arrangements, and concerns about strength of covenant, in connection with a major proposals for a voluntary aided school, was the creation of a special account to enable the trustees, the governors, the LEA and the DfEE to contribute to the capital and revenue components of the unitary charge under the PFI.

20.30 Under the new financial system for maintained schools, as from 1 April 1999, local education authorities must determine a 'budget share' of its 'individual schools budget'[1] for every school it maintains. Authorities must consult upon and obtain the approval of the Secretary of State for a scheme for financing of schools, which sets out the financial relationship between the authority and the school. Every maintained school must have a delegated budget, under which the majority of recurrent expenditure funded by the LEA is delegated to the school (this delegation now covers major items such as building repairs and maintenance). Schools are entitled to decide how to spend the delegated budget for the purposes of the school, subject to any requirements imposed by the scheme for the financing of schools. The funding arrangements for schools, and the arrangements for delegation of budgets to them, is of key significance in any PFI proposal involving a maintained school and has been an especially difficult area in the transition between the old and new frameworks for schools.

1 The individual schools budget is the local schools budget (ie the total budget which authorities decide to spend on schools) less the authority's planned expenditure which it retains centrally.

20.31 As PFI contracts generally involve payments for services, they cut across the areas in which budgets have been delegated to schools. Consequently there is normally an agreement between the governing body[1] and the LEA under which the governing body undertakes to meet part of the costs over the life of the contract. There may also be a 'charging provision' in the LEA's scheme for financing of schools, under which the LEA is entitled to take certain amounts directly from a school's delegated budget[2]. The governing body may well wish to ensure that if monies are withheld from the contractor on account of poor performance, that will be reflected in the contribution they are required to make to the costs of the scheme.

1 The power of a governing body to contract is contained in the School Standards and Framework Act 1998, Sch 10, para 3(c).
2 See the School Standards and Framework Act 1998, s 48(2)(b), and the Financing of Maintained Schools (England) Regulations 2000, SI 2000/478, reg 5(1) and Sch 2.

C The Secretary of State and funding authorities

20.32 The Education Act 1996, ss 10–11 places a duty on the Secretary of State to promote the education of the people of England and Wales.

20.33 The Secretary of State is required to exercise his powers in relation to bodies in receipt of public funds so as to promote primary, secondary and further education; and to improve standards, encourage diversity and increase opportunities for choice in schools and in the further education sector. Most functions, which include wide regulation-making powers over schools and further and higher education institutions, are outside the scope of this book[1].

1 See P M Liell, J E Coleman and K P Poole *The Law of Education* (Butterworths 9th edn, 1999) to which this chapter is much indebted.

D Local education authorities

20.34 All local education authorities ('LEAs') are required –

> '. . . so far as their powers extend, to contribute towards the spiritual, moral, mental and physical development of the community by securing that efficient ... education ... shall be available to meet the needs of the population in the area.'[1]

1 Education Act 1996, s 13.

20.35 The LEAs in England and Wales are the councils of counties, metropolitan districts, London boroughs and the City of London.

20.36 LEAs are financed mainly by revenue support grant, which is a general grant to local authorities, unallocated to particular functions, from the aggregate of which, before it is distributed, deductions are made to meet expenditure incurred by certain national educational (and other) bodies[1]. They receive full reimbursement of expenditure on mandatory awards for students on first degree and comparable courses and payments by Health Authorities in respect of expenditure incurred in performing functions for the benefit of disabled persons[2]. Local authorities may in certain circumstances receive grants from the European Social Fund for educational purposes.

Part VIII of EA 1996 (ss 484–494) specifies the several kinds of grant payable by the Secretary of State under that Act, the circumstances in which he is obliged to pay school fees and expenses, and the arrangements for recoupment of expenses by one LEA from another.

1 Local Government Finance Act 1988, Pt V. See the Revenue Support Grant (Specified Bodies) Regulations 1992, SI 1992/89, under which deductions from revenue support grant finance, inter alia, the National Foundation for Educational Research and the National Institute of Adult Continuing Education.
2 National Health Service Act 1977, s 28A(1),(2)(c).

20.37 LEAs are to allocate budget shares for each financial year for all their maintained schools (including new schools with temporary governing bodies). Budget shares are determined by the LEA, in accordance with regulations, and derive from the LEA's 'individual schools budget'. This is the amount remaining once they have made prescribed deductions from their 'local schools budget': the amount they appropriate annually for meeting prescribed expenditure on schools or otherwise. Regulations also set limits to the amounts to be deducted and, alternatively, specify other conditions[1].

1 School Standards and Framework Act 1998, ch IV. See para **20.20**.

20.38 The regulations about budget shares, in particular[1] –

(a) set the time when the shares for the year are to be initially determined;
(b) specify the factors or criteria which LEAs are to take into account and other requirements with which they are to comply;
(c) require LEAs to make adjustments to a school's share for pupils permanently excluded or admitted having been excluded from other schools (the amount of deduction from one school's share and addition to the other's in respect of any one pupil not necessarily being the same);
(d) specify how new schools are to be treated;
(e) authorise or require LEAs to take account of, or disregard, matters arising during a financial year, in the former case by changing shares or adjusting them for the following year;
(f) require LEAs to consult, as specified, about proposed allocation factors and criteria; and
(g) enable the Secretary of State to substitute an LEA's arrangements which he approved for the prescribed arrangements under which shares are determined[1].

1 School Standards and Framework Act 1998, s 47.

20.39 LEAs are to finance their maintained schools in accordance with the 'scheme' dealing with relevant matters specified in regulations and in SSFA 1998, Pt II, ss 20–83. The scheme prevails over rules and regulations made by an LEA on funding or financial management of schools which are inconsistent with it. In preparing the scheme and submitting it to the Secretary of State for his approval an LEA is to take into account any guidance he gives and consult governing bodies and head teachers as specified. The Secretary of State may, after consultation, modify schemes before approving them, attach conditions to approval, or, exceptionally, again after consultation, impose his own scheme upon an LEA which fails to submit one, or whose scheme cannot, he believes, be modified so as to comply with his guidance. There are procedures for revision. Schemes are not to come into force until approved or imposed. They are to be published as prescribed.

20.40 Regulations may require schemes to deal with –

(a) carrying forward to a school's budget share surplus or deficit from one financial year to another;
(b) amounts chargeable against budget shares;
(c) miscellaneous income received by schools, and its use;
(d) management of delegated budgets; and
(e) the terms on which LEAs provide services and facilities for their schools.

E Delegated budget responsibility

20.41 The governing bodies of maintained schools have a delegated budget responsibility for their schools budget share. LEAs may not delegate the power to spend from the local schools budget to governing bodies otherwise, except –

(a) when budget delegation is suspended;
(b) in connection with education standards grant; and
(c) when their scheme so provides.

In spending from amounts the LEA make available, governing bodies and head teachers are, with specified exceptions, the LEA's agent, and the amount unspent remains the LEA's property[1].

1 School Standards and Framework Act 1998, s 49.

20.42 Where a school has a delegated budget the governing body may spend their budget share (for the whole or part of the financial year as appropriate) for any 'purposes of the school' or other prescribed purposes, subject to the LEA's scheme. The 'purposes of the school', unless so prescribed, do not include providing –

(a) part-time education suitable for persons of any age over compulsory school age; or
(b) full-time education for persons of 19 and over.

Payment of allowances to governors beyond those otherwise authorised is not permissible. The governing body may delegate their powers, so far as the scheme permits, to the head teacher. Governors are not personally liable for anything done in good faith[1].

1 School Standards and Framework Act 1998, s 50.

20.43 LEAs may suspend financial delegation when the governing body have either failed substantially or persistently to comply with any requirement or restriction, or have mismanaged the delegated budget. At least one month's notice is to be given to the governing body (with a copy to the head teacher and the Secretary of State) except in circumstances of gross incompetence or mis-management or other emergency. The grounds for the proposed suspension are to be specified in the notice and the governing body informed of their right of appeal to the Secretary of State[1]. Suspension deprives the governing body of staffing powers.

1 School Standards and Framework Act 1998, s 51.

20.44 Suspension is ordinarily to be reviewed by the LEA before the beginning of each financial year, but may be reviewed at any time. The LEA are to give the governing body and head teacher an opportunity to make representations. If the LEA decide to revoke the suspension following a mandatory review, the revocation is to take effect from the beginning of the financial year following the review; otherwise at an earlier date. The governing body may appeal against the suspension (or failure to revoke it) to the Secretary of State, who in deciding whether to allow or reject the appeal is to have regard to the gravity of the default and the likelihood of its continuance or recurrence. During suspension the LEA may permit the governing body, under conditions, to make some decisions about spending from the school's budget share and to delegate spending powers to the head teacher[1].

1 School Standards and Framework Act 1998, s 51 and Sch 15.

20.45 LEAs are now required to publish budget statements before the beginning and after the end of each financial year in the form, manner and time prescribed. Such statements are to contain prescribed information about planned expenditure; the end of the year statement is also to contain prescribed information about expenditure actually incurred and about other resources the LEA allocated to maintained schools. LEAs are to send copies of statements (or prescribed parts) to school governing bodies, who are to make a copy available for inspection of the school at all reasonable times and free of charge[1]. If the Secretary of State so directs, LEAs are to require the Audit Commission to make arrangements for certifying all or part of financial information statements. Copies of certified statements are to be sent to the Secretary of State[2].

1 School Standards and Framework Act 1998, s 52.
2 SSFA 1998, s 53. For England see the Education (Budget Statements) (England) Regulations 2000, SI 2000/576.

F Grants

20.46 The regulations under which most of the specific grants mentioned below are paid from the Exchequer to LEAs and others may make payment depend on the meeting of conditions and provide for compliance with requirements or requests[1]. Special provision is made for grants in respect of nursery education[2], and grants for the Fellowship of Engineering and the Further Education Unit[3] and in respect of ethnic minorities[4] are not made under regulation.

1 Education (No 2) Act 1986, s 50; Education Act 1996, s 489. See the Education Standards Fund (England) Regulations 2000, SI 2000/703.
2 See para **20.55**.
3 Education Act 1986, s 1(1).
4 See para **20.56**.

20.47 To assist in the training of teachers and others in prescribed classes the Secretary of State or the Teacher Training Agency[1] pay grants, under regulation, to prescribed persons other than LEAs. 'Training' includes further (not necessarily post-qualification) training, the provision of experience beneficial to a person's employment, training for a change of employment in education and the study of matters related to education[2].

1 Education Act 1994, ss 1–2.
2 Education (No 2) Act 1986, s 50; Education Act 1994, s 13.

20.48 The Secretary of State pays an education standards grant on an annual (financial year) basis to LEAs in aid of expenditure on activities which he wishes to encourage. Regulations may (a) prescribe the type of expenditure eligible; (b) determine the rate of grant, and when and how it is payable[1] and (c) may oblige LEAs to delegate decisions to prescribed persons[2]. Eligible expenditure includes that incurred by LEAs on the implementation of their education development plans and under regulations about teachers' induction periods. England and Wales may be treated differently.

1 Education Act 1996, s 484 and Education (Grants for Education Support and Training) (England) Regulations 1997, SI 1997/514 as amended. For the Welsh Regulations see SI 1998/392 as amended.
2 Education Act 1996, s 489.

20.49 The Secretary of State has power to pay grants under regulation to persons other than LEAs in respect of educational services and research as follows[1]:

(a) non-LEA special schools;
(b) a special, limited, category of further and higher education institutions;
(c) specified bodies providing tuition for adult education courses;

(d) educational services provided by national adult education associations;
(e) vocational, social, physical and recreational training;
(f) specified courses for training youth leaders and community centre wardens;
(g) expenditure by specified learned societies and on certain educational services and research;
(h) training abroad of teachers and others;
(i) certain music and ballet schools, to reimburse them for operating the aided pupils scheme for pupils at those schools, and the Choir Schools' Association Bursary Trust;
(j) city technology colleges[2];
(k) voluntary aided sixth-form colleges, preparatory to their entering the further education sector[3];
(l) higher education corporations[4], for a limited period after establishment;
(m) proprietors of independent schools in respect of education provided to certain five-year-old children, and in connection with training programmes at independent schools in Wales;
(n) expenditure incurred by the Engineering Council on bursaries for standards on engineering degree courses;
(o) approved expenditure on services provided by early excellence centres.

1 Education Act 1996, s 485.
2 EA 1996, s 482.
3 Further and Higher Education Act 1992, s 28.
4 Education Reform Act 1988, ch II.

20.50 The Secretary of State may by order modify an institution's trust deed or other regulating instrument, after consulting the persons responsible for its management, to enable them to comply with the requirements of regulations[1].

1 Education Act 1996, s 482.

20.51 The Secretary of State has power to pay grants under regulation on approved expenditure to 'partnership projects' of groups of schools in England co-operating for specified purposes, and on research into partnership projects. There is to be at least one maintained and one independent school in each group[1].

1 Education Act 1996, ss 484–485.

20.52 The Secretary of State has power to pay grants under regulation to bodies other than LEAs whose main object is the promotion of learning or research[1].

1 Education Act 1996, s 486.

20.53 The Secretary of State has power to pay grants under regulation to LEAs and other persons in aid of the teaching of the Welsh language or the teaching of other subjects in that language[1].

1 Education Act 1996, s 487.

20.54 The Secretary of State has power to pay grants under regulation to LEAs or institutions within the further education sector in aid of prescribed descriptions of expenditure on the education of persons –

(a) whose (or whose parents') way of life is, or was recently, such that they either have no fixed abode or leave their main abode to live elsewhere for significant periods each year; or

(b) who are for the time being resident in accommodation provided for refugees or displaced or similar persons[1].

1 Education Reform Act 1988, s 210; Education Act 1996, s 488.

20.55 Nursery education in this context is education provided for children from a prescribed time until they reach compulsory school age. The Secretary of State may make (or delegate the task of making) arrangements for grants in respect of nursery education to be paid (a) to LEAs for nursery education provided at their schools and (b) to others as prescribed. The amount of grant and related matters are settled by regulation, and the recipients are to comply with requirements imposed by the arrangements which, under conditions the requirements specify, may call for repayment of grant. Breach of a prescribed condition in relation to a child may justify refusal to provide a nursery education place at a maintained school, without right of appeal[1].

1 Nursery Education and Grant-Maintained Schools Act 1996, ss 1–2.

20.56 The Secretary of State may pay grants to city colleges and to governing bodies of institutions within the further education sector towards approved expenditure on employing extra staff where, in his opinion, they make special provision to meet the needs of persons belonging to ethnic minorities within the locality of the school or institution whose language or customs differ from those of the rest of the community[1].

1 Education Reform Act 1988, s 211; Education Act 1996, s 490.

G Payment of schools fees and expenses

20.57 The Secretary of State is to make provision, by regulation, to pay all or part of the fees and expenses of children attending fee-paying schools so as to enable them to take advantage of the educational facilities without hardship to themselves or their parents. Payment depends on compliance with prescribed conditions and requirements[1]. The Assisted Places Scheme was abolished by The Education (Schools) Act 1997.

1 Education Act 1996, s 491.

H Recoupment

20.58 To settle responsibility for expenditure as between LEAs the Secretary of State has made regulations to establish the area to which a person receiving education belongs: this is normally the area of the LEA in which he is ordinarily resident, otherwise that in which he is resident for the time being[1]. Under separate regulations one LEA can recoup from another the costs of providing education (and related benefits and services) for: (a) children with statements of special educational needs, (b) persons attending special schools, and (c) persons under 19 receiving education in hospital special schools or otherwise than in school. The amounts are to be agreed between the LEAs or, failing agreement, determined by the Secretary of State. The amounts may, but are not required to reflect average costs incurred by LEAs. In all other cases of primary, secondary and further education and part-time education of those under compulsory school age recoupment is voluntary, and depends on agreement between the LEAs concerned[2]. The Secretary of State may make regulations to meet cases where education is provided by an LEA in England and the paying authority is in Scotland, and vice versa, but he has not yet done so[3].

1 Education Act 1996, s 579(1).
2 EA 1996, s 492; Education Act 1997, s 57(1) and Sch 7.
3 Education Act 1996, s 493.

20.59 Where a pupil is permanently excluded from one LEA's school and, within the same financial year, his education, at school or otherwise, is provided by another LEA, regulations determine the amount payable by the one to the other. Provision is made for circumstances in which an 'intermediate authority' provides education at a pupil referral unit or otherwise than at school. Any inter-authority dispute about entitlement to payment is settled by the Secretary of State[1].

1 Education Act 1996, s 494.

Glossary

This glossary contains some of the expressions which are commonly encountered in connection with local government finance, including those used:

(a) in legislation relevant to this work (and in which case, the references are given and should be referred to for the full definition);
(b) for accounting, as opposed to legal, purposes; and
(c) in the connection with the administrative arrangements for local government finance.

The following abbreviations are used:

- 'LGHA 1989' means the Local Government and Housing Act 1989.
- 'LA(CF)R 1997' means the Local Authorities (Capital Finance) Regulations 1997 SI 1997/319 as amended by SI 1997/848, SI 1998/371, SI 1998/602, SI 1998/1937, SI 1999/501, SI 1999/1852, SI 1999/3423, SI 2000/992 (Wales), SI 2000/1033, SI 2000/1474, SI 2000/1553 and SI 2000/1773.
- 'LACO 1995' means the Local Authorities (Companies) Order 1995 SI 1995/849 as amended by SI 1996/621.
- 'The DETR' means the Department of the Environment, Transport and the Regions.

Account is not defined in the relevant legislation, but its ordinary meaning is a record setting out details of income and expenditure in a structured manner. Various enactments relevant to local government require local authorities to maintain special accounts in respect of particular activities (such as the separate account to be kept in relation to agreements made with other local authorities or public bodies for the supply of goods or services, pursuant to the Local Authorities (Goods and Services) Act 1970, s 2(2)) and may prescribe the items to be included in the special account (see, for example, the **Housing Revenue Account** under LGHA 1989, ss 74 and 75 and Sch 4); cf **fund**.

Accounting Standards Board (ASB) is a body whose role is to set accounting standards in the United Kingdom. It is supported by, but is independent of, central government, being part of the private sector process of self-regulation. It took over the role of setting accounting standards from the Accounting Standards Committee (ASC) in 1990. The ASB collaborates with equivalent organisations in other countries to ensure that the standards it develops have due regard to international standards. The Code of Practice on Local Authority Accounting in Great Britain produced annually by **CIPFA**, which constitutes **proper practices** for accounting by local authorities, is developed in accordance with the ASB's code of practice for the production of Statements of Recommended Accounting Practice (SORPs).

Accruals basis is an accounting convention sometimes described as the 'matching principle' in which a transaction is reflected in the accounts for the period in which the substance of the arrangement takes place (eg when a service is provided or when goods are delivered) as opposed to the period during which a contract is entered into, or in which payments are made or received. Since the financial year 1994/1995, local authority revenue accounts have been compiled on an accruals basis (cf **cash basis**).

Adjusted cost is an amount which an authority is required to calculate if a **credit arrangement** is varied. It is one of the factors used to assess the amount of any further **credit cover** which must be made available as a result of the variation. See LGHA 1989, s 51(4) and (5) and LA(CF)R 1997, regs 46–50.

Adjusted credit ceiling (ACC) is based on an authority's overall **credit ceiling** and provides a basis for the calculation of the amount of **minimum revenue provision** the authority must make each year. See LGHA 1989, Sch 3, para 18 and LA(CF)R 1997, regs 124–129.

Aggregate credit limit (ACL) is the total of: (a) an authority's temporary revenue borrowing limit; (b) its temporary capital borrowing limit; (c) its **credit ceiling**; and (d) the excess of its cash and **approved investments** over its **usable capital receipts**. (See LGHA 1989, s 62(1)). It is one of the most important financial limits under LGHA 1989, Pt IV. It places an upper limit on a local authority's borrowing and credit arrangements, which must not be exceeded at any time. See LGHA 1989, ss 44(1), 50(4) and 62.

Aggregate External Finance (AEF) is financial support provided by central government towards local authority revenue expenditure based on **Total Standard Spending**. AEF comprises **revenue support grant** (RSG), **national non-domestic rates** (NNDR) and certain specific and special grants for local authority services.

Amortisation period is a period during which a debt or other credit liability is to be discharged. Under the provisions of LGHA 1989, Pt IV, the effect of an amortisation period being specified is normally that the liability must be discharged over the specified period by making provision from revenue for the full amount through equal annual instalments, rather than at the usual rate of 4% per annum (or 2% for housing) by way of **minimum revenue provision**.

Annual capital guidelines (ACGs) are guideline figures used by central government in calculating **basic credit approvals**. They represent the government's assessment of the appropriate level of capital expenditure by local authorities in a particular year, based on national expenditure plans. ACGs are determined for separate services such as housing, education, transport, social services, fire and other services and are applied at both a national and individual local authority level. (Authorities are not, however, required to keep their spending within the level of the ACG for any particular service block.) Basic credit approvals are calculated by deducting **receipts taken into account** from total ACGs.

Annuality is used to refer to the principle under which budgets are allocated and expenditure is authorised only for one financial year.

Appointed auditor is an external auditor appointed by the Audit Commission to audit the accounts of a local authority (or a national health service body) under the Audit Commission Act 1998, s 3, being either an officer of the Commission (a **district auditor**), or a private individual or firm.

Approved investments for the purposes of the regime under LGHA 1989, Pt IV are investments of particular kinds approved by the Secretary of State in regulations. They include gilt-edged securities, Treasury bills, and short-term deposits with banks, building societies and other local authorities. Approved investments are given preferential treatment under the capital finance system to encourage authorities to invest their surplus funds in them rather than in other, more speculative, forms of investment (for example, the receipts from their disposal are not treated as capital receipts for the purpose of LGHA 1989, s 58 and consequently they are not subject to any **set-aside obligation**). See LGHA 1989, s 66(1)(a) and the Local Authorities (Capital Finance) (Approved Investments) Regulations 1990 SI 1990/426 as amended or modified by SI 1991/501, SI 1992/1353, SI 1992/3218, SI 1994/2567, SI 1995/850, SI 1995/1041, SI 1995/1982, SI 1996/568, SI 1997/319, SI 1999/1852 and SI 2000/1033.

Asset for *accounting purposes* under **FRS 5**, means rights or other access to future economic benefits controlled by an entity as a result of past transactions or events. See **FRS 5, on balance sheet, off balance sheet** and **recognition**.

Asset management revenue account (AMRA) is an account a local authority is obliged to maintain under capital accounting arrangements instituted from the financial year 1994–1995 onwards. This account is credited with **capital charges** levied on individual services and debited with **debt charges** and **minimum revenue provision**.

Audit Commission is a body corporate established under the Local Government Finance Act 1982, s 11 and continued under the Audit Commission Act 1998, s 1, intended to be independent of both central and local government, which is responsible for the appointment of auditors to audit the accounts of local authorities and national health service bodies. The Commission consists of between 15 and 20 members appointed by the Secretary of State.

Balances surplus of income over expenditure which may be used to finance expenditure. Balances are not normally earmarked in the **accounts** for specific purposes, but represent resources set aside for such purposes as general contingencies and cash-flow management. See also **reserves**.

Basic credit approval (BCA) is a notice in writing issued annually to each local authority, in advance of the financial year to which it relates, which may be used to authorise borrowing or entry into, or variation of, a credit arrangement. The amount of BCA may be nil. See LGHA 1989, s 53. See also **credit approval** and **supplementary credit approval**.

Best value refers to the new regime under the Local Government Act 1999, Pt I and in particular, to the obligation of a local authority as a 'best value authority' under s 3, to make arrangements to secure continuous improvement in the way in which its functions are exercised, having regard to a combination of economy, efficiency and effectiveness.

Billing authority is a local authority empowered to set and collect council taxes and manage a **collection fund**. In England, unitary authorities, shire and metropolitan district councils, the Council of the Isles of Scilly, London borough councils and the Common Council of the City of London are all billing authorities. In Wales, county and county borough councils are billing authorities. See the Local Government Finance Act 1992, s 1(2) and s 69(1).

Budget requirement is an amount which must be calculated by **billing authorities** and **precepting authorities** in advance of each financial year pursuant to the Local Government Finance Act 1992, ss 32, 43 and 50. It is broadly the amount of revenue expenditure which is to be met from **council tax** income, redistributed **national non-domestic rate**, **revenue support grant** and certain additional government grants, having allowed for other revenue income and any reserves.

Capital charge is a charge to a service revenue account to reflect the cost of fixed assets used in the provision of services.

Capital cost is used by accountants to refer to the **capitalised** value of an income or expenditure stream. It is also used, distinctly, to refer to the amount of an item of capital expenditure.

Capital cost of leases is a defined expression for the purposes of LA(CF)R 1997 (see reg 14) used to calculate, inter alia, the **initial cost** of a lease entered into by a local authority and the amount of **credit cover** which must be provided. In general terms, the capital cost of a lease is the **capitalised** value of the rental payments and other consideration given by the authority after they become the lessee (although certain consideration may be excluded from the calculation in specified circumstances). It is calculated by aggregating all such payments and consideration, applying a prescribed discount formula to payments made in subsequent years, in order to estimate their total value as at the date the arrangement is entered into (cf **capital value of a lease**).

Capital expenditure (or **expenditure for capital purposes**) is defined for the purposes of LGHA 1989, Pt IV by s 40 of that Act and by LA(CF)R 1997, regs 2–10. Under s 40, expenditure for capital purposes comprises expenditure relating to tangible assets on:

- the acquisition, reclamation, enhancement or layout of land;
- the acquisition, construction, preparation, enhancement or replacement of roads, buildings and other structures; and
- the acquisition, installation or replacement of moveable or immoveable plant, machinery and apparatus and vehicles and vessels.

Under LA(CF)R 1997, regs 2–8, expenditure on various additional items is treated as being expenditure for capital purposes (whether or not it would otherwise be so), eg expenditure on the repayment of a capital grant to a Minister of the Crown, expenditure on the acquisition or preparation of a computer program (including rights to use the program) and expenditure under a **private finance transaction**. Conversely, under regs 9 and 10, certain expenditure which would otherwise be treated as being for capital purposes is treated as if it were *not* for such purposes, eg expenditure on certain financial assistance for officers. Under LGHA 1989, s 40(6) the Secretary of State is empowered to give a direction to authorise a local authority to treat specified expenditure as if it were expenditure for capital purposes (ie to **capitalise** that expenditure so that it can be met from **capital resources**). An example of the use of this power has been in relation to redundancy costs.

Capital Programme Working Party (CPWP) is a group comprising representatives of the DETR and local government which meets to consider issues concerning local authority capital finance (and in particular its regulation) and produces a number of papers on topical issues and developments in this field.

Capital receipts are defined by LGHA 1989, s 58 and LA(CF)R 1997, regs 56–63. They include sums received by a local authority in respect of the disposal of an interest in land, or from the disposal of other capital assets. Sums received from the disposal of shares and other investments (other than **approved investments**) and in respect of repayment of capital grants and loans, are also capital receipts.

Capital Receipts Initiative (CRI) was a central government initiative described in guidance issued by the DETR on 1 October 1997. The broad aim of the Capital Receipts Initiative was to allow phased spending by authorities of their reserved capital receipts on the improvement of local authority housing stock, through the issue of **supplementary credit approvals** (SCAs). It required amendment to LGHA 1989, s 55 which was given effect by the Local Government Finance (Supplementary Credit Approvals) Act 1997. The Secretary of State is now able to take into account the extent to which a local authority has available to it set-aside capital receipts as one of the criteria for deciding the amount of any SCA (an impermissible factor prior to the amendment under the 1997 Act). Under the Initiative, SCAs were distributed between authorities partly on the basis of the extent to which they had built up set-aside receipts since the introduction of the system under LGHA 1989, and partly in accordance with their assessed need to spend on housing. In the financial year 2000/2001 there was no CRI as such, but the resources were built into local authorities' **basic credit approvals**.

Capital resources is a colloquial term used to refer to the sources of funding **capital expenditure** which cannot be used to fund revenue expenditure. These resources include **usable capital receipts**, borrowing or **credit arrangements** in reliance on **credit approvals** and capital grants from central government. (Revenue may, however, also be used to fund capital expenditure.)

Capital value of a lease is a defined expression for the purposes of LA(CF)R 1997 (see reg 80), which concerns leases granted by a local authority and is used in various of the concessions for specified transactions under Pt VIII of the Regulations. Capital value is the authority's estimate, made at the time it 'disposes' of the lease, of the value of the monetary and non-monetary consideration the authority is to receive before or during the financial year when the lease is granted, plus the discounted value of all such consideration to be received in subsequent years (using a prescribed discount rate); cf **capital cost of leases**.

Capitalise broadly means treating a revenue cost, normally falling to be met over a number of years, as if it were capital expenditure met in a single year, or treating an income stream as if it were a capital sum. The Secretary of State has power to make regulations (applying to all local authorities), or to issue directions (to individual local authorities), authorising local authorities to capitalise expenditure which would otherwise be treated as revenue expenditure (See LGHA 1989, s 40(5) and (6)). Such expenditure does not need to be charged to a revenue account and can be met from **usable capital receipts**, grants, or in reliance on a **credit approval**.

Capitalised value is the total estimated present day value of payments to be made over a number of years, often calculated by applying a prescribed discount rate to future payments. See also **net present value**.

Capping was used to refer to the former regime under the Local Government Finance Act 1992, Pt I, Ch V under which the Secretary of State set a limit or 'cap' on the budget requirement of each local authority, so as to restrict the amount of

council tax which could be set. The capping regime was abolished by the Local Government Act 1999, Pt II. However, under the replacement regime, the Secretary of State has retained extensive reserve powers to intervene if a local authority sets a **budget requirement** which he considers to be too high.

Cash basis is an accounting convention in which transactions are recorded in the period in which payments are made or received, which was used by local authorities prior to April 1994 to record capital expenditure and receipts. These are now to be accounted for on an accruals basis (cf **accruals basis**).

Charge is used in different contexts with different meanings, but as applied to property or other assets, signifies that the asset is the security for the payment of a debt or the performance of an obligation. In this sense, 'charge' is a general term covering various forms of security, such as mortgages and liens. (Local authorities may not charge their property as security for their borrowing: see LGHA 1989, s 47.) In relation to accounting, items which are debited to a particular account are said to be 'charged' to that account. 'Charge' is also used to refer to the price which is charged by an authority for a service, where this is authorised by statute (as in 'fees and charges').

CIPFA is the Chartered Institute of Public Finance and Accountancy. It is a professional accounting body whose origins date back to the 19th century. Originally primarily for local government accountants, in recent years its membership has included accountants for health, housing and commercial entities.

Collection fund is a fund a **billing authority** is required to maintain pursuant to the Local Government Finance Act 1988, s 89. **Council tax** and **national non-domestic rate** collected by the authority (and residual Poll tax) are paid into the fund, and payments are made out of the fund to the national pool of non-domestic rates, to precepting authorities and to the **general fund**.

Commutation and commuted payments are single or other 'lump sum' payments made in lieu of an annual or other periodic payment. See, for example, the general power of the Secretary of State to make commuted payments to a local authority under LGHA 1989, s 157 in cases where there is a statutory power or duty to make periodic payments. Certain commuted payments are given special treatment under the capital finance system (see LGHA 1989, s 63(2) and (3)).

Contingency is a provision made in a budget for unforeseen expenditure, a shortfall in income, or inflation in excess of any other budgetary provision which has been made.

Contingent liability is either a *possible obligation* arising from past events, which will only be confirmed by uncertain events in the future which the local authority cannot control, or a *present obligation* arising from past events, where it is not probable that payment will be required, or the amount of the obligation cannot be measured with sufficient certainty.

Council tax is the main form of local taxation levied on households within the area of a **billing authority** to meet its budget requirement and cover **precepts**. It must be paid into the **collection fund**. See the Local Government Finance Act 1992, s 1.

Council tax base of an area is equal to the number of band D equivalent properties. It is calculated by counting the number of properties in each of the eight council tax bands and then converting this into an equivalent number of band D properties (eg a band H property pays twice as much council tax as a band D property and is therefore equivalent to two band D properties). For the purpose of calculating **revenue support grant**, the Government assumes a 100% collection rate. For the purposes of calculations made by a local authority of the basic amount of **council tax** for its area for each financial year, the authority makes an estimate of its collection rate (to allow for non-recovery): see the Local Government Finance Act 1992, s 33 and the Local Authorities (Calculation of Council Tax Base) Regulations 1992, SI 1992/612, regs 3 and 4 (as amended).

Council tax benefit is a means tested benefit provided by **billing authorities** to **council tax** payers on low incomes pursuant to the Social Security Contributions and Benefits Act 1992, s 123 and administered in accordance with a prescribed scheme made under the Social Security Administration Act 1992. The Secretary of State provides council tax benefit subsidy to local authorities pursuant to the Social Security Administration Act 1992, s 140A to reimburse 95% of their expenditure on council tax benefit (subject to limitation under the Council Tax Benefit Subsidy Limitation Scheme, if the authority has increased its council tax in excess of a guideline figure issued by the Secretary of State).

Council Tax for Standard Spending (CTSS) is, approximately, the level at which **council tax** for a band D property would be set if all local authorities spent at the level of their **Standard Spending Assessments** (and assuming a 100% council tax collection rate). It is used to calculate how **revenue support grant** should be distributed between local authorities.

Credit approvals are issued to individual local authorities by the Secretary of State. They provide limited authority to enter into credit arrangements and borrowing. **Basic credit approvals** are issued annually (but may be a nil amount), and **supplementary credit approvals** are given for specific purposes. See LGHA 1989, ss 53 and 54 concerning the issue of credit approvals and s 56 regarding their use.

Credit arrangements are an important feature of LGHA 1989, Pt IV and cover a variety of transactions which are considered to have a similar economic effect to borrowing, but which do not in law amount to borrowing. In simple terms, credit arrangements include:

(a) leases of land and goods taken by local authorities;
(b) a broad category of transaction, sometimes described as 'extended credit', which covers deferred purchase, contractor credit and other arrangements under which local authorities defer payment for assets and other benefits for more than a full financial year; and
(c) the newly created category of **private finance transaction** (if such a transaction does not constitute a credit arrangement within (a) or (b) above).

Local authorities have only limited authority to enter into credit arrangements. Together with borrowing, they are subject to certain common limits. See LGHA 1989, s 48 and LA(CF)R 1997, reg 17.

Credit ceiling, in simplified terms, gives an indication of an authority's net indebtedness in relation to capital transactions, being the difference between its total liabilities for borrowing and credit arrangements and the provision it has made to meet those liabilities. This ceiling is not constant, but rises when additional capital commitments are taken on and reduces when **provision for credit liabilities** is made. An authority's **adjusted credit ceiling** forms an essential component of the calculation of the amount of **minimum revenue provision** that an authority must make for its credit liabilities each year. See LGHA 1989, s 62 and Sch 3, Pt III and LA(CF)R 1997, Pt X.

Credit cover—when entering into a **credit arrangement**, a local authority is required to provide credit cover equal to the **initial cost**. Further credit cover may be required if the arrangement is subsequently varied. See LGHA 1989, ss 50(2),(3) and 51(4). Under LACO 1995, Pt V, a special form of credit cover must be provided by a local authority in respect of certain transactions and increases in liabilities of a **regulated company**.

Credit liabilities for the purposes of LGHA 1989, Pt IV are broadly liabilities in respect of the principal of borrowed money and liabilities in respect of credit arrangements including notional interest. Local authorities are required and empowered to make various kinds of provision for their credit liabilities, but there is no explicit obligation to *apply* this provision to *discharge* credit liabilities. See LGHA 1989, s 64.

County fund is the principal fund maintained by a county council which is *not* a unitary authority (and consequently is not a **billing authority** required to maintain a **general fund**). All receipts of such a county council are carried to the county fund and all payments are made out of it. See the Local Government Act 1972, s 148.

Current expenditure is expenditure on running costs such as those in respect of employees, premises, services and supplies.

Debt charges are charges to the revenue account made in respect of principal and interest on loans raised for capital expenditure.

Debt-free is a brief way of describing local authorities with only limited forms of outstanding borrowing, and who have made sufficient (or more than sufficient) provision to cover their **credit liabilities**, so that they have a **credit ceiling** of a nil or negative amount. The main benefits of debt-free status apply only when the authority has no external borrowing (other than certain disregarded borrowing). Debt-free status may be defined in different ways for different purposes. See, for example, LA(CF)R 1997, reg 65(2) and the definition of 'relevant authority' in reg 154(2).

Defray—expenditure is normally 'defrayed' when the payment constituting the expenditure is made (cf **incur** and **discharge a liability** in respect of a payment).

Direct labour organisation (DLO) and **direct service organisation (DSO)** are terms which were applied to parts of a local authority's workforce which undertook construction or maintenance work or 'defined activities' under the former compulsory competitive tendering regime of the Local Government Planning and Land Act 1980 and the Local Government Act 1988 (and the Local Government Act 1992). The former legislation required that separate accounts be maintained in respect of these activities, to show whether specified rates of return or financial objectives had been met. (The **CIPFA** Best Value Accounting Code of Practice (Section 2, Annex D) recommends that continuing 'trading accounts' be maintained for in-house 'contracts' won by DSOs under the former legislation.)

Discharge a liability for the purposes of LGHA 1989, Pt IV: a local authority 'discharges' a liability in respect of a payment at the time when it actually makes the payment, whether or not it has, at that time, become unconditionally liable to do so (LGHA 1989, s 66(2)(b); cf **incur** and **defray**).

District auditor is an officer of the Audit Commission who may be appointed by the Commission to audit the accounts of a local authority (or a health service body). See the Audit Commission Act 1998, s 3(1)(a). See also **appointed auditor** and **external audit**.

Enhancement for the purposes of LGHA 1989, Pt IV, means the carrying out of works which are intended to lengthen substantially the useful life of an asset; or increase substantially the open market value of an asset; or increase substantially the extent to which the asset can or will be used for the purposes of, or in connection with, functions of the local authority. The definition excludes any expenditure which would not, in accordance with **proper practices**, be regarded as **expenditure for capital purposes**. See LGHA 1989, s 40(3).

Excluded credit arrangements are a special class of **credit arrangement**, described in regulations made by the Secretary of State under LGHA 1989, Sch 3, para 11(2), as being excluded from the normal rule that the **credit ceiling** is to increase when a **credit approval** is used as authority to enter into or vary a credit arrangement. Thus there is no increase in the amount of **minimum revenue provision** an authority must make each year under s 63 in respect of an excluded credit arrangement. The practical effect of the special rules on excluded credit arrangements is that liabilities (other than any initial premium on a lease) are charged direct to revenue, rather than being met from **provision for credit liabilities**. Under LA(CF)R 1997, reg 122, a lease of land at a full open market rent (with no premium) is an excluded credit arrangement. Under reg 123, a **private finance transaction** entered into by a **debt-free** authority is an excluded credit arrangement, if the authority uses a **supplementary credit approval** to provide credit cover.

External audit is an independent examination of a local authority's accounts undertaken by a **district auditor** or a private individual or firm appointed by the **Audit Commission** pursuant to the Audit Commission Act 1998, s 3(1), aimed at establishing whether the accounts have been prepared in accordance with the statutory requirements and **proper practices** and whether the authority has made proper arrangements to secure economy, efficiency and effectiveness in the use of its resources. (See the general duties of auditors under the Audit Commission Act 1998, s 5).

Finance lease is a lease on terms which are such that substantially all the risks and rewards of ownership of the leased asset are transferred to the lessee, and the lessor recovers its outlay, plus a return equivalent to interest at a commercial rate on the asset. In economic substance, a finance lease is considered to be equivalent to a secured loan (cf **operating lease**).

Financial regulations are financial guidelines produced by local authorities to regulate their financial affairs. They usually include detailed administrative requirements for contracts and financial transactions, budget, accounting and internal audit requirements.

FRS 5 (Financial Reporting Standard 5) is an accounting standard produced by the **Accounting Standards Board**, which sets out the general principles for reporting the substance of transactions, ie their commercial and economic effect, as opposed to simply their legal form. The standard gives guidance on how to identify the effects of a transaction on the **assets** and **liabilities** of an entity and whether any resulting assets should be included in a balance sheet. **Proper practices** for local authority accounting embody requirements for accounting statements to reflect the reality or substance of the transaction or activity underlying them, rather than just their legal character, except where there are conflicting statutory requirements. Since 1 April 1999, Application Note F to FRS 5: 'Private Finance Initiative and Similar Contracts', has been incorporated in summary form in the proper practices for local authority accounting (see Appendix E to the Code of Practice on Local Authority Accounting in Great Britain 2000, produced by **CIPFA**). From 1 April 2000, Application Note F to FRS 5 has been used, indirectly, to assess eligibility for the main capital finance concession for local authority **private finance transactions** under LA(CF)R 1997, reg 40. The new test under reg 40 turns on the **off balance sheet** treatment of the assets in accordance with **proper practices** for local authority accounting (which practices now incorporate the principles of Application Note F to FRS 5).

Fund is not defined in the relevant legislation. Its relevant ordinary meaning would be a stock of money set apart for a particular purpose. Local authorities are required by statute to establish and maintain a number of funds, including the **collection fund**, the **general fund** and the **pension fund**. They have no authority to establish or maintain funds other than those specifically prescribed by statute and trust funds. Funds are distinct from **accounts**.

General fund is a central fund which all **billing authorities** (other than the City of London, for which special provision is made) must establish, from which all payments must be made and to which every payment must be received, other than **collection fund** and any trust fund liabilities. See the Local Government Finance Act 1988, s 91. This is subject to specific requirements for establishment of other accounts or funds, such as the ring-fenced **Housing Revenue Account** or the **pension fund**.

Guarantee is an agreement under which a person (the guarantor) is liable for the debt or default of another person (the principal debtor). The validity of a guarantee is dependent upon the validity of the primary contract and is contingent upon the principal debtor's default. It requires independent consideration and must be evidenced in writing. A guarantee is one form of contract of surety (cf **indemnity**).

Housing benefit is a means-tested benefit paid or allowed by local authorities to meet the whole or part of rent payments by people on low incomes, pursuant to the Social Security Contributions and Benefits Act 1992, s 123 and administered in accordance with a prescribed scheme made under the Social Security Administration Act 1992. Benefit is payable both to private sector tenants (rent allowance) and to local authority tenants (rent rebate). Most of the benefit costs are met by the Department of Social Security. Local authorities receive housing benefit subsidy from the Secretary of State pursuant to powers under the Social Security Administration Act 1992, s 140A. The subsidy on rent allowance payments is 95%. Rent rebate subsidy forms part of the overall **Housing Revenue Account Subsidy**. Authorities are given further support towards the costs of administration of housing benefit.

Housing investment programme (HIP) is a submission made annually by a local authority to the government office (usually by the end of July), outlining proposals to meet housing need and capital expenditure on housing in the forthcoming financial year. Resources are allocated by central government partly on the basis of a needs index and partly on the basis of discretion.

Housing Revenue Account (HRA) is a separate account in which local housing authorities are required to credit specified income and debit specified expenditure relating to dwellings and other land and buildings within the account. Authorities are required to take steps to prevent any deficit arising on the HRA. See LGHA 1989, ss 74–76 and Sch 4.

Housing revenue account subsidy is a government grant paid by the Secretary of State to local housing authorities towards the costs of providing, managing and maintaining dwellings and providing **housing benefit** (rent rebates) for its tenants. See LGHA 1989, s 79.

Incur a liability for the purposes of LGHA 1989, Pt IV—a liability in respect of a payment is 'incurred' when the local authority becomes unconditionally liable to make the payment (s 66(2)(a)). The authority may subsequently **defray** the expenditure and **discharge** the liability.

Indemnity has several meanings, the main one being a form of surety under which one person agrees to pay to another sums which are owed, or may become owed, to that other person by a third party. A contract of indemnity (as a form of surety) is distinct from a contract of **guarantee** because, amongst other things, the indemnifier is liable regardless of whether the third party defaults and even if the primary obligation is unenforceable (for example, because of lack of capacity of the primary obligor). Unlike a guarantee, an indemnity need not be evidenced in writing. 'Indemnity' is also used in connection with:

- the relationship between a principal and an agent, which requires the principal, unless otherwise agreed, to indemnify the agent against all expenses and liabilities the agent incurs in carrying out the agency; and
- cases where one party to a contract is entitled to be indemnified against a specific loss or liability caused by the default of the other party (often by operation of law), even though there would be no claim to damages.

Indemnity also has the more general meaning of a promise to compensate or reimburse a party for any harm done, or for any cost or loss incurred.

Individual Schools Budget (ISB) is that part of the **Local Schools Budget** which must be delegated to schools under the Fair Funding system introduced for financial years beginning on or after 1 April 1999. See the Financing of Maintained Schools (England) Regulations 2000, SI 2000/478 as amended by SI 2000/1090 and in relation to Wales: SI 1999/101, made under various provisions of the School Standards and Framework Act 1998. The ISB corresponds with the Aggregated Schools Budget under the former system of Local Management of Schools.

Initial cost is an expression used in LGHA 1989 and in LA(CF)R 1997 in connection with **credit arrangements**. In simple terms, initial cost represents the total of the **net present value** of all payments due to be made (and non-monetary consideration to be given) by a local authority over the life of a credit arrangement. It provides a measure of the amount of money an authority would have had to borrow if it had funded the transaction through a loan. LA(CF)R 1997 make special provision for the calculation of the initial cost of certain kinds of credit arrangement, particularly leases and **private finance transactions**. Initial cost, combined with the obligation to provide an equal amount of **credit cover**, are vital elements of the mechanism for controlling the extent to which local authorities can enter into leases and other credit arrangements. Regulations are issued annually by the Secretary of State to prescribe a discount rate to be used in calculating initial cost. See LGHA 1989, s 49 and LA(CF)R 1997 regs 26–45 and SI 2000/259 which prescribes a discount rate of 7.9% for the financial year 2000/2001 for local authorities in England, and SI 2000/825 which prescribes a rate of 7.5% for that year for local authorities in Wales.

Internal audit—local authorities are required to maintain an adequate and effective system of internal audit of their accounting records and control systems by virtue of the Accounts and Audit Regulations 1996 SI 1996/590, reg 5.

Intra vires means within the powers of a corporate body or person (cf **ultra vires**).

Levy is, in effect, a demand for payment made by a **levying body** to a **billing authority**, or to a county council, in order to meet expenditure of the levying body. A levy differs from a **precept** in that a levy may be issued against a **precepting authority** or a **billing authority** and the amount of the levy is treated as expenditure of the authority to which it is issued and is built into that authority's budget, (rather being a separate item which is demanded by a billing authority from local tax payers on behalf of a levying body).

Levying body is a body on whom the Secretary of State has conferred the power to issue a levy to a **billing authority** or to a county council by virtue of regulations made under the Local Government Finance Act 1988, s 74. Levying bodies include metropolitan county passenger transport authorities, the National Rivers Authority (in respect of local flood defence districts) and National Park authorities.

Liability, for the purpose of **FRS 5**, means an entity's obligation to transfer economic benefits as a result of past transactions or events.

Local Government Finance Settlement (LGFS) is the annual financial settlement made by central government for local government in respect of its general revenue expenditure. The settlement is based on central government's determination of **Total Standard Spending**, which is the amount it considers local authorities should spend in the light of national economic policies, and provides the basis for calculation of government support through grants. Importantly from the perspective of local authorities, the Settlement indicates how central government support is to be distributed between individual authorities (and certain other local government bodies) for the forthcoming financial year. A provisional financial settlement is normally announced by the Secretary of State in Parliament and to local authorities in late November or early December. Following a period of consultation, the final settlement is normally approved by the House of Commons in late January or early February, to enable local authorities to set their budgets for the next financial year.

Local Schools Budget records all planned expenditure on local authority maintained schools, comprising the local education authority's central budgets and the **Individual Schools Budget** to be delegated to schools. See the Financing of Maintained Schools (England) Regulations 2000, SI 2000/478 as amended by SI 2000/1090 and in relation to Wales: SI 1999/101, made under the School Standards and Framework Act 1998.

Minimum revenue provision (MRP) is the minimum amount a local authority is required to set aside from revenue as **provision for credit liabilities** under LGHA 1989, s 63 in relation to principal in respect of all its credit liabilities and notional interest on credit arrangements. MRP in respect of principal is based on the **adjusted credit ceiling** as at the last day of the preceding financial year and consists of 2% of the housing amount and 4% of the non-housing amount. See LGHA 1989 s 63(1) and Sch 3, Pt IV and LA(CF)R 1997, regs 124–153 and Sch 2.

National non-domestic rate (NNDR) (also described as business rates, the uniform business rate or non-domestic rates) is levied on businesses and is based on a national poundage set by central government. It is collected by **billing authorities** on behalf of central government and is pooled centrally and then redistributed among local authorities and police authorities in proportion to resident population.

Net present value (NPV) is an estimate of the current value of payments to be made (or received) and of non-monetary consideration to be given (or received) at future dates, involving the use of a discount formula.

New Deal for Communities (NDC) is a government regeneration initiative targeted at deprived neighbourhoods (of between and 1,000 and 4,000 households) in the very poorest areas of the country, aimed at tackling social exclusion and issues such as employment, crime, education and health. 17 local authority districts in England were selected as pathfinders in the first round and a further 22 areas were selected to participate in a second round. Resources of £800 million have been made available for a three year period and are allocated following a bidding process. Schemes are led by 'local partnerships'.

Non-approved investments is used colloquially to refer to investments, such as company shares, which are not **approved investments** for the purposes of LGHA 1989, Pt IV.

Notional capital receipt is defined in LGHA 1989, s 61. Notional capital receipts arise in circumstances where, if money had been paid to a local authority, the sum would have been treated as a **capital receipt** under LGHA 1989, s 58. They include non-monetary consideration (for example, where an asset is received in exchange for the disposal of local authority land), and cases where a local authority requires that the purchase price for its land is paid to a third party, rather than to the authority itself. See LGHA 1989, s 61 and LA(CF)R 1997, Pt IX.

Non-scoring credit approval (NSCA) was an expression used to describe a means of providing special revenue support (or **PFI credit**) for a **private finance transaction** which did not satisfy LA(CF)R 1997, reg 40 and was not eligible for **notional credit approval**, but was nonetheless considered worthy of special support. NCSAs were not used in practice, but the present administrative arrangements for revenue support for PFI schemes continue to incorporate a special means of offering support for **private finance transactions** which do not satisfy the **off balance sheet** test in reg 40. This support is now described simply as **supplementary credit approval** (which is what, in substance, an NSCA would have been).

Notional credit approval (NCA) is an expression used to describe the main form of approval (or **PFI credit**) given to local authorities by central government for **private finance transactions** which meet the criteria under LA(CF)R 1997, reg 40 and have an initial cost of nil. Under administrative arrangements, the issue of an NCA triggers special revenue support. The original intention was that it should lead to an increase in the local authority's **Standard Spending Assessment** in a similar way to a normal **credit approval** leading to an increase in the authority's **revenue support grant**. However, to date, **special grant** has been used to provide revenue support for local authority PFI projects. (See also **non-scoring credit approval**.)

Off balance sheet is used to describe the accounting treatment where no asset in a property is to be **recognised** in any balance sheet of an entity in respect of a transaction. In deciding whether the entity has an 'asset of a property' under **FRS 5**, accountants consider whether that entity has access to its benefits and bears the risks inherent in those benefits, such as changes in its value and risks of profit and loss, as opposed to solely who owns the legal title. Accountants are required to consider the overall effects of a range of factors to establish the true commercial and economic effects of a transaction, beyond its legal form and to consider the combined effects of a group or series of transactions designed to achieve an overall economic effect.

On balance sheet is the converse of **off balance sheet**, ie the situation where an asset is **recognised** in a balance sheet of an entity because that body has all (or most of) the risks and rewards inherent in that **asset**.

Operating lease, in general terms, is a lease of an asset (normally for a term which is shorter than the useful life of the asset), where the lessor accepts the risk that the asset might depreciate faster than expected and stands to gain if the asset retains value better than expected. For the purpose of LA(CF)R 1997, an 'operating lease' is a lease taken by a local authority of any vehicle, vessel, plant or machinery or apparatus, which is given special treatment if it meets the criteria specified in reg 20. For example, the termination value of the asset must be no less than 10% of its value on the commencement date and there must be no provision under which the authority can acquire the asset at the end of the lease. Such a lease is excluded from being a **credit arrangement** under LGHA 1989, s 48 (cf **finance lease**).

Pension fund or **superannuation fund** is a fund which must be maintained by 'administering authorities' (eg non-metropolitan county councils, London borough councils and designated district councils) as part of the provision made by the Secretary of State for pensions for local government staff pursuant to the Superannuation Act 1972, s 7 and the Local Government Pension Scheme Regulations 1997, SI 1997/1612 as amended.

Precept is a request for money, made by a **precepting authority** to a **billing authority**, which requires the billing authority to collect money from local tax payers (cf **levy**).

Precepting authorities include county councils, police authorities and fire and civil defence authorities ('major precepting authorities') and parish and community councils ('local precepting authorities') See the Local Government Finance Act 1992, s 39.

Private Finance Initiative (PFI) was launched in the Chancellor of the Exchequer's Autumn Statement in 1992, with the underlying aim of increasing private investment in public assets and reducing the amount which would count against the public sector borrowing requirement. The basic principles of the PFI were said to be value for money, appropriate allocation of risk between the public and private sectors and open competition. The PFI was intended to represent a new approach to the combined procurement of assets and services by the public sector. For local government, the PFI did not gain momentum until 1997, following a number of changes including the introduction of the Local Government (Contracts) Act 1997, the amendment of the capital finance regime and the introduction of new administrative arrangements to provide special revenue support for local government PFI projects in the form of **PFI credits**.

PFI credits are part of the administrative arrangements under which central government provides special revenue support for **private finance transactions** entered into by local authorities and other bodies subject to LGHA 1989, Pt IV.

They now take two forms: **notional credit approval** and **supplementary credit approval.**

Private finance transaction (PFT) is defined in LA(CF)R 1997, reg 16. In simple terms, a PFT is a transaction under which a local authority receives both a capital asset which the authority needs for its statutory purposes, and services in relation to the use of that asset. (Dwellings within the **Housing Revenue Account** are excluded.) At least part of the consideration given by the authority must be in the form of annual or more regular fees, which vary according to the standard of performance of services by the contractor and/or the degree of use of the asset. LA(CF)R 1997 contain various concessions in relation to the initial cost of a PFT which meets specified additional criteria and for connected leases and notional capital receipts. In so far as they would not otherwise be credit arrangements for other reasons (ie under LGHA 1989, s 48(1)(a) or (b)), PFTs constitute a new category of credit arrangement created by the Secretary of State under LGHA 1989, s 48(1)(c). See LGHA 1989, s 48(1)(c) and LA(CF)R 1997, reg 16 (for the full definition of a private finance transaction) and regs 8, 17, 28, 37, 40–42 and 112. The administrative arrangements for revenue support for certain PFTs were described in the DETR publication: 'Local Government and the Private Finance Initiative' (updated September 1998), and have since been revised by letters from the DETR to local authorities.

Proper practices, for the purposes of the LGHA 1989, Pt IV, all subsequent enactments and the Local Government Finance Act 1988, mean accounting practices which an authority is required to follow by virtue of any enactment or which, by reference to any generally recognised published code or otherwise, are regarded as proper practices to be followed in the keeping of the accounts of local authorities, either generally or of the description concerned (LGHA 1989, s 66(4)). **CIPFA** publishes a Code of Practice on Local Authority Accounting in Great Britain each year, which constitutes 'proper practices' for the purposes of s 66(4). This Code of Practice is based on approved accounting standards (such as those produced by the **Accounting Standards Board**), except where these conflict with specific statutory accounting requirements.

Provisions (cf **reserves**) are amounts set aside in the accounts for a financial year to cover future expenditure on liabilities or losses that have been incurred, but are of uncertain timing or amount.

Provision for credit liabilities (PCL) is required (or permitted) to be made by local authorities in various circumstances specified in LGHA 1989, Pt IV. These circumstances include the obligation to reserve part of a **capital receipt** (s 59), to make provision in respect of a **notional capital receipt** (s 61), to make **minimum revenue provision** annually (s 63) and to provide special credit cover in respect of financial transactions of **regulated companies** under LACO 1995, Pt V. Voluntary provision may be made under LGHA 1989, s 60(2) and s 63(1). PCL may only be used for the specified purposes listed in LGHA 1989, s 64, which include the repayment of the principal of borrowed money, to meet liabilities under a **credit arrangement** or, in effect, as an alternative to new borrowing, where a credit approval is used.

Public Works Loan Board (PWLB) is a statutory body whose functions are derived primarily from the Public Works Loans Act 1875 and the National Loans Act 1968 to consider loan applications from local authorities and other prescribed bodies and to collect repayments. The moneys are drawn from the National Loans Fund and rates of interest are determined by the Treasury. Local authorities are allocated annual quotas for loans for capital purposes from the PWLB, at a lower rate (just above that of the cost of government borrowing) and at a higher rate (slightly below market rates).

Qualifying purposes for the purposes of LA(CF)R 1997, are specified in Sch 1 to the Regulations. They comprise 10 categories of use of land eligible for disposal and replacement under reg 99. Eight of these categories (concerning various kinds of buildings) are also used in connection with the **private finance transaction** concessions for replacement, improvement and new buildings under regs 41 and 42.

Receipts taken into account (RTIAs) are intended to reflect the extent to which a local authority is able to fund capital expenditure from its own resources in the form of built up **usable capital receipts**. Central government deducts an amount in respect of RTIAs from each local authority's **annual capital guidelines** when the amount of any **basic credit approval** is calculated.

Recognised, recognition, for the purposes of **FRS 5**, means the process of incorporating an item into the primary financial statements of an entity under the appropriate heading. It involves the depiction of the item in words and by a monetary amount and the inclusion of that amount in the statement totals.

Regulated company is a term used in LACO 1995 made under LGHA 1989, Pt V to refer to a company (or an industrial and provident society) in which a local authority participates by way of shares and/or the appointment of directors to such a degree that the authority's relationship with the company is subjected to the main financial and propriety controls imposed by the Companies Order. All companies which are 'controlled' by a local authority for the purpose of LGHA 1989, s 68 and some companies which are treated as 'subject to the influence' of an authority for the purpose of s 69 are treated as 'regulated companies' unless they are specially exempt. See LACO 1995, art 1(4)–(8).

Reserves (cf **provisions**) are amounts set aside in the accounts for future purposes which fall outside the definition of **provisions**. They include general **balances** and reserves which have been earmarked for specific policy purposes. Expenditure is not charged directly to a reserve, but to the appropriate service revenue account.

Reserved part. See **set-aside obligation**.

Revenue support grant (RSG) is a grant from central government to local authorities towards the cost of services which is calculated on the basis of the shortfall between an authority's **Standard Spending Assessment** (SSA) and the amount the authority will receive in **council tax** and redistributed **national non-domestic rates** (NNDR). RSG = SSA – redistributed NNDR – (**Council Tax for Standard Spending** x the **council tax base**). No allowance is made for any shortfall in collection of council tax. See the Local Government Finance Act 1988, ss 78–83.

Risk for the purpose of FRS 5 means uncertainty as to the amount of benefits. The term includes both potential for gain and exposure to loss.

Set-aside obligation and **reserved part** are brief ways of describing a local authority's obligations to set aside the reserved part of its (cash) **capital receipts** under LGHA 1989, s 59 and to set aside an amount equivalent to the reserved part in respect of its **notional capital receipts** under s 61. The reserved part is usually expressed as a percentage. The set-aside obligation refers to what must be done with the reserved part, ie it must be set aside as **provision for credit liabilities.** Where a set-aside obligation greater than nil percent applies, a local authority cannot re-use 100% of the capital receipts to apply to a new project and it would have to make special provision if, instead of cash, it received non-monetary consideration for disposing of land or any other capital asset. Various regulations give concessions from the usual set-aside or reserved part requirements. See LGHA 1989, ss 59 and 61 and LA(CF)R 1997, Pts VII–IX. The rules on set aside have generally been less onerous since 1 September 1998 when the rules were, in effect, abolished for most (but not all) non-housing capital receipts and notional capital receipts by the reduction of the proportion required to be set aside to 0% (by SI 1998/1937). Set-aside obligations continue to apply to receipts from the disposal of housing revenue account assets and **non-approved investments** other than shares or loan capital in eight specified kinds of company.

Single Capital Pot is the name given to the method by which central government is to allocate capital support to local authorities as from the financial year 2002–2003. In preparation for the new system, local authorities are being required to prepare Asset Management Plans (AMPs) by November 2000, containing information about the authority's assets and aimed at optimising their maintenance, utilisation and development and to identify surplus assets for disposal.

Single Regeneration Budget (SRB) is a government initiative launched in 1994 which brought together a number of earlier programmes based on various statutory provisions, to offer special funding for regeneration in deprived areas of the country for periods of up to seven years. Funds from the SRB have been awarded following annual bidding rounds under which local partnerships comprising members of the public, private and voluntary sectors have competed for resources for their proposals. Some £4.4 billion of SRB funding has been earmarked over the lifetime of the currently approved schemes.

Special grants are grants given by the Secretary of State to local authorities with the consent of the Treasury under the Local Government Finance Act 1988, s 88B. Such grants must be specified in a Special Grant Report laid before and approved by the House of Commons. The report must be preceded by a determination of the Secretary of State and contain specified information, such as the authority or authorities to which special grant is to be paid and the purposes of the grant. Special grant is being used as a means of providing special revenue support for **private finance transactions**, rather than building the support into the **Standard Spending Assessment** system immediately as originally indicated.

Specific grants are grants paid to local authorities by the Secretary of State for specific purposes under a variety of statutory provisions relating to local government. Examples include grants for National Parks, extra places in pre-school education or projects aimed at reducing drug abuse.

Specified capital grants (SCG) are grants, contributions and subsidies which are paid to local authorities in support of certain capital expenditure, which are specified by the Secretary of State by regulations made for the purpose of LGHA 1989, s 57. See LA(CF)R 1997, Pt V which specifies certain housing and disabled facilities grants. The amount of any SCG is taken to reduce or extinguish any **credit approval** which is relevant to that grant.

Standard Spending Assessment (SSA) is an assessment made by central government of the appropriate level of spending by a local authority to provide a 'standard level of service' in respect of their various services. It is an essential component of the calculation of **revenue support grant**.

Statement of accounts—local authorities are required to prepare, in accordance with **proper practices**, a statement of accounts in respect of each financial year, which contains an explanatory introduction, summarised statements of income and expenditure on funds and of capital expenditure, a statement of accounting policies, consolidated revenue account, balance sheet and cash flow statement and notes as prescribed in the Accounts and Audit Regulations 1996 SI 1996/590, reg 6. The statement must be approved by a resolution of a committee or the full council of the local authority as soon as reasonably practicable and in any event within six months after the end of the financial year in question. The statement must be published by 1 January following the end of the financial year, regardless of whether the external audit of the accounts has been completed.

Structural Funds are the source of grant assistance provided by the European Community to member states to assist areas or groups most in need of assistance with economic and social development to make the most effective use of their resources. The Structural Funds comprise the European Regional Development Fund (ERDF), the European Social Fund (ESF), the European Agricultural Guidance and Guarantee Fund (EAGGF/FEOGA) and the Financial Instrument for Fisheries Guidance (FIFG). See SI 2000/589 which has reformed the treatment of grants from the Structural Funds for the purposes of the capital finance regime under LGHA 1989, Pt IV.

Superannuation fund. See **pension fund.**

Supplementary credit approval (SCA) is a notice in writing which may be issued to a local authority by the Secretary of State at any time, giving approval for **credit arrangements** or borrowing for **expenditure for capital purposes** of a particular description specified in the approval (although the Secretary of State may specify 'all capital purposes'). See LGHA 1989, s 54. See also **credit approvals** and **basic credit approval.**

Total Standard Spending (TSS) is the amount which local government as a whole would spend if all local authorities spent at the level of their **Standard Spending Assessments.**

Ultra vires means 'beyond the powers'. Local authorities can only do those things which they are authorised to do by statute, either expressly or by reasonable implication from the terms of the statute. If a decision or action is beyond the powers given to a local authority by Parliament, it will be 'ultra vires' and it will be void and of no effect (subject to the powers of the court to give effect to an ultra vires contract which has been certified under the Local Government (Contracts) Act 1997 in prescribed circumstances: see s 5(3) of that Act); cf **intra vires.**

Usable capital receipt or **usable part** is that part of a (cash) **capital receipt** which is left once a local authority has complied with its **set-aside obligations.** The usable part normally augments an authority's capacity to engage in capital projects. See LGHA 1989, s 60.

Vire, virement refer to the transfer of resources from one budget head to another. Virement is usually regulated by a local authority's **financial regulations** and requires authority from the appropriate committee(s) or officer(s) with delegated authority.

Vires means powers. See **intra vires** and **ultra vires.**

Index

Adjudication Panels
adjudication by, 6.41
appeal from, 6.43
appointment, 6.40
findings, 6.43
hearings, 6.42
members of, 6.40
Agricultural land and buildings
rating, exemption from, 2.25
Airport
companies, local authorities' interest in, 16.14, 16.30
Approved investments
controls, 10.22
debt-free authorities, treatment of, 10.29
disposal, receipts from, 14.20
list of, 10.24
purpose of, 10.21
qualification as, 10.25
regulations, 10.23
specification of, 10.23
Art gallery
fund for, 3.38
Asset sales
reinvestment of proceeds, 1.34
Audit
auditors. *See* AUDITORS
best value. *See* BEST VALUE
bodies subject to, 8.21–8.24
Commission. *See* AUDIT COMMISSION
current account, 8.54, 8.5
District Audit Service, 8.11
documents, inspection by interested persons, 8.78–8.81
extraordinary –
direction for, 8.110–8.112
objector, rights of, 8.114
statutory provisions, 8.113
use of, 8.115
framework, 1.57
history of, 8.2
internal –
annual report, 8.10
draft code of practice, 8.7–8.10
guidance on, 8.6
independence, 8.9
objectives, 8.8
Audit—*contd*
internal—*contd*
overall strategy, 8.8
regulations, 8.4
scope of, 8.5
system, requirement to maintain, 8.4
local government electors, rights of –
meaning, 8.82, 8.83
objection to accounts, 8.91–8.101
questions to auditor, 8.87–8.90
statement of accounts and auditor's report, inspection of, 8.84–8.86
objection to accounts –
appeal against auditor's decision on, 8.102–8.107
determination of, 8.99
notice of, 8.93
party other than objector, appeal by, 8.108
procedure on, 8.91–8.100
right of elector, 8.91–8.101
time limit, 8.101
vexatious, 8.95
Pension Funds, of, 3.33
public interest reports, 8.68–8.71
reports and recommendations, duty of local authorities to consider, 8.72–8.77
requirement, 1.20
year end –
annual audit letter, 8.66, 8.67
certificate, 8.62
completion of, 8.58
conclusion of, 8.62–8.46
delay in conclusion, 8.65
duties relating to, 8.61
opinion of auditor, 8.62–8.46
sequence of events, 8.57
timing, 8.56–8.60
Audit Commission
auditors, appointment, 8.26
best value authorities, functions as to, 1.45
best value inspection, 7.44–7.55. *See also* BEST VALUE
codes of practice, 8.15, 8.16
directions to, 8.13
establishment of, 8.12
extension of functions, 8.14
information, publication of, 8.19

Audit Commission—*contd*
members of, 8.13
National Health Service, functions relating to, 8.14
origins of, 8.12
proper standards, maintenance of, 8.17
role of, 1.21
studies, reports and recommendations, 8.18
Auditors
advisory notice –
power to issue 9.95
prohibition order distinguished, 9.96
purpose of, 9.97
appointment, 8.25–8.28
audit process, duties in. *See* AUDIT
confidentiality, duty of –
criminal sanctions, 8.39
exceptional circumstances, 8.40–8.42
generally, 8.39
personal information, of, 8.43
transactions not reflected in accounts, 8.43
controlled company, of, 16.67
decisions and action, by, judicial review of, 8.49–8.51
decisions of local authority, notification to, 8.75
district, 8.28
documents, access to –
body subject to audit, of, 8.122
computerised records, 8.123
failure to comply, 8.118
information, scope of, 8.120
privileged information, 8.121
requirement of, 8.116
scope of power, 8.119
statutory provisions, 8.117
duty of care, 8.53
exercise of discretion, intervention in, 8.48
external –
code of practice, 8.32, 8.36
common law functions, 8.29, 8.30
confidentiality, duty of, 8.39–8.43
independence, 8.35–8.38
statutory functions, 8.31–8.34
view on legality, etc, expressing, 8.38
facilities, provision of, 8.125
fees, 8.124
illegality and irregularities, investigation of, 8.109
independence, 1.21
judicial or quasi-judicial capacity, acting in, 8.44–8.46
judicial review, seeking, 9.98–9.105
jurisdiction, nature of, 8.44–8.47
liabilities of, 8.52, 8.53
local authority, reference to, 8.4
local government elector, questions by, 8.87–8.90
parties other than local government electors, information obtained from, 8.109
prohibition order –
advisory notice distinguished, 9.96

Auditors—*contd*
prohibition order—*contd*
appeals, 9.91, 9.92
certified contract, in relation to, 15.103
effect of, 9.90
expenses, recovery of, 9.88
indemnity, 9.94
introduction of provisions, 9.86
power to issue, 9.84, 15.102
repeal of provisions, proposal for, 9.85
report from chief finance officer, 9.89
summary of provisions, 9.87
third party's entitlement to damages, not affecting, 9.93
public interest reports, 8.68–8.71
qualifications, 8.27
reform of functions, proposals for, 9.3
report, consideration of, 1.22
reports and recommendations, duty of local authorities to consider, 8.72–8.77
roles of, 8.47
unlawful expenditure and action, duties and powers relating to –
principles of, 9.4
proposals, 9.3
statutory provisions, 9.2
See also LOCAL AUTHORITY ACCOUNTS

Beacon council scheme
proposals, 1.62–1.64
Best value
application of requirements, 7.7
Audit Commission, inspection by –
direction for, 7.46
discretion as to, 7.45
existing specialist inspectorates, working with, 7.48
fees, 7.52
guidance, 7.55
housing benefit and council tax inspections, and, 7.53
inspectors, 7.49
notice of requirements, 7.50
police authorities, of, 7.54
recommendations of auditor, having regard to, 7.47
report, 7.51
requirement of, 7.44
audit –
amendment of provisions, 7.43
code of practice, 7.41
fees, 7.42
requirement of, 7.36
role of auditor, 7.37–7.42
authorities –
accounting regime, 7.76
Audit Commission functions, 1.45
classification of, 7.12, 7.13
companies, power to form, 7.70
concept of, 1.40
continuous improvement, arrangements for, 1.41

Best value—*contd*
authorities—*contd*
exemption, 7.14
information, publication of, 7.77
non-commercial matters, powers as to, 1.44
orders, 1.43
compliance, securing –
audit, 7.36–7.43. *See also* audit, *above*
inspection, 7.44–7.55. *See also* Audit Commission, inspection by, *above*
continuous improvement, template for, 7.80
detailed system, provision for, 7.4
duty to secure –
arrangements, making, 7.16
consultations, 7.17
core, 7.15–7.17
external service provision, 7.5
guidance, issue of, 7.78, 7.79
initiative, 1.37
need to ensure, 1.32
non-commercial matters, 7.73
overview, 7.1–7.7
performance indicators, 7.18–7.20
performance plan –
audit, 7.37–7.42
contents of, 7.32, 7.33
Order, 7.21
recommendations of auditor, statement in response to, 7.34, 7.40
requirement to prepare, 7.32
statement of responsibility in, 7.35
performance standards, 7.21
pilot projects, 7.9
proposals, government comment on, 7.6
regime –
creation of, 7.1
emphasis of, 7.2
implementation, 7.81
statutory framework, 7.3
review –
competition and in house provision, guidance on, 7.29–7.31
conduct of, 7.27
cross-cutting, 7.25
first, conduct of, 7.24
Order, 7.21
purpose of, 7.23
requirements for, 7.28
specified matters, 7.26
scope of duty, 7.7
Secretary of State, intervention by –
contracting out powers, extension of, 7.68
disapplication or modification of enactments, 7.58, 7.64–7.72, 16.118, 16.119
extensive powers of, 7.56
framework for use of powers, 7.63
procedural matters, 7.71
representations before, 7.60, 7.61
statutory powers, 7.57
urgency, as matter of, 7.62
Wales, in, 7.59
Secretary of State, powers of, 7.3

Best value—*contd*
statutory provisions, 1.39–1.45
targets, 7.22
timetable, 7.8
Wales, in, 7.10, 7.11
Borough councils
establishment of, 1.2
functions of, 1.2
Borrowing
approvals, 13.9
creditors, protection of, 13.18–13.21
debt management, 13.37–13.40
European Investment Bank, from, 13.9
general powers, 13.1–13.6
interest, rate of, 13.6
lender outside UK, from, 13.10
limits on –
authority, determined by, 13.26, 13.29–13.31
credit arrangements, common limit, 13.23
exceeding, 13.28
factors, 13.31
forms of, 13.22–1324
generally, 11.28
regulations, 13.25
short-term borrowing, for, 13.27, 13.36
loan instruments, 13.13–13.17
period of, 13.4
permitted means of, 13.7–13.12
Public Works Loan Board, from, 13.41–13.50. *See also* PUBLIC WORKS LOAN BOARD
revenue or capital purposes, for, 13.5
security for, 13.18–13.21
short-term, 13.8
ACL, within, 13.35
limits, 13.27, 13.36
period of, 13.33, 13.34
revenue purposes, for, 13.33
timing differences, covering, 13.32–13.35
statutory functions, to fulfil, 13.3
Boundary Commissions
alterations to boundaries, suggesting, 1.3

Capital expenditure
approved investments. *See* APPROVED INVESTMENTS
controls, replacement of, 10.27
definition, 10.15
enhancement, 10.17
exceptions, 10.18–10.20
permitted sources of, 10.26
regulations, 10.18–10.20
system, overview of, 10.26
Capital finance
approved investments. *See* APPROVED INVESTMENTS
capital expenditure. *See* CAPITAL EXPENDITURE
controls, introduction to, 10.8
credit approvals. *See* CREDIT APPROVALS
current system –
background to, 10.4–10.6
subordinate legislation, importance of, 10.7

Capital finance—*contd*
debt-free authorities, treatment of –
approved investments, 10.29
capital receipts, reserves and notional, 10.34
commutation loss, 10.33
meaning, 10.28
minimum revenue provision, 10.30, 11.48
private finance transactions, 10.35, 15.60
provision for credit liabilities, application of, 10.31, 10.32, 11.63, 11.66, 11.67
regulated companies, 10.36
European Community grants, 10.37–10.39
local authorities, definition, 10.8
provisions applying to, 10.9
public sector housing, for, 19.43–19.45
reform proposals, 10.1, 10.3
revenue account, expenditure not charged to, 10.14

Capital receipts
definition, 14.4
items not being –
approved investments, disposal of, 14.20
late payment, interest for, 14.22
leases, payments under, 14.19
regulations, 14.23
statutory provisions,14.18
superannuation fund receipts, 14.21
land disposals, from –
reduced, 14.51–14.55
reserved part, 14.39–14.41
legal capacity, provisions not addressing, 14.50
notional –
concessions, application of, 14.60
housing assets, disposal of, 14.62
land disposals, from, 14.40
private finance transactions, in connection with, 15.57–15.59
reliefs, 14.57–14.62
reserved part, 14.35–14.38
set-aside provision for, 14.17
special provisions, 14.13–14.17
regulated companies, abolition of set aside, 16.70
regulations, 14.1
reliefs –
background, 14.44–14.50
development of rules, 14.48, 14.49
housing assets, disposal of, 14.56, 14.62
land disposals, from, 14.51–14.55
methods of, 14.45
notional receipts, for, 14.57–14.62
original need for, 14.44
reasons for, 14.49
special treatment, categories given, 14.46, 14.47
reserved part –
housing assets, 14.27–14.29
land disposals, from, 14.39–14.41
meaning, 14.24
non-housing receipts, 14.26
notional receipts, of, 14.35–14.38
percentages, 14.25

Capital receipts—*contd*
reserved part—*contd*
set-aside percentages, 14.30–14.34
significance of, 14.3
statutory provisions, 14.1, 14.2
sums being –
advance, relating to, 14.9
disposal of interest in asset, for, 14.6, 14.33
disposal of investment, for, 14.7, 14.33, 16.17
grants or other financial assistance, relating to, 14.8
received, meaning, 14.10, 14.11
sums treated as, 14.12
treatment of, 19.45
usable part of, 14.42, 14.43

Charities
rate relief, 2.26

Chief Finance Officer
accounts, preparation of, 5.15
appointment, 5.9
delegation by, 5.17
duties of, 5.1, 5.10
guidance, 5.18
monitoring officer, not being, 5.1, 5.19
politically restricted post of, 5.9
qualifications, 5.9
security, 5.15
unlawful conduct, reports on, 5.11–5.14

City of London Common Council
Fund, 3.6

Communities
system of, 1.3

Community charge
introduction of, 2.11
replacement of, 1.16, 2.11
uncollected, provision for, 3.14

Community council
members' allowances, 6.5, 6.6

Community meeting
transacting business of, 4.31

Company
authorised –
controls on, 16.91–16.93
meaning, 16.47, 16.48
minority interest, as, 16.49
controlled –
arms' length, 16.37, 16.38
auditor, 16.67
meaning, 16.35
means of exerting control, 16.36
minutes of general meetings, availability of, 16.68
regulated. *See* regulated, *below*
statutory provisions, 16.32
directors. *See* DIRECTOR
economic development, sale of shares in, 17.38
influenced –
associated person test, 16.40–16.43
business relationship test, 16.44–16.46
meaning, 16.39

Company—*contd*
influenced—*contd*
regulated. See regulated, *below*
statutory provisions, 16.32
local authorities' interest in –
background, 16.1–16.7
consultation papers, 16.3–16.6, 16.117
funding, 16.5
operational advantages of, 16.6
statutory controls, background of, 16.7
Widdecombe Committee, 16.1, 16.2
participation by local authorities –
airports, commercial undertakings for, 16.14, 16.30
assumptions, 16.16–16.18
authorised. See authorised, *above*
best value obligations, 16.118
change, proposals for, 16.116–16.120
classification, 16.31, 16.32
controlled. See controlled, *above*
development company trading in land, 16.18
economic development, for, 16.9
enabling legislation, 16.19
exemption from regulatory regime, 16.28–16.30
express authorisation of, 16.8–16.15
further education, in relation to, 16.15, 16.16
housing associations, 16.11
housing for homeless people, for, 16.20
influenced. See influenced, *above*
leisure development, for, 16.20
more than one authority, 16.34, 16.94–16.98
non-charitable trusts, 16.26
non-compliance with provisions, sanctions for, 16.99–16.101
orders, 16.23
playing fields, transfer of, 16.20
powers, case law on, 16.19–16.21
regulated. See regulated, *below*
regulation of, 16.22
sale of shares, receipts from, 16.17
statutory provisions, application of, 16.24
transport, for, 16.13, 16.30
trust, formation of, 16.19, 16.20
types of body corporate, 16.25, 16.26
waste disposal, for, 16.12
regulated –
capital receipts, abolition of set aside, 16.70
complexity of, 16.50
concept of, 16.33
conditions, 16.53, 16.59
controlled company as, 16.52
controls on –
basic credit approval, increase in, 16.80
credit cover, requirement to provide, 16.76–16.79
financial, 16.69–16.90
non-compliance, sanctions for, 16.65, 16.99
receipts, contracts and liabilities, on, 16.70–16.75
regime, 16.64

Company—*contd*
regulated—*contd*
debt-free authorities, of, 16.90
dominant influence over, exercise of, 16.53–116.58
group accounts, applicable provisions as to, 16.59–16.63
importance of classification, 16.50
liabilities of, 16.81–16.89
local authority expenditure on, 16.102
meaning, 16.51
propriety, 16.66–16.68
Comprehensive Spending Review
results of, 1.31, 1.33
scope of, 1.30
Compulsory competitive tendering
abolition, 3.43
accounting provisions, relevance of, 3.43
accounting requirements –
councils to which applying, 3.45
defined authorities, 3.46
cessation of effect, 1.42
defined activities, for, 3.44
direct labour and service organisations. *See* DIRECT LABOUR ORGANISATIONS; DIRECT SERVICE ORGANISATIONS
repeal of regime, 7.7, 7.75
Compulsory purchase
transfer under, VAT provisions, 18.59, 18.60
Contracts
certification –
certificate –
challenge to, 15.100, 15.101
contents of, 15.95
model, 15.96
public inspection, 15.105
signature, 15.97, 15.98
procedure, 15.92–15.101
requirements –
consent, 15.99
period for satisfying, 15.93
scope of, 15.94
validity, 15.92
certified –
contracting out of functions, 15.115
judicial review, application for, 15.90
novation, 15.104
private law protection, extent of, 15.106–15.108
prohibition orders, 15.103
public and private law position, 15.89
public law proceedings, discretion of court, 15.114
relevant discharge terms, 15.109–15.111
absence or invalidity of, 15.112, 15.113
scope of provisions, 15.88
services, for, 15.89
special treatment, 15.83, 15.89
types of, 15.88
loan, with person making, 15.86

Contracts—*contd*
Local Government (Contracts) Act 1977 –
assets, meaning, 15.85
background, 15.73–15.81
conclusion, 15.116
first strand, 15.84–15.87
overview of, 15.82, 15.83
second strand, 15.88–15.91
power to enter into, clarification of, 15.83–15.87

Council members
allowances –
authorisation of, 6.3
financial loss, 6.5
parish or community council members, of, 6.5, 6.6
regulations, 6.4
scheme for, 6.4
travelling expenses, 6.6, 6.7
behaviour, statutory provisions –
code of conduct –
compliance with, 6.23
requirement to adopt, 6.23
general principles of conduct, development of, 6.21, 6.22
council tax, effect of failure to pay, 6.12
directors, as. See DIRECTOR
disqualification for financial irregularities –
discretion to order, 9.34
restrictions on, 9.35
wilful misconduct, loss through, 9.73
documents, access to, 6.2
ethical framework for –
components of, 6.19
proposal for, 6.18
Wales, in, 6.20
National Code of Local Government Conduct, 6.13–6.15
pecuniary interest, having –
beneficial interest in securities, arising from, 6.8
code of conduct, 6.14
disclosure of, 6.8, 6.14
dispensation, grant of, 6.10, 6.11
married persons, of, 6.8
meaning, 6.9
Nolan Report, provisions of, 6.16, 6.17
number of members disabled by, 6.10
offences, 6.10
public register, proposal for, 6.17
reasonable apprehension or suspicion of bias, 6.15
record of, 6.9
voting, refraining from, 6.8
statutory duties, 6.1

Council tax
appeals, 2.19
bands for, 1.16, 2.12
placing property in, 2.13
basic amount, 2.12
billing authorities, 1.16
Collection Fund, 3.9–3.20. See *also* FUNDS

Council tax—*contd*
calculation of, 2.12, 2.15
capping, 1.33
statutory provisions, 1.46, 1.47
collection, 2.18
Collection Fund, 1.17
community charge, replacement of, 2.11
discounts, 2.16
grants, 2.8
instalments, payment by, 2.19
introduction of, 2.12
levy of, 1.16
levying bodies, 1.18
liability to pay, 2.14
precepting authorities, 1.17
setting, 1.19, 2.17
timetable for setting, 1.25, 1.26
valuation list, 2.13

County councils
County Fund, 3.7, 3.8
establishment of, 1.2
functions of, 1.2, 1.10

Credit approvals
Annual Capital Guidelines, 11.21, 11.22
application of, 11.6
basic, 11.12, 11.13
capital financing costs, revenue support for, 11.27
credit ceiling, increasing, 11.3, 11.38
determination of, 11.25
forms of, 11.2, 19.44
individual authority, share of, 11.23
issue of, 2.10
criteria for, 11.17–11.20
current practice, 11.21–11.26
national total available for, 11.21
priority of use or reduction, 11.7
purpose of, 11.1
Receipts Taken into Account, 11.23, 11.24
reform of system, 11.26
regulated companies, for, 16.80
revenue support, provision of, 11.4
specified capital grants, 11.9–11.11
supplementary, 11.14–11.16
transfer, 11.8
use of, 11.1, 11.5

Credit arrangements
arrangements not being –
de minimis provision, 12.50
licensing contracts, 12.55, 12.56
local government reorganisation, property transactions arising from, 12.53, 12.54
operating leases, 12.52
regulations, 12.86
significant premium, lease with, 12.51
statutory provisions, 12.47, 12.48
superannuation investments, 12.57
three per cent disregard, 12.58
background, 12.2–12.6
categories of, 12.4, 12.5, 12.84

Credit arrangements—*contd*
complex transactions, 12.27
consequences of, 12.7–12.10
credit cover for, 12.85
need to provide, 12.7–12.10
economic development, guarantees for, 17.37
equipment replacement scheme, 12.107–12.111
excluded –
consequences of entering into, 12.46
meaning, 12.45
excluded contracts, 12.6
extended credit –
analysis, 12.17
complex transactions, 12.27
cost at any time of, 12.79
estimates, assumptions for, 12.23, 12.24
guarantees, 12.29
guidance on, 12.28
initial and subsequent cost, calculation of, 12.73–12.79
multiple contracts, 12.19–12.22
one complete and part year, covering, 12.25, 12.26
options, treatment of, 12.23, 12.24
statutory provision, 12.16
time of creation, 12.19–12.22
variation of, 12.20
financial effect of, 12.10
goods, lease of –
adjusted cost of, 12.125–12.133
analysis, 12.13
initial and subsequent cost, calculation of –
capital cost, 12.64–12.66
general rule, 12.63
regulations, 12.62
special provision for, 12.87, 12.88
statutory provision, 12.12
time of creation, 12.15
variation, 12.125–12.133
guarantees, 12.29
heating, lighting and street lighting contracts, 12.107–12.111
initial cost, 12.8, 12.11
calculation of –
basic provisions, 12.60, 12.61
exceptions to rules, 12.82, 12.83
extended credit arrangements, 12.73–12.79
leases, 12.62–12.72
minimum revenue provision, 12.80, 12.81
private finance transactions, 12.73–12.79
special provision for, 12.87, 12.88
transitional arrangements, 12.80, 12.81
meaning, 12.59
initial cost of nil, where, 12.106
land, lease of –
adjusted cost of, 12.125–12.133
analysis, 12.13

Credit arrangements—*contd*
land, lease of—*contd*
initial and subsequent cost, calculation of –
capital cost, 12.64–12.66
cost at any time, 12.72
exceptions to rules, 12.82, 12.83
general rule, 12.63
nil, initial cost of, 12.89–12.102
regulations, 12.62
special cases, 12.67–12.71
special provision for, 12.87, 12.88
nil, initial cost of –
consecutive leases of non-housing land, 12.95
credit cover, not requiring, 12.89
fire authority, of, 12.97, 12.98
homeless persons, accommodation for, 12.92
leases subsequent to, 12.102
National Park authority, of, 12.99, 12.100
non-housing purposes, for, 12.93, 12.94
private finance arrangements, under, 12.90
re-acquired, 12.96
subsequent cost of, 12.101
term not exceeding three years, for, 12.91
variation of, 12.102
reduction in initial cost of –
regulations, 12.103
released credit cover, transfer of, 12.104, 12.105
statutory provision, 12.12
time of creation, 12.15
variation, 12.125–12.133
meaning, 12.2
power to enter into, limits on, 12.135–12.138
private finance transactions. See PRIVATE FINANCE TRANSACTIONS
reform of system, 12.1
statutory provisions, 12.3
subsequent cost of –
calculation of –
basic provisions, 12.60, 12.61
exceptions to rules, 12.82, 12.83
extended credit arrangements, 12.73–12.79
leases, 12.62–12.72
minimum revenue provision, 12.80, 12.81
private finance transactions, 12.73–12.79
transitional arrangements, 12.80, 12.81
transitional –
adjusted cost of, 12.134
entering into, 12.43
exclusion from provisions, 12.44
initial and subsequent cost, calculation of, 12.80, 12.81
power to enter into, limits on, 12.138
practical significance of, 12.42
variation, 12.134
variation –
adjusted cost, calculation of, 12.116–12.119
credit cover, provision of, 12.120

Credit arrangements—*contd*
variation—*contd*
deemed, 12.122
effect of, 12.115
general rules, 12.112–12.124
initial cost –
decreasing, 12.124
increasing, 12.121, 12.123
leases, 12.125–12.133
option, consideration being, 12.114, 12.122
statutory provision, 12.112
transitional arrangements, 12.134
Credit liabilities, provision for
application of, 11.62
capital expenditure, use for, 13.12
commuted payments, 11.68–11.70
debt-free authorities, treatment of, 10.31, 10.32, 11.63, 11.66, 11.67
excluded uses of, 11.64
meaning, 11.45
minimum revenue provision. *See* MINIMUM REVENUE PROVISION
reasons for, 11.60
use of amounts set aside, 11.61–11.67
Credit limits
aggregate –
borrowing, limiting, 13.22
calculation of, 11.32, 11.33
control on credit, significance for, 11.29
exceeding, 11.31
increase in, 11.35
increasing, 11.3
internal lending, allowing for, 11.35
operation of, 11.29–11.36
rise in, 11.34
temporary borrowing within, 13.33, 13.35
credit ceiling –
adjusted, 11.43, 11.44
calculation of, 11.37
credit approvals increasing, 11.3, 11.38
excluded credit arrangements, effect of, 11.39
transactions having neutral effect on, 11.42
transactions leading to decrease in, 11.41
transactions leading to increase in, 11.40
Crown property
rating, exemption from, 2.23

Development Board for Rural Wales
housing subsidies, 19.42
Direct labour organisations
accounts –
amounts in excess of relevant amount, 3.52
construction or maintenance work, for, 3.53, 3.54
exclusion from requirements, 3.51
failure to comply with provisions, 3.55
general highway works, for, 3.49
revenue, 3.47, 3.53
where required, 3.48
works of new construction, for, 3.50
functional work by, 3.43
Direct service organisations
accounts –
defined activities, for, 3.56
failure to comply with provisions, 3.58
true and fair picture, showing, 3.59
annual report, 3.57
functional work by, 3.44
Director
conflicts of interest, 16.107
council members and officers as –
duties of –
company, vis à vis, 16.103–16.07
council, vis à vis, 16.108
indemnity, 16.109–16.112
shadow, 16.113–16.115
external body, representing interests of, 16.105
nominee, 16.106, 16.107
shadow, 16.113–16.115
Disabled persons
rating, exemption from, 2.27
District Audit Service
foundation and functions of, 8.11
District councils
functions of, 1.10
large metropolitan areas, in, 1.11

Economic development
companies, sale of shares in, 17.38
express powers, creation of, 17.6
financial assistance –
conditions of, 17.34, 17.35
definition, 17.13
excluded forms of, 17.21–17.25
financial results, calculated on, 17.24
guarantees, 17.37
matters being, 17.14
repayment, 17.36
state aids, notification of, 17.40–17.42
local –
context of, 17.1–17,3
Widdecombe Committee report, 17.3–17.5
local authorities –
ability to spend, criticism of, 17.7
promotion, power of, 17.2. *See also* promotion of, *below*
review of proper role, 17.5
role of, 17.1, 17.3
spending, proportion of, 17.4
plans, 17.30–17.32
promotion of –
accounting requirements, 17.33
consultation, excluded steps in absence of, 17.26–17.28
consultation paper, 17.43
excluded activities, 17.18–17.20
extent of powers, 17.12–17.15
financial assistance. *See* financial assistance, *above*
guidance, 17.29
new power, limits on, 17.49
objectives, 17.46

Economic development—*contd*
promotion of—*contd*
power of, 17.2
proposals for change, 17.43–17.53
regulations, 17.10
relevant authorities, 17.11
restrictions on, 17.16–17.32
significance of provisions, 17.15
statutory provisions, 17.8–17.11
White Paper, 17.44
strategy for, 17.50
Education
departmental inspectors, 1.14
further, local authorities' interest in companies, 16.15, 16.16
grants –
city colleges, for, 20.56
education standards, 20.48
educational services and research, for, 20.49, 20.50
ethnic minorities, for, 20.56
further education, for, 20.56
homeless or travelling persons, for, 20.54
learning or research, for promotion of, 20.52
nursery education, for, 20.55
partnership projects, for, 20.51
refugees, for, 20.54
regulations, 20.46
teacher training, for, 20.47
Welsh language, in respect of, 20.53
local education authority –
Asset Management Plan, 20.9
bodies being, 20.28, 20.35
budget shares, allocation of, 20.37, 20.38
budget statements, publication of, 20.45
duties of, 20.8, 20.9, 20.34
financing, 20.36
funding of schools. *See* SCHOOLS
goods and services, supply of, 3.61
grants to, 20.36
maintained schools, financing, 20.39, 20.40
role of, 20.8, 20.9
Private Finance Initiative in respect of, 20.27, 20.31
recoupment of expenditure, 20.58, 20.59
responsibility for expenditure, 20.58
school fees and expenses, payment of, 20.57
schools. *See* SCHOOLS
Secretary of State, duty of, 20.32, 20.33
trust, formation by local authority, 16.19, 16.20
Ethical standards officers
cases referred to, 6.30
disclosure to, 6.35, 6,36
functions of, 6.31
information and documents, right of access to, 6.34
interim report, 6.39
investigation of allegations by, 6.32, 6.33
reports, 6.37, 6,38
European Community grants
special treatment of, 10.37–10.39
Expenditure planning
annual process, 1.27, 1.28
capping procedure, 1.24
central and local government, relationship of, 1.19
consultations, 1.27, 1.28
Consultative Council on Local Government Finance, role of, 1.27
key processes, 1.24
Local Government Finance Report, 1.24
statutory framework, 1.24–1.26

Fire service
departmental inspectors, 1.14
Funds
block grant, 1.19
City of London, 3.6
Collection –
billing authorities, establishment by, 3.9
General Fund –
transfers from, 3.12, 3.14, 3.16
transfers to, 3.18, 3.20
liabilities, sufficient to meet, 3.14
payments into, 3.11
precepting authorities –
payments from, 3.13
payments to, 3.19
regulations, 3.12
schedule of instalments, 3.15
sums paid from, 3.18
use of, 3.17
consolidated loan pool, 3.1
County, 3.7, 3.8
General –
Collection Fund –
transfers from, 3.18, 3.20
transfers to, 3.12, 3.14, 3.16
payments from, 3.4
receipts paid into, 3.3
regulations, 3.12
requirement to establish and maintain, 3.3
sums paid into, 3.1
local lottery, for, 3.38
museum or art gallery, for, 3.38
Pension –
administration expenses, payment of, 3.28
admissions agreement, 3.26
audit, 3.33
employees covered by, 3.25
individual adjustments, 3.34
investment manager, 3.31, 3.32
investment, 3.29
management and investment, 3.27–3.33
payments on account, 3.35
payments to, 3.36
pension increases, provision for, 3.37
proper advice, Administering Authority taking, 3.30
rates and adjustment certificate, 3.34, 3.35
Police Authority, 3.39
pooling provisions, 3.1
requirement to establish and maintain, 3.1

Funds—*contd*
statutory authority for, 3.38
superannuation –
administration, 3.23, 3.24
maintenance of, 3.23
provision for, 3.21
receipts, 14.21
regulations, 3.22
Trust, 3.38
types of, 3.1
Wales, for, 3.2

Grants
block, system of, 2.1
council tax, 2.8
distribution, 1.59
education. *See* EDUCATION
European Community, 10.37–10.39
Rate Support, replacement of, 2.2
Revenue Support. *See* REVENUE SUPPORT GRANT
special, 2.9
specified capital, 11.9–11.11
transport, 2.8
Greater London Authority
creation of, 1.65
precepting authority, as, 1.17

Highways
private street works, accounts, 3.69
Housing assets
disposal, receipts from, 14.56, 14.62
Housing associations
local authority, promotion or formation by, 16.11
Housing finance
budget, 19.30, 19.31
capital, 19.43–19.45
housing repairs account. *See* HOUSING REPAIRS ACCOUNT
housing revenue account. *See* HOUSING REVENUE ACCOUNT
reform, proposals for –
resource accounting, 19.49, 19.50
single capital pot, 19.46–19.48
special rules for, 19.29
statutory provisions, 19.1, 19.2
subsidies –
Development Board for Rural Wales, for, 19.42
new town corporations, for, 19.42
statutory provisions, 19.32
See also HOUSING REVENUE ACCOUNT
Housing repairs account
power to maintain, 19.7
practice and procedure, 19.8
Housing revenue account
basic principles for, 19.9
categories of property excluded, 19.5
categories of property for which kept, 19.4
credits –
bad or doubtful debts, reduced provision for, 19.16

Housing revenue account—*contd*
credits—*contd*
expenditure, contributions to, 19.13
housing benefit transfers, 19.14
housing repairs account, transfers from, 19.15
previous year, balance from, 19.19
rent, 19.10
Secretary of State –
sums calculated as determined by, 19.17
sums directed by, 19.18
services and facilities, charges for, 19.11
subsidy, 19.12
debits –
bad or doubtful debts, provision for, 19.26
capital purposes, expenditure for, 19.21
housing repairs account, transfers to, 19.25
previous year, balance from, 19.28
rent rebates, 19.23
rents, rates, taxes and other charges, 19.22
repairs, maintenance and management, expenditure on, 19.20
Secretary of State, sums calculated as determined by, 19.27
subsidy, sums payable by way of, 19.24
disposal, meaning, 19.6
expenditure, items of, 19.3
practice and procedure, 19.8
requirement to keep, 19.3
subsidy –
calculation of, 19.33
determination –
average gross rent per dwelling, 19.40
capital, charges for, 19.36
details in, 19.35
interest, 19.41
items of reckonable expenditure, 19.38, 19.41
notional rents, 19.39
qualifying expenditure, items of actual expenditure excluded from, 19.37
items in, 19.34
statutory provisions, 19.32

Inner London Education Authority
abolition, 1.6
Interest swap transactions
power to enter into, lack of, 13.38, 13.39
ultra vires, 15.78

Joint boards
powers of, 1.12
Judicial review
auditor seeking, 9.98–9.105
auditors, decisions and actions of, 8.49–8.51
certified contracts, relating to, 15.89, 15.90
financial activities of local authorities, intervention in –
annual accounting, 4.23–4.26
broad principles, 4.5
charges, levy of, 4.9
financial motives, 4.9

Judicial review—*contd*
financial activities of local authorities, intervention in—*contd*
forward funding, 4.23–4.26
improper purposes, 4.20, 4.21
irrationality, 4.7
jurisdiction, 4.4
profit, trading for, 4.10
quasi-fiduciary duty, 4.8
unlawful delegation, 4.22
unlawful fetters on discretion, where, 4.11–4.19
Wednesbury unreasonableness, 4.6, 4.7
Revenue Support Grant, of, 2.7

Lease
capital receipts, rents not being, 14.19
land and goods, of. *See* CREDIT ARRANGEMENTS
operating, nature of, 12.52
private finance transaction, as part of, 15.52–15.56
significant premium, with, 12.51
value added tax. *See* VALUE ADDED TAX
Licensing contracts
credit arrangements, not being, 12.55, 12.56
Loan instruments
borrowing by, 13.13–13.17
meaning, 13.13, 13.14
register of, 13.16, 13.17
terms of, 13.15
Local authorities
accounts. *See* LOCAL AUTHORITY ACCOUNTS
capital finance. *See* CAPITAL FINANCE
charges, levy of, 4.9
chief finance officer, 1.23
company, power to charge, 4.31
corporations, as, 1.8
economic development by, 3.71
economic, social or environmental wellbeing, promotion of –
modification of enactments, 1.55
power of, 1.49
ethics, 1.56
executive –
discharge of functions, 1.52
forms of, 1.51
overview and scrutiny committee, 1.53
public consultation, 1.54
finance –
capital, 1.60, 1.61
credit approvals, 2.10
further government proposals for, 1.58
grants. *See* GRANTS
Select Committee report, 1.66–1.68
financial activities –
express statutory powers, 4.2
ultra vires doctrine, relevance of,
financial duties, discretion in exercise of –
annual accounting, 4.23–4.26
auditor, intervention by, 8.48
broad principles, 4.5
charges, levy of, 4.9

Local authorities—*contd*
financial duties, discretion in exercise of—*contd*
decision-making process, intervention in, 4.4
financial motives, 4.9
forward funding, 4.23–4.26
improper purposes, 4.20, 4.21
irrationality, 4.7
profit, trading for, 4.10
quasi-fiduciary duty, 4.8
scope for, 4.3
unlawful delegation, 4.22
unlawful fetters on –
areas of concern, 4.11
contract, entering into, 4.13, 4.14
current elected body, commitment outliving, 4.15
informal representations, by, 4.16
meaning, 4.12
non-contractual undertakings, by, 4.16
party political discipline, by, 4.18
policies, adoption of, 4.17
Wednesbury unreasonableness, 4.6, 4.7
financial motives, 4.9
forward funding, 4.23–4.26
function, activities being, 4.27–4.32
funds. *See* FUNDS
goods and services, supply of –
contracts for, 3.60
education, for, 3.61
incidental powers, 4.27–4.32
incurring expenditure in interest of area, power of –
annual limit, 4.46, 4.47
conditions, 4.48
discretion in, 4.41
exercise of, 4.38–4.43
funds, contributions to, 4.45
interests, nature of, 4.42
limiting, 4.35
local bodies, contributions to, 4.39
overhead costs, 4.43
publicity, not including, 4.44
statutory provision, 4.34–4.37
trust, creation of, 4.40
loans by, 3.72
members. *See* COUNCIL MEMBERS
monitoring officer, 1.23
political structures, 1.50–1.55
profit, trading for, 4.10
publicity –
accounts –
exemption from requirements, 3.65
expenditure, of, 3.64
inspection of, 3.66
authorities subject to restrictions, 3.63
statutory restrictions, 3.62
quasi-fiduciary duty, 4.8
ultra vires doctrine, subject to, 4.27
Local authority accounts
annual accounting, 4.23–4.26
audit. *See* AUDIT

Local authority accounts—*contd*
direct labour and service organisations. See DIRECT LABOUR ORGANISATIONS; DIRECT SERVICE ORGANISATIONS
economic development, in respect of, 3.71
failure to account, duty to certify for –
appeals, 9.77–9.79
auditor, procedure by, 9.76
bribes and sums received, payment of, 9.51
decision not to collect fees or charges, 9.48
future developments, 9.80–9.83
members of local authority, conduct of, 9.64–9.67
officers, conduct of, 9.68, 9.69
rebuttal of, 9.50
recovery action, 9.74, 9.65
repeal of provision, 9.42
sanction by Secretary of State, 9.52
statutory provision, 9.41–9.47
sums due, assessment of, 9.70–9.72
sums not paid over, 9.49
goods and services, supply of, 3.60, 3.61
heat, etc, provision of, 3.68
item of account contrary to law, declaration of –
aggrieved objector, appeal by, 9.40
application to court, 9.5, 9.6
auditor –
exercise of discretion by, 9.38
procedure by, 9.39
contrary to law –
decisions in previous financial years, re-opening, 9.18
ex gratia payments, 9.17
examples of, 9.13
expenditure not being, 9.21
gratuities, 9.16
imprudence, 9.12
income, items relating to, 9.22
meaning, 9.10
redundancy payments, 9.19
retirement packages, 9.20
retrospective payments, 9.16
substitution of view, 9.11
unlawful decision, expenditure or income relating to, 9.14
Wednesbury failings, 9.15
court, powers of, 9.27–9.29
disqualification of members –
discretion to order, 9.34
restrictions on, 9.35
item of account –
meaning, 9.7, 9.8
omissions, 9.9
rectification of accounts, 9.37
repayment –
persons liable to make, 9.30, 9.31
restrictions on, 9.35, 9.36
responsibility for incurring or authorising, 9.32, 9.33
sanction, 9.23–9.26
statutory provision, 9.5

Local authority accounts—*contd*
loans, of, 3.72
loss through wilful misconduct, duty to certify for –
appeals, 9.77–9.79
auditor, procedure by, 9.76
disqualification for, 9.73
expenditure lawful in itself, 9.59
future developments, 9.80–9.83
intentional or reckless defiance of law, 9.56–9.58
members of local authority, conduct of, 9.64–9.67
misconduct, examples of, 9.60–9.63
officers, conduct of, 9.68, 9.69
omissions, 9.54
recovery action, 9.74, 9.65
repeal of provision, 9.42
standard of proof, 9.55
statutory provision, 9.41–9.47
sums due, assessment of, 9.70–9.72
wilful misconduct, meaning, 9.53
objection to –
appeal against auditor's decision on, 8.102–8.107
determination of, 8.99
notice of, 8.93
party other than objector, appeal by, 8.108
procedure on, 8.91–8.100
right of elector, 8.91–8.101
time limit, 8.101
vexatious, 8.95
parking, in respect of, 3.70
private street works, for, 3.69
publicity –
exemption from requirements, 3.65
expenditure, of, 3.64
inspection of, 3.66
purposes not otherwise authorised, for, 3.67
statutory requirements, 3.40
surcharge, repeal of provisions relating to, 9.3, 9.83
Local education authorities. See EDUCATION
Local government
administrative structure, development of, 1.1
central control, appointments subject to, 1.14
central government hold on, 1.1
central government, relationship with –
audit, 1.20–1.22
public expenditure planning, 1.19
default powers, 1.14
expenditure planning. See EXPENDITURE PLANNING
functions, allocation of, 1.9, 1.10
Golden Age, 1.1
income and expenditure, central government stranglehold on, 1.14
London, in. See LONDON GOVERNMENT
Modern Local Government White Paper –
areas of proposed change, 1.37
publication of, 1.35
modern system, ancestor of, 1.1

Local government—*contd*
modernisation, policy on, 1.29
options for change, 1.36
restructuring, 1.2
structure, 1.2, 1.3
Local Government Finance Report
available grant, setting out, 1.24
Local Government Improvement and Development Agency
creation of, 1.65
Local government officers
Chief Finance Officer. *See* CHIEF FINANCE OFFICER
code of conduct, 5.27
directors, as. *See* DIRECTOR
ethical standards. *See* ETHICAL STANDARDS OFFICERS
financial affairs, administration of –
Chief Finance Officer. *See* CHIEF FINANCE OFFICER
monitoring officer. *See* MONITORING OFFICER
proper administration, meaning, 5.7, 5.8
regimes, application of, 5.2–5.6
requirement of, 5.1
statutory duty, 5.7, 5.8
monitoring officer. *See* MONITORING OFFICER
paid service, head of, 5.24–5.26
security, 5.15
London Fire and Civil Defence Authority
establishment of, 1.11
London government
administrative area, 1.4
borough councils, 1.4
education, responsibility for, 1.6
London Pensions Fund, 1.5
metropolitan district councils, 1.4
Residuary Body, 1.4
structure of, 1.4
Lottery
local, fund for, 3.38

Metropolitan counties
creation of, 1.3
Minimum revenue provision
debt-free authorities, treatment of, 10.30, 11.48
initial and subsequent cost, calculation of, 12.80, 12.81
notional interest on credit arrangements, in respect of, 11.58, 11.59
principal, in respect of –
additions to, 11.56
aggregate amounts, 11.51
calculation of, 11.57
debt-free authorities, treatment of, 11.55
items added to, 11.54
main element of, 11.52
reducing balance, 11.53
replacement of system, 11.46
requirement to make, 11.47
revenue account, set aside from, 11.50
types of, 11.49

Monitoring officer
Chief Finance Officer not being, 5.1, 5.19
duties of, 5.20
failure to report, 5.22
post of, 5.19
reports, 5.20–5.23
Museum
fund for, 3.38

National Assembly for Wales
creation of, 1.65
New town corporations
housing subsidies, 19.42
NHS Trusts
Private Finance Initiative, application of, 15.81
Non-domestic rate
appeals, 2.32
basis of, 2.21
collection, 2.33
Collection Fund, 1.17
exemptions and reliefs –
agricultural land and buildings, 2.25
charitable and other organisations, 2.26
Crown property, 2.23
disabled persons, 2.27
generally, 2.22
personal, 2.29
places of public worship, 2.24
unoccupied property, 2.28
instalments, payment by, 2.33
levy of, 2.21
rateable value, 2.30
rating list, 2.21, 2.31
appeals, 2.32
system of, 2.20
valuation for, 2.31
Non-metropolitan counties
creation of, 1.3

Parish
continuation of, 1.3
meetings, requirement to hold, 1.3
new, constitution of, 1.3
Parish councils
establishment, requirement of, 1.3
functions of, 1.10
members' allowances, 6.5, 6.6
Parish meeting
transacting business of, 4.31
Parking
accounts in respect of, 3.70
Pensions
Funds –
administration expenses, payment of, 3.28
admissions agreement, 3.26
audit, 3.33
employees covered by, 3.25
individual adjustments, 3.34
investment, 3.29

Pensions—*contd*
Funds—*contd*
investment manager, 3.31, 3.32
management and investment, 3.27–3.33
payments on account, 3.35
payments to, 3.36
pension increases, provision for, 3.37
proper advice, Administering Authority taking, 3.30
rates and adjustment certificate, 3.34, 3.35
superannuation funds –
administration, 3.23, 3.24
maintenance of, 3.23
provision for, 3.21
regulations, 3.22
superannuation investments, nature of, 12.57
Places of public worship
rating, exemption from, 2.24
Planning
VAT provisions, 18.61, 18.62
Police
authorities. *See* POLICE AUTHORITIES
departmental inspectors, 1.14
Police authorities
areas, 1.13
arrangements for, 1.13
funds, 3.39
joint committees, 1.13
members, 1.13
own right, in, 1.13
Private Finance Initiative
adoption of, 15.6
approval of schemes, 15.10
background, 15.1–15.11
basic criteria, 15.3
contractor, 15.6
contractual arrangements, 15.8
Design, Build, Finance and Operate schemes, 15.7
development of, 1.33
education, in respect of, 20.27, 20.31
encouragement of, 15.73
forms of, 15.4
Guide, 15.74
launch of, 15.1
local government, introduction for –
additional measures, 15.16
capital finance concessions, 15.16
DBFO schemes, concessions for, 15.17–15.21
evolution, 15.12, 15.13
further measures, 15.17–15.21
initial measures, 15.14, 15.15
outputs and results, concentration on, 15.9
Private Finance Panel, 15.5
promotion of, 15.5
Public Private Partnerships Programme Limited, 15.11
rationale, 15.2
Ryrie Rules, 15.1
Private finance transactions
background, 12.32–12.40
certified contracts –
certificate –
challenge to, 15.100, 15.101
contents of, 15.95
model, 15.96
public inspection, 15.105
signature, 15.97, 15.98
certification requirements –
consent, 15.99
period for satisfying, 15.93
scope of, 15.94
contracting out of functions, 15.115
judicial review, application for, 15.90
novation, 15.104
private law protection, extent of, 15.106–15.108
procedure, 15.92–15.101
prohibition orders, 15.103
public and private law position, 15.89
public law proceedings, discretion of court, 15.114
relevant discharge terms, 15.109–15.111
absence or invalidity of, 15.112, 15.113
scope of provisions, 15.88
services, for, 15.89
types of, 15.88
validity, 15.92
cost at any time of, 12.79
credit arrangement –
creation, time of, 12.41
treatment as, 12.30, 12.31, 12.35–12.40
credit cover, need for, 12.36
current arrangements for, 15.20
DBFO contracts, 12.37
debt-free authorities, treatment of, 10.35, 15.60
definition, 12.33, 15.22
entering into, 12.30
example of, 12.34
exclusion from definition, 15.24
initial and subsequent cost, calculation of, 12.73–12.79
exceptions to rules, 12.82
leases as part of, 15.52–15.56
leases of land under, 12.90
legislation, need for, 15.80
non-scoring credit approval, 15.69–15.72
notional capital receipts, 15.57–15.59
notional credit approval, 15.66–15.68
PFI credits –
availability of, 15.62
framework for, 15.63
meaning, 15.61
promissory notes, 15.64
total amount of, 15.65
Private Finance Initiative. *See* PRIVATE FINANCE INITIATIVE
reduced or nil initial cost –
building, procurement of, 15.49, 15.51
building, replacement or enhancement of –
qualifying purposes, 15.44–15.48
spend to save schemes, 15.43

Private finance transactions—*contd*
reduced or nil initial cost—*contd*
capital assets or services, transactions involving procurement of –
contract structure test, 15.29–15.33
criteria, 15.28
from 1 April 2000, 15.34–15.42
initial requirements, 15.27
variation, 15.38–15.41
heating services, procurement of –
equipment replacement scheme, 15.51
qualifying purposes, 15.44–15.48
spend to save schemes, 15.43
regulation of, 12.31
requirements, 15.23, 15.24
revenue support, administration of –
non-scoring credit approval, 15.69–15.72
notional credit approval, 15.66–15.68
PFI credits –
availability of, 15.62
framework for, 15.63
meaning, 15.61
promissory notes, 15.64
total amount of, 15.65
special arrangements for, 15.61
supplementary credit approval, 15.69–15.72
technical measures, 15.25, 15.26
ultra vires transactions, 15.75–15.79
Public finance
Comprehensive Spending Review, 1.30
Economic and Fiscal Strategy Report, 1.31
elements of reform, 1.31, 1.32
spending plans for 1999–2002, 1.33
Public Works Loan Board
additional quota loans, 13.48
aggregate loans, limit on, 13.44
capital payments, loans financing, 13.49
change in arrangements, 13.50
debt, amount of, 13.41
functions of, 13.43
loans by, 13.45
non-quota loans, 13.45, 13.46
origins of, 13.42
quota loans, 13.45, 13.47

Rate Support Grant
replacement of, 2.2
Rates
community charge replacing, 1.16
Rating
history of, 2.11
non-domestic rate. *See* NON-DOMESTIC RATE
Regional Development Agencies
creation of, 1.65
Registered social landlord
local authority, promotion or formation by, 16.11
Regulated companies
debt-free authorities, treatment of, 10.36
Revenue account
expenditure to be charged to, 10.11, 10.12
exceptions, 10.13, 10.14

Revenue Support Grant
challenging, 2.7
distribution, 2.2, 2.4
introduction of, 2.2
payment of, 2.6
population report, 2.5
statutory provisions, 2.2
total amount of, 2.3

Schools
assets, ownership of, 20.22
classification –
pre-1998, 20.2
Schools Standards and Framework Act 1998, under, 20.7
closure –
direction for, 20.24
disposal of assets, 20.25
liabilities, discharge of, 20.26
procedural requirements, 20.24
delegated budgets, 20.20, 2021
disposal of assets –
discontinuance, on, 20.25
restrictions on, 20.23
exclusion of pupil from, recoupment of payments, 20.59
foundation, 20.11
funding –
community schools, 20.13, 20.29
community special schools, 20.13
county and maintained nursery and special schools, of, 20.3
foundation schools, 20.14, 20.15
foundation special schools, 20.14, 20.15
grant maintained schools, 20.6
maintained nursery schools, 20.13
maintained schools, 20.12, 20.29, 20.39, 20.40
voluntary schools, of –
aided, 20.5, 20.16–20.18, 20.29
controlled, 20.4, 20.14, 20.15, 20.29
special agreement, 20.5
governing bodies, 20.10
maintained –
assets, ownership of, 20.29
budget share, 20.30
categories of, 20.29
delegated budget responsibility, 20.41–20.45
financial delegation, suspension of, 20.43, 20.44
funding, 20.12, 20.29, 20.39, 20.40
management responsibilities, 20.29
revenue support, 20.29
provision of, 20.1
Standards Boards
appointment, 6.28
general powers, 6.29
members of, 6.28
staff, 6.29
status of, 6.29
written allegations to, 6.30

Standards committee
authorities required to establish, 6.25
composition, 6.25
establishment of, 6.25
functions of, 6.27
regulations, 6.26
State aids
notification of, 17.40–17.42

Transport
companies, local authorities' interest in, 16.13, 16.30
grants, 2.8
Trust
local authority, formation by, 16.19, 16.20

Ultra vires
doctrine, object of, 4.1
financial activities of local authorities, relevance to, 4.1
interest swap transactions, 15.78
local authorities subject to, 4.27
local authority contracts being, 15.75–15.77
Unitary authorities
establishment of, 1.7

Value added tax
administration of, 18.2
appeals, 18.63–18.66
basis of, 18.1
charge of, 18.5
exempt business supplies, recovery for, 18.14, 18.26–18.34
exempt supplies, 18.11, 18.12
input tax, 18.7
land, property and construction supplies, treatment of –
assignments, 18.54
compulsory purchase, 18.59, 18.60
election to waive exemption, 18.45–18.50
exempt supplies, consequences of making, 18.42–18.44

Value added tax—*contd*
land, property and construction supplies, treatment of—*contd*
exemption, 18.40
generally, 18.35–18.41
option to tax, 18.45–18.50
planning functions, 18.61, 18.62
rent-free periods, 18.58
residential and non-residential property, rules for, 18.35
reverse assignments, 18.55, 18.57
reverse premiums, 18.56, 18.57
reverse surrenders, 18.53
surrenders, 18.52
zero-rating, 18.37
legislation, 18.1
local authorities –
activities of, 18.15–18.20
exempt business supplies, refunds for, 18.26–18.34
non-business activities, refunds for, 18.21–18.25
non-business supplies, 18.13, 18.21–18.25
output tax, 18.6
partial exemption, 18.33
payments and refunds, 18.9
person bearing, 18.10
publications, 18.2
reduced rate, 18.11
Reference Manual, 18.3
registration, 18.17
returns, 18.8
zero-rated supplies, 18.11, 18.12

Wales
county council petitioning for county borough status, 1.15
principal councils, Council Fund, 3.2, 3.5
residuary body for, 1.15
Waste disposal companies
local authorities' interest in, 16.12